THE
ROMAN REPUBLIC

IN THREE VOLUMES
VOLUME TWO

THE
ROMAN REPUBLIC

BY

W. E. HEITLAND, M.A.

FELLOW OF ST JOHN'S COLLEGE

VOLUME TWO

GREENWOOD PRESS, PUBLISHERS
NEW YORK

First published in 1909 by the Cambridge University Press
Reprinted by permission of the Cambridge University Press

First Greenwood Reprinting 1969

Library of Congress Catalogue Card Number 69-13930

SBN 8371-2078-0

PRINTED IN UNITED STATES OF AMERICA

TABLE OF CONTENTS

VOLUME TWO

Book V.

Rome an Imperial Republic.

Book VI.

Revolution. The Gracchi to Sulla. 133—79 B.C.

LIST OF MAPS

ADDITIONAL NOTES AND CORRECTIONS, 1922

VOLUME TWO

§ 418. The formation of the Macedonian kingdom under a Greek dynasty is emphasized by Isocrates, *Philip* §§ 107—8, pp 103—4.

§ 450. The evacuation of the 3 Fetters was in harmony with the policy of the Scipionic party in Rome, which was opposed to eastward expansion. Nitzsch, *Röm Rep* p 14.

§ 470. The 'faith' of the Roman people. The concept may be illustrated by the notion of *fides* underlying the relation of client and patron in Roman Law. See Mommsen, *Staatsrecht* III 76.

§ 488. Interference of Rome in Achaean League. See Freeman, *Federal Government* ed II p 504.

§ 525. Polybius XXXII 15 remarks that Paullus' son Aemilianus saw much hunting sport in Macedonia under his father, and kept it up to his benefit in later life.

§ 540. Galatians and Pergamum. See Polybius XXIX 22, XXX 3, 20, XXXI 2, 6.

§ 543. Macedonian timber. The importance of this trade may be illustrated by Andocides *de reditu* § 11, p 21, and Jebb on Theophrastus *char* 6 [23].

§ 578. Greece is spoken of as a Province by Valerius Max VII 5 § 4 in a characteristically loose passage.

§ 579. Decline of population in Greece. Polyb XXXVII 9.

§ 581. Attalus III a bad king. Diodor XXXIV 3.

§ 597. Africa a Province. Appian, *Punica* 135. The Punic tongue. Cf Apuleius *apol* 98.

§ 601. No walled strongholds. Diodor XXXI 39.

§ 642, note 1. Soldiers carrying money with them were no new thing. See Thucyd VI 31 § 5.

§ 660. Demoralization. Polyb XXXI 24, XXXII 11, Diodor XXXI 24, 26 §§ 2, 6, 7.

§ 704. That the action of Nasica was viewed in a much more favourable light by senatorial partisans, is clear. See Velleius II 3 § 1 and Orelli's onomasticon to Cicero.

§ 709. Phrygia. See Justin XXXVIII 5, Appian, *Mithr* 57.

§ 718 (p 295 note 1). It should be added that Greenidge *History* p 150 agrees with Mommsen in attributing the increase of numbers in the census of 125—4 to the operation of the land law.

§ 750. The law of 111 BC is by some identified with the *lex Thoria*. See Ferrero, *Greatness and decline* Eng trans I pp 62—3, 180. In any case, the general result, as set forth in this section, is the same. See Hardy, *Six Roman Laws* (Oxford 1911).

§ 757. From Polybius III 39 it appears that the road through southern Gaul to Spain had already been made into a regular line of communication and considerably improved, before the reconstruction by Domitius.

§ 787. Arausio. The name finds a passing mention, with no reference to the battle, in Strabo IV 1 § 11 page 185.

§§ 823, 825. The trials of Norbanus and Rutilius Rufus, and their dates, are dealt with in Greenidge and Clay's *Sources* (1903) pages 96 and 226.

§ 848 (p 439 note 2) an interesting parallel to this military story occurs in S R Gardiner's *Great Civil War* II 218, where the two characters are Baillie and Montrose.

§ 853. See on § 1067.

§§ 855—6. Mommsen in *Hermes* XXII pp 101—6 cites the recorded Tribes of a number of Italian communities, shewing that all the 31 rustic Tribes had some new citizens enrolled in them. If this conclusion is right, it seems to me a confirmation of the statement of Velleius.

§ 858. That it was in earlier times possible to choose Patricians as *tribuni plebis*, at least by the method of cooptation, is indicated by the tradition preserved in Livy III 65 § 1, v 10 § 11, as is pointed out by Ed Meyer, *Kleine Schriften* p 480.

§§ 863, 910. The truth as to these augmentations of the Senate by Sulla is a matter still in question. See an article by D[r] Hardy in Journ Rom Stud 1916.

§ 891. It seems that the compact of Sulla with the Italians in 83—2 was not fully kept. See Cic *de domo* § 79. The passage in the speech of Lepidus (Sallust *hist* I 55 § 12 Maurenbrecher) implies that the law referred to by Cicero was still in force in the year 78.

§ 915. It may be that Pompey's capture of Carbo was at the beginning of 81. But the detailed chronology is not easily ascertained.

§ 920. I do not mean that the *lex Cornelia de provinciis ordinandis* formally and expressly separated the magistracy and pro-magistracy. But that such was its effect in working is surely a safe inference. See § 1178.

§ 921. See on § 1067.

§ 922. Nitzsch *Röm Rep* II 40 traces the beginning of this qualification by tenure of quaestorship to the policy of the censors of 179 BC.

BOOK V

ROME AN IMPERIAL REPUBLIC

CHAPTER XXVII

411. THE 'world's debate' was over, for the overthrow of Carthage left Rome without an effective rival in the regions of the Mediterranean. This is clear to us from our knowledge of the sequel: but the generation then living can hardly have guessed that within forty years all Mediterranean peoples and powers would be looking to Rome as their actual or prospective mistress, at least as a resistless umpire. To Polybius, who lived to see the change, it presented itself as the beginning of a world-history, an unification of human affairs that went so far as to make the local histories of other peoples meaningless and uninstructive unless considered in relation to the central history of Rome. As for Rome herself, even after recent triumphs she could hardly as yet be conscious of her imperial destiny. The lesson of the Hannibalic war had been differently learnt by Senate and People. In the eyes of the ordinary citizen the exhaustion produced by long strain and sacrifices suggested the need of a long period of rest: to the Senate, capable of wider views, it seemed a prime necessity to forestall the development of other powers, rivals perhaps even more keen and dangerous than Carthage. An enemy and provocation were not far to seek. Philip of Macedon had left no opening for doubt as to his hostility. But before we enter on the story of the second Macedonian war we had better take a brief glance at the condition and relations of the peoples outside the Roman dominion with whom Rome had been, or was soon to be, brought into contact.

412. In welcoming and helping the Punic invaders the Gauls and Ligurians of northern Italy had written their own doom. Rome

[1] Beside the valuable fourth volume of Holm's *History of Greece*, there are a number of English works bearing on the subject of this chapter. I will only name Freeman's *History of Federal Government*, Hogarth's *Philip and Alexander of Macedon*, Mahaffy's *Empire of the Ptolemies*, Bevan's *House of Seleucus*. For illuminative criticism Mahaffy's *Greek Life and Thought* is a most useful work.

well understood that she must conquer these districts sooner or later, but for the present she was in no urgent hurry, and had much else to do. No great power existed or was likely to arise there. The Gauls of the rich plain and the Ligurians in their rocky strongholds were alike in devotion to a tribal system which made firm combination impossible and their native valour of no effect. And so, slackly and wastefully, the conquest went on. In Spain the situation had changed since the final expulsion of the Carthaginians. Rome felt bound to keep her hold on the country that it might not again become a base of operations for the Punic enemy. But the Spanish natives were restive under any yoke, and had no marked preference for their new masters as compared with the old. And here too the tribal system prevailed: there was no great power the overthrow of which might ensure or promote the submission of its subjects. Hence war, open or smouldering, soon became normal in Spain. Victories achieved little permanent result: any Roman disaster undid the work of years of fighting, and so the weary struggle went on. The final conquest of Spain was not completed till the time of Augustus. Africa presents a different picture. Humbled and crippled as she was, Carthage soon began to recover wealth and strength. Nothing seemed able to impair her commercial vitality, and the jealous fears of Rome awoke. But Roman forethought had provided an effective means for checking the enemy's reviving power. The reduced territory of Carthage bordered on the Numidian kingdom over a frontier of some 200 miles. Masinissa gladly took to a policy which he well understood to suit the real wishes of his Roman allies, and worried the Carthaginians with border forays and claims which the Punic government dared not actively resist. The sequel of this miserable state of things will be dealt with below. Thus from North West and South Rome had for the present nothing serious to fear: it was to the East that she looked uneasily. Here were the great kingdoms formed out of the remains of Alexander's empire, and a number of minor powers: even Greece, though torn by dissension as of old, was for the most part organized in Federations, larger units than the brilliant city-states of her days of glory. Of the real weakness of the eastern powers the Romans could as yet form no adequate notion, and the aggrandisement of any one of them, particularly by encroachments in Greece, was to the Senate a natural cause of alarm.

413. To begin from the South, the greater part of Peloponnesus was now incorporated in the Achaean League. This famous federation had grown up to meet the needs of communities anxious to preserve their autonomy but unable to stand alone. The several members of the League retained the fullest freedom in their internal affairs.

But the central power suffered from the weakness common in Federal governments. The yearly change of persons in office was a disadvantage not neutralized as at Rome by the presence of a Senate of experienced men holding their places for life. To secure prompt obedience on the part of the federated cities to the decisions of the League Assembly was not always easy, and we need not wonder that the military forces of the League sometimes fell to a low level of efficiency. The disastrous results of this slackness had been seen at the time of the collision with Sparta (227—221 B.C.). Sparta still existed as a city-state, and underwent a military revival in the hands of the reforming king Cleomenes III. Aratus, the subtle intriguer to whom the greatness of the League was chiefly due, could make no head against Cleomenes, and at last he was driven to seek the help of Antigonus (Doson) the reigning king of Macedon, rather than come to terms with his Peloponnesian rival, the king of Sparta. The step was a fatal one. For the time, Antigonus crushed Sparta and drove Cleomenes into exile. But he exacted the citadel of Corinth as his price, and so held the key of the Peloponnese. From that time the Achaean League lost its freedom of action. However little the king might interfere with the Achaeans, they could take no important step in disregard of his wishes: and the League built up in an interval of Macedonian weakness, largely as a check on the domination of Macedon, was now in its foreign policy a Macedonian client. Nor was the Spartan question really settled: the military tyrants who ruled there after a period of revolution were a thorn in the side of their neighbours. But the Achaean cause was better upheld by their new leader Philopoemen. He was more soldier than statesman, and his military reforms raised the position of his country for a time: it was a last flicker of Greek freedom, soon destined to be quenched. But he had fallen on evil days, for the possible policy of the League soon narrowed itself to the choice between taking part with one of the great belligerents or waiting in trembling neutrality to become the victor's prize. The situation in the Peloponnese was further complicated by the fact that Elis and some places in Arcadia, for some time even Mantinea, stood in more or less close relations with the great Federation of Aetolia, to which we must now turn.

414. The Aetolian League, a league of cantons rather than cities, had existed from very early times as a loose union of mountaineer tribesmen whom kinship and common interests led to combine, chiefly for purposes of war. As the brilliant age of Greece came to an end, and a tamer patriotism left the defence of civilized states to professional mercenaries, the backward peoples came more to the front, being able to supply large numbers of hardy recruits fit and

willing to face the strain and perils of a soldier's life for a soldier's pay. These 'aliens' (ξένοι) were far more efficient as fighters than the amateur citizens: they seem normally to have kept faith with their paymasters, and after the East had been opened up by Alexander the vast treasures put into circulation gave a great stimulus to the employment of these hireling troops. Many were drawn from other parts of Greece, but the most plentiful source of supply was Aetolia. The high pay earned, not to mention gains of looting, brought money into the country. As the League grew in importance, its constitution became more definite, and its area was extended by the addition of new members. Some of these were far distant places, such as coast-towns on the Propontis, others were districts of Greece itself or islands near. They had in Naupactus a good harbour and a fairly good fleet, and kept touch with their outlying members. Our knowledge of this League is mainly derived from the Achaean writer Polybius, a prejudiced witness. It is clear that they were not a mere reckless band of robbers, as he makes out: but their methods were often rough, and between them and the more formal Achaeans there was a deep-seated antipathy. Their heads may have been somewhat turned by their rise to a leading position in the Greek world: but they were at least a free people with a policy of their own, and too highspirited to play adroitly the secondary part allotted them in the course of events. They had on more than one occasion come to the front as champions of Greek freedom against Macedonians or Gauls, and it was as opponents of Macedon that they became entangled in the coiling diplomacy of Rome.

415. In most other parts of northern and central Greece confederations existed closer or looser according to the various degrees of common sentiment and interest and the pressure of external danger. Such were Epirus, Locris, Phocis and Boeotia. In Acarnania was a League which probably resembled the Aetolian. Suffering from the violence of their stronger neighbours, they had at one time looked to Rome for help, but relief came through the mediation of the Macedonian king, who set in motion the pirates of Illyria. The Acarnanians are depicted as a brave and loyal people: it was unlucky that their connexion with Macedon involved them in a losing cause. In Thessaly too Aetolians and Macedonians competed for power. What recognition of unity there was among the Thessalian cities was slight and inefficient. The country was generally a Macedonian dependency, but the Aetolians had made conquests there: and the reconquest of some of these places by king Philip at the end of the so-called Social war (221—217) left the Aetolian League ready to join any power in opposition to Macedon. Of the old city-states

Athens still remained, an unfederated unit, dreaming of her old imperial splendour now long departed. Weak in her isolation, celebrated only as the centre of the philosophic schools, spared by the great powers in reverence for her former achievements in literature and art, she enjoyed on sufferance a freedom that she knew not how to use. Aratus had bought out the last Macedonian garrisons in 229, but Athens only became an ally of the Achaeans: she would not forget her pride and become a member of the League. Her vain democracy thought it more dignified to earn by subservience and flattery the patronage and largesses of foreign kings. In no community did the intervention of Rome in Greek affairs meet with a readier welcome.

Powers in eastern Mediterranean about 200 B.C. Epidamnus (Dyrrachium), Apollonia and Corcyra are dependents of Rome. Macedon (M) holds Euboea, also Corinth and a few other places in Peloponnesus, and dominates Achaean League (Ach). Southern Thessaly (T) had been won from the Aetolian League (Aet) in the peace of 205. Byzantium (B), Heraclea (H), Rhodes (R) and Crete (Cr) are free Greek states. P = Pergamene kingdom. S = Seleucid kingdom of Syria. E = dependencies of Lagid kingdom of Egypt. C = Carthaginian territory. Ep = Epirus.

416. Two of the Aegean islands call for mention. Rhodes had been a prosperous maritime state for some 200 years. Into her interesting history we cannot enter here. Her chief interests were of course commerce and banking, but as a seat of Greek culture she ranked very high. Good faith, and the absence of grasping ambition, made the Rhodians contrast favourably with other powers, and they

were so thoroughly trusted and respected that international disputes
were sometimes submitted to their arbitration. Their fleet was better
equipped and handled than other naval forces of the day, and its
chief employment was the suppression of piracy, already a serious
evil in the eastern Mediterranean. When a great earthquake in 227
wrecked their splendid city, kings and princes sent rich gifts to aid
its restoration: so frankly was it recognized that the welfare of
Rhodes was the interest of all. But, while the Rhodian republic kept
on good terms with all civilized powers, it had a policy of its own,
and an old particular friendship[1] with the governments of Egypt and
Rome. Nor was it found inconsistent with their unambitious scheme
to hold a province on the mainland of Asia Minor, the revenue derived
from which was a help in the maintenance of their position. For the
remaining free cities and islands of the Aegean and Euxine looked
generally to Rhodes as their leader, and there was a sort of confeder-
ation with some of them for the protection of seaborne trade. Very
different was the condition of Crete. Here there were a number of
separate communities organized on a common model, a chief feature
in which was the support and training of a dominant military caste.
They and their followers found insufficient occupation in the internal
wars long chronic in the island, and numbers of them served for hire
in foreign armies. Beside the horse and foot of Aetolia might
commonly be seen the bowmen and slingers of Crete. Others took
to the sea and infested the trade-routes. For lying and treachery
the Cretans were proverbial: and it may be said of them that they
were pests abroad, though powerless at home.

417. We cannot pause to sketch the vicissitudes through which
the great empire of Alexander had passed since his death in 323.
Within its vast bounds there now remained three kingdoms held by
dynasties descended from some of the Successors (διάδοχοι), the
Marshals who won thrones in the partition of the empire. In
Macedon were the Antigonids, in Syria and lands to East and West
of Syria were the Seleucids, in Egypt were the Lagids or Ptolemies.
Beside these there was the kingdom of Pergamum in western Asia
Minor, ruled by Attalus I (241—197). But Attalus was not descended
from one of the genuine Successors. For him there was no share of
the mantle of Alexander, and the Attalids were not recognized as equals
by the occupants of the three great thrones. The same may be said of
the kingdom of Bithynia, at this time ruled by Prusias. This was a
meaner power, and need not detain us here. The bulk of northern
Asia Minor had never been really conquered by Alexander, nor are
we at present concerned with Pontus and Cappadocia. But the large

[1] See note at end of this chapter.

inland district traversed by the upper waters of the Sangarius and Halys was held by intruders of Celtic race known as Galatians. Here they had settled down in the first half of the third century B.C., after long wanderings in the course of which they had devastated Macedonia and penetrated far into Greece. They brought their families with them, for their movement was a popular migration : and when they reached their Asiatic home they were still numerous enough to form three strong tribes and to become the plague of their neighbours. Like their brother Gauls in Italy, they inspired terror by their wild charge in battle and their habitual ferocity. We hear of them everywhere as mercenaries : whole armies of them could be hired to fight on any side in any quarrel. So their employers made no scruple of sending them to certain destruction when it served the purpose in view, or even massacring them if troublesome. They are in short a barbarian type quite different from the Asiatic, a disturbing element in the history of Asia Minor.

418. To return to the three great Successor-kingdoms and the lesser monarchy of Pergamum. They had many common characteristics. There was in each an established Royal House, and the reigning king was absolute : if the Macedonian king had to consider the wishes of assembled chiefs, this check, seldom in operation, was practically void through the existence of a national loyalty. If Macedon was an exception to the rule that the seat of government was a splendid capital city, the residence of the royal court, this was simply the outcome of local circumstances. In general, the efficiency gained by the concentration of power in a single hand was neutralized by the mistakes of a monarch unaccustomed to hear the truth. The less assured position of the Pergamene kings made them keener than others to discern their interest. An unscrupulous diplomacy, based on deep mutual distrust, was common to all. The common language of the royal courts was Greek, and their tone cosmopolitan, as was perhaps only natural when the governments were dynasties imposed from without, not national organs developed from within. In this last respect the case of Macedon is again exceptional. The generally free tone of the courts is illustrated by the bold self-assertion of the princesses. That royal marriages were matters of dynastic interest and ambition was a principle well understood and accepted. The royal ladies could not change this even if they wished to do so : but they could and did make their influence felt in the policy of the courts, and bear an active part in intrigue and crimes. The contrasts were not less striking than the resemblances. The king of Macedon differed from his neighbours in having a real nation at his back, in

fact the only community of ancient times to which we can apply the
name of a nation in a fully significant sense. It was Philip II,
Alexander's father, that had welded together the discordant tribes
with masterful force and judgment, till they became a nation in
virtue of what has been well called 'community of tradition and hope.'
When Alexander's conquests were over and his empire divided, the
Macedonians sank back into their previous condition as a nation of
farmer-folk. But they enjoyed little rest. Wars between claimants
of the throne (for the old royal house was soon extinct), followed by
the disastrous inroad of the Gauls (279) left exhaustion behind them,
but the reign of Antigonus Gonatas (277—239) was marked by a
revival. This king was grandson of old Antigonus, one of the great
Marshals of Alexander, and in him we see the Antigonid dynasty
firmly established in Macedon. His grandson Philip V reigned from
220 to 179, a king ambitious unscrupulous passionate clever and
unwise, who played a great part in the politics of Greece and the East
and achieved his own ruin in collision with Rome.

419. Very different was the Asiatic realm over which Antiochus III ruled for 35 years (222—187). He had succeeded to
what was left of the vast dominions of his ancestor, the great Seleucus. The core of his kingdom was Syria. Of the lost eastern
provinces he reconquered some, and recovered part of the 'Hollow
Syria,' which in the weakness of the Seleucid monarchy had been
annexed by the Ptolemies. Styled 'the Great' by his admirers, and
convinced of his own competence and power, he turned his ambitions
to the West, to restore the shaken authority of his house in that
direction. The Seleucid kings claimed a long strip of country
running westward from Cilicia and the Taurus, and a considerable
territory beyond. How the determination of Antiochus to confirm and
extend his power in Asia Minor led him into Europe and into conflict
with Rome, we shall see below. In 203 he made an infamous compact with Philip of Macedon to rob the boy king of Egypt of some
of his possessions, but the Rhodians and Attalus in fear for themselves took the part of Egypt, and time was given for Rome to get
her hands free and humble Philip. The Syrian monarchy was in
extent much the largest of the Successor-kingdoms, and the house
of Seleucus was firmly seated on the throne: but the loyalty of its
subjects was the sectional loyalty of various peoples bound together
by allegiance to a common master, not the national loyalty that
sees in the nation's king an embodiment of the nation's vital unity.
Thus the fabric of Seleucid power was territorial: provinces could
be lopped off without rendering it necessary for the conqueror to

fell the main stem. The capital city, Antioch on the Orontes, was famed for its beauty and its luxuries: and the whole atmosphere of the Syrian court was more Oriental than Greek.

420. The Egyptian kingdom rested on the material foundations of security and wealth. Its founder, Ptolemy son of Lagus, had with far-sighted judgment chosen this wonderful country as his share of Alexander's heritage. Its resources were enormous, and in those days wealth gave the command of mercenary soldiers according to need. Nor were the natives, patient tillers of the Nile-dressed soil, of themselves inclined to rebel: and it was the policy of the Ptolemies to conciliate the priests of the ancient worship, whose hostility was the one serious source of danger from within. Against foreign invasion nature had provided barriers, for the belts of desert were an obstacle to the passage of armies. The rapid growth of Alexandria as the successful rival of Tyre and Sidon made easy the creation of a powerful fleet. Thus not only was the country secured against an attack by sea but the possessions of the kingdom were extended abroad. Cyprus and the Cyrenaic district became appanages of the Egyptian crown, and a number of places in southern and western Asia Minor, Aegean islands and towns on the Propontis, were gradually added as dependencies. The earlier Ptolemies acquired much influence in Greece, and from Egypt more than any other kingdom came the royal subsidies by which Greek statesmen were enabled to prosecute their designs: for instance, both Aratus and Cleomenes were in the pay of Ptolemy III. Speaking generally, the Antigonid and Seleucid kings were hostile to the Lagid house, the former jealous of Egyptian influence in Greece and the Aegean, the latter as rivals in the control of ˙˙ ˙llow Syria and Palestine. With Rhodes and Pergamum, powers interested in peace and trade, the Ptolemies as a rule were good friends. Their policy was to make useful alliances, and we have seen how Ptolemy II became a friend if not an ally of Rome before the first Punic war: he did not however break with Carthage, also his nominal friend. The land forces of the Lagids were what money and management made them: strong and efficient, or the opposite, at various times. There was a Macedonian body-guard, privileged, and important at least in the earlier days of the dynasty: the Greek mercenaries, Aetolians, Peloponnesians, Cretans and others, beside the barbarians from Galatia and Thrace. But there was a growing tendency to train and use native troops, and the increase of this element was one of the symptoms of the decay of the Graeco-Macedonian government. For after the death of Ptolemy III (in 222 or 221) a degeneration of the Lagid house sets in: only the protection of Rome delays for nearly two centuries the

inevitable end. The great capital of Ptolemaic Egypt, Alexandria, has been described by several modern writers. It was the most splendid populous and cosmopolitan of all the imperial cities, and contained among its motley throng a large colony of Jews living according to their own customs, and in a separate quarter of their own. The Museum, a sort of great college of professors, with its library observatory and natural history collections etc., was the greatest centre of learning and research in the world. It was the home of Greek mathematics and kindred sciences, and, on the literary side, of criticism and grammar. It was in short a world's university of special and technical studies.

421. The kingdom of Pergamum had its origin in the enterprise of an eunuch who was holding that fortress for Lysimachus king of Thrace. When his master lost throne and life in 281, the fort and the treasure stored there were at the governor's disposal. He raised more troops, and gradually won a considerable territory. He courted the favour of his powerful neighbours, and in troubled times it was more their interest to keep on good terms with the upstart than to take arms and eject him. He was succeeded by his nephews, the second of whom, the famous Attalus (241—197), was the first to assume the title of king, after his victory over the Galatians. Pergamum now became a considerable power both on land and sea, and the capital an art-centre with a fine school of sculpture. But the growth and pretensions of Pergamum (for Attalus had no small influence in Greece) roused the jealousy of the kings of Syria and Macedon, and the need of a powerful ally threw him into the arms of Rome. The Pergamene kingdom, having no national cohesion and only a moderate extent of territory, depended on sheer wealth: so far as its geographical position was concerned, it was, unlike Egypt, insecure.

422. Such in brief outline was the state of things in Greece and the East about 200 B.C. The Roman Senate was afraid to stand aside and let things settle themselves: at present they had allies and owed those allies a duty. It was not for Rome to abandon her traditional policy by leaving her allies to perish, with the prospect of having to fight their conqueror single-handed. The fatal slackness shewn in the case of Saguntum was fresh in men's memories, and not to be repeated for the present. The first need was to put an end to the aggrandisement of Philip of Macedon and confine him to his hereditary domains. But it was not likely that the responsibilities of Rome would end here. From Rhodes Alexandria and Pergamum came news of the movements of the 'Great' Antiochus, pushing boldly to the West. An important factor in the Roman policy in the time now coming on was the attitude of leading Romans towards

Hellenism. Hellenism may be used as a convenient term to connote the aggregate of striking Greek qualities regarded from the point of view of their influence on peoples not Greek. Suppleness, versatility, subtlety, imagination, the turn for seeking and questioning that led to rationalism, the sense of proportion that gave immortality to their literature and art, in short, their brilliant competence in body and mind, had long made the Greeks the admiration of all with whom they came into contact. Alexander, most magnetic of conquerors, had carried many Greek influences far into the East, stimulating the growth of cities, and, though the house of Seleucus no longer ruled those distant provinces, Greek influences were not extinct. The Bactrian kings still issued beautiful coins, the Hindoo went on carving in stone, the Parthian kings were proud to bear the title of 'Greek-lover' ($\phi\iota\lambda\acute{\epsilon}\lambda\lambda\eta\nu$), and Greek cities long existed in their empire, notably Seleuceia on the Tigris. The Lagid and Seleucid courts were as Greek as they could contrive to be, though the reaction of the passive Orient was seriously affecting them both. In western Asia Minor and the Aegean the Greek had been at home for centuries.

423. The main problem presented by Hellenism is to account for its utter failure to give any vital strength to the governments most subject to its influence. Why did the Hellenized world crumble under the half-hearted touch of Rome? We may perhaps answer that the military monarchies had extinguished any national feelings that may have existed in the peoples of the East, while the Hellenism they introduced was no sort of working compensation for the loss, small though that loss might be. The moral weakness of the Greek character had ruined the Greek city-states in their prime. Greek classic literature is a golden treasury of wise saws and warnings. It was not for want of knowing that union is strength that the states had worn themselves out in quarrels, nor ignorance of the virtue of moderation that made states and the parties within them habitually go too far. The lesson of the pride that goes before a fall lies like a cloud upon many of the Greek masterpieces. But the parable was of no avail, and the everlasting contrast between principles and practice was and remained the canker of public life. Mutual confidence was impossible, and things were in these later days rather worse than better, if we may believe the witness of Polybius. And in its extension over the East after the conquests of Alexander Hellenism was subject to an unwholesome development. It was not the finer exceptional Greek types, the representatives of Pericles and Socrates, of Thrasybulus and Timoleon, for which there was a demand at the courts of the Successors, but rather the slippery rogues who outdid the tricks of Themistocles and Lysander. And not only did autocrats

prefer flattery to honest truth: the worse qualities of the Greek adventurers were ripened by their surroundings, in contact with oriental suspicion and guile.   And so in course of time there grew up a mongrel race of Oriental Greeks, chiefly in the cities, not devoid of a kind of base ability, a blend of the rich vices of the parent stocks. We shall meet these people later on, sapping Roman morality and propagating corruption.   For the present we need only remark that their influence was a source of weakness to the East, in particular to the Seleucid kingdom.

424.   But at Rome Hellenism was in a fair way to become the fashion.   Leading men like Scipio Africanus and his circle were fascinated by Greek literature, and enjoyed the stimulating society of accomplished Greeks.   Younger men such as Titus Quinctius Flamininus, who had served with old Marcellus in the Hannibalic war, lay under the same potent charm.   The age was the age of Plautus and Ennius, who were the means of popularizing Greek ideas in Rome.   It is not to be wondered at that the Senate did not understand the situation and, as we shall see, made blunder after blunder. There was a philhellene party eager to relieve Greece from the pressure of the Macedonian king, and who honestly believed that freedom would bring about a Greek revival.   It was an idle dream.   If there had ever existed political forces adequate to achieve the regeneration of Hellas—which may be doubted—they had perished in the lamentable history of the last 200 years.   But Rome was drawn into the tangle of Greek and Eastern affairs, and, once in, she found it impossible to get out: nor could she find a tolerable halting-place till she had established herself as the dominant power in the whole Greek-speaking world.

425.   It was a momentous step, nor could anyone then have guessed that the reflex action of the East on Rome would be not less important than that of Rome on the East.   Yet so it certainly was.   It may help to clear our observation of the series of events now opening, if we consider briefly in advance the main influences to which the Romans were in due course subjected.   We will take first the points in which existing tendencies were developed, then those in which new ones were brought in.   Roman diplomacy had always been far-sighted and astute, with a tendency to quibble and to regard the end as justifying the means: contact with the Hellenistic world did not change its essential character, but left it more unscrupulous than ever.   Romans had always been grasping in money matters, insisting closely on their legal rights, but not apt to exceed them: upright poverty was traditionally held in honour.   Even after half a century of exposure to the temptations of Oriental wealth

Polybius still found the average Roman far more honest than the average Greek: but he already detected symptoms of degeneracy, and the rampant greed and worship of wealth that marked the men of the later Republic contributed not a little to its ruin. Rome had already Provinces, and in Sicily at least had set up a system of taxation modelled on that of her predecessors in dominion. But in the art of extracting revenue from subjects she learnt much from Asiatic examples, and from the spectacle of the Ptolemies sitting at Alexandria and taking toll of the bounty of the Nile.

426. It may seem far-fetched to lay stress on the familiarity with monarchic rule acquired in the East as a new influence, boding no good to the Roman Republic. It is true that this familiarity quickly bred contempt in the Roman mind, if not for monarchy, at least for the monarchs. But I think it did tend to blunt the once keen antipathy to kings, traditional in Rome since the expulsion of the Tarquins. The tradition was still there, but it became more and more a hollow cry in the- interest of a ruling clique jealous of individual eminence. Far more important and speedy in its effects was the action of Greek thought upon Roman ideas of religion and morality. The old Italian polytheism, with its shadowy gods and precise ceremonial, had sufficed for the conquerors of Italy as they went forward, incorporating new gods, or rather new worships. But during their recent struggles the Romans had taken to importing new worships from beyond the seas, and the process was destined to continue. So also the time-honoured rule of conduct had been conformity to ancestral custom (*mos maiorum*). A man did or refrained from doing this or that, not as the outcome of an inward moral debate, but in obedience to what had become an instinct. It suited the Roman nature, practical rather than speculative, but under the influence of Greek questionings it melted away. Nor did the Greek philosophic systems supply any substitute for the old worships and traditional morality. For the Academic school, claiming descent from Plato, had arrived at no positive results, and hesitation and agnosticism did not meet Roman needs. The true strength of the Peripatetic school lay in specializing inquiries into all manner of subjects, and by its influence much positive knowledge was attained: but this could not fill the place of the ancient guides of Roman life.

427. The issue really turned on what we may perhaps call Enthusiasm, the recognition of something that men might think it worth while to live and die for. Either this must be proved unnecessary, or the something must be found. The system of Epicurus attempted the former solution, and offered a doctrine of acquiescence. A man should take things as they come, and make the best of them from the point of view of his own comfort and pleasure: he should avoid all perturbations of mind, particularly superstition: the gods have no other function than that of self-satisfied and unruffled existence. But this Quietism was a dangerous guide of life for Romans, citizens of the great imperial Republic, built up by stubborn active patriotism: nor was the average Roman likely to interpret 'pleasure' in the refined and intellectual spirit of a gentle sage lost in thought beneath Athenian trees. The doctrine of the Stoics dealt with the question differently. There is one great divinity, of which the gods of the popular worships are partial manifestations. All is God, and God is all: he is the soul of the Universe: the soul of man is part of the universal soul, and so is divine. All things are ordered by universal law, to live in conformity with which is the true nature of everything. Herein is found the duty of Man, and complete conformity, fulfilment of Duty, is perfection, only attained by the Wise Man. The difficulty of knowing when this standard has been reached was got over by what has been well called the doctrine of Assurance—for it has indeed a strong savour of Puritanism. The Wise Man is convinced of his own perfection. The inner court of appeal thus set up is the Stoic machinery of conscience: what is good or bad is not the act, but the intention of the actor. In such a system as this there was much that might blend with the traditional moral atmosphere of Rome. Its clear conception of Duty, its recognition of personal dignity as essential to happiness, might have seemed not uncongenial, though perhaps unnecessary, to Fabricius himself. That the Stoic love of paradox gave their teaching a somewhat hard litigative character, was assuredly no obstacle to its reception in Roman society, and no class took to it so readily as did the Roman lawyers. And while Stoicism, like Epicureanism, appealed to the needs of the individual, the former had the advantage that its principles did not withdraw men from an active participation in public life. True, it appealed only to the Chosen Few, and could not be strong in the number of its adherents. But the governing class at Rome was not large, and the stronger natures who embraced the Stoic tenets exerted an influence out of all proportion to their numbers.

I cannot think that the above topics are out of place in a consideration of Rome's eastward movement, or that the frequent anticipatory references to things that had not yet happened need any apology. In the narrative of the wars of the next half century these general remarks cannot find a place: and the wars themselves are only of interest as illustrating the advance of Rome and the gradual degeneration of Roman life that accompanied it.

428. Note on *socii* and *amici*.

Since the above was written, an article by Miss Matthaei (*Classical Quarterly*, vol. 1) has thrown much new light on the alliance-relations of Rome in the period after the second Punic war. I think it well to give an abstract of some of the chief points of her conclusions, recast to suit my purpose.

The position of the Italian *socii* (to whom I always refer as Allies, with initial capital) was regulated by treaties which varied in detail, but which (*a*) created a permanent relation and (*b*) always required a fixed yearly amount of military contingent from the state bound to Rome by the *foedus*. No neutrality was possible. Rome and each Ally were bound to mutual defence, but the contingents of Allies were to serve under the command of Roman generals, and liable to be employed in offensive wars. These permanent *foedera* had grown up under the old Italian international law (*ius fetiale*), a complex formal system that proved unsuitable for use beyond the bounds of Italy, and indeed decayed rapidly after the time of the war with Pyrrhus.

It was especially the contact with Greece and the East that introduced the Romans to a new set of ideas. Permanent alliances and fixed yearly contingents were held inconsistent with freedom, that is state-existence, as in truth they were. The Greek custom was (*a*) temporary alliance for a definite purpose, (*b*) friendship, that is diplomatic relations, in time of peace. The position of neutrality was fully recognized. We must remember that Rome was by no means prepared to set out on a career of conquest, and so to compel the powers of the Greek East to accept permanent alliance, equivalent to subjection. To secure and extend her power she had to fall in with Greek notions and develop a new international system on these lines.

This she did through the recognized relation of Friendship ($\phi\iota\lambda\iota\alpha$, *amicitia*), and she wasted no time over this change of policy. Beginnings had indeed already been made. Her .Friendship with the Ptolemies dated from 272 B.C., that with Rhodes is said to have been even earlier (306 B.C.). The relation between Rome and her *amici* may then be stated thus. Neither party was to fight against the other. Neither was bound to send help to the other. This meant a compact for permanent neutrality in time of war, so long as the Friendship lasted. No formal declaration of neutrality was needed. But it was open to either party to send help to the other, in such amount and for such time as might be settled between them by special agreement. Any such force was commanded by a general of its own, not subordinate to the Roman commander save by special agreement. And further, the war being a joint war, all Friends represented in the field had a right to be represented in negotiations with the joint enemy.

Of Rome's *amici*, some were *foederati*, some not. A *foedus* could not be terminated at will by one party. An *amicitia* could coexist with a *foedus*, but was not created by it. If both were broken off, the former could be renewed without the latter. Where we find the two together, the *foedus* was meant to define special points in the relations between the parties, generally temporary arrangements, such as the settlement after a war, the effect of which lapsed with fulfilment. Treaties made with *amici* contained no clause binding them to supply a yearly contingent. The phraseology of later writers (e.g. Livy) is often very loose, but careful examination shews that the distinction between *amici* and *socii* was well understood. It was one of military status, and applied to the *amici* whether they had treaties with Rome or not.

It is obvious that the system of voluntary help would tell in favour of the Great Power. The small must shew zeal in helping her, if they wish (*a*) her to help them, (*b*) not to arouse her jealousy. This was in fact what happened. Rome soon began to look askance on neutrality. The case of the Achaeans in 192 B.C. illustrates the downward progress of free Friends towards the position of subject allies. Those of Pergamum and Rhodes in 171—168 B.C. shew the relation of Friendship decaying into virtual subjection. The later Friendships approximate to the old Alliances, and generally bind the *amici* to a defensive league with Rome.

The turning-point in Roman policy, from the procedure by *societas* to that by *amicitia*, was the second Punic war. In Sicily, the Carthaginian province ceded in 241 B.C. became Roman and the people[1] *socii*. Hiero of Syracuse was *amicus*, and help from him was voluntary. He died in 216 (215), and war delayed a settlement till 210, when all Sicilian communities became *sociae* on various terms. The peace of 201 not only bound Carthage to cessions and indemnities; it made her foreign policy dependent on Rome, and bound her to supply a naval contingent, like the Greek cities in Italy and Sicily. She became *socia*. Then comes the case of Philip of Macedon. With him too peace was made by a *foedus* in 196. But he was not yet accepted as *socius amicusque* (the usual expression) of Rome. After the treaty, he was advised by a Roman commissioner to apply for this recognition; if he did not, he would seem to be waiting for the coming of Antiochus, that is for an opportunity of revenge on Rome. The recognition seems to have been sought and granted. But on becoming a Friend he found that he was expected to send help to the Romans against the Syrian king, and ended by doing so. He never became *socius* in the old sense. Weissenborn's note on Livy XXXIII 30 § 6, to which Miss Matthaei does not refer, supports her view.

The transition clearly marked in the above selected cases was, I may add, of vast importance. The old Roman love of formality and punctilious interpretation (see Livy XXXVI 3) did not die out, and misunderstandings arose. The tortuous policy of Rome was perhaps often rather litigious in spirit than intentionally unfair. But in dealing with her Friends all turned upon their persuasion of her superior power, and the necessity of keeping her prestige was the main underlying motive of her wars in Greece and Asia Minor during the period 200—168 B.C. This note will be referred to in the notes on the following chapters.

An article by the same writer (*Class. Q.*, vol. II) on the place of Arbitration and Mediation in Ancient Systems of International Ethics is also of much interest as illustrating the legal-religious formalism of Roman policy.

---

[1] Surely only in name. If they had *foedera* (as a very few had) they certainly furnished no contingents to the Roman army, and were not encouraged to bear arms. They did provide ships marines and oarsmen, but this was only when needed. In practice Rome could require anything, such as men to form a local militia in emergencies, and she did. Moreover the tithes levied in Sicily had no precedent in Italy. The name *socii* was a courtesy-title for 'subjects' as used in Sicily. Holm, *Geschichte Sicil* III pp. 363—5, treats this matter well. For the *foedera* of Messana Tauromenium etc. see the interesting passage Cic. II *in Verr.* V §§ 49 foll.

CHAPTER XXVIII

THE SECOND MACEDONIAN WAR AND THE SEQUEL
200—194 B.C.[1]

429. WE have seen that in 205 B.C. Philip of Macedon made peace with the Aetolians and with Rome. He had not backed up Hannibal, and Hannibal was now not in a position to help him. For the present therefore he gave up the notion of war with the western Republic, of whose power he began to be seriously afraid. Even his designs on Greece offered no good prospect of success unless he first increased his resources by acquisitions in some other direction. His ambition was restless, and he was already much corrupted by the influence of bad advisers and absolute power. He had been some fifteen years on the throne and had been engaged in several wars, in some of which he had shewn considerable ability and vigour. But the fruits of his exertions were very small, and his conduct had been such as to earn him the fear and mistrust of most of the Greeks. In 205 Ptolemy IV died and was succeeded by his son, who was a mere child. A long minority, and competition for the control of Egypt and its boy-king among the worthless courtiers of Alexandria, were clearly in prospect. So Philip and Antiochus of Syria at once prepared to take advantage of Egyptian weakness. The royal robbers entered into an infamous compact to divide between themselves the outlying portions of the Ptolemaic empire. What Philip wanted was the Greek cities on the coast of Thrace and Asia Minor and the hellenized strip of land behind them, the islands, and in short the control of the Aegean. To Antiochus the Hollow Syria with Phoenicia and Palestine were the immediate objects. The main point with each was to secure himself against the interference of the other until he had got what he wanted: future divergence of interests was no doubt in the calculations of both, and each from the first intended to play a selfish game. To neither king does it seem to have occurred that this scheme could not be carried out without the leave of Rome and

---

[1] Our best authority for the events contained in this chapter, Polybius XV—XVIII, exists in a fragmentary state. Livy's narrative, XXXI—XXXIV, is complete. In many parts he followed Polybius closely. It is unnecessary to give references in detail save on a few notable points.

that this leave would not be given.   In Antiochus this blindness
may be excused.   Antioch was far from Rome, and in 204—3 the
second Punic war was not yet ended.   That Rome had now got the
upper hand was perhaps not clear to him: that Rome was far the
strongest power of the day, he could hardly guess, nor would he
learn the unwelcome truth from his courtiers.   Rome was no doubt
an ally of the Ptolemies, but hitherto it was from Egypt, not to
Egypt, that help had come.   To judge the situation aright might
have puzzled a wiser man.   But that Philip, near to Italy, following
the fortunes of Hannibal with keen interest, and having himself
already had a taste of the quality of Rome, should fancy that he
could assail Roman allies without having to fight Rome herself
sooner rather than later, is astounding.   Truly this warlike king
was no far-sighted statesman.   But he set briskly to work preparing for his intended conquests.   He had created a sort of fleet
for the operations of his late war with Rome: this he now enlarged
and improved so much that we shortly find him possessed of a navy
as well as an army of great strength.   Meanwhile, if Livy's authority
is to be trusted, he rashly sent a Macedonian corps to the aid of
Carthage and shared the disaster of Zama.

430.   The development of Philip's schemes at once brought about
a coalition to resist them.   The Rhodians, long friendly with Egypt,
and deeply interested in keeping open the maritime trade-routes,
could not look on and see the control of the Aegean and the gate
of the Euxine pass into the hands of a greedy king.   Attalus of
Pergamum was directly threatened by the advance of Philip.   For the
moment these two powers stood alone against him, and Philip lost no
time.   While an emissary of his set fire to the arsenal of Rhodes, he fell
upon the Hellespontine cities and took or destroyed several of them.
In particular, Cius in the Propontis was treated with shameless barbarity.   Now this and other towns of those parts were attached to
the Aetolian League, with which Philip was then at peace.   So his
conduct not only shocked the Greek world generally but enraged
the Aetolians.   Still they were exhausted with recent war, in which
they had been roughly handled by Philip, and their leading men,
acting in the king's interest, kept them quiet for the present.   He
next turned to the islands, took a number of the Cyclades, and then
attacked Chios and Samos.   He fought two sea-fights against the
allied fleets of Rhodes and Pergamum, and seems to have had the
best of it in the second encounter.   He laid waste the Pergamene
territory.   But the city itself was too strong for him to besiege, and
his resources were now failing.   Though he made some rapid conquests in Caria, he could not hold them, for want of supplies.   To the

great relief of friends and foes he withdrew from Asia towards the end of 201. Rome had just got her hands free, and he might at any moment have to face a much more dangerous coalition. It seems to have been in the winter of 201—0 that a congress was held at Athens. Attalus appeared in person, and delegates came from Rhodes. A Roman embassy was also present, the members of which seem to have been charged to warn both Philip and the neutral powers against meddling with Roman allies, and thus to make a fair show of un-willingness to begin the inevitable war. Athens joined the coalition, and one of the king's generals invaded Attica, but retired when warned off by the Romans. The latter then proceeded to warn the Achaean and Aetolian Leagues and also the Epirotes and other peoples in the North: this done, they took ship for the East in hope to make peace there and save their Egyptian ally from the encroachments of Antiochus. Philip must now have seen his danger, but his spirit was high, and in mad obstinacy he pursued his course. While the Rhodians and Attalus won back his southern conquests, he rapidly made himself master of the Thracian coast cities and the Hellespont. Abydos offered a stubborn resistance, but fell at last: to escape slavery, most of the inhabitants sought a voluntary death. To a Roman ambassador, who came just then to bid him desist, he would give no satisfactory answer. And indeed for pacific concessions, short of complete submission, it was perhaps already too late.

431. The Roman Senate was resolved on war, but the people were war-weary. When one of the consuls for 200, P. Sulpicius Galba, called upon the Assembly to declare war against Philip, the motion was rejected by a great majority of the Centuries. It is said that he then summoned a second Assembly, from which he managed to secure the necessary vote. It may be true that there was thought to be force in the dilemma 'you must either choose to fight abroad or be compelled to fight in Italy,' which is the gist of the harangue put into the consul's mouth by Livy. But it presently appears that in the arrangements for the year the forces destined for the irksome and unprofitable service in the armies of occupation employed in Gaul Bruttium Sicily and Sardinia were to be drawn exclusively from the Italian Allies. Mommsen acutely suggests that this was meant to conciliate the Roman citizens and had much to do with the Assembly's change of mind. Old legions were to be disbanded and new ones enrolled, six in number, and of these two only were for the Macedonian war, supported by a corps of veterans serving as volunteers. For a war to be waged in Greek lands the Senate meant to gain every possible Greek ally and to make the utmost use of those allies when gained. This was nothing but the same

old policy that had made Rome mistress of Italy. The enemies of Philip had now a firm rallying-point. The coalition could grow in numbers without losing its efficiency.

432. Yet for some time the intervention of Rome led to no decisive result. In 200 Galba[1], in 199 P. Villius, were operating against the king in the mountains of Illyria, and the former even drove Philip to retreat into Thessaly. But Galba was not able to follow up his success. At this time Macedonia was invaded by some of the northern tribes, and the Aetolians, after much bickering and doubt, joined the coalition. But Philip, beset on all sides, rose to the occasion: the northern raiders were driven out with loss, and he himself surprised and cut up the Aetolians in Thessaly. Earlier in the year he had invaded Attica, and thence made a flying expedition into Peloponnesus. Here there was as usual trouble between Nabis of Sparta and the Achaeans. Philip proposed to undertake the chastisement of Nabis, if the Achaean army would furnish garrisons for Corinth and his strongholds in Euboea. This trick failed, for the Achaeans saw that he meant to get their men into his power and practically compel the League to declare for him. So he withdrew north again by way of Attica: again he laid waste the country and destroyed buildings, even the venerable tombs of the Athenian dead. Athens he could not stop to besiege, and the Roman fleet was hovering off the coast: indeed they had already by a sudden attack taken his fortress of Chalcis, but were unable to find a garrison to hold it. Later in the year the combined fleets of the allies made a few more captures. Philip's fleet seems to have been quite unable to face them, and he was himself busy with the land campaign. We have seen that he was successful in Thessaly. At this point he met with a piece of good luck, which illustrates the condition of Greece[2] at this time. Mercenaries were badly wanted at Alexandria: a recruiting agent visited Aetolia with a large sum of money, and in spite of the war in which the League was involved at home, a great part of the fighting men of Aetolia, induced by the offer of high pay, went off to serve in Egypt. As to the events of the year 199 we are singularly ill informed, but it seems that very little was effected on either side. The consul Villius was sorely hampered by a mutiny of the so-called 'volunteers,' who declared that they had been sent to the war against their will. Perhaps the experience of last year's cam-

---

[1] It seems more probable that Galba was continued in command as proconsul for at least part of 199, but the confusion of the chronology is quite unimportant.

[2] Philopoemen the Achaean general had recently returned from a second term of service as a hired captain in Crete. Philip, in addition to his Illyrian and Thracian mercenaries, had Cretans also.

paign, richer in hardship than in booty, had something to do with their discontents. Villius advanced into the interior to meet the enemy, but before he had matured his plans he received news that his successor, the new consul Flamininus, was not only already appointed, but had already reached Corcyra. It would seem that Villius' march was early in 198. The chronology is difficult to follow. Meanwhile Philip had been mainly busy with preparations for the coming struggle. He hired and drilled mercenaries, and recruited and trained his national army. But above all he strove to win back his lost popularity at home and abroad, in particular by ceding Macedonian possessions in the Peloponnese to the Achaean League. But this interested generosity was too late.

433. At Rome the elections for 198 gave some trouble, for objection was taken to the candidature of Titus Quinctius Flamininus. He was not yet 30 years of age, and had never been aedile or praetor. But as yet there was no law to prevent his proceeding direct from quaestorship to consulship. No doubt the Senate was well aware that a system of regular sequence in the tenure of offices tended to keep power in the hands of the governing class (that is, themselves), but it was urgently necessary to bring to an end the war now dragging on, for the conduct of which it had proved so difficult to provide. So they overruled the objection, and the young Patrician was elected consul. He understood Greek, and as governor of Tarentum in the latter days of the Hannibalic war had had experience in dealing with Greeks. That well-worked institution, the lot, assigned him the Macedonian command: he raised troops, mostly veteran volunteers, to reinforce the army in the field, and took ship early in 198 for the seat of war. The anxiety of the Senate with regard to the Graeco-Macedonian war was not lessened by the news from the East. King Antiochus had beaten the Egyptian army, and won the upper hand in the Syrian districts which it had been his first object to annex. It now suited his policy to patch up a peace with Egypt on easy terms, and a secret treaty left him a free hand in Asia Minor. He trusted neither Philip nor the Romans, and hoped to take advantage of their embroilment to reassert and extend the power of the Seleucids to the West. The Pergamene kingdom was of course directly menaced by this move, and the invasion of his territory by a Syrian army at once caused Attalus to despatch an embassy to Rome. He begged the Romans either themselves to send a force for the defence of his kingdom, or to allow him to withdraw his own contingent[1] from the allied armies for that purpose. The Senate was

---

[1] Rome was on terms of *amicitia* with Antiochus Ptolemy and Attalus. The last was actually helping her, of course voluntarily. See § 428.

in no mind to provoke a conflict with Antiochus just then, so chose the second alternative. But Rome, though allied to Egypt, was on friendly terms with the Syrian king, and it was an important object to keep him quiet if possible. So an embassy was sent to explain that Attalus was at present engaged in warfare as an ally of Rome against Philip, and to beg Antiochus as a favour not to molest him. Antiochus withdrew his invading army, moved by this wily humility and his own interest. But this did not imply the abandonment of his designs.

434. When Flamininus reached the front, he found Philip posted strongly in the mountains on the northern border of Epirus. After due consideration he decided to force the pass. A futile conference shewed that Philip was not ready to concede the Roman demands. But a local guide was found who led a Roman detachment by night to a point that commanded Philip's position. The success of the frontal attack was secured, the king's army routed and driven to fall back in flight to Thessaly. It was characteristic of Philip that he destroyed towns and laid waste the land as he retired. The people were his own subject allies, but he made them leave their homes and follow his march, taking with them such movable property as his soldiery had spared. It was a lesson that to be his friend was much the same as being his enemy. After these acts of despair he withdrew into Macedonia, for the Aetolians and Athamanians now broke into Thessaly and took town after town. Flamininus too advanced through Epirus into Thessaly, but slowly: he kept his army well in hand and stopped plundering, and hence was delayed by the work of bringing up supplies. Meanwhile the allied fleet was busy taking two fortresses held for Philip in the south of Euboea. The consul took several Thessalian towns, but had to raise the siege of Atrax. The year was now far spent, and he wisely determined to seize a port on the Corinthian gulf, where he could fix his winter quarters and draw supplies by sea. Accordingly he moved into Phocis and occupied the district with its port Anticyra.

435. In the course of these operations Flamininus had shewn a steady forbearance and considerateness that made him popular with the inhabitants of the districts traversed. The Greeks began to see in him a liberator, and to hope that Rome would really set them free from the yoke of Macedon. At this moment great was the perplexity of the Achaeans. Hitherto they had observed strict neutrality[1], but it was fast becoming necessary for all Greeks to take a side. The League had accepted many favours from the Macedonian kings. But their most precious possession, Corinth, had been the price

---

[1] See § 428.

exacted for saving them from Cleomenes in 221, and it was still in Macedonian hands. And the general distrust of Philip was growing stronger and stronger in most of the cities of the League. He was held to have poisoned Aratus, and recently to have attempted the assassination of Philopoemen. To be at his mercy, in the event of his victory, was an alarming prospect for his friends. And, while they doubted what to do, the wily Flamininus made them a most tempting offer. The allied fleets were just preparing for a combined attack on Corinth: if the Achaeans would only join Rome, Corinth should when taken be restored to the League as a member. The autumn meeting of the Federal Assembly was now close at hand, and the question of the League policy in the present crisis was brought before it. Envoys from the combatant powers were heard, Roman, Pergamene, Rhodian, and Philip's agents in reply: last came the speakers from Athens with a rejoinder to the king's case. An important factor in the situation was the pro-Roman influence of the President Aristaenus. At last, after formal hindrances had been overcome and open opposition was manifestly hopeless, three states (of which Argos was one) that lay under special obligations to Macedon withdrew from the meeting, and the Achaean League joined the coalition against Philip.

436. The siege of Corinth was now begun and vigorously pressed. But the hope of a betrayal from within was not fulfilled. It is said[1] that the Macedonian garrison partly consisted of Italian deserters, either refugees from Hannibal's army or Allies who had run away from the hated service of the Roman fleet. And when a Macedonian reinforcement was successfully thrown into the town, the siege had to be abandoned for the time, and the expectant Achaeans were left to wait for their reward. Meanwhile Argos left the League and openly joined Philip. The king, embarrassed by the adhesion of faithful allies, who were not strong enough to stand alone, much less to help him, presently handed over Argos to the ruffian Nabis of Sparta, whom he wished to use as a check upon the Achaeans. Nabis took over Argos, where with robbery and violence he acted again the horrors of Sparta: but he kept no faith with Philip. He was already negotiating with the Romans, and now definitely joined the coalition, keeping Argos, though Attalus made a strong protest. In contrast with the service of Italian deserters under Philip, we hear that an auxiliary force was this year sent by Masinissa[2] from Numidia to join the Roman army in Greece: also that supplies of food and clothing were forwarded from Sicily and Sardinia. The relations between

[1] Livy XXXII 23 § 9. The *socii navales* would include freedmen.
[2] As a *rex socius et amicus*. See Livy XXXI 11.

Rome and the Italians were changing for the worse, but Rome was now no longer a merely Italian power.

437. The elections for 197 were held. The new consuls however were neither of them sent to take the place of Flamininus, who was continued as proconsul in charge of the Macedonian war. The news of this could not reach him without some delay, and the fear of being shortly superseded was for a time an anxiety to the successful general. But during the winter he was extending his influence in central Greece, and a conference was at Philip's request held to discuss conditions of

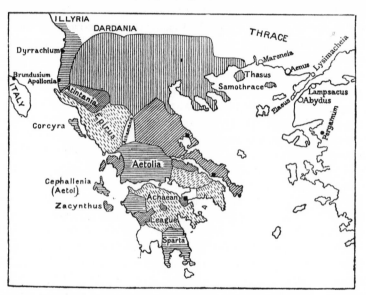

Sketch map of Balkan peninsula **200** B.C. Macedonian kingdom ▨ . ▨ Macedonian dependencies. ▨ States inclined to Macedon. ▬ Anti-Macedonian or allies of Rome. ▨ Inclined to Rome or joined Rome for various reasons. ■ The three 'Fetters.'

peace. Nothing came of it, for the king made reservations to which the Greek powers, who mistrusted him, would not agree: the chance of getting rid of Macedonian tyranny, while the Romans were there to help, was too good to be lost. But an armistice was granted him, and envoys were despatched by both sides to Rome to request the decision of the Senate on the points in dispute. Philip hoped to gull the wary Fathers, but they had been well primed by the agents of the coalition, and put a test-question to the king's envoys. Was he prepared to surrender the three 'fetters of Greece,' the commanding strongholds of Demetrias Chalcis and Corinth, or was he not? On their replying that they had no instructions on the point, the Senate sent them about their business, and left the proconsul a free hand to fight and negotiate as he judged best. He at once broke off all communication with Philip, and set to work to make an end of the war by a decisive victory. The Boeotian confederacy had hitherto taken neither side in the war: they were dependent allies of Macedon, and the general sympathy inclined to Philip. But by a rather mean ruse Flamininus managed to introduce a Roman force into Thebes on the day before the meeting of the Boeotian diet. There was an end to freedom of voting, and the coalition was joined by an unwilling ally. Old king Attalus was taken with a fit or stroke while making a speech to the Boeotians, and returned to Pergamum to die. The proconsul gathered in the allied contingents as he moved northwards. Nabis sent some Cretan mercenaries, while his wife wrung gold and jewels and rich clothes from the Argive ladies by torture. Philip too recruited and trained his army as best he could, enlisting boys and old men to fill up the ranks of his Macedonians, thinned by the constant warfare of recent years. In the spring of 197 we find the two armies feeling for each other in Thessaly. The numbers on each side seem to have been about 25000, but in the case of Philip this was practically the whole of his fighting strength, mercenaries included. The nucleus of each army was a national force, Roman or Macedonian: and the conflict of two contrasted military systems gave a peculiar interest to the following battle.

438. The term Phalanx, which had formerly meant 'line of battle,' became specialized in the sense of a large tactical unit, consisting of infantry all armed alike with heavy equipment, in a formation of considerable depth. The Macedonian modification of the phalanx, famous in the campaigns of Philip II and Alexander, consisted mainly in a change of weapon. The object of the phalanx formation was to break through an enemy's line by the sheer force of impact. For this special purpose it had to be stiff and heavy, and to present an irresistible array of points in front. Elasticity and the separate efficiency of individuals were quite secondary considerations. So the old Greek spear (δόρυ) was discarded and a long heavy two-handed pike (σάρισα) took its place. That the old shield also disappeared cannot be doubted: but it seems that some kind of target was still worn on the left arm. That the best way of using the phalanx was to combine its frontal onset with charges oi horse on the enemy's flanks, has been well pointed[1] out. But this does not seem to have been the practice of the later Macedonian kings. In course of time the phalanx came to be regarded as valuable in itself

---

[1] By Mr Hogarth in *Philip and Alexander of Macedon.* But in several points I cannot follow his account of the phalanx.

rather than as a part of the general military machine.   In the time of
Philip V the pike in use was over 20 feet in length.   The shaft was
thicker near the butt, or possibly weighted, to make some counterpoise
to the longer part projecting in front of the bearer when he brought
it down to the charge.   Only the five foremost ranks, out of a total
of 16, could thus lower their pikes: five rows of pike-heads projected
in front of the front-rank men: the eleven rear ranks had to keep
their pikes tilted upwards, and are said to have found in them some
protection from missiles.   Their weight, when in close order, added
greatly to the momentum of the charge.   But what actually happened
in the crush, how the hinder ranks ever got the chance of using their
pikes, how it was possible (if at all) to manœuvre the phalanx in any
other way than as a charging mass, are points of great obscurity.   It
is admitted that on hilly or broken ground it fell into disorder and
was helpless.   Even on level ground the least exposure of its flanks
was apt to be fatal: an enemy getting to work upon a crowd, where
every man's hands were cumbered with a pike that he could not use,
had simply to cut and stab at leisure.   Very different was the organization of Roman troops.   Trained to act not only in the legion but in
the smaller units of the cohort and maniple, not to stake all on the
issue of a single rush, going into battle in comparatively open order
with room to ply their arms, elastic in tactical movements, each man
an effective combatant, covered with his shield, hurling his javelin at
the foe and then coming to close quarters with the sword—here was
a force able to act efficiently anywhere and not be thrown out of gear
by the common accidents of war.   The Roman maniples could easily
retreat, reform, and return to the charge, and a partial repulse by no
means implied a defeat.   Nor was it a small matter that the weapons
of the legionary were small and handy compared with the pike of the
phalangite, who plodded through weary marches encumbered with a
clumsy spar.   Hence it was found that, when it was necessary to take
palisades with the column of march for purposes of encampment,
the Roman soldier had the advantage in a greater power of carrying
stakes.

439.   The weather in Thessaly turned to rain and fog, and the
leaders strove to avoid a battle till they could see what they were
doing.   But the armies were close together, and one misty morning
they came to blows on a range of hills known as Cynoscephalae or
'Dog's Heads.'   Reinforcements sent to the parties engaged gradually
brought on an undesigned and disorderly battle.   The place and the
hurry necessarily told against Philip.   The part of his phalanx on his
right wing succeeded in routing the Roman left.   But on his left there
had not been time for proper formation of the phalanx, and it was

thrown into utter disorder by the broken ground. His cavalry had
been sent to beat off the Roman attack on this wing, but had themselves been driven back by the Aetolian horse. Flamininus now
pushed the attack on this side, leaving his own left to make what
fight they could, and was completely victorious. Lastly a clever
officer, seeing that all was going well with the allies in this quarter,
led 20 maniples away to the left, and took Philip's successful phalanx
in the rear. It was now all over with the king. Unable to resist, his
men were cut down fast, and the rest dropped their pikes and ran.
In his flight to the North he managed it is said to secure the burning
of the letters and documents in his headquarters at Larissa, which
were of a nature to compromise both himself and his partisans in the
Greek states. The Macedonian losses are given at 8000 killed and
5000 prisoners: the victors lost about 700 men. The plunder of the
king's camp was no doubt an object of desire to the Roman troops,
and they were enraged to find that it had been seized by the Aetolians before they arrived on the scene. The victory was in the main
a Roman victory. It is true the elephants sent by Masinissa had
done good service, and the Aetolian horse had given most valuable
support at a critical moment of the battle. But it seems that the
Romans had done most of the fighting, and it was their doing
that the great coalition had been effectively held together. No
wonder then that when the Aetolians gave themselves airs as the
heroes of the day, and shewed that they aimed at taking the place
of Macedon as the dominant power in Greece, Flamininus ignored[1]
them and went his own way. The proconsul granted Philip a truce
(for a bribe, said the Aetolians), and arranged a conference with him.
Meanwhile he held a meeting of the allied leaders to discuss conditions of peace. The chief feature of this gathering was the implacable
bitterness of the Aetolians. Nothing, they urged, short of the death
or dethronement of Philip, would ensure peace to Rome or freedom
to the Greeks. At this the Roman, himself unaffected by the deadly
antipathies of Greece, and with wide views on the international situation of the moment, cut them short. He told the meeting that it was
not the object of Roman warfare to destroy their enemies. To make
Macedon harmless to the Greeks was a question of conditions, and it
would be kept in mind: meanwhile, to have it as a bulwark against
Gaulish or Thracian invasion would be in the interest of Greece. He
did not it seems expose his chief motive for desiring an early peace,
which was the news of the warlike preparations of Antiochus and his
contemplated advance into Europe.

---

[1] This was really a slight, for the Aetolians as *amici* of Rome had a right to take part in
negotiations preceding this truce. See § 428.

440. At the peace conference Philip wisely made a dignified submission, conceding all the demands hitherto refused by him, and leaving all doubtful matters to the decision of the Roman Senate. This meant the surrender of all his possessions in Greece and the Aegean. And now broke out an open quarrel between the proconsul and the Aetolians as to the disposal of the fruits of victory. The Roman declined to hand over to the League Thessalian towns that had surrendered on the faith of Roman protection. When they appealed to the terms of their former treaty with Rome in 211, he reminded them that they had themselves annulled this treaty by making peace with Philip separately in 205 without the consent of their Roman allies. The firm stand made by Flamininus on behalf of the freedom of Greek cities (for the once Aetolian towns in Thessaly had only been annexed to the League by force) was approved by the rest of the allies: the exasperation of the Aetolians was extreme. It was now arranged that Philip should send an embassy to Rome to seek confirmation of the peace from the Senate, and in the meantime pay a large instalment of a war-indemnity and give hostages, among them his son Demetrius. Operations of minor importance had been or were taking place at other points. The Achaeans surprised the garrison of Corinth engaged in a careless raid and defeated them with loss. The loyal Acarnanians, now the only Greeks faithful to Macedon, were called upon by the admiral of the fleet, the proconsul's brother Lucius, to join Rome. But the pro-Macedonian party got the upper hand, and it was necessary to attack them. Their chief city Leucas was taken, the news of Cynoscephalae came to hand, and this brave little people were forced to submit. Beyond the Aegean, in Caria, a motley force kept there by Philip was soundly beaten by a not less motley one in the pay of Rhodes. Macedonians were the nucleus of one army, Achaean mercenaries of the other: and the stiff phalanx and clumsy pike were as hopeless a failure as they were on the Thessalian hills. So Rhodes won back some of her lost possessions on the mainland. And now, in Philip's hour of defeat, a host of barbarous Dardani poured over his northern frontier, wasting and plundering the land. The king rose in wrath, hastily raised a small army, beat them in battle with great loss, cut up the straggling maurauders, and drove out the survivors in headlong flight.

441. Rome had a deep interest in what was passing in the East during the season of 197. Antiochus was at last on the move westwards. His sons were busy concentrating an army at Sardis, while he himself with a large fleet transported another force along the southern coast of Asia Minor, landing here and there to receive or compel the surrender of one of the Egyptian forts.   This process was clearly meant to be continued all along the seaboard, and every step brought him nearer to his ally Philip.   But the faithful Rhodians barred the way: embassies were exchanged, for neither side really wished to fight.   The king tried hard to reassure the Rhodians as to his intentions, and pointed to his friendship with Rome, attested by the complimentary letters of the Senate and the reception given to his agents.   Just then came the news of Cynoscephalae.   The Rhodians no longer felt it their duty to stand between Antiochus and Philip, but they did not omit to warn and succour the cities of their own neighbourhood that belonged to the Egyptian connexion; and they seem to have thwarted the ambition of the Syrian king.   Well may Livy[1] (no doubt following Polybius) reckon their bold action on this occasion as one of the most splendid of the many proofs of their loyalty to Rome.   Greece was apparently quiet since the defeat of Philip.   Flamininus had his winter quarters in Phocis, and all were waiting for the answer from Rome.   But the fires smouldering beneath the surface were not extinct, and serious trouble arose in Boeotia.   The Boeotians wanted to get back a body of their citizens who were in Philip's service.   This they effected through the consent and good offices of the proconsul.   The Macedonian party gained the upper hand, and the Roman partisans, in fear for their own safety after the departure of the Romans, assassinated Brachylles the pro-Macedonian leader.   Vengeance taken on the chief culprits was not enough: it was generally believed that Flamininus had been privy to the murder.   Open rebellion was impossible, but assassinations of Roman soldiers became frequent, and at length violent repression became necessary.   The Boeotians had to deliver up the assassins and pay a fine: and the moderation of this punishment was partly due to the intercession of Achaean deputies.

442.   The Boeotian affair seems to belong to the beginning of the year 196.   The news of the great victory had reached Rome about the time of the elections for that year.   The usual ten commissioners, among them Galba and Villius, were appointed to settle and carry out the details of the peace under the presidency of the proconsul.   The new consuls desired the Greek command for one of themselves, but Flamininus was left to finish the business.   Great rejoicings took place, and the 35 Tribes unanimously approved the peace.   It was indeed well-timed: beside the menacing attitude of Antiochus, news was at this time received of grave disasters in Spain.   When the ten commissioners reached headquarters, they brought with them the decree of the Senate on the conditions of

[1] Livy XXXIII 20.

peace. The chief points in it were (*a*) a general declaration in favour of the freedom of the Greeks, (*b*) all the cities subject to or held by Philip were to be handed over to the Romans before the date of the Isthmian games, (*c*) he was to evacuate and set free a number of cities in Asia Minor, (*d*) to hand over all prisoners and deserters, (*e*) to give up his fleet, (*f*) to pay 500 talents down, and 500 more in ten yearly instalments, as a war-indemnity. That he was forbidden to engage in foreign war without the consent of Rome is possible: but the case of Carthage is not analogous, and this clause is not preserved[1] in Polybius. The limitation of his army to 5000 men (which seems at least not to have been enforced), and the territorial rewards of Pergamum Rhodes and Athens, are probably added by Livy from inferior authorities.

443. It seems certain that these terms were more severe than the settlement contemplated by the Greek-loving proconsul. A number of details were reserved for the decision of the commissioners, and of these none was more important than the question of the policy to be followed in dealing with the three ‘fetters.’ It was feared, not without reason, that the evacuation of these strongholds would simply leave them open to be used as military bases by Antiochus in an invasion of Greece. Flamininus, stung by complaints of the Aetolians that Greece was being handed over from an old master to a new one under the vain pretence of freedom, fought hard for giving them up at once. But the unsentimental committee of hard-headed hard-fisted Romans would, in the present position of affairs, give up nothing more than the city of Corinth: its citadel, Acrocorinthus, together with Chalcis and Demetrias, was to be retained until things looked less threatening in the East. And now came on the Isthmian festival : a greater crowd than usual gathered together at the precinct of the sea-god : for peace was restored, and gossip as to the intentions of Rome had aroused the native curiosity of the Greeks. Flamininus, whose appetite for applause was keen, prepared for them a dramatic surprise. A herald came forward and proclaimed that a number of Greek peoples (whom he mentioned by name) were, by order of the Roman Senate and the proconsul, declared free under their own laws, and not liable to receive garrisons or pay tribute. The proclamation was repeated by request, and it came home to the mighty throng that the peoples named were just those that had been subject to Philip. Rome was not flaunting in the world’s eye her patronage of rescued Greece, but restoring to those enslaved by Macedon their heritage of Greek freedom. In the hysterical outburst of joy that followed, the events of the games lost their interest, and Flamininus

---

[1] Polyb. XVIII 44, Livy XXXIII 30 (Weissenborn).

was nearly mobbed to death. But Rome could not give to the Greeks the moral qualities tending to peace and unity, qualities the very salt of political and social life, and without which freedom is rather a burden than a boon.

444. The second Macedonian war was ended, but the sequel down to 194 is really part of the same series of events. The commissioners first dealt with an embassy from king Antiochus. Circumstances had enabled them to take a firm tone. They took the position of protectors of Greek freedom, and ordered him to evacuate the Greek cities he had already taken and leave others alone. They forbade him to invade Europe, and said that some of their number would shortly visit him. Meanwhile they went on with the details of the settlement of Greece. These were in part arrangements to gratify allies, such as the Achaean League and the king of Illyria, who both received extensions of territory; the king of Athamania, who kept his conquests; and recognition of freedom in the cases of the Orestae (a Macedonian tribe) and some cities in Thessaly. The Aetolians were allowed to take back Phocis and Locris into their league, from which Philip had detached them : but they clamoured for concessions in Acarnania and Thessaly, and were referred back to the Senate for a final decision. The same body decided that some towns in Euboea should not fall to Attalus' successor Eumenes, but be free. The commissioners now divided their functions locally and went their several ways. King Philip, advised to seek alliance[1] with Rome and prove his loyalty in the face of the movements of Antiochus, agreed to the proposal. In the Aetolian diet the commissioner was less well received, and the general dissatisfaction was by some speakers violently expressed.

445. The mission to Antiochus was a much more serious matter, and the ambassador specially assigned to this business was reinforced by the support of three members of the commission of ten for Greek affairs. The king had spent the winter of 197—6 at Ephesus, and was busy establishing his authority in the Greek cities of the seaboard, in fact taking the place of the now powerless Egypt. Only Smyrna and Lampsacus, perhaps relying on Roman protection, refused to submit. He laid siege to both, and himself sailed northwards early in 196, took his army over the Hellespont, and made himself master of the important tongue of land known as the Thracian Chersonese. The Roman representatives found him engaged in restoring the city of Lysimacheia, which commanded the isthmus. He was in Europe, and had manifestly come to stay. After the formal courtesies, the parties soon came to loggerheads. The Romans required him to give

---

[1] See § 428.

up all the cities lately subject to Ptolemy or Philip, of whose embarrassments he had been taking advantage.   The other (free) cities
he must let alone : and they would thank him to explain his presence
in Europe at the head of such a powerful force : if it was not an act
of war against Rome, pray what did it mean ?   But Antiochus, flushed
with recent successes, and ignorant of the real power at the back of
these uncourtly republicans, was in no humour to draw back and take a
second place before the eyes of the impressionable East.   He replied
that he represented Seleucus, to whom the kingdom of Lysimachus,
which included Thrace, had passed by conquest some 85 years before.
His claims in that part of the world were paramount.   He was now
recovering from the real grabbers, the kings of Macedon and Egypt,
the possessions of which they had robbed the Seleucids, distracted by
urgent matters elsewhere.   As for Ptolemy, they were now the best
of friends.   If any cities in Asia were to be free, this must be an act
of his royal grace, not the effect of foreign dictation.   As he was not
menacing Italy, and had no designs hostile to Rome, perhaps the
Romans would explain by what authority they intervened in the
affairs of Asia, with which in his opinion they had no legitimate
concern.   He does not seem to have boasted of his present relations
with Philip.   Naturally : to Philip Antiochus was the mean ally who
had left him to his fate and then greedily profited by the misfortunes
of his accomplice.   And Philip was not the man to forgive or forget.
The conferences were brought to an end by the introduction of the
envoys from Smyrna and Lampsacus[1].   The king found that the
Romans took the position of umpires, and flatly declined to be put on
his defence before them.   The conferences thus ended with mutual
exasperation would probably have been broken off sooner but for
rumours of the death of the reigning Ptolemy, which reached both
sides.   Each affected ignorance.   The ambassador from Rome was
instructed to bring about peace between Ptolemy and Antiochus, and
made his duty of visiting the former a pretext for going to Alexandria :
Antiochus wanted to seize Egypt in the moment of confusion certain
to accompany the demise of the crown.   Each wanted to forestall the
other.   The king started with his fleet to the southward and then
worked eastwards along the southern coast of Asia Minor.   On the
voyage he heard that the rumour of Ptolemy's death was false, but he
still designed to annex Cyprus.   But first a mutiny, then a storm,
left his force in no condition to attempt the conquest.   So he

---

[1] The interesting embassy from Lampsacus to Massalia to invoke their support (both cities
being colonies of Phocaea), the influence exerted at Rome on their behalf by the Massaliots,
the letter from Massalia commending the cause of Lampsacus to the Asiatic Gauls, etc.,
should be read in Bevan's *House of Seleucus*, Vol. II p. 45.

pushed on to Seleuceia on the Orontes, and retired to winter in Antioch.

446. In order to appreciate the grounds for the uneasiness of the Romans with regard to Antiochus, we must return for a moment to the affairs of Carthage. The mere existence of the great Phoenician city was a thorn of anxiety in the side of Rome. And now, when the pacification of northern Italy was being taken in hand, it was intolerable to learn that the resistance of Gauls and Ligurians was being organized[1] by a Punic leader. So in 200 an embassy was sent to Carthage to demand, among other matters, the recall and extradition of this man. The Roman dissatisfaction with Carthage was emphasized by compliments to Masinissa, and a request for the help of a Numidian contingent in the Macedonian war. The Punic government did everything in its power to satisfy the Roman demands, and also sent large consignments of corn to Rome and to the army in Macedonia. In 199 Punic envoys brought the first instalment of the war-indemnity to Rome. The silver was assayed by the methods then used at the Roman treasury, and the quaestors reported that it was 25 $^{\circ}/_{\circ}$ short of the proper value. The Carthaginians made up the deficiency by raising a loan in Rome, and we may fairly assume that they had to borrow at a rate remunerative to Roman lenders. Some concessions relative to the Carthaginian hostages in Italy were granted them. Years went by, and things steadily improved at Carthage under the influence of Hannibal. While Rome was busy dealing with Spaniards and Gauls, and trying to produce equilibrium in Greece and Macedon, the great Carthaginian was serving his country as a patriot statesman. Abroad, his policy towards Rome was that of the soft answer. At home he was the champion of retrenchment and reform. The Board of the 104 'judges' had by unscrupulous use of their powers become in these latter days the dominant body in the state. They held office for life, and were now a close self-regarding clique, careless of the general interest. Hannibal gained the support of the mass of citizens, reduced the Judges to a yearly tenure, with reelection only allowed after an interval of at least a year, thus weakening their power for mischief and earning the hatred of the disturbed oligarchs. He then turned to finance. Bribery, the canker of Carthaginian politics, rested largely on peculation, by which the state was regularly defrauded of a large part of its revenues. Taxation was clearly in prospect, to make up for a wholly unnecessary deficit. Hannibal checked the waste of the public resources, compelled the robbers to disgorge some at least of their plunder, and placed the finances of Carthage on a

---

[1] Livy xxxi 11 §§ 4—6.

sound basis of solvency. No act of his life shewed more effectively his magnetic power over the people: none more surely led up to his ruin.

447. For some time past influential men in Rome had suggested uneasy doubts as to the designs of Hannibal. They were primed with Carthaginian gossip by letters from their correspondents there, members of the wealthy governing families. Now that the enterprising Barcid party were under the cloud of defeat, these gentry recovered some of their former power, and had no mind to be once more humbled through the reviving popularity of Hannibal. They knew that the Romans feared him, and they basely invited the help of the public enemy to destroy their own great citizen. They wrote that he was bent on kindling another great war, and already intriguing with Antiochus. True or false, the story found belief, appealing to Roman fears. And when Hannibal carried through his constitutional and financial reforms, the efforts of his enemies were redoubled, and they succeeded in getting the matter brought up in the Roman Senate. Scipio Africanus generously denounced[1] the meanness of entering into the party grudges of Carthage, and placing Rome in the position of prosecutor of a defeated enemy. But he spoke in vain : it was carried that an embassy be sent to accuse Hannibal before the Carthaginian senate of having intrigued with the Syrian king. Settlement of disputes between Carthage and Masinissa was made the pretext of their visit, but Hannibal knew better, and he knew too that the complaisance of the pro-Roman plutocrats would stoop to anything. By clever strategy he escaped safely from Carthage and made his way to Tyre, from Tyre to Antioch, from Antioch to Ephesus, where he found the king busy with plans and preparations for war. In response to the Roman demands for punishment, the wretched Punic government confiscated the estate of the fugitive, razed his house to the ground, and passed on him sentence of banishment. The greatest general of the age was warmly welcomed by the Great King of the East. The combination of these two filled Roman statesmen with alarm : they knew Hannibal, and did not know Antiochus.

448. Greece was at this time (195) enjoying an interval of peace and prosperity, but two storm-centres threatened a disturbance of the unwonted calm. The Aetolians were restless and sulky, and the Spartan question could hardly be shelved much longer by a Roman proconsul who posed as the liberator of Greece. Flamininus summoned a conference of delegates from the Greek states at

---

[1] Livy XXXIII 47 §§ 4, 5, Valer. Max. IV 1 § 6.

Corinth. Even the Aetolians attended. The issue to be decided was whether the allies should or should not free Argos from the yoke of the ruffian Nabis. The fury of the Aetolians broke out in bitter obstruction. It was maddening that while their own claims were held in suspense, Senate and proconsul each referring them back to the other, they, the first champions of Greek freedom against Macedon, should now, after a victory largely due to Aetolian prowess, be asked to bear a hand in adding Argos to the Achaean League, which, though it deserted Philip in adversity, was once a Macedonian satellite. But the other states would not be browbeaten by their denunciations of Rome, calling for the immediate evacuation of the three 'fetters,' and insisting that the Spartan question was being used as a pretext for keeping a Roman army of occupation in Greece. They all voted for the war, and the Aetolians seem to have left the conference in disgust. They like others were called upon for a contingent, but sent none. Philip of Macedon on the contrary sent 1500 men. A premature rising in Argos was cruelly suppressed, and Flamininus had some trouble to induce the allies to let Argos wait and march straight on Sparta. But it was done, and the combined fleets of Rome Rhodes and Pergamum beset the Laconian coast. Nabis was completely outmatched: beside his 2000 Cretans and 3000 other mercenaries, he had only the mass of emancipated peasants, descended from the old Helots, and his case seemed desperate. But two circumstances fought for him. The proconsul was in a hurry to get the business ended before worse complications with Antiochus ensued, and before a successor came to supersede him. And his object was the liberation of Argos and the coast towns, not the rooting out of the latterday tyranny of Sparta. He hoped for a rising against the tyrant in Sparta itself, but Nabis quenched in blood all inclination to rebel. The tyrant however was beaten in one or two fights, a number of coast towns, his port of Gytheum among them, were taken by the allied fleet, and his governor at Argos abandoned the city and fell back on Sparta. He now opened negotiations for peace.

449. At the following conference he defended his conduct, particularly in relation to Rome, and his impudence is said to have been rebuked by Flamininus. But, when it came to a question of concessions, Nabis only offered to yield on a few points, and asked to have other demands put in writing for his consideration. This was done, and meanwhile Quinctius discussed the situation with the Greek delegates. They were mostly concerned to destroy Nabis, and he only checked their warlike ardour by reminding them of the expense and other sacrifices that a winter siege of Sparta would

entail. Livy[1], no doubt following Polybius, gives a sketch of their reflexions, as each thought over the matter from the point of view of his own state. They well knew the general slackness, the jealous tendency of the stay-at-home citizens to find fault with the men at the front, the obstacles to unanimity arising from 'equal rights,' the emptiness of the public exchequers, the stinginess of taxpayers. These things gave them pause, and in order to shirk responsibility they left the decision in the hands of the proconsul. He at once drafted proposals for peace, the chief points of which were (a) the usual restitutions compensations and war-indemnity, (b) special details of the same kind, called for by the peculiar robberies of Nabis, (c) the evacuation of Argos and other towns, (d) withdrawal of the right of making war or alliances, intercourse with Crete being particularly forbidden, (e) surrender of the fleet and abandonment of all naval activity. These terms were severe, but it is clear that Flamininus meant to cripple the tyrant, not to destroy him. Nabis skilfully used the hard terms to nerve his hireling ruffians to a resistance of despair. They clamoured for a renewal of the war rather than give up all they had gained in the tyrant's service, and it is said that he held out hopes of succour from the Aetolians and Antiochus. After some conflicts outside they were driven back into the city, which Quinctius now assaulted with a force of 50,000 men. Sparta in these latter days was a fortified town, but in spite of stubborn resistance the assailants would have completed their task, had not the besieged had recourse to fire. The flame and smoke of the burning houses caused Flamininus to draw off his troops. In a few days Nabis found it necessary to accept the terms offered, and the war was at an end. When the Nemean festival came on, the Roman proconsul was appointed to preside, and the freedom of Argos was proclaimed amid general joy: the Achaeans welcomed the return of an old member of their League. But their satisfaction was marred by seeing Sparta left in the hands of Nabis, who from the nature and conditions of his power was never likely to be other than a troublesome neighbour. The Aetolians made Greece ring with denunciations of Roman inconsistency and the lenient treatment of the tyrant.

450. In the winter of 195—4 the peace with Nabis was confirmed at Rome. For 194 Scipio Africanus was elected consul for the second time, with Tiberius Sempronius Longus. These two were sons of the two consuls of 218, the first year of the Hannibalic war. It seems that the arrangement of 'provinces' for the year led to great intriguing and wirepulling, in which the ambition of Scipio played a part. But the key to these manœuvres is lost. We can only make out that the

---

[1] Livy XXXIV 34.

Senate decided to recall and disband the armies serving in Macedonia and Spain. Flamininus, who had spent the winter in promoting political reforms calculated to strengthen the pro-Roman party in various Greek states, made a theatrical exit from the scene of his labours. He held a 'durbar' at Corinth, and delivered a farewell address to the assembled delegates. The mercy shewn to Nabis he defended as better than the only alternative, the destruction of Sparta: the rest of his policy was approved by all. He now told them that he was about to return home with his army: in a few days the Roman garrisons of all fortresses, even the 'fetters,' would be withdrawn, and they would be able to estimate Aetolian slander at its proper value. Here the part of Rome would end, and he hoped that her work would not be wasted. But 'Greece for the Greeks' was an ideal only to be attained by harmony and moderation: citizen must pull together with citizen, state cooperate with state. The practice of calling in external aid to overcome domestic rivals was the one real danger to Greek freedom. The impressionable Greeks were moved to tears by this fatherly oration, and the proconsul took advantage of their melting mood to make a request on his own part. He reminded them that of the Roman prisoners, whom the Senate had refused to ransom from Hannibal in the great war, a large number were still slaves in Greece. To redeem these men, and hand them over to him, would give him his heart's desire. It was done, though at great expense, for they were not less than 1200 men. Flamininus now sent on his army to the Illyrian coast to be transported to Italy. He withdrew all the garrisons, and gave another lecture to the delegates of the Euboean cities. Last of all he undertook a constitutional reform of the turbulent cities of Thessaly. He acted on the principle followed by the Romans in Italy, of putting power in the hands of the propertied classes, presumably interested in peace and order. His return to Rome was signalized by a splendid triumph. The crowd stared at Macedonian pikes and targets, Grecian works of art, vast quantities of specie, rich gifts of compliment, illustrious prisoners and hostages, and a whole army of soldiers rewarded with liberal largess. But the most striking feature of the scene was the liberated slaves following their liberator, with heads shorn and wearing the cap of freedom, according to the custom of the newly emancipated at Rome.

At this point, when Greece was for a moment left to itself, we may pause and look round to see how Rome had been faring in other parts of the world. For the present it is enough to remark that the achievements of Flamininus redounded rather to his personal glory than to the lasting benefit of Greece.

CHAPTER XXIX

NORTH ITALY AND SPAIN 201—194 B.C.

451. IN dealing with the affairs of Greece and the East we have had the inestimable help of the well-informed reasonable and honest Polybius. Where his text is lost, we have a Latin adaptation[1] of it: for such is the character of Livy's treatment of this section of his subject. When we turn to the foreign affairs of Rome in the West, we pass into a sort of historical twilight. What Livy tells us seems to rest almost wholly on the authority of Roman annalists and writers of memoirs, with whom not only were carelessness and ignorance causes of error, but partiality and prejudice impaired the devotion to truth. Many no doubt were the shades of colouring between the slight perversion and the downright lie, but it is seldom that we have any means of checking these doubtful stories. As for trustworthy accounts of what happened in northern Italy or Spain, we have none. In this as in previous periods there are a few main facts to be accepted with reserve. The essential character of the wars of this period is their utter want of finality. Northern Italy had to be conquered sooner or later as a measure of security, but the exertions called for in Spain and the East, not to mention the watching of southern Italy Sicily and Sardinia, diverted a large part of the Roman forces elsewhere. Spain must be held, but that this could in the long run only be effected by a thorough conquest and civilizing of the Spanish tribes was for some time not understood. Nor could sufficient forces be spared for the continuous development of the necessary forward policy, and the pitiful alternation, of wrongdoing and slackness that provoked native rebellions, with outbreaks of cruel energy in suppressing them, only produced mutual exasperation and horrible bloodshed. Rome had in short too many things to do at once, and did nothing thoroughly.

452. In 201 we read of a disaster to a Roman force in northern Italy, 7000 men being killed by the Boian Gauls. Next year the praetor Furius was sent with a force of 5000 Allies, but a great rising

---

[1] Of course not to be trusted implicitly: from surviving passages of Polybius we know that Livy now and then misunderstood him, and sometimes added details taken from other sources.

of Gauls and Ligurians took place. Placentia was taken and sacked, and Cremona besieged: it was said that a certain Hamilcar, a survivor of Hasdrubal's expedition of 207, was the moving spirit of this rising. A regular consular army had to be sent to the rescue of the colonies on· the Po. A great battle resulted it is said in the crushing defeat of the barbarians with the loss of 35,000 killed or taken prisoners, and Hamilcar was among[1] the dead. But the victorious army was under the command of Furius, the consul Aurelius having been detained in Rome by public business. Hence arose an unseemly struggle over the question of a triumph, which Furius claimed and the formalists and partisans of Aurelius strove hard to prevent. It was eventually granted, but the absence of soldiers prisoners and spoils of the enemy, detained by the sulky consul, made the procession but a poor show. In the arrangements for 199 we find that a praetor with 5000 Allies was to be posted at Ariminum, thus guarding the Roman citizens planted in the *ager Gallicus*. It seems that this officer also took over the army of the late consul, until he should be relieved by one of the new consuls with a new army. Eager to win glory, the praetor ventured to invade the Insubres, who quickly beat him back with the loss of the greater part of his force. The consul hurried to the seat of war, but achieved no great success. In 198 there was again a praetor in the district, and a consul with two armies at his disposal: but again little was done beyond the restoration of Placentia and Cremona, and driving back[2] the colonists to homes where they had as yet enjoyed small comfort and peace. In the season of 197 a more serious attempt was made to pacify the country. The Insubres Boii and Cenomani were in arms, and some Ligurian tribes in league with them. Both consuls took the field, one marching against the Gauls by the ordinary route, the other starting from Genua and moving northwards through the Ligurian hills, making some conquests on his way. The two effected a junction in the plains of the Po. The Boii were drawn off by a raid into their territory, the loyalty of the Cenomani was sapped by Roman[3] diplomacy, and the now isolated Insubres cut to pieces in a pitched battle. The Boii and Ligurians were then dealt with, and general submission gave a deceptive appear-

---

[1] Livy XXXI 21. In the battle of 197, see XXXII 30, the slain were 35,000, prisoners 5200, and among these last according to one story was Hamilcar, who was led in the consul's triumph, XXXIII 23. Such is the record.

[2] Livy XXXII 26 § 3, compare XXXIV 22 § 3, XXXVII 46 §§ 9—11, 47 § 2.

[3] The treaty with the Cenomani and Insubres, referred to by Cicero *pro Balbo* § 32, was probably made about this time, perhaps in 196. A clause in it seems to have forbidden the granting of Roman citizenship to members of these tribes, probably a stipulation on their part to hinder absorption. Rome was glad to grant terms that would keep these tribes friendly while she absorbed other neighbours. The Cenomani had not joined Hannibal. See § 268.

ance of lasting peace. The successes of the consuls were probably much exaggerated. Minucius was even refused a regular triumph in the city, and had to content himself with the makeshift substitute, a procession on the Alban mount. Cornelius was followed by colonists[1] of Placentia and Cremona, wearing caps of liberty. That he had relieved them from siege, and recovered some of them from bondage among the Gauls, was made much of: but this was almost an open confession that the necessary pacification of the country had not been effected as yet. Indeed in the next year (196) we hear again of both the consuls operating in the same districts with even less decisive result. In 195 Spain was the chief field of activity, and the forces sent to northern Italy were meant to be armies of observation. A praetor was posted in northern Etruria to threaten the Ligurians on their rear, and keep them from supporting Gaulish movements on the Po, while the consul L. Valerius Flaccus overawed the Gauls and continued the restoration of the two colonies. But the Gauls were not so completely cowed as had been thought. Flaccus had to fight and beat them before they would be quiet. Again, early in 194, before the arrival of his successor, he had to fight a pitched battle with the Boii and Insubres near Mediolanum. When the consul Sempronius came, he was even assailed in his camp, and seems to have held his ground with the greatest difficulty. Such was the state of things at the time when the Senate was ordering the recall and disbandment of the army of Flamininus and the chief army in Spain. We shall see below how shortsighted and costly this policy proved to be. As for northern Italy, the futility of such half-measures was once more evident at the beginning of 193, when a great Ligurian rising took place. One army invaded Etruria, another laid waste the land up to the walls of Placentia, and the Boii were on the move once more. So serious did the outlook appear, that emergency measures were adopted to meet the danger, as in the old days when Rome was a struggling Italian power.

453. We now turn to Spain, where we find much the same course of events. After the departure of Scipio in 206, the Carthaginians being now driven out, it was hoped that the country would quiet down, and for some years it was the practice to leave Roman interests in the charge of two proconsuls. The one had his 'province' in the North-East of the peninsula, the other further South, the districts being known by the respective names of Hither and Further Spain. These proconsuls were not men of the first rank, ex-consuls, but men who had held minor offices or none at all. Each had under him a small army to maintain his position, but it was not intended that

[1] Livy XXXIII 23 § 6.

these governors should have the conduct of serious wars. Wars however broke out, Rome was far off, and the Home government preoccupied with other cares: the proconsuls had to do their best to meet the needs of the hour with the forces at hand. Thus, when L. Cornelius Lentulus (one of Scipio's successors) came home in 200, it was recognized that his military services were up to the standard of a regular triumph: only formal reasons stood in the way and caused the Senate to grant him no more than an ovation. In the same year Gaius Cornelius Cethegus is said[1] to have won a great victory in eastern Spain, killing 15,000 natives, a very doubtful story. For the next year (199) two proconsuls were appointed as before. Shortly after a deputation from Gades visited Rome. That important city had voluntarily submitted to Rome when the Carthaginians left Spain, apparently on favourable terms. It seems that the Romans had lately been in the habit of sending[2] a sort of resident magistrate (*praefectus*) to Gades as a representative of the paramount power. We must remember that the approach by land was liable to be cut off by native risings. But the Gaditanes regarded this tutelage as an infringement of their rights, and petitioned the Senate for withdrawal of the prefect. The Senate, at this time anxious to get their hands free to deal with more urgent matters elsewhere, granted the request. It was indeed an old principle of Roman policy to secure loyalty of subject allies, wherever possible, without interfering with local government. The return of another proconsul is recorded in this year. Of events in 198 we hear nothing. At the elections for 197 a novelty appears. It seems that the plan of appointing praetors for duties outside Italy was extended. Six praetors[3] were elected instead of four, and two were assigned to Spain. Each was provided with a force of 8000 foot and 400 horse, all drawn from the Allies. An important instruction given them by the Senate was the order to determine the boundary between the two provinces. The exact line taken is uncertain, but it was probably a good distance to the south of the Ebro. These new arrangements shewed plainly that Rome meant to stay in the Iberian peninsula, and may have been in some degree the cause of the risings that now followed. Late in 197 bad news came from the praetor in the Further Spain. A number of the southern tribes were up in arms, and it was practically certain that the insurrection would spread. The Senate well knew that there was no army on the spot able to put down a widespread rising, and at last

---

[1] Livy XXXI 49 § 7. This is a good instance of the utter uncertainty of our record. Beside the exaggeration of annalists, errors of MSS. (frequent in the case of numbers) must be taken into account.

[2] Livy XXXII 2 § 5.   [3] Livy XXXII 28 §§ 6, 11.

began to treat Spanish affairs seriously. Before the arrangements
for 196 were made, their anxiety was increased by news of a great
disaster in the Hither Spain. Beside reinforcements of Allies, a
Roman legion was set apart for each province, and these new troops
were despatched to the front with all speed. At this juncture we
read of the return of two former proconsuls with Spanish booty.
One of them even had a belated ovation for successes the hollow-
ness of which was now manifest, Rome being face to face with the
necessity for a regular war.

454. Of the consuls for 195, L. Valerius Flaccus and M. Porcius
Cato, one was to go to Spain, and the lot fell on Cato. He was to
have two Roman legions, and the praetors each one: there were also
large contingents from the Allies. The total strength of the forces
is not clear, but it was probably about 50,000 men. News came of a
success in the nearer province, but the worth of these successes seems
now to have been better understood: anyhow the plans made were
carried out, and Cato sailed for the Hither Spain. The passage of
the great convoy seems to have been uneventful. Rome's old ally
Massalia was the head of the remaining Greek settlements in those
parts, and it was at one of these, Emporiae[1], that the landing of the
army took place. The actual Greek quarter of the town was small,
strongly fortified with a wall of its own, jealously guarded: for the
Greeks, though only peaceful traders, dared not put themselves in the
power of the natives, and lived under the conditions of a military
camp. Cato set to work to collect intelligence of the enemy, while
he trained his raw troops. He sent back to Rome the corn-con-
tractors who were with the army, meaning to feed his men on the
enemy's corn, and made a start by engaging in a local raid. He soon
had an illustration of the unsafe state of the country. A praetor
returning victorious from Further Spain reached his camp: but it
appeared that he had only fought his way through with difficulty,
though guarded by a strong escort. And now Cato's real campaign
began. A friendly chief, hard pressed by the insurgents, sent a
pitiful appeal for help. The consul had barely enough men for his
main task, and was driven to the miserable shift of promising relief
and breaking the promise. But he gave relief in another and better
way. After trying the temper of his men in successful raids, he
marched inland and brought to battle the main army of the rebels.
The cool tactics of the Roman general and the discipline of his troops
gained a great victory. The advantage was followed up, and in a
short time the district north of the Ebro was once more submissive to
Rome. A number of prisoners were recovered from captivity. Minor

[1] Livy XXXIV 8, 9, Strabo III 4 § 8 (p. 159).

rebellions were promptly put down, but forgiveness was not repeated: after a second revolt he simply took the survivors and sold them for slaves. News soon came of a great victory over the less warlike tribes of the South gained by the praetor of the further province. Meanwhile Cato was busy disarming the tribes north of the Ebro, and dismantling their walled towns. This last measure[1] he is said to have carried out by a ruse. The order was delivered to all the towns on the same day: instant compliance was required, under threat of war. Each town fancied that it alone was affected, and general obedience was the result. The story somewhat strains our belief, but it seems at least not to be a late invention. Like the number of towns thus dealt with (400), it is probably a contemporary exaggeration, perhaps derived from Cato himself. That the difficulties with which he had to contend were very great, and that his success was attained by remarkable energy and self-control, we have no reason to doubt. Of the war in the South we only hear that the defeated natives hired a force of Celtiberians, the race of mixed blood who held a large part of central Spain. The consul was unable to win over this mercenary host, and in the Further province things seem to have been at a standstill. He now withdrew with a small force to the Ebro, and effected some minor conquests in the North. Not content with pacifying the country by force, he increased its prosperity by the promotion[2] of mining, which became an important feature in the economic life of Spain. In the last stages of his administration in the West Cato may have been hampered by the workings of party intrigues at Rome. Scipio Africanus and Cato had been enemies ever since their quarrel in Sicily. The great man had done little since his return from Africa: his glory was growing stale, while Flamininus and Cato were winning fresh laurels in the East and West. The elections and the assignment of provinces for 194 were within sight, and it seems certain that Scipio aimed at securing for himself a second consulship, and with it some important charge out of Italy, in which he might find an opportunity to revive his wasting renown. He won the consulship, but the majority of the Senate, with whom he was unpopular, treated the troubles in Greece and Spain as ended, and recalled and disbanded both armies. What actually followed it is, in the confusion of our authorities, impossible to tell. It would seem that the thwarting of Scipio's ambition was complete, but that the determination to keep him out of Spain as well as Greece led the Senate to recall Cato also. Two praetors were appointed as before, and Cato returned to a well-earned triumph.

[1] Frontinus *strat.* I 1 § 1, Livy XXXIV 17.
[2] Livy XXXIV 21 § 7. From Pliny *N. H.* XXXIII 96, 97, we learn that in this he was only following the precedent set by Hannibal. For Spanish mining see Strabo III 2 §§ 8—11.

CHAPTER XXX

WARS IN GREECE AND THE EAST 195—187 B.C.[1]

455. WE dropped the thread of Eastern affairs at the point where Greece was for the moment free from actual war, though the discontent of the Aetolians was extreme. Antiochus had already gained a footing in Europe, and controlled the Hellespont: he was now returning from Antioch to pursue his designs in the West, and had been joined by Hannibal. Philip was no doubt watching the situation with keen interest. It could hardly escape his notice that the Roman conqueror had on the whole dealt with him kindly, and shielded him from Greek vindictiveness, while his ally or accomplice Antiochus was taking advantage of his weakness to lay greedy hands on the very places which it had been his own ambition to annex. Clearly a decisive struggle was at hand to settle the question, who was to be master in the lands round the Aegean;—who in short was to be the effective leader of the Greek-speaking world. In this struggle the two principals must be Rome and the Great King of Syria. Philip of Macedon could not now compete with either. But there would be no harm in husbanding the kingdom's resources, fulfilling with decency his treaty obligations to Rome, and waiting to see whether the combat might not end in the exhaustion of both combatants and an opportunity for asserting the claims of a third party. Meanwhile, of the powers of the second order likely to bear a part in the coming struggle, the Aetolians alone were hostile to Rome: and Philip certainly at this time preferred Rome to the Aetolians. We do not of course know exactly how Philip argued. But the above were obvious considerations suggested by notorious facts, and they correspond with the actual course of Macedonian policy, which is one of the most interesting circumstances connected with the following war.

456. A good deal of negotiation was attempted in the year 193, for each of the rivals wished to have at least the appearance of maintaining a just cause and appealing unwillingly to arms. The Roman

---

[1] Our chief authorities are Polybius XVIII—XXII, Livy XXXIII—XXXVIII. On various points help is given by Appian (*Syr.*), Plutarch (*Flamininus* and *Philopoemen*), fragments of Diodorus XXVIII, XXIX, and stray notices elsewhere. Only a few references are given on points of special interest.

position was that, if the king entered Europe, then they had a just ground for intervening in Asia: if he was to have a free hand in Asia, he must leave them the same in Europe. On the part of Antiochus it was replied that he had hereditary rights in Europe, while they had no right at all in Asia. To him it seemed only natural and proper that he should win back all the places that had at any time belonged to the house of Seleucus. To the Romans, speaking as the champions of Greek freedom, it seemed more important to uphold wherever possible the cherished autonomy of Greek cities than to allow the king to reestablish an obsolete overlordship by the sword. There was no possible way of reconciling the two contentions; but neither party was as yet ready to fight, and the exchange of futile embassies went on. Meanwhile the Greek envoys at Rome were assured that Rome did not intend to leave them in the lurch.

457. Antiochus had no mind to abate his demands, and was seeking to strengthen himself by various means. In the dynastic policy of the eastern courts matrimonial alliances played a considerable part, and the king saw in his daughters a valuable asset, which he resolved to employ to the best advantage. One was married to the young Ptolemy, another to the king of Cappadocia. A third was offered to Eumenes of Pergamum, but declined with thanks. That judicious ruler knew better than to weaken his connexion with Rome. Another important step was to utilize the willing service of Hannibal. Now in order to do this with effect it was first necessary to give the great general full powers, and leave in his competent hands the direction of the coming war. But this was just what could not in practice be done. Autocrats are apt to be jealous of those whom they employ, and in particular to look askance on great military distinction. They are as a rule ill informed, for their dependents curry favour by colouring or suppressing unwelcome truths. And Antiochus was as others. Indeed circumstances made it exceptionally difficult for him to form a sound judgment of the situation. Of the three royal houses that claimed to share the mantle of the great Alexander, that of Egypt had sunk very low, that of Macedon had just suffered crushing defeat: only the house of Seleucus enjoyed with its wealth the prestige of recent victories. And the Seleucid kingdom embraced that part of Alexander's empire in virtue of which he had stood before the world as successor of the Persian monarchy, as the Great King, an institution congenial to the East and for centuries impressive to the West. As for Rome, she had only with extreme difficulty overcome Carthage: and the Phoenician motherland of Carthage was but a small segment of the sea-fringe of Syria. No wonder then that Antiochus underrated the real strength of

Rome, and mistook her studied moderation for conscious weakness: or that Hannibal, jealously thrust into the background, toiled and suffered in vain.

458. When the great Carthaginian was invited to express his views, he laid stress on what seemed to him the first condition of success, a vigorous offensive movement into Italy. There they could live at the enemy's cost, and rouse his unwilling subjects to revolt. This was the only practical way: to leave the Romans free to employ the resources of Italy in war abroad would mean giving them the victory. For himself, with ships and a small army he was ready to visit Carthage. Whether they rose in rebellion or not, he would land somewhere in Italy and stir up a war. The King could cooperate by invading Greece in force and watching the turn of events. But to let all the world see that the credit of success really belonged to Hannibal was not to the taste of Antiochus and his courtier favourites. It seems however that the exile was allowed to communicate with his friends at Carthage. This, fearing to put his thoughts into writing, he did by means of a trusty agent. But the man was recognized and his purpose suspected. The pro-Roman plutocrats wanted to arrest him and hand him over to Rome: but he made his escape and cleverly contrived not to get Hannibal's sympathizers into trouble. The Punic rulers (such was Carthage at this time) obsequiously reported the affair to the Roman Senate and thought this a good opportunity to complain of the encroachments of Masinissa. That troublesome neighbour had seized Carthaginian territory and was drawing tribute therefrom. The Senate heard envoys from both parties and sent commissioners to settle the boundary questions raised. But these umpires, acting probably under secret instructions, settled nothing; which meant that Rome left the king of Numidia free to repeat the process at will. Evidently not much was to be hoped for from Carthage in the way of help against Rome: and nothing whatever, unless Hannibal himself were sent with a fleet and army. Hannibal's advice had been disregarded, and the first hope of Antiochus had failed.

459. There remained his project of crossing over to Greece and making that country the seat of war. Hannibal had warned him against this as a separate plan, but the king had a blind belief in his own strength, and temptations to adopt this course were not wanting. The Aetolians had been put in the background by Rome, and were resolved to take their revenge. They succeeded in stirring up Nabis to local warfare for the recovery of the lost coast towns of Laconia, but the Achaeans were watching the tyrant, and took precautions to check his movements, and reported his outbreak to Rome. With

Philip the Aetolian emissary seems to have had no success. The king of Macedon had little reason to trust his old enemies, and the Romans held his favourite son as a hostage. He had probably also observed that the friends of Rome as a rule fared better than her enemies. Antiochus however lent a willing ear to their proposals: his own designs pointed to a campaign in Greece, and his vanity was flattered by the Aetolian appeal. He had only to appear, they told him, and he would find ample support: Philip and Nabis were only waiting for the right moment to join in the war of liberation. The success of the Romans hitherto had been really due to Aetolian aid, and the whole force of the League would now be at the disposal of the king of Syria. Antiochus only too readily believed this rubbish, and in some form or other gave them to understand that he would come.

460. The exact order of events is not clear, but it must have been about this time (early in 193) that a final embassy from Rome to Antiochus landed in Asia. Their instructions were to visit king Eumenes on the way. Eumenes was all for war, and indeed the security of his throne was involved in the overthrow of Antiochus. The latter was for the moment engaged in a local war, asserting his sovranty in Pisidia. Conferences took place with the king himself and with one of his trusted ministers. But nothing came of these meetings, for neither side was willing to make material concessions: at last there was an end of idle bickering, and they parted. Incompatible claims were now to be settled by the sword. At this point it is not out of place to revert to the grave disadvantage under which Antiochus lay through ignorance of the facts of the situation. His Greek advisers either did not know, or did not dare to tell him, that no trustworthy support awaited him in Greece, and that his only chance of success lay in taking with him a large and efficient army of his own. The Romans on the contrary were regularly furnished with the latest intelligence from Pergamum and Rhodes, and from their partisans in the Greek states, whose fortunes were bound up with the stability of Roman influence. In one quarter alone could Antiochus learn the truth: but Hannibal was out of favour at court, all the more as he had not shunned social intercourse[1] with the Roman ambassadors during their sojourn at Ephesus, and malicious rivals put the worst construction on his civility. It was at this juncture that he is said to have regained the royal confidence by telling the story of the

[1] Whether there is any truth in the story (apparently derived from Polybius) that Scipio Africanus came on an embassy to Ephesus and there conversed with Hannibal, it is hardly possible to tell. It is a picturesque episode in the Scipionic legend, and is at the least highly coloured. See Weissenborn on Livy XXXV 14, Appian *Syr.* 9—11.

oath sworn in childhood to his father Hamilcar, that he would be
Rome's enemy till death. He was once more summoned to councils
of war: but the foolish plan of campaign, based on false assumptions,
was already approved, and the use to which the greatest strategist of
the age was turned was no more than the charge of minor operations
without effect upon the general result.

461. While the king's courtiers were inflating their master with
brave words and assurances of easy victory, grim business-like preparations were being made at Rome. The actual hostilities begun
by Nabis afforded a pretext for raising unusually large forces in 192.
After providing for Spain and Gaul, special care was taken to hold
southern Italy and Sicily in strength, for fear lest Antiochus or
Hannibal should suddenly appear in the West. Coast towns were
garrisoned, ships were built, and a fleet and army held ready to cross
the sea to the help of their allies in Greece. The total number of
troops raised is not certain, but the Allies were (as now usual) far
more numerous than the Roman citizens. As the great crisis was
looked for in the next year, it was arranged that one of the consuls
should keep himself ready to come to Rome and hold the elections
for 191 at an early date. The building of reserve ships went on, for
no one knew how soon it might be necessary to have a strong navy at
the front. The tension of anxiety at Rome was extreme, no doubt
due in great measure to the dread of Hannibal. The year wore on in
uncertainty, fed by a succession of rumours true and false. The
elections for 191 were held, and the army raised for service in Greece
was sent over to Epirus, to be ready for the coming campaign.

462. In Greece fighting had already begun, for the Achaean
League could not stand by and see Nabis recovering the coast-land
of Laconia and becoming dangerous once more. A Roman fleet had
been ordered to their aid, but they could not wait. Their great
general Philopoemen was in office as President. He was no seaman,
but it seemed that the relief of Gytheum, then besieged by Nabis,
could best be effected by sea. His naval expedition was a ludicrous
failure, but he soon turned the tables on his opponent by land.
In a brilliant little campaign he destroyed most of the tyrant's forces
and laid his country waste. He returned home in triumph, leaving
Nabis shut up in Sparta and controlling little beyond the walls.
So far the success of Rome's allies was satisfactory, but it was well
known that an anti-Roman feeling was widely prevalent in the Greek
states, and that the rumoured strength of Antiochus would encourage
many to follow the lead of the Aetolians. When therefore a Roman
embassy, headed by Flamininus, came over to warn the suspected
communities against making war on Rome and her allies, they found

work to do. In general the wealthier citizens were for Rome and the existing settlement, while the poor hoped to be gainers by any change. Such was the state of things in the important fortified city of Demetrias. Here Quinctius succeeded for the moment in suppressing disaffection, and the leader of the Aetolian party fled to Aetolia, where all was now in ferment. Thoas, the chief agitator and evil genius of the Aetolians, had just returned from a mission to Antiochus, bringing with him an agent of the king, and the easily inflated Aetolians were wild with hopes and excitement. The restraints of Roman patronage would be swept away by a prince coming with vast fleets and armies, with elephants and gold. It was now too late for warnings, but Quinctius resolved to make manifest to all that Rome desired peace and was forced into war. He got with some difficulty a hearing in an Aetolian diet, but was insolently received. Before his face they passed a resolution inviting Antiochus to Greece, and, when the Roman asked for a copy of the document, the President replied that he could not give it him just then, but would do so shortly from his camp on the Tiber.

463. The Aetolians had now taken the plunge, and it only remained for them to carry out vigorously the war-policy to which they were committed. The first thing was to seize and hold important strategic positions in readiness for the coming of Antiochus. Corinth was no doubt strongly held for the Achaean League, but Demetrias and Chalcis were obviously suited to the purpose, and the former was by a ruse occupied without serious opposition. In Euboea the Aetolians were unpopular: with help from neighbouring towns the attempt on Chalcis was foiled. The third enterprise was the boldest: it was no less than the occupation of Sparta. In Peloponnesus the Eleans and Messenians were on the Aetolian side. Nabis of Sparta was also their ally, and was calling for support against the Achaean League, to weaken which was an object of Aetolian policy. By an act of gross treachery a force of Aetolians was sent to Sparta apparently in response to the appeals of Nabis. At the first opportunity the tyrant was murdered, but the Aetolians fell to plundering in the general confusion, and the citizens had time to look round them. None lamented Nabis, but Aetolian methods of liberation seemed to call for supplementary action: so they rose and massacred the Aetolians. While they deliberated on the next move, Philopoemen appeared at the head of an Achaean force and offered a solution of his own, which was that Sparta should become a member of the League. He procured some kind of vote to this effect, and the immemorial separate existence of Sparta was at an end. War was now begun, but neither of the principals had as yet appeared in

full force upon the scene. The watchful Eumenes was there, but Flamininus and he could not even garrison Chalcis effectively, much less recover Demetrias.

464. It was now high time for Antiochus to shew himself. Thoas hurried off to report to him the capture of Demetrias and entice him over by lying promises of the allies and the general enthusiasm that would greet the coming of the deliverer of the Greeks. It is said that he used all his arts to dissuade the king from employing Hannibal in the war, and succeeded. We may at least be sure that nothing could have brought the true natural genius of Hannibal into harmony with the false braggart of Aetolia, and we know that the one great man was thrust into the background. Antiochus now drew together what forces he had within reach and set sail for Greece. He received it is true a warm welcome at Demetrias, but the smallness of his force— only 10,000 foot 500 horse and 6 elephants—was not calculated to inspire either confidence or fear. In a few days an assembly of the Aetolian League was held, in which the king was elected to the supreme command of the federal forces. In a speech to the meeting he held out promises of huge armies and fleets, and boundless supplies to feed them: for the moment he asked his allies for food. It seems that there were two views as to the extent of the authority to be vested in Antiochus. In the end Thoas and his party prevailed: but, while the king was given the absolute control of the war, he was requested to bring up his forces. This seems a sign of a very natural uneasiness. If the Aetolians were to profit by the exertions of their ally (and this was their design), that ally must exert himself. On the other hand Antiochus saw in the League his most sure and hearty ally: but from this time forth there was an Aetolian party to whom the powers entrusted to the king seemed excessive. This would not tend to quicken the cooperation on which Antiochus relied.

465. It was however necessary to procure adherents in Greece without delay, and a beginning was made with Chalcis. But the rulers of the city politely declined alluring offers of 'freedom.' They were free, and liked the Roman alliance. The king had but a handful of men with him, and, when invited to prove his professed friendship by going away, had to do so. Such was his first taste of general eagerness to welcome the liberator. But Amynander, king of the Athamanians, was won over by vain dreams of aggrandisement, and hopes were entertained of winning the Boeotians, and even the Achaean League. The Boeotians did not love Rome, but they had had more than enough of troubles in recent years: for the present their answer was that they would wait till the king came in person,

and then consider the matter. The general diet of the Achaean League heard speeches from agents of Antiochus and the Aetolians, boasting of vast resources or past prowess, and speciously inviting them to stand neutral in their own interest. Flamininus replied on behalf of Rome, scoffing at the grand talk and meagre performance of these ill-assorted partners, who, having imposed upon each other, now sought to impose upon third parties. He pointed out that neutrals[1] would be the victor's prize, and appealed to their experience of the good faith of Rome. Now the Achaeans had never been attached to the Seleucid house, as they had to the Antigonids of Macedon, while the Aetolians were old enemies. On the other side, there was thought to be a personal jealousy between Flamininus and Philopoemen: but the Achaean general was too genuine a patriot to let this interfere with his public duty. The Assembly without hesitation voted to follow the lead of Roman policy and declared war against Antiochus and the Aetolians. They sent small reinforcements to the garrisons of Chalcis and the Piraeus, and Quinctius himself took advantage of the moment to put down some rising disaffection at Athens. But at this juncture the luck suddenly turned. A detachment of Roman troops on their way to form part of the garrison of Chalcis was surprised and cut up at Delium: a second attempt of the king on Chalcis was successful: and in a short time he cleared the neighbouring mainland of his opponents, and made himself master of all Euboea.

466. The Romans had dallied long enough, indeed too long. It is true that they had an army in Epirus, but the consul to command it was not yet appointed, and delay was inevitable. Meanwhile in this winter of 192—1 much mischief might be done, and in fact was done. However, war was at làst formally declared, and the command in Greece allotted to the new consul Manius Acilius Glabrio. Religious observances and other formalities were attended to[2] with more than ordinary care, ior the war was not entered on with a light heart. As before, the defence of southern Italy and Sicily was provided for, and the fleet in Greek waters was strengthened. Reserves, both military and naval, were to be kept ready for emergencies. Supplies were ordered from the provinces of Sicily and Sardinia, and agents sent to buy corn in Numidia and at Carthage and arrange to have it shipped to Greece. A consular edict[3] restricted the senators' ireedom of movement: at any moment questions might arise not suitable for decision in a thin house, and the men on whom the responsibility oi government rested must be

---

[1] See § 428.

[2] Livy XXXVI 3.   [3] Livy XXXVI 3.

kept within reach. The importance of having the fleet manned with trustworthy crews[1] was recognized in the raising of men from the citizen colonies on the coast. Some claimed to be exempt from service abroad, but the Senate overruled the claim. The forces newly raised for the war were ordered to assemble at Brundisium, and Rome was now ready to act. At this time Roman confidence must have been a good deal restored by the striking manifestations of zeal on the part of allied powers, some of which had probably been the subject of misgivings as to what course they would take in the present crisis. Ptolemy (who was now Antiochus' son-in-law) offered to take part in the war on the Roman side, and sent a large sum in cash. Philip offered troops money and corn. But the Senate thought it wise to decline these offers with thanks, only inviting Philip to support the consul in the coming campaign. Carthage was ready to contribute[2] and deliver free a large quantity of corn, to raise and equip a naval contingent, and to discharge at once by a single payment the balance of the war-indemnity due in instalments. From Masinissa came a similar offer of supplies, and of cavalry and elephants for the war. The corn was in both cases accepted, but as a purchase, not as a gift. The cash proposal from Carthage was refused, the ships[3] accepted in some form. Our information is far from clear. Of a Numidian contingent we hear later on. From the guarded responses made to these various offers we may perhaps infer a resolve not to place any ally in a position to act as the Aetolians had lately done, assailing the dignity of Rome by claiming the chief credit of victory.

467. While Rome was thus busy, Antiochus was not idle. The source of our knowledge of his doings, directly or indirectly, is Polybius; but he was not with the king, and some details may be matters of hearsay. He was approached by the Eleans asking for help to repel the expected attack of the Achaean League. In order to do this—and as Liberator he could hardly refuse—he had to detach troops from an army already too small. Next came envoys from Epirus, whose chief object was to find out whether the king could effectively protect them or not. If he could and would, the Epirotes would eagerly welcome him: if not, they begged him to excuse them from taking his part openly in a war where they would be exposed helpless to the first rush of Roman vengeance. Antiochus wisely shirked this

---

[1] These were no doubt to act as armed sailors (*nautae*), not rowers (*remiges*). This distinction is clearly brought out in Cic. II *in Verr.* v §§ 51—102 *passim*. The exemption from field service overruled in 207 seems to be quite another thing. See §§ 217, 363.

[2] Carthage was *socia*, the other powers *amici*. See § 428.

[3] Only the fixed contingent, not the extra ships offered. Livy XXXVI 4.

treacherous dilemma, and promised to send ambassadors to discuss their common interests. He proceeded to Boeotia in person, and it was doubtless his presence that emboldened the anti-Roman party to demonstrate in his favour. He only asked for the friendship of the Boeotian confederacy, not for a declaration of war against Rome: but the silly people, in passing a colourless resolution of this kind, knew well enough that they were virtually declaring war. Polybius draws a picture of the utter social disorganization of the Boeotia of that period, a political legal administrative and economic degeneracy, which in its main features is probably true. If so, we need only remark that the prospects of great and enthusiastic support with which Antiochus had been lured over to Greece had as yet not been verified. The present adhesions were rather an embarrassment than a help. The need of more allies was urgent, and the obvious place to look for them was Thessaly. So at least the Aetolians thought. But it would seem that the king had now begun to doubt the wisdom of following their lead: for we hear that the advice of Hannibal was sought once more. Naturally he took a larger view, urging that to waste time over these smaller powers, who would always go with what seemed to be the stronger side, was bad strategy. The key of the situation rested with Philip: if he were once won over, he dare not draw back, and they could then enter upon the only rational policy in dealing with Rome, an aggressive war. If the Aetolian account of Philip's inclinations was false, and he adhered to Rome, the only thing to be done was to order the army now in Thrace to invade Macedonia from the East and so draw him away from the war in Greece. In any case the forces left in Asia must be brought over without delay, and ample supplies with them: at present the forces within reach were too few for their purpose though too many for the resources of the commissariat. Whether Hannibal ever actually spoke to this effect we do not surely know. But the situation was at least such as the advice attributed to him implies. Antiochus was in an utterly false position through having given ear to the selfish liars from Aetolia. Yet nothing more was done than to send for the forces in Asia. Warnings were wasted on an autocrat unconscious of his imminent danger.

468. So they moved into Thessaly with what forces they could muster. One of the first acts ordered or approved by the king was the burial of the bones of the Macedonians still lying on the field of Cynoscephalae. The exact motive for this is uncertain. Its direct result was to inflame the wrath of Philip, who saw in it a reproach aimed at himself, and that by the selfish ally who had left him to his fate. It was probably after this affair that he made the offers of help

to the Romans of which we spoke above.   He also warned the officer
in charge of the army in Epirus, and proposed to cooperate with him
against Antiochus in Thessaly.   But Antiochus was there already.
Larisa, the chief of the Thessalian cities, remained true to the Roman
alliance, but the fall of Pherae, which defied the king and was forced
to surrender after a siege, caused other towns to submit.   For a time
Antiochus and his allies marched about receiving the submission of the
frightened cities.   But just as they were about to besiege Larisa, a
Roman detachment came to its relief, and the king, deceived by the
'bluff' of the Roman officer, thought he had before him the main
army of the enemy.   It occurred to him that the weather (it was
about mid-winter) was too inclement for campaigning.   So he raised
the siege and drew off his men to winter quarters.   The Aetolians and
Athamanians dispersed to their homes.   Surely they must have begun
to doubt whether this sort of fitful and pottering warfare would serve
to check the advance of Rome.

469. Now comes the story of Chalcis, the Capua of king Antiochus,
perhaps highly coloured by Greek gossip.   We hear that the king
passed the latter part of the winter there in heedless luxury.   Though
over 50 years of age, and engaged in a great enterprise, he married
with lavish display a quite young girl of Chalcis, and gave himself up
to uxorious and convivial living.   The army did much as their king,
and were quite unfit for active service when the spring came round.
The momentous season of 191 opened with a campaign in Acarnania,
which was at first successful, but was abandoned when news came
that the consul and his army were in the field.   Meanwhile the
propraetor Baebius and Philip of Macedon had entered Thessaly,
and their combined operations led to the speedy recovery of some
of the places recently surrendered to Antiochus.   Soon Glabrio
arrived with a fresh army of 22,000 men, and town after town
returned to its former allegiance.   King Amynander took to flight,
and Philip made himself master of Athamania.   Antiochus was now
aware that he would shortly be attacked.   He had been reinforced
from Asia, but apparently not so as to raise his army to a strength
sufficient for a pitched battle in the open.   Naturally he called upon
the Aetolians to join him in full force.   But their government was
unable to induce individuals to serve in a cause where the prospects
of victory were more than doubtful: probably the affair of Larisa had
bred a general mistrust of Antiochus' nerve.   About 4000 Aetolians
were all that responded to the call.   The unhappy king had now
no resource left but to take advantage of a strong position, and
accordingly fell back upon Thermopylae.   This famous pass, a narrow
way between Callidromus, a spur of Mount Oeta, to the South, and

the shoal waters of the Malian gulf to the North, had its traditions of the heroic resistance of the Spartans in 480. But tradition also recorded that the pass had been turned by a detachment following a mountain path. The Romans had recently used the same strategic move against Philip in Epirus. Antiochus therefore, as the consul and his army drew near, sent to the Aetolians then garrisoning Heraclea and Hypata, begging them to hold the mountain paths and not let the Romans turn his position. Only half of them obeyed, and these 2000 were broken up into three weak parties. Glabrio sent detachments to force the mountain paths, one of which under Cato, late consul in Spain but now serving as lieutenant (*legatus*) under Glabrio, dislodged the careless Aetolians from Callidromus. The frontal attack had not been successful, but the appearance of Cato's men on a height commanding the king's position soon turned resistance into headlong rout. The king fled to Chalcis, and so to Ephesus, with the 500 men who alone remained to him: the sword and the slave-market accounted for the rest.

470. The result of the battle promptly brought to their senses the weak and flabby allies whose adhesion Antiochus had been at such pains to procure. In Phocis and Boeotia all was repentance and pleading for mercy as Acilius and his army marched through. Chalcis and the rest of Euboea were recovered without a blow. The fleet too was active, and surprised a great convoy of corn-ships off the island of Andros, capturing most of them. The consul now turned to Heraclea, but, though he held out some hopes of pardon in case of immediate surrender, the bold Aetolians defied him. A siege pushed with great vigour by very superior numbers at last overcame their stubborn defence. At the same time Philip was besieging Lamia, but could not take it, and the town surrendered to the Romans after the fall of Heraclea. The hearts of the Aetolians now failed them, and they sent to the consul to open negotiations for peace. A few days earlier they had despatched envoys over to Asia to beg Antiochus not to desert them, but to return in force or at least support them with men and money. They were as yet far from an abject submission, and the lieutenant whom the consul sent to meet them warned them that they must take a very different tone. At last they were persuaded to 'entrust themselves to the faith[1] of the Roman people,' a technical expression of Roman diplomacy meaning unconditional surrender. This the Aetolian delegates did not understand or mean, and when Acilius, acting on the Roman sense of the phrase, proceeded to order them to hand over certain persons, they replied that they could not in honour do so, and the

[1] Polyb. xx 10, Livy xxxvi 27, 28.

mistake became clear, even to the angry consul. In order to procure
a decision from their Assembly, the delegates were granted a ten days
truce: but nothing came of it. Their senate saw that they must submit
sooner or later, and were ready to accept the situation: the mass of
the people would not hear of surrender, and no vote could be taken,
so the truce ran out and the war went on. Their determination to
fight on rather than submit had been strengthened by the return of
one of their envoys bringing money and promises of help from
Antiochus. On his way home this man had fallen into the hands
of Philip, who to his surprise and relief received him kindly, and told
him to chide the folly of the Aetolians in bringing first the Romans and
then Antiochus into Greece, and to suggest that cooperation rather
than hostility was the true interest of Aetolia and Macedon alike.
In short, the king was watching chances and playing for his own
hand.

471. The Aetolians now concentrated at Naupactus, and prepared to make a stand. The consul with infinite difficulty led his
army over mount Corax and laid siege to the place. While he was
thus busy, things were happening in Peloponnesus that shew how full
of awkward questions Greece then was, and the sinister spirit that
was beginning to shew itself in the policy of Rome. The Achaeans
had been on the winning side, and their statesmen—we must remember that the Greeks were 'free'—seem to have thought themselves
at liberty to take their share of the spoils by annexing Elis and
Messene to the League. But these states were willing members of
the Aetolian League, and objected to the change. In the case of
Messene open war was the result, and the Messenians, finding themselves hard pressed, sent delegates to Flamininus to say that they
were ready to surrender to Rome but not to the Achaeans. Quinctius,
who seems to have been kept in Greece during the war as the representative of Roman diplomacy on the spot, at once interfered. He
called off the Achaean force, and gently explained to the President
that such an undertaking ought not to have been begun without
his previous sanction. While he ordered the war to cease, he also
ordered the Messenians to join the Achaean League and to recall
their own exiles. That after seven years experience of Greek politics
this able man acted thus in pure innocence, is hardly to be believed.
Surely he had learnt that the return of exiles, thirsting for compensation and revenge, had been for centuries a notorious source of
seditions in the Greek states. Surely he could see that nothing was
more likely to weaken the ties of the Federal Leagues than the
inclusion of unwilling members. And, when we read of the jealousy
which he soon after shewed in dealing with Philip, we are justified in

detecting the first steps in the cynical policy that Rome certainly employed after this in her treatment of the Greeks. To divide her allies and weaken them by promoting internal discord, to prevent any one power from becoming too strong, were no new moves: but she had hitherto acted towards the Greeks with more sympathy and candour. Flamininus followed up his coercion of the submissive League by raising the question of Zacynthus. The island had once been occupied for a time by the Romans: since then it passed into various hands, and the Achaeans had just arranged to buy it from a Sicilian Greek who commanded there for the last owner, not in his own right. Quinctius claimed it for Rome as a forfeit of the war, the Roman victory being the real cause of the present vacancy of ownership. Some Achaeans demurred: whereupon the Roman spoke in a parable. As a tortoise[1] is safe so long as it is huddled under its shell, but cannot thrust out a limb without risk, so the League would be wise to confine its extensions to the Peloponnese with its natural seaboard frontiers, capable of being easily unified and treated as a political whole. This it is said convinced the Achaeans, and the island passed to Rome. Meanwhile Philip was not idle in the North. He got leave from the consul to proceed with the reconquest of the rebel states. Demetrias submitted at once, and he went on to occupy large districts, such as part of Perrhaebia, the Dolopian mountain country, and Aperantia on the north-western frontier of Aetolia. But Flamininus was watching him, and when he joined Glabrio, now pressing the siege of Naupactus, he called the consul's attention to the matter. In the interest of Rome, he argued, it was more important to check the excessive aggrandisement of Philip than to weaken the Aetolians further: and Glabrio saw the force of this. A truce was arranged to allow time for an embassy to visit Rome, and the siege of Naupactus was raised.

472. When Quinctius ordered the Messenians to join the Achaean League, he had added that, in case they found cause of complaint, they might lay the matter before him. This claim to take cognizance of internal questions was a direct weakening of the federal sovranty of the League over its members, and opened up a prospect of Roman interference in future. No wonder that patriotic Greeks regarded it with uneasiness. At the meeting of the Achaean diet in the autumn of 191 two important questions came up. The incorporation of Elis was deferred: it seems that the Eleans (old allies of the Aetolians) made their application independently, declining Roman mediation. The matter of the Spartan exiles was more serious. Sparta was already making trouble in the League,

[1] It appears that the figure of a tortoise was used on coins to represent the Peloponnese.

and several questions had been recently laid before the Roman
Senate, among them that of the recall of exiles. The Senate had
expressed wonder that this restoration had not taken place. Flamininus now wanted the League Assembly to vote it. The patriot
party, headed by Philopoemen, prevented this, but carried out the
measure themselves later as an act of grace, when Philopoemen
was again President. Very different was the position of the Epirotes.
They lay under reasonable suspicion of disloyalty, owing to their
dealings with Antiochus. When they approached the consul, he
referred them to the Senate, who gave them not an acquittal but
a pardon. An embassy came from Philip also, to bring congratulations on the victory. They were kindly received, and allowed to make
sacrifice and offering to Capitoline Jove. The king's son Demetrius
was set free and sent back to his father. In truth Philip had been an
useful ally, and deserved some favour. We must also remember that
further service was soon to be required of him, and this the Senate
doubtless foresaw. While matters were thus being arranged in
Greece so as to promote a general dependence on Rome, Antiochus
was hoping that he would at least be unmolested at Ephesus. Hannibal is said to have opened his eyes to the unpleasant truth, and he
made ready to fight for his kingdom. He had great hopes that his
large fleet, commanded by a Rhodian exile, would give him the
control of the Aegaean. But the Romans had mobilized a large fleet
also, and appeared off the Asiatic coast. The chief islands and most
of the cities were on the side of Rome: in her fleet, among the allied
contingents, were a Pergamene squadron under Eumenes himself
and even a few ships from Carthage. The fleets met off the coast
between Chios and Phocaea. After a sharp fight, in which grappling
and boarding played a part, the king's ships were put to flight with
loss and took refuge in the harbour of Ephesus. The Romans were
now joined by a Rhodian fleet, and had the command of the sea: but
the land army was not yet ready. So Eumenes and the Rhodians
were sent home, and the fleet laid up for the winter, leaving that of
the enemy still in being.

473. The Aetolian embassy to Rome met with a harsh reception.
They were offered a choice of two alternatives. The one was an
immediate payment of 1000 talents and the conclusion of an alliance
which would make them dependent on Rome in all foreign policy.
This was impossible: to begin with, they could not find the money.
The other was to place themselves unreservedly in the power of the
Senate. They inquired to what matters this power would be held to
extend: but the Senate declined to limit its scope by definition.
For an unconditional surrender the Aetolians were not yet prepared,

so the war went on. The resolve of Roman statesmen to achieve a solid result and be rid of the menacing power of Antiochus is shewn in the preparations made during this winter. Of the two consuls for 190, L. Cornelius Scipio and Gaius Laelius, it was arranged that the former should have charge of the war in Greece and Asia, his brother the great Africanus having offered to go with him as his lieutenant (*legatus*) or Chief of Staff. As before, careful precautions were taken for the protection of Italy and Sicily, for reinforcement of the fleet, and for supplies of corn. A force was provided to hold the Aetolians in check and leave the main army free to operate against Antiochus in Asia. But in fact things were for the most part quiet in Greece during this next season. The Scipios were anxious to push on and finish the war in Asia before Lucius' year of office came to an end. Publius therefore prompted the Athenians to intercede for the Aetolians, whose position was steadily getting worse, and himself supported the application. At last the consul yielded so far as to grant them six months truce for another embassy to Rome. The brothers had now secured quiet in their rear, and could deal with Antiochus.

474. The question before them was, were they to advance into Asia by the direct sea route, or to march round by Macedonia and Thrace. The land route was chosen, probably from fear of what might happen if a squadron of the enemy's ships or a sudden storm should catch the laden transports in an awkward place. The king's fleet had not been destroyed, and the Romans perhaps knew that he was making great preparations for the maritime war. But on the other hand the land route was wholly controlled by Philip. It seems that the king of Macedon had been warned that his co-operation might be required: but, before putting their army at his mercy, the Scipios sent an officer in advance to pay him a surprise visit and see what he was doing. This man, travelling express, reached Pella unexpected, and found the king carousing at ease in the style of the Macedonian court. Next day he ascertained that all manner of preparations were already made to facilitate the passage of the Roman army, and hastened back to report the manifest loyalty of Philip. The army at once started for the North, and was well received and helped on its way by the king. Philip had chosen his line of policy, and carried it out thoroughly. The former ally of Carthage and Antiochus was now the ally of Rome. No doubt he hoped that this alliance would turn out more to his advantage than had the others. Antiochus had not shrunk from profiting by the disaster of Macedon: might not Philip get some pickings out of the empire of Seleucus? Anyhow he left nothing undone to help the

Romans on their way, and the long march to the Hellespont was thus successfully accomplished. We hear[1] of one attack made by Thracian raiders and repulsed by the Numidian contingent. Philip was rewarded for his services by the remission of the balance of the war indemnity still due.

475. And now for a short time fortune smiled on Antiochus. He had raised new troops in Asia, some even from the Galatians, and his son Seleucus was able to keep a hold on the coast districts and to detach some cities, such as Phocaea, from the Roman cause. As usual, the wealthier citizens inclined to Rome, while the mass (in the Asiatic cities a mongrel mob) were ready for change. To strengthen his fleet he drew upon the naval resources of the Syrian seaboard. Hannibal was sent to fetch a contingent from Phoenicia and probably from the Cilician coast. On the Roman side too the fleet had been early at work, but duty called them to the Hellespont, to make ready for the army known to be approaching, and clear the way for its crossing to Asia. While it was thus engaged, a disaster befel the Rhodian contingent near Ephesus. The king's admiral, a typical Asiatic Greek, beguiled the Rhodian admiral by a pretence of betraying to him the king's fleet, and led him into a trap from which few of the Rhodian ships escaped. Rhodes lost the flower of her navy, but the gallant islanders soon sent another fleet to sea. The check however was a serious one: more cities joined Antiochus, and the minor naval operations which followed were fitful and indecisive. The praetor Aemilius now arrived to take command of the Roman fleet. On the advice of a Rhodian it was decided to attack the coast of Lycia, in the hope that by quieting the district belonging to Rhodes the Rhodians might have their hands more free for the general war. It was also an object to prevent the fleet coming from the East from joining the king's other fleet at Ephesus. The expedition was a failure, and the armament soon returned to Samos.

476. In all the earlier movements of the season of 190 Eumenes had borne a part: indeed none had been so active as he. But Seleucus now led the king's army against Pergamum. Attalus, who commanded there, found the enemy too strong for him, and the city was virtually besieged. Eumenes hastened thither, and the Roman-Rhodian fleet moved northwards in support. Antiochus soon appeared in person, and Pergamum with its port Elaea became the centre of interest. And now the king opened negotiations, being anxious to bring the war to an end before the main Roman army came up. But it was the interest of Rome, now that things had gone so far, not to make peace till she could dictate terms, and the clear-

[1] Livy XXXVIII 41 §§ 12, 13.

sighted Eumenes stoutly opposed any such concession. The answer sent was a refusal to negotiate in the absence of the consul. Antiochus then went off on a raid to the North, and presently a small but efficient force of Achaeans reached Pergamum. These troops were so skilfully handled by their commander that they soon compelled Seleucus to withdraw his army. He and his father now frittered away their time and strength in minor operations, unimportant in relation to the main issue, while the Roman and Rhodian fleets watched the seas, and Eumenes was busy preparing the various appliances for transporting the consul's army over the Hellespont. At this time the king's new fleet under Hannibal was expected from the East, and the Rhodians raised another force to prevent its junction with the other fleet at Ephesus. Off the coast of Pamphylia a battle was fought, in which the losses were small, but Hannibal's design was thwarted.

477. Antiochus was meanwhile busy organizing his forces for the war by land. He tried in particular to gain the support of Prusias king of Bithynia, whose territory lay on the flank of the Roman advance. But Prusias heard the representations of both sides, and judiciously inclined to Rome. So another hope had failed the unhappy Antiochus. He returned to Ephesus and ordered his fleet to sea while he himself operated on land. And it seems that his Rhodian admiral came very near to catching his opponents in a trap: accident or Rhodian skill took the Roman-Rhodian fleet out of danger just in time. The great sea-fight of the war followed, known as the battle of Myonnesus, near the city of Teos. Rhodian seamanship, aided by the use of fire-pots hung out from some of their ships, gained a decisive victory, and the king's fleet fled to Ephesus with the loss of 42 ships. Antiochus now saw his enemies in command of the sea, and his nerve seems to have given way under the strain of his disasters. The one serious obstacle to the advance of the Scipios was the strong fortress of Lysimacheia which he had recently restored and garrisoned. It stood in a commanding position, and the Romans would probably not wish to leave it in their rear. He withdrew the garrison, and gave up his last hold on Europe. A pitched battle in and for Asia could not now be long delayed. He saw no resource but to try once more the time-honoured methods of the East and put his trust in numbers. He sought help from the king of Cappadocia, and gathered in forces from any and every quarter. But it was too late to impart any effective cohesion to bodies of men devoid of common feeling or interest, and the product of his exertions was an armed mob, not an army.

478. The Scipios occupied Lysimacheia, where it is said they even found a welcome store of provisions. The army was rested and fed, and crossed over into Asia unopposed. Africanus was delayed on the European side some days by a matter of religion, and when he rejoined his brother he found an embassy from Antiochus in the Roman camp. The king offered to pay half the cost of the war to Rome, and to give up a number of Asiatic cities the cession of which he had hitherto refused. The Roman reply was that he must pay the whole cost of the war and give up his Asiatic possessions as far east as mount Taurus: that range must henceforth be his north-western frontier. Here was a deadlock, perhaps not unexpected on the king's part: for his agent bent his chief efforts to the indirect attainment of his object by winning the support of Africanus, one of whose sons had somehow fallen into the hands of the king. Not only did he offer to restore this youth, but he endeavoured to bribe[1] Publius by promising immense sums of money as the price of his procuring the acceptance of the king's terms. Scipio it is said thanked him for offering to restore his son, an act which would earn his gratitude as from man to man. The offer of money he declined: as a representative of the Roman state his policy was not for sale. He advised the king to accept the Roman terms at once. Now that their army had been allowed to enter Asia, there was no hope of successful resistance. But to Antiochus the advice was unpalatable. He could hardly be worse off if defeated in a great battle, and accordingly he made ready to fight it out. He fell back to a position in the low country between Thyatira and Magnesia[2], and constructed strong lines to stop the onset of the enemy. Meanwhile he thought it wise to conciliate Africanus, who was lying sick at Elaea. So he sent him back his son as a free gift. At this point a strange story meets us. It is said[3] that in sending his thanks Scipio repaid the good turn · by advising the king not to join battle until he heard of his return to the Roman headquarters. If true, this is hard to explain. That it amounted to a suggestion of readiness to betray the interests of Rome on the battlefield is quite incredible. Perhaps the grateful invalid was thinking of the chance of intervening to protect a beaten adversary on the morrow of victory. Flamininus had stood between Philip and the vindictive rage of his own allies: Africanus himself had acted generously to Hannibal. Other Romans might treat Antiochus with impolitic severity, and Eumenes was likely to egg them on. Another story relates to Hannibal, and assumes that he had left his fleet and rejoined the king. After a grand review

---

[1] Livy XXXVII 36, Polyb. XXI 15.
[2] The Magnesia near mount Sipylus. There was another on the Maeander.
[3] Livy XXXVII 37.

of the army, equipped with oriental splendour, Antiochus asked him whether he did not think so great and magnificent a force enough for the Romans. The skilled eye of Hannibal saw only prospective Roman booty in the standards and trappings flashing with gold and silver. Sadly and grimly he replied 'yes, enough, however greedy they may be.' If an invention, it is at least an appropriate one: but it may be true, for Hannibal had a way of being wise before the event.

479. The foreboding was quickly verified. In the absence of Publius the consul Lucius Scipio, who appears as a somewhat helpless man, was mainly guided by Gnaeus Domitius, who doubtless had his own ambitions. To be the virtual commander in the decisive battle was a tempting prospect. Winter was coming on: the consul was not likely to wish for delay, which might transfer the glory of victory to another: the army was in high spirits and eager to engage. So Domitius forced on the battle. In the accounts given by Livy and Appian (probably from Polybius) the exact numbers of the two armies are not stated, but the Romans with allies seem to have been about 30,000, while Antiochus mustered about 65,000 (perhaps 70,000) men. The Romans had 16 African elephants, but kept them idle in their rear: Antiochus had 54 of the more powerful Indian breed. It is curious that we hear nothing of a Numidian contingent, referred to elsewhere. But there were Achaean and Pergamene troops, light skirmishers from Crete and Illyria, and a body of volunteers raised in Macedonia and Thrace. The main strength of the Roman line was the 23,000 Romans and Italians, mostly foot. Antiochus too had his Cretan and Illyrian mercenaries, but the bulk of his forces were drawn from his own empire or from neighbouring peoples. Asia Minor sent Carians, Lycians, Pisidians, Pamphylians, Mysians, Phrygians, Lydians, Cappadocians, Galatians: from beyond the Taurus came Cilicians, and Syrians of various kinds: there was a camel-corps from Arabia, and bowmen and slingers from the land of the Medes and Persians: even Central Asia was represented by some Dahae, wild horsemen from the Scythian border. This list is not complete, for beside the Indian mahouts in charge of the elephants there was a body of mixed auxiliaries. The kernel of the army was a phalanx of 16,000 men armed and drilled in the Macedonian manner. But it was broken up into ten sections or columns each of which had a depth of 32 men. Thus, if we allow for five pike-heads projecting in front of each front-rank man, there would be 2500 pikes more or less effective in a charge, while the other 13,500 pointed up into the air and were more troublesome to their bearers than to the enemy. We have seen above that in the phalanx formation order was all-important. An-

tiochus placed a pair of elephants in each gap between the sections of
his phalanx, as if to make sure of having the order broken. The
other troops, light and heavy, horse and foot, were posted in detachments on the flanks of the phalanx: but the variety of equipment
nationalities and tongues made the motley array of doubtful value as
a fighting line, however brave individuals might be. The scythed
chariots, an old oriental arm, had to be placed in front, for to bring
them forward through their own battle-line was out of the question.
It was hoped that their onset would throw the enemy's ranks into
disorder.

480. Such in brief was the patchwork mass of discordant races
gathered together to do battle for Antiochus: to such a level of
muddled futility had the military pedantry of a few generations brought
the once famous system of Alexander. The accounts of the battle are
not very clear. It seems that Eumenes played a leading part. By
plying the horses of the scythed chariots with missiles he drove them
back upon their own line and threw it into confusion: the disorder
spread from corps to corps as the attack developed: the king's left
wing was rolled up, and the legions began to assail the phalanx.
Meanwhile Antiochus had gained an advantage over the Roman left,
but a prompt rally checked his advance, and he fled from the field.
The men in the phalanx tried to make a stand: but the storm of
Roman javelins and the rush of wounded elephants soon left them,
a helpless mob, to the mercy of the Roman sword. The flying
masses of light troops, horsemen, chariots, camels, elephants, were
chased and cut up by the Pergamene and Roman cavalry. The
losses of the beaten army were estimated at 50,000 men or more.
Of the victors there fell some 350 men. The vain show of military
pageantry had collapsed at the touch of real discipline and efficiency.
One blow had placed the long dreaded Orient at the feet of Rome.
It was her reward for organizing the powers of cohesion and progress
that existed in the peoples of the West.

481. We need not enlarge upon the rush of cities owned by
Antiochus to transfer their allegiance to Rome. Africanus returned
to his brother's headquarters at Sardis about the time when a humble
embassy arrived from the king to sue for peace and ask to know the
terms. It was thought by some that the effect of the restoration of
Scipio's son was to be traced in the unexpected mildness of the terms
dictated. Eumenes too shewed a surprisingly conciliatory temper,
and all went smoothly. The new frontier was to be the Taurus, the
money to be paid to Rome now or in instalments was fixed at 15,000
talents in all, 400 talents due to Eumenes were to be paid him,
and the surrender of Hannibal, of Thoas the Aetolian, and a few

other dangerous characters, was demanded, in addition to the usual hostages selected by the Romans. These terms were accepted and an embassy sent to Rome to get them ratified. To Rome also the consul's messenger hastened with the great news of victory, followed by Eumenes, by envoys from Rhodes and Smyrna, and from a number of eastern principalities and powers. All now knew where to pay their court and seek favour. The true centre of power was no longer in doubt, and the facile recognition of accomplished fact exposed the profound difference, moral and political, of the eastern and western worlds. We must not forget that Rome was still at war with the Aetolians, though truces and embassies had kept open hostilities at a standstill. But the League, never remarkable for its good faith, used the respite to injure Rome's ally, Philip of Macedon. An Aetolian force invaded Dolopia and, taking advantage of the local discontent with Macedonian government, drove Philip's garrisons out of Athamania and replaced Amynander on the throne. While these northern aggressions were going on, the Aetolian embassy mentioned above was in Rome to negotiate for peace. But their tone was so offensive that the Senate promptly sent them packing. When the new consuls, M. Fulvius Nobilior and Gnaeus Manlius Vulso, entered on office, the Senate assigned Aetolia and Asia as the consular provinces for the year (189), and provided strong armies for both. Aetolia fell to Fulvius, Asia to Manlius. The Roman government was in earnest, and the arrival of the news of the decisive victory of Magnesia caused no slackening in their resolve. The eyes of the foolish Aetolians were at last opened to their danger; they despatched another embassy to sue for peace, and begged Athens and Rhodes to intercede for them.

482. Before considering the ratification of the peace with Antiochus, the Senate gave audience to the various embassies present in Rome. Generally speaking, all questions raised on points of detail were left for the decision of commissioners, according to the usual practice. But a question of principle[1] arose out of the speeches of Eumenes and the Rhodians. In rewarding these allies for their signal services it was clear that grants of territory would be made. What was to be the status of the Greek cities planted here and there? The Rhodians begged to have them declared free, and cited the action of the Romans in Greece as a worthy precedent. Eumenes asserted that to do this would make them virtually dependencies of Rhodes, and hinted that the island republic was seeking her own inordinate aggrandisement. He urged that these cities, having stood by Antiochus (those that had joined Rome were of course not in

[1] Polybius XXI 19—24, Livy XXXVII 52—55.

question), deserved no favour, and asked that they might be made tributary to himself as they had been to their late master. The decision was given against him on the whole case, but he was left in possession of all cities that had paid tribute to his father Attalus. In the assignment of territory he was treated with lavish generosity. All the lands to the North and East round to the South-East and South, up to the borders of Bithynia Galatia Cappadocia Cilicia and Lycia, were granted to him, with a strip of Caria north of the Maeander. The area of these new possessions was roughly about ten times that of his present kingdom. Lycia and Caria south of the Maeander formed the portion of Rhodes. So remarkable a transaction must excite our surprise. To strengthen Rhodes was a natural step from the standpoint of Roman interests. It was important to have the eastern Mediterranean controlled by an ally not only loyal but able to maintain a powerful navy. But the object of conferring so vast an empire upon Eumenes is not so clear. We can hardly set it down to mere ignorance, for there were then in Rome many envoys from Asia well able to give the Senate an idea of the countries whose sovranty was to be vested in the Attalids by a vote of the House. If we look at the effect of the measure, we see that (*a*) Rome was not burdened by the retention of territory which she did not want, and which it would strain her resources to occupy and protect, (*b*) this burden was laid upon Eumenes, and in so far as he made his sovranty effective in his new provinces he would be an useful buffer-state against Antiochus and a rival to watch Philip, (*c*) in marked contrast to the treatment of Eumenes, Philip, whose cooperation had been of the greatest service, received no reward, (*d*) the numerous free Greek cities, and the states whose frontiers touched those of Eumenes, were pretty certain to afford occasion for border quarrels, and thereby pretexts for Roman interference. When we review the situation thus created, and compare it with the policy already followed in Africa and Greece, it seems most reasonable to conclude that it was the outcome of cool-headed and far-reaching design. In raising the upstart dynasty of Pergamum to an equality with the reigning houses of Macedonian origin Rome fostered jealousy[1] by a balance of power: she gave away what she did not want to keep, in such a manner as to leave her own hands free for future action, while to friends and foes alike she applied the diplomatic principle of the greatest embarrassment of the greatest number.

[1] In granting to Eumenes at this time the outlying port of Telmessus in Lycia, it may well be that the Romans had an eye to the friction that it would create between the King and Rhodes. To keep these two from combining was an object quite in keeping with the Roman policy of the time.

483. We must turn to the Aetolian war. The consul Fulvius[1] landed in Epirus and opened hostilities by laying siege to Ambracia. The city was strongly fortified and noted for its fine buildings and works of art. It had once been the royal capital of Pyrrhus, but now belonged to the Aetolian League. The defence was conducted with great ingenuity and vigour, and the Aetolians made desperate efforts to relieve the place, but in vain. Meanwhile they were suffering from a Macedonian invasion of the northern districts lately wrested from Philip, and to the South their seaboard was harried by a squadron of Illyrian and Achaean ships. So they were driven to beg humbly for peace, and Ambracia surrendered. Luckily they found influential friends in the Roman camp: we may perhaps infer that the consul himself was somewhat of a sentimental philhellene, from the fact that he brought the poet Ennius as a member of his suite. Stubborn and proud to the last, they reluctantly accepted the terms offered by Fulvius. But at Rome they encountered more difficulty: Rhodian and Athenian deputations pleaded for them, but envoys from Philip were there to denounce them, complaining bitterly of their recent acts of aggression. At length they got the peace[2] confirmed. It placed the League in a position of marked inferiority: its foreign policy was to be wholly dependent upon that of Rome, and its freedom of action restricted: the usual clauses as to war-indemnity, hostages, restitution of prisoners, and so forth, were included. Cephallenia was, though a member of the League, excepted from the treaty: Rome's regular policy was to keep islands in her own hands as a means of securing the passage of the seas. On the whole the treatment of the Aetolians seems lenient. This was partly due to intercession and the goodwill of the consul, partly perhaps to a reaction against Philip, who, himself lately protected against Aetolian vindictiveness, now sought to take extreme vengeance on the prostrate League. It is not unlikely that the principle of balancing powers had also some weight: it might not be amiss to have the growing Achaean League watched by a rival.

484. To return to Asia. In 189 the consul Manlius took over the army, and the praetor Q. Fabius Labeo the fleet, while their predecessors returned to celebrate a splendid triumph in Rome. Fabius found occupation in an expedition to Crete, where he achieved little beyond rescuing from bondage a number of Roman and Italian captives. On the Thracian coast he removed Antiochus' garrisons from the Greek cities of Aenus and Maronea, and declared them free. These places were coveted by king Philip. Manlius, a rising

---

[1] See inscriptions given below § 688 (c).
[2] Polyb. XXI 32, Livy XXXVIII 11.

ambitious man, had a good excuse for an active campaign. The pacification of many of the districts ceded by Antiochus was desirable in itself, if not necessary: but a still more important object was the humiliation of the Asiatic Gauls. They had sent forces to help Antiochus, and were the most notorious disturbers of the peace of Asia: Eumenes had no doubt taken good care to keep their misdeeds before the eyes of the Romans. According to Livy[1] the Senate, in making the arrangements for 189, had had in view the possibility of a Galatian war: and he may have had authority for this statement. Anyhow Manlius, nothing loth to grasp at the chance of a triumph, and finding his troops eager for what seemed to them an easy undertaking, resolved to conduct a punitive expedition into the interior. Eumenes being still in Rome, his brother Attalus was called upon to contribute by his knowledge of the countries and peoples, and by furnishing a contingent, to the success of the enterprise. The army advanced eastwards through Caria into Pisidia and Pamphylia and then turned northwards through Phrygia up to the Galatian border. The consul's progress through these ceded districts was not a mere military parade. He had to settle disputes between communities, to receive submissions, and now and then to coerce the contumacious, as he passed along. He punished resistance by exacting heavy fines of money and corn. He also came upon stores of food in towns deserted by the people at his approach. But a chief source of supply lay in the corn which Antiochus was bound to provide until the formal execution of the treaty expected to arrive from Rome. Manlius extended this obligation to include the feeding of Attalus' men as well as the Roman troops, and the exaction had to be submitted to: no doubt the exercise of supremacy in the name of Rome was in its way worth as much as the extra corn. In short the whole expedition served as a practical assertion of the truth that Rome was the real overlord of the lands wrested from the Seleucid empire. It impressed these Oriental peoples and princelets: as for Eumenes himself, he knew well enough that he was a tenant-at-will But it also impressed the Roman officers and men, who saw in passing the wealth of the country and the weakness of the local powers. Henceforth it was a commonplace in Roman military circles that gain and glory were the fruits of service in the East, a striking contrast to the dangers and disappointments of campaigning in Liguria and Spain.

485. It was a far cry to Galatia, but the actual fighting there did not take long. Negotiations through a friendly chief led to no result, and the consul pushed on to find the enemy, boasting that the Manlian house were the hereditary conquerors of the Gauls. The

[1] XXXVII 51 § 10, with Weissenborn's note.

three tribes or cantons lay from west to east in the order Tolistobogii Tectosages Trocmi. They had it is said hoped that in their distant uplands they were beyond the reach of Rome : but even now, in the presence of immediate danger, they did not form one great army of defence. They reverted to their old method of concentration, used in their migratory days. The Tolistobogii and Tectosages each chose a position on a hill and constructed a stronghold: into these strongholds they severally gathered their families and movable stock. Cooperation went this far, that the Trocmi left their non-combatants in charge of the Tectosages, while their warriors marched to aid the Tolistobogii, who had to bear the first brunt of the war. All had ample supplies, and in their simple strategy fancied that they could indefinitely protract the war and expose the invaders to the destructive inclemencies of a winter in the heart of Asia Minor. But Manlius knew better than to dally with his task. He had prepared an immense store of missile weapons, and delivered a skilful assault upon the Gaulish lines. The position was carried with great slaughter. The Tectosages now opened treacherous negotiations and tried to entrap the consul at a conference, but the project failed. Manlius now attacked their stronghold also, and gained another great victory. The booty taken was enormous. Some three generations of robbers had gathered in the plunder and black-mail of wealthy neighbours: the Gaulish love of ornament and habit of hoarding precious metals have been noted elsewhere. The consul seems to have had trouble with his own men, whose propensity to looting it was not always possible to check. In later times the weakening of Roman discipline was commonly traced to the demoralizing experiences of the Galatian campaign. Envoys now came to sue for peace. Manlius ordered them to make their application at his headquarters in Ephesus. The season was far advanced, and he withdrew his army from chilly Galatia to winter in the genial coastlands of the Aegean.

486. The expedition of Manlius had been carried through with great military skill. His year of office was running out, but he was continued in command as proconsul. During the winter of 189—8 embassies from all parts visited him. Many came to present congratulations and complimentary gifts. The Gauls were kept waiting for their treaty till Eumenes and the ten commissioners should arrive. Ariarathes, king of Cappadocia, sent to make his peace: this was granted on payment of 600 talents fine. In general it seems that the joy expressed at the chastisement of the turbulent Galatians was more spontaneous than that at the overthrow of Antiochus. In the spring of 188 the commissioners and Eumenes reached Ephesus.

Manlius, who was busy in Pamphylia, hastened back to meet them at Apamea, and in that city the settlement of eastern affairs[1] was transacted. The treaty with Antiochus in its final form followed the lines already laid down. It had the usual clauses binding both parties to the friendly duty of allies, the surrender of prisoners and deserters, provision for arbitration in case of disputes, and the like, but with the superior position of Rome clearly marked. What arbitration would mean in practice was shewn by the dispute[2] about Pamphylia, which was referred to the Roman Senate. The king's power for mischief was curtailed by making him give up all his elephants (which were handed over to Eumenes) and nearly all his ships of war (which were broken up or burnt). He was not to send a fleet beyond a fixed point on the Cilician coast. He was so rigidly excluded from the western world that he might not even receive exiles or enlist mercenaries from countries subject to Rome. If attacked by powers in alliance with Rome, he might wage a defensive war, but not receive them as allies or annex territory. Such were the chief points of the treaty. Rome was determined not to be taken at an advantage and forced into another war against her will. The general settlement effected by the commissioners was of course that sketched by the Senate, but went more into detail, favouring wherever possible the cities that had deserved well of Rome. An important new point was that Lysimacheia and the part of Thrace which Antiochus had occupied were granted to Eumenes—a fresh disappointment for Philip. A little piece of dynastic by-play[3] illustrates the situation of the moment. Ariarathes of Cappadocia betrothed a daughter to the king of Pergamum, who used his interest to get the Cappadocian's fine reduced to 300 talents. Thus Eumenes gained an ally to the East of his new territory, and Ariarathes got his pardon 50 % cheaper.

487. It would seem that some kind of settlement or treaty had been made with the Gauls at Apamea. But it was thought well to summon the Galatian chiefs to meet Manlius and the commissioners at the Hellespont. They received a farewell warning that in future they must settle down quietly in their own land, and give up the habit of wandering abroad and disturbing the peace. The Roman army was on its way home. Why the land-route was chosen[4] for

---

[1] Polyb. XXI 45—48, Livy XXXVIII 38.

[2] The district being partly on one partly on the other side of Taurus, the question was to whom it belonged. In point of form the issue lay between Antiochus and Eumenes. So too the Galatians were bound to keep the peace with Eumenes, not with Rome. Rome kept her hands free and posed as umpire.

[3] Livy XXXVIII 39 § 6, Weissenborn.   [4] Livy XXXVIII 40, 41.

their return we do not know: Rome was now mistress of the sea. It can hardly have been a whim of the proconsul. Possibly it was meant as a demonstration to overawe Philip. This is a mere guess: but it is suspicious that the king of Macedon was thought to have encouraged the Thracian tribesmen to attack the column of march. Vast sums of money and other valuables, the property of the state or of individuals, were being hauled Romewards along a difficult country side in long trains of waggons. In an army whose work was done discipline might be somewhat relaxed: the proconsul's enemies said that his slackness and bad management were to blame. Anyhow the victorious troops were at times in serious danger, and did not force their passage through the wilder parts without loss of men and booty. At last they reached Epirus, but it was winter, and they had to wait at Apollonia and did not cross the Adriatic till the spring of 187.

488. We must glance briefly at the course of affairs in Greece. The Aetolians were now quiet, but the consul Fulvius did not take possession of Cephallenia without a struggle. In this petty warfare four months were wasted. About the end of 189 he had to proceed to Rome to preside at the elections for the next year. On his return he found troubles in the Peloponnese. An important reform carried through by Philopoemen had increased the federal harmony and strength of the Achaean League. This Fulvius had not seen his way to prevent, though Roman jealousy was beginning to look askance on anything that tended to solidify the League's power. We must remember that the Achaeans, though careful to avoid collision with Rome, had acted with a certain independence and dignity, and that the League was in the exceptional position of having shewn a capacity for growth since the Romans began to interest themselves in the affairs of Greece. Hence there had already been shewn on the part of Rome an inclination to pose as umpire in the internal disputes of its members: and a fresh out-break of disturbances in Laconia supplied a pretext for intervention. An Achaean force entered Laconia to stop the aggressions of Sparta. Sparta openly seceded from the League, and sought Roman protec-tion. Fulvius forbade further fighting, and referred both parties to the Senate: the Senate gave an ambiguous decision, and the war broke out again. After many acts of violence had taken place, the coercion of unruly Sparta was effected. The old 'Lycurgean' insti-tutions of Sparta were abolished, and the system assimilated to the ordinary Achaean type. Thus a refractory member was subdued and restored to the League: but the sulky conformity of Sparta brought no strength to a Federation whose life-blood was mutual good-will, and was sure to give opportunities to Roman malignity, now more vigilant than ever.

489. The events of five years had made a vast change in the position of Rome both at home and abroad. The anxieties of the outlook in 192 had given place to unquestioned predominance and confident dictation to friends and foes. In 187 there was no present fear operating to hush internal dissensions, and induce men to abstain on public grounds from attacking evil-doers, if personally disposed to arraign them. The private animosities among the Roman nobles were habitually keen, and there was at this time in the Senate a strong conservative reform-party, who sincerely believed that the old Roman virtues were the cause of their country's greatness, and who viewed with alarm the appearance of new principles of action. Their ideal types were Cincinnatus, Fabricius, Manius Curius, and other such heroes of Roman history or legend: many would remember old Fabius the slow antagonist of Hannibal, and had mourned Aemilius Paullus who fell at Cannae. It was true that men such as Scipio Africanus, Flamininus, Fulvius Nobilior, Manlius Vulso, were very different from the old types. But change of circumstances was largely the cause of the change of type. The old narrowness and stiffness of the conquerors of Italy was bound to broaden and become more supple in the conquerors of a world. Contact with Greeks, Macedonians, and the mongrel populations of the semi-hellenized East, required and developed a more versatile character. Contact brought with it new temptations, and familiarity with a new moral code, less simple and rigid than that which had sufficed for the old-time worthies of Rome. In particular, the wars and the diplomatic settlements thereby necessitated were steadily pouring money into the Roman treasury and private purses. Increase of wealth and luxury made life more expensive, especially for public men, while a source of riches apparently inexhaustible had been found. The plunder of camps and towns, the complimentary presents offered to commanders by princes and city governments, tended to blunt the old-fashioned honesty of Roman patriots. Nor was direct bribery lacking; and east of the Adriatic to take bribes was no more than to confess a share of the common frailty of mankind. Thus, when enormous sums, the property of the Roman state, passed through a general's hands, it was suspected, not without reason, that a large part never reached the treasury in Rome. Whether the money deducted to meet the costs of a campaign had all been applied to the ostensible purpose, who could tell? If subordinates knew, they had doubtless shared the peculations. These evils were only beginning in the period under consideration, but they were already so manifest as to rouse the indignation of Romans of the old school. Hence the attacks now made on several successful men: attacks which sometimes found support in the influence of personal grudges or the jealousy of those who had been denied the like opportunities of easy self-enrichment and renown.

490. The first to be attacked[1] was M. Fulvius Nobilior, who was still as proconsul on duty in Greece. One of the new consuls for 187, M. Aemilius Lepidus, thought himself aggrieved by acts of Fulvius, who happened to have been presiding officer at consular elections for 189 and 188. On both occasions Aemilius had been a defeated candidate, and attributed his rejection to Fulvius' misuse of official power. He now sought to avenge himself by arraigning the conduct of Fulvius in connexion with the affair of Ambracia. He laid the matter before the Senate, and brought into the House a deputation of Ambraciots well prepared with a woful story. Though they were obedient to Roman commands, Fulvius had attacked them unprovoked, had forced them to stand a siege, taken their city, carried off their goods and works of art, and exposed them to the brutal extremities of war. But the absent proconsul found a defender in Aemilius' own colleague Gaius Flaminius, son of the popular reformer who fell at Trasimene. He and Fulvius had a few years before held simultaneously the provincial praetorships in Spain, and he now spoke up for his old colleague, and gave notice that he would block all proceedings in the matter till the proconsul's return. But Flaminius fell sick, and in his absence the Senate was induced to pass an order granting autonomy to the Ambraciots and making reparation for their wrongs, and adding a resolution slurring the military achievement of Fulvius. Of the merits of the question we cannot certainly judge. That Fulvius meant to have war when he sailed for Aetolia seems fairly certain, or why did he take out Ennius? The sequel[2] of this attack is worthy of note. Later in the year, when Fulvius came home, he applied to be allowed a triumph. A tribune, acting on behalf of Aemilius, then absent on duty, gave notice that he would block all motions on the subject until the consul's return. But he was opposed by another tribune, and eventually the triumph was granted. In short, the assailants of Fulvius were able in the first rush to carry a resolution assuming his guilt: after a little delay they were not able to affix a mark of disgrace to Fulvius himself.

491. The next to be called to account[3] was Manlius. When he asked to be allowed a triumph for his victories over the Galatians, strong opposition was offered by the majority of the ten commissioners with whom he had had to work in Asia. One of the leading opponents was L. Aemilius Paullus, a man of the old-Roman type, virtuous and poor, whose sister was married to the great Scipio. All

[1] Livy xxxviii 43, 44.
[2] Livy xxxix 4, 5.   [3] Livy xxxviii 44—50.

the chief acts of Manlius were denounced.   His progress through the
ceded districts of Asia and his war with the Galatians as unauthorized
and unnecessary, in fact no better than private brigandage: the mismanagement of his homeward march as having exposed a Roman
army and Roman interests to extreme danger.   The answer of
Manlius to these charges would not, it is said, have availed to save
him from the disgrace of a refusal.   But an adjournment following
the debate gave his supporters time to use influence with individual
senators: precedents for refusing a triumph were rare, and the Galatian war was no trivial affair: and, when it came to voting, leave was
granted by a handsome majority.

492.   More significant than either of the above attacks, was the
movement resulting in the trials[1] of the two Scipios.   Of Cato, who
had spoken against Fulvius, and had probably joined the opposition
to Manlius, we shall say more below.   He had been an opponent of
Publius ever since the latter days of the second Punic war, and it was
now his intense zeal that gave vigour to the attack.   Unluckily the
accounts of the affair are more than usually untrustworthy.   They
rest on the evidence of careless and probably partial annalists: some
details are inconsistent with each other, and the order of events
doubtful in themselves cannot be restored with any reasonable certainty.   We must bear in mind that Africanus was beyond question
the first man in Rome, a fact of which he seems to have been only too
conscious.   His behaviour at times betrayed this consciousness, and
gave offence to the nobles, whose aristocratic principles approved a
more gracious pretence of equality among themselves.   Hence, though
censor after censor placed his name at the head of the senatorial roll
(indeed they could hardly have done otherwise), it was in the Senate
that an attack upon him was most sure of a sympathetic hearing.
Ordinary citizens were less disposed to resent the assumption of
preeminence, and to rouse their hostility it was necessary to bring
against Scipio a serious and plausible charge.   This was found in the
circumstances of the conclusion of peace with Antiochus.   We hear of
a motion in the Senate, followed by a bill before the Assembly, to
appoint a commission to inquire into the application of the moneys
received from the king in the course of the war—the state-booty.
The story of Publius Scipio tearing up the account-books produced
by his brother Lucius perhaps refers to the proceedings in the Senate.
At some stage of the proceedings before the people he is said to have
used violence in resisting the tribunes: when, is not clear.   The
actual trials held seem to have been at least two: that of Lucius and
that of Publius.   The form of the charges brought against each, and

[1] Livy XXXVIII 50—60, Weissenborn.

even the names of the accusers, are no longer to be ascertained. It seems that eventually Lucius was condemned to pay a heavy fine, either in a trial before the people or by a special court of inquiry. Publius withdrew from Rome before the clumsy procedure of a popular trial was complete. A tribune, Tiberius Sempronius Gracchus, who though opposed to the Scipios had protected Lucius from arrest, stopped proceedings by his veto, and the great Africanus, high-handed and impatient, too touchy and self-conscious for the rude jostling of republican politics, passed the rest of his days in retirement at his Campanian villa, a soured and disappointed man. He gave his younger daughter in marriage to Gracchus, and from this union sprang the two famous reformers of the failing Republic. On the affair of the Scipios in general we can form no sure judgment. But that there was some wrongdoing on their part seems probable. Publius was exposed to suspicion through the favour received from Antiochus in the matter of his son. As for Lucius and the money, there was apparently no working system at Rome by which the accounts of a general would be audited on his return from a war, nor was there an independent officer to be responsible for finance abroad. The quaestor was a mere subordinate of the commander: even Cato had not been able to turn that office into an effective check on his superior. It was not surprising that under such conditions Roman generals sometimes proved unable to withstand temptation.

We have now reviewed in their main features the wars waged by Rome between 195 and 187 B.C. in Greece and the East, the settlements resulting from those wars, and the party struggle in Rome to which they immediately gave rise. The light thrown by these events on the condition of the Greek and Oriental powers, their relations to each other and to Rome, is great. The condition of the Roman state, which they illustrate from many points of view, will be discussed in a later chapter.

CHAPTER XXXI

THE FALL OF THE MACEDONIAN KINGDOM AND THE SETTLEMENT OF 167. 187—167 B.C.[1]

493. THE settlement that followed the wars in Greece and Asia Minor was dictated by Rome in her own interest. She rewarded lavishly those allies whose services she was likely to need in the future. to the calls of mere gratitude she was less ready to respond. Philip of Macedon in particular had laid her under great obligations, but in the hour of victory she had treated him with marked neglect. To have increased his strength would indeed have been contrary to the policy consistently pursued by the Roman government, of maintaining a balance of power. To aggrandise Eumenes was safe enough: the geographical position of his kingdom made it certain that he must continue to depend on Roman support. The case of Philip was very different. As a 'buffer' against the barbarians of the North Macedon seemed to be sufficiently strong already, for Philip had (perhaps unwisely) given proof of its remaining vigour in the course of the recent war. Not only had he shared the campaign in Greece, but by his action in securing the transit of the army of the Scipios he had shewn complete control of his kingdom and its resources. He was master in his own house, and defeat had not impaired his people's loyalty. Moreover Philip was hardly the kind of man to settle down into a tame dependence on the Roman Republic, and he had behind him the imperial traditions of the Macedonian crown. Thus it was natural that the Senate and its emissaries should incline rather to curtail than to enlarge the king's possessions: it was also natural that Philip, resenting overlordship, and what seemed to him ingratitude, on the part of Rome, should look round for the means of revenge.

494. Time would enable him to raise another army, as the younger generation grew up to manhood. To increase the supply of men, he settled a number of Thracians on some of his vacant lands, and by

---

[1] Our chief authorities are Polybius XXII—XXX, Livy XXXIX—XLV. Plutarch (*Aem. Paul.* and *Cato maior*), the fragments of Diodorus XXIX—XXXI, Appian (*Maced.* and *Illyr.*), with stray notices in other writers, supply help here and there. I have only given references on a few points of interest.

careful taxation and the development of mines he began to accumu-late large funds for the purposes of war. But he was watched, and the news of his doings soon reached Rome. It quickly got abroad that the Senate viewed him with suspicion: now was the time for complaints of his enemies to find a hearing. During the war with Antiochus Philip had been allowed to take possession of Athamania and a number of places in Perrhaebia and Thessaly, of Magnesia including Demetrias, and since then he had occupied some towns in Thrace. These conquests he expected to retain, but deputations from the several peoples concerned now raised an outcry against him at Rome, backed up by the supple Eumenes, who well under-stood the situation and did what was required. A commission was appointed to visit Macedonia and decide the various questions after inquiry on the spot. Rome appeared as the umpire in the interests of order freedom and justice. On various pretexts the commissioners deprived the king of most of his recent acquisitions. Philip was of course indignant, but the matter of the Thracian cities was the most serious of all. He had laid hands on Aenus and Maronea. Eumenes claimed that these cities, if not left free, should belong to him: this was implied in the settlement made after the overthrow of Antiochus, of whose European possessions they had formed part. Philip pro-tested loudly, but to no purpose, and there was much to be said on both sides. The decision given was evasive in form, for the lordship of the cities was not definitely assigned to either king: but the order for withdrawal of Philip's garrisons pending the final decision of the Senate shewed what was really meant,—Philip at least was not to have them. In the course of these inquiries he had incautiously let fall the remark that his sun was not yet set for ever. The threat was noted, and it told against him. He was now mad with rage, and under the influence of passion broke out into an act of blind brutality. More embassies had been heard at Rome during the winter of 185—4, and Philip learnt that the last hope of his being allowed to retain the Thracian cities was gone. He wreaked his vengeance on the unhappy people of Maronea, of whom a great number were butchered in cold blood by a band of barbarians in the service of the king. A new commission was on its way from Rome, and Philip tried to keep from them all knowledge of this transaction. But they heard of it, and promptly called him to ac-count. The excuses given were brushed aside, the matter reserved for the judgment of the Senate, and the chief agents of the crime ordered to Rome. Casander, who had been in command at Maronea, and could have proved the guilt of Philip, opportunely died on the way, perhaps (as Polybius says) of poison. But it was in truth useless to suppress evidence: the commissioners were fully convinced that the king was guilty of the massacre and plotting mischief. But he was not yet ready for open war, so to gain time he sent his son Demetrius to Rome. During his former sojourn there as a hostage the young prince had been a favourite companion of the Roman nobles: if any one could procure Philip's forgiveness, it was he. Meanwhile the restless king was not idle. On pretence of succouring the Byzantines, he attacked some Thracian tribes, and on the strength of the influence thus gained he is said to have tried to bring about an invasion of Italy by the northern barbarians. About this time he seems also to have sent aid to Prusias of Bithynia, who was at war with Eumenes, and had in his service no less a general than Hannibal.

495. But the affairs of Macedon, where the frequent visits of commissions only made worse the friction they were ostensibly meant to allay, were not the sole occupation of Roman diplomacy in Greece. Much the same line of policy was being followed in relation to the Achaean League. That body strove hard to avoid giving offence to Rome, but had not yet thoroughly grasped the fact that the 'freedom' of the Greek states was in effect the freedom to do nothing without Roman leave. In 185 the League received embassies from Pergamum Alexandria and Antioch. With the reigning Ptolemy and with Seleucus IV (who had just succeeded his father Antiochus III) they renewed former friendship, but cautiously declined a present of ships of war, offered by the latter. Eumenes offered them[1] a large sum of money the interest of which was to provide the expenses incurred by the members of the federal council in attending meetings of the League. After sharp criticism this offer was rejected as unconstitutional and unworthy. The League therefore had as yet done nothing of which Rome (where the whole story would at once be reported) had any right to complain. But, if we reflect that the leading principle of Rome's policy had been to bind her allies to herself and isolate them from each other, we shall see that the Senate would hardly be pleased at the news. That a Roman ally should hold diplomatic intercourse as an independent power with the eastern kings, and receive splendid offers—even though only to refuse them—was certain to arouse Roman jealousy. Again, why was Eumenes so eager to get officials of the League into his pay? We may be sure that this question was asked, and the difficulty of finding a satisfactory answer from the Roman point of view may have laid the first foundations of the doubts afterwards entertained as to the simple good faith of the ruler of Pergamum.

[1] See Polyb. XXII 10—12, Freeman, *Federal Government*, c. 9.

Eumenes was certainly a man prone to exact good value for his money. But, having made the offer, he would not like to be met with a refusal, and the League would have one enemy the more. The Senate might suspect Eumenes, but they would give ear to anything that he might insinuate to the disadvantage of the League. It is true that we have in the fragments of Polybius no direct warrant for thus treating the sequel as partly the consequence of this episode, and that Livy ignores the whole story. But that the Senate regarded the matter with indifference is most improbable. They were keeping a jealous watch on the affairs of Greece, and becoming more and more addicted to the cynical policy of promoting divisions among their allies as the cheapest method of control.

496. Into the internal troubles of the Achaean League we need not enter in detail. The main difficulty was that members had been attached to it against their will, and Sparta in particular was in a state of chronic discontent. As parties successively gained the upper hand, the leaders of the beaten side were driven into exile, and no ingenuity could have enabled the federal government to restore this afflicted member to the ways of prosperity and peace. Nor were the federal authorities always judicious in their action when compelled to interfere. And it was known that complaints against the League would be listened to at Rome. The visits of Roman commissioners only made things worse: their decisions lacked the finality which would have strengthened the League. Sparta was not to be allowed to secede and go her own way: but the federal authorities were not allowed a free hand to assert the sovranty of the central power. Forms were observed, of course: the League was nominally dealt with as an independent state. But the nice balance of powers in a federal constitution, necessary for combining united efficiency with local freedom, was unfamiliar to the Roman mind. Nor was the immediate interest of Rome, as understood by Romans, likely to induce the Senate and its agents to treat the Achaean constitution with genuine respect. When a commissioner requested the League officials to call a general meeting[1] under conditions forbidden by the law, and they politely declined an unconstitutional compliance, a rebuke from Rome soon followed. The Achaeans were advised to pay attention to Roman ambassadors and give them a proper reception, just as their ambassadors were received at Rome. This has a plausible sound, but the foreign affairs of Rome were transacted by a resident Senate, to summon which was an easy matter, and which was constantly in session. The seats in the Senate were held on what was practically a life-tenure, while the legal powers of

[1] See the remarks of Freeman, *Federal Government*, chapter 9 § 2.

the Assembly were fast dwindling by disuse. The League had no such organ. Its officials formed no doubt a sort of 'Government,' but they were changed from year to year, and the power of final action lay with the general Assembly. The real effect of the Roman 'advice' was therefore a very broad hint that Achaean constitutional law must be ready at any time to give way to Roman will. For the present the Achaean patriots were strong enough to refuse mere abject compliance with the orders of the emissaries of Rome. But in the League, as in all the 'free' states of Greece, a party was growing up whose policy was one of unquestioning obedience to Roman orders: a party which tended to grow stronger, and was more and more led by mean men basely pursuing their own private interests. Lycortas (the father of Polybius), who succeeded Philopoemen as leader of the patriot party, fell upon evil days. For in 183 Philopoemen died. · Messene had seceded from the League, and in the war against the rebels the old general fell into the hands of the enemy. Fearing a popular reaction in favour of a man so universally respected, the separatist leaders poisoned him. Such were the pleasant ways of decaying Greece.

497. Before we return to the story of Macedon, we must glance at the diplomatic activity of Rome in other quarters. Accident has preserved a fragmentary record of intervention in Crete. It appears that a Roman commission put an end to one of the chronic local wars in the island, by adjudicating in a question of disputed territory. But we gather from the words of Polybius[1] that they went further, and interfered to regulate the mutual relations of the Cretan cities. Of course it was the same old story as in continental Greece. So much care was taken to prevent coercion of individual cities by the general body, that unity in distracted Crete was further off than ever. In 183 an embassy headed by Flamininus was sent to call Prusias of Bithynia to account for making war upon Eumenes and harbouring Hannibal. Prusias, basest of rulers, allowed the old hero to be surrounded in his castle by the soldiers of Flamininus' escort. All chance of escape being gone, Hannibal eluded capture by taking the poison which he kept by him for the last resort. Plutarch says that the bloodthirsty zeal of Flamininus was disapproved by most of the Roman Senate, and contrasted with the generous behaviour of Scipio towards his fallen enemy. There were however some to defend the act on the plea of necessity. About this time, perhaps[2] in this very year, Scipio Africanus also passed away.

498. In the year 183 there was a rush of embassies to Rome, mostly for the purpose of denouncing Philip. Demetrius was there

---

[1] Polyb. XXII 19.　　　　[2] See Weissenborn on Livy XXXIX 52.

also, to make answer on behalf of his father.   The task was too much
for the young prince, and Philip's own draft of his defence neither
convinced nor pleased the Senate.   But they treated Demetrius with
marked respect and shelved the awkward questions, adding that they
would send out another commission to see that the previous orders
were being carried out.   In fact they gave the king a period of grace
in which to carry out orders that were notoriously being evaded.   But
they took care to leave their own hands free, and their conciliatory
tone only served to cloak an ingenious and malignant device.   In
their reply they mentioned that their gentle dealing was due to
Demetrius, whom it was their wish to honour.   And the reception
of the prince by the Roman nobles was altogether so cordial and
complimentary, that the youth's head was somewhat turned.   He
seems however not to have failed in loyalty to his father.   According
to Polybius[1], some at least of those who paid marked attention to
Demetrius were deliberately seeking to produce an estrangement
between father and son, and a chief figure among these intriguers
against the peace of the Macedonian court was T. Quinctius
Flamininus himself.   Reports of the doings at Rome soon reached
Pella, doubtless not minimizing the compliments showered upon
Demetrius; and the king, irritable and prematurely old, needed little
prompting to arouse his jealous suspicions.   But a watchful prompter
was at hand.   Of his two recognized sons Demetrius was the younger,
but undoubtedly legitimate.   The elder, named Perseus, was supposed
to be Philip's child by a concubine: it was even uncertain whether
he were Philip's child at all.   In unscrupulous ambition he took after
his reputed father: in his nerveless propriety, his avarice, and his
sneaking meanness, he was foreign to the type of the royal house.
Demetrius was the king's favourite, and more generally popular than
his brother, but Perseus meant to be king, and set to work to achieve
the ruin of Demetrius.   The news of the ostentatious favour shewn
to the latter at Rome played into his hands.   It was clear that Roman
interest would support Demetrius at the next vacancy of the throne:
so Perseus endeavoured to meet this by posing as the champion of a
strictly Macedonian interest.   Prudence dissuaded him from open
demonstrations, but there were in and about the court men who felt
their position threatened by the growth of Roman influence.   Perseus
soon had plenty of agents and spies committed to his service and
depending upon his succession for their security and reward.   Meanwhile Philip continued to prepare for war with Rome.   A campaign
in Thrace served as a pretext and improved the efficiency of his
troops.   Next he took to transplanting the city populations of the

[1] Polyb. XXIII 3.

coast into the wild interior, and filling up the towns with Thracian and other barbarians, less accessible to the attractions of Rome. This caused general indignation: but, as if to make himself more hated, he set about hunting down and murdering the children of former victims. In fact he was blood-mad, fearing revenge and not knowing whom to trust. About this time Demetrius returned from Rome, and the tragedy of the Macedonian court began in earnest.

499.   It was not wonderful that the heedless youth should boast of his splendid reception. He may easily have acquired a genuine admiration for the Romans, with whose leading men he had enjoyed such pleasant intercourse. Things were not cheerful at Pella, where a sour old tyrant was surrounded by dependants each of whom was chiefly concerned to promote his own fortunes and to save his own neck. Philip's cruelties had made him detested by the common people, but they were loyal to the king as such: indeed from time immemorial they had known no other government than royalty. The personality of Demetrius was attractive, and in various ways the people shewed their liking for him. In the prospect of his accession to the throne they saw a hope of better times and a revival of the glories of Macedon. Unwittingly they thus helped on the destruction of their favourite. Perseus could only defeat the combination of Roman interest and local popularity by compassing his brother's death. It was easy to alarm Philip by insinuating that Demetrius had designs upon the throne. But Philip preferred Demetrius to Perseus, and the end in view was not reached without long and patient plotting. The rivalry of the princes was well known, and at times broke out openly, with the sole result of enraging Philip. But Perseus had his spies even among the companions of Demetrius: each unguarded word was reported, every act misconstrued: traps were laid for the unwary victim, to bring him into compromising situations. At last Philip was induced to send envoys to Rome to inquire into the truth of certain allegations. What had taken place between Flamininus and Demetrius in reference to the Macedonian succession? Two men supposed to be partisans of neither prince were selected, to discover the exact truth. They were corrupted by Perseus, and brought back a forged letter purporting to come from Flamininus, artfully worded so as to lend colour to the suggestion that Demetrius had thoughts of taking his father's life. The young man, seeing himself out of favour, had of late been more careful to avoid offence: but this devilish trick completed his ruin. Philip now gave orders for his death, and Perseus saw to it that he was murdered without delay.

500.   For two more years the king lived on, gnawed by unavailing

remorse. Perseus now felt secure, for all looked to him as the coming king, and did his will. Philip had one true friend left, named Antigonus. In 179 this man gave him proof of the plot that had led to the death of Demetrius. He had been duped into destroying his favourite son: at least he would try to prevent the survivor from enjoying the fruit of his crime. He roused himself and set about making arrangements for placing Antigonus on the throne. But grief and rage and nightly horrors ended him before he could carry out his plans: Perseus, warned by the court physician, came and assumed the royal power at once without challenge. The passionate savage was gone, and the plausible villain reigned in his stead[1].

501. Among the schemes of Philip interrupted by his death was a compact with the Bastarnae, a barbarous people, probably Celts or Teutons, who were migrating from the North. They were to be given free passage through Thrace, and let loose upon the Dardani, always enemies of Macedon. Something went wrong with the scheme in consequence of Philip's death. When the horde reached Thrace, they fell foul of the Thracians, and it seems that they encountered a terrible storm somewhere in the mountains. In a very forlorn plight they parted off into two bodies, one of which turned back and recrossed the Danube, while the other penetrated into Dardania, where we lose sight of them for the present. Perseus was sending an embassy to Rome to announce his accession and renew the 'friendship' existing between the republic and his father: and he managed to procure his recognition. Meanwhile he put Antigonus to death and made other arrangements for his own safety and comfort. He found himself possessed of an efficient army, and considerable accumulated wealth: of his father's designs he might take over more or less as he pleased. So at least it might seem. But Rome was never likely to trust him, considering his past: and it was impossible for his ambition to move freely without first shaking off the control of Rome. So he quietly went on with his father's preparations for inevitable war. He was probably well aware of his great enemy's weak points: of her fears of barbarian invasion from the North, of the growing discontent of her Greek allies, of the yearly system under which her troops were changed as often as possible, and in which it seemed to be a main object not to train professional soldiers. At all events we shall see that he set himself to alarm the Romans for the safety of their northern frontier, to seduce their Greek allies, and to give a perfect professional finish to his army. And all

[1] The wars (183—179) of Pharnaces, the aggressive king of Pontus, are omitted here. Most of the powers in Asia Minor were involved. Rome only intervened in 179 to keep Syria quiet and to restore peace, the terms of which are given in Polybius XXV 2.

the while he piled up hoards of money with the zest of natural appetite. As to the weak points of his own position he seems to have been less clear-sighted. The barbarians might (and did) prove to be a broken reed. For gaining allies it was above all things necessary to be open-handed with money and to inspire confidence: Perseus was nothing if not stingy and mean, and his character was such that he could hardly be suspected of good faith. The sovranty of a Macedonian king, ruler of both the nation and the army, gave him all the familiar advantages of concentrated power. But to be responsible for civil government and general policy, and at the same time to command the army in the field, is an undertaking that has only been successful in the case of a very few monarchs of abnormal capacity and nerve. Now the capacity of Perseus seems to have been a genius for collecting means, without the nerve to use them for the attainment of his end. He was subtle in strategic design, but unable boldly to carry through a well-devised plan, fatally wavering when all turned upon decision. Of fine appearance, and a marked contrast to his passionate and licentious father in the sober decency of his life and the dignity of his manners, he gradually gained a considerable amount of credit and sympathy among the Greek-speaking world, though few ventured openly to support him.

502. Some time in the years 176—5 the affair of the Bastarnae came to a head. An embassy from the Dardani reached Rome, to report that these invaders were too strong for them, and doubtless to ask for help. What happened we do not know, for our authorities are nothing but stray references in fragments. It seems that the news led to the despatch of a Roman embassy, that after serious fighting the Bastarnae withdrew to their former haunts in the North, and (if we may trust the assertion[1] of a late writer) perished through the breaking of ice in the attempt to cross the Danube. Perseus denied that he was in any way responsible for the movements of these barbarians: it is more probable that, not being yet ready for war, he disowned his handiwork. He was busy at home. Once established on the throne, he wanted to have at his disposal a number of adherents whose fortunes depended on his own. With this aim he recalled to Macedonia men who had run away or been banished, debtors, criminals, and political suspects. The presence of these men in the country would be no small help to an industrious ruler, eager to be informed of everything. As time went by, and he consolidated his power at home, he began to act with more confidence abroad. He dethroned a Thracian king who inclined to Rome, and procured

[1] Orosius IV 20, writing in the 5th century A.D., perhaps here following Livy, whose 41st book is in a very fragmentary state.

the assassination of an Illyrian chief and two of the leading men in Boeotia, for the same reason. So at least it was said. He gave a sister in marriage to Prusias of Bithynia, the enemy of Eumenes and (so far as he dared) of Rome. He married a daughter of Seleucus IV, and thus opened up a connexion with the court of Antioch. He had previously given to the Rhodians a great quantity of timber from the famous Macedonian forests, and the fleet of Rhodes had been brought up to great strength. At his request the Rhodians undertook the safe conveyance of the royal bride from Syria to Macedon, and seem to have carried out their undertaking in a style worthy of a great naval power. They, like others, had perhaps not yet grasped the truth that Rome was more inclined to be jealous of her allies[1] than afraid of her enemies, or they would have been less forward to display their forces in a great naval review. Roman policy ran its usual course. The Rhodians were busy organizing the territories assigned to them in 189. The Lycians, a people long used to freedom and bound together in a federal union, resented the introduction of a Rhodian system of government, the practical effect of which was doubtless very different from the shadowy and intermittent suzerainty of eastern rulers. They rose in rebellion, but the Rhodian forces put down the rising. This however was not the end of the matter. On the outbreak of war an embassy[2] had been sent from Lycia to Rome. Their complaints of oppression formed an opportune excuse for interference. The award of the settlement commission of 189 was looked into as bearing on the question, and Roman envoys were sent to announce to the Rhodians the decision of the Senate. They came just when the Lycian trouble seemed to be well ended, and gave their message, the gist of which was that the Lycians had been handed over to Rhodes as friends and allies, not as a free gift. The effect of this announcement was instantaneous. Rhodes was filled with confusion and alarm: the Lycians again revolted. The Rhodian government thought, or at least hoped, that the Senate had made a mistake, misled by Lycian representations, so they sent an embassy to Rome to explain matters. But the Senate knew very well what they were about, and it does not appear that they retracted what was really part of a settled policy. This affair seems to belong to the year 177. It laid the foundation of an estrangement between Rhodes and Rome, which, so far as it went, was all in the interest of Perseus. Never again, while Rhodes still retained any freedom of action, were

[1] Strictly speaking, the relation of Rhodes to Rome was 'friendship,' not alliance, but this only left Rhodes more freedom of action, which was hardly the wish of Rome. See § 428.
[2] Polyb. xxv 4—6.

the Roman party in the island republic the unquestioned rulers of the
state. Rhodes still followed the lead of Rome, but the old hearty
cooperation was gone.

503. In 174 we find Perseus considerably bolder. It seems that
he sent an embassy[1] to Carthage. Masinissa, a prejudiced witness,
declared that a Punic embassy had been sent to Pella. Nothing,
beyond the keeping alive of Roman suspicions of Carthage, seems
to have come of this move. Perseus next invaded Dolopia, a district
generally dependent on Macedon, and coerced some discontented
subjects, after which he made a progress through northern Greece,

Sketch map of Balkan peninsula about 170 B.C. Roman dominions in black. Aetolia
a dependent ally of Rome since 189. Greece in 'free' Leagues, the Achaean now
including the whole Peloponnesus. The 'free Laconian' district dotted. The divisions
of Macedonia 167—148 B.C. roughly indicated by dotted lines.

visiting in particular the oracle of Delphi, and passing with scrupulous
avoidance of all damage through Achaia Phthiotis and Thessaly.
He took every pains to make friends with the Greeks as he passed:
but his most serious effort to win Greek favour was addressed to the
Achaean League. All through the recent wars the League had been
on the Roman side: their hostility to Macedon was marked by a
decree still in force, excluding all Macedonians from Achaean territory.
But Perseus knew that they were becoming restive under the slow
pressure of Rome, and hoped to make them remember that they had

[1] Livy XLI 22.

once been the allies of Macedon. He wrote a letter[1] to the authorities of the League, offering to restore to the Achaeans a number of their runaway slaves who had taken refuge in Macedonia. His first object no doubt was to open friendly communications with the League and to procure the repeal of the hostile decree: thus he would be able to send ambassadors and use his diplomatic arts to undermine the influence of Rome. The President was friendly, and laid the letter before the Assembly of the League. Some thought well of it, but after a debate the Council managed to block the matter, and nothing was done. The Roman party took further precautions, so that, when soon after an embassy came from Perseus, it did not get a hearing. But the seed of dissension was sown: the more hot-headed patriots had now the hope of external aid to quicken their growing dissatisfaction with Rome. At this time we hear[2] of troubles in Aetolia, amounting in fact to civil war. Polybius, a witness hostile to the Aetolians, traces this outbreak to the pressure of Rome on a lawless people. No longer permitted to bully and rob their neighbours, unused to patient industry, they turned upon each other the arms they had formerly employed abroad. The explanation sounds malignant, but it is supported by the occurrence of much the same state of things in Crete. These had been the two chief breeding-grounds[3] of mercenaries. Commissioners were sent from Rome to heal these disorders, apparently with no lasting success. The war between the Rhodians and Lycians was also still going on. All these troubles were of course to the advantage of Perseus. He was also, we may conjecture, encouraged by the knowledge that the Romans had plenty to occupy them in the West. The slow smouldering wars consumed men, and a plague at Rome[4] had interrupted public business and even made it difficult for the moment to raise recruits for the legions.

504. In 173 the commissioners for Aetolia, charged also to visit Macedonia, returned with the news that Perseus meant mischief and that war was now near at hand. His popularity in Greece was growing fast: the promises of Perseus were more regarded than the solid benefactions of Eumenes. This could only mean that the spread of disaffection was rendering the king of Pergamum unpopular as being identified with the cause of Rome. It was not that men admired Perseus, whose personal reputation was as bad as it could

---

[1] Livy XLI 23, 24, evidently following Polybius.

[2] Livy XLI 25, Polyb. XXX 11.

[3] The great hiring-place for mercenaries had been in Laconia, near the cape of Taenarum. The practical suppression of this market was one of the grievances of latter-day Sparta. See Holm, *Gk Hist.* IV cc. 10, 18.

[4] Livy XLI 21.

be. And now further news came of the troubles in Aetolia, which
had continued and spread to Thessaly and even Perrhaebia. It was
said[1] that they were the outcome of a general rising of debtors against
creditors, an old cause of seditions in Greece. Once more the Senate
sent commissioners to try and restore order. Some kind of peace
was patched up, at least for the time. Whether these disturbances
were fomented by emissaries of Perseus, or were mere phenomena
of Greek distress, we have no means of judging. At this time a
broad hint was conveyed to the Achaeans that they did well in
making no advances to Macedon. Another embassy, headed by
C. Valerius, was despatched to keep an eye upon Perseus, with orders
to pass on to Alexandria and renew the old friendship with the
young Ptolemy VI (or VII) Philometor, who had come to the
throne in 181. During their absence an embassy from Antioch
appeared in Rome. Antiochus IV, son of Antiochus III, had
recently (175) succeeded his brother Seleucus IV. In his youth
he had been at Rome as a hostage for his father. Madness, as yet
only half developed, caused him to be notorious for eccentricities
from the very beginning of his reign. He utterly lacked consistency
and dignity, and his pranks were so extraordinary that his official
surname Epiphanes (Notable) was perverted to Epimanes (Crazy)
by the wags of Antioch. His flighty brain had been greatly impressed
by Roman customs and institutions, and he had a mania for re-
producing them in his Syrian capital: only the outer forms, for in
oriental surroundings the elections and law-courts of Rome were
a childish travesty of the originals. One evil thing, the fights of
gladiators, he introduced in all its grim reality. Such was the king
who now sent one of his chief ministers with costly gifts and promises
of loyal service, to renew the alliance made by his father. This was
done, and the embassy received with special honour.

505. But the Senate had other visitors[2] also, whose errands had
more direct bearing upon the questions of the hour. Eumenes
appeared in person. He strove to impress upon the House the
danger of the present situation and the urgent necessity of war.
Indeed the growth of Perseus' resources, the completeness of his
preparations, the spread of his influence, and the evidence of his
far-reaching designs, were sufficient grounds for rational alarm. Nor,
it seems, were the senators in any doubt as to the coming struggle,
but under the Roman system it would take some time to prepare
for war and place an army in the field: for the present they deliberated in secret and would not shew their hand. Next came envoys

---

[1] Diodorus XXIX 33, Livy XLII 5, 13.
[2] Livy XLII 11—14, Weissenborn.

from Perseus, who were ill received: their tone was less conciliatory than that of previous missions, and they wound up with what amounted to a defiance. Then there were a number of minor embassies from Greek and Asiatic governments, sent on various pretexts, really to gratify the general curiosity by finding out what was happening at Rome. Rome was the centre of things: but was this going to continue? Would she dally with the situation till it was too late? If Perseus became supreme in Greece and had well-wishers in Asia, what were the prospects of the Roman allies in the two continents? Such questions were no doubt troubling all the minor powers, whom no sympathy or gratitude could absolve from the manifest duty of being on the winning side. There was also an anxiety to know what the crafty Eumenes had been about. In particular, the Rhodian envoys assumed that he had been maligning Rhodes, and attacked him for his policy in Asia, declaring that he had encouraged the Lycian rebellion. But the Senate cared for none of these things. They kept their own counsel, though in fact resolved on war. As for Eumenes, Cato and some others viewed him with suspicion, but with the majority he only rose in favour through the attack made upon him, and he started for home under a shower of compliments.

506. The agents of Perseus reported to him that war was now certain, and he resolved to get the start of his enemies. First he laid a plot to assassinate Eumenes as he visited Delphi on his way to the East. But, though a Cretan was put in charge of the business, Eumenes was only stunned and eventually recovered, though reported dead. When he reached Pergamum he found his brother Attalus in possession of his wife and crown, but this caused only a temporary coolness, for it was not the way of the Attalid House to indulge in family quarrels. Shortly after this affair Valerius returned to Rome from his mission mentioned above. He not only confirmed the allegations of Eumenes against Perseus, and brought evidence of the king's guilt in the matter of the attempted murder, but had with him a leading citizen of Brundisium who charged the king of Macedon with attempting a still more audacious crime. This man, one Rammius, had been in the habit of entertaining envoys both Roman and foreign as they passed through the port-town on the regular route to and from Greece. Perseus had made his acquaintance through some of his own ambassadors, had induced him to visit Pella, and, after a most friendly reception, endeavoured by splendid promises to persuade him to undertake the poisoning of such Roman generals or envoys as would be pointed out to him by letter. Rammius escaped from Perseus' court by a pretended compliance, and hastened to Rome in the company of Valerius. It was abundantly

clear that no terms could be made with a king of this sort: so the Senate voted Perseus a public enemy, and set one of the praetors to raise some troops—at last. This was in 172. The war was to begin in the following year, when one of the new consuls would organize the expeditionary army. Such was the leisurely Roman way: but there was now no Hannibal to forestall them with his deadly spring.

507. While the Senate was taking stock of alliances, and wondering how far they might rely on the support of the eastern kings, an embassy arrived from Ariarathes IV of Cappadocia, bringing a prince of the same name, the king's reputed son. This youth he begged the Senate to take in charge[1] as a ward of the state, in short to bring him up as a Roman. The compliment was just then welcome, and arrangements were made at once. Thus the Senate and people of Rome appeared for the first time in a new capacity, as the drynurse of kings. Still more welcome were envoys from some Thracian tribes, with whom an alliance was made, thus threatening Perseus on his rear. But the anxieties of the time led to the despatch of a travelling commission[2] with orders to find out the truth about the intrigues of Perseus and generally to learn the temper of the island powers and the eastern kings. Their attention was particularly directed to Rhodes. At this time too we hear of another of the disputes between Carthage and Masinissa. Punic envoys came with bitter complaints of the king's aggressions. Their pitiful story was listened to, but just now the Roman Senate was more than usually concerned to keep Masinissa in a good humour. So the final decision asked for was not given: the awkward question was shelved by an evasive reply. Before the end of the year an embassy sent to make formal demand for redress of wrongs and to break off friendly relations returned from Macedon. They reported that Perseus was practically ready for war, and that an angry interview with the king had ended by his ordering them to quit his territory. Arrangements were at once made for holding the elections at an early date. Some ambassadors from Gentius of Illyria were found to be in Rome, deferring the disclosure of their mission while they picked up information for their master. They were promptly sent about their business, and Roman envoys were sent to call Gentius to account for a recent attack upon some allies of Rome. Gentius, who ruled a large part of Illyria, was feeling his way to discover which side it would be his interest to take in the coming war. And now the travelling commission returned from the East. They had found

---

[1] Livy XLII 19 §§ 3—6, Diodorus XXXI 19 § 7.

[2] This is drawn from Liv. XLII 19, 26, by a combination of the two passages. But the numerous commissions of this time make a very confused story.

traces of Perseus' diplomatic activity everywhere, but no reason to suspect the faith of allies, with the single exception of Rhodes. The loyalty of that republic had been somewhat shaken.

508. The time before the elections came on was spent in preparations for war. Ships were repaired, crews enrolled, troops raised among the Italian Allies, and a whole legion of seasoned Romans, with Allies to match, withdrawn from the army in Liguria. Agents were sent to purchase corn. This was of course only a force to act in advance, crossing the Adriatic under a praetor in temporary command and occupying a good landing-place, ready for the coming of the consul with the main army. The elections were held, and special religious observances ordered in view of the approaching crisis. We are not however to suppose that the Senate was greatly afraid of Perseus. The sequel clearly shewed that defeat and danger were needed to make them take the revived power of Macedon seriously. But Rome had many other calls upon her energies. Spain could never be trusted to remain quiet for long: Ligurian warfare was an open sore: the condition of Italy was not wholly satisfactory, and a number of lately planted colonies no doubt were needing time to become thoroughly established: Sicily Sardinia and Corsica all had to be firmly held. The situation generally was a serious one: but it was assumed that an ordinary consul would soon conquer Perseus and set the Roman republic free for the completion of other designs.

509. At this point in the story Livy[1] gives us a review of the various attitudes of the kings and free states. It is manifestly an adaptation from Polybius, whose text is here lost. On the Roman side were ranged Eumenes, and with him Ariarathes of Cappadocia: Antiochus and young Ptolemy both made loyal promises of aid, but the pending struggle between them for the Hollow Syria left little to be expected from either Syria or Egypt. Masinissa was preparing to give material help: if Rome won, his present position was safe: if she suffered defeat, he would conquer Carthage and be lord of Africa[2]. On Perseus' side Cotys, king of the Thracian Odrysae, stood openly. Neutral were Prusias of Bithynia, who thought he saw his way to excusing himself with either side: and Gentius of Illyria, suspected by Rome, but at present genuinely unable to make up his mind. The free states are treated as a group of communities presenting essentially similar phenomena. The contrast of rich and poor—the Haves and the Have-nots—was the main line of division in them all. In general the needy were in

[1] Livy XLII 29, 30.
[2] That is, of the Punic territory, later the Roman province of Africa. But if he got a free hand, so would Carthage.

favour of Perseus, for Roman policy habitually favoured the wealthy
few in communities subject to Roman influence.   Perseus represented
royal power, naturally jealous of leading men, and the prospect of
change, always attractive to those who have nothing to lose or who
hope to cancel debts in revolution.   But the simple issue, a struggle
between rich and poor, the Few and the Many, for mastery and
the direction of the policy of each community, was complicated by
the divisions among the wealthier citizens themselves.   These are
classified as follows.   First, the partisans of Rome, either genuine
admirers of the Roman system or seeking their own advancement.
Secondly, the partisans of Perseus, either flighty men lured by the
fair promises of the king or seeking in change relief from private
embarrassments.   Thirdly, the patriotic statesmen, who, while preferring Roman overlordship to Macedonian, wished to secure for
their own states the greatest attainable freedom of action: and who
therefore desired that neither of the belligerent powers should crush
the other.   This analysis needs to be received with some reserve,
highly instructive as it is.   The point of view is that of a patriot
statesman of the Achaean League, in fact of Polybius.   Either he
did not see that the waiting attitude ascribed by him to his own
virtuous and prudent party was practically ineffective in presence
of a death-struggle such as that now beginning; or he underrated
the power of Rome and her determination to put down the Macedonian kingdom for good and all; or he saw these things, but did
not deal with them in writing; or he wrote, and Livy has left the
passage out.

510.   The formal act of declaring war now took place in the
Assembly, and the Senate drew up its scheme for the armed forces
of the year.   The details are not quite clear, but the chief points[1]
seem to be these.   The army of Macedonia was to include two
legions of extra strength, and a larger force of Italian Allies.   Strong
pressure was to be used to fill the legions with old soldiers: veteran
centurions were particularly in request.   It appears that the troops
already taken across the Adriatic numbered only some 5300 men,
not a third of the force ordered.   Later we hear of foreign auxiliaries
being employed.   The total strength of the forces at the consul's
disposal may have amounted to about 40,000 men, exclusive of the
allied contingents from Greece and the East.   The backbone of the
army was the two choice legions.   To ensure efficient officers the
rule, by which their military tribunes had to be elected by the
Assembly, was suspended for the year, and the consul was left free

---

[1] We have to depend on Livy XLII 30—35, who is again dabbling in the inconsistent
narratives of Roman annalists.

to nominate men on the sole ground of merit.   Beside the land
forces, there was a powerful fleet raised by Rome and her maritime
allies.   It is noted that of the fighting crews two thirds were to be
citizens, one third Allies.   But the citizens drafted off for this unpopular service were Freedmen, that is, either liberated slaves or
men of servile extraction.   The 'province' of Macedonia fell by lot
to the consul P. Licinius Crassus: the praetor C. Lucretius Gallus
commanded the fleet.   We hear of some senior centurions objecting
to be called out for service unless guaranteed a seniority equal to the
highest rank reached by them in previous campaigns, but an appeal
to their patriotism got over the difficulty, and the veterans left their
claims to the judgment of the military tribunes.   A reserve army, of
four city legions and a smaller force of the Allies, was also raised.

511.   The mingled nervousness and trickery of Perseus was just
now shewn by the appearance of another embassy from him, asking
for explanations of the Roman acts of war, and protesting that he
was ready even now to make reparation for any wrong that he might
have done.   But evidence was produced to prove that the king's
deeds were wholly inconsistent with his plausible offer.   The season
of artifice was past, and the envoys, who had not been admitted into
the city, were ordered to quit Italy.   The consul at the head of the
field army was for the time the representative of Rome.   But before
the arrival of Crassus in Greece Roman commissioners traversed the
country, calling on the states to declare for Rome and raise[1] contingents.   Their reception varied.   In Peloponnesus they contrived
to offend the Achaeans: in Thessaly they were warmly welcomed.
Q. Marcius Philippus, the leading man of the commission, was one
of those acting in the northern district.   There was some tie of
friendship between him and the royal house of Macedon, and Perseus
now made yet another attempt to negotiate: a letter sent to meet the
commission on their journey from Rome had been left unanswered.
The timid king, whose courage was just then ebbing, now hoped
much from Marcius.   After a conference, Marcius, who insisted on
asserting his precedence of Perseus and took a confident tone, as a
great favour granted him a truce to send another embassy to Rome.
Thus the wily Roman duped[2] the wily king.   Time was what the
Romans wanted, for Perseus was ready and they were not.   During
this respite the commissioners had the affairs of Boeotia[3] to deal
with.   After many disagreements (for the Boeotian cities were
divided) the Romans managed to come to terms with the several

---

[1] Nominally a voluntary act, but at this time Rome scorned to allow a declaration of
neutrality on the part of her *amici*.

[2] Livy XLII 43, 47, Diodor. XXX 7.   [3] Polyb. XXVII 1, 2, Livy XLII 43, 44, 47.

cities and break up the Boeotian confederacy, thus carrying out the traditional policy of Rome in dissolving unions wherever possible. An Achaean contingent was set to garrison Chalcis, and the commissioners returned home. Marcius boasted of having tricked Perseus: it is said that the proceeding was severely criticised in the Senate as unworthy of Rome, but that eventually scruples were overcome by expediency, the act approved, and Marcius sent back to Greece on a diplomatic mission with large general powers. The truce was turned to account by the occupation of some important posts. How the slippery tricks of Perseus could have been successfully met without some dissembling, is very hard to see.

512. Not less important was the work of a commission sent to the Greek cities in Asia and the islands, calling upon them to join Rome and get their contingents ready. Rhodes[1] in particular was expected to furnish a strong fleet, and her example would give a lead to a number of hesitating minor states. All passed off well: the Rhodian President just then was a Roman partisan, and the envoys were gratified to find 40 fine vessels ready for sea. This was a practical reply to the charges of disloyalty made against them by Eumenes, with whom they were still on unfriendly terms. But Perseus had not given up his hopes of drawing some of the Greek powers over to his side, or at least of inducing them to remain neutral. He used the interval of the truce to send letters round, describing the conference with Marcius in a sense favourable to himself. To the Rhodians he sent a formal embassy, and artfully urged them to stand neutral for the present, and then to come forward energetically as mediators. But the Rhodians, though desiring peace, were fully committed to the cause of Rome, and perhaps did not think Perseus so certainly in the right as he would fain make out. They civilly declined to do anything inconsistent with the long-standing friendship and comradeship in arms that bound them to Rome. One or two Boeotian towns rashly declared for the king: he sent them no garrisons, and told them to stand neutral, a request not likely to rouse enthusiasm for his cause in Greece.

513. Perseus' last ambassadors had nothing to tell the Senate that the Senate cared to hear. They were ordered out of Italy, and the consul Crassus and the praetor Lucretius ordered to go at once with their army and fleet to the seat of war. This they did. The consul encamped in Epirus. He seems to have been a man of small military experience, and the Senate took care to see that he was provided with skilled advisers on his staff. The defects incidental to the Roman system had been exposed by Hannibal, but they still

[1] Polyb. XXVII 3—7, Livy XLII 45, 46.

remained and had to be patched up somehow. The curt dismissal of Perseus' envoys shewed the king that the only choice left him was that of fighting or submitting. The majority of his councillors urged him to fight. He now gathered his army together and held a grand review. Beside the national forces of Macedon, he had Thracians, Cretans, Greek mercenaries, and Gauls[1]: troops various in kind, but all good in quality. The kernel of his army, the infantry of the phalanx, seem to have been about 21,000, and the total amounted to 43,000 men. They were eager to fight: the king was well supplied with money, provisions, and missiles of the latest patterns. He now crossed the Cambunian mountains. City after city fell into his hands by surrender or capture, and in a short time he was master of Perrhaebia and most of northern Thessaly. As he had always held Demetrias, the Magnesian district was at least partly in his power. But, instead of using to the full the prestige of initial success, he encamped at Sycurium, a healthy spot near the foot of mount Ossa, where he drew supplies from the rich lowland and awaited the Roman advance. This lack of enterprise left the consul free to cross the Pindus range into Thessaly unmolested. He reached Gomphi safely, after a terrible experience in the mountain passes, and moved on towards Larisa. Eumenes now joined him with 5000 men, having left 2000 more in garrison at Chalcis. Various auxiliary Greek contingents also came, all weaker[2] than they should have been, some quite insignificant. The fleet reached Chalcis, but there was no naval war, and the men were employed in an attempt to capture Haliartus, a town in Boeotia, held for the king. Naval contingents[3] from Carthage and some of the eastern Greek cities came dribbling in, but the praetor did not want them, and let them go home. Meanwhile Perseus extended his raids in Thessaly, hoping to draw the Romans into the open to protect their allies. But Crassus stuck to his camp by the Peneus, and the days went by.

514. The Romans seemed to be afraid: the king's men grew all the bolder. Perseus advanced and appeared unexpectedly before the consul's camp. A small and indecisive affair of cavalry and light troops took place, in which the Roman force (Galatian Mysian and Cretan auxiliaries) seems to have had somewhat the worst of it. Anyhow the king moved his camp nearer, and soon brought on a more serious engagement of the same kind, in which he was clearly victorious. But on this occasion also the heavy infantry took no part in the battle. Perseus hoped to achieve important results through

---

[1] Whether from Galatia or from the North, is not clear. Perhaps they were really Bastarnae. Note of Weissenborn.

[2] Livy XLII 55 §§ 8—10.   [3] Livy XLII 56 § 6.

the moral effect of his present success, and kept the precious phalanx
for a later day. The consul withdrew his army in the night to the
left bank of the river to restore their morale. The blame of the defeat
was laid upon the Aetolian horse, falsely, some said: the Thessalian
contingent were highly praised. It seems as though the Romans
looked for a scapegoat: it is not unlikely that some of the Greek
auxiliaries were lukewarm in the cause of Rome. The victory of
Perseus was welcomed, secretly or openly, by numbers of people in
Greece, but they remained spectators of the struggle and contributed
applause. About this time the Numidian contingent[1] reached the
Roman camp, 1000 horse, 1000 foot, and 22 elephants: an opportune
evidence of Rome's far-reaching power. And now the plausible king,
ever seeking to evade the necessity of putting his all to the hazard,
and not having grasped the truth that the prospect of a decisive issue
was an essential factor in the determination of the Romans to go to
war, made an offer to conclude peace on the terms granted to his
father after Cynoscephalae. But Rome had not yet come down to
this. The answer was that they would grant him peace on condition
that he surrendered himself and his kingdom to be dealt with as the
Roman Senate should think fit. Most of his advisers were for breaking
off the negotiations at once. But Perseus, cowed by the firmness of
the Romans, went on bidding for peace, vainly offering more and
more tribute-money, till he was at last compelled to return to his
camp under Ossa, having wasted his chances and fooled away the
moral effect of his victory. Meanwhile the suppression of Macedonian
partisanship in Boeotia was being carried out. Haliartus, after a stout
defence, was taken and utterly destroyed. Other places[2] were dealt
with by purging them of the leaders of opposition to Rome. In
Thessaly Perseus tried to surprise and set on fire the Roman camp,
without success. On another occasion he surprised and captured a
number of foragers, and surrounded a Roman outpost. But the men
held out bravely under a terrible fire of missiles, and were relieved in
time by the main army. The king ordered the phalanx to the front,
but it got jammed in a narrow way among captured forage-carts, and
was too late. The consul had an opportunity of dealing a severe blow
to the enemy, but cautiously abstained, thankful for a small success.
Perseus now withdrew to winter quarters in Macedonia, and Crassus
won back most of the towns that had been lost earlier in the year.
In Boeotia the consul acted with great barbarity, particularly at
Coronea, where he sold the people into slavery as though they were
prisoners of war. In Epirus[3] the news of the success of Perseus, and

---

[1] Livy XLII 62 § 2.　　　[2] See Hicks, *Greek Historical Inscriptions*, Index under *Thisbae*.
[3] Polyb. XXVII 15, 16.

the tyranny of the Roman partisans in power there, led to a revolution in favour of Macedon. Only the southern part of that country remained under the control of Rome, and the consul, alarmed no doubt for his communications with Italy, sent a garrison to occupy the important city of Ambracia. Even on the water, where Perseus was confessedly weak, there was disaster. A fleet of transports laden with corn for the army was surprised off the north of Euboea, and all either taken or sunk. This looks as if Greek sympathy with the king had gone so far as to furnish information of the Roman movements. In short, the winter of 171—170 left the Romans in Greece worse off than when the war was declared. Their military reputation was dimmed, and most of the population among whom the campaigning must be done were becoming more and more hostile :—a great disadvantage in war, and one not easily removed.

515. The elections for 170 had been held and official duties assigned. The consul A. Hostilius Mancinus was to succeed Crassus, the praetor L. Hortensius to take over the fleet. The Senate, on hearing of the doings at Coronea, ordered the action of Crassus to be cancelled, the enslaved to be restored to freedom, and all possible reparation to be made to the sufferers. But no redress can wipe out a committed wrong : the fact of the outrage remained, and the redress was doubtless incomplete. Our authorities about this time are even more fragmentary than usual, but we learn enough of the events of the year 170 to see that the incompetence and cruelty of the new commanders were fully up to the standard of their predecessors. On his way to the seat of war Hostilius narrowly escaped being kidnapped in Epirus and sent as a present to the king of Macedon. In the course of the summer he seems to have made two attempts to invade Macedonia, the first of which was repulsed, and the second checked by the bold attitude of Perseus. The utter failure of the consul's campaign is shewn in the leisure enjoyed by Perseus, who found himself free to give the troublesome Dardani a beating, thus relieving the pressure on his northern frontier ; also to invade Illyria and Epirus, apparently with the view of displaying his power and encouraging actual or prospective partisans. He was especially anxious to gain the support of Gentius.

516. At Rome indignation was aroused by the reports of the misdeeds of Roman commanders. Lucretius, who had done many bad things[1] with his marine forces, was threatened by the tribunes. He had wound up his season of command by allowing his rough company to insult and bully the Greek citizens, when quartered for the winter at Chalcis. He was now living at ease at Antium, close

[1] Livy XLIII 4, 7, 8.

to Rome, earning local popularity by the public employment of his ill-gotten gains.   He had not yet been brought to justice, when the news of an exploit of his successor diverted the attention of the Roman public.   This time the bitter cry came from the Greek city of Abdera on the Thracian coast.   It was a tale of an enormous requisition of corn and money, of a truce granted for sending an embassy and broken on some pretext or other: of an assault and capture, followed by executions and a slave-market.   The Abderites were probably free allies of Rome, at least harmless people, and this barbarity was in the highest degree ill-timed.   The Senate took up the matter and passed orders for redress as they had done in the case of Coronea.   Nor were these gross instances of brutal misconduct confined to Greek cities.   On the north-eastern borders of Italy the consul C. Cassius had behaved with equal barbarity[1] to Gaulish and other tribes in the preceding year.   The Senate heard the story from envoys and repudiated the consul's acts: but the man was now out of reach, serving on the staff of Hostilius in Greece.   The House promised that on his return, if the injured peoples would then raise the question, steps should be taken to exact reparation.   Meanwhile they did what they could to soothe the chiefs with gifts and sent an embassy with sympathetic messages and so forth.   The fact remained that the Senate, for all its immense power, could not or would not exercise an effective control over the commanders of the armed forces of the state.   And now we hear of a number of embassies[2] from various cities in Greece and Asia, all grovelling before their masters with abject humility, tendering their poor little services or asking little favours.   The envoys from Athens even mentioned that they had been subjected to requisitions by the Roman commanders.   From Carthage came a humble offer of corn, from Masinissa the same, and of a fresh contingent as well.   From Crete came a notice that the force of bowmen demanded by Crassus had been despatched to the seat of war.   The envoys took back a message that, if the Cretans wished to be recognized as allies of Rome, they must cease to furnish bowmen to Perseus, and contrive to withdraw from the king's service those they had already sent him.   If the Senate could not control the acts of Roman commanders, it could at least put pressure on the free Cretans to abandon their most cherished privilege.   To keep up the cash value of their services to each belligerent by also serving the other side was the Cretan ideal of good business: limit him to the support of one cause, and what was a poor Cretan to do?   Most important of the embassies was that from Chalcis, complaining of the wrongs endured at the hands of the praetors in command of the

[1] Livy XLIII 5.   [2] Livy XLIII 6, 7.

Roman fleet. Hortensius was following the example of Lucretius: spoliation and violence and injuries of every kind were the portion of Rome's faithful allies. Chalcis was an important post, and no effort was spared to redress the wrongs of the Chalcidians and prevent their continuance. Hortensius himself could not be reached at present, but Lucretius was brought before the court of the Assembly and condemned to pay a heavy fine by the unanimous sentence of the Tribes.

517. In the present position of the Macedonian war it was natural that both sides should be interested in Illyria. The ambiguous attitude of Gentius caused the Romans some uneasiness. Troops were sent there from Italy and from the army in Greece, and local levies were raised in that part of southern Illyria where Roman influence prevailed. But an attempt to extend the influence of Rome by an advance up the country was a failure. The officer in command fell into a trap and only escaped with heavy loss. The Senate heard of this disaster with alarm. Things were in a bad way, and a thorough change was needed if they meant to carry this tiresome war to a triumphant end. So they sent out two commissioners[1] to report the actual state of things at the front: they made arrangements for holding the elections for 169 at an early date: and all senators not then serving abroad were recalled to Rome. The commissioners on their return brought no cheerful news. Discipline in the army was slack: numbers of men were absent on furlough: the consul blamed the legionary officers, who in their turn blamed the consul. Meanwhile the successes of Perseus were remarkable, and the allies of Rome were losing heart. Preparations were now made for the coming campaign. Even now, in the third year of the war, a reserve army was to be kept ready for emergencies, after the ordinary field armies and fleet had been brought up to their proper strength. So little had as yet been accomplished towards the suppression of the power of Macedon. The general uneasiness expressed itself in the report of a number of prodigies, which were carefully expiated by the usual ceremonies. In this year censors were elected. This eventful census will engage our attention below, but we are concerned here with its bearing[2] on the military levy. The consuls found great reluctance on the part of the citizens to come forward for enlistment. Two praetors declared that it was the consul's fault for not using compulsion, and offered to see the business through. The Senate consented, thus reflecting on the popularity-hunting weakness of the chief magistrates. The censors backed up the praetors by adding to the regular oath taken by every citizen a special clause solemnly

[1] Livy XLIII 11. [2] Livy XLIII 14.

binding all men under 46 years of age to present themselves for enlistment whenever required. This brought home to defaulters the imminent risk of their forfeiting the privileges of citizenship if they continued to shirk its burdens, and the levy was completed within eleven days. By the use of censorial powers the absentees from the army now on furlough in Italy were compelled to return to Greece. In short, the old republican machinery for realizing the identity of citizen and soldier was set going again, and was for the moment (that is, till the next census) effective. But it was already beginning, in the need for such extreme action on the part of the censors, to betray the unwelcome truth that times had changed and the old military system was out of date.

518.   In connexion with the recent cases of cruelty and extortion on the part of Roman officers the Senate had passed a general order, forbidding the allies to supply anything whatever[1] for the purposes of war without a vote of the Senate to that effect. This direct attempt to put an end to unauthorized requisitions was well received, particularly at the diet of the Achaean League. It was formally published by two delegates sent round by Hostilius, now proconsul, early in 169 before the new consul arrived. In Aetolia the delegates found the country full of quarrelling and mutual recriminations, and ripe for civil war. They took hostages and passed on to Acarnania, where things were almost as bad. In fact the unexpected successes of Perseus had unsettled the Greeks more than ever. The overlordship of Rome was an onerous fact; that of Macedon might be even more onerous some day, but at present it did not exist. The Achaeans however, though suspected of slackness by the Roman delegates, soon decided to cooperate actively with Rome. Meanwhile Perseus had been using the winter months to push his designs in Illyria. He invaded the districts next to his own frontier, where he bore down all resistance, and made prisoners of a number of Roman soldiers scattered in various garrisons. Having given sufficient proof of his power, he sent ambassadors to Gentius, inviting his alliance in the war with Rome. Gentius was not unwilling to join him, but to mobilize the rude hill-men of Illyria for any serious purpose was an undertaking that required money. The gist of his reply was therefore a request for a subsidy. Perseus, bent on doing the thing cheaply, ignored this essential point, and several embassies passed between the parties, the one demanding, the other shirking. While this contest of obstinacy went on, Perseus crossed the Pindus range in hope of drawing the Aetolians to his side by a demonstration. But Stratus, the first place aimed at, was occupied in the nick of time

---

[1] Livy XLIII 17, Polyb. XXVIII 3—6.

by a Roman garrison, and a body of Aetolians, sent by his friends to support him, seeing what had happened, joined the Romans instead. The king had to return home with some loss of prestige. On some unsuccessful minor operations of Roman officers in Illyria and Epirus we need not dwell: the chief feature of the situation was that the spring was come, and Gentius still unemployed.

519. Q. Marcius Philippus, who now took over the command as consul, was a striking instance of the inadequacy of the Roman system to provide for the management of a serious war. He had been consul in the year 186, when he made a short campaign in Liguria; in the course of which he contrived to lead his army into a trap, and only brought back a remnant of them in disgraceful flight. Most of his public life had been spent in civilian duties of a judicial or diplomatic kind. His sharp practice in the recent negotiation with Perseus had been disapproved by the more scrupulous and old-fashioned senators. But the Senate as a body seems to have condoned an act that might be regarded as excess of zeal in the interests of Rome. He was over sixty, but still full of energy, and insisted on doing his military duty in person, though old and fat. On reaching Thessaly he found things in a good state for immediate action. His predecessor Hostilius had restored discipline in the ranks, and had loyally carried out the Senate's orders for the protection of the local allies. It was decided to dally no longer in Thessaly but to invade Macedonia, while the praetor C. Marcius Figulus made a parallel movement with the fleet against the enemy's coast. Perseus soon knew of this design, and occupied all the passes. But he ventured on no bold move, and waited for the Romans to strike, accepting the moral disadvantage of the mere defensive. At last the consul made his choice of route, by a pass over the southern spurs of mount Olympus. The way was difficult, but the army reached the top, and the light troops of Perseus could not stop them. But retreat was now out of the question, and the perils of the descent were such that the whole force were at the mercy of an enemy. Only the faint-hearted neglect of Perseus allowed them to reach the bottom in safety. But when they had time to look round they found themselves in an awkward fix. To retrace their mountain journey was impossible. Hemmed in between Olympus and the sea on a narrow strip of ground, they had but two ways open to them: retreat by way of the famous gorge of Tempe, a very narrow passage along by the river Peneus, or advance along the coast-road in the direction of Dium and Pydna. Marcius, true to his military record, had again fallen into a trap, for the backward route was held by a Macedonian force, while a forward movement was barred by the king and his main army. Only a little patience was needed, for time to

make the Roman position unendurable : but the nerve of Alexander's successor was not equal to the strain. He drew in his detached posts, abandoned all the advantages of his position, evacuated Dium, taking with him some golden statues and removing the population, and the Roman army, without any exertion of its own, was free to advance with its communications safely open to the rear. The strategic results of moral strength and moral weakness were never more strikingly exemplified.

520. Marcius now pushed forward and occupied Dium without opposition, but was soon driven to retreat by want of supplies. He now devoted his attention to securing the line of communications by the Tempe pass. The supplies left in the Macedonian forts relieved his commissariat. Perseus now took heart to advance again, but only to fortify a position between Olympus and the sea and stand on the defensive as before. He allowed the Romans to storm and take a town within sight of his lines. In his late panic he had sent orders that his treasure was to be sunk and his arsenal at Thessalonica burnt. The former part had been carried out, the latter not. He now recovered the treasure : and it is said that he put to death both the officers to whom the orders had been sent, and even the divers who raised his gold. Thus he hoped to suppress the evidence of his abject fright. The blame for letting the enemy break into Macedonia he laid upon his generals. But even with the help of such an adversary as this the Roman cause did not make much headway. The fleet was active, first along the seaboard of Macedonia and Chalcidice, then off Magnesia : a number of descents were made, and some sieges undertaken, in most cases without success.

521. We are now come to a stage in this war at which we must more than ever lament the fragmentary state of the text of Polybius. Rome and her allies are, or seem to be, at cross purposes : and a series of suspicious intrigues and negotiations are the result. We have no sufficient clue to guide us to the truth through the complicated maze. Nor can we safely draw back-inferences as to these affairs from the important consequences that followed them : those consequences were the outcome of the Roman view of these affairs, and it is by no means certain that the Roman view was right. The situation was briefly as follows. The war in the East was practically decided in favour of Syria. Antiochus IV had advanced into Egypt, and the Egyptian government was in disorder. This war, more than that between Rome and Perseus, was unfavourably affecting the trade of Rhodes. The Rhodians were uneasy. The Romans, for whom they had made so many sacrifices, seemed to be almost at a standstill in their Macedonian war : meanwhile all commercial interests were

suffering, and Rome could hardly restore peace in the East till she had done with Macedon. Importation of corn was checked, and the populous island could not subsist on its home produce. No doubt the Macedonian partisans used the rise of prices to foster discontent, but the Roman party were still in power. What the government did was to send a double embassy. The envoys to Rome were to renew[1] the old friendship and to defend the Rhodians against the current charges of disaffection: they were also to ask for leave to buy corn in Roman territory. So far all went well; they were kindly received, and were authorized to buy a definite quantity[2] of corn in Sicily. Those sent to the consul Marcius were only concerned with the diplomatic errand, and their visit at once introduces us to other complications.

522. When the Achaeans, as we saw above, decided to give active support to the Romans in Thessaly, they sent envoys[3] to Marcius, to inform him of their decision and ask him to fix time and place for their forces to join him. At the head of this mission was Polybius, now the second official of the League. He found the consul preparing to cross the mountains, and so busy that he put off for the moment the matter of his errand. When the army was safely over the pass, he delivered the proposal of the League, and pointed out that they had from the outset of the war conformed to all the requirements of Rome. Marcius expressed his satisfaction, but declined the proffered aid on the ground that it was no longer needed, and he did not wish to put them to trouble and expense. Yet it seems certain that the Roman army was in a by no means favourable position. And he went further than this. News came that in consequence of recent defeats the Roman position in Epirus was imperilled: at least the officer commanding there had sent a request for the help of 5000 Achaeans. Marcius sent off Polybius at once to see that this help was not granted, declaring that there was no need for it. But his instructions were private, and when the matter came before the Achaean Assembly Polybius was in great difficulty as to executing his commission. He solved the problem by adducing the Senate's recent prohibition of unauthorized demands, and got the question referred to the consul. But why did Marcius act in this strange manner? Polybius rather half-heartedly throws out two suggestions—first, he may have desired not to burden the Achaeans; secondly, he may have desired not to promote a successful campaign in Epirus. Of these, the former is hardly consistent with what we know of the career and character of Marcius: the disloyal jealousy of the latter is perhaps conceivable. But Marcius knew that the

---

[1] See Livy XLIV 14.   [2] Polyb. XXVIII 2.   [3] Polyb. XXVIII 12, 13.

Senate was anxious and displeased at the slow progress of the war, and it is hardly credible that he deliberately used his authority to protract it.   That Polybius in forming opinions sometimes missed the inner truth of things we know from his criticism of the Roman constitution.   It is perhaps more likely that Marcius mistrusted the Achaeans, and did not wish to see them mobilize an army which might pass over to the enemy at some critical moment.   He probably knew that Eumenes had been treating with the League through his brother Attalus for the restoration of his 'honours' (statues, inscriptions, etc.) in Peloponnesus.   Once numerous, these honours had lately been annulled for some reason now obscure.   The proposal had been kindly received, a result which Polybius himself[1] attributes mainly to a speech of his own.   Intimate relations between Roman allies without Roman intervention were never pleasing to Roman statesmen : and that the designs of Eumenes included something more than mere honours would be a natural suspicion on the part of a diplomatist like Marcius. For at this time the loyalty of the king of Pergamum was beginning to be doubted.   A Cretan officer in his employ was said[2] to have had communication with others in the Macedonian service.   At present this seems to have been all that was alleged, but the mention of Cretans always suggested the idea of treachery.   And from a fragment of Polybius we learn that Eumenes had lately been interfering[3] in one of the endless internal quarrels of Crete.   If then Marcius mistrusted the Achaeans, he did nothing out of keeping with Roman policy and his own character.

523.   To return to the Rhodian envoys.   They found the consul[4] in his camp near the coast north of the pass of Tempe.   His reception of them was most friendly.   He was not the man to listen to slanders against Rome's old friends—not he !   Only let the Rhodians do the same by Rome.   The Greek envoys were charmed with this open goodwill.   But history has known of bluff hearty deceivers : and we are invited to accept as fact that the genial frankness of Marcius was but the cloak of infamous guile.   He privately suggested to the leader of the embassy that it would be well if the Rhodians would make an effort to bring the present state of war to an end : such an act would be in keeping with the traditional policy of Rhodes.   In this matter also the motives of the consul were dark, and gave rise to various[5] explanations.   Polybius offers two: perhaps

---

[1] Polyb. xxviii 7.   [2] Polyb. xxix 6.
[3] Polyb. xxviii 15.   [4] Polyb. xxviii 16, 17.
[5] See Polyb. xxviii 17, Appian *Mac.* 17.   That the question of the eastern war was discussed between the Rhodians and Marcius is very probable.   From Polyb. xxviii 1 we learn that Marcius had been authorized by the Senate to write to Ptolemy and settle the eastern question to the best of his judgment, and at the end of xxviii 17 we hear that

he wanted to end the war with Perseus for fear lest its protraction might prevent Rome from dealing effectually with the eastern question: things were moving fast in Egypt, and Antiochus might get beyond control. This theory seems to have been accepted by Appian, who attributes timidity to Marcius. On this hypothesis the advice would be sincere. But Polybius leans to the other view, that Marcius was confident of a speedy decision of the Macedonian war, and wanted to put the Rhodians in such a position that they would be at the mercy of Rome. The Romans would be certain to resent their interference, and in the settlement after the war could deal with the 'old friends' of Rome just as they saw fit. The subtle malignity of this design was credible enough to a Greek of the second century B.C., and this explanation may be the true one: but certainty is not attainable in the darkness of the transaction, nor is it likely that we shall ever lift the veil.

524. If we may believe Livy, whose patchwork narrative is about this time in great confusion, an offer of auxiliary troops[1] came to Rome from some Transalpine Gauls, probably tribes NE of Italy, during the season of 169. It was courteously declined. Interference, even help, from beyond the mountain barrier was of course not to be encouraged. But as the year wore on the necessity of bringing the Macedonian war to an end was more and more brought home to men's minds. The consul wrote reporting his progress, such as it was: he asked for winter clothing for his men, and some remounts for the cavalry: there was besides a large quantity of corn, bought in Epirus, which had still to be paid for. All these requirements were at once met, and another little matter[2] dealt with. This was the rewarding of a Macedonian deserter. His story was that he had tried in vain to deter Perseus from going to war. Falling under suspicion in consequence of his advice, he sought safety in flight, and had been of great service to the Roman commander. He was hospitably received, and granted an allotment out of the state-domain in the district of Tarentum, probably some of the land forfeited by the Tarentines for their conduct in the second Punic war. He became, not a Roman citizen, but a *socius*, that is an (Italian) Ally. He seems to have been a man of some standing in the country of his birth. By what acts of betrayal he had earned his reward, we do not hear. The story shews us the sort oi thing that was going on. And now the time for the elections drew near, and all Rome looked round for a man.

a Rhodian embassy was also sent to Alexandria on an errand of mediation. But this move seems to be quite distinct from the general mediation suggested by Marcius. Appian clearly understood this to refer to the war with Perseus, rightly, I think.

[1] Livy XLIV 14.   [2] Livy XLIV 16.

525. The man[1] was found in L. Aemilius Paullus, son of the consul slain at Cannae. The Aemilii, an old Patrician house, had long held an honourable place in the history of the Republic. In the life of Paullus we see combined the conflicting tendencies of the age, a singular harmony of old and new. His family traditions seem to have been of the old Roman school, while the marriage of his sister to Scipio Africanus suggests that he soon was brought into touch with members of a more modern circle. He early served the state in minor offices: as aedile he seems to have been active. He was made an augur, and was noted for the minute precision with which he conned and applied the lore of that sacred college. In military life he shewed the same bent by maintaining the strictest discipline. His campaigns, as praetor in the Further Spain[2] and in Liguria as consul, had not been unchequered by reverses, but had ended in victory. Both in military and civil life he scorned to court popularity. His honesty amid many temptations was attested by the smallness of his means: his justice and mercy to conquered peoples, by his being chosen to uphold the cause of his former province when the oppressed folk of Spain sought redress of their wrongs. To schemes of conquest and spoliation he was firmly opposed, and he was one of the commissioners who in 187 objected to the triumph of Manlius Vulso for the unwholesome glories of the Galatian war. He was not unambitious, but the good of his country was his first consideration: and this in an age when ambition was fast becoming rather self-regarding than patriotic in character. Though an able speaker, judged by the standard of his day, he was not addicted to oratory either at meetings of the people or in support of clients in their actions at law. After his first consulship (182) it is said that he more than once shewed a wish for a second, but was overlooked: once he appeared as a candidate, and was defeated. Hereupon he devoted himself all the more to his augural duties and to his most absorbing interest, the education of his sons. These fortunate youths, beside the traditional Roman training, had Greek masters (no doubt carefully selected) to instruct them not only in riding and field-sports but in rhetoric and general culture and the arts of design. Thus it would seem that he carried the education of his sons beyond the standard of his own, though he too was a liberally-educated man: we find that when he chose (it was a condescension in a Roman

---

[1] Plutarch's life of Paullus is one of the best of his Roman biographies. Among the authorities used by him were Polybius and a letter of Scipio Nasica describing the Macedonian campaign. He refers also to a certain Posidonius, who wrote a history taking the side of Perseus. In some points Plutarch differs from Livy, not always for the worse, I think. See H. Peter's *die Quellen Plutarchs in den Biographieen der Römer*, Halle 1865.

[2] See the inscription quoted § 688 (*b*).

magistrate) he could converse with Greeks in their own tongue, and that he took a cultivated interest in the glorious past of Greece. How highly this generous father and upright citizen was valued by men of discernment may be gathered from his intimate relations with the leading men of different schools. Of four children by his first wife Papiria, he gave the elder son in adoption to a Fabius, son of the old slow-going hero of the Hannibalic war: the younger to a Scipio, son of his brother-in-law Africanus. The elder daughter was married to the son of the famous Cato, the younger to Aelius Tubero, a man of simple and exemplary life, poor and incorruptible, who held together in unity a compound household of 16 kinsmen with wives and families, a pattern of primitive Roman virtue. But Paullus for some unknown reason put away Papiria and took another wife, by whom he had at least two sons. It was the feeling that his own family succession was now secure that led him to transplant the sons by his first wife into other houses. We shall see that by the irony of fate he thus provided for the continuance of those families to the extinction of his own.

526. Such was the man who at the age of 60 consented under pressure to accept a second consulship for the purpose of retrieving the blunders of others. The chosen of the people, men of the ordinary type, had spent three years in not doing what they were sent to do. The appointment[1] of Paullus to the Macedonian command—for the lot of course fell on him—was felt to be an important step. The new general was a man of good abilities and a real soldier. Above all, whatever he could do for his country would actually be done: neither greed nor jealousy nor slackness nor want of moral courage would impair the efficiency of his powers. He seized the reins at once. By his directions three commissioners were despatched to the seat of war, to find out the true state of things and report to Rome with all speed. During their absence an embassy from Alexandria was heard, appealing for help[2] against Antiochus of Syria, who had made himself master in Egypt and was now besieging the capital. The matter was urgent, for interest and duty alike forbade Rome to allow the invader to appropriate the resources of Egypt and overthrow the kingdom of the Ptolemies. An embassy was sent, headed by C. Popilius Laenas, armed with a peremptory decree ordering both parties to cease hostilities at once. Of this embassy we shall

---

[1] According to Plutarch, who followed good authorities, lots were not drawn, but the command specially voted to him.

[2] It appears from Polyb. xxix 23—5 that the Ptolemies also applied for help to the Achaean League. Perhaps it was feared that Rome was too busy elsewhere to give serious help at once.

hear again. Soon the commissioners returned from Greece, and delivered a most unfavourable report. The operations of the main army had been futile, and the situation at the front was a deadlock: as for the army in Illyria, it was not strong enough to threaten Macedonia from the West, and was in fact itself in danger of destruction: it must either be brought up to a proper strength or withdrawn. The condition of the fleet was deplorable: the remains of the ships' companies were unpaid and unclad: disease and desertion had removed the rest. The winter had been severe, the armies were short of supplies, and Perseus still held the field in full strength. The Pergamene fleet had been strangely casual in its movements, and, though Attalus was loyal enough, there was reason to doubt the good faith of Eumenes.

527. Guided by a strong man, the Senate set to work to change all this. The praetor L. Anicius was taken from judicial duties and appointed to command in Illyria. For him a strong army was provided. It was arranged that Paullus should have a free hand in the selection of his legionary tribunes, and his legions were to be made up to a strength of 6000 foot and 300 horse in each: all ineffective men were to be discharged. The fleet also received reinforcements. Among the Allies levied for service we hear[1] of an interesting novelty: 600 auxiliary horse were to be raised in Cisalpine Gaul. The circumstances of Paullus' appointment, his address to the people before leaving, the grand 'send-off' that the people gave him, became part of the patriotic tradition of Rome, the stock material used to edify the young with dramatic lessons from the past. And it may very well be true that he declined to render thanks for the consulship as a favour, but accepted it as a burden of public duty: and that he bade the people to leave the conduct of the war to the general in command, and mind their own business, not hampering the man at the front[2] by wagging their irresponsible tongues in Rome. He set out at once for Macedonia with Cn. Octavius the commander of the fleet.

528. Rome was at length in earnest, but Perseus too had not been idle during the winter months of 169—8. He came to terms with Gentius, who agreed to join him for a sum of 300 talents (about £70,500), and also agreed to send envoys to Rhodes with those sent by Perseus to induce the Rhodians to join the coalition against Rome. All was arranged, hostages given on both sides, and agents of Gentius forwarded to Pella, to receive the money promised by Perseus. But to part with so much specie was agony to the miser of Macedon. He allowed the Illyrian agents to put their official seal on the parcels of money, and sent on at once an instalment of ten talents, while the

---

[1] Livy XLIV 21 § 7.   [2] Polyb. XXIX 1, Livy XLIV 22.

rest followed slowly and was stopped altogether at the frontier. On
receipt of the ten talents the foolish and drunken Gentius was induced
to seize and imprison two Roman ambassadors newly arrived at his
court. He was thus committed to war with Rome; and Perseus,
whose notion of cleverness was to receive value and to shirk payment,
promptly fetched back the 290 talents to Pella—for the Romans.
A negotiation of much the same kind was carried on with a horde of
barbarians who about this time crossed the Danube and appeared in
the North. It was desirable in any case to keep them employed, and
there was work for them to do in stopping the Roman advance. But
while they named their price and stuck to their demand, Perseus
tried to wriggle out of payment by complimentary presents to their
chiefs: and a conflict of insistence and evasion ended in their marching off in disgust. Thus, in order to hoard some of his treasure a
little longer, the greedy king threw away the chance of securing the
services of 20,000 hardy fighting men.

529. These affairs were bad enough as instances of blind in-
fatuation. In some respects the negotiation with the king of Pergamum was an even more lamentable proof of folly, and it involved
Eumenes as well as Perseus. We have no sufficient ground for
doubting the general truth[1] of Polybius' story, which is as follows.
Eumenes knew better than to trust Perseus: he did not wish him to
win the day and become dangerous. But of this result there seemed
to be no prospect. On the other hand the Romans too were not
doing well, and an Aetolian rising in their rear might happen at any
time. He fancied that he saw a chance to mediate between the weary
combatants, and to pocket a handsome commission in the character of
honest broker. So he negotiated secretly with Perseus, who met
his advances eagerly, scenting the material for a successful swindle.
Two offers were submitted as alternatives to Perseus by Eumenes.
Either he would cease cooperating with the Romans, or he would
bring about a peace. For the first accommodation the price was
500 talents (about £117,500); the second, which we may guess implied
the possibility of war with Rome, could not be done for less than three
times the sum. The first plan was rejected—the transaction would
not look well—, the second accepted, but at this point the royal
higglers came to a deadlock. Perseus proposed to deposit the
1500 talents in the famous Samothracian temple, to be paid over
for value received on the conclusion of peace. Samothrace belonged
to Perseus. Eumenes would not act on the faith of a deferred remittance,—he knew his man—and insisted on ready money. Thus
the negotiation failed, ending, as Polybius says, in a drawn game.

[1] Polyb. XXIX 7—9.

The utmost secrecy had been maintained, but the coming and going of ambassadors could not be concealed. It was indeed a legitimate ground of suspicion, all the more as Antiochus of Syria was approached at the same time. So the Romans more than ever looked askance at Eumenes and shewed favour to Attalus: this was the one practical result of the crooked intrigues of Perseus.

530. The spring months of 168, before the new consul and praetor arrived, were employed by the Macedonian fleet in naval operations. Their light handy vessels scoured the Aegean, escorting convoys of corn-ships to their own ports, and intercepting those of the enemy. A body of 1000 Galatian cavalry, horses and all, just shipped by Eumenes to reinforce Attalus, were cut off by this cruising squadron and all killed or taken. A notable feature in this cruise was the use of Delos as a naval base. A few Roman and Pergamene vessels were there too, unmolested: for the island was sacred, and the permanent truce of the god protected them. But they could do nothing, and the fleet of Perseus held the mastery of the sea for the time, and spared only the commerce of Rhodes. These proceedings were having their natural effect on public opinion in that republic, when the joint embassy from Perseus and Gentius appeared. The Roman partisans could no longer control the popular excitement. A favourable answer was sent to the two kings: embassies were appointed to visit Rome and the consul in command, and give both Senate and consul to understand that the war must come to an end: the Rhodian republic had made up its mind on that point. Negotiations were at once opened in Crete, the mother-land of mercenaries: and for a little while the Rhodian Demos enjoyed the dream of playing a great part on the stage of international politics.

531. But events now moved fast; the fabric painfully built up by diplomacy gave way at the stroke of the sword, and the builders, and others with them, were involved in the disaster of its fall. Gentius was the first victim. In a campaign of thirty days the praetor had beaten his forces, taken his capital, rescued the imprisoned envoys, and received the surrender of the king and most of his family. By judicious lenity and fair dealing the subjects of Gentius were conciliated: order was maintained, the chief prisoners forwarded to Rome to adorn a triumph, and the danger from the side of Illyria was at an end. It was now the turn of Perseus. His army was strongly posted on the northern bank of a mountain stream, the deeply-cut channel of which, itself a great protection, was so defended by a system of works as to defy a frontal attack. Small bodies were detached to resist expected descents on the Macedonian coast, for the Roman fleet was cruising near, ready to cooperate with the

movements of the consul. The difficult pass on the NW of Olympus, by which the king's position could be turned, seems not to have been occupied at first. The camp of Paullus lay to the south of the stream, on land apparently waterless: indeed one of the disadvantages by which Perseus hoped to wear out the Romans was this notorious difficulty of getting water on such ground. But Paullus had eyes, and from the vegetation on the hillsides inferred the existence of water below. By sinking wells through the porous soil, no doubt the detritus of the mountain, he obtained an abundant supply. This elementary display of commonsense greatly impressed the rank and file, whom his firm discipline brought to a high pitch of efficiency. Improved methods of passing orders, of relieving outposts, and other details, all helped to promote smartness and confidence, worthy of the best traditions of the Roman army.

532. While the two armies lay watching each other in ominous calm, the Rhodian envoys arrived in the Roman camp. The news of the victory in Illyria had just come to hand. A council of war heard their message with furious indignation: the consul promised them an answer in fifteen days' time. He had got information and guides, and was maturing plans for a turning movement. The charge of this expedition he entrusted to Scipio Nasica, a son-in-law of the great Africanus, and his own son Q. Fabius Maximus. Meanwhile frontal attacks, not driven home, and other feints served to keep Perseus employed. However he got wind of the real operation against his rear through the inevitable Cretan deserter, and sent a force to hold the pass. Nasica and his men met and routed this force, and safely reached the open country. The king's line of communications was threatened and he at once fell back, leaving the strong lines constructed with so much trouble. He took up a well-chosen position in front of Pydna, where on the advice of his staff he decided to accept battle. Paullus followed at his heels, picking up the corps of Nasica on the way. When the army found itself face to face with the enemy, officers and men were for falling on at once. The self-reliant consul knew better, and with his habitual secrecy kept his plans to himself. With much ado he held in his eager troops, formed a camp, and took a day for foraging and for resting his men, wearied with a dusty march under a Mediterranean sun near the end of summer. That night there was an eclipse of the moon, a phenomenon traditionally portending evil to some person or persons unknown, and thus liable to inspire misgivings in all persons conscious of their own importance. It is said that in the Macedonian camp there was utter consternation, such as would have paralysed any army in earlier times: men whispered that the fall of

the kingdom was at hand. But Greek astronomers had not calculated, and able Romans had not studied Greek lore, for nothing: a military tribune, C. Sulpicius Gallus, by leave of the consul (himself interested in such phenomena) addressed the troops, foretelling the eclipse and preventing a panic. It seems that the time-honoured custom of beating kettles and brandishing torches was not omitted, and Paullus himself offered sacrifices. Next morning he lavishly slaughtered and inspected victims in the good old style until the signs were favourable, and made a vow of games and further offerings in the event of victory. It was thought that he dallied over these formalities purposely: even after their completion he lingered in his tent. He was in fact resolved not to fight in the forenoon, for in the afternoon the sun would be in the faces of the enemy.

533. The battle was brought on by the collision of the advanced parties on both sides. The tactics are obscure, and do not concern us in general. The appearance of the phalanx, in two or more deep columns, bristling with pikes, was as usual most impressive: and it was irresistible in front, charging in compact mass, as some brave Italian Allies found to their cost. But motion soon dislocated its ranks, and Paullus threw small bodies of his swordsmen into the gaps, with the usual result. Once the armies were actually engaged, the victory was won in about an hour. Perseus suddenly remembered that he had omitted to sacrifice to Heracles at Pella, and rode off in hot haste to perform this ceremony. The royal horseguards and other cavalry followed: the foot were butchered till nightfall. The slain on the Macedonian side were estimated variously at 20,000 or 25,000, the Roman losses are put at about 100 men. All was over: the famous kingdom of Macedon was at an end. And the result had been attained, not by surpassing military genius, nor by some unaccountable stroke of luck, but by the superior efficiency of the Roman officers and men and the greater elasticity of the Roman tactical system. Timidity, slackness, and general unfitness for high responsibilities,—some or all of these defects had caused three successive consuls to fail. But the task was easy enough for the vast power of Rome: no sooner was it undertaken by a competent and determined man, a man whose staff were not advisers but subordinates, than the tone of the army was restored and the enemy completely overthrown. The battle of Pydna was decisive, because it was the military expression of the great political fact of the age.

534. We need not follow Perseus in his flight, doffing his royal robes and querulously blaming others for his own fault, while on various pretexts his friends slipped away. Nor need we inquire whether he did or did not at Pella slay his chief treasurers with

his own hand. The troops with him mostly dispersed to their homes, but a body of Cretans attended him to Amphipolis, with an eye to the treasure that the king took with him. It is said that he purposely left out plate to the value of 50 talents (£11,750) for them to plunder: later, as his first panic abated, he offered to redeem some cups that had belonged to Alexander the Great. Those who knew him well did not respond to this offer: those who were weak enough to surrender their booty were cheated out of the cash. The story may be a work of Greek imagination: it is at least in character. His last refuge was the island of Samothrace, where with his family he took sanctuary in the temple of the Dioscuri. He had with him treasure amounting to 2000 talents (£470,000). Octavius blockaded him with the Roman fleet, but respected the sanctity of the temple. Perseus made a last effort to escape with some of his money in a ship of Crete, but the Cretan skipper, having got the money on board, put to sea and left the royal party behind. He is said to have been mean and faithless to the few companions who were still with him. At length one of these betrayed his children to the Romans, and he surrendered. All his hopes were gone. Paullus had refused to treat with him as king, and he had to appear as a private applicant for mercy. He was generously received by the consul, but reserved to grace the coming triumph. By his own acts he had furnished rich material to the moralists of after times: Paullus himself is said to have made him the subject of 'a few earnest words' on the mutability of human things.

535. From time immemorial kings had ruled in Macedon, and all the traditions of national·unity and glory were bound up with the initiative vigour of a monarchic power. Accordingly the flight of Perseus was the end of national resistance. We are told that in two days the whole of Macedonia (that is, no doubt, the vital centres) made submission to Paullus. What happened at Amphipolis illustrates the situation. This strong town was held by a Greek governor with a garrison of Thracians. The overthrow of their employer left these barbarians without a master, and it seemed likely that they would turn to looting on their own account. Such a result would please neither the Roman consul nor the fugitive king nor the citizens. So the wily Greek forged a letter purporting to be an appeal from a coast-town for help against a raid of the Roman fleet. In hope of surprising the raiders laden with booty the Thracians were induced to set out for the supposed scene of action: whereupon the gates of the fortress were closed. Perseus and his Cretans soon after arrived: they were got rid of, money and all, as soon as possible, and the town surrendered to the Romans.

The consul allowed his victorious troops so much licence as to let the horse plunder the neighbourhood of Pydna while the foot divided the spoils of the enemy's camp. But he seems to have kept his army in hand, and to have done his best to make the conquest final by protecting the people of the country. His gentle treatment of the wretched Perseus made a good impression, says Diodorus, and his influence on his officers, who imitated his example of justice and mercy, served to reconcile the world to the dominant primacy of Rome. In considering this influence it is well to notice the way in which Paullus transplanted his family circle to his camp. Beside Scipio Nasica, a marriage-connexion through the family of Africanus, he had with him his sons, Fabius Aemilianus and Scipio Aemilianus the hero of the next generation: and his two sons-in-law, young Cato, who distinguished himself at Pydna, and the incorruptible Tubero. When we reflect that a Roman magistrate commanding an army in a foreign land was for the time civil governor as well as general, we need not wonder that the scrupulous consul made a point of leavening his staff with relatives whose characters he knew and had helped to form. Only Scipio was a boy. He had shewn his keen fighting mettle at Pydna, and was so forward in the pursuit that he was for a time supposed to be dead.

536. Among the dramatic elements with which the story of the fall of Macedon abounds, no episode is more striking or more numerously attested than that of the supernatural transmission[1] of the news of victory to Rome. The variations of the accounts are so remarkable, that we need not inquire what (if any) is the basis of fact underlying them. We may gather that a vague presentiment of a great victory spread through the city, and that none knew how or whence the rumour arose. It may serve as an index of the extreme tension of mind prevailing at the moment, itself a highly significant fact. It was several days before the news came to hand, and rejoicings and thanksgivings were the business of the hour. The first care of the Senate, after the duties of religion were done with, was to provide for the gradual disbanding of the forces held in reserve. These were considerable, and seem to have been kept in full readiness, though the earlier success in Illyria might, one would think, have eased the strain to some extent. Another dramatic scene that seems to belong to this stage of events is the reception of the Rhodian ambassadors who had been sent to put an end to the war. They had not arrived, or at least had not delivered their message, before the news of Pydna made their rash errand not only

---

[1] Cicero *de deorum natura* II § 6, Livy XLV 1, 2, Valer. Max. 1 8 § 1, Plin. *nat. hist.* VII § 86, Plutarch *Aemil.* 24—5, Florus 1 28 § 15.

out of date but disastrous. They had to admit that their original mandate was the restoration of peace, but on their own responsibility they changed it to a message of congratulation. Why the war had been allowed by Rhodes to go on while Perseus was campaigning with success in Thessaly, and yet was to be stopped so soon as the Romans had gained a footing in Macedonia, was the question to which they could give no answer consistent with friendly devotion to Roman interests. The Senate therefore held that the intervention of Rhodes was prompted by a wish to help Perseus out of an awkward predicament, and according to Polybius they seem to have been fully entitled to take this view. The envoys were dismissed with no definite answer. A great settlement was coming, and the turn of disloyal friends would come with it: for the moment there was no hurry.

537. Meanwhile proceedings at Rhodes[1] itself were illustrating the revival of fear of the long arm of Rome. The collapse of the Macedonian kingdom put an end to the control of the Aegean by the king's fleet, and Popilius and his colleagues started again from Delos on their mission to Egypt. On their way they met a deputation of leading Rhodians, who entreated them to put in at Rhodes and satisfy themselves as to the recent and present policy of the state. It was feared that hearsay reports might unjustly damage Rhodes in the eyes of the Romans. The Roman envoys objected, but at length agreed to come. The hard uncompromising Popilius made the unhappy Greeks tremble as he bullied and browbeat them, charging their state and statesmen with disloyal words and deeds during the war. In abject terror the Assembly voted to put to death all persons convicted of having taken the part of Perseus. The leaders of the Macedonian party took to flight or committed suicide. The envoys went on to Alexandria, but the Rhodians, with all the cruelty of fear, proceeded to commit a series of judicial murders. Even more impressive was the effect of the battle of Pydna in Egypt. Antiochus had withdrawn from that country, but kept the fortress of Pelusium commanding the only practicable approach from the East. Clearly he meant to have Egypt at his mercy. So the quarrelling members of the Lagid family[2] came to terms with each other. Antiochus took this in high dudgeon and again entered Egypt. Nothing would satisfy him but territorial cessions which they were not prepared to make. He was close to Alexandria, and there seemed no hope for the Ptolemies, when the Roman ambassadors met him. He held out his right hand to Popilius, who did not take it, but gave him the copy of the Senate's decree and told him to

---

[1] Livy XLV 10, Weissenborn.　　　　[2] See below § 587.

read it. It was an order to put an end to the war at once, and of course to evacuate Egypt. The king said 'I want to lay the matter before my councillors.' Popilius with his stick drew a circle round Antiochus on the ground, and replied 'Your majesty will please to give your answer before you step out of that circle.' Antiochus hesitated for an instant, dazed by the insolence of the Roman: but a moment's reflexion convinced him of the impossibility of resistance, and he answered that he would obey the orders from Rome. The Romans then shook hands with him as a friend. They presently took ship again for Cyprus, where they found a Syrian force victorious. This force they ordered out of the island, and waited to see the evacuation carried out. Cyprus remained a dependency of Egypt, and Rome had, so far as possible, restored the kingdom of the Ptolemies. But the brutal frankness of Popilius shocked the Greek world, long used to the empty and ceremonious etiquette of royal courts. Only to small peoples, interested in shaking off the control of unsympathetic monarchies, was the crude assertion of Roman supremacy welcome. Antiochus on his way home, disappointed of his Egyptian prey, outraged the feelings of the Jewish people by sacrilege and religious persecution, which led to the famous revolt of the Maccabees[1] in the year 167. A few years later we find Rome in alliance with the Jews: and, if Rome did not actually send armies to support them in their struggle for independence, the mere countenance of the great republic was a help.

538. And now embassies[2] began to pour into Rome from the East, thanking, grovelling, begging forgiveness, above all congratulating. Antiochus was grateful for the blessed boon of peace, that is, for being kicked out of Egypt: the Ptolemies for their rescue from Antiochus. Then came a son of Masinissa to express his father's devotion to Rome his patron, and his joy in their victory. Another son, on his way home with the Numidian contingent from the seat of war, lay sick at Brundisium. All these were received in a friendly and hospitable manner, and special care taken of the invalid prince. A suggestion that Masinissa himself would like to visit Rome was discouraged. He was wanted in Africa: the Senate had not forgotten or abandoned the policy of watching Carthage. In the arrangements for the year 167 the new consuls were provided with provinces in northern Italy, to keep an eye on Ligurians and Gauls. Paullus and Anicius were to stay on in their provinces as proconsul and propraetor, and bodies of commissioners were appointed to assist them in carrying out the detailed settlement of the conquered countries. The main outlines of the settlement were laid down by

---

[1] See 1 Maccabees cc. 1, 8.   [2] Livy XLV 13, 14.

the Senate. In fixing these the party of which Cato was a leading member played a great part. The object in view was to advance Roman interests without weakening old Roman virtues. The wholesale extension of Roman dominion over transmarine provinces east of Italy was not contemplated. First, it was agreed that the conquered peoples were to be 'free.' That is, they were to have no kings,—in other words, no central powers to which they might rally and perhaps again give trouble to Rome. Secondly, as a further security against troublesome combinations, the countries were to be cut up into districts, each district having an independent local government. Thirdly, the several districts were to pay a fixed tribute to Rome, but this tribute was to be only half the amount of what they had hitherto paid to their sovrans. A special proviso dealt with the case of the Macedonian mines, the development of which had enriched the kings. It was held that to leave them in Macedonian hands would promote jobbery, and only lead to disputes and civil war. On the other hand, to take them over and work them as state property would open the door to intolerable abuses. The state could only operate through contractors[1], whom it could not effectively control. The contractors would either not do their duty by Rome, or would cruelly oppress the natives, who were Roman allies. It was therefore agreed that the mines must be shut down. A similar decision was arrived at in the matter of the state domainlands. The Senate seems to have been sincerely desirous to do nothing that might hinder the conquered from settling down quietly under the new state of things, and fully convinced that the difficulty of restraining the greed and tyranny of their own countrymen at so great a distance from Rome was insuperable.

539. These countries then were not to be annexed and made into Roman Provinces. But the principle applied in the settlement is essentially the same as that underlying the provincial system in several most important respects. Rome had succeeded to the sovranty of previous rulers, as of king Hiero and Carthage in Sicily. She habitually interfered as little as possible with local government, partly to conciliate subjects, partly to save trouble. In Macedonia, and to some extent in Illyria, she found large united areas. To break up these, and artificially create local governments, was to leave

---

[1] Livy XLV 18, Diodor. XXXI 13. I can only explain this by supposing that two kinds of contract are referred to. First, the state paying contractors to do the work, itself taking risks and profits. This would be an *ultro tributum*, and the state would lose by slackness of contractors. Second, concessions to lessees paying a fixed rent and taking risks and profits. This would be a *vectigal*, and the lessees would exact forced labour from natives. The former alternative may have been an approximation to the system employed by the kings, who would probably dislike the plan of concessionary leases.

herself in the position of the virtual sovran. The arrangements
rested on her authority: all questions arising out of them must
inevitably be referred to her sovran power, for there was no other.
We can see that to pass from this condition to that of a regular
Province would be a short and easy step, indeed little more than the
appointment of a governor. This may have been present to the
minds of some senators at the time; that it was, we cannot affirm.
What came of the arrangement we shall see below.

540. The relations between Rome and her friends the king of
Pergamum and the republic of Rhodes now came up for consideration.
It was not seriously intended to suppress these suspected powers, but
it was felt by many that the great accessions of territory granted
to them after the defeat of Antiochus III had not answered the
purpose, and the Senate was in no mood to condone offences.
Attalus came on behalf of Eumenes, to bring congratulations and
to complain of a recent invasion of his territory by the Galatians.
This last annoyance may have been a 'pin-prick' administered with
the connivance of some powerful Romans, to teach the king his
dependance on Rome. Anyhow some leading men took Attalus in
hand and egged him on to ask favours for himself, to wit a kingdom of
his own, of course carved out of his brother's. Attalus had ambitions,
and was very nearly persuaded to adopt this sinister advice. But
Eumenes, forecasting the danger, sent a trusty agent after his brother,
and this man arrived just in time to dissuade Attalus from a step
that would at once ruin the Attalid kingdom: a kingdom of which
Attalus was himself the apparent heir. The prince drew back in
time, and in his official capacity adhered to his original errand, only
asking for himself the lordship of the coast-towns Aenus and
Maronea. This gift the Senate granted, and promised to order the
Galatians to retire. Polybius[1], rightly or wrongly, declares that the
senators regarded the moderation of Attalus as the insincere decency
of a public utterance, and expected that he would push his own
claims by private intrigues. But he gave them the slip, and their
disappointment vented itself in declaring Aenus and Maronea free
cities, and (to judge from the sequel) in instructing the ambassadors
to Galatia to let the barbarians understand that for all Rome cared
they might be a thorn in the side of Pergamum.

541. The grovelling embassies came and went, and the Senate
became daily more familiar with the self-abasement of the eastern
world. In the temper developed by this degrading spectacle they at
first refused to give an audience to the wretched Rhodians. To add
to the terror of the envoys, a praetor gave notice of a bill for de-

[1] Polyb. xxx 1—3.

claring war against Rhodes, and harangued the people on the subject. Two tribunes blocked this proposal, but Rome was upset by the elation of the moment and the reaction from recent anxieties, and precedent was disregarded[1] in the procedure of both sides. At length the Senate condescended to hear them: they humbly prayed to be allowed to exist, and prostrated themselves on the floor of the House. The debate on their case was memorable. Some of the better and more far-seeing members opposed the brutal spirit only too prevalent in that hour of victory: a famous speech[2] delivered by Cato in behalf of the Rhodians was the chief feature. He urged that to punish hostile intent, when no act of hostility had been committed, was not worthy of the Roman people. He warned the House not to lose its head, and appealed to its sense of justice, probably also to the true interest of Rome. The envoys got off with a grim rebuke, and the answer left them in a very ambiguous position. But there was clearly no actual declaration of war to be dreaded, and some of the envoys hastened back to Rhodes with the news. What might befal them under the coming settlement none could tell. For the present they were relieved from fear of the worst extremities; it seemed now a small matter, compared with the past agony, that they had to withdraw their governors from Lycia and Caria, the recent gifts of Rome. They sent off a new embassy with a costly offering, to beg for admission to the Roman alliance. Hitherto they had avoided[3] alliances: now it was important to get their relation to Rome clearly defined. But their troubles were not over. In their old possessions on the mainland their subjects rose in rebellion. It was an affair of life and death, for the resources of their own island were not enough to support the population. A force was promptly despatched, and the rising put down.

542. In Illyria the propraetor Anicius had little trouble, and soon set out to conquer those parts of Epirus that had taken part with Perseus. This was an easy task: the people saw that the time for resistance was past, and the anti-Roman leaders manfully met their cruel fate. Returning to Scodra, he met the five commissioners, and with them settled the affairs of Illyria. The scheme of the Senate[4] was followed. The number of districts was to be three. Some communities received special favours, in accordance with time-honoured Roman practice, so that the conquered people might not

---

[1] Livy XLV 21.

[2] The fragments of this speech, preserved by Gellius VI 3, are given in Jordan's collection pp. 21—5, and discussed in his Introduction pp. lvi, lvii. Gellius' article is well worth reading.

[3] Polyb. XXX 5, Livy XLV 25.   [4] Livy XLV 26.

be too closely bound together by exact identity of interests. It is to be noted that we hear of no similar settlement in Epirus. Paullus, after punishing a few rebellious towns, set out for a tour in Greece, to see temples oracles antiquities and works of art. Athens Corinth Sparta and Olympia were among the places visited. He admired greatly the statue of Olympian Zeus, and with a costly sacrifice acknowledged the creation of Phidias as the imaged godhead of Roman Jupiter. His suite was very small, and the hospitality and courtesy of the proconsul charmed the Greeks, all the more as he carefully shut his ears to charges of sympathy with Perseus: for Paullus bygones were to be bygones. In Macedonia too, whither he now returned to preside over the settlement-commission, it was observed that he kept his hands off the royal treasures. He only took the royal library, for the sake of his cultivated sons. The treasure was treated as state property. Discipline had suffered in his absence: it was now firmly restored.

543. In due course delegations from the Macedonian communities were assembled at Amphipolis. Public documents and all moneys due to the royal treasury were likewise called in from outlying places. No pains were spared to bring home to the multitude of spectators the fact of a great and irresistible change. From his seat among the ten commissioners the proconsul rose and announced the final decisions of the Senate and the commission. He spoke in Latin, being the official mouthpiece[1] of Rome: an interpreter rendered his utterances into Greek. The settlement followed the lines laid down by the Senate. The country was divided into four districts, to each of which a capital city was assigned as the seat of the local government. The four republics thus formed were to be independent of each other. To isolate them more effectually, it was enacted that the mutual exercise of private rights was barred as between the citizens of the different republics. No member of any one could contract a legal marriage (*conubium*) or acquire and hold[2] real property (*commercium*) save in his own district. Beyond an arbitrary boundary line his family connexions and proprietary rights ceased. Gold and silver mines[3] were to be closed: those of copper and iron might be worked, at a payment[4] to Rome of half what the kings had been used to exact. The import of salt[5] was forbidden:

[1] Not from inability to speak Greek.
[2] If the words of Livy XLV 29 § 10 are accurate, *commercium* in movable property was not forbidden.
[3] It appears that they were reopened in 158, probably to gratify Roman capitalists.
[4] Whether this was a rent or a royalty does not appear.
[5] Mommsen sees in this a blow dealt at Rhodian trade. Perhaps it in some way favoured operations of Roman capitalists.

why, we are left to conjecture. The felling of timber for shipbuilding was also forbidden, probably in order to discourage local maritime enterprise, perhaps also to cut off the supplies of other[1] maritime peoples: for Rome was always nervously suspicious of doings on the water, since she kept no navy in commission to guard the peaceful traffic of the seas. Those districts which had barbarian tribes for neighbours were allowed to maintain armed forces on the frontier, an exception to the general disarmament dictated by the interests of Rome. We hear that the Macedonians received the settlement with mixed feelings. So far as having less taxes to pay, they were pleased: the division of the country was a painful shock. In fact Rome was dealing with a state of things foreign to her experience. In cutting up a kingdom she was on this occasion cutting up a nation: the process was painful, and led to troublesome consequences, as we shall see. It was no light thing to violate a national unity that had overcome local and tribal diversities and hardened into habit in the course of nearly 200 years. That the people were pleased with ‘freedom,’ that is, with the abolition of the monarchy, was plainly nothing but a Roman fiction. This was no doubt partly due to sheer misunderstanding, partly to cynical indifference, for the policy of Rome was to pose as the universal benefactor while acting from purely selfish motives. It was a cruel mockery when the people of the four districts were called upon to elect an administrative council for each of them. Notice was given that all those named in a published black list were to leave the country and report themselves in Italy under pain of death; a measure which at one stroke removed every one conversant with affairs of government, and left the people without their natural leaders. That constitutions were served out to the unhappy republics was no compensation for the destruction of the system to which, such as it was, the people were accustomed. These proceedings were followed by a scene surpassing the usual indecency of ancient conquerors. Amphipolis witnessed a magnificent festival, performances of actors and athletes, horse-races, sacrifices, feasting, a bonfire of spoils, a grand show of all the works of art and other valuables of which the cities of Macedon had been stript. Of the destination of these outward and visible signs of a growing civilization there was no doubt: the ships to bear them away to Rome lay ready in the Strymon.

544. And now the hand of the commission[2] was laid upon the Greek states. Roman partisans, men for the most part base and cruel, were now in power everywhere. In Aetolia a massacre of the

---

[1] Such as Rhodes, to which Perseus had lately presented timber.
[2] Livy XLV 31, Weissenborn.

chief men had taken place, and a Roman officer had lent his troops to help in the bloody work. This man was condemned (*damnatus*), but we do not hear what (if anything) was done to him. Numbers had been driven into exile and their goods confiscated. The commissioners condoned everything. It was not for them to discourage honest fellows who had perhaps been a little rough in excess of zeal. This specimen of Roman justice and mercy stirred up the leaders of the Roman party elsewhere to the foulest iniquities. They had the ear of the commission, and the names of all the best men of position in the several states, Aetolia Acarnania Epirus and Boeotia, were placed on a black list with orders to appear and stand their trial in Rome. Other details are mentioned, all aimed at producing weakness and disunion. The Achaeans, as the chief power, were separately dealt with by two of the commissioners in person. There was no evidence among the captured correspondence of Perseus that implicated any Achaean: the behaviour of the League had been most correct. But the infamous Callicrates[1] persuaded the commissioners that disloyalty abounded, and 1000 Achaeans, the flower of latter-day Greece, were deported to Italy on the pretext of being tried in Rome. One of these was the historian Polybius himself. Such was the Roman assize of loyalty in Greece. The once glorious Hellas had now come down to this, that a man's betrayal of his fellow-citizens was the first condition of political power.

545. To the just and humane Paullus all these harsh and malign proceedings were distasteful: but he had to bear a part in still worse doings on his way home. A raid in Illyria, to punish the hostile districts for supporting Perseus, was perhaps nothing more than the usual mark of disapproval, expressed in terms of fire and sword. But the treatment of the inland parts of Epirus[2] sent a shudder through a world not easily shocked by treachery and horrors. A deliberate decree of the Senate ordered that disloyal Epirus should be given over to plunder for the benefit of the returning army. Paullus had no choice but to carry out the order speedily and effectively with the least possible expenditure of Roman lives. Seventy towns received simultaneous instructions to have all their gold and silver ready on a certain day, and a detachment of soldiers was sent to each town to take over the local treasure. But the precious metals were not plentiful in these poor communities. The Epirotes themselves had a market value, and in their persons the Roman soldiery found most of the expected reward. At a preconcerted time they fell to work, looted the houses, and in one day carried off into slavery 150,000 people. What was the exact amount realized by the whole

---

[1] Polyb. XXX 13.   [2] Polyb. XXX 16, Livy XLV 34.

transaction we do not know: but we are expressly told[1] that those who shared the profits were not satisfied with the dividend.

546. The discontent of the greedy soldiers was turned to account by an officer who owed Paullus a grudge. When the time came for the people to vote triumphs to the victorious commanders, no opposition was offered to the claims of Anicius or Octavius the praetor of the fleet, but those of Paullus[2] were resisted. By great exertions on the part of leading men this scandal was averted, and the great proconsul was allowed to triumph, though he had maintained discipline and brought home for the state treasury money that rightfully belonged to it. No such spectacle as this famous triumph had ever been seen in Rome. For three days the procession filed along the streets. Greek works of art, destined to adorn the city; waggon-loads of splendid armour piled up, with points of swords showing here and there, and bristling with the celebrated pikes of Macedon; vessels of silver and masses of silver coin, and, separated from these, a like array of gold; the king's chariot and regalia: his little children, too young to understand their fate: Perseus himself, with his suite: cars laden with golden crowns, the gifts of fawning cities: then the conqueror in triumphal dress, followed by a staff of distinguished officers, his own Fabius and Scipio among them: last of all came the soldiers of his victorious army, singing as they marched along. Yet that time of thanksgiving and sacrifices, of joy and feasting, was of no good omen for the future of the republic. The largess distributed was small (an ordinary foot soldier got about £4 of our money) and sullenly received. Since the Galatian campaign of Manlius the mercenary taint had fast infected military life. Paullus was still able to keep up some of the traditions of the old citizen army. But he was already an exception, and awful consequences were to follow from the fact that men were finding the plough less profitable than the sword.

547. For the present the Roman commonwealth stood before the world in unexampled prosperity and power. The supremacy gained in previous wars had been challenged, with the result of the challenger's destruction. All over the civilized world, wherever organized government existed in Europe or western Asia, the hand of Rome made itself felt. A few years earlier it had found some difficulty in reaching Hannibal: henceforth even minor enemies found it impossible to escape. Polybius tells[3] the story of the flight of a Rhodian partisan of Perseus. Being 'wanted,' he took refuge in one place after another: nobody liked to surrender the suppliant,

---

[1] Plutarch *Aem.* 29, compare Livy XLV 34 § 7.
[2] Livy XLV 35—9, Weissenborn.   [3] Polyb. XXX 8, 9.

but nobody dared to shelter him : four times he was surrendered, and finally forwarded to Rome in a Rhodian ship. Hardly less remarkable was the relief of financial pressure. The forced war-loans had hitherto been a regular feature of the Roman system. Men were yet living who could remember the exhaustion and the desperate shifts necessitated by the Hannibalic war. Paullus now paid into the treasury a sum variously stated—from £1200,000 to £3000,000 of our money. War-indemnities and provincial taxation had no doubt in recent years reduced the burden formerly borne by Roman citizens in time of war. Henceforth the *tributum civium Romanorum* ceased[1] to be levied, and the financial fruits of conquest enabled the government to pay its way. It was noted that Paullus himself was none the richer for all this. But it mattered not. One of his remaining sons died just before his triumph, the other just after it, and his house was left unto him desolate. He was censor in 164, and some four years later he died.

548. Perseus and Gentius were placed in custody in Italian country towns. The former was thought a poor coward for clinging to life, and stories gathered round him as he passed to his dishonoured end. The Latin colony of Alba by the lake Fucinus was his prison, and there he died. A surviving son of his afterwards served the local magistrates as a clerk. More deserving of pity were the numerous Greeks, not prisoners of war, deported to Italy as 'suspects.' The Roman government did not want them to return home. They were picked men, and their detention in Italy meant the withdrawal of so much intellectual and moral vigour, so much political force, from states that had given trouble or uneasiness to Rome in the past, and might do so again. They were not brought to trial, but placed out in the charge of Italian towns. In uncongenial surroundings they lived a homesick existence : as their hopes died out, so did they. The story of the few survivors who returned to Greece will meet us below. A very few had the good fortune to find protectors among those more enlightened Romans in whom the expansion of Roman dominion produced an expansion of their general interests. Chief of the favoured few was Polybius, a man of much thought and knowledge, and of large political experience. His entertaining and instructive company was soon highly valued, and he found a noble patron in Scipio Aemilianus. In the cultivated circle that in a few years gathered round this distinguished man Polybius was a familiar figure. In such surroundings he learnt more of the politics and history of Rome than was given to any other Greek. No doubt he learnt to magnify the Scipios, and to admire

[1] See Marquardt, *Staatsverwaltung* vol. II, under *tributum*.

Rome and the Romans overmuch: but he seems never to have forgotten his own people or lost sight of his duty as a statesman of the Achaean League.

549. I have in this chapter recounted the events that led directly up to the third Macedonian war, the story of the war itself, and its immediate consequences. I have tried to bring out the meaning of this highly significant series of events. It remains to add a few words on the general drift of the foreign policy of Rome since the end of the second Punic war. We have now reached a point at which this may profitably be done: and we cannot shirk a topic upon which authorities of note have expressed divergent views. In the first place, how far was Rome in earnest (as Mommsen holds) in the liberation of Greece? Secondly, does Roman diplomacy change in this period, becoming infinitely subtle and treacherous—Macchiavellistic, as Carl Peter[1] calls it? Thirdly, to take a particular case, are we with Mommsen to dismiss the story of the wavering and the contemplated intervention of Eumenes as a silly fabrication, or not? These questions, involving closely connected issues, have been partly dealt with in the course of our narrative, but need some answer of a more direct kind. To the present writer it appears that the first and second of them must be considered in relation to the Roman Senate, its composition and its powers. There were in that body a number of old men, and a few young, but the majority would probably be between 40 and 60 years of age. Some, a slowly decreasing number, would be men of the old Roman school, hard and narrow: there were the reformers, Cato and others, never a numerous band, but strong in energy: also a growing new school, philhellenes and others. There were many of the great noble houses, Cornelii and others, to whom public office was rather a family incident than an evidence of popular approval: there would be some (a minority no doubt) members of less important houses, even a very few who had themselves by attaining public office first made their families 'noble.' All or nearly all would in this period have had some experience of military service. All would be men of some property, some even rich: the influence of wealth was steadily growing, and by the time of the war with Perseus there must have been many greedy senators watching for opportunities of making money in ways other than the closed thoroughfare of commerce. With the spread of Roman dominion and the greater complexity of public business the Senate more and more put on the character of a governing body, and gave orders to magistrates whom it was originally meant to advise. It controlled state patronage, and directed state policy: but

---

[1] C. Peter, *Studien zur Römischen Geschichte* (Halle, 1863).

there was at least one department in which the Assembly still exercised its constitutional right—the declaration of war. Already in the year 200 it had been no easy matter to get war declared against Philip, and the difficulty of raising legions and keeping them efficient in campaigns abroad was getting worse and worse.

550. The Senate then found itself in an awkward position. All would agree that the primacy of Italy (that is, of Rome) in the Mediterranean world must at all costs be upheld. No rival must be left in a condition to contend with Rome on equal terms. True, after the failure of Hannibal there was no power at all comparable to Rome: but this superiority had to be demonstrated, and now, when the will of Rome had to be enforced in distant lands, it was found that her strength could not be made available so readily as of old. From the necessities of this situation two marked consequences followed: the wars demoralized the soldiers, and the Senate strained the resources of diplomacy to the utmost, in order to achieve its objects without resort to war. To keep in obedient dependence so many kingdoms and republics was a gigantic task, and wars could not always be avoided. But they were always reluctantly undertaken, and it regularly took some time to produce both an efficient army and a capable general. Then, when the war was over, Rome was not prepared to take over the conquered countries and rule them herself as provinces. For that practical and intelligible step things were not yet ripe. The experience of her provinces in the West was not wholly satisfactory, but she could not safely abandon them. This experience, coupled with the fear of attempting too much, and the mutual jealousies of members of the Senate, for the present checked the policy of provincial extension. Another solution of the problems created by conquest was found in the policy of handing over ceded districts to allies, or of allowing them to make conquests on their own account. Pergamum and Rhodes are instances of the former practice, Philip and the Achaean League of the latter: Greek city-communities were generally declared 'free.' But when Rome had strengthened a Friend so far as to hold an enemy in check, the fear immediately arose that too much power had been granted, power that might be used against Roman interests. There was nothing quixotic in the relations of states: Rome was no more wicked than others. Her aim was to produce equilibrium in Greece and the East, so that she might enjoy the maximum of supremacy with the minimum of exertion. To anything that threatened to disturb the equipoise she was nervously alive. That Rome was at first in earnest with the liberation of the Greeks is probable enough, if we bear in mind that she meant them

to give her no further trouble: so far the sentiment of the philhellenic clique might prevail in the Senate, there being for the moment no alternative before the House. But, once it became clear (as it soon did) that the wretched communities of Greece, incapable of peace and freedom, were ever ready to embroil their neighbours by intrigues and seditions, Roman policy became less considerate. It more and more took the line of backing up the Roman partisans in the several states. Whatever nobler sentiments may at first have guided it, they were now cast aside, and Rome's treatment of the Greeks became unscrupulous and cruel. Aetolia and Boeotia were the scene of horrors in northern Greece: in Peloponnesus, jealousy of the League's stability and power led Rome to foment the Spartan troubles and condone the atrocities of Nabis. The ambiguous decisions and underhand dealings of the Senate tended to prevent Greece from settling down in quiet, even had the Greeks been so inclined.

551. In relation to the kings Rome played her old game. She divided her enemies, and smote them one by one. In this there was nothing beyond the common processes of statecraft. But the methods employed to deceive an enemy and lull him into security never have a gracious appearance. Both Philip and Perseus lost points in the game through Roman guile. The attempts to set Demetrius against his father and Attalus against his brother were also ugly affairs, and speak ill for the honour of Roman senators. What shall we say of such double-faced diplomacy as appears in the secret encouragement of the Galatians to worry Pergamum as Masinissa worried Carthage? What, but that the kings were no more scrupulous in their dealings with Rome, or indeed with each other. And here we come at once to the question about the intrigue of Eumenes. It is simply this. Polybius[1] got the story by hearsay. At the time it leaked out in the form of gossip, but he tells us that other details were afterwards communicated to the inner circle of Perseus' friends. Thus he may have got at these confirmatory pieces of evidence when he and some of the king's friends were detained in Italy. Next we must consider whether Polybius was competent to judge the genuineness of these revelations, or not. He was not infallible, but to reject the whole story as a fiction is to credit him with a mere gaping simplicity. We have no sufficient warrant for doing this. The affair is consistent with the characters of the two kings, and we must not forget that the basis of the Attalid kingdom was money. We shall do well to accept the story in its main outlines.

552. To sum up our conclusions as to the drift of Roman policy. That it had always been wily, we know. That its diplomacy became

---

[1] Polyb. XXIX 4—9, Livy XLIV 24—5 is merely an adaptation of Polybius.

in this period more double-faced and treacherous can hardly be denied. But this was only a natural development promoted by the internal changes in the Roman state. And, when we read of the infamous duplicity imputed to such a man as Q. Marcius, we must reflect that all Rome's emissaries had to stand the criticism of the Senate on their return. They were not principals, but agents, and their first business was to succeed. Failure might have passed muster with a select few, on the plea that Greek subtlety had been too much for Roman frankness: when it came to voting, double-dealing was more readily condoned. The really significant fact in the foreign policy of the period is not that there was so much craft employed, but that, considering the greatness of the results attained, there was so little direct action of the sword.

Note. While this book is passing through the press, there has appeared *The Client Princes of the Roman empire under the Republic* (Cambridge Historical Essays Nº XVI) by Mr P. C. Sands. The collection of evidence in Appendix A is most useful. The methods and effect of 'recognition' by Rome are fully dealt with. One important point comes out very clearly, that a potentate officially addressed as *rex* by the Senate was on a wholly different footing from the petty princes or chiefs, tributaries of Rome, of whom the literary language often speaks as *reges*.

CHAPTER XXXII

WARS AND POLICY OF ROME IN THE WEST, 193—167 B.C.

553. IT may be thought a clumsy and confusing method to devote several short chapters to the wars and policy of Rome in the West during the period 200—133 B.C. There is so much sameness in their phenomena that this long period is sometimes treated as one, only dividing the narrative on a principle of locality. And it is true that the wars in Istria and the plains of the Po are not connected with those in Spain. They are however connected with the inland warfare in Liguria, and in the other direction the communications of Rome with Spain had to be kept open: Ligurian piracy had to be suppressed, and Sardinia and Corsica reduced to a final submission. And these wars have also a common character in that they were essentially aggressive. Hence we find them smouldering or breaking out according as Roman policy is more or less active. Not having any great organized power to face, Rome could choose times and seasons to suit her own convenience. Her hand was not forced, as it was in the East by Antiochus and Perseus. Rebellions in Spain were generally the outcome of Roman misdeeds: the wise and just policy of Gracchus in 179 was so effective that the peninsula enjoyed comparative peace for some 25 years. If we turn to Liguria, we find war practically continuous for 20 years (193—173), in half of which we find both consuls appointed to that 'province,' pecking away at the hills with little result. We read of victories and defeats, of which the latter at least are credible. Then from 172 to 168 Rome had more urgent business, settling accounts with Perseus, and accordingly we hear that Liguria was comparatively quiet. After Pydna the conquest was slowly and intermittently resumed, until resistance died out and Roman influence prevailed. And not only were the wars in the West carried on at Rome's good pleasure and in obedience to the larger considerations that governed her general policy, but our fragmentary knowledge of them is indirectly derived from Roman annalists and historians, in whose honesty we can place no confidence. If then the piecemeal treatment may seem somewhat clumsy and confusing, it may fairly be pointed out that herein it corresponds to

the nature of the events and the darkness of the record. For the present we will only continue the story down to the year 167 or thereabouts. The confirmation of Roman supremacy effected by the ruin of Macedon forms a convenient halting-place.

554. From 193 to 167 we find in Livy some reference to Spain under the events of each year. Doubtful successes, barren of result, and less doubtful defeats, avenged in due course by victories; submission of tribes, soon cancelled by new rebellions; triumphs or ovations of returning governors; such is the matter of most of these references. The details more important in magnitude or significance may be summarized as follows. In 190 Aemilius Paullus met with a disaster in the Further Spain, his army being badly cut up by the Lusitanians. But he managed somehow to reorganize it and to quiet the southern natives by a great victory[1] in the following year. Under the year 184 we read of grave discontent in the armies: the long and irksome service so far from home was the cause, and a mutiny had at all costs to be avoided. Indeed the Spanish service was wholly inconsistent with the military system of Rome. Yet it was felt to be impossible to recall the seasoned troops and trust only to raw levies. The Senate sent out strong reliefs and only allowed time-expired men and others of special merit to come home. In 181 a great rising took place among the Celtiberi. These were a race of mixed blood, who combined the dash of the Gaulish Celt with the tendency to recoil characteristic of the stubborn Iberian. To them is due a great part of the resistance experienced by the Romans in the peninsula. But a great victory of the praetor Flaccus, well followed up, restored quiet in central Spain, and we hear that most of the Celtiberi made their submission. In this campaign local levies are said[2] to have fought for Rome. In 180 the complaints of the long service came up again, and were dealt with on the same lines as before. The new praetor for the Hither Spain was Tiberius Sempronius Gracchus, the father of the two famous reformers, himself one of the best public servants of Rome. He was kept at his post in 179 as propraetor, and entered upon a new course of policy[3] beneficial to Rome and the Spaniards alike. He made treaties with the native tribes on fair terms, and tried to lead them to more settled and peaceful habits by the promotion of urban life. We hear that when Flaccus was (early in 180) withdrawing his army from the interior, and was attacked by the Celtiberi, the local levies had shewn a lack of steadiness. But Gracchus continued the system of raising native forces, and wisely encouraged

---

[1] So Livy XXXVII 46, 57. Plutarch *Aemil.* 4 knows nothing of the defeat. See the inscription given below § 688 (*b*).

[2] Livy XL 30—32.   [3] Appian *Hisp.* 43, 44, Plutarch *Tib. Gracc.* 5 § 3.

chiefs[1] to enter the Roman service. So long as these men were kept loyal, they would make valuable officers, understanding the temper of their countrymen: no doubt by this move the auxiliary forces were greatly improved. The government of Gracchus marks an epoch in the relations between Rome and Spain. And when he returned home he did not forget those whom he had governed, but used his influence to prevent evasion or violation of the treaties, so that the Spanish peoples might learn to put some trust in the Roman honour.

555. In 176 we meet with a curious[2] story. When the 'provinces' for the year were allotted, Crassus, the praetor to whom Hither Spain had fallen, objected to go. He declared that duty required him to perform (in person and at Rome) certain fixed sacrifices: it was therefore impossible for him to go abroad. A few years later (171) he was consul, and the religious scruple did not hinder him from accepting the Macedonian command, and enriching himself at the expense of the wretched Greeks. He was also in 167 chief of the infamous embassy to the Galatians. Clearly he was a man of great influence and unscrupulous character. On the present occasion he was allowed to make oath publicly of his conscientious objection, and so released from an unwelcome duty. The concession made to Crassus aroused a similar desire in M. Cornelius Maluginensis, who had drawn the Further Spain. That he pleaded sacrificial obligations we are not told, but it was probably some pretext of the kind. He seems to have been a man of bad character. Two years later the censors of 174 struck him off the roll of the Senate, whether for perjury or for some other offence, we do not hear. On the whole it is a fair inference that these two rogues shirked service in Spain because the prospects of enriching themselves there by plunder and extortion were small. Perhaps the opportunities had been curtailed by the recent arrangements of Gracchus. We now come to the time of the third Macedonian war, when Rome was preoccupied with eastern affairs, and had little spare energy for conquests in the far West. In 172 we hear of much reluctance on the part of the Senate to vote the reinforcements needed for the army in Spain, and in the years 171—168 we find the whole provincial charge of Spain entrusted to a single praetor. This course was partly adopted in order to leave one praetor free to take command of the fleet in the East, but partly no doubt to check the forward policy in the West until a more convenient season.

556. In 171 envoys from both the Spanish provinces[3] appeared

---

[1] Livy XL 49 §§ 4—7.   [2] Livy XLI 15, with Weissenborn's note on § 10.
[3] Livy XLIII 2. The brevity of expression makes the interpretation of this chapter very

in Rome. They laid before the Senate a sad tale of the extortions practised by recent governors, and begged redress of their wrongs. It was a critical moment. Some remedy must be found to soothe the Spaniards, for none doubted that extortion had taken place: on the other hand it was not a moment for new and heroic remedies that might cause a disturbance in public life, when the attention of the state was otherwise engaged. A public trial before the Assembly was avoided, perhaps for this reason. There existed a civil court for settlement of claims between parties, who need not both be Roman citizens, known as the 'Recoverers' or court of Recovery, speedy and simple in its procedure. It could at any time be called into active life by appointing certain persons as *recuperatores* to try a definite issue. They were nominees of an officer holding *imperium*. The institution is supposed to date from early times, and to have had a sort of international origin, being devised to settle disputes between citizens of neighbouring states. Turning to this as a way out of the present difficulty, the Senate instructed the praetor who had just drawn Spain as his province to take up the matter. As claims were presented against this or that ex-governor, he was to name five senators as the Recovery court to try that particular case, and to allow the claimant party to choose counsel (*patroni*, Roman citizens of course) to conduct the pleading on their behalf. It is a significant fact that the protectors chosen by the Spanish delegates all belonged to what we have called the Reform party in the Senate, that is, the men who admired the old traditional Roman virtues and strove to counteract the evil tendencies of the day. Cato and Paullus were two of the four. So far all went well; in the abstract virtuous indignation prevailed. When it came to concrete cases, it was found less easy to punish individual offenders. The first trial resulted in adjournments and an acquittal. In two following cases the claims were supported by evidence of most heinous acts: adjournment followed in each case: and when the courts reassembled neither defendant[1] appeared. They had gone into voluntary exile, and there was an end of the means of redress. It seems to have been thought that the delegates would gladly have gone on to take proceedings against some offenders of higher rank and importance, but that their

difficult. I have taken into consideration von Keller's *Civilprocess* 1 § 8 *recuperatores* and § 16 *litis aestimatio*.

[1] To discuss the technicalities possibly involved in this part of the story is out of the question here. The consequences that the defendants ran away to avoid must have been connected with the proceedings that would follow the civil action. Either these would be assessment of damages (*litis aestimatio*), or a prosecution before the Assembly (*iudicium populi*) might be threatened. The exile of these two offenders was only a change of residence to Latin towns. One went to Praeneste, the other to Tibur.

protectors had warned them not to venture on such an undertaking. The conduct of the praetor lent some colour to this surmise. He dropped the business, set about raising troops, and slipped off to his province. This may be slanderous gossip reported by some hostile annalist. Still we are not far from the time when to screen each other's misdeeds was a normal occupation of the inner circle of the Roman nobles. But it does seem strange to find Paullus, even stranger to find Cato, interfering to burke proceedings for redress. A more detailed judgment of this affair seems quite out of reach: the materials are lost. As for misgovernment of the Spanish provinces in future, the Senate tried hard to prevent it. Three great abuses were dealt with. First, there was the valuation of corn: when it was to be bought, or taken as part of the fixed tribute, the governor would put a low price[1] on it, and so exact more corn: the corn received would then be charged to the state at a higher figure, and the governor took the difference for himself. On the other hand, if a temporary requisition[2] was made, beyond the tribute, it paid him to require so much corn, to value it at a fancy price and then commute the contribution in kind for cash, reckoned on the fancy valuation. Lastly, it had become the practice to collect the fixed tribute by means of officers sent for that purpose to the several towns: the Spaniards preferred to collect it themselves and pay it over to the Roman officials. So far as ordinances of the Senate could put a stop to these abuses, the thing was done. But of course to get the new regulations carried out in good faith was the really important point. The bold assertion of their rights by the Spaniards was however not wasted: we shall see later on that provincial taxation appeared in its least oppressive and irritating form in the provinces of Spain.

557. Another Spanish question[3] now came up. Long service in a distant land had led to a not unnatural result. Soldiers had taken to themselves wives of the daughters of the people, and a generation of half-breeds was growing up. Delegates representing more than 4000 of these asked for the grant of a town in which they might settle and form a community. Their present position seems to have been this. Between their fathers and mothers there existed no right to contract a legal marriage. Thus on the principles of Roman law they were illegitimate, that is, they would have the legal status of their mothers. But they had been brought up in or about Roman

---

[1] If this part of the story is to be trusted, it would seem that this valuation trick began very early in the history of the Roman provinces. Later it became a common abuse.

[2] For what is known or inferred concerning the obscure *vicesima* (5 %) mentioned by Livy, see Marquardt, *Staatsverwaltung* index under *vicesima*.

[3] Livy XLIII 3.

camps, and had no wish to belong to the subject race. We may guess also that their maternal tribes would not have received them on an equal footing. The Senate solved the problem cleverly. They selected Carteia in the South of Spain for the residence of these camp-children. It lay on the coast, and had been a Phoenician colony. There was probably a mixture of bloods there already. The praetor was instructed to found a colony there, consisting of the half-breeds and such of the present inhabitants as were willing to stay on and amalgamate with the new-comers. The place was to become a Latin colony, with the usual provision for allotments of land, and doubtless for a local government on the Italian model. But a remarkable distinction appeared in its title: it was to be called the colony of the freedmen. The name seems intended to mark it off from the ordinary Latin Colonies in Italy, and at the same time to recognize the exceptional position of the new colonists. By regarding their mothers as virtually slaves, the children would be slaves also: to treat the children as free was to treat them as freed slaves or the children of freed slaves. Thus they were brought into an existing status as *libertini*, but it was arranged that the freedom thus initiated should be that of Latin Allies, not that of Roman citizens. Carteia was the first colony founded by Rome outside Italy. The Spanish natives would probably see in it a fresh proof that the Roman occupation of Spain was meant to last.

558. The islands of Sardinia and Corsica had been seized by Rome soon after the end of the first Punic war. If the action was dishonourable in the circumstances of the moment, it must at least be admitted that the position of the islands made it necessary for the dominant Italian power to occupy them some day. Sardinia was supposed to have been conquered in 235, Corsica in 231. They were formed into a province under a single governor, and took their place in the Roman system as one of the departmental duties entrusted year by year to one of the praetors. Yet it seems clear that the conquest had as yet been only superficial, and in this period we hear of serious warfare in both islands. Under the years 181, 178, 177, we read of fighting and Roman victories. In 177 we find the province entrusted to a consul, and a strong army assigned him, in order to effect a thorough pacification. The duty fell to Gracchus, who here as in Spain shewed himself efficient. But there was so much to be done that he was kept on in charge as proconsul in 176. He conquered Sardinia so thoroughly that no more great general risings occurred. He carried off a vast number of prisoners to Rome when he returned for his triumph in 175: so many indeed that there was a glut in the slave market, and 'Sards for sale' (*Sardi venales*)

became a proverbial expression connoting excess of supply over demand. Corsica was taken in hand by the praetors who succeeded to the province. In 173 it was fairly pacified by conquest. In general we may remark that when a praetor was wanted for some special temporary duty, such as the holding of an inquiry or the command of a force raised for some emergency, it was usual[1] to employ the new Sardinian praetor for this purpose, leaving the province under his predecessor as propraetor. No doubt the nearness of the province to Rome and its insular character were the considerations that determined this choice: it was not in general so engrossing a charge as Sicily or the Spains.

559. The country known as Liguria was chiefly a mountainous district formed by the junction of the Apennine range (here running almost east and west) with the south-western or Maritime Alps. The tops of the hills furnished a series of natural fortresses, and most of the country was cut up by deep ravines. The greater part slopes towards the North, and its streams are mostly tributaries of the Po. Its connexion by land was thus mainly with Cisalpine Gaul. Its seafront was what we now call the Riviera: in parts a narrow strip of lowland edges the water, while for a considerable distance the mountain spurs abut in cliffs upon the sea. The physical features of the land were the great obstacle to the Roman conquest, for in such a country the possession of the strongholds and local knowledge of the paths were advantages worth many thousands of men. The Ligurians seem to have been the survivors[2] of an ancient race, driven into the hills by later invaders. It is thought that they had once occupied all the southern part of what is now France, and were akin to the Iberians of Spain. The Basques of the Pyrenees are supposed by many to be a remnant of this stubborn race. The Romans came into contact with them first in northern Etruria. The hill country to the North of the Arno was in their hands, and probably the friction that usually arises between highlander and lowlander was chronic from the first. But it was not until Rome began to occupy the great plains of the Po and conquer the Cisalpine Gauls that the real struggle with the Ligurians began. It soon came home to the leaders of Roman policy that the low country could not be peacefully and securely held so long as the hill tribes were free to raid it at pleasure and even (as sometimes happened) to send down armies of hillmen to aid the resistance of the Gauls. So when Philip of Macedon had been punished the Senate took in hand the conquest of Liguria as a necessary part of the Roman advance to the northward. For about forty years (193—154) Ligurian wars were going

---

[1] See Weissenborn on Livy XLV 16 § 4.   [2] See above § 16.

on, with obscure alternations of success and disaster. The general
scheme was to assail the country from both sides whenever Rome's
eastern relations were such as to leave her free to operate more
vigorously in the North. But the work was never wholly abandoned:
at the least there were corps of observation holding advanced posts
on the borders. From the northern side the hills seem to have been
more easily pierced, and the power of the Gaulish tribes was no
longer what it had been. It was generally possible to watch them
with a detached force while the main army entered Liguria. On the
South invasion was more difficult. Pisae was generally held in force
as a base of operations, but an advance along the coast to the fine bay-
harbour known as *portus Veneris* (Spezia) brought the Roman forces
more within striking distance of the heart of the country. The
advance was marked by the foundation of colonies[1] as bases of
operations. In 180 a Latin colony was planted on land offered for
the purpose by the people of Pisae. This was almost certainly Luca.
In 177 a strong citizen colony was planted at Luna near (but not
on) the bay just mentioned. It is evident that these posts were
designed to facilitate the movement northwards. Luna was placed
on land taken from the Ligurians, and the road made in 109 from
Pisae to Genua ran through it. But expeditions were also made
up the country from points further along the coast. To put down
the piracy still occasionally troublesome in those parts was an object
in itself: but how difficult it was found to do this thoroughly we may
gather from what happened in 189. A praetor on his way to Spain[2]
fell in with some Ligurians, and was so severely wounded that he died
at Massalia a few days later. Apparently he had landed with a small
party on the Ligurian coast and was surprised by a party of natives.
Such was the state of the seaboard between the dominions of Rome
and those of Massalia.

560. The years 187 to 179 inclusive seem to be the time when
the warfare in Liguria was at its height. Two consular armies were
regularly employed in the work of conquest, and the policy of transplanting the hillmen, seriously begun in these years, was probably
more effective than the actual fighting. In 182 we are told[3] that
after some Roman victories 2000 Ligurians begged to be allowed to
settle in Cisalpine Gaul. How this matter was settled is not clear.

---

[1] This is a matter of much dispute. After long consideration of the evidence I am
convinced that Livy XL 43 § 1 and Velleius I 15 § 2 refer to the same event, the foundation of
Luca, and Livy XLI 13 §§ 4, 5, to *Luna.* Thus I do not accept the emendation *Luna*
for *Latina* in Livy XL 43, made by Mommsen on the inscription CIL I 539 (given below,
§ 688 *g*). This conclusion is due to the arguments of Beloch, *Ital. Bund* 147—8, and
Nissen, *Landeskunde* II 287.

[2] Livy XXXVII 57.   [3] Livy XL 16 §§ 4—6.

It was no part of Roman policy to destroy the Ligurian people, but rather to acquire control over them and make them use their fine military qualities[1] in the service of Rome. They might be converted into a valuable barrier against the Gauls beyond the Alps, from whose teeming population swarms were beginning to find their way over the passes as in earlier times. But after the great exertions found necessary in 181 transplantation was freely resorted to. In 180 we hear[2] that 40,000 Ligurians were torn from their homes and settled on some vacant state lands in Samnium, and soon after 7000 more. In 179 we are told that 3200 were removed from the hill country to the lowlands, whether within the boundaries of Liguria or in Cisalpine Gaul is not clear. An earlier instance of this occurred in 187. As years went by, the mutual exasperation of the combatants naturally gave a more ferocious turn to the warfare. Triumphs for successes in Liguria were becoming too common and were derided in Rome as cheaply won by victories on a small scale and inconclusive to boot. Some doubtless were too easily granted, and the victories perhaps fictitious. But the difficulties of the task were probably underrated by the home-staying people, as the dangers of eastern wars were overrated. The strength of the Ligurians was not yet broken. In 177 they made a bold descent into the lowlands and took the colony of Mutina. True, it was retaken in 176, and some Ligurian land confiscated as well. But the war went on. By 173 the prospect of war with Perseus began to influence the Senate, and cause a change in its northern policy. In that year a consul attacked the most inoffensive of the Ligurian tribes and defeated them in battle. The survivors surrendered, hoping for moderate treatment, but the consul, after disarming them, brutally sold them for slaves. For the aggressors to apply the hard laws of war was seen to be an extreme step. It would put a stop to surrenders in future, and make the war bloodier than ever. The Senate promptly sent orders to the consul, that he must refund the purchase-money to the buyers, set free the enslaved captives, and generally make redress, putting the sufferers so far as possible back into the position they occupied before he took them in hand. This reproof drew the consul back to Rome in a fury. He tried to bully the Senate into recalling their decree and approving his conduct, but in vain.

561. This consul was Marcus Popilius, one of a hard[3] family. Their influence was evidently great about this time: his brother Gaius was elected consul for 172, and on entering office took up

---

[1] They are specially referred to as able to endure hardships in Verg. *Georg.* II 168 *adsuetumque malo Ligurem.*

[2] Livy XL 38, 41 § 3, 53.

[3] Livy XLII 7—10, 21, 22.

the quarrel with the Senate.   For some time there was a sort of
deadlock in the administration.   Gaius Popilius and his colleague
would not proceed to Liguria: Marcus stayed there as proconsul, and
went on with his aggressions and bloodshed.   But the Senate was in
earnest on one point.   It would not allow the Ligurians to be provoked into a general rising at a moment when war with Perseus was
imminent.   The tribunate supplied the means of coercing the refractory Popilii.   Two tribunes threatened to fine the consuls if they
delayed going to their province, and brought forward a bill for the
trial and punishment of any state officer charged and found guilty of
preventing the redress of the wrongs of the enslaved Ligurians.   The
bill passed into law, but Marcus Popilius kept away from Rome.
The tribunes gave notice of a bill providing for his trial and sentence
while absent.   This move at last brought back the contumacious
proconsul.   The Senate received him angrily, and appointed two
praetors to see that all Ligurians enslaved during the last seven
years were set free and provided with lands in the Gaulish districts
beyond the Po.   We may infer from this measure that the enslavement of Ligurians was no new thing, and that the Senate was quite
aware of it.   It is also probable that the settlement of Ligurians
beyond the Po was a piece of artful policy, meant to create a division
of interests between them and the Transpadane Gauls.   The trial of
the offender illustrates the underlying hypocrisies of Roman public
life.   Two hearings, followed by adjournments, were solemnly gone
through.   Then the matter was getting stale, and the influential
Popilii were putting great pressure on the praetor presiding at the
trial.   He, like others, had no wish to incur the animosity of a
powerful clique, who might do him many an ill turn.   So at the
second adjournment he fixed a date for the next hearing on a day
when he would himself be no longer in office, and his successor
would not have been as yet put in charge of the trial.   Thus proceedings fell through, and were not resumed.   In fact the punishment
of the misdeeds of powerful men was under the changing conditions
of Roman life becoming more and more a farce.   Probably the order
for restoration of their goods to the injured Ligurians was not much
more real in its effect.   The treatment of the Ligurians by Rome was
in this period generally bad, probably far worse than our meagre and
partial record enables us to learn.   To the Romans the hill tribes
seemed fickle and faithless.   But this accusation is always heard
whenever a civilized power comes into touch with tribal barbarism.
The barbarian submits to superior force with the mental reservation
that, when his chance comes, he will not let it slip.   The civilized
man, familiar with contract and other legal conceptions, is shocked at

barefaced repudiation, not veiled in the decent clothing of a legal quibble. He is apt to think that no terms can be kept with such people, and to become doubly barbarous himself. Such was the position of Rome and the Ligurian tribes. For the moment there was almost peace. From 171 to 168 the Romans seem to have ceased from troubling and the persecuted hillmen were at rest.

562. It is convenient to speak of the Cisalpine Gauls after the Ligurians, because, while at first Gallic and Ligurian wars run together, as time goes on they separate again, and any anxiety felt by the Romans in regard to the Gauls was rather connected with the Istrian war and with the risk of further Gaulish swarms from beyond the Alps. In this period the resistance of the Gauls is practically broken. We hear of a hard-won victory over the Boii in 193, and a few smaller affairs later. But we have reached a point at which progress is rather the effect of Roman policy than of victories in the field. In 192 we hear[1] that the Boii submitted, particularly all the men of wealth and position. We may fairly see in this notice a trace of the traditional Roman practice of favouring the aristocratic party in communities with which they had relations. Half the Boian territory was confiscated. These Gauls were not poor barbarians. At the triumph over them in 191 there were displayed a number of silver articles, but the show of gold was even more remarkable. In 190 the Latin colonies of Placentia and Cremona were reinforced with contingents of fresh colonists. At the same time it was agreed to plant two new colonies in the land taken from the Boii. The Romanizing of the country was to be begun in earnest. Hitherto the last permanent post on the north road had been Ariminum : the colonies on the Po were advanced posts not connected with a military road. In time of war communication with them had sometimes been kept up by way of the river, and this approach may have been used in time of peace. In 189 was founded the Latin colony[2] of Bononia, and we can hardly doubt that some kind of track existed or was then made between this place and Ariminum. In 187 two important roads[3] were undertaken by the consuls of the year. One, the *via Flaminia*, led from Arretium in Etruria over the Apennine range to Bononia : this gave the Romans a route to Cisalpine Gaul, alternative to the old north road by Ariminum, also *via Flaminia*, the work of the famous popular leader (220 B.C.), father of the present consul. His colleague carried the *via Aemilia*[4] parallel with the Apennine from Ariminum to Bononia and on to Placentia, where

---

[1] Livy XXXV 40. [2] Livy XXXVII 57.
[3] Livy XXXIX 2. [4] See inscriptions given below § 688 (c).

the fortress-colony secured the passage of the river. Rome could now effectively defend the Po colonies, and their prosperity was thus guaranteed. She could control the Ligurians of the lowland and the hill slopes, and overawe the Insubrian Gauls.

563. But the Roman government did not trust to material measures only: the use of moral influences was not overlooked, and its policy in this period shews at its best in dealing with the Gauls. In 187 an officious praetor, seeking to gain credit for a public service, disarmed the Cenomani, a Gaulish tribe who dwelt at the foot of the central Alps. The relations between Rome and the Cenomani had long been peaceable or even friendly. To make enemies of them by wilful maltreatment was an unpardonable piece of blundering. They complained to the Senate, and the Senate instructed the consul Aemilius to hold an inquiry into the matter and decide upon the case. The result was[1] that the praetor was ordered to give the Cenomani back their arms and quit the province: another version of the story says that he was fined. Here we seem to have a genuine case of effective redress. In 186 we begin to hear of the inroads of Transalpine Gauls on the North-East frontier, which caused some uneasiness[2] at Rome for a few years. A body of them crossed the eastern Alps and entered the land of the Veneti, a lowland district which the Romans regarded as already within their sphere of influence. They came in peace, but prepared to build a town at the head of the Adriatic. This could not be tolerated: without the leave of Rome none must settle south of the Alps. The Senate sent an embassy to the parent tribe or tribes to complain of the intrusion, the authorities of which disowned all connexion with the enterprise. This was probably their usual procedure. It was one thing to send out a swarm to occupy foreign lands: quite another thing to accept responsibility for the adventurers' acts. In 184 the newcomers were building, and clearly meant to stay. The praetor in Gaul was ordered to try and induce them to depart in peace (183): if they would only go under compulsion, one of the consuls was to bring his army from Liguria and take the business in hand. On the approach of an army they submitted, and sent delegates to Rome to complain of hard treatment, they being harmless inoffensive immigrants. But the Senate would not make a precedent by condoning the intrusion, and so they were civilly shewn out of Italy. It is said that another embassy was sent beyond the Alps, and that their reception was friendly: the Gaulish elders wondered or affected to wonder at the

---

[1] Livy XXXIX 3, Diodor. XXIX 14.
[2] Livy XXXIX 22 §§ 6, 7, 45 §§ 6, 7, 54 § 1—55 § 4.

indulgent and moderate conduct of the Roman people. But the firm and consistent policy now being pursued in the North shews that the Roman leniency was not due to weakness.

564. In this year (183) the colonies of Mutina and Parma[1] were founded, and the conquest of Istria begun. The two colonies were planted on the Aemilian road at convenient distances between Bononia and Placentia, in the land lately taken from the Boii, and the hold of Rome on the country was greatly strengthened thereby. They were citizen colonies, but served the purpose for which Latin colonies had formerly been employed, the maintenance of inland communications. Accordingly they received 2000 colonists each, being new fortress-towns, very different from the citizen colonies of the old type. It was agreed also to found a colony, to be called Aquileia, at the head of the Adriatic. This was in connexion with the advance into Istria, and the plan was not carried out[2] till 181. It was a Latin colony, the last of the old sort, and had 3000 colonists: none too many for their important task of guarding the approach to Italy from the North-East. Why colonies of different classes were planted in these different districts we are left to guess. The purpose of Latin colonies had been to cover and facilitate the Roman occupation of Italy. Ariminum had in its time (268) done duty as frontier post in the North. Bononia marks the firm resumption of the advance by land. Placentia and Cremona were outposts (218) accessible by water, and such now was Aquileia. But with the making of the Aemilian road the two Po colonies were brought into regular connexion with the system of land-communications, and the stretch of road between Bononia and Placentia was too long to be left undefended. If two Latin colonies had been planted in the gap, there would have been six strong communities of that class holding the country from Ariminum to the Po. It is highly probable that Mutina and Parma were made colonies of Roman citizens partly in order to break the line of Latin communities. This would be in agreement with the general course of Roman policy, the essence of which was a jealous watching and isolation of those whom they meant to control and from whom they required great services. There was of course also the difficulty of finding men willing to be planted out as colonists without enjoying the Roman franchise. But that it could be done, if sufficient inducements were offered, is shewn by the case of Aquileia: there the allotments of land were exceptionally large. That colony was planted just in time. Rumours, current in 182, of the approach of another swarm of Transalpine Gauls, were verified[3]

---

[1] Livy xxxix 55.   [2] Livy xl 34 § 2. See inscription given below § 688 (f).
[3] Livy xl 53 §§ 5, 6.

in 179, when a body came in peace asking to be admitted as settlers. They were simply ordered out of Italy. In 178 we hear[1] of an auxiliary corps of Gauls employed with the Roman legions in the Istrian campaign, under the command of an officer appointed by their own chief, and in a moment of panic, caused by a disaster in Istria, a further contingent was raised. Nothing could shew more clearly that Rome was now mistress[2] up to the Alps, and the long weary struggle at an end.

565. Rome had been on terms of friendship, if not of actual alliance, with the Veneti[3] as with the Cenomani since before the Hannibalic war. No doubt this was a part of the northward movement which that conflict interrupted, and was another instance of the traditional policy pursued by Rome from very early times—that of securing allies on the flank or rear of the enemy. But at the present stage of Roman progress the want of a scientific frontier in the lowlands of Venetia was sure to be felt. Moreover there were rumours that Philip of Macedon aimed at directing a horde of barbarians upon Italy from the north-east. To forestall any such move by gaining the control of a better line of defence was a rational precaution, and the peninsula of Istria (or Histria)[4] would at least to some extent supply what was needed. Its conquest also would fit in very well with the naval operations for suppression of Illyrian piracy which had to be undertaken about this time. The Istri were probably Illyrians, and anyhow some of the corsairs sailed from their ports. The war did not last long, though there seems to have been a good deal of the usual blundering on the part of the Roman commanders, and the Senate was apparently satisfied with establishing Roman supremacy in the district. A new province was not wanted, but it was a real gain to control the harbours and to be able, whenever necessary, to use them as naval bases on the flank of the Illyrian pirates. By about the end of 177 the objects of Rome had been attained. In 171 an affair occurred in these parts that well illustrates[5] the way in which Roman generals provoked inoffensive neighbours in this period. The consul C. Cassius, vexed at not getting the command against Perseus, looked round to find an opening for distinguishing himself. His 'province' was Italy, including Gaul. There was nothing to be done against the Gauls, and conciliation was just then the policy in Liguria. He turned eastward, and set out

---

[1] Livy XLI 1, Weissenborn.
[2] A map of Cisalpine Gaul is given in § 759.
[3] Strabo V 1 § 9 (p. 216) says συνεμάχουν. See above § 17 and index.
[4] For conquest of Histria see index to Livy under *Histri, Histria*.
[5] Livy XLIII 1, 5.

on a wild expedition into northern Illyria, meaning to break into Macedonia from the North-West, and gather for himself some of the laurels to be won in the eastern war. News of this move reached the Senate, who in hot haste sent three commissioners after the consul to forbid the enterprise. Thus thwarted, he vented his disappointment on several of the Alpine tribes of the neighbourhood, wasting their lands with fire and sword. This unprovoked aggression caused an appeal to the Senate in the following year. The guilt of Cassius seems to have been certain, but for the moment he could not be got at, for he was now serving under the consul in Greece. The Senate received the envoys kindly, and did all they could to soothe the chiefs with messages and presents. But it was not likely that the chiefs could send another embassy to wait for the return of Cassius and get him brought to justice. So the redress of wrongs was as usual evaded.

566. Of Italy in general, regarded as a part of the dominion of Rome, we will speak below. We must say a few words here of the process by which the Romans secured their dominion, restored after the rude shock of the second Punic war. The conflict with Philip of Macedon for a time delayed matters, but in 194 the planting of colonies began in earnest. From 194 to 192 no less than ten of these were planted in southern Italy, on the coasts of Campania Lucania Bruttium and Apulia. Eight of the ten were citizen colonies. What with these and the colonies of earlier date, and the allied Greek cities such as Neapolis and Rhegium, the southern seaboard was now well watched. That smouldering discontents still gave some cause for uneasiness is shewn by the precautions[1] taken against invasion by sea during the eastern wars. Hannibal had proved how dangerous a small invading force could be if backed by revolt of Roman subjects, or even by their passive goodwill. After the war with Antiochus, the North was taken in hand. From 189 to 180 we find nine colonies planted in Etruria Picenum Umbria Cispadane Gaul and even on the Istro-Venetian frontier. Seven of the nine were citizen colonies. That this series of plantations was the result of a fully thought-out policy, needs no further demonstration. But we have no ancient account of this policy as a whole. So far as we know, this is a specimen of the way in which the Senate made history that was probably never written.

[1] See §§ 461, 466, 473, 508.

Citizen colonies	Latin colonies	Where situated	Remarks
[before 191 Pyrgi]	... ...	Etrurian coast ...	See §§ 256, 269
194 Puteoli ...	... ...	Campanian coast ⎫	
194 Volturnum ...	... ...	Campanian coast ⎪	
194 Liternum ...	... ...	Campanian coast ⎪	
194 Salernum ...	... ...	Campanian coast	Founded in the
194 Buxentum ...	... ...	Lucanian coast ...	process of securing
194 Sipontum ...	... ...	Apulian coast ... ⎬	southern Italy. For Puteoli see below
194 Tempsa ...	... ...	Bruttian coast ...	§ 688 (*k*).
194 Croton ...	... ...	Bruttian coast ...	
	193 Copia[1] ...	Lucania ... ... ⎫	[1] = Thurii
	192 Valentia[2]...	Bruttian coast ... ⎭	[2] = Vibo (Hipponium)
	189 Bononia ...	Cispadane Gaul ...	Connected with *via Aemilia*.
184 Potentia ...	... ...	Coast of Picenum	
184 Pisaurum ...	... ...	Coast of Umbria	
183 Parma ...	... ...	Cispadane Gaul ... ⎫	On *via Aemilia*.
183 Mutina ...	... ...	Cispadane Gaul ... ⎭	
183 Saturnia ...	... ...	Etruria	
181 Graviscae ...	... ...	Etrurian coast	
	181 Aquileia ...	Venetia	An outpost on NE. frontier.
	180 Luca ...	N. Etrurian border	
177 Luna	... ...	Coast of Etrurian north frontier	
	[171 Carteia] ...	S. coast of Spain...	⎧ An exceptional case, of different character from ordinary colonies.

After this it seems that no more Latin colonies were founded, for Dertona was probably no exception to the general practice, though direct information is lacking. The citizen colonies of the later Republic were as follows

157 Auximum ...	... ...	Picenum	
124 Fabrateria ...	... ...	Latium (Volscian land)	To supersede Fregellae, destroyed.
122 Minervia ...	... ...	Bruttian coast	
122 Neptunia ...	... ...	Tarentum	
? Dertona ...	... ...	Liguria	⎧ Commanding roads from Cisalpine to Ligurian coast.
122 Junonia ...	... ...	Carthage... ...	An abortive venture of Gaius Gracchus.
118 Narbo Martius ...	... ...	Southern Transalpine Gaul	
100 Eporedia ...	... ...	Transpadane Gaul	Guarding an important Alpine pass.

The later colonies were military settlements, a form of pension for soldiers on their discharge.

567. We must say a few words here in continuation of the story of Carthage. If this subject turns up now and then as a sort of intermittent accompaniment to the narrative of other events, that is just what it seems to have been in reality. The Senate did not lose sight of Rome's old enemy, but was so busy elsewhere that it seldom interfered in Africa. In 188 two Romans are said to have assaulted some Punic ambassadors. The outrage seems to have occurred in Rome: what the ambassadors were there for does not appear. It was a breach of the recognized law of nations, and the offenders were formally handed over to the envoys and carried off to Carthage in expiation of their crime. Of course it was well known that the Punic government dared not treat them with severity. A fragment of Dion Cassius[1] tells us what Livy omits, that they were let go unharmed. In 182 we hear of one of the usual territorial disputes between Carthage and Masinissa: the king was the aggressor, but the Roman arbitrators sent to decide the question, acting no doubt under secret instructions, contrived to leave him in possession and refer the question of right to the Senate. What happened we are left to guess, as we well may. If the Carthaginians had any chance of a favourable award on the spot, it surely disappeared when the matter became one of hard swearing in Rome. In 181 we are told[2] that hostages were restored to the Carthaginians, a confused and perhaps erroneous notice: also that Rome not only refrained from war with Carthage (no pretext for which is suggested) but actually kept Masinissa quiet. He however was still in armed occupation of the territory in question. So the unsettled dispute seems to have dragged on. I have elsewhere referred to the suspicions of Carthaginian intrigues with Perseus in 174. In 172 we find Punic envoys in Rome once more on the old errand, and a son of Masinissa there to oppose them. The king had gone on with his aggressions, and now held a number of towns and posts in Carthaginian territory, recently seized. Carthage was bound by treaty not to wage war against a Roman ally, and so might not resist him. They begged[3] that Rome would settle the frontier by a final award and guarantee it: or that they might be allowed to take up arms in self-defence. If they had done any wrong, let the Romans exact punishment themselves, and not expose them to the mercies of a tormentor whom nothing would satisfy. The Numidian prince appealed to Roman interests, and compared his father's loyalty with the undying hostility of Carthage. The Senate had the war with Perseus before them, and preferred to temporize till that struggle was over. They invited both parties to send delegates to argue out the

---

[1] Dion Cass. fragm. 61, Livy XXXVIII 42 § 7.
[2] Weissenborn on Livy XL 34 § 14.　　　　　　　　[3] Livy XLII 23, 24.

question at Rome, and declared their firm intention to do no more than justice to Masinissa and no less than justice to Carthage. Hospitality and presents were granted to both the parties' representatives now in Rome, and for the time the matter was shelved amid an odour of sanctity that was a masterpiece of hypocritical decency.   In the next year (171) we read of two Carthaginian battle-ships serving with the Roman fleet in Greek waters.   In 191 their naval contingent had been five ships: why it was smaller now, we are not told.   But later in the year, when a Punic embassy came to offer a gift of corn for the campaign of 170, they are said to have expressed regret that in their reduced circumstances they had not more to offer. This is supposed[1] to have been a side-thrust at Masinissa, whose encroachments had lessened their resources.   But it was useless to complain at Rome of a king who was sending contingents to the Roman army, and corn as well.   The story of the last days of Carthage will be told below.   It is clear that her fate after the fall of Perseus depended, not on what she might do or abstain from doing, but simply and solely on the will of Rome.

Livy XLIII 6 §§ 11—14.

CHAPTER XXXIII

568. IT is convenient to carry on the story of Rome's external development, the spread of her dominion and influence, from the settlement following on the victory of Pydna down to 133 B.C. During those years the destiny of the now imperial people was working itself out with the continuity of a mighty stream, drawing near to falls and rapids, but for the present flowing well above the level of the sea. Of the evil tendencies at work in Rome and Italy we have already caught glimpses. The importance of the period 167—133 is to be sought in the steps by which the Roman power, now without a rival, removed the remaining obstacles to its absolute dominion, only to enter upon a century of revolution. That revolutionary period begins with the reaction headed by the Gracchi : by the time the agony is over, the destiny of the commonwealth is revealed: the Roman people, in whose name imperial power is exercised, has politically ceased to exist. Our present business is to note the gradual suppression of the powers of which the governing class at Rome might entertain any suspicion or jealousy, a process so far complete that it cleared the ground for civil wars of unexampled magnitude to be carried on undisturbed by foreign intervention. It has been the custom to mark off this period at the year 146, when Carthage and Corinth were destroyed. But it is better to include the important Spanish wars down to 133, partly because there is no sufficient reason for putting them into a later chapter, partly because in the history of Rome the attempt of Tiberius Gracchus is the manifest opening of a new series of events.

569. In entering upon this period we part from the historian Livy, whose extant text ends with the year 167. The epitomes of his later books, supposed to be a work of the fourth century A.D., are perhaps the abstract of a previous abstract, and are in any case no substitute for the work that is lost. With all Livy's faults, we miss him sadly. A continuous narrative by a Roman writer gives us at the least a Roman point of view : and Livy has preserved to us many details not recorded in our other authorities and yet probably trust-worthy, certainly significant. For the present period we have to

depend mainly on Greek[1] writers.   The fragments of Polybius, which
take us down to 145 B.C., are of course good material so far as they go.
Of Diodorus, who wrote under Augustus, we have a good many
fragments, and he is probably better informed in reference to this
period than in some of the earlier portions of his work.   He has the
largeness of view characteristic of Greek historians after the example
set by Polybius, and he is not, like that writer, composing under the
direct fascination[2] of Scipio Aemilianus and his clique.   Appian, who
wrote in the second century A.D., was probably honest enough, but his
method is faulty and his narrative often untrustworthy or obscure.
Strabo the geographer (Augustan age) is often helpful.   Of the great
Roman History compiled by Dion Cassius in the third century A.D.
little survives bearing on this period.   There are of course many stray
references in the works of other authors, Roman and Greek.   Of these
the chief are Cicero and Plutarch.   But the orator and the moralist
are never historical witnesses of the first order: facts adduced for
a temporary and non-historical purpose are peculiarly liable to be
coloured and distorted, and Cicero at least was not the man to weaken
a convenient argument by historic scruples.   Pausanias, whose book
of travels in Greece belongs to the second century A.D., recounts the
loss of Greek independence with a certain difference in detail from
the fragmentary notices of other writers, but the story is essentially
the same.   Instructive as this period is, connecting as it does the century
in which Rome became the dominant power of the Mediterranean
world with that in which the Republic perished through internal
maladies, the events which it includes are not in themselves of the
first importance.   The destruction of Carthage and of Corinth, highly
dramatic scenes, are of the nature of a sequel, the outcome of past
dealings with Africa and Greece: the shameful episode of Numantia,
in its exposure of the inadequacy of Roman character and Roman
institutions, gives us also a forewarning of the coming period of
revolutionary change.   It will be best to describe the external action
of Rome in this period according to localities: as before, we will begin
with Greece and Macedon.

570.   We left the Greek states prostrate before the victors of Pydna,
and Rome, weary of their quarrels, weary also of the Macedonian war,
seeking to ensure a little quiet in these parts by depriving Greece and
Macedon alike of their natural leaders.   To the Achaean League this
policy was a fatal blow.   The moderate party was paralysed by the

---

[1] Polyb. XXXI—XXXIX, Diodor. XXXI—XXXIII, Appian *Hisp.* 44—98, *Pun.* 67—135,
Illyr. 10, 11, *Syr.* 67, 68, *Mithr.* 3—7, Pausanias VII cap. 7—16.

[2] But comparison of the fragments clearly shews that Diodorus in this period often
followed Polybius very closely as an authority for facts.

loss of its best men. The Roman partisans, naturally a self-seeking gang, were for the time in power, able to tyrannize over their fellow-citizens. As time went on these men provoked a violent reaction, a bitter hatred of Rome and all her works. But the League still existed, and the general soundness of public sentiment is shewn by the persistent efforts made to obtain the restoration of their lost leaders. Time after time Achaean embassies vainly pleaded at Rome for the release of these men, or at least for their speedy trial. We must remember that they were the picked men of an allied state, a state that had stood by Rome in the late war, and that nothing had been proved against them. To confine them year after year without trial was an arbitrary act of the grossest injustice. And in refusing the Achaeans' prayer, on the ground that the restoration would not be good for either Rome or the League, the Senate with subtle malignity tried to sow discord among the members of the federation. Their answer was so drafted[1] as to refer only to the interest of the several cities, with which Rome had no concern, ignoring the federal union, which was Rome's ally. We have before had occasion to note the jealousy with which allies possessed of strength were regarded by the Roman government. The League was now perhaps, after Rome, the most powerful state within the Roman horizon; and this was enough. International justice and the claims of faithful service went for nothing: was not Rome the protector of the Greeks?

571. A quarrel between Sparta and Megalopolis gave an opportunity for further mischief-making in Peloponnesus under the pretext of arbitration. But the League still held together, and even discontented members knew their true interest too well to respond to insidious suggestions of secession. In 153 war broke out between the Rhodians and Cretans; both sides sent to ask Achaean help. The League would have taken part with Rhodes. But the leader of the Roman party, Callicrates, warned the Assembly against engaging in war without Roman leave, and this was enough to put a stop to the design of independent action. And now an event happened which made a change in the policy of the League. The exiled Achaeans— all that was left of them—were in the year 150 at last[2] allowed to return. Out of 1000 barely 300 were now left: most of the best men were gone. They came home after a dreary confinement of some sixteen years in Etruscan towns, and it is not to be wondered at if the sudden change, from pining and repression in a foreign land to the sympathy of relatives and friends, somewhat upset their judgment. Their influence on the popular sentiment would be out of all proportion

---

[1] Polyb. XXXI 8. See Freeman *F. G.* chap. ix § 4.
[2] Pausan. VII 10 § 12.

to their numbers, and the fretting Achaeans had yet to learn that the hand of Rome in effect lay as heavy on them as on the decaying cities of Etruria. Polybius soon went back to Italy. He was now thoroughly acclimatized in the best society of Rome, and he probably saw that there was at present no place for him in Greek politics. If he was convinced of the necessity of submission to Roman power, as he was, this did not lessen his abhorrence of the policy of Callicrates and his gang, whose base cringing to Rome and persecution of their fellow Greeks was converting subjection into slavery. So he returned to Rome, where at the centre of things he could at need more effectually serve his country, and enjoy what was to him a chief pleasure and interest of life, the close contact with great affairs.

572. To discuss the complicated series of events by which a quarrel between Athens and Oropus led to dissensions among the leading Achaeans, and a war between the League and Sparta, is beyond our present purpose. Suffice it that all Roman intervention was conducted on the principle of promoting disunion among the Greeks wherever possible. From 156 to 150 unrest prevailed in various ways. In 149 the dispute with Sparta came to a head. A decision of the Roman Senate was reported to the two disputants by their representatives in contradictory terms. It had probably been so framed as to be ambiguous. Sparta had now to face the whole force of the League, for no other members could be induced to secede. The League was now led by violent anti-Roman partisans, whom nothing but the instant fear of a war with Rome could restrain. And at this juncture it may have seemed to hot-headed men that there was an opportunity for pursuing an independent policy without serious risk of punishment: at any rate they thought it worth while to make a bid for the retention or increase of their own importance. Rome was indeed not in a position at the moment to issue plain orders and enforce them at once. She had on hand the wasteful warfare in Spain, and was just entering on her third war with Carthage. She was also confronted by a national rising in Macedonia: for the present therefore she was compelled to temporize, and the Achaean leaders presumed on her weakness.

573. We may now turn for a moment to the Macedonian[1] rising. The people had never taken kindly to the system of the four republics, with their officials and assemblies and machinery of more or less popular government. They were a rustic population, used to obedience in military service and unrestrained freedom in country life. They were a real nation, but in civilization had not advanced beyond the stage in which the effective maintenance of unity is the only visible

[1] Polyb. xxxvii 1, 2, 9, Diodor. xxxi 40a, xxxii 15, Livy epit. 49, 50.

guarantee of independence and order.   This unity was expressed in
the monarchy, on which the national sentiment set great store.   The
reduction of taxation granted by the Romans in 167 was probably
found by experience to be a delusive boon, for the destruction of
national unity and the restrictions on the intercourse of the four
districts were disadvantages that far outweighed it.   They had lost
more than they had gained, and the general disarmament of the
people wounded the national pride.   In 164 their discontent and
unrest were already known at Rome, and the Senate ordered a
commission of three, then starting for Syria, to take Macedonia on
their way and inquire into the state of affairs.   What came of this
visit we do not know, but it is clear that the Macedonians did not
become contented with their lot.   In 149 the appearance of a pretender
gave occasion for a general rising.   A certain Andriscus had been
watching his opportunity.   He seems to have been an Asiatic Greek
adventurer, who took the name of Philip and gave out that he was
a son of Perseus by a concubine, and had been handed over to the
Romans by Demetrius I king of Syria.   He escaped from Rome and
raised a band in Macedonia: when the people found that he was in
earnest, they rallied to him.   He was soon at the head of a considerable
army, and even attempted to enter Thessaly.   We hear that this
attempt was repulsed by an Achaean[1] force employed by Roman
commissioners.   In 149 a Roman praetor was sent with an army to
put down the rising, but was defeated and slain.   His successor
Q. Caecilius Metellus was a competent soldier, and was furnished
with a full consular army.   The False Philip since his previous victory
had lapsed into tyranny and cruelty, and in 148 Metellus defeated
and captured him.   For the time quiet seems to have been restored
in Macedonia.   But the existing arrangements were evidently found
very unsatisfactory, and in 146 the country was made the 'province'
of a resident Roman official.   This change seems to have put an end
to the four districts, so that as a Roman Province a certain unity was
recovered, and the hated local restrictions removed.   But in drawing
up the provincial charter (the *lex provinciae*) it seems that the regulations drafted by Paullus[2] and the commission of 167 were in most
respects followed.   We hear of at least one small rising a few years
later, but Macedonia was henceforth simply a portion of the provincial
empire of Rome.

---

[1] Livy epit. 50 Thessalia...per legatos Romanorum auxiliis Achaeorum defensa est.   This
detail at least serves to shew how defective is our knowledge of the events of this critical
time.   It is so out of keeping with what we learn of Achaean politics from other sources that
it can hardly be a mere invention.

[2] Weissenborn on Livy XLV 32 § 7.

574. To resume the story[1] of the Achaean League. Early in 148 Metellus on his way to Macedonia heard of the state of war in Peloponnesus and sent word to the Achaean leaders, asking them not to attack Sparta but wait the arrival of commissioners coming from Rome. It was too late to save the Achaeans from themselves. Victory over the Spartans only led to internal quarrels. The President Damocritus was charged with treachery and driven into exile. He was succeeded by Diaeus, who according to Polybius was especially the evil genius of the League in its latter days. This man also was warned by Metellus, and made some show of obedience. And now (147) the Roman commission under L. Aurelius Orestes appeared. The war with the sham Philip being over, Rome had available forces at hand to enforce her will. The commissioners disregarded the lawful procedure of the League and simply declared the will of the Senate, that certain cities should no longer be members of the Union. Of these cities Corinth, where the meeting was being held, was one. The anti-Roman party raised a riot, and the commissioners were perhaps insulted, certainly alarmed. On their report to Rome, a new commission under Sextus Julius Caesar came over and delivered another warning in a more conciliatory tone. It may be that Rome was temporizing once more, staggered by the unexpected duration of the siege of Carthage. Many put this construction on the milder manner of the commission, and the protest of Polybius[2] is not of sufficient weight to prove that their opinion was wrong. The great historian had his full share of Greek vanity, and was deeply gratified by his own flattering reception in the best houses of the chief city of the world. He saw the events of this time through Roman glasses. Diaeus (148—7) was succeeded as President by Critolaus (147—6), another desperate anti-Roman partisan, under whom the hapless League moved onward to its doom.

575. What followed is in several points obscure, and the details hardly concern us. On insincere pretences the Roman commission was rendered futile, and the Achaean President set to work to promote mob-rule in the League cities, relieving debtors, and generally upsetting the political balance. Once more Metellus tried to prevent a war, but his envoys were insulted in a League Assembly at Corinth, and Critolaus induced the multitude to take a step only resorted to in great emergencies, conferring on himself a practically monarchic power. War was declared nominally against Sparta, virtually against Rome. The last efforts of Metellus, who was now on the point of being superseded in his command, were met with contempt, and

---

[1] Full authorities in Freeman *F. G.* chap. ix § 4.
[2] XXXVIII 7, well criticised by Freeman.

indeed it was now hardly possible to avoid an appeal to arms. The Roman Senate was determined to make an end of opposition in Greece, and L. Mummius, a soldier of the old Roman school who had served with some distinction in Spain, had been appointed to the command. Critolaus led the army of the League, supported by allied contingents from Thebes and Chalcis, to coerce Heraclea on the Malian gulf. This city, an outlying member of the League, had seceded, and was now besieged. Metellus advanced with his forces and raised the siege. The Achaeans fell back beyond Thermopylae, but were caught at Scarphea in Locris, where the Romans put them to the rout. Critolaus was not seen again, and Diaeus succeeded to the command. By violent measures, such as the liberation of slaves, he raised more troops: but the League was now at its last gasp, as the tortures and executions of its squabbling leaders plainly shew. At last Mummius came, and the gentle pressure of Metellus was exchanged for more drastic methods. At Leucopetra on the Isthmus the army of the League was defeated. Diaeus fled and took poison: Mummius marched into Corinth, and gave the inhabitants found there to the slave-market or the sword. The city, famous for centuries as a centre of commerce and navigation, of luxury and wantonness, was plundered of its artistic and other treasures and given to the flames.

576. Corruption and the mad fury of leaders, who saw no hope of pardon for themselves, had given the death-blow to what little yet remained of Greek freedom. But Polybius may have judged these men too hardly. We are tempted to compare the sack of Corinth with that of Syracuse in 212. But at Corinth we hear of no foreign mercenaries ruling the city. The ruin of the city was a natural episode of ancient warfare: those responsible for the result were Greeks. The example made of Corinth put an end to all resistance. The horrid work of Mummius was not without its element of mercy, for it was a message understood by all. And the general himself was incorruptible, and as lenient as was consistent with the duty of finally pacifying Greece. Now was the time for Polybius to use his influence on behalf of his country. With pride he tells us[1] how the conqueror listened to him and forbade the destruction of the statues and other monuments of Philopoemen. Nor does he omit to record his own virtue in refusing an offered share of the confiscated goods of Diaeus and other misguided men. Meanwhile Mummius[2] was busy with dismantling and disarming cities that had borne a part in the war. Thebes and Chalcis were laid waste, and he had now cleared the ground for the work of the inevitable settlement-commission which soon afterwards appeared.

[1] Polyb. xxxix 14—16.　　　　[2] See below § 688 (*i*).

577. In this settlement we detect the time-honoured principles that had guided Roman policy ever since Rome entered on her imperial course. To ensure effective subjection with the least possible trouble was always her end: to prevent large and close political unions her means. Accordingly she dissolved the remaining Leagues: Hellas became once more a collection of small communities. But they became independent of each other to a degree probably surpassing all previous experience. There was to be no *commercium* between them, for to allow the citizen of one community to own property in another would tend towards the growth of common interests. But if the several communities in relation to each other enjoyed a full measure of the 'autonomy' to which the Greek cities had so often aspired in vain, their servitude to their one mighty mistress was not less complete. Another old-established practice used in the extension of Roman dominion was graduation of privileges. As in Sicily, so in Greece, the treatment of different communities differed greatly. Of the cities destroyed, the site of Corinth was cursed and left to lie waste, its territory together with the Boeotian and Euboeic lands became domain-land of the Roman state. Some few, at least Athens and Sparta, were recognized as Free States. The former had even a little subordinate empire of her own: beside Lemnos Imbros and Scyros, which had usually belonged to her, she had received Delos, the importance of which island will presently appear. Between these extremes came the mass of the Greek cities. There was no doubt a great deal of work to be done in the fixing of boundaries, and therewith in deciding what places should be recognized as separate communities, what others should rank as hamlets of some more favoured or important city. Preexisting local relations would of course count for much: the outlying hamlets of Sparta, detached in recent times, seem to have remained separate. But favour was shewn to cities known to have been less inveterate than their neighbours in opposition to Rome, or backed by influential patrons: thus a slice of the forfeited land of Corinth was granted to Sicyon. Whether bribes passed, we cannot surely tell: from the fragmentary notice of Polybius it would seem that they did not.

578. There were also the constitutions of the several communities to be regulated in the traditional Roman style. All democracies were suppressed, and the franchises limited to owners of a certain property: magistrates and law-courts remained, but local administration and local law were no longer to be dependent on the political support of men with nothing to lose. We must not underrate the importance of this measure in Greece. A decline of wealth had long been in progress, and with it doubtless a decrease in the

number of slaves. Poor freemen were perhaps more numerous in proportion to the total population than they had been formerly, at least for a very long time. And the Roman conquest only strengthened these tendencies. We hear of trouble arising in connexion with the slaves armed by Critolaus, and we have vivid pictures of the local mobs in the latter days of the Achaean League. Furthermore we are told by Pausanias[1] that Greece was made subject to tribute. There is nothing strange in this. Eastern experience had already familiarized the Romans with the practice of raising revenue by taxation of dependants, and from 167 to 146 a tribute had been exacted in Macedonia, that is for twenty years before it became a Province of the Roman people. This leads us to the question, whether Greece did or did not become a Province in 146, a question which has been long debated. We have no direct statement to help us, and the path of inference is beset with pitfalls. Perhaps the soundest solution[2] is that of Holm, who shews that the evidence relied upon to prove an affirmative does not prove it at all. It would seem that the little communities of Hellas were still left in nominal 'freedom' but rendered impotent by isolation, that the governor of Macedonia was charged[3] with the duty of exercising any supervision that might be necessary. The subjection to Rome was no longer a matter of doubt, and unscrupulous Roman officials might in years to come contrive to rob and oppress the Greeks: but the formal creation of the Province of Achaia was a logical conclusion due to Augustus. For the present it was enough to break up political unions: religious unions for the purpose of festivals and worships were probably not suppressed.

579. Many regulations on points of detail were doubtless made by the commissioners for the several cities. To explain these, and smooth over the transition to the new constitutions, it was a happy thought to employ Polybius. After Mummius and his colleagues left for Rome in 145, the good man stayed behind and did his best to make the new institutions work easily. No part of the career of this sincere and fussy patriot was more truly to his credit. Pausanias[4] tells us that not many years after the settlement of 146 the Romans took pity on Hellas, allowing the federal leagues to be revived, and granting the right of *commercium*; whether between league and

---

[1] Pausan. VII 16 § 9. Holm thinks that this applied only to the Greeks recently at war with Rome, but I do not think that this is made out.

[2] A. Holm, *Hist. of Greece* vol. IV c. 19 and notes. We may call it a *Protectorate*.

[3] The language of Cicero, *de domo* §§ 23, 60, may be fairly regarded as a confirmation of this view. The governor of Macedonia had a wide sphere of authority outside his proper province. Illyricum and Crete in later times were for a while placed under his care.

[4] Pausan. VII 16 § 10.

league or only between the several members of a League, does not appear. On the whole it does not seem that the Roman treatment of pacified Greece was unfair or harsh. But the state of peace imposed by Rome brought neither prosperity nor happiness. Already population was declining, and it continued to decline. To the Greek race in its prime a true political life, with all its glories and errors, was a necessity of existence, and with it a certain economic well-being went hand in hand. Henceforth the Greeks of old Hellas have practically no part in the great political movements of the ages: even in mental achievements it is the Greeks and half-Greeks of other countries that take the first place. Wars do take place on Greek soil, but they are Roman wars. The philosophic schools of Athens lived on, but the nerve and originality of Greek thought had departed, and the Demos of Athens was a population of Quidnuncs, fawning on influential Roman visitors and catering for the wants of students and tourists. In general we may say that the flat deadness of parochial politics weighed heavily on a naturally gifted race: the rustics, never numerous in a mountainous country, became more than ever absorbed in the mere satisfaction of bodily needs, while the city folk degenerated under the influence of materialism and vice. A great apathy, a silence of decay, fell upon the land from which there had once issued so much of the intellectual stimulus of the world.

580. In the islands and eastern coasts of the Aegean Roman sovranty was undisputed, but the old life chiefly commercial went on as of old. We have already spoken of the punishment dealt out to Rhodes and Pergamum after the overthrow of the Macedonian kingdom. Both powers still existed, though weakened. They were allies of Rome, 'free' to obey her orders, and in faithful obedience they now steadily remained. That Rhodes had still some freedom of action is shewn by her war with the Cretans of which we hear in 153. But the loss of nearly all her territory on the mainland sadly reduced the revenues of the state, and a further blow to her prosperity was the rise of Delos. The Romans opened the sacred island as a free port. In point of form[1] it was made a dependency of Athens, but Roman influences were completely dominant there. As a maritime sanctuary it had long been a place of common resort, and indeed it had been the centre of a 'League of the Islanders' formed to promote the security of sea-borne commerce: but the suppression of piracy was mainly carried on by Rhodes. Delos was no doubt well known to the enterprising Italian traders who followed

---

[1] A good account of this, with details from the discoveries of the French school, is given in Mahaffy's *Silver Age of the Greek World*.

or even preceded the extensions of Roman dominion, eager to exploit for their own profit the various turns of political change.   These men had the means of influencing Roman policy from time to time, being connected as agents or partners with the capitalist class now growing powerful at Rome.   The Senate did not take over Delos as a Roman provincial possession: it was less trouble to place it in the hands of subservient Athens.   But they could prevent Athens from levying dues on the shipping and trade of the port, and this was done, probably under capitalist pressure.   The position of the island in mid-Aegean was highly favourable to its development as a commercial centre, and it quickly became one of the chief markets of the world.   Merchants from East and West dealt on its Exchange in great numbers, and numerous inscriptions unearthed in recent years have shewn that they formed themselves into organized unions or companies for promotion of common interests.   The trade of the Euxine formed an important part of the business transacted, and the leading article for sale was slaves.   The depression of Rhodes was not the only consequence of the rise of Delos.   No doubt the destruction of Corinth threw more trade into the Delian mart: and it may well be that in ordering its destruction the Roman government was consciously influenced by the capitalists interested in Delos.   But the prosperity of the new free port did not reach its height until the Pergamene kingdom became the Province of Asia, and corrupt officials usurious financiers and grasping dealers swarmed over to enrich themselves iniquitously by the plunder of that unhappy land.   Then the halfway house of Delos was at the zenith of its infamous splendour.   Of its later misfortunes we shall speak below.

581.   In Pergamum Eumenes II was left on the throne till his death in 159.   About the end of 167 he went to Italy in hope of being allowed to make a personal defence before the Senate and get acquittal or forgiveness for the disloyalty laid to his charge.   But the Senate would have none of his explanations, and sent him back from Brundisium.   He left a son, but his immediate successor on the throne was his brother Attalus II, who reigned till 138.   Being in good odour with the Roman government, and playing with zeal and discretion his secondary part, he enjoyed a prosperous reign.   A contingent sent by him served in the Achaean war.   When the chief spoils of Corinth were being picked out for transmission to Rome, Mummius gave the less valuable objects to Attalus' general, and Pausanias[1] tells us that even in his day Corinthian spoils were still on view at Pergamum.   At his death the kingdom passed to his nephew Attalus III, who reigned till 133 and at his death bequeathed

[1] Pausan. VII 16 § 8.

his kingdom to the Roman people as a 'free' protectorate[1], thus declaring the monarchy at an end. But we may suspect that his will was executed under the influence of Roman diplomatists or of Roman financiers operating from Delos. It is at least unlikely that Rome would in any case have allowed the Pergamene kingdom to fall into the hands of any ruler who could not be trusted to carry on the policy of subserving Roman interests. Attalus II in particular had been a most useful instrument. He had supported the Roman nominee in Cappadocia, and had been a check on troublesome movements in Bithynia, where he is said[2] to have helped Nicomedes II (149—95) to dethrone and murder his father Prusias II (185—149). He had also intervened in the affairs of the Syrian succession in obedience to Roman wishes. But the third Attalus seems to have been a poor creature, and the Romans may very naturally have preferred to take over the wealthy kingdom as a Province rather than let it pass to some irregular claimant with the risk of provoking a war of succession. What actually happened in the sequel we shall see below.

582. To glance hastily at the less important powers of Asia Minor, we may note that Rome could not afford to neglect Bithynia. The people of the country (or at least the dominant race) were of Thracian origin, rough and strong, and the wealth of the kingdom grew with the development of Greek or semi-Greek cities, encouraged by the wily and ambitious kings. It lay on the line of Euxine trade, and the Bithynians themselves took kindly to the sea. But the Bithynian kings were often in trouble with their neighbours, and this kingdom never became a power of the first rank. The menacing rise of Pontus belongs to the next period, but it was steadily developing under Mithradates III (169—121), who was on friendly terms with Rome. This is probably another trace of the traditional far-sighted Roman policy of alliances with powers commanding the rear or flank of enemies or allies whom it was an object to watch. Cappadocia was in this period ruled by Ariarathes V (163—130), who was also a friend of Rome, and indeed met his death in battle fighting for a Roman cause. The troubles of this country were chiefly due to its becoming mixed up with the succession-wars of Syria, and for a short time Ariarathes lost the half of his kingdom. In all these four kingdoms Greek civilization was spreading. Pergamum was indeed one of the great centres of Greek culture. Art, particularly sculpture, and literature, though in a less degree, flourished there under the Attalid dynasty, and the prosperous inland cities were almost as Greek as the old Hellenic cities on the coast. In

[1] See Livy epit. 59, and the inscription quoted in Sands' *Client Princes* p. 190.
[2] Livy epit. 50.

Bithynia, beside the coast cities, there were the royal foundations of Nicaea and Nicomedia inland, both famous in after days, but in this country the hellenizing leaven worked more slowly. The Pontic kings also greedily absorbed the Greek cities of the coast, but favoured Hellenism. Clever Greeks organized their army and navy: as they pushed to the West, Sinope became their capital. In Cappadocia too the hellenizing efforts of Ariarathes were not without success. Nor is it to be supposed that the Galatians were wholly unaffected by the general movement around them. But their importance as a power would seem to have been on the decline, partly perhaps owing to their retention of a politically weak tribal system, partly because the growing influence of Rome tended on the whole to reduce the number of wars. A slack demand for mercenaries would constrain many an honest cut-throat to become a tiller of the soil. Wars of course there were, but Rome was not involved in them, and to treat of these obscure conflicts is outside our subject.

583. The relations between Rome and Syria were in some respects peculiar. The treaty made with Antiochus III in 189 was their basis, and it supplied sufficient pretext for diplomatic action whenever Rome saw fit. But a further precaution (not, it seems, stipulated in the treaty) was taken to ensure the good behaviour of the Seleucid kings. A prince of the royal house was required to reside in Rome. Antiochus IV (175—165) had in his time been thus virtually a hostage. His younger brother Seleucus IV succeeded to the throne at their father's death in 187, and reigned till 175. Shortly before his death he sent his own son Demetrius to Rome in exchange for Antiochus, who was allowed to return to Syria. Antiochus succeeded his brother and reigned ten years. Of his strange career we have already spoken. When the news of his death reached Rome, Demetrius asked leave to go and claim the throne of his father and uncle. But the Senate chose rather to recognize the son of the fourth Antiochus, a child of nine years, as Antiochus V (164—162). Trouble however was not avoided by this device. The minister Lysias, who was the real governor of the country, took to increasing the military forces beyond the limits fixed by the treaty of 189. The Senate at once sent out commissioners with orders to destroy ships and elephants and arrange matters in the interest of Roman supremacy. Deaf to the warnings of the loyal king of Cappadocia, these men refused his offer of an armed escort, and entered Syria in sublime reliance on the majesty of the Roman name. But Syria was full of unrest, and Lysias and his followers had no mind to be set aside so easily. When the commissioners got to work riots ensued, and one of them was murdered.

To an embassy sent to protest the innocence of the young king and his friends the Senate gave no heed.   At this juncture (162) the hostage-prince escaped from Rome with the help of Polybius[1] and other friends.   He reached Syria safely and was well received.   He put the boy king to death and reigned till 150 as Demetrius Soter. When settled on the throne he tried to propitiate the Romans by sending a costly gift and handing over the murderer of the Roman envoy.   The Senate accepted the gift but refused the criminal, preferring not to close the incident but to keep open a pretext for interfering at some convenient season.   Demetrius unwisely tried to gain influence in Cappadocia.   This offended Rome, and brought upon him a number of enemies let loose by Roman diplomacy.   A pretender appeared, a certain Balas, who took the name Alexander and claimed to be a son of Antiochus IV Epiphanes.   With the support of the kings of Pergamum Egypt and Cappadocia this Balas overthrew Demetrius and reigned in his stead (150—145).   But he was a worthless creature, and was in his turn ejected by Demetrius, son of Demetrius I, to whom the king of Egypt had transferred his favour.   The career of Demetrius II was a chequered one.   He was king in some sense from 145 to 139, but his tenure was disputed. In 145 or 144 an adventurer, one Diodotus, raised a son of Balas to the throne, but in 142 seized it himself and ruled as king Tryphon till 137.   He was overthrown in 137 by Antiochus the younger son of Demetrius I, who reigned 137—129 as Antiochus VII Sidetes. When he committed suicide in disgust at failure in a Parthian war, Demetrius II, who had been for ten years a prisoner in Parthia, came back and ruled till 126.

584.   So much for the outline of Syrian chronology.   It is very confused, and authorities differ.   But the difference of a year or two here and there is of no importance for our purpose.   What concerns us closely is to remember that the Syria of which we are speaking was nothing but a petty remnant of the once enormous empire of Seleucus.   Armenia had revolted from Antiochus III after his defeat at Magnesia.   Antiochus IV had recovered it, but we do not find it forming an effective part of the Syrian kingdom.   Rome had shorn away the provinces west of the Taurus.   To the East even vaster territories had been lost.   Alexander's Punjab province had long ago become part of an Indian kingdom.   Bactria had been independent under princes with at least Greek names for about 100 years (255—150), when it fell under the dominion of the Parthian king.   The Parthian monarchy founded by Arsaces about 250 was a thorn in the side of the Seleucids.   In this period Mithradates I the ruling

[1] Polyb. XXXI 19—23.

Arsacid added not only Bactria but Media Persis Susiana and Babylonia to his empire. His reign (174—136) and that of his son Phraates (136—127) cover our present period. Parthia was now the great disturbing force in the political relations of the Orient. The circumstances of the Seleucid empire had from the first been such as to deny it permanence. Times were bad for the house of Seleucus. True, they still (when not ousted by pretenders) reigned in Antioch over Syria proper and neighbouring districts, and were regarded as the legitimate royal family for many years yet. The root of their power was in the semi-Greek cities founded or fostered by Seleucid kings, cities for the most part enjoying considerable privileges, and destined to hellenize the country in a very remarkable degree. The spread of Hellenism was an object of royal policy, as tending to promote a common standard of civilization and lessen the differences among the many peoples still comprised in their shrunken realm. This policy brings us to the question of the Hollow Syria Phoenicia and Palestine.

585. These districts had long been a bone of contention between the Syrian and Egyptian kingdoms. We have already spoken of their occupation by Antiochus IV, of his expulsion from Egypt by Rome, and have referred to the rising of the Maccabees provoked by that eccentric king's tyranny and sacrilege in Judaea. Heavy taxation, caused by the financial necessities of the impoverished Seleucid court, was another Jewish grievance, and the rebellion took more and more an aggressive character as time went on. What concerns us is that among all the ups and downs of this period the Jewish leaders profited by the distresses of their nominal overlords to extort concessions, and the disputed successions to the throne of Antioch strengthened the hands of the High Priests of Jerusalem. Their policy is well illustrated by the episode of Balas. When this pretender appeared in 152, the Jews took his part, thus cooperating with Ptolemy Philometor and playing the power of Egypt against the Syrian. In the war between Balas and Demetrius II they still clove to Balas, but Ptolemy changed sides and Demetrius succeeded. Punishment seemed near, but the clever negotiation of the reigning High Priest turned the financial straits of the new king to good account. The Jewish tribute was redeemed for ever by a ready-money payment. That the bargain was a judicious one we need not doubt. And by it a principal sign of dependence, useful to the one party, galling to the other, was taken away. Enough has been said to shew that the Jews were well on their way to independence, which was practically achieved when in 141 the garrison in the citadel surrendered, and Jerusalem was free. Antiochus VII Sidetes re-

conquered it, but only for a moment, and after his death in 129 the independence of the Jews continued till the coming of the Romans and Pompey's settlement of the East.

586. In Judaea then the attempt to hellenize a small but stubborn people by force called forth a resistance in which religion played an important part, and it failed. But quietly and gradually Greek influences made their way even here. And even the old Phoenician cities, decayed but still existing and doing business on their little strip of coast, were affected thereby. Business-Greek was now the trade language of the eastern Mediterranean, and the Phoenicians were close pressed by hellenistic neighbours. Not only were there the cities of Syria proper at their back: close by to the north lay Cilicia, the level eastern part of which was the site of numerous cities, all hellenistic centres, favoured by the rulers of Antioch. The chief of these was Tarsus, famed as a seat of education and learning. But while Hellenism, that is not merely the use of the Greek tongue but the assimilation of intellectual and social influences—'Greek is that Greek does' gives the note of this mongrel Hellenism—was spreading in these regions of the East, it was decaying[1] in Egypt. There it had never taken hold of the native population, and indeed was chiefly confined to the one great centre of Alexandria. But Alexandria was from the first a cosmopolitan city, and contained, besides a number of native Egyptians, a large colony of Jews. Even the mercenary troops were not all Greeks. Their presence marks the artificial nature of the Graeco-Macedonian kingdom of the Ptolemies. Greek influences centred in the famous Museum, but in the country at large they had no effect. The permanent influence there was that of the priests, who in spite of Persian or Macedonian conquests had from time immemorial swayed the people of the Nile. The Ptolemies had early discovered that it was necessary to conciliate this powerful caste, and in the present period things had gone so far that in Alexandria itself Egyptian influence was fast gaining ground.

587. The situation in Egypt during this period is most difficult to grasp. The Lagid dynasty had seen its best days, and the affair of Popilius and Antiochus IV shews that the continuance of the monarchy depended on the protection of Rome. Rome however did not desire to see a great independent power built up again in Egypt. To save an allied kingdom from its enemies, and then to keep a check on its development, were but two parts of the same normal policy. The claims of two Lagid brothers gave ample opportunity for the effective assertion of the Roman protectorate guided by Roman interests. In 181 Ptolemy V Epiphanes died, and his eldest son,

[1] See Mahaffy, *Empire of the Ptolemies.*

Ptolemy VI, very soon after. Two sons remained, the elder of whom (181 or 180) succeeded as a minor, Ptolemy VII Philometor, under the guardianship of his mother Cleopatra I. He attained his majority in 174, when he became actual king at the age of 14, but with the death of his mother in 173 his troubles began. Defeat in a war with Antiochus for the possession of the Hollow Syria weakened his position at home, while his younger brother came to the front in the resistance to the Syrian invasion of Egypt, and was in fact joint ruler with Philometor from 170—163 under the name of Ptolemy IX (or VIII) Euergetes II, whom we will speak of under the nickname[1] of Physcon. The brothers quarrelled in 163, and Physcon ejected his milder brother. Philometor went to Rome and got the Senate to order his restoration. But they assigned the outlying Egyptian province of Cyrene to Physcon as a separate kingdom. Physcon then put in a claim to the other detached province of Cyprus. Philometor protested, and a Roman commission reported against the claim. But Roman interests were in favour of the change, and commissioners were sent to transfer the island to Physcon. Roman intervention was needed again later to restore him to the kingdom which he had forfeited by his barbarity. On one occasion he seems to have fallen into the hands of Philometor, who spared his life. After Philometor's death (146) in the Syrian war, Physcon succeeded to the whole empire of the Lagids, and held it till death (117). On the revolts produced by the hateful cruelties and abominations of his reign, and the massacres by which he restored what passed for order, we need not enlarge. The points to notice are that he thinned out the Greek element in the population of Alexandria, and that in spite of all his enormities he enjoyed to the last the countenance of Rome. As throwing light upon the principles that guided the policy of the Senate, no passage of history is more deeply significant than the career of this bloated criminal. It can hardly be maintained that Roman action in Greece and the East shewed qualities worthy of a great people now the unquestioned leaders (and, wherever they chose, rulers) of the most civilized parts of the world. Lamentable as is the use of force in determining the mutual relations of peoples, its evil effects are small compared with those of a continuous policy of dominating (not governing) by the promotion of divisions and weakness among subordinate communities. To abstain from conquest is admirable when the motive for the abstinence is good and when the stronger power treats the best interests of the weaker

---

[1] This is the notorious monster to whom the Alexandrians gave the contrary name of Cacergetes (malefactor) in parody of his official style of Benefactor. In middle life he became monstrously fat, and is now best known by his nickname of Physcon (swag-belly, fat-paunch). His remarkable career is set forth in Mahaffy's *Empire of the Ptolemies*.

as consistent with its own.   But when a tortuous diplomacy is preferred, merely to save trouble for the moment and to shirk responsibility, the result is apt to be bad for all parties.

588.   We next turn to consider the course of events in Africa. The name Africa was anciently applied to the middle part of the northern coast-lands of the great southern continent, the part which was ruled or influenced by Carthage when at the height of her power. Things were now sadly changed with the great city.   Her actual territory was only the block of land about 200 miles from east to west and 300 from north to south, lying to the south-west of Sicily. Beside this she retained also the strip of coast to the east, stretching between the bights known as the Greater and Lesser Syrtis.   But, having no longer a navy, her hold upon the seaboard was weakened, and of her embarrassments advantage was constantly taken by the Numidian king.   Masinissa was rewarded for his services in the second Punic war with the eastern half of Mauretania, and we have already seen that he was always seeking to enlarge his kingdom at the expense of Carthage.   Having at command any number of hardy and active fighting men, he pushed eastward bit by bit till he had got behind the coast-towns of the eastern Carthaginian province. Some he seems to have occupied, but the economic pressure exerted by commanding inland routes probably gave him a sufficient control of the rest.   This would affect the revenues of Carthage: and Carthage could neither defend herself nor induce the Roman government to redress her wrongs.   The hypocritical commissions came and went, and nothing came of the solemn farce.   Meanwhile in spite of all her sufferings the merchants of Carthage made great profits in trade, and the agriculture of the Home province flourished exceedingly. And so it was that, when a commission was sent in 157 to arbitrate once more between Carthage and Masinissa, the manifest signs of wealth filled the ten Romans with wonder, some of them at least with alarm.   Was it for this that Rome had bled and suffered? had the persecution of a twice-humbled rival been of no more effect than this? And what was the meaning of the stores of timber[1] in the dockyards? Was Rome to be again compelled to raise great fleets and do battle for the empire of the seas?   An army was in the field to resist Masinissa: was not this a mere pretext, the real enemy being Rome?

589.   What might have been the outcome of this commission, had the members of it all been ordinary men, we cannot tell: that one of them was old Cato was a fact of evil omen for Carthage.   He went out prejudiced against Rome's old enemy: he came back bent upon her speedy destruction.   When the commission made their

[1] Livy epit. 47.

report to the Senate, Cato called for an immediate declaration of war. He was opposed[1] by P. Cornelius Scipio Nasica, one of the first men in Rome, who was also one of the old Roman school, but on this point of policy took a larger view. Nasica succeeded in getting another commission sent out to keep an eye on affairs. They censured the proceedings of the Punic government, and at least made a show of patching up a peace between them and Masinissa. Perhaps the terms on which the king was to evacuate the land in dispute were too unfavourable to Carthage. At any rate we hear that a democratic magistrate roused the fury of the mob by urging them to war, and that the Roman envoys, in fear of outrage, fled for their lives. This episode enraged the Roman Senate more than ever. But indeed, ever since Cato took up the matter in earnest, the destruction of Carthage was a burning question of Roman politics. The encroachments of Masinissa went on till the patience of the Carthaginians was exhausted. In 152 they began to prepare seriously for armed resistance. The Punic government may have been encouraged to bolder action by observing the reluctance of Rome to use force in Greece and the East, and by rumours of the unrest in Spain. But the policy of Rome might be fitful or lethargic elsewhere: Africa was jealously watched. Masinissa's son Gulussa reported the doings at Carthage to the Roman Senate. Cato again clamoured for war. The old man's devotion to a fixed idea was probably turned to account by the Roman capitalists, now becoming a powerful class. The merchants would be glad to destroy their commercial rivals: financiers and speculators would scent the chance of bargains and profitable investments, sure to follow the conquest of a rich country. Fortunes were being made in Sicily, and greedy eyes were turned to Africa. Cato therefore was probably backed up by many who had not the smallest sympathy with the general political aims of the old reformer. And the secret influence of the capitalist is always far more potent than his open claims. For the moment however Nasica managed to get another commission sent to make further inquiries. On their return with confirmation of the report of the mobilization at Carthage, the debate broke out afresh. But Nasica so far prevailed that an ultimatum was sent ordering the Punic government to burn their fleet and disband their army, and a declaration of war, inevitable in case of a refusal, was still avoided.

590. In some form or other the Carthaginians did refuse to obey this order, and in 151 they began open war with Masinissa without the leave of Rome. Even now they may have fancied that the Senate was not in earnest, and that its weak temporizing displayed in Syria

[1] Livy epit. 48, 49.

would be repeated in Africa. If so, they were soon undeceived. Rome
vacillating and Rome tenacious exhibited only the same temper in
various moods: the mood of vacillation it is true was becoming more
habitual.   Before this period she had dealt firmly with Pyrrhus
Hannibal Philip and Antiochus.   In later years her hesitation was
not less fatal to Jugurtha and Mithradates.   It seems to have been
in 150 that war was actually declared against Carthage and an army
and fleet prepared.   Just when the armament was about to start, an
embassy appeared in Rome on an important errand.   It came from
Utica[1], once the headquarters of Phoenician colonization in Africa,
a city which, though long subordinate to Carthage, had never forgotten
the claims of superior antiquity.   Under what influences the Uticans
now acted, we do not know.   What they did was to abandon Carthage
in her distress, and place themselves wholly in the hands of Rome.
The Roman forces had thus from the first a harbour and a base of
operations.   To Carthage the loss was but one more blow.   Already
the old Numidian king had defeated their army with great loss.   To
withstand Rome and Masinissa combined was impossible: so they
sent envoys to offer submission on any terms.   The Senate ordered
them to furnish 300 children of their first families as hostages and
obey the orders of the new consuls (149), who were coming.   Accordingly a deputation met the consuls at Utica, and received orders
that all arms engines and other material of war must be delivered up.
This was done, and the quantity is said to have been enormous.   The
ships of war appear to have been previously surrendered or destroyed.
Carthage was now helpless.   The resource of old days, a host of
foreign mercenaries, could no longer be employed: Rome commanded
the waterways, and the coasts of Spain and Gaul.   And now the
consuls issued the final order.   The population must remove to some
inland spot not less than ten miles from the sea: the present city was
to be razed to the ground.   It is said that this population numbered
700,000 persons.   Nothing but the trade made possible by that
advantageous site enabled such a vast multitude to exist.   The order
was of course not meant to be obeyed: it was to furnish a pretext
for the ruthless execution of the secret instructions brought by the
consuls from Rome.   No entreaties found a hearing, and the Carthaginians, after an outburst of fury and despair, settled down to shew
the Romans what a tortured Semitic people could do and suffer in
their last agony.

591.   The story of the siege is given very fully by Appian.   The
chief authority followed by him, and by Livy also, was certainly
Polybius.   No doubt the exploits of Scipio did not lose in the telling

[1] Polyb. xxxvi 3, Appian *Pun.* 75, Livy epit. 49.

at the hands of his devoted admirer. But that nearly everything done in workmanlike fashion during that weary siege was done by Scipio, is a conclusion we may accept without reserve. He had but lately returned from Spain, where he had done inestimable service under a corrupt and incompetent commander. He was now military tribune in the army before Carthage, and again it devolved on him to retrieve the blunders of his superiors. Both consuls were there, but two consuls were not better than one. Confident that they had but to appear and take possession of the defenceless city, they made no haste to begin the siege: and while they dallied the Carthaginians laid in stores of food and made shift to forge weapons and construct new engines of defence. They organized a field army of over 30,000 men, and a flying column of light horse scoured the country. The Romans thus found the gates of Carthage closed and the walls manned. Their attempts to carry the place by storm were easily repulsed. When a party did effect an entrance at an ill-guarded point, they were driven out again with heavy loss. The enemy managed to set fire to a number of Roman ships. Meanwhile foraging parties were harassed or cut off by the Punic cavalry, the camp itself was threatened by a nightly sortie from the city, the activity of the field army was causing great uneasiness, and the haughty attitude of the consuls towards Masinissa had for the time interrupted the old king's cordial support. In all these troubles it was the wisdom and bravery of Scipio that saved the Roman army from serious disasters. It was his watchfulness and skill that the enemy feared, his good faith that they could trust. When an expedition was made into the country for the purpose of destroying the Punic army, it was Scipio who extracted the force from a position of great peril, into which it had been brought in defiance of his advice. The fame of his services soon reached Rome, and it is said that old Cato quoted a line of Homer[1] meaning 'the rest are but flitting shadows, he alone has wits.'

592. Before the end of the year 149 Cato and Masinissa both died. The old king, who lived 90 years in the enjoyment of vigorous health, distinguished as a ruler a warrior and a promoter of agriculture, left three legitimate sons. He meant them to share his now extensive kingdom, named Scipio as umpire, and charged them to make the partition by the Roman officer's advice. Scipio did not break up the kingdom, but arranged a partnership[2], assigning to each prince a particular department; to Micipsa the general presidency with Cirta the capital, to Gulussa the command of the army, to Mastanabal the administration of justice. We may fairly guess that

---

[1] *Odyssey* x 495 adapted.   [2] Livy epit. 50, Appian *Pun.* 106, 107.

Roman interests dictated this curious award. It was not easy to quarrel with Gulussa, and he would surely be content, having the power of the sword: the army was kept together, and Rome thus could and did summon to her aid the undivided force of her ally. Hearty concord between the three brothers was hardly to be looked for, and we find Gulussa actively cooperating with the Romans, while the other two made promises[1] of arms and money which they were in no hurry to fulfil. Besides settling the question of the Numidian succession, Scipio performed a most useful service by inducing Phameas the leader of the enemy's cavalry corps to desert to the Romans with a number of his men. The year 148 was now begun, and a new consul was coming. Leave was given to the successful subordinate to visit Rome and introduce Phameas to the Senate, who greeted the deserter with rewards, and sent him back to make himself useful at the seat of war. The new consul did not do better than his predecessors. He spent most of his time in besieging and not taking several coast cities. Meanwhile a Numidian leader deserted from Gulussa's service, and brought over to that of Carthage a valuable body of 800 horse. The Carthaginians took heart at the inefficiency of the Roman operations, and sent embassies to tempt Micipsa and Mastanabal to support them, to rouse in arms some of the desert tribes, and even to encourage the pretender then fighting for the crown of Macedon. They had now also built a considerable fleet, ready to take advantage of any opportunities that might occur. They knew no doubt that Rome, beside her preoccupations in Macedonia and Greece, had now to face the rising of Viriathus in Spain. At this stage of the war there might seem a hope that Carthage would survive the shock. In Rome indignation at failure caused men to look to Scipio. But according to the present constitutional law he was too young (37) to be consul, and it was a standing rule that a man must be consul to command a consular army. On the other hand it was not the Roman way to strain a principle to the cracking-point. So, when this most orderly and conformable of men stood for the aedileship, means were found[2] (perhaps a relief-bill passed by the Assembly) to elect him consul. It is said that he was specially assigned as his 'province' Africa, that is the Punic war. With his arrival in camp, bringing reinforcements and some volunteers from foreign allied states, the effective siege of Carthage began.

593. His first experience was a familiar one. The outgoing admiral tried to surprise the city on the sea side. The attack miscarried, and Scipio had to extricate the Roman force from a position

---

[1] Appian *Pun.* 111.

[2] Livy epit. 49, Cicero *Philipp.* XI § 17.

of great peril. But by far the most important step now taken was the expulsion of the horde of non-combatant undesirables, traders and others, whose presence impaired the efficiency of the army. Luxury and wantonness gave way to simplicity and discipline: through business to pleasure was again the note of military effort. The first attack was made on the great suburb of Megara or Magalia. This seems to have been larger than all the older quarters of the city together: it consisted mainly of gardens and was thinly inhabited. In these respects, and in being fortified, it resembled the Epipolae of Syracuse. To man walls of so great a circuit was not easy, and the suburb was eventually carried by escalade. But, barring the inconvenience caused to the besieged, this success did not bring the Romans much nearer to taking Carthage. What went on inside the wall of the old city was more in their favour. The Punic general Hasdrubal tortured his Roman prisoners to death on the top of the walls, thus depriving his people of all prospect of mercy, and proving to them that their leader had himself lost all hope. He became a cruel tyrant, ruling only by fear. And now Scipio constructed a long line of siege works, by which he cut off the communications of the city with the interior. Hitherto—which shews the incapacity of the Roman commanders—the besieged had been drawing most of their supplies by this route, for sea-borne traffic was checked by the presence of a Roman fleet. A fitful blockade-running, exposed to great risks and depending on wind and weather, now served to feed the fighting men: the women and weaker folk were no longer certain of a meal.

594. Observant and methodical, the consul set about the next great step, to get command of the harbour mouth. He first with great labour built a long bank or dam through the shallow water towards the mouth, which he hoped to close. As this work advanced and it seemed that it might effect its purpose, the Carthaginians changed their plans and secretly cut a new outlet to the sea, not from the outer or commercial harbour, but from the inner or naval harbour, a circular basin surrounded by the sheds of the military dockyard. Out of this their fleet issued: we are told that the Romans were completely taken by surprise when it appeared. But the Punic admiral let slip the moment of advantage, and in a sea-fight three days later the Roman fleet, no doubt better found and better manned than the makeshift vessels of Carthage, gained a decisive victory. We learn that on the Roman side the ships most cleverly handled were five voluntarily sent to Scipio's support by the city of Side[1] in Pamphylia.

---

[1] Appian *Pun.* 123.

The success was followed up by an attack on a long wharf or quay which commanded the harbour.   After a severe struggle Scipio retained a lodgment on this spot.   He was now superior in the most accessible part of the sea-front.   The next thing was to destroy the field army through which the Carthaginians kept a hold on the inland country.   This he effected with the cooperation of Gulussa in the winter of 147—6.   General submission was the result, and nothing now remained of the great Punic power save the starving and desperate thousands standing at bay behind the city walls.

595.   The Roman government had the sense to let Scipio stay on in command as proconsul to finish his work.   First he seized the harbour-quarter and the marketplace, in short the old commercial part of the city.   After this came a long exhausting struggle in which the streets leading up to the citadel were captured house by house, amid scenes of frantic daring and incomparable horrors.   When gained, this block was set afire: portable things of value had no doubt been looted: the flames consumed the rest, and with them bodies alive or dead.   The assault of the Byrsa or citadel was to follow, when suppliants appeared to beg for their lives.   This the proconsul granted them, and the poor faint remnant marched out into slavery, in number about 50,000.   The Byrsa was now occupied, but one last refuge within it was still left.   This was the temple of Aesculapius (Eshmun) the god of healing, perched upon the highest point of the hill.   In its precinct were gathered a band of some 900 Roman deserters, probably not Roman citizens but Italians and foreign auxiliaries, to whom all mercy was denied.   At this last moment the mean and brutal Hasdrubal left them, and with them his wife and children, to beg his life from Scipio.   They set fire to the temple and perished by sword or flame.   Such was the end of Phoenician Carthage.

596.   The closing scenes of this horrible drama must have produced a profound impression throughout the Mediterranean world.   For this thing was not done in a corner.   Nor did the story merely pass from mouth to mouth: competent eye-witnesses recorded it in writing, and for centuries no event was more widely or accurately known.   Polybius was present during great part of the siege, and a Roman historian, C. Fannius, a man of high repute for honesty and ability, was one of Scipio's fighting officers.   It was he that attested in his narrative the gallantry of young Tiberius Gracchus, who was the first man to mount the wall.   Among the good men of the consul's staff was of course his inseparable friend C. Laelius, who acted as second in command.   But the most striking figure was the general

himself. Mild humane and firm, he had assuredly small pleasure in his brutal task : but he did it as a workman obedient to his country's will. In carrying out his duty, we must not attribute to him more compunction than was within the scope of a Roman in that hard and selfish age. In the wave of feeling that came upon him when all was over, and the once imperial city was a heap of smouldering ruins, Polybius heard him quote the lines[1] of the *Iliad* in which Hector forebodes the fall of Troy, and saw him weep to think of the mutability of human things. But the Greek observer is careful to express his admiration of the great conqueror who did not lose his balance in the hour of victory. What made Scipio for the moment sick at heart was not remorse for the destruction of Carthage, but misgivings as to the future of Rome.

597. We need not describe the rejoicings in Rome on receipt of the news. The usual ten commissioners[2] were sent out by the Senate to arrange with Scipio the settlement of Africa. Meanwhile the proconsul was busy enough, rewarding the brave, selling captives, and claiming for the Roman state its share of the booty. It seems to have been before the arrival of the commissioners that he took a remarkable step[3] in reference to certain works of art. There were in Carthage a number of statues brought from Greek cities in Sicily, sacked by Punic armies in the old wars. Bronzes had all been melted down owing to the dire need of metal, but many works in marble had escaped the general wreck. Scipio now sent notice round the Sicilian towns inviting them to send over delegates to identify and receive back their own. No wonder Appian (after Polybius, surely,) remarks that this kind and courteous act made him immensely popular. To us this act is especially interesting, for Scipio could have given no more striking proof of the genuineness of his Hellenism than by shewing that he understood the Greek feeling on such matters. The settlement of Africa proceeded on the usual lines. Friendly towns, Utica in particular, were rewarded with lands and privileges. Those faithful to Carthage were punished with confiscation of lands or dismantled. The site of Carthage, particularly the citadel, round which Phoenician associations most richly centred, was cleared and laid under a curse, as a spot where man's foot might tread but no man might dwell. The territory actually owned by Carthage at the beginning of the war became the Roman province of Africa. It was to pay a fixed tax and to be administered by governors in the usual way. It remained a very wealthy country, even under Roman

[1] *Iliad* VI 448—9, Polyb. XXXIX 5. [2] See Mommsen, *Staatsrecht* II 624.
[3] Appian *Pun.* 133, Cic. II *in Verrem* II § 86, IV *passim*, Diodor. XXXII 25.

rule. A large share of the trade of the country now fell to the 'free city' of Utica, which enjoyed Roman favour, and till the revival of Carthage as a Roman city was the chief town of the province. A considerable number of Roman business-men settled there, attracted by the openings for making money in so rich a country. It seems probable that the restrictions on land-tenure introduced long ago in Italy, and later in Sicily, were applied to Africa also. The effect of giving to Roman citizens the right of acquiring and holding land anywhere, while the provincials, unless endowed with a privilege seldom granted, were confined each within the bounds of his own particular community, was steadily to transfer proprietary rights into Roman hands. Hence the formation of immense provincial estates, a state of things not peculiar to Africa and Sicily, but of which these two provinces supplied a notorious example. The Carthaginian systems of tillage were retained, but the slave-gangs toiled for other masters. A more interesting witness of the former domination of Phoenicians in northern Africa survived in the Punic tongue, which lived on even after the use of Latin had become general: the emperor Severus (A.D. 193—211), himself an African, spoke it fluently.

598. Whether the destruction of Carthage was a great loss to the world from an intellectual moral or spiritual point of view, may be doubted. We have no reason to think that art or literature would have gained much from Phoenician influences. What little we can gather of their politics does not give a favourable impression, and as inquirers and active fertilizers of other peoples' genius they will hardly bear comparison with the Greeks. Their position in history is singular. Bearing the oriental stamp, they are yet not a monarchy but a republic, at least during their historical period. We have met them as a check upon Greek expansion: in this function they could hold their own. Rome then took up the competition, and Carthage, led by the great men of the house of Barcas, was for a time a check on Rome. That check had now been finally removed, and there is no more to be said.

Numidia seems to have been left as a joint kingdom under the sons of Masinissa. How Scipio's settlement worked we do not know. It is probable that the Senate interpreted his award as a fresh acknowledgement of the right of Rome to arbitrate in internal disputes whenever she saw fit. When a few years later the curtain rises again on Numidian affairs, we shall see how troublesome a client-kingdom could be.

599. TABLE SHEWING SYNCHRONISM 167—133 B.C.

Macedonia and Greece	Africa	Spain	N. Italy, Liguria, Dalmatia &c.
164 Commission of inspection to Macedonia.			166—155 Local outbreaks in Liguria and Corsica suppressed.
164—151 Wretched state of Greece, repeated appeals for restoration of deported Achaeans.			
	157 Commission (Cato) visits Carthage.		
156—5 Quarrel of Athens and Oropus.			156—5 Dalmatian war.
153 War between Rhodians and Cretans.		155—150 Local risings lead to wars, Romans often defeated. Treacherous massacres by Lucullus and Galba.	155—4 Ligurian tribes invade territory of Massalia, but are beaten and quiet restored.
151—0 Return of Achaean exiles.	152 Carthage prepares to resist Masinissa.		
	151—0 War of Carthage against Masinissa.		
	150 Preparations at Rome. Utica joins Rome.		
149 War between Achaeans and Sparta.	149 Deaths of Masinissa and Cato.	149—140 War with Viriathus, who is only overcome by assassination.	
149—8 Pseudophilippus in Macedonia put down with some trouble.	149—146 Third Punic War. Carthage destroyed. Roman province *Africa*.		148 *via Postumia* from Genua into Cisalpine Gaul.
148—7 Troubles in Greece. Two Roman commissions.			
146 Macedonia made a province. Achaean war. Destruction of Corinth.			
142 A pretender in Macedonia easily put down.		143—133 Numantine war. Numantia destroyed.	143 Salassi wantonly attacked by Claudius.
135 Scordisci defeated in Thrace by the praetor of Macedonia.			135 Vardaei (Illyrians) conquered.

600. If we turn to the West we find, as in the preceding period, different circumstances and a different course of events. Rome has had to set up provincial government in Spain, and therefore to use force: diplomatic methods would avail her nothing here. But in her halting inadequate policy we detect the same fundamental weakness as in the East. She has got to govern, but to govern she must effectively conquer. She takes no sufficient steps to effect this. Mutual misunderstandings, not to mention misgovernment, cause trouble in her provinces, and the still independent tribes naturally bear a hand in checking the advance of Roman dominion. Mutual exasperation, as we saw in Liguria, leads to treachery and barbarities in which the officers of the more civilized people completely outdo the Barbarian. And this conclusion is based on Roman evidence: we have not the Spanish version of the story. The conquest, carried on with insufficient means, was a bloody and wasteful process, of which we can only recover a general outline. The wise and conciliatory policy of Gracchus in 179 was successful in keeping the country generally quiet for a number of years. But the effects of firm conquest and good government died away, and about 156 or 155 we hear of Lusitanian inroads and Roman defeats in the Further Spain. The year 153 saw the beginning of the great Celtiberian war which dragged on to the disgrace of Rome for 20 years. This kept central Spain in a ferment, and was more directly an affair of the Hither province. But side by side with it went on the Lusitanian war, which belonged to the sphere of the Further province. Under the leadership of Viriathus (149—140) a certain amount of common action was achieved by the Spanish tribes, and the Roman supremacy was rudely shaken. After the death of the Lusitanian hero the disasters of the Romans were simply due to gross mismanagement, and the employment of capable generals at last brought the war to an end. Before proceeding to set forth some of the more significant details of the Spanish wars it will be well to say a word on the authorities. A very small part of Polybius' 35th book survives. The epitomes of Livy supply very little, and that not always clear. A few fragments of Diodorus remain. Stray references in Cicero and Velleius are not as a rule very helpful. In general we depend on late writers, Appian, Dion Cassius (fragments), Orosius, and the like: these took at least part of their matter from contemporary witnesses such as Sempronius Asellio, or writers of somewhat later date such as Claudius Quadrigarius (early 1st century B.C.); and a few other fragments are preserved in Gellius and elsewhere. Much was no doubt taken direct from Livy. In general we may say that the numbers given are not to be trusted. And it is impossible to guess whether, and if so how far, the failures and misdeeds of the earlier generals may have been exaggerated in order to throw into relief the virtues and successes of the hero of the period, Scipio Aemilianus.

601. The first four years (153—150) form a kind of prelude to the great struggle. In Further Spain the praetor L. Mummius did something, but not much, to restore the credit of the Roman arms. His successor M. Atilius (152) did fairly well at first, but a winter rebellion swept away what little he had achieved in west-central Spain. Next came Servius Sulpicius Galba (151), who met with disaster, but seems to have stayed on as propraetor during the next year. Meanwhile there had been war in the Hither Spain. It had for some time been the policy of Rome in the Peninsula to allow no walled strongholds to be formed, since they were found to serve as bases of rebellion. A quarrel over a question of this kind arose in 154 up in the Celtiberian country. The rights reserved[1] under the treaty of Gracchus were differently interpreted by the natives and by the Senate, and war was the result. That nothing less than the sovranty of Rome was in jeopardy seems to have been well understood and seems proved by the change in the official year. We are told[2] that the consuls of 153 began their term of office on the first of January instead of the first of March, and that the reason for this step was the rising in Spain. But the consul Q. Fulvius Nobilior had no success. He was badly beaten, a further rising at Numantia broke out, other disasters followed, and a cruel winter played havoc with his troops, short of food and fuel and cooped up in a cheerless camp in central Spain. Next came the consul M. Claudius Marcellus (152), whose firm and cautious strategy brought the Spaniards to desire peace. But the Senate refused, and the consul L. Licinius Lucullus (151) was sent out with further reinforcements, which seem[3] to have been raised with great difficulty. We hear that recourse was had to the drawing of lots, apparently to settle who should be enrolled in the forces destined for Spain. But not only was it far from easy to fill up the ranks for this hated service: officers also were not to be had. All hung back, for the dangers and hardships of Spanish warfare were notorious, and the pessimistic views of Marcellus were known. The consuls tried to enforce the levy: unwilling recruits appealed to the tribunes, who intervened to prevent the coercion of some of their own friends: the consuls disregarded their opposition, and the tribunes, falling back upon their traditional rights, seized the consuls and threw them into prison. At this pinch

---

[1] Appian *Hispan.* 44. [2] Livy epit. 47.

[3] Livy epit. 48.

matters were suddenly and dramatically mended by the offer of
P. Cornelius Scipio Aemilianus, who came forward and said that
he was ready to serve in Spain whether as a member of the consul's
staff (*legatus*) or as a military tribune, as the consul might direct.
His patriotism[1] set others volunteering, and the crisis was at an end.
When Lucullus reached Spain he found the war concluded, Marcellus
having forced the Numantines to come to terms and pay an indemnity.   But the new consul wanted money and glory, and found
a pretext for attacking the Vaccaei, further to the West.   One town
he forced to surrender on terms: he then improved the occasion by
breaking faith and butchering the people.   This taste of Roman
mercies hardened the resistance of the natives.   Intercatia stood out
bravely, and the want of supplies caused great suffering in the
Roman camp.   In vain did Scipio kill a Spanish champion in single
combat and lead a storming party into the town: they were driven
out again and the breach repaired.   Both sides were short of food,
but terms were only arranged through Scipio.   He pledged his word
that faith should be kept, and a peace was patched up.   The consul
moved on to Pallantia, where he was able to effect nothing, and a
long and painful retreat to winter quarters further south ended a
disastrous and shameful campaign.   The geography of all these
events is very obscure, but it would seem that both Lucullus and
Galba passed the winter of 151—0 in the south of Spain.   Both were
seeking to retrieve disasters, and both turned upon the restless
Lusitanians.   The proconsul took a number of prisoners, the sale of
whom brought in money.   Galba laid the country waste and concluded a treaty with the barbarians humbled by distress.   Then, on
a promise[2] of finding them lands, he divided them into three bodies
at some distance from each other.   He then led his army to each
party in turn, took away their arms, and cut them to pieces.   The
number of 30,000 may be an exaggeration, but there is no doubt
that this treacherous massacre was one of the foulest episodes in all
the blood-stained conquest of Spain.   Galba and Lucullus between
them had exhibited the fair dealing and clemency of Rome to some
purpose.   Both had enriched themselves, and indeed had waged war
with a single eye to their own interests.   The cause of Rome in
Spain was certainly left by these men weaker than they found it,
and this at the cost of a vast outlay of money and lives.   They
returned to Rome in 149.   Lucullus was saved by influential friends

---

[1] How far this story is to be trusted we cannot tell.   That the troops sent to Spain were
now (as before) mainly contingents of Italian Allies is highly probable, though we have
no direct statement to that effect.

[2] Appian *Hisp.* 59, 60, Livy epit. 49.

from a richly-deserved impeachment. Galba was brought to trial before the Assembly, and even Cato[1] in extreme old age vehemently supported the prosecution. But by the use of his ill-gotten wealth, and by the tears of his little sons, the butcher of the Lusitanians escaped. Five years later he was consul.

602. From Galba's massacre a few had managed to escape, among them Viriathus, a hardy shepherd of the western hills. Highly gifted in body and mind, and possessed of moral qualities that enabled him to inspire and command, he drew to him desperate and patriotic men, resolved to assert their freedom with the sword. For some four years he ran a course of victories; praetor after praetor met with defeat or death in Further Spain. Viriathus understood how to turn to account the superiority of his men in enthusiasm, in mobility, in knowledge of the country and its climate. He did not give away his advantages in pitched battles and sieges, where a Roman army was at its best. By cutting off detachments, laying ambushes, alarming the camps by night, breaking communications, capturing supplies, and the like, he foiled the Roman generals and destroyed the confidence of the rank and file. He seems to have penetrated far into the Roman provincial districts. A concerted rising of the Spanish tribes might perhaps have changed the whole history of Spain. But such a cooperative effort was evidently out of the question. On the contrary we get glimpses during these later wars of native contingents serving on the Roman side. And by the end of 146 the Senate seem to have become awake to the fact that they were face to face with a war-problem of a most serious kind. Macedonia Greece and Carthage had just been dealt with: they now set to work more earnestly to effect a lasting settlement in the West. Accordingly they reverted to the plan of sending consuls with full consular armies. The greatest of the Roman noble houses supplied most of the commanders during the last thirteen (145—133) years of the war, consuls or proconsuls. Succours from Numidia had been often employed elsewhere and in Spain (153): we now hear of fresh contingents (142, 134). And yet the course of events was hardly glorious for Rome, though dogged tenacity gave her victory in the end.

603. In 145 the consul Q. Fabius Maximus Aemilianus took over the Further province. He had learnt enough of war under his father Aemilius Paullus to act with caution, and spent some time in imparting tone and discipline to his raw troops. When he had made them into an efficient and well-found army, he advanced

---

[1] A matter several times referred to by Cicero. See Piderit's index to his edition of the *Brutus*. Livy XXXIX 40 § 12.

and took some towns and drove before him Viriathus, who knew better than to give him battle. But while he wintered in the South Viriathus was busy in the North, and induced some Celtiberian tribes to rise in arms. This was the beginning of the miserable ten years' struggle (143—133), known as the Numantine war. It will be best to finish our sketch of the war in Further Spain and then return to the story of Numantia. Who commanded in 143 is not clear: it seems that after a success at first the campaign ended in failure. In the year 142 the consul Q. Fabius Maximus Servilianus, brother by adoption of Fabius Aemilianus, came to try his hand at the business. He too gained some successes, but suffered serious losses. His army lost heart, and he had to give ground. But in 140 as proconsul he maintained the traditions of Roman governors in Spain by slaughtering 500 out of 10,000 prisoners and selling the rest into slavery. Shortly after this Viriathus caught him engaged in a siege, defeated him utterly, and penned the beaten army in a corner. But instead of destroying them he let them go on terms which meant the independence of the Lusitanians. Of course this humiliating treaty was evaded. Q. Servilius Caepio, brother by birth of Servilianus, succeeded him (140—139). For some reason the forces of Viriathus were weakened. Perhaps the recent compact had encouraged the dispersal of his guerrillas, always impatient of continuous service. Anyhow Caepio more than held his own, though greatly embarrassed by discontents in his army, and on one occasion by open mutiny. Resolved at all costs to accomplish something, he opened negotiations with Viriathus, his real object being to tamper with the trusted agents of his adversary. At last he found his men, and with bribes and promises secured their help. The dastardly murder of the shepherd-hero soon followed. One version of the story[1] adds that the lofty principles of Caepio induced him to cheat the traitors of their covenanted reward. With good reason the Lusitanians mourned the lost leader: their chances of freedom were at an end. A new chief was chosen, but he soon met with disaster. His men had to surrender, and it is said that the proconsul simply disarmed them and settled them on lands sufficient to support them, a wise and merciful policy, if the tale be true. No doubt there were at this time only too many brigands in Spain. The actual assignment[2] of the lands seems to have been carried out by Caepio's successor D. Junius Brutus in 138. He followed the precedent created in the Ligurian wars, transplanting these western folk to a district on the east coast. Brutus stayed on in Spain for several years, engaged in the pacification of the West. And now at last we begin to see signs

[1] Eutropius IV 16, Orosius V 4 § 14, Appian *Hisp.* 74.   [2] Livy epit. 55.

of a more humane and consistent treatment of the natives, a sort of reversion to the old methods of Gracchus. The proconsul beat down resistance, and took the strongholds of Lusitania, but he refrained from needless massacres, and apparently kept faith with the enemy. Bit by bit the superior power of Rome made itself felt: it was found possible to surrender without being handed over at once to the executioner or the slave-dealer: and the resistance, at first desperate in the extreme, gradually died away. But a further blow was necessary to secure what had been gained. The Callaici or Gallaeci of the far North-West had supported the Lusitanians, and a large army (60,000, says[1] Orosius, probably following Livy) appeared in the field. Brutus defeated them with great slaughter. Whether he penetrated into the heart of Gallaecia we do not know, but some kind of Roman suzerainty seems to have been recognized, or at least claimed, in that distant land.

604. We must now turn to the Celtiberian war which centred in Numantia and was connected with Rome's Hither province. In the years 143—2 Q. Caecilius Metellus, who had put down the Macedonian rising in 148, held the command. He is said to have been on the whole successful, and we hear that severe discipline in his army and kind treatment of the natives marked his governorship. His conduct as a servant of the Roman state was however not blameless, if we may believe the story[2] that, in order to satisfy a personal grudge against his successor, he purposely ruined the efficiency of the army he was about to hand over. It is said that this successor, Q. Pompeius, gained the consulship[3] by a trick. He promised to support Scipio's friend C. Laelius, and then turned his opportunity to account on his own behalf. Thus he incurred the hostility of Scipio and his clique, whose resentment told against him later. This resolute man, who first raised the Pompeii to a place among the great noble houses, may have been maligned by Roman scandalmongers: in any case his campaigns in Celtiberia (141—140) were a failure. Such accounts of them as have come down to us are more than usually confused, but his ill fortune seems certain. Even when he took a number of prisoners, with true Spanish perversity they killed themselves to escape Roman slavery, and this waste of valuable property added to the annoyances of the sorely-tried consul. After marches and sieges, much labour and little profit, we find him at length concentrating his efforts on the siege of Numantia, in hope

---

[1] Oros. v 5 § 12, Livy epit. 56.

[2] Valerius Max. IX 3 § 7. The version in Appian *Hisp.* 76 amounts to a direct contradiction of this. One version must be derived from a tainted partisan source : perhaps both.

[3] Plutarch *apophthegm Scip. min.* 8, Cicero *Laelius* § 77.

by its capture to end the war. But he could make no progress, and a commission from Rome presently appeared in camp. This shews that he had not the confidence of the Senate. It had also been discovered[1] (not, we may guess, by Pompeius' friends) that a number of his men had just served the usual time (6 years) in Spain, and a draft of raw troops were sent to relieve them. The winter of 140—139 was too trying for these new levies in the lines before Numantia, and in small affairs with the enemy the proconsul lost both men and officers, young nobles whose deaths would make an impression in Roman society. At last he drew off his army and went, commissioners and all, to winter elsewhere. But he made peace with the Numantines, and this on terms not likely[2] to be ratified at Rome. And when M. Popilius Laenas (139—8) appeared to take over the command, Pompeius repudiated his own act. The Numantines, who had fulfilled their part even to the payment of an indemnity, protested: and Laenas referred the whole matter to the Senate. At Rome the business ran its usual course. The treaty, denied by Pompeius, was ignored by the Senate, who meant to make an end of Numantia. But Pompeius lied, and the Senate knew it. How was the state to stand clear of guilt before heaven, and yet not perform the oaths sworn on its behalf? The Senate had a motion made in the Assembly for handing over Pompeius to the enemy. But he had partisans, and somehow, perhaps by connivance of the tribunes, the bill was thrown out. We hear that in the next year he was tried on a charge of extortion. But this also failed. Politics were brought into the case, and he was acquitted. It would not do to make him a victim of the scruples or jealousy of the leading nobles.

605. The exploits of Popilius in Spain consisted of at least one disaster, probably more. What an ill name the Spanish service had at this time was well shewn[3] in 138. It seems that party-spirit was rising in Rome, and the tribunes of the year were weary of the misgovernment of the great nobles and the growing discredit of the western wars. A man was brought before them charged with being a deserter from the army in Spain. He was flogged with special ignominy and sold for a small coin. This would carry with it the loss of civic rights, if he were a Roman citizen, but we cannot be sure on the point. Side by side with this story we are told of a renewal of the interference of the tribunes with the military levy of the year. They claimed the right of excusing from service ten men each, that is 100 in all, if they chose. And they did choose, for their friends did not want to go to Spain. This right, of which we have no other evidence, must have

---

[1] Appian *Hisp.* 78.   [2] Livy epit. 54, 55, Appian *Hisp.* 79.

[3] Livy epit. 55.

been a survival, the fruit of some encroachment of the tribunate in its earlier and more vigorous days. The consuls declined to recognize it, and the tribunes, as in 151, threw them into prison. The story is only preserved in an epitome of Livy, so we get no details, not even a word as to how the dispute was settled. But we have traces of differences[1] at this time between the consuls and tribunes on other questions: and it may well be that these are signs of the coming struggle between the ruling nobility and the 'people's men' (*optimates* and *populares*), in which is centred most of the historical interest of the next period.

606. The year 137 was famous for an exhibition of Roman incompetence, and 136 for a crowning triumph of Roman hypocrisy. The consul C. Hostilius Mancinus set out for Spain amid bad omens. The army was in bad order, the active Numantines had the best of it in many small encounters, and a force was said to be coming to relieve the town. An attempt to withdraw the besieging army unobserved was detected. The Romans, 30,000 in number, were pursued by 4000 Spaniards, who harassed them on the march and drove them into a corner. To save his hungry and helpless army Mancinus had to sue for terms. The Numantines were probably unwilling to provoke Roman vengeance by pushing their present advantage too far: we must remember that Viriathus was dead, and Rome triumphant in the South, while Brutus was conquering the West. But to expect good faith from an average Roman governor like Mancinus was impossible for men with memories. They knew however that Tiberius Sempronius Gracchus, son of the good governor of 42 years before, was with the army as quaestor. Through this young officer[2] they consented to negotiate. A treaty was made in which the lives of the Roman army were bought with the independence of Numantia, Mancinus swore to it on behalf of Rome, but the real trust of the Numantines was in the quaestor's word of honour. They shewed him special courtesies: meanwhile the report of the transaction was forwarded to Rome. The other consul, M. Aemilius Lepidus, was sent out to relieve his unlucky colleague. The record of his doings is most obscure. It would seem that he could not wait for events and so perhaps have to return home without gain or glory. Accordingly he picked a quarrel with the Vaccaei to the west of Numantia, laid siege to Pallantia without proper supplies of food, and in an attempt to extricate a part of his army, thinned by hunger and sickness, he met with a great disaster. He was recalled and punished.

---

[1] Valerius Max. III 7 § 3. The story is probably quite distinct from the one given above from Livy epit. 55, as Long has pointed out.

[2] See Holden on Plutarch *Tib. Gracc.* 5.

Mancinus' treaty had now been discussed and repudiated. The Senate instructed the consuls for 136 to move the Assembly to annul it and to vote that the parties to the transaction should be handed over to the enemy. One version of the story is that Gracchus had sworn to the treaty, and so was involved in this provision, and that he escaped only by the help of Scipio. Anyhow it was agreed to make Mancinus the only scapegoat, and it is said that the ex-consul himself spoke in favour of the bill. So he was sent out in charge of the consul P. Furius Philus. He was solemnly stripped of his outer garment, and conducted by a special officer of religion to a spot in front of Numantia, and left bound and helpless to the mercy of the foe. But the Numantines would have none of him. After spending the day half-naked between the armies, he was fetched back: the religious scruples as to this course were got over somehow. The frequent references to the story of Mancinus in Cicero and elsewhere surely betray the difficulty felt by later generations in justifying the conduct of their fathers. The question as to his loss of civic rights (settled eventually by a declaratory law in his favour) seems to have been keenly debated. It became a stock case, cited in discussions concerning *civitas*.

607. Philus (136) and his successor Q. Calpurnius Piso (135) could make no way with the Numantine war. There can be no doubt that this was largely due to the state of the army. Discipline had been relaxed under recent governors, and these men were not equal to the task of restoring efficiency. In Rome public indignation at the scandalous mismanagement of the war became irresistible, but there was only one man in whom all had confidence. Scipio Aemilianus had been sent out not many years before this to redeem the failures of others in the third Punic war. Even then it had been necessary to suspend the statutory limit of age in order to elect him consul. A clause forbidding reelections now stood in the way. But arrangements were made[1] to exempt him from its operation, probably by a special enactment. He was then reelected consul without appearing as a candidate, and commissioned to make an end of the business in Spain. Whether the Senate, now alarmed at the slave-war in Sicily, made a difficulty about further levies, or whether Scipio saw himself that quality, not quantity, was the need of the moment in the army at the front, is not quite clear: it seems that he raised no fresh troops in the ordinary way. Volunteers were sent by allied states and kings, picked men, no doubt, to the number of about 3500. He had besides a corps of 500 raised among his own friends[2] and dependants. This was a sort of private cohort, a general's bodyguard: their relation to

---

[1] Livy epit. 56.   [2] Appian *Hisp.* 84, Marx, *Lucilius, prolegomena* p. xxv.

Scipio was in fact a personal one. Such a guard was needed to secure the reforming commander while he carried out his unpopular duty. The fact was big with consequence: in it we have the germ of the later *cohors praetoria* and the famous Imperial Guard. Scipio lost no time in reaching the army, and set to work vigorously purging it of corruption. Idleness, laziness, luxury, disobedience, debauchery, had made it a worthless mob. He sold off unnecessary animals and restored the soldier's burden to his back. Dealers in dainties, soothsayers, camp-followers generally, were sent packing: it is said that 2000 women were thus driven to abandon a military career. When he had thus pruned away the growths of previous license, he began to train his men to endurance and obedience in a course of practical campaigning under strict field-service conditions. The actual campaign, in the land of the Vaccaei, was of minor importance: it was everything that the men became soldiers, that they learnt to move in heavy marching order, to scout and forage cautiously and systematically, to encamp according to the traditions of the Roman service, and to use the pick and shovel as well as the *pilum* and the sword. Having thus remade his army, he led them back to Numantia and constructed an elaborate system of lines to isolate the city. He meant to reduce it by famine, a slow process, but there was to be no mistake this time. The position of the place was very strong, the people desperate. From the first Scipio discouraged combats, not wishing to spend the blood of his men in reducing the number of hungry mouths in the beleaguered town. That supplies might not reach the defenders by way of the river, he contrived a barrier that boats, and even swimmers, could not pass. Contingents from allied Spanish tribes were called out, and judiciously distributed among the detachments of the besieging force. The ground was mostly commanded by forts armed with the artillery of the day. Signalling was brought to great perfection, and a reserve force could quickly be summoned to threatened points. It is said that Scipio had in all about 60,000 men: the Numantines were perhaps about one eighth of that number.

608. Before the end of 134 the investment was complete, and from that time the city was held in a firm grip. The siege of one Spanish stronghold was in itself not an event of the first magnitude. But circumstances gave it exceptional importance. The fate of the Peninsula turned upon that of a single community that had hitherto defied the arms of Rome. Scipio, like his father Paullus, had gathered round him a number of remarkable men. His own brother Fabius Aemilianus acted as second in command. Among the military tribunes were P. Sempronius Asellio and P. Rutilius Rufus, who both wrote histories of the Numantine war. The latter was a good soldier

and a student of military affairs: his honesty was remarkable in that age, and turned to his disadvantage in his later years. Serving in the cavalry was a young man from Arpinum, one Gaius Marius, a hard keen soldier, smart and sure. Scipio, it is said[1], detected in him the germs of future eminence and honoured him with approval. The general's elder brother-in-law Tiberius Sempronius Gracchus, who had distinguished himself at the siege of Carthage and recently in Spain, was detained in Rome by political business. But his younger brother Gaius (age 21—2) was there, and served with credit. Polybius is known to have written a separate history of this war, and it is probable that he also visited the headquarters of his protector and pupil. One of the most noteworthy figures of the company was a person of a very different type. He was a young Numidian, natural son of a prince lately deceased. His uncle, king Micipsa, disquieted by the vigour and ambition of the youth, had sent him in command of an auxiliary contingent, hoping, it is said[2], that he might fall in some rash enterprise and so cease to cause anxiety at home. But he escaped all perils, and gained glory and experience. Scipio discerned his merits, and employed him in services calling for judgment and daring. Repeated successes proved his competence, and he became one of the most popular men in camp. Thus he was admitted to the company of officers who belonged to the first families of Rome, whose unguarded gossip betrayed to his eager ear the symptoms of decay in the great republic, the rottenness of politics, the growth of hypocrisy, the greed and venality of even the most respectable leaders. This was all laid to heart, perhaps taken too literally. It was destined to have serious consequences in later years, for this young Numidian was Jugurtha.

609. That the Roman nobles were not all corrupt, is said to have been exemplified during the siege by the commander himself. The story[3] is that Antiochus VII of Syria, desiring to win favour at Rome, and judging Romans by the standard of eastern experience, sent to Scipio magnificent presents, in short a bribe. It had become usual for Roman generals to accept such gratifications and say nothing about them. Scipio made public declaration of his acceptance, and ordered his quaestor to enter the amount as a receipt in his account-books, announcing at the same time that he meant it to form a fund for providing rewards of bravery. The Numantines still made attacks on the Roman lines, and on one occasion a few broke through. At length under pressure of hunger they sent to beg for terms, but Scipio would accept only unconditional surrender. So they held out a while longer, feeding on bits of leather and finally on each other. Whether

---

[1] Plutarch *Mar.* 3.   [2] Sallust. *Jug.* 6—9.   [3] Livy epit. 57.

they ended by mutual slaughter to escape slavery, or whether after a last despairing attack on the Roman lines the miserable remnant, foul and brutalized by the horrors of their long agony, gave themselves up to the mercies of Roman slave-drivers, does not matter now. The city fell after a laborious siege of fifteen months, and its destruction was so complete that its exact position has only lately been determined by Schulten. The lesson of its fate was not lost upon the tribes of Spain. The supremacy of Rome was seen to be inevitable, and no more great risings took place. Minor revolts there were, and a part of the North was not conquered till the days of Augustus: but the only important war, that of Sertorius, was essentially a part of the civil wars of Italy. A settlement of the country was now made in the usual course by a senatorial commission. The taxation took the form of a fixed[1] tribute, a plan by which the irritation caused by varying tithes and greedy collectors was avoided. Roads gradually opened up the inland districts, and, in the absence of a self-conscious common civilization of Spain, Roman civilization steadily made itself felt and gradually achieved the conquest of the land. Settlers from Italy gathered round the garrisons. Roman capitalists pushed on the development of the mines. The native Spaniards were peacefully Romanized, and those who returned from service in Roman armies brought Roman influences with them. Of all the parts of the great Roman empire of later times, none were more thoroughly Roman or more uniformly prosperous than the provinces of Spain. The work of Brutus and Scipio had brought the period of wasteful and hesitating conquest to an end.

610. In conclusion we will briefly sketch the course of events in northern Italy (Cisalpine Gaul and Liguria) and the neighbouring countries. Our stock of information is small and fragmentary, but enough remains to shew that the old stubborn resistance of the tribes to Roman supremacy was broken. Only small local outbreaks now interrupt the steady progress of Romanization in these parts. In 166 the consuls waged a war of some kind with Ligurian and Gaulish hill-men. In 163 an obscure rising in Corsica was put down. In 160 one consul watched the Ligurians. In 159 a consul subdued a rebellious tribe, and in 155 much the same is said to have happened. At this point we begin to hear of extensions of the field of operations east and west beyond the geographical bounds of Italy. This was inevitable. To secure the coasts of Italy, Rome was compelled to keep the peace of the Adriatic on the one hand and to support her old and useful ally Massalia on the other. The former necessity led to the invasion of

---

[1] *stipendium.* Cic. II *in Verr.* III § 12.

Dalmatia, the latter to the entry of Roman armies into Transalpine Gaul. In 156 we hear[1] that a consul attacked the Dalmatians, to chastise these wild folk for their raids upon Illyrians under Roman protection. At first he met with reverses, but retrieved them later in the campaign: in 155 the consul P. Cornelius Scipio Nasica broke their resistance and took their stronghold Delminium and perhaps other towns also. He sold his prisoners for slaves, and the lessons of the war sufficed to keep the Dalmatians quiet for a time. Rome did not at present occupy the country, but she had asserted her supremacy in the Adriatic. Meanwhile Massalia needed help. This flourishing old Greek colony owned the coast now known as the western or French Riviera, where a long straggling narrow strip of lowland extends between the mountains and the sea. In this favoured district they had dependent towns and hamlets. The towns of Antipolis and Nicaea[2] were molested, if not sacked, by some of the Ligurian mountaineers from the highland behind. Q. Opimius consul in 154 made a brilliant little campaign, encountered the enemy in two divisions and beat them in detail. As they had not only attacked Roman allies, but maltreated Roman commissioners, there was some excuse for severity. He disarmed the guilty tribes, confiscated some of their territory, which he gave to the Massaliots, made them send hostages to Massalia (an arrangement which saved Rome trouble), and himself wintered with his army in the neighbourhood. This little affair seems to have been seriously and wisely managed and peace established in the hill-country. The war was followed up by a practical measure, the construction of a road through the heart of the disturbed district. The *via Postumia*[3] built by Spurius Postumius Albinus, consul in 148, led from Genua on the coast into Cisalpine Gaul, eventually reaching Verona by way of Placentia and Cremona. This useful connexion made it easy for a Roman force to operate southwards from the region of the Po as well as in other directions. In 143 the consul Appius Claudius Pulcher, the Spanish war having fallen to his colleague, was looking out for a chance to distinguish himself. In his 'province' of Italy, including Cisalpine Gaul, he could find no better opening than to attack the Alpine dalesmen. The Salassi in the north-west had a dispute with neighbours lower down the stream (the Duria, now Dora Baltea) in reference to the water supply[4] needed for some gold-washings. Claudius was instructed to find a settlement of the dispute, a commission which he tried to execute with fire and sword. At first

---

[1] Livy epit. 47, Appian *Illyr.* 11. [2] Livy epit. 47, Polyb. XXXIII 7—11.
[3] See Tacitus *Hist.* III 21, inscription given § 688 (*h*) below.
[4] Strabo IV 6 § 7 (p. 205), V 1 § 12 (p. 218), Pliny *N. H.* XXXIII 78.

he suffered a defeat, but afterwards gained a victory, and claimed, what was indeed his sole object, a triumph. This was very properly refused, but with a Claudian disregard of the proprieties he actually did triumph after a fashion at his own expense. An indignant tribune tried to drag him from the triumphal car, but his daughter, a Vestal virgin, flung herself between them and protected her father. Such is the story[1], perhaps corrupted in detail, but hardly a mere fiction. It shews the weak point of the system in use at this time, of treating Cisalpine Gaul as an appendage to Italy. It was not made into a regular province, though the population were really provincials: at the same time raids of Alpine tribes made it necessary to keep some troops there, and this arrangement was a great temptation to an ambitious consul who drew Italy as his charge and who wanted a little cheap glory.

611. At the beginning of this period Rome had only four Provinces in the special territorial sense (1) Sicily (2) Sardinia with Corsica (3) Hither Spain (4) Further Spain. These had all been either taken from Carthage, or occupied to shut Carthage out. In the present chapter we have seen three added (5) Africa, the Home Province of Carthage, which Rome was compelled to take over and govern; (6) Macedonia, also a necessary annexation, not made till an alternative plan had completely failed; (7) Asia, the treatment of which belongs to the next period. The case of Illyricum is doubtful. In 59 B.C. it was already organized as a province. When this step had been taken is not known, but it is at least not likely that it was until after 146. The kingdoms of Perseus and Gentius had been broken up into separate districts on the same principle. In Macedonia the new system broke down, therefore it was made a province: in Illyria it seems to have worked better, for there was no vital unity of a national kind. It would seem then that for the present the Illyrians paid their fixed tribute and Rome left them in peace. That the Senate was anything but eager to annex provinces is clear enough, and was no doubt mainly due to the known difficulty of controlling distant governors: there was also the pressure of Cato and the 'old Roman' party, who strove to keep out un-Roman ideas and customs. It cannot be doubted that the wealth or poverty of a country was an important consideration in deciding whether it should be taken over as a province or not. The mountainous lands peopled by the rude and hardy Illyrian race offered small attraction: how troublesome warlike tribes prematurely annexed could be had been learnt at great

---

[1] Dion Cassius fragm. 74, Cic. *pro Caelio* § 34, Suet. *Tib.* 2, Val. Max. v 4 § 6, Orosius v 4 § 7 probably after Liv. 53.

cost in Spain. But Africa and Asia were rich, and broken-in by subjection to earlier lords, nor could the former safely have been handed over to the sons of Masinissa, or the latter left to fall under the sway of some new dynasty, perhaps more powerful and aggressive than the house of Attalus. These considerations would assuredly have great weight, urged as they would be by men greedy of power and money, who sniffed the plunder from afar. Accordingly Africa and Asia were made provinces at once, and these two governorships became the most sought after of all the appointments in the patronage of the Roman people.

CHAPTER XXXIV

INTERNAL HISTORY, 201—133 B.C.

612. BEFORE we pass on to the century of revolution, ushered in by the movement of the Gracchi, we must review generally the internal history of the Roman Republic in the period following the second Punic war. Side by side with the events abroad, through which Rome found herself at the end of the period 200—133 B.C. in possession of a great empire outside Italy, a not less important development was going on within. The position of the Gracchi in the next period shews this. They had not only to deal with questions different from those that had occupied Flaminius a century before: the forces that a reformer could bring to bear, or with which he had to contend, differed not less widely in the two cases. Changes political, military, economic, social, intellectual, moral, had transformed the state to a far greater extent than contemporary observers were able to perceive. There were still the old magistracies, the Senate, and the Assemblies, but the relations between them had been profoundly modified by events. The position of the Roman people in the world had changed, and the character of the people had been changed with it. The constitution was no longer sufficient for the needs of the time: to amend it was practically impossible, nor indeed do we find the Romans conscious that it required reform.

613. To begin with the Magistrates. The tendency of the Senate to overshadow and control them had long been at work. The strain of the great war had made it necessary to entrust exceptional power to competent individuals, but with the defeat of Carthage the necessity came to an end. This was assuredly a great relief to the Roman nobles, whose ideal of government was a system under which they (or the leading men among them) divided among themselves year after year all the most important offices. It was now once more possible to prevent those frequent reelections to the consulship which had given old Fabius and Marcellus an unrepublican preeminence among their peers. If the members of the great houses had been in general inclined to view with indifference the dwarfing of ordinary

nobles by the elevation of a few competent men, the triumphant
return of Scipio from Africa was sure to arouse their jealousy. The
conqueror of Hannibal was beyond question the first man in Rome,
and he was still young and credited with far-reaching ambitions.
Accordingly we find a clearly-marked tendency to revert to the old
system of yearly commands held by the consuls, and to keep the
consuls within reach. They could thus be regularly superseded by
their successors in office, and the continuation of their military powers
in the form of the proconsulate was prevented from becoming normal.
Exceptions had of course to be made in the greater wars of the
period, when a Flamininus a Paullus or a Scipio was employed on
some service needing special authority and skill. We must bear in
mind that the dictatorship had been quietly dropped, and that a
consul was no longer liable to be suddenly thrust into the background by the appointment of a temporary king. It was therefore
only natural that the nobles should turn a jealous eye on the consulate. To keep that office in subjection to the influence of the
Senate was the keystone of the constitution from the point of view
of the nobility, for they controlled, and in effect composed, the Senate.
Nor was this jealousy groundless: we have had to note instances of
consuls who grew restive under the control of a body to which they
themselves belonged and whose weak points they doubtless knew.
The chief means by which the consulate was held in check were the
restrictions on reelection and the employment (in ordinary circumstances) of praetors and propraetors for the performance of continuous
duties at a distance from Rome. The latter is best illustrated by
the history of the Spanish provinces in this period, and by the course
of Graeco-Macedonian affairs 148—6 B.C., where we see the successful
propraetor Metellus not superseded by the consul Mummius until it
was understood that important changes were inevitable in the Roman
policy. The reelection question was a more serious matter still, and
calls for a more particular treatment.

614. We must first remark that the question[1] was essentially
one concerning the consulship. To repeat the tenure of the lower
offices was never likely to be an object of ambition to many. It
seems that even the praetorship was seldom held more than once,
though the variety of functions assignable to praetors made this
office suitable for repeated tenure. Further, it concerned the regular
yearly offices of the state, those that is for which Patricians as well
as Plebeians were eligible: the tribunate therefore does not come
into account here, nor yet extraordinary offices like the censorship.

---

[1] This subject is thoroughly treated in Mommsen's *Staatsrecht* vol. I, chapter on
Qualification for the Magistracy.

Since the number of praetors had been raised to four (227 B.C.) it had become the usual practice for a man to pass on[1] from the praetorship to the consulship, not immediately, but after an interval of at least a year.   There was no statutory rule, and in critical times an exception might occur: thus Scipio Africanus and Flamininus (consuls 205 and 198) had never been praetors, and there were other cases.   The quaestorship had from the first been regarded as a subordinate post in which young men gained their first practical experience of public affairs.   There is some reason to think that Scipio Africanus had never served in this office, but his whole career was quite exceptional, and so were the times in which he would naturally have held it.   That a man must pass through the quaestorship was a rule of usage as rigid as a rule of law.   The order, quaestorship praetorship consulship, was at the beginning of the period 200—133 B.C. established as a normal succession, only to be departed from in critical emergencies.   Another office must be mentioned here, the Aedileship.   As there were but four aediles (2 curule, 2 plebeian), while from 197 onward the number of praetors was six, it is clear that tenure of the office, which came before the praetorship, could not be made a condition of election to the higher post: there would not have been enough qualified candidates.   But the aedileship was much sought after.   The chief function of aediles was now the provision of the costly games and shows customary at festivals.   A lavish outlay on these entertainments was the sure means of winning the favour of the city mob, now more and more becoming the voting exponents of the Roman people's will.   In short the tenure of this office was in this period regarded as an electioneering appliance which an ambitious man could not venture to neglect.   The exception of Flamininus, consul 198, who had held neither the aedileship nor the praetorship, was a mere matter of emergency: an unpopular war had to be ended with all speed.   The regular official course was thus, quaestor, aedile, praetor, consul, and the regular interval between any two offices a year or more.   An anomaly had existed in the case of the Plebeian aediles: as strictly plebeian officials they had not been brought under the interval-rule, and so could[2] while in office, with their popularity still fresh, stand for the praetorship.   After 196

---

[1] Immediate continuation of offices seems to have been allowed, though disliked, in the earliest days of the Republic. Mommsen concludes that successive consulships were forbidden in 342, or perhaps 330, when an interval of ten years was prescribed. Immediate passage from one office to another seems to have been forbidden before the second Punic war, but no interval fixed : a clear year was a common interval.

[2] The case of Cato, plebeian aedile 199, praetor 198, is notable. The aediles had a large and varied jurisdiction, and Cato was not the man to spare offenders. Probably his fearless action pleased the poorer citizens. Of course he gave his *ludi* like others.

this practice suddenly and finally ceases, and it is not easy to resist the conclusion of Mommsen that it was forbidden by a law passed in that year, though the record of it (as of many another event) has not survived.

615. The above is a brief outline of the position of the Roman magistracies, the stage reached in their development, after the close of the second Punic war. The experience of the next twenty years seems to have convinced the nobility that something more was needed if they meant to keep their power as a body. They were threatened on the one hand by the influence of a few over-powerful families: there would be little room left for smaller men, if such as Scipio Flamininus or Fulvius Nobilior were allowed to gain a monopoly of power. But, if the nobles aimed at maintaining the aristocratic principle of the greatest possible equality among members of their own class, they were on the other hand no less determined to discourage the intrusion of 'new men' into their charmed circle. Nobility conferred by the tenure of office was a quality attainable by popular election: it naturally tended to become in effect hereditary, and those whose fathers had been consuls or praetors, and who were themselves bent on climbing the ladder of office, were especially unwilling to see the number of possible competitors increased. Meanwhile the old-Roman or conservative reform-party desired to check the ambition of the young nobles, mostly men of the new school, who were over-eager to secure their own advancement in disregard of the claims of tried merit and riper age. It seems that an attempt was made to reduce the number of yearly offices by electing four[1] praetors instead of six in alternate years: but this was no remedy. In the year 180 the attempt to regulate and fix by statute the sequence of official promotion assumed a practical form in the 'law of years' (*lex annalis*) carried by the tribune L. Villius. This is one of the most significant enactments in the history of the Republic.

616. The main points of this law seem to have been as follows. The practice of leaving an interval between the tenure of the regular yearly magistracies (for to these only it applied) was recognized, and the interval fixed at a space of not less than two years. A regular sequence was enjoined, probably in the form of declaring that only one who had held office A was to be eligible for office B. Thus, if the lowest office could only be held at a certain minimum age, a scale of age-qualification would be operative throughout the series. And it was probably in this thoroughly Roman indirect way that

---

[1] Livy XL 44 § 2. Of this very obscure matter no clear account can be given. For conjectures see Mommsen *Staatsrecht* II 190, Lange *RA* II 243.

the determination of the ages[1] at which the several offices could be held was attained. We have now the *certus ordo magistratuum* which is a characteristic feature of the later Republic. The official career thus regulated worked out in practice as follows.

		Regular or normal number of posts	Completed age
Age of liability to military service	17		
Military tribunate.....................	22	24	
10 years service.......................			27
quaestorship	28	12 [or 8 ?][2]	
biennium	2		30
⌈aedileship	31	4 [2 + 2]	
⌊biennium...........................	2		33⌉
praetorship...........................	34 [31]	6	
biennium	2		36 [33]
consulship	37 [34]	2	

617. This table shews how a man began by submitting to the military levy, and serving in the field if required. Ten years was the term of compulsory service in the cavalry, and most (if not all) young Romans who looked to an official career would undoubtedly serve as *equites*. Whether contained in the Villian law or not, the ten years service[3] was certainly a statutory requirement in this period. The young man could then hold the office of quaestor, that is, serve an apprenticeship in military or civil affairs and gain the general all-round competence expected in a Roman magistrate. He then could (and if possible did) pass on to the aedileship, but this step was optional. The praetorship offered him either an important post of jurisdiction at home, or a provincial governorship, or the command of an army in a minor campaign: an extension of his *imperium* in the form of propraetorship was possible, and he was henceforth *nobilis* not merely in the sense of belonging to a noble family. The attainment of the consulship placed him in the highest

---

[1] Livy XL 44 § 1, Weissenborn.

[2] The number of quaestors is not certain, but it is very probable that the number (8 about 267 B.C.) had been raised to meet provincial needs before the time of Sulla. See Tacitus *ann.* XI 22 and Mommsen *Staatsrecht* II 556.

[3] Polybius VI 19.

position at this time open to a Roman. He and his colleague for
a year stood before gods and men as representing the majesty of
Rome at home and abroad. Not every act of the home government
needed a consul to perform it; but, the more solemn and important
the act, the more imperatively was the presence of a consul required.
On the military side, the armies operating in northern Italy during
this period were commonly commanded by consuls; but, whenever
a serious war called for the concentration of Roman power to meet
some enemy beyond the seas, consuls and full consular armies were
sent to Greece or Asia Minor, to Africa or Spain. And the consul
victorious in a distant war stood every chance of being continued
in command as proconsul, and of presiding over the momentous
settlement that followed on a Roman conquest. Under his chair-
manship and influence proceeded the reward of allies and the
punishment of rebels, the fixing of boundaries and establishment
of institutions, the organization of subject provinces or the award
of dependent thrones. Over immense areas all trembled before him
who could sell thousands into slavery and whose word could set in
motion the sword not borne in vain. No wonder that proconsuls
often supplemented their share of military booty by exactions on
their own account and by receiving gifts the outcome of gratitude
or fear. Then came the return and the triumph, in the case of
eastern wars a gorgeous spectacle: the feasting of the people, the
largess to the soldiers, whose claims it was more and more difficult
to satisfy: the offering of sacrifices, the discharge of vows, and the
payment of captured gold and silver into the treasury: everywhere,
in the Senate-house, in the Forum, in the family circle, thanksgivings
and congratulations: a surfeiting orgy of glory, the manifestations
of an imperial Rome gone mad.

618.   And yet the very conditions of a triumph in Rome carried
with them a reminder of a reaction to come. None but[1] a consul (or
praetor) could strictly speaking triumph in Rome. Most of the
greater triumphs in this period were those of proconsuls or propraetors returning from distant wars. But the *imperium* thus extended
did not include the right to exercise it in its full military sense within
the city walls. To do so would trench on the sphere of the acting
magistrate of the current year. This difficulty was got over by
carrying a short bill through the Assembly conferring on the victorious pro-magistrate the full right of military *imperium* in the
city for the period of the triumph only. On the morrow he would
be once more *privatus*, a simple citizen, a man of mark no doubt,
with a fresh flavour of burnt-out official power, at least for a time.

[1] We are dealing with regular magistrates: the dictator was exceptional.

In the Senate he took his place among the ex-consuls or ex-praetors: but he found beside him men who had reached the same standing before him and whose reputation was already staled, or who had risen by the mere force of office-holding undistinguished by note-worthy achievement.   As years went by, he too would be pushed on into the like galling seniority by younger men, soured by dis-appointed ambition or bearing fresher laurels to wither in their turn.   From the first he would be watched jealously by all who felt oppressed by a superior or crowded by an equal.   Such was the inevitable result of the republican system as now worked by the Roman nobility.   A cold bath of reaction awaited the conqueror flushed with victory, and the old simple habits, that made instinctive and cheerful conformity to this levelling process a second nature in the Roman worthies of earlier days, were fast dying out.   And it was well for him if his conduct abroad had not included acts on which, justly or unjustly, the malignity of personal enemies might fasten to do him hurt.   We hear charges of embezzlement of booty, of taking bribes, of extortion barbarity and ill-faith, crimes sure to impair the reputation of Rome abroad and make heavier the task of her officers in days to come.   What we do not gather is that punishment surely followed guilt or that the great offenders were attacked in preference to smaller men.   Instances of these attacks, and their inconsequent results, have come before us in the preceding chapters: and we have had occasion to note the disturbing effects of politics and party-spirit in such cases.   In this respect too things were getting worse during this period.

619.   The *lex Villia* did not put an end to intrigues among the Roman nobles.   As Rome became more imperial, the ambition of individuals widened, the young nobles pushed forward, not to serve the state but to reap the fruits of empire, while many of the elder men of distinction were ill-content to be shelved as heroes out of date.   But the law passed, apparently supported by Cato and the old Roman school and at least not seriously opposed by the nobles in general.   The latter perhaps foresaw what its effect would be— to establish a rigid rule of official promotion, exceptions to which would be almost impossible, a plan certain to work in the direction of recruiting the dominant cliques rather than of checking the rise of young nobles in favour of 'new men' of merit.   How truly it expressed the prevailing tendency of the period is shewn[1] by its long permanence.   The notion of a fixed sequence of offices was adopted by Sulla in a stricter form, and is a feature in the ideal

---

[1] It became a recognized object of ambition to hold each office in the candidates 'own year' (*anno suo*), that is, at the earliest date allowed by law.

constitution of Cicero. But the nobles went a step further in their eagerness to secure a maximum of opportunities for average members of their class. They got a law passed to forbid reelection altogether, thus superseding the old law that required a ten-year interval between two consulships. From the facts, that a man who had been consul in 166 and 155 was reelected consul for 152, and that a special exemption[1] from an established rule of law was needed to enable Scipio Aemilianus to hold a second consulship in 134, after which reelections cease till the days of Marius: and from the fact that Cato (who died in 149) spoke for the bill, it is inferred[2] that it was carried in the year 151. But Marius broke it all to pieces: the old ten-year interval was reenacted by Sulla, to little purpose in an age of revolution.

620. I have said that the strictly Plebeian offices were not touched by the Villian law. The position of the Tribunate calls for a few remarks. This once powerful office had greatly declined in importance since the equalization of the Orders and the growth of the mixed patricio-plebeian nobility. It had fallen under the control of the Senate, and the period of great wars naturally lowered the prestige of an office that did not qualify the holder for military command. During the Hannibalic war, or even earlier, we find it customary to hold it before the aedileship, and this seems to have become a rule of practice from which no one thought of departing. Yet in their origin the aediles were merely assistants of the tribunes. As for reelection, so long as the tribunes were the leaders of the struggling Plebs, that is down to 367 B.C., they were freely reelected. After 367 we no longer find immediate reelection from one year to the next. Perhaps, as Mommsen conjectures, some concession in this direction on the part of the Plebs was extorted by the Patricians as a consideration for the abandonment of opposition to the Licinian laws. At any rate we find continuation of this office represented as illegal[3] in the days of the Gracchi, though reelection after an interval was not barred. In the period 200—133 there was nothing to tempt men to seek reelection to an office that was a mere step to something higher, an atrophied organ of a commonalty itself degenerate.

621. How completely the old distinction of Patrician and Plebeian had died out and given place to the common interest of the nobility in keeping official power to themselves, chiefly for the benefit of a few great families, is shewn by stray facts that have come down to us. Cases of 'new men' attaining the consulship are very rare, but we have Cato in 195, M'. Acilius Glabrio (backed by the Scipionic

---

[1] Livy epit. 56.   [2] Mommsen *Staatsrecht* I 502.
[3] See below §691.

influence) in 191.   Later on these cases do not meet us, save that
Q. Pompeius was elected for 141, defeating C. Laelius the friend of
Scipio Aemilianus: but he is said to have succeeded only by a gross
breach of good faith.   That family interest could and did override
the claims of friendship is shewn in the case of the consuls of 190,
if it be true that Scipio Africanus induced the Senate to assign the
coveted command against Antiochus to his incompetent brother
rather than to C. Laelius (the elder), his own old friend and comrade
in arms.   That in 194 the two consuls were sons of the two consuls
of 218, and that in 179 two brothers (sons of a Fulvius, one of them
by adoption a Manlius) held office together, are interesting facts and
thoroughly illustrative of Roman ideas.   In 172 for the first time
both consuls were Plebeians.   The same thing happened in the years
171, 167, 153, 149, 139, and often afterwards.   The ranks of the old
Patrician houses were becoming thin.   Times were indeed changed
since the days when two Patricians not seldom held the two consulships in defiance of the Licinian law.   This decay of the genuine
aristocracy of old Rome boded no good to the commonwealth.   The
nobility of the later Republic were in the main a set of moneyed
mediocrities.   Sulla and Caesar, the two mighty men of the revolutionary age, were both Patricians.   In the period of rigid office-rules
from 180 to 133 one man alone was dispensed from their operation,
in 147 to make an end of Carthage, in 134 to make an end of
Numantia.   The Patrician son of Paullus, adoptive grandson of
Africanus, was in short employed at a pinch, regardless of the law,
to relieve the anxiety of a self-condemned nobility, and to free their
hands for the congenial occupation of plundering and misgoverning
a luckless world.

622.   It can hardly be too often repeated that the real government
of Rome in this period was the Senate as the organ of the nobility,
provided that we never lose sight of the fact that their power rested
on no foundation of law.   Circumstances had long played into their
hands: as compared with the magistrates they supplied the element
of continuity, as compared with the Assembly they were always in
working order, able to deal with emergencies.   But they were well
aware of the difference between a gradual *de facto* usurpation and
a deliberate concession *de iure*, and that it was necessary for them to
control not only the magistrates but also the Assembly, the constitutional source of the sovran power.   This control was on the face
of it an easy consequence of their having at their disposal the
now subservient tribunate.   Whatever questions came before the
Assemblies, legislation, popular trials, or issues of policy, the tribunes (or rather any one of the ten) could at some stage or other

'intercede': and an officer empowered to block other proposals was surely in a strong position for promoting the passage of his own. But another point had to be considered—was it certain that the character of the Assembly would remain the same, and that the old devices for manipulating it would still answer their purpose? This question was perhaps not new, but that it was a serious one was shewn in the year 200, when it was found very difficult to induce the exhausted people to declare war against Macedon. Yet this was a matter for the Centuries, in which the wealthier classes still had a favoured position. The influence of the nobility would make itself felt more easily under those conditions than when the people (as they most often did) voted by Tribes. The composition of the citizen body and its organization for voting purposes are important matters in every state in which ordinary citizens are entrusted with any share of power. At Rome their importance was greater than in most of the Republics of antiquity, owing to the capricious operation of the group-system. Now it was the duty of the censors to decide from time to time who should be placed on the register of citizens, and in which of the 35 Tribes each individual should be enrolled. When we remember that these officers also revised the list of the Senate, and by their management of state contracts had a certain power over the capitalist class now pushing to the front, it is not wonderful that the importance of the censorship is a striking feature of this period. The succession of censors at intervals of five years is perfectly regular[1] from 199 to 154, and a large part of the political interest of the period is connected with their various acts. The two burning questions for which different censors found different solutions were (*a*) the claims of Latins to be placed on the register as Roman citizens (*b*) the old dispute as to the position of citizens of servile extraction, whether they should be enrolled in all the 35 Tribes or only in a limited number. From the senatorial point of view, that of keeping the voting Assemblies amenable to the influence of the governing class, the decision of these issues in one way or another was all-important, and it became more and more vital as time went on.

623. Of the general position of the Latins and other Italian Allies we shall speak below. What concerns us here is the way in which their claims were treated as compared with those of the freedmen. It is on the face of it clear that the latter would as a class tend to follow the lead of their wealthy patrons, the heads of the houses whom they or their fathers had served and to whom they owed their

---

[1] This was an essential part of the supremacy of the Senate, which expressed itself more clearly in this way than in any other. Cf. Nitzsch, *Gracchen* p. 149.

freedom. The freed bondman took the name of his patron's *gens*, and a close relationship, recognized both by custom and by law, bound him to the family of his former master. In an age of great wars, followed by a great influx of wealth, the number of slaves, and with it the number of manumissions, increased : and the powerful social tie of patronage placed in the hand of the Roman nobles a force capable of being turned to account in the region of politics. When Latins were placed on the Roman register the effect was very different. The Latin thus enfranchised would generally be one of the most pushing members of his native stock, perhaps even a descendant of a Roman citizen included in some Latin colony. He might be a real gain to the Roman state, an element politically sounder than the freedman : but it was useless to expect from him a like subservience. The precarious tie of friendship might influence his vote, but there was no certainty as to who his friend or friends might be. Now all through this period the Roman nobles were becoming more and more conscious, if not of an imperial mission, at least of imperial opportunities of enrichment and glory. They were becoming more and more cosmopolitan in thought and life ; and the old-Roman school with its narrow outlook, its conception of Rome as essentially an Italian power, was gradually losing ground. Scipio Africanus might be disgusted with public life and end his days in scornful retirement : but it was the new school, of which he was the first and most shining light, that gave the master-bias to the progress of Rome. The reactionaries led by Cato could secure no permanent tenure of power, and their unpractical opposition was productive of little fruit. We find both sections interested in the matter of registration as carried out by the censors from time to time, and both their difference and their agreement are instructive. The new imperialists, wishing to secure a free hand by controlling votes in the Tribes and Centuries, were inclined to put freedmen into any of the 35 Tribes: the old-Roman school opposed this as a degradation of the citizen body, holding the traditional conservative view that the 31 country Tribes at least should not be tainted by the intrusion of an alien element. But neither section favoured the inclusion of resident Latins in Roman Tribes : the new school as suspicious of voters probably difficult to control, Cato and his followers from taking a narrowly legal view of the relation between Rome and her Italian Allies. Thus their rigid principles made no allowance for the change of circumstances, and stiff legality played into the hands of interested opportunism.

624. When we look at the fragmentary records[1] of the censor-

---

[1] These censorships are discussed by Lange *RA* §§ 105—110, who instructively brings them into connexion with all the movements of the period.

ships from 199 to 136 inclusive, we find traces of the working of different principles, but on the whole a general tendency clearly marked. Those of 199[1] and 194 belong to the time of the wars with Philip and Antiochus. The Scipionic party was in the ascendant, and a certain slackness in home policy not unnaturally accompanied the action of a government preoccupied with war. This slackness shewed itself not only in finance but in the census. It seems that Latins removed to Rome and found their way on to the register. That there was no intention of favouring the Latins was shewn in 194. Citizen colonies were being founded, and, in default of citizens willing to make up the complement of these coast-garrisons, 'Latins' were in certain cases received as colonists. Applicants from Ferentinum, a Hernican town which in 306 B.C. had declined the offer of Roman citizenship, claimed that the membership of a citizen colony made the colonist a Roman citizen. This claim was disallowed[2] by the Senate: whether the applicants drew back or went out nevertheless we do not know. The rise in the value of the Roman franchise, and the reluctance to extend it, are significant of the changed relations between Rome and her Italian confederates since the Hannibalic war. It was an evil sign, and it was an ill-managed policy that, while a Latin could not win the *civitas* by bearing a citizen's burdens in a new colony distinctly Roman, he could migrate to Rome and acquire it by stealth in the very place where he could make the most profitable use of its privileges. The census of 189 was in several respects notable. It seems that all Latin communities were at this time compelled to undergo a census corresponding to that of Rome, and to furnish each of them an official copy of their local return to the Roman censors. The main point was no doubt the roll of men fit for military service when required. The rule was originally a burden[3] on the twelve colonies which shirked their duty in 209 and were punished in 204. It was now made binding on the rest (18) whose record was unbrokenly loyal. Perhaps some step in this direction had been taken by the censors of 194. It has at least been pointed out[4] that in 193 a consul summoned contingents of Allies in proportion to the totals of men fit for service in each community, not according to the terms of the old fixed quotas. Be this as it may, the old Latin towns and the 18 colonies seem now to have been brought down to the position of the faithless twelve.

625. And, as if to mark even more clearly the gulf that parted the *civis* from the *socius* at a time when the blood-tax was sweeping

---

[1] Scipio Afr. censor 199. See inscription given below § 688 (*d*).
[2] Livy XXXIV 42.
[3] Livy XXIX 15, 37. Above § 378.   [4] Livy XXXIV 56, Lange *RA* II 206.

off Allies wholesale to perish in distant wars, the condition of the remaining half-citizens was deliberately raised. None of the southern rebels in the Hannibalic war had seemed to Rome more guilty than the Campanians. But the bloody vengeance taken in 211 and the destruction of Capua as a community had put the real offenders out of the way. The country folk had probably been little to blame for the deeds of the misguided city, and the Senate now held out the hand of forgiveness. They were allowed to present themselves for registration at the Roman census, where they would no doubt for the present be enrolled among those whom the censors recorded as 'payers of poll-tax' (*aerarii*), men in no Tribe, and so unable to vote in the Assemblies. But in a sense they were citizens of Rome, and in 188 they were granted[1] the right of intermarriage with full Roman citizens. As they had probably never wholly lost the right of trading, they were now in the position of ordinary half-citizens, as they had been before their fall. At the same time the three half-citizen communities of Fundi Formiae and Arpinum were granted the full franchise of Rome. There is also reason to think[2] that some step was taken in the direction of allowing freedmen's sons to be enrolled in the 31 country tribes. Thus, while there was a marked tendency to equalize *cives* of every degree by promoting the lower grades, the reverse process was applied to the Allies. We may faintly guess how galling this would be to the Latins and other *socii*, who in their isolation had to submit, and to whom the coveted franchise seemed now further off than ever. It is not to be wondered at that the migration of Latins to Rome, and their stealthy registration as Romans, went on as before. Thus far then the effect of censorial slackness had been to degrade the Latins as a whole, and yet to leave open a door through which as individuals they could pass to complete equality with Roman citizens. It put a premium on migration to Rome: the Latins that suffered were just those who stayed in the towns to which they belonged and duly discharged the duties assigned them by the central power.

626. Various causes produced widespread discontent with the administration of the dominant party, and the jealousy of some nobles strengthened the hands of those who acted with Cato. The year 187 saw vigorous attacks made by the opposition upon Fulvius Nobilior and Manlius Vulso for their conduct in Aetolia and Asia. Failure only whetted the appetite of the assailants, and they proceeded to attack the Scipios themselves. The condemnation of L. Scipio, and the withdrawal of Africanus from public life, were a victory for the

[1] Livy XXXVIII 28, 36.
[2] Plutarch *Flamin.* 18, Lange *RA* II 218—9, Nitzsch, *Röm. Rep.* p. 37.

Catonian opposition. Their power was shewn in the expulsion[1] from Rome of 12,000 Latins, who had left their towns and illegally crept on to the Roman register. This high-handed measure compelled them to resume their former domicile for the time, but of course its effectiveness would depend on the firm continuous enforcement of the rule: and of this the working of the Roman constitution offered little prospect. For the present however the reform party triumphed, and the alarm caused by the affair of the Bacchanalia still further strengthened them. The commission for dealing with this alleged conspiracy was appointed in 186, and the business occupied Roman officials for more than five years. But corrupting influences were telling against the reformers. The splendid triumphs and largesses of Nobilior and Vulso in 187, the great shows (lasting ten days) given by L. Scipio in 186, and the general influx of wealth, go far to explain why elections to the consulship went against the reform party, and why Aemilius Paullus was more than once defeated. But the indomitable Cato did not give up the struggle. He was elected[2] censor for 184 together with his steady supporter L. Valerius Flaccus, defeating L. Scipio, Nobilior, and Vulso. He now set about his famous attempt to use the censorial powers as an active engine of reform.

627. The action of the censors was nothing but a reaction against the slackness of their predecessors in recent years. Severity in preparing the list of the Senate and the muster-roll of the Knights was in itself a good thing. It was well that no family influence could protect unworthy members of great houses from being deprived of senatorial or equestrian rank. But the censors fell into an error of judgment to which men 'acting on principle' are especially liable. They did not distinguish between minor breaches of social decorum and gross immoralities or crimes, and this pedantic disregard of common sense doubtless destroyed much of the moral effect of their fearless policy. Sound economy was promoted by punishing robbery of state property and undertaking useful public works. The strict care of state interests in the matter of public contracts raised a storm from the companies of contractors, whose cause was taken up by leading men irritated by the censors' severity. The contracts were cancelled, but Cato relet them to other contractors on terms little less favourable to the state. In the valuation of citizens' property an attempt was made to check luxury by assessing fancy articles (such as favourite slaves) at ten times their already high market price: these things were then also made liable to taxation at an abnormally high

---

[1] Livy XXXIX 3.　　　　　　　　　　　　[2] Livy XXXIX 40.

rate in the event of a war-loan[1] being needed. So far as it displayed
the boldness of the reforming censors, the censorship of Cato and
Flaccus was a success: but the acts of censors were only valid until
their successors took office five years later, and the number of persons
interested in upsetting the work of these reformers, coupled with the
inevitable cooling of the enthusiasm that had placed them in office,
might foretell the certainty of a counter-reaction. In regard to the
treatment of freedmen and resident Latins we are reduced to inferences
from what happened a few years later. It seems probable that Cato
and Flaccus registered citizens of servile descent in the four city tribes
only, and that they excluded Latins altogether. This is quite of a
piece with the rest of their policy.

628. We can only review briefly (with one exception) the policy
of later censors as illustrating the internal history of this period. The
reformers under Cato had for the time weakened the Scipionic party.
Scipio died in retirement (185 or 183), but the tendencies of the age
favoured the new school to which he belonged, and this section was
still powerful, led by Fulvius Nobilior. The middle party under
M. Aemilius Lepidus seems to have ruled the Senate for a little
while, and the election of Paullus as consul for 182 marks their
influence. They had hitherto inclined towards the Catonian section,
but in 179 we find them coming over to the other side. In that year
Lepidus and Nobilior were censors. These two had long been at
feud, but a reconciliation was now brought about by some leading
nobles. In the coalition thus signalized it was only natural that the
policy of the new school should preponderate. From our fragmentary
record we can only gather that the censors did not proceed on the
same lines as Cato, but returned to the milder methods. They made
some changes[2] in drawing up the citizen roll, perhaps partly to the
advantage of freedmen. That their slackness allowed Latins again
to creep on to the register appears from the outcry raised in 177. A
movement of migration was going on. Latins went to live in Rome
and passed for Roman citizens: meanwhile numbers of the non-Latin
Allies, Samnites and others, moved into the Latin towns and passed
for Latins. Thus various allied communities were being depopulated,
while their liability to provide military contingents remained. The
means employed to stop this migration were highly significant. A
law was carried[3] in the Assembly, ordering the Latin immigrants of
recent years to return to their homes. The proceeding by way of an

---

[1] The last instalment of the *tributum* raised in the second Punic war had only just been
repaid out of the Asiatic booty of Manlius Vulso. See Livy XXXIX 7.
[2] Livy XL 51. The details are very obscure. Cf. Cic. *de legibus* III § 41.
[3] *Lex Claudia de sociis.* Livy XLI 8, 9.

order of the Senate had given place to regular legislation: the exclusion of Latins was now no longer a mere act of policy on the part of
the governing nobles, but a statute passed by the votes of the Roman
mob. At the same time measures were taken to prevent various
evasions, and the policy of exclusion may be taken as henceforth
adopted by both Senate and people, only to be abandoned some
80 years later in consequence of the great Italian War.

629. In fact the one great practical question in the internal
politics of this period was that of the Roman franchise. How eagerly
the franchise was desired is illustrated by one of the evasive processes
used for attaining it. A Latin, wishing to make his son a Roman
citizen, sold his son to some Roman under a private compact that the
purchaser should emancipate the young man and so make him a
citizen. It seems that to rank among Romans even as a freedman
was thought a better status than that of a Latin citizen free from the
beginning. Indeed such a transition was so closely analogous to the
method of adoption that it can hardly have imparted to such a freedman any marked servile taint. Individual Romans, poor or unscrupulous, were found willing to act the part of patrons in these
operations: and the success of the device served to encourage other
Latins to migrate and claim the franchise without going through this
roundabout process. We must not suppose that the right of voting
in Roman Assemblies was the effective object of desire. Those bodies
were in this period steadily losing power. It was rather the material
advantages attached to Roman citizenship, and becoming ever greater
and greater, that were the real attraction. Formerly the Latin
colonies, with their large land-allotments and their local self-government, had drawn off numbers of Allies; even Romans had been found
to join them, becoming Latins for the sake of a livelihood. Now
things were changed. In 183 the new large inland foundations began
to take the form of citizen colonies. Very few Latins seem to have
been allowed[1] to join these and so to acquire Roman citizenship. And
after the foundation of Aquileia in 181 no more Latin colonies were
founded in Italy. At the close of a war it had been the custom to
give equal largesses to citizens and Allies. But in 177, at the triumph[2]
of the consul Claudius Pulcher, the reward of the discharged Ally was
only half that of the citizen. This Claudius was the author of the *lex
Claudia* referred to above. In 174 the same policy was followed. The

---

[1] The commissioners for founding colonies were allowed to admit a few outsiders to a new
foundation as citizens. But it seems that the number of such admissions was strictly limited.
See the case of Ennius above § 407.

[2] Livy XLI 13 § 8.

consul[1] L. Postumius Albinus, brother of one of the censors of that year, put forth a stringent edict ordering Latins to leave Rome and be registered in their own cities. And the censors seem to have continued the favour previously shewn to freedmen, while one of them gave a specimen of Roman insolence by robbing[2] the famous Lacinian temple of its marble tiles to adorn his new temple at Rome. This was too much: the Senate ordered their restoration, and the tiles were carried back, but never replaced in position. In the temple court they lay, a memorial of the outrage offered to southern Italy with its Greek traditions. What Pyrrhus and Hannibal had spared, the censor Fulvius, an officer of the great central power of Italy, had wantonly destroyed.

630. In this censorship we hear of a sudden waking-up to the fact of encroachments on the state lands in Campania and the neglect of lessees to pay their rents. It may be that the yearly payments[3] of the Syrian war-indemnity had kept the treasury full and caused preceding censors to overlook these abuses. But the last remittance from Antioch was now due. The Campanian boundaries[4] were now verified, and provision made in 172 for the regular exaction of the rents. Clearly the finances were at this time causing some anxiety, and the Senate no doubt had an eye to the coming Macedonian war. More mysterious still are the motives of the censors of 174 in slack dealing[5] with the state contracts, while they revised the list of the knights (the stronghold of the capitalist class) with severity. It may be that personal grudges or party bias are explanation enough, but we do not know. At this time occurred an event[6] which doubtless added to the discontents of the Latins and of the other Allies as well. The consul L. Postumius was instructed to proceed to Campania and settle the questions of boundary between the public and private lands. He travelled by way of Praeneste. Praeneste was one of the few remaining old Latin cities, once members of the great Latin League. Since the dissolution of the League in 338 it had been a Roman Ally of the first rank, proud of its position as enjoying full internal sovranty, and had rendered many valuable services to Rome. If any allied city deserved good treatment, it was this. But times were changed, and Postumius had a grudge against the people of Praeneste. It seems that on a visit for purpose of sacrifice (a purely personal matter) the local authorities had taken no notice, official or private,

---

[1] He was consul in 173. Thus he would be in office during the latter part of the official term oi the censors. A Sp. Postumius was consul in 174. Livy XLII 10 § 3.

[2] Livy XLII 3.

[3] Lange *RA* § 108 (II 260).

[4] Livy XLII 19 §§ 1, 2.

[5] Livy XLIII 16 §§ 2—7, Weissenborn.

[6] Livy XLII 1 §§ 6—12.

of the honour conferred on them by the presence of a Roman noble. He was now consul, full of the arrogant self-importance characteristic of his class, and he resolved to teach these Allies a lesson. He wrote ordering the Praenestine chief magistrate to give him a public reception, to entertain him at the public cost, and to provide ample conveyance for him on the next stage of his journey. This was in effect grossly to exceed his rights. There was probably no law or decree of the Senate directly forbidding this particular offence against a Latin Ally. The Roman state provided its officers with the means of travel as required. The notion that a consul would so maltreat Roman Allies, putting them to such trouble and expense in gratification of his own vanity, would never have occurred to the Romans of an earlier day. The sound rules of healthy custom were enough: and the private friendships between the leading men of Rome and allied cities ensured mutual courtesies and willing entertainers. Postumius had given his orders. If the Praenestines objected, there was the Senate to whom they might appeal. But that the Senate of this time would censure or check one of their own peers in defence of Latin Allies was surely to be doubted: that Postumius and his friends would do them an ill turn on the first opportunity was certain. The Praenestines, probably for this reason, chose what seemed at the moment the less of two evils, and did as they were bidden. Their submission served to register a stage in the encroaching development of Roman Imperialism, and to create an evil precedent for the days to come.

631. We must bear in mind that about this time a number of grave scandals occurred, surely not unremarked by thoughtful men. The years 179 to 169 witnessed many episodes shameful to the Roman government, in particular betraying its weakness and inability to control its agents abroad. In Istria, in Liguria, in Spain, Roman officers had been guilty of gross disobedience cruelty or misgovernment, and punishment of offenders and redress of wrongs had been evaded or rendered vain. And to these evils were now added the failures of the Macedonian war and the extortions and barbarities in Greece. Such were the fruits of the reaction against the party of reform, now powerless. Cato had not ceased to thunder against the corruption of the age, but vainly. Now however the more serious of the nobles were alarmed, and another counter-reaction once more brought the Reformers into power. For 169 two strong censors[1] were chosen, C. Claudius Pulcher and Tiberius Sempronius Gracchus. They had been consuls together in 177. The former, a vigorous but hot-headed man, was the author of the recent *lex Claudia*; the latter,

[1] Livy XLIII 14—16.

who as tribune in 187 had protected the Scipios, had commanded
with distinction in Spain and Sardinia. Their action in support of
the weak consuls, enabling the military levy to be carried through
and discipline to be restored in the army abroad, has been referred
to[1] above. In revising the roll of the Senate they were more severe
than had been usual in recent years. So too in the revision of the
Knights; but before this business could be taken in hand they were
involved in serious difficulties owing to a quarrel with the capitalists.
They thought that the state contracts of the last censors had either
been let on terms too favourable to the contractors or had been
carried out badly. So they put forth an edict announcing that any
tenders from these contractors would on the present occasion not be
considered. The capitalists were furious. In the course of surveying
public property Gracchus had ordered the demolition of an encroaching wall. The offender was a client of Rutilius, a tribune of the year
and himself of equestrian rank. The angry patron tried to protect
his client. But the other tribunes held back, and the censors fined
the builder of the wall, probably for disobedience. This defiance
further enraged the tribune. He took up the cause of the excluded
capitalists, and gave notice of a bill cancelling the action of the
censors in regard to contracts and enacting that the contracts should
be put up afresh to public competition from which no one should be
excluded. Before this proposal came on for voting it was discussed
at an informal meeting (*contio*), and opposed by the censors. And
here Claudius came into collision with the tribune. In ordering his
herald to call for silence he might seem to invade the prerogative
of the tribune who had brought together the unruly mob. Rutilius
caught at the pretext, declared that the censor had come between[2]
him and the meeting he had summoned, and with this protest withdrew. He followed up this step by accusing both censors of high
treason (*perduellio*). This accusation they were not bound to face
while still in office, but it seems that they judged it better to meet
the danger at once. They sealed up all their official documents,
dismissed their staff of attendants, and left the resumption of public
business to await the issue of their trial before the Centuries. When
the voting-day came, the influence of the capitalists was seen: the
majority of the First Class was against Claudius, whose case came on
before that of his colleague. He would have been condemned but
for the exertions of the leading nobles, who by abject entreaties
turned the hearts of some of the poorer voters, whose Centuries had

[1] See § 517.
[2] To interrupt a tribune addressing the Plebs (*avocare contionem*) was forbidden by the
Icilian law in the early days of the Republic (492 B.C.).

not yet polled, and the loyalty of Gracchus. Gracchus was personally popular. His anxiety, it seems, was manifest: the people tried to relieve him by assurances of his own acquittal. Then he swore solemnly that if Claudius were condemned he would not await the result of his own case, but would go with his colleague into exile. Even so Claudius only escaped with eight Centuries to spare. The case against Gracchus was then dropped.

632. There are several points in this strange story that illustrate the state of Roman politics at the time. First, it seems clear that we have here a conflict between two great interests, the senatorial nobles and the equestrian capitalists, and that the former only prevail in the end with great difficulty. In truth the capitalist class were fast gaining ground: in a few years Carthage and Corinth were to feel their power. Secondly, it is the mass of poorer citizens that decides the issue of the conflict, the wealthier being divided against themselves. Thirdly, the power of the tribune, once irresistible within the city walls, is after all defied with impunity. That is, while nominally endowed with all the immense powers of the tribunes of old, the tribune of these days cannot exert those powers in practice. When censor and tribune, both broken-in to normal dependence on the Senate, get to loggerheads, and the Senate backs up the censor, the tribune no longer ventures to seize the censor and imprison him, and his nine colleagues apparently do nothing on either side. The censor, feeling the Senate at his back, is bold: so bold, that he narrowly escapes an unpleasant surprise. Lastly, with the mob the dignity of the nobles, men whom they had been used to see in authority, still has weight: but we have nothing to disprove a very natural suspicion that bribery may have been employed by both sides. In any case the affair was a strong reminder of the need of watching carefully the constitution of the Assembly, for that the mob could not be safely trusted to vote consistently in the best interest of the state was only too plain.

633. The censors resumed business[1] with stern energy. In revising the list of Knights they struck off a number of members as unfit for various reasons, among them their opponent Rutilius, whom they placed on the black list of *aerarii*. But their most important task was in drawing up the roll of citizens, for they were resolved to deal with the question of the place of freedmen in the Tribes. The

---

[1] The account of this notable census survives in three detached passages of Livy, XLIII 16, XLIV 16, XLV 15. There are defects in the text, but in the main the story is clear. It would seem that the business took an unusually long time, owing no doubt to the amount of friction developed. It is not unlikely that Livy is following different authorities in different parts of this narrative.

existing arrangement was that freedmen who had sons[1] over five years old were allowed to be placed in any of the 31 country Tribes, while the rest were confined to the four city Tribes. This arrangement was left undisturbed in regard to those already on the register. But the numbers of freedmen were growing fast with the growth of slavery, and it was an object to put some check upon their influence, for the nobility were beginning to see its dangers. As their numbers grew, they would probably become less amenable to the guidance of patrons, a form of control not likely to remain unimpaired by time. The principle followed was to favour those possessed of considerable country properties, estates valued at more than 30,000 sesterces (over £300), those, that is, qualified by their assessment to be placed in Centuries of the first or second Class. These were allowed to be registered in any of the country Tribes. As for the rest, it seems that Gracchus would gladly have excluded them from the Tribes altogether. Claudius held that to do so would be to exceed their powers, and a compromise was found. The new freedmen-citizens of the poorer classes were placed in one only of the four city Tribes : this Tribe, the Esquiline, was chosen by lot. We hear that the censors acted together in perfect harmony, and that the Senate voted them the thanks of the House for the wisdom and firmness of their official conduct. But when they asked for an extension of their official term to enable them to see to the proper execution of the public works for which contracts had been made (the interruption of their activity by Rutilius doubtless furnished a pretext), a tribune blocked[2] the proposal, and it fell through. This was done in revenge for a slight, the censors not having put his name on the senatorial roll.

634. So ended this notable attempt to counteract the tendencies of the age by censorial action. Nothing, it seems, was done to redress the grievances of Latins, nor was the author of the *lex Claudia* a person likely to take up their cause. And the acts of any censors were only in force till the next census. It was to little purpose that an effort to check growing luxury and license had been made early in 169 by the *lex Voconia*, passed to check the accumulation[3] of pro-

---

[1] These sons would be freeborn (*ingenui*), but of course marked with social inferiority. See index under *Freedmen*, and § 661 below.

[2] Whether this *intercessio* took place in the Senate or the Assembly is not clear. While in office the tribune would have access to the Senate, but not afterwards, unless his name had (as usual) been put on the roll.

[3] For this and the *lex Furia testamentaria* which preceded it see Poste on Gaius II §§ 225, 226, 274, Lange *RA* II 239, 280. Livy epit. 41, with Weissenborn's note at end of book XLI, Orelli's *index legum* under *Voconia*, Cicero *pro Balbo* § 21, *de republ.* III § 17. This law was supported by Cato. See below §§ 649—651.

perty in the hands of women. The victory of Pydna in 168, followed
by a general sense of security and a fresh influx of wealth, set the
tide of demoralization flowing again with renewed strength, and all
the vain barriers of reactionary reform were speedily swept away.

635. Of the later censorships in this period we know very little,
owing to the loss of the rest of Livy's great work. What can be
gathered justifies the inference that their general tendency was that
of a weak and drifting policy. It seems that the freedmen regained
most of what they had lost. Nor can it be doubted that their numbers
continued to increase: that the roll of citizens on several occasions
recorded a decrease was due to the melancholy fact that the numbers
of trueborn Romans were falling. Meanwhile the exclusion of the
Latins, and the illtreatment of the Allies generally, went on as before:
any move towards incorporation of the wholesome Italian elements
with the Roman state seemed further off than ever. The power of
the capitalist class was growing: while Roman Knights were ceasing
to furnish cavalry corps for the wars, the non-noble men of property
hung together, and their influence was often irresistible. They were
virtually an Order: in the next period we shall find them (*equester
ordo*) openly recognised as such. In 164 Paullus was censor. Even
in good health he would probably have been able to effect little, with
the masterful Philippus for colleague. But the good man's health was
broken. His death in 160 left a gap in the ranks of the better nobles:
another check on the men of the new school was removed, and a
selfish and greedy clique dominated the Senate more than ever.
Passing over the censors of 159, 154, 147, we come to those of 142,
of whom Scipio Aemilianus was one. He was the most trusted man
in Rome, and a true patriot; but L. Mummius was his colleague, and
the destroyers of Carthage and Corinth could not agree. Anything
that Scipio might have done to improve public or private life therefore remained undone. It is probable that things had by this time
gone too far for even concordant censors to undertake reform with
any chance of success. With the death of Cato in 149 the most
whole-hearted supporter of remedial measures had passed away.
Aemilianus was reduced to preaching, vainly, as he well knew. At
the general purification of the *lustrum* he went so far as to change
the wording[1] of the solemn concluding prayer. He prayed the gods,
not to make Rome greater, but to keep her safe. He saw that Rome's
imperial task was already beyond her powers: that Roman character
and Roman institutions could not be expanded under existing conditions to meet the growing needs of the empire. Pessimistic as he

---

[1] Valer. Max. IV 1 § 10.

was in temperament, he had nevertheless but too good reason to fear that the commonwealth would break down under the strain.

636. Indeed the sincerest Roman patriot of that time might well have been puzzled to discover what he might undertake with a reasonable hope of doing good to his country. To raise none but good men to the magistracies, and keep them loyal and obedient to the central government, worthily representing Rome at home or abroad: to restrain the intrigues of self-seeking nobles, and provide the Senate with far-sighted leaders devoted to the common weal: to arouse in the mongrel mobs that generally made up the Assemblies some feelings worthy of Roman citizens, some steady appreciation of the true interests of the state: to enforce honesty in contractors and discipline in the armies: these and the like were patriotic aspirations, but aspirations without effect. For there was no point at which to make the beginning of a fruitful crusade: each element of the political compound was progressively corrupting the others. Nor need we look far for the main cause that made the outlook hopeless. The vigour and growth of the old Rome had been due, not to intellectual eminence or to perfection of political machinery, but to a devotion to duty that endured all sacrifices and a vital harmony that survived all civil strife. It was a moral force that was the mainspring of the whole machine, and it was precisely this moral force that was now failing fast. History knows of nations humbled by defeat and suffering, to whom disaster has been a stimulus and a cause of national revival. But such a situation could hardly arise in the case before us: the wholesome fear of rival powers was at an end. Nor indeed was Rome a true nation or an organic state. The chances of such a consummation had been extinguished by her conquests, and her present treatment of the Italian Allies was a mere confession of the fact. Of old she had gained greatly by incorporating aliens to be sharers of the burdens, and eventually of the privileges, of Roman citizenship. But in this period the Roman was fast learning to shirk burdens and monopolize privileges. Perhaps no single privilege was so distinctive of the citizen as that conferred and extended by the Porcian laws.

637. Of these three laws, sometimes referred to as one, the one certain characteristic is that in some form and some circumstances or other they relieved the Roman citizen from liability to cruel scourging. The dates cannot be fixed, but they probably belong to this period, and it is not unlikely that the author of the earliest was Cato himself. Mr Greenidge[1] argued that one at least of these enactments took the form of allowing the citizen to appeal to the people against

[1] *Classical Review* XI 437.

the exercise of the magistrate's compulsory powers (*coercitio*) on the occasion of a military levy. This conclusion at any rate agrees well with what we know of the growing reluctance of citizens to serve abroad, and the tendency to lay an undue share of this burden on the Allies. Whatever may have been the detailed provisions of the Porcian laws, it seems certain that their general effect was to protect the citizen's back (*pro tergo civium*) in some way, and thus to mark him off more invidiously than ever from the unprotected Ally. Nor was it in military matters only that the Ally was made to feel his inferiority. We have referred to this subject above; and there is preserved[1] a fragment of a speech of Cato describing the public flogging of the chief men of some allied town for a trivial offence by order of a Roman magistrate. A stray notice has reached us of an application to the Senate from the town of Patavium for help in restoring order there. Party-strife (*seditio*) ran high, and it had come to actual fighting. A consul setting out for Gaul was commissioned[2] to intervene, and did so with good results. But we have no details, and it is more than likely that the civil strife was between rich and poor, and that the consul supported the former. This in a Roman view would be quite satisfactory. When Roman interference in local affairs was invited we may fairly assume that it was for party reasons.

638. But, if the disadvantages of their position were galling to the Latins and other Italian Allies, the instances of flagrant wrong were probably rare, and friendships and exchange of hospitality might often tend to keep their relations with Romans fairly smooth. Nor had they yet lost all hope of an improvement in their position. Far more helpless and hopeless were the subject peoples in the Roman Provinces. We have already spoken of the origin of the provincial system and of the acquisition of six dependencies of this kind, (1) Sicily, (2) Sardinia with Corsica, (3, 4) the two Spains, (5) Africa, (6) Macedonia. All had this in common, that the Roman governor of each was a temporary absolute ruler, in whose hand were united both civil and military power. True, he was supposed to do nothing contravening the constitution or charter (*lex*) granted to the Province: but the governor and governed might put different constructions on its provisions. His view would prevail, and many matters essentially civil might be deemed to fall within the range of unlimited military law.

---

[1] Gellius x 3 § 17 (Jordan's *Cato* p. 41). The scene was probably somewhere in the north of Italy. See Weissenborn on Livy XXXVII 46. That the people were Allies seems clear from the reference to *societas*. Cato speaks as an accuser, of course, but the main fact is hardly to be doubted.

[2] Livy XLI 27 *Patavinis saluti fuit adventus consulis.*

Before entering on office he (following the practice of the judicial praetors at home) put forth[1] an,'edict' in which he gave notice of the principles that would guide him in administering the law.   But there was no check on him in the Province during his term of office, and all depended on the good faith with which his promises were kept.   A good instance of the importance of this may be found in the various degrees of privilege enjoyed by various communities in a Province. Towns that welcomed the coming of the Romans, such as Messana or Utica, were highly favoured, while rebellious Syracuse was placed in the lowest grade of subjection.   The highest grade enjoyed autonomy in local government, retained their territory and their local law, and had *commercium*[2] throughout the Province, enabling their citizens to acquire and hold estates outside their own borders.   A scrupulous respect for the rights of the various grades was dictated by Roman interests.   Rome profited by the peace and prosperity of tributary lands.   Provincial disorders were a source of trouble and expense, and the central government, practically the Senate, was not guilty of the folly of intentional cruelty or oppression.   But to carry out the Senate's scheme of administration with due regard to local circumstances was a matter of delicate discretion and care, and the governors had no special training to fit them for the charge.   Romans of the great office-holding families had indeed an early introduction to public affairs by way of the Roman method of apprenticeship, and this had sufficed while Rome was merely an Italian power.   But an imperial position brought imperial needs.   There was no civil service of trained permanent officials to watch the details of administration with expert eye.   If, as I have pointed out, the armies suffered from the lack of professional skill in their commanders, not less did the provincial government suffer from being entrusted to amateurs.   Even a well-meaning man must have been hampered by the want of a competent staff to manage the routine, and the short period of office made it impossible for him to become an expert himself.

639.   Precedent always went for a good deal with Roman statesmen, and the provincial edict of a new governor was in the main copied from that of his predecessor, with occasional modifications suggested by recent experience.   But the practice of governors varied far more than their principles.   To subject peoples it was all-important that the practice of their rulers should be firm and consistent, such that men could understand it and rely on it.   Then they could adapt themselves to its requirements.   Uncertainty kept them uneasy, and

[1] See §§ 991, 1373—1377, and Index.
[2] See Cic. II *in Verr.* III §§ 93, 108, and above § 252.

was bad for business. As yet the instances of gross oppression and extortion seem to have been rare, but we have seen that they did occur in the cases of Sardinia and Spain. No doubt many a wrong was endured in silence, for it was a very difficult matter to obtain redress. It was a far cry to Rome, and no effective machinery had been provided for dealing with abuses that had not been foreseen. We have seen[1] attempts to get justice done by use of existing procedure with the help of powerful patrons: but offenders contrived to elude punishment, and the sufferers had to be content with a vain show of justice. As time went on, things were getting worse in the provinces, a fact assumed and confessed in the year 149 by a notable attempt[2] at remedial legislation. A tribune, L. Calpurnius Piso Frugi, famed for his upright character and afterwards an annalist of repute, carried through a law establishing a new permanent court for the trial of cases of extortion. The *lex Calpurnia de repetundis* was meant to provide for the restitution (*pecuniae repetundae* = moneys to be reclaimed) of wrongful exactions. The *praetor peregrinus* was in each year to prepare a list of jurors (*iudices*) chosen from the senators. On demand he was to form a court selected from this list for the trial of a particular case. The procedure seems to have followed very ancient lines. A claim made by one party was denied by the other: both parties then deposited a sum in court, and the trial took the form of deciding which party's deposit (*sacramentum*) should be forfeited. If the accused lost his case, he had to restore to the accusers the amount claimed by them. But, so far as we know, this was all. Later laws attached further penalties of disabilities and disgrace to a conviction, and from a civil action the extortion-process became in effect a criminal prosecution: but extortion was still practised. It does not appear that the old methods of redress, by a special commission-court, or in the Recovery court, were forbidden by the new statute: they had been a failure, and had to be supplemented for this purpose by a new machine. As for trials before the Assembly, they were far too clumsy and quite unsuited to the purpose. These processes were in effect set aside indirectly by the new statute. The new juries acted under statutory powers granted by the Assembly. Their decisions were final. There could be no appeal to the people from the decision of its own delegates, and with the development of the new courts (for they were soon extended to deal with other offences) appeals virtually ceased. Magistrates could still impose penalties subject to appeal, but the practice died out. We see that in passing this law the

---

[1] See above § 556.

[2] Cicero *Brutus* § 106, and Orelli's *index legum* under *Calpurnia*.

Assembly of Tribes had been induced to abdicate one of its earliest functions. It must also be noted[1] that, as the Tribe-Assembly could not condemn a man to death, so neither could the juries to whom it had delegated its power. The power of life and death still rested with the Centuries, but the disuse of the death-penalty was an established fact, and indeed the Centuries seem to have been only called together now for certain elections, for declarations of war, and for the very rare trials for high treason. Further, with the new jury-system disappeared the 'intercession' of tribunes in public trials. The *iudex* in civil suits had never been regarded as a magistrate, so his verdict was not exposed to be blocked[2] by a tribune. And the new courts were, as Mommsen[3] points out, in their origin merely a development of the old court of Recovery.

640. The year 149 was one of many anxieties. The wars and troubles in Spain Africa Macedonia and Greece no doubt helped to incline both Senate and people towards an act of reform. The unchallenged supremacy of Rome was already developing the two parties, or rather factions, whose strife became the bane of the Republic in the next period. The supporters of the 'best' element in the state (*optimates*) and the champions of the 'people' (*populares*) were alike politically worthless. Both were led by men of the governing class, seeking their own advantage; the one being the faction of the rich, resting on its majority in the Senate, the other nominally that of the poor, earning power in the Assembly by base pandering to the mob. They represented no honest difference of patriotic opinion, but a selfish struggle for the emoluments of office, and were both an effect and a cause of the growing degradation of Roman politics. Between them wavered the capitalist class, the most selfish of all, strong in wealth and cohesion, valued as adherents, and selling their adhesion dear. In such a situation as this, we must ask, how came the *lex Calpurnia* to be passed? We can only guess. It can hardly have been a move of the senatorial majority. But they may have seen that the 'popular' party would in any case support a measure ostensibly designed to check the noble governors of Provinces, whom the Senate was no longer able to control. To have it carried in spite of the Senate was a rebuff not to be courted: and, so long as the court consisted of senators, the law would be no great blow to the nobility. If then they assented to the proposal, only keeping a keen eye on the jury-clause, they would shew themselves good tacticians: and this would explain why we hear of no great conflict arising over the bill of honest Piso. Anyhow the law passed, and may for a time

---

[1] Maine's *Ancient Law*, chapter 10.   [2] Cic. II *in Verrem* II § 30.
[3] *Röm. Staatsrecht* I 259—60.

have done some good. But from the first it was difficult to put the law in operation owing to the distance of Rome from the places where extortion had been practised and whence witnesses had to be brought. Delays were inevitable, Roman patrons had to be got to plead the case, and the ablest of pleaders might easily fail in persuading a senatorial jury to condemn a guilty member of their own Order. We must remember that the capitalist Knights, who were probably already beginning to exploit the Provinces, were not touched by the law. The general effect of it seems to have been slight. The Senators had as a rule either done much the same as the accused, or were waiting for the chance of doing so, and accordingly acquitted each other. The redress of grievances became a mockery of justice, and the 'possession of the courts' (*iudicia*), the privilege of condemning your enemies and acquitting your friends, became a prize competed for by factions. But the *lex Calpurnia* was not barren. Juries were at least more workable than Assemblies, and the application of the jury-system to non-political offences made possible the creation of criminal courts and the development of criminal law.

641. A governor had under him a staff of officials and subordinates. In this staff we see clearly the close adherence to a military model. First came the quaestor[1] in charge of finance, a young man serving an official apprenticeship. He could and did act as a deputy for the governor, to whom he stood in the relation of a temporary son. He was expected to shew perfect obedience and loyalty to his chief. Next came the official legate or legates, subordinate deputies appointed by the Senate, and a number of experts clerks orderlies and attendants. Besides these, the governor was allowed to take out a number of companions (*comites*) of his own choice, just as a general in the field had a number of select friends attached to his headquarters. All the Romans who went abroad did so in view of some personal advantage, immediate or prospective: thus the governor was surrounded by men eager for money or preferments practically reserved for the wealthy. The money wanted could only be got by fleecing the provincials, and the greedy crew about him could command immense influence at Rome. His future career was at stake, and in most cases he yielded to temptation, extorting money himself and winking at the extortions of others. Small exactions, submitted to at first, soon became normal, and were extended under the stimulus of impunity thus were established the colossal abuses of the following period. The methods of extortion were ingeniously varied. A favourite plan was to evoke voluntary offerings by hints of a contemplated official visit

---

[1] In Sicily there were two quaestors. The island had been acquired in two parts at different times, and the original duality was so far retained.

or the coming of troops to be quartered on a town. Pretexts could generally be found for such threats: the expense of such visits was certain to be great, and to the presence of the soldiery all parents of families and quiet people in general entertained a singular aversion. And to buy off the visitations of one governor was only to call the attention of his successor to the town, so that the voluntary compounding for exemption was apt to become a customary burden. Nor was it long before the courts of justice began to be used by bad governors as a means of enrichment. A Province was for administrative purposes divided into districts (*conventus*). The centre of each district was a town in which the governor held his periodical assize. The courts for the district were held there, and complaints petitions and local business dealt with. When jurors were required, they were chosen from the Roman citizens resident in the district. Over them he had no power of life and death, but over all others his power was absolute. By unfair management of trials, even by mere delay, he could make it worth the while of litigants to gratify his rapacity. The time was to come when a Verres would sell justice without shame. Into these matters we need not now enter further. The next age saw the provincial system in all its glory, teeming with abominations that no reformer could check. For the present these abuses were in their infancy: but those connected with exactions of corn seem to have been already in full swing.

642. Of Roman citizens in the Provinces there were several classes. Even before the country was organized as a Province, traders (*mercatores*) were generally on the ground. Alleged ill-treatment of merchants was not seldom a pretext for campaigns and annexations. More important still were the business-men (*negotiatores*), partners in or agents of companies, or acting for themselves, who did the banking and money-lending. They swarmed into every new Province and monopolized financial transactions, backed by the favour of governors. The largeness of their numbers is probably to be taken in connexion with the decline of Italian agriculture. If a man sold a farm that did not pay, and did not wish to become a mere city-loafer, what was he to do with himself and his little capital? The average Roman had a native gift for the management of money. In a Province he might start in a small way of business, and build up a fortune by usury and by the various opportunities that his right of *commercium*, coextensive with Roman rule, might be trusted to supply. He was sure of a favourable hearing in the courts and the countenance of those in authority. There can be little doubt that many of those who dropped out of Italian life as farmers, and especially those who had served

in campaigns abroad[1] and seen foreign lands, took to this line of life. And, as richer Provinces were opened up to this form of enterprise, the emigration flowed in fuller and fuller stream. Among the *negotiatores* there were of course also many men of large means, Knights and others, who from the first did business on a larger scale.

643. These classes had no official connexion with the provincial system: the *publicani,* though not officials, represented the employment of capital under contracts made with the Roman state. The custom, widely prevalent in ancient times, of leasing the right to collect various dues, had long been used in Italy, and was applied to the Provinces. Where the yearly returns varied from year to year, it was thought convenient for the state to take a lump sum and make over its rights for a certain term to contractors, who took the risks of a rise or fall. Taxes[2] by percentage, royalties, customs-dues and other tolls, are specimens of revenues thus dealt with. In the case of the Provinces a marked distinction must be drawn between the two systems[3] on which their tributary relations with Rome were organized. Strictly speaking, it was payment of a fixed tribute (*stipendium*) that distinguished the Subject (*stipendiarius*) from the Ally (*socius*). And it was this kind of tax that Rome was instinctively inclined to impose on the conquered, an invariable impost suited to the simplicity of Roman finance. It seems to have been the form of taxation adopted in the Spains Africa and Macedonia. The amount was not excessive, and it was a good working plan. But in Sicily, both in the Punic province and in the kingdom of Hiero, the Romans found existing[4] a system of exactions in kind, a yearly percentage of the crops, good or bad, and hence ever varying. They doubtless knew that this system was in vogue in the kingdoms of the East, and with their usual reluctance to change existing organizations they adopted it. But it suited ill with Roman character and republican institutions. The collection of these tithes[5] (*decumae*) had to be farmed out: there was no trusty force of civil servants to whom the work might be safely

---

[1] That soldiers on foreign service carried money about with them seems certain, and those returning from eastern wars probably a good deal. In Livy XXXIII 29 we hear of soldiers carrying money *negotiandi ferme causa,* and being murdered by Boeotians for the sake of gain, and this in B.C. 196.

[2] See Cic. II *in Verr.* II §§ 169—171, III §§ 167, 168.

[3] In Sardinia both systems seem to have been in use, as Marquardt points out. But this unhappy island was a great sufferer early in its history as a Province, see Livy XXXII 27 (B.C. 198). Hence no doubt the risings so cruelly put down. The Province contained no towns enjoying special privileges and immunities as several did for instance in Sicily and Africa.

[4] Cic. II *in Verr.* III §§ 12—20.

[5] We hear of double tithes exacted in Sicily and Sardinia in 191 and 190 under pressure of the needs of the war with Antiochus. See Livy XXXVI 2, XXXVII 2.

left. So they were put up to auction, and knocked down to that company of capitalists who made the highest bid in ready money. These *publicani* stipulated for sundry privileges and exemptions, and it was of course part of the bargain that the state should facilitate collection. Now dealing with tithes in kind is necessarily a troublesome process. Many agents had to be employed in the business, which came with a rush[1] at the season of harvest: the provincials had to be sharply looked after to prevent fraud. To get in the full amount, whether taken in kind or commuted, was the agents' duty, and they were not likely to forget the unsentimental court by whom their accounts would be audited. The shareholders in the company would overlook many things, but not an unsatisfactory dividend.

644. Under such conditions it is not wonderful that the exaction of not less than the amounts due led to the exaction of a little more, to leave a margin of security: or that the collectors should be tempted to exact something further for their own profit. Governors, mostly praetors hoping to attain the consulship, would be ready to oblige the great companies at Rome with an eye to future elections. Hence the services of their staff would be at the tithe-collectors' disposal, and in the next period at least the loan of a squad of soldiers was not unknown. To the complaints of their subjects they too often lent an unwilling ear. In such matters as customs-dues the greed of the *publicani* was notorious, but the department in which their villainy was most effectively matured was the farming of the tithes. Things were already going from bad to worse before the kingdom of Pergamum became the property of the Roman people and gave to this iniquitous system a great extension. No laws—and they were many, more and more severe—availed to put down the abuses. In practice there was but one means of bringing the governors to justice, to secure the help of influential Romans and the ablest pleaders of the day. This help was generally granted for one of two motives, or both. A personal grudge against the offender, or a desire to win credit for eloquence and skill, were enough to induce a rising orator to prosecute or a man of position to support the cause. Mere indignation at wrong or compassion for the sufferings of provincials were doubtless not extinct feelings in Roman society. But the Free-lance who would act vigorously on the impulse of such motives as these must always have been a rare type. Even Cato had an eye to Roman interests quite as much as to Roman honour. And he did not live to use the new machinery of the new statute. His death and the *lex Calpurnia* fall in the same year.

645. At this point we may pause to observe that the growth of

[1] See Cic. II *in Verr.* V § 29.

the provincial system is strictly a part of Rome's internal history. At Rome was decided the policy to be followed in the treatment of her subjects: the defects of Roman society were the main cause of the evils we have noted : on Roman society fell evils, less obvious but more incurable, as the misgovernment of the Provinces reacted on Rome. In particular the worship of wealth led to most serious consequences. The great wars enriched many and raised the standard of expenditure all round. Larger incomes were needed, and whoever would not drop behind in the social and political race must enrich himself without delay. Now with the end of the great wars no other source of speedy enrichment remained but the Provinces, and the robbery of enemies (or people treated as such) gave place to the fleecing of subjects. This was more continuous, and even more demoralizing. We are on the threshold of a time when public office will be chiefly valued, not for its powers and dignities at home, but for the prospect of gaining wealth by extortion abroad. And hand in hand with unscrupulous greed went a development of lawless pride, an impatience of restraint engendered in the Roman nobles by the temporary enjoyment of a practically monarchic power. It was no easy thing for an ex-governor to resume quietly a place among his peers and submit to the magistrates of the year : yet this was his duty as a good citizen, and indeed the very corner-stone of the aristocratic Republic. The hard virility of the Roman stock was not exhausted, and growing luxury and vice did not quench ambition. By fair means or foul the nobles contended for preeminence: jobbery in the Senate, bribery in the Assemblies, had already begun and became worse with time. Patriotism was more and more sapped, and general inefficiency enhanced. In promoting the private self-seeking and public impotence that foiled all efforts for reform, the provincial system played a great part, and it was through the influence of the Provinces that the Roman Republic came to a violent and unlamented end.

646. In this period the Roman treasury was constantly receiving supplies of the precious metals. Some war-indemnity or other was generally coming in by yearly instalments, and the payment of large sums into the state chest was the regular sequel of a triumph. This was the state's share of the booty. Some no doubt was intercepted by greedy commanders, but what reached its destination was enough. It is recorded[1] that in 157 the accumulations of gold and silver in bars and coin were large. Mommsen estimates the total at nearly £860,000 of our money, and draws attention to the smallness of the amount. Small it is, according to modern ideas, when we consider the vast area already under Roman rule. But the expenses of the

---

[1] Pliny *NH* XXXIII 55.

state were large and ill controlled, and, as Cato once said, the theft of private property landed the thief in the stocks and fetters, but the state-thief swaggered in purple and gold. Money, however got, was become the dominant influence in Rome: of the business-qualities noted by Polybius, the honesty was becoming rare, while the grasping keenness was as strong as ever. When Scipio Aemilianus[1] treated his relatives liberally, paying dowries before they were legally due and resigning an inheritance to a poorer brother, his quite exceptional disinterestedness was at first supposed to be a mere mistake. An evil sign of the age may be detected in the increase of legislation, of which there can hardly be a doubt. If laws seldom heal the maladies of a degenerating state and people, they at least record them: and we have already referred to various enactments on constitutional matters such as the sequence of offices, restriction of reelection, the franchise question, and the like, narrow-minded attempts to stop irresistible tendencies, destined to fail utterly in the coming period of revolution. As instructive specimens of the attempts to combat corruption and luxury we may speak briefly of some laws dealing with bribery and undue influence in the Assemblies, and others of a sumptuary character.

647. In 181 we hear of a *lex Cornelia Baebia de ambitu.* The term *ambitus*[2] had by this time come to mean 'corrupt practices' used in canvassing for office, particularly bribery of any kind. This was the first of a series ever increasing in severity, all alike futile: the Roman people went on selling their votes till the end of the Republic, that is, so long as there were buyers. This law had the approval of the Senate and the support of Cato. Its penalty, ten years exclusion from office, seems to have been raised in 159 by a *lex Cornelia Fulvia* to what Polybius[3] calls 'death,' that is in effect exile. Twenty years later, when the opposition of the *populares* to the rule of the nobility had become developed, a *lex Gabinia* introduced the ballot[4] instead of open voting, but for elections only. This was to be a check, not only on direct bribery, but on the use of a prevailing influence by great men on their various dependants. In 137 a *lex Cassia* extended the principle to the voting in trials before the Assembly (*iudicia populi*), which, though now of rare occurrence, had not been abolished. The Tribes were meant, for the law left untouched the jurisdiction of the Centuries in cases of high treason. In spite of the opposition

---

[1] Polyb. XXXII 12—14.

[2] If Livy VII 15 is to be trusted, there was a law against *ambitus* so early as the year 358. It then seems to have meant canvassing of an undignified kind, an outrage on republican simplicity; not bribery.

[3] Polyb. VI 56.

[4] The *locus classicus* on Roman ballot-laws is Cic. *de legibus* III §§ 33—39.

of the nobles the law passed : a tribune blocked it, but was induced
by Scipio Aemilianus to reconsider his position. The object of the
law[1] was no doubt to revive the power of the Assembly over erring
Magistrates. The use of the *tabella* or *tessera* for voting in legislative
Assemblies was not introduced till a few years later (131), and in
treason trials not till 107. But the ballot was of no avail in restoring
the purity and independence of Assemblies. The voters were corrupt,
and no *lex tabellaria* could purify them.

648. A preface to the sumptuary legislation was the repeal[2] in
195 of the Oppian law restricting the finery and luxury of women.
Passed in 215, when Roman resources were strained by the pressure
of war, even Cato in his consulship could not save it. In 181 a *lex
Orchia* limited the number of guests that might be entertained at
a single party. Even if this were not evaded it still left the outlay
per head unlimited. It registers the fact that the pleasures of the
table were taking hold of the rich nobles, chiefly no doubt the men of
the new school, and that there were still many to whom this luxury
was an abomination. Cato declared that it was evaded, and we may
well believe it. It is said[3] that gluttony grew fast, with disastrous
effect on the morals of young men, and that the example of their
betters led to an epidemic of drunkenness among the common people.
In 161 the *lex Fannia* imposed a limit on the cost of dinners and
forbade the use of certain viands. This also was futile. It would
seem that one difficulty in the way of enforcing it was that it only
applied to Rome. On this pretext a *lex Didia* was passed in 143
to extend the provisions of the Fannian law to all Italy : at the
same time the guests as well as the host were made liable to the
statutory penalties. But the evil continued, as later legislation, itself
also vain, sufficiently attests.

649. Closely connected in its aim with the sumptuary laws was
the legislation[4] dealing with inheritances. The old family system,
which tended to keep estates in the hands of males, and discouraged
legacies to persons other than the heir who took over the rights and
duties of his predecessor, had been breaking down. Men's ideas on

---

[1] So Lange *RA* §§ 110, 122.

[2] Livy XXXIV 1—8.

[3] See Macrobius *Sat.* III 16, 17. He quotes from a speech of one C. Titius in support of
the Fannian law, a fragment which (even allowing for exaggeration) gives us a very unfavourable impression of the behaviour of the men acting as *iudices* in the civil courts of the
day. They appear as utterly debauched and lost to all sense of propriety. For the question
as to the identity of this Titius see Piderit, indices to Cic. *Brutus*, Teuffel-Schwabe *Rom.
Lit.* § 141 note 7. That the Didian law applied to Allies, as well as to Roman citizens
scattered over Italy, is hardly to be inferred from the loose language o. a late writer (about
400 A.D.), and so wanton an encroachment on their local liberties seems very improbable.

[4] See note on § 634 above.

the subject had changed, especially since the end of the second Punic war and the growth of foreign influences, mainly Greek. The weakening of the position of the *pater familias* was finding expression in the frequency of large bequests, and in the greater freedom of women, to whom many of these bequests were made. In a period when the desire of individuals for wealth at their personal disposal was superseding the claims of civic duty in other ways, it is not wonderful that undue influence on testators and misuse of the power of bequest should become common enough to alarm old-fashioned Romans, who set great store by the permanence of families. The right of a testator to the free disposition of his estate, recognised in the Twelve Tables, was assuredly never meant to be used so as to break the proper family succession. If no natural heir existed, the testator was free, but the right course for a Roman was to secure an heir by adoption. To impoverish an existent heir, by leaving him to succeed to all the family obligations with only a fraction of the family property, bequeathing the rest in legacies according to personal liking, was contrary to family religion and ancestral custom. But under the influence of new ideas the old family-basis of society was wasting and the individual becoming more important. The uneasiness of the old-Roman party shewed itself in an attempt to reestablish the ancient practice by statute. The *lex Furia testamentaria*, generally assigned to the year 183 and connected with the censorship of Cato, limited bequests to not more than 1000 *asses* each in cases where the legatee was outside a certain degree of affinity. But by making numerous bequests it was still possible to exhaust the estate and leave the heir penniless. The law missed its aim. And, while its failure was being proved, the progressive emancipation of women was also attracting the notice of social reformers.

650. The traditional position[1] of the Roman woman had been one of lifelong tutelage. The wife was in the 'hand' of her husband, the unmarried woman or widow was the ward of a guardian (*tutor*), who was generally her nearest relative in the male line. But the introduction of less complete forms of marriage (plebeian) had slowly weakened the stringency of the marriage tie even in Patrician houses. Many wives were now no longer their husbands' property in the old full sense. And those who had no husbands were contriving to evade the restraints of wardship and gain no small freedom of action. The means were found by the ingenuity of jurists. A husband was induced to insert a clause in his will leaving his wife free to nominate[2] her own

---

[1] See in particular Gaius I §§ 108—115 *b*, 142—58, with Poste's notes.

[2] In 186 we read of *tutoris optio* being granted to a woman as part of her reward for giving information about the Bacchanalia. See Livy XXXIX 19.

guardian in the event of his decease, a guardian of course selected for the purpose of leaving the lady a free hand.   Unmarried women and widows not entrusted with this discretionary power were desirous to acquire the same practical liberty, and their wishes were met by the device of a sham sale (*coemptio*).   A woman wheedled or worried her present guardian into letting her sell herself to another man, and did so under a fiduciary contract binding him to transfer her by resale to a third man, the person whose ward she intended to be.   In this person's hands the function of guardianship became merely formal, and the lady enjoyed a high degree of freedom in dealing with her property: whether this as yet extended (as it did later) to the power of disposition by will, is doubtful.   The economic independence thus gained might have been a good thing, if the Roman ladies of the period had not fallen away from the solid moral type of earlier days. But their extravagance and love of display were becoming a marked feature of the age.   In the scandal of the Bacchanalian orgies (186) women of position had played a leading part, and it was believed that in that affair vice had been followed by crime: those whose secrecy was doubted had been silenced by poison.   In 180 a consul died, poisoned, it was said, by his wife[1] in order to get her son by a former marriage made consul in his stead.   This succession actually took place: but a special commission to try this and other suspicious cases found the lady guilty and sentenced her to death.   When such things were possible we need not wonder that several cases of divorce in high places are recorded in this period.   The most notable was that[2] of Aemilius Paullus.   There were of course good people, and there were happy marriages, as that of Gracchus the censor[3] and the famous Cornelia.   But the general tone was certainly declining, and it was no mere narrow-minded prejudice that saw in the excessive enrichment of women a social evil.

651.   We come now to the famous *lex Voconia* of 169, supported by Cato and the reform party in the hope of checking the growing extravagance of women.   It applied only to testators possessed of sufficient property to entitle them to a place in the first of the property-classes, for it was only among the wealthy that the trouble arose. The law forbade[4] any such testator to make a woman his heir.   As for legacies, it provided that no one could take as legatee a larger sum than what the heir received.   Thus a male succession was secured, and the maximum bequest to a woman limited to half the estate.   But it was still possible by numerous bequests to bring down the share of

---

[1] Livy XL 37.　　　　　　[2] Plutarch *Aemil.* 5.　See too Valer. Max. VI 3 § 10.
[3] Cicero *de divin.* I § 36, II § 62, Pliny *NH* VII § 122.
[4] See in particular Gaius II §§ 226, 274, with Poste's notes.

the heir to an amount that, considering the obligations to be discharged, made it not worth his while to take. In course of time another mode of evasion[1] was devised, by leaving the heir subject to a trust to transfer the estate to a person named. This however he was under no legal liability to do, and the temptation to profit by strict observance of the law, rather than follow the dictates of moral rectitude, still existed in full force in the time of Cicero. Until trusts of this kind were made legally binding, a change which seems to have begun in the time of Augustus, the *lex Voconia* remained an important statute. But that it effected any change for the better in the conduct of women or men of the wealthy classes we have no reason to believe.

652. In connexion with legislation we must glance at the attempt to regulate by statute the management of signs from heaven, the effect of which on the holding of Assemblies has been referred to above. It certainly belongs to this period, and has been probably assigned to the year 153, when the date of entering on office for consuls and other officers was shifted from the first of March to the first of January. Two laws[2] dealt with the subject, the *leges Aelia et Fufia*. They seem to have given statutory force to existing rules resting on custom. No Assembly could legally be held in the face of the announcement of unfavourable auspices. Any one might report an unlucky occurrence to the presiding magistrate. This was *obnun-tiatio*: in any case of doubt, an augur was at hand to say whether the occurrence was of evil import or not. But the regular magistrate had a further right, that of deliberate watching for a sign to occur (*spectio*), and, while he was known to be thus engaged, the public right of meeting was in abeyance. Thus, by giving notice that he was keeping watch on the heavens (*de caelo servare*), he could stop business. On the other hand the higher magistrate could prevent a lower magistrate from using the right to thwart his projects. It was customary for a consul in giving notice of an Assembly to put a clause in his edict forbidding lower magistrates to watch for signs. He then had only to run the chance of what might turn up at the Assembly, such as a clap of thunder. What were the detailed provisions of the Aelian and Fufian laws we do not know, but we do know that after this time the use of the auspices as a political engine, to check movements to which the nobles were opposed, becomes common : indeed in the days of Cicero we find it a public scandal. It is perhaps not too rash to infer that some of those who supported these measures did so with an eye to their

---

[1] See Gaius II §§ 246—59, Cicero *de fin.* II § 55.

[2] See Lange *RA* index, Greenidge in *Classical Review* VII 158—61, *Roman Public Life* 162—3, note p. 409 of Vol. I[2] of Tyrrell and Purser's *Correspondence of Cicero*.

political effect. Tradition[1] says that there was a clause providing that in any year the elections of magistrates must be got over before legislative Assemblies could be held. In any case it was chiefly legislative action that was meant to be checked. And these laws, so eminently liable to shameless misuse, were certainly not the outcome of a genuine revival of old religious ideas in Romans of the governing class. It is possible that, as Lange thinks, the Licinian and Aebutian laws, by which the proposer of a law creating any extraordinary office (such as a commission) was, himself and all closely connected with him, debarred[2] from holding the appointment, belong to this time. It was evidently a time of reorganization. I have already pointed out that the law to prevent reelections to the consulship is most likely to be assigned to the year 151.

653. As in the matter of auspices, so in general religious observances we find no slackening in this period. Ceremonies are performed with minute care, vows punctiliously discharged, prodigies expiated, temples built and restored, all scruples considered and doubts resolved by the colleges of experts, the Sibylline books consulted at need, sacrifices and festivals repeated rather than the state should suffer for a possible oversight or flaw. The Fetials[3] still directed the nice formalities of international contact, in particular the exact details of a declaration of war. Though new worships were finding their way into Rome, though the identification of old Italian gods with foreign divinities, chiefly Greek, was now beginning, accompanied by a personal mythology conveyed in literature and anthromorphic notions commended by works of art: still the spirit in which the Senate and the sacred colleges guided religious observances was Roman enough. Whatever had been distinctively Roman in the ancient worships had lost much of its interest since the Plebeians had invaded the Patrician heritage, and the adaptation of old cults and the introduction of new[4] have always been common phenomena in polytheistic systems. Imperial extension was bringing Rome into

---

[1] Through the Scholiast of Bobbio. Rejected by Mommsen *Staatsrecht* I 108. Certainly the later practice does not confirm it, for legislation was chiefly effected early in the year.

[2] If so, they were of course broken by Gracchus in 133. But it is perhaps more probable that they were carried in consequence of the Gracchan family-commission, as A. W. Zumpt on Cic. *de leg. agr.* II § 21 thinks. See index.

[3] See above § 428. Livy XXXI 8, XXXVI 3.

[4] A notable event is the appearance of *Roma* as a goddess. In 170 the people of Alabanda sent to say that they had built a *templum urbis Romae* and founded a yearly festival in connexion therewith. Smyrna had done much the same in 195. See Livy XLIII 6, Tac. *Ann.* IV 56. Such an act came naturally to Asiatics, accustomed to deify kings. On the other hand we hear of leave granted to Asiatics to sacrifice in the *Capitolium*. Liv. XLIII 6, XLIV 14. See § 472 above.

touch with foreign religions, and a remodelling of the Roman pantheon was in progress. But the state kept a firm hand on religion. The new patricio-plebeian nobility were well aware of the importance of such an influence: even when rationalism began to sap the beliefs of educated men, it was an object to guide and control those of the common people, to suppress worships of doubtful tendency and admit innovations not open to suspicion. They thus regulated the supply for which timid ignorance and superstition created an unfailing demand. The arrangement suited both the nobles and the masses: the latter were satisfied and calmed in anxious crises, while it placed in the hands of the former a power that they were able, and soon very willing, to use for political ends. There were no doubt in this period a good many among the nobility to whom traditional religion with its rules and forms still appealed as a necessary condition of wellbeing. Such were Cato and Paullus the studious expert in augury. And an age of great conquests, the fall of Rome's enemies one after another, seemed to attest the satisfactory relations of the conquering people to the supernatural powers. Rome had done her duty by the gods, and the gods had done their duty by Rome.

654. And yet the state religion, though modernized, was surely dying. If its precise forms and ceremonies, its righteous dealing towards the gods, had in earlier times reacted[1] upon the conduct of man to man and citizen to state, this influence was fast losing its effect. It was being turned into a mere political engine, and any scruples that men of the governing class might feel in making this use of it were being swept away by destructive criticism. The questioning bent of the Greek mind had for centuries challenged popular mythology, and suggestions that the gods were no more than glorified men had not been wanting. Near the end of the fourth century B.C. Euhemerus treated the subject systematically from this point of view, doing away with the supernatural element in theology. The book had a great vogue, for Greek religion had by then lost its vitality: and thus floating notions among the cultivated classes hardened into a sort of creed. Euhemerism was no very profound theory, but easily understood, and it thus appealed to the average man. Choicer spirits, dissatisfied with its negative results, strove hard to rebuild theology on a new basis and so to attain fresh confidence in a divine government of the universe. But those who came nearest to success, the Stoics[2], did so at the cost of making their belief in the supernatural too refined and sublime to be within the reach of common minds. There was true grandeur in Pantheism, but it could not really blend with mythology or be expressed in works of art. The general effect on

---

[1] See above §§ 24, 408.　　　　[2] See above § 427.

educated Greeks of the second century B.C. is probably indicated by the attitude[1] of Polybius, who believes in an essential difference between right and wrong, in the rule of a divine providence manifested in the punishment of evil doers, but who has no definite theology to take the place of the old polytheism.　We have now to sketch the influence of Greek views of religion on the society of Rome.

655.　When Polybius described the patriotism and honesty prevailing in Rome as compared with other states he was at pains to account for the general atmosphere of self-restraint and good faith that he admired.　He found the main cause of Roman virtue to be the fear of the gods, and regarded the promotion of this fear as part of a deliberate policy by which the governing class held the multitude in check.　This explanation seems itself to admit that faith in the state religion was based on ignorance.　Later on he plainly admits the decay of public and private virtues, and points out that Paullus and his son Aemilianus were exceptional men.　He may have written some passage attributing this decay to the decay of religious belief: if he did, the passage has been lost.　In any case his utterance above referred to does not prove much as to the solidity of Roman religious beliefs.　The first great blow to the current theology was dealt by Ennius, who lived into the middle of this period.　He translated into Latin the work of Euhemerus, and drove home the sceptical attack by applications in his own works.　The existence of evil and the prosperity of the wicked emboldened him to deny that the gods were in any way concerned with the doings of mankind, and to publish this opinion in one of his tragedies.　That he dared do this is highly significant.　What he was propounding in the god-fearing society of Rome was nothing less than the veiled atheism of Epicurus.　But this attack was of a kind to affect the weightier and more thoughtful minds: meanwhile another leaven was working on the more passionate and emotional natures, a large percentage of all communities.　The importation of the worship of the 'Great Mother' in 204 had probably rather stimulated than satisfied the craving for excitement which found little or no vent in Roman ceremonies.　The worship of Bacchus had long been domiciled in Italy as a simple cult of the wine-god, but of late it had tended to put on a more advanced character, developing into mysteries, secret rites performed only among the initiated, and initiations of novices under the strictest vows of secrecy.　The Greek districts, particularly the Tarentine neighbourhood, and degenerate Etruria, always addicted to superstition, were the chief seats of the movement, but it soon spread to Rome, and gained many adherents there.　For some time the

[1] Polyb. VI 56, XXXVII 9. See Mahaffy, *Greek Life and Thought* chapter XXII.

state took no steps to suppress it, though it was matter of common knowledge, and in impunity it took worse and worse forms: wild nightly orgies, with immoralities that shocked a not too squeamish public, and, it was said, occasional murders. Such an organization offered facilities for secret conspiracy, a danger that the Roman government was prone to suspect and prompt to encounter. At last certain information[1] was laid before one of the consuls, who secured his evidence and laid the matter before the Senate. That body was thoroughly alarmed. Here was a secret association, including persons of all classes, extending over Italy no one knew how far, consisting largely of women, indeed in its early stages confined to women, at least in Rome. Its influence might have stolen into any man's house, and he not know it. The consuls were commissioned to hold an inquiry with full powers in Rome and through Italy: arrests, rewards to informers, and executions of the guilty, went on with ruthless energy: but it took about five years before the evil was stamped out. Thousands were put to death, and strict regulations made to prevent excesses in the future. The last district purged was the South of Italy. It so happens that the famous bronze tablet inscribed with a copy of the order of the Senate on the subject was found in that very neighbourhood.

656. Hardly had this scandal been suppressed with a heavy hand, when a strange story of another kind bore witness to the unseen influences at work beneath the surface of Roman life. This was the unearthing of what purported to be[2] the 'Books of Numa,' buried in a stone chest in a garden beyond the Tiber. They were written on paper (*charta*), a material probably not used in Italy in the traditional age of the priest-king; and looked like new, which could hardly be reconciled with a burial of some 500 years. Seven were in Latin, dealing with religious institutions, particularly the duties of the pontiffs: seven in Greek, of a 'philosophical' character, probably concerned with interpretation of rules ascribed to Numa. A praetor glanced at their contents, and, when the matter came before the Senate, offered to declare on oath that their tendency was subversive of the state religion. The House voted this enough, and by its order the books were publicly burnt. It was said that the principles of the 'philosophy' were Pythagorean. This must be taken in connexion with the fact that Greek writers who made up the current narratives of Regal Rome strove to gain credit for an asserted intercourse between Numa and Pythagoras, in defiance of received

---

[1] The story of the discovery in Livy XXXIX 8 foll. is an interesting romance.

[2] The various versions of this story may be found in Livy XL 29 with Weissenborn's notes.

chronology. The mystical Pythagorean school, once very powerful as a brotherhood in southern Italy, had hardly died out in Tarentum Ennius had perhaps come into contact with it there during his boyhood. Some of his works shewed traces[1] of its influence and one book, the *Epicharmus*, was distinctly Pythagorean. That the 'Books of Numa' were a forgery admits little doubt. That they represented an attempt to smuggle 'philosophy' into Rome, as a substitute for ancestral precedent and religious law, is an inference[2], but a probable one.

657. The uneasiness of the Senate, aroused by these discoveries, strengthened the hands of those who would gladly have got rid of Greek influences altogether, and were at least resolved to check the promulgation of doctrines tending to upset the state religion and perhaps the state itself. A stray notice[3] tells us that in 173 two Epicureans were expelled from Rome for introducing strange pleasures, that is for preaching Pleasure as the rule and guide of life, a philosophy deemed unwholesome for the Roman youth. Again in 161 we hear[4] of a decree of the Senate instructing a praetor to expel philosophers and rhetoricians generally. In 155 occurred the famous embassy[5] of the three philosophers from Athens. While the business of their mission hung fire, they gave lectures in the city, to which the Roman youth flocked, attracted by the intellectual treat of listening to ingenious discourses, particularly those of Carneades. But the sceptical tone of these addresses—Carneades maintained a principle one day and refuted it the next—became known, and Cato persuaded the Senate to hasten its decision, in order to send the envoys home and allow the unsettled youths to resume obedience to Roman magistrates and laws. The story is quite credible, and the alarm of the old-Roman school was fully justified, but it was a hopeless task to strive against the stream. Cato[6] might warn his son to beware of the slippery incorrigible Greeks, whose literature was on the way to taint the Roman mind, while their physicians avenged on Roman bodies the subjection of Greece. Nothing could be effected by measures of exclusion or words of warning: the hard shell of old Romanism was cracked, and Hellenism, entering from many sides, conquered its conquerors with its native charm.

658. In the first place there were the two general influences

---

[1] Reid on Cic. *Acad. pr.* II § 51, Conington on Persius VI 10.

[2] Preller, *Röm. Mythol.* vol. II part 12.

[3] Preserved in Aelian *var. hist.* IX 12 and Athenaeus XII 68 (547 *a*).

[4] Sueton. *de rhet.* I, Gellius XV 11.

[5] Lactantius *Inst.* V 14, Plut. *Cato* 22, Pliny *NH* VII 112, and references in Ritter and Preller, *hist. phil.*

[6] Jordan's *Cato* p. 77.

of Art and Literature. At intervals new consignments of works of art, acquired in wars, reached Rome: by the end of this period they must have been very numerous. Appreciation of these treasures grew more slowly, but at least they aroused some interest. Latin adaptations and versions of Greek plays were plentiful. Tragedy was represented by Ennius (died 169) and Pacuvius (died 132), comedy by Plautus (died 184), whose plays kept the stage, and Terence (died young 159), not to mention minor writers. P. Terentius Afer, born at Carthage, was a slave at Rome. His indulgent master educated him and gave him his freedom. As freedman he turned playwright, working as a close imitator of the Athenian New Comedy: at least four of his six plays are from Menander. His talents gained him admission to the select circle that gathered round Scipio Aemilianus. His chief literary merit was the purity of his Latin style. Scandal suggested[1] that he was helped by Scipio and Laelius: his ambiguous defence was to welcome the suspicion as a compliment. What concerns us here is that he kept up the supply of Greek ideas to the Roman public, and that the morals of the New Comedy were essentially lax. Even more important was the rapid spread of the Greek language in the homes of the upper classes. The Roman nobles were becoming conscious that they had to deal with a far wider world than that open to their fathers, and the better men desired to enlarge the mental horizon of their sons. The elder Scipio and Flamininus were both greatly influenced by contact with Greek books and men. Paullus[2] gave his sons, in addition to their Roman training, a thorough education by Greek teachers. Cato himself, who scented corruption in everything Greek, knew something of Greek literature, and learnt to read the language: whether this was only in his old age, as we are told, is more than doubtful. The two Gracchi, the active reformers of the next period, were trained under Greek tutors in the present. Such was the fashion of the time, and no doubt many parents left their sons in the hands of the teachers and did not, like[3] Cato Paullus and Cornelia, supervise their education themselves. We need not wonder that Greek philosophers lecturing in Rome found in the Roman youths an intelligent audience.

659. Whatever Cato and others might say, the superiority of the Greeks in the world of thought had ceased to be a matter of question. Gallus, who foretold the eclipse before Pydna, was undoubtedly a student of Greek astronomy as well as literature. Indeed all special

---

[1] Teuffel-Schwabe §§ 108, 109. See prologue to the *Adelphoe*.

[2] Plutarch *Aemil.* 6.

[3] The devotion of Cato to his son's education was remarkable. Plutarch *Cato* 20. His literate slave Chilon was no doubt a Greek.

technical studies, with perhaps the exception of agriculture, were now based on Greek research, of which the great centre was Alexandria. But the discussion of questions relative to man as an individual or as a member of society was more momentous than any other innovation of Greek origin, for it involved the reconsideration of the traditional standards of duty. Public lectures might be forbidden. But it was not possible to regulate the conversation in private houses or to prevent serious and responsible men from enjoying the company of clever and well-informed Greeks. The most famous centre of the new enlightenment was the 'Scipionic circle,' a gathering of friends, chiefly at the house of Aemilianus, where some of the best men in Rome met to talk over ethical and political questions. The leading mind was Panaetius of Rhodes, a Stoic philosopher versatile enough to tone down the stiffness of his school and adapt its principles to the practical needs of society. The subtle Greek no doubt knew that to make his hearers pleased with themselves was the surest means of influence, and to draw him out on his special topics would be a main feature of these social gatherings. Another notable figure[1] was Polybius, inferior to no man of the age in varied experience of affairs, and an acute observer of the qualities of states and men. He too knew how to handle his Roman patrons, and his admiration of Rome would disarm all suspicion of any criticisms he might offer. Other talented Greeks would now and then as guests bear a part in the intellectual picnic, but these two were themselves well able to set the company a-thinking. The centre of the circle was the rich virtuous and dignified Scipio, earnest and accomplished, but apt at times to dissemble his powers, and master of a dry humour that suited well with his position as the unofficial chairman. Good temper and good manners were promoted by the presence of the gentle and cheerful Laelius, whose mellow discretion became a proverb. Among the other lights of this constellation were P. Furius Philus (consul 136), an orator of some repute, M'. Manilius the jurist, Terence and Pacuvius the dramatists, Lucilius the maker of Roman satire, and some younger men such as C. Fannius the historian, P. Rutilius Rufus the soldier lawyer and historian, and Q. Aelius Tubero, one of the most perverse of the perverse Roman Stoics. The juniors mostly made their mark in the next period, but this was the time in which their characters were developed. Stoicism especially gave the tone to this society, and some of its members, such as Rufus, made it the guide of an upright and noble life. This system, more easily than others, blended

---

[1] Mahaffy, *Greek Life and Thought* chapter 22, points out that Polybius never mentions Panaetius, and acutely suggests jealousy as the cause. I think he is right, but the fragmentary state of Polybius' history is not to be forgotten.

with Roman notions of steadfastness and duty, and was destined to
a long and glorious career in Rome as the creed of choice spirits
in evil times.   But none the less it acted as a solvent of old notions,
for its rationalized theories superseded inherited rules, and the very
men most fitted to uphold the *mos maiorum* were those whom Stoicism
was most likely to attract.

660.   If Romanism was dying in the best society, overpowered by
influences in themselves wholesome and refined, it was threatened
with speedy destruction from below.   It was bad enough that in rural
life the free farmer was giving place to that hopeless and desperate
chattel, the rural slave.   Far worse was the foul corruption that the
increase of slavery was bringing into domestic life.   In the houses
of the rich the demand for sturdy men servants was as yet small:
a porter and one or two able-bodied attendants to see their lord safe
through the racket and scuffle of the streets or meetings (litters
were hardly in use in Rome as a vehicle till later, at least for men)
would about make up the list.   The service of the kitchen, the table,
and the toilet, was beginning to employ numbers of menials, who had
endless opportunities of ingratiating themselves with the master and
mistress.   Young handsome slaves of both sexes were already beginning to be kept as pets, and to command prices in the market
at which Cato held up hands of horror.   And all this pampered crew,
Graeco-orientals for the most part, were wholly at the mercy of their
owner.   Slave-owners recognise their common interest, so no help
was to be looked for near at hand: the bondman's old home was far
away; his relatives powerless: in a few years he would be forgotten
even there.   Supple and submissive, they accepted their lot, and set
themselves to lighten the yoke by ingenious use of their talents.
From gratifying the wishes of their owners it was an easy step to
create in them new desires and then provide the satisfaction.   Vainly
did Cato lament the passing away of good old times when a man
paid more for a horse than a cook.   Gluttony and other vices spread
apace, for the Roman once roused was apt to take his pleasures with
a riotous appetite, to which his slaves ministered with the mature
vitiosity of the East.   But in no respect were the oriental slaves more
mischievous than in their treatment of the young.   It was their
immediate interest to curry favour with the rising generation, and
their means of doing so was a course of indulgence and secret con-
nivances, demoralizing from the first, and becoming worse as the
children grew up.   Such parents as Paullus and Cornelia would keep
good slaves and watch them sharply.   Cato, hard and indifferent
as a master, was most careful to guard his son from all corrupting
influences.   But these were exceptional cases, and it is because they

were remarkable that the record of them has survived. In the matter of religious innovation there can be little doubt that the influx of eastern superstitions took place largely by way of the slave-market. The ladies were most affected by this influence, which probably had something to do with the spread of the Bacchanalian rites.

661. While we are speaking of slavery, it may be well to note the way in which that institution pervaded all departments of life. The Greek physician or surgeon had his staff of trained slaves as assistants, the shipowner his slave-seamen, the banker his clerks, the contractor his men skilled in the engineering and building trades: already capital was beginning to seek returns by developing the individual aptitudes of slaves. Caught young and trained as artisan, clerk, cook, actor, dancer, gladiator, elementary teacher, or what not, the slave could be either sold at a price that gave a good profit or let out at a rent to anyone in need of his services. Some slaves were allowed to ply their trade for themselves, the owner having of course a first charge on the profits: only trustworthy fellows would be allowed to hire themselves from their masters like this. By time-honoured custom a slave was allowed to acquire by industry and thrift a little property (*peculium*) of his own, with which he could buy his freedom, or, if his master waived all claim to the recovery of capital sunk, employ to start himself in business on his own account. Manumission was common, for it suited both parties: the slave was naturally eager to become his own[1] owner, while his master might find a considerable balance of advantage in his own favour. He had reaped the profit of the best working years of the man's life, and was spared the expense of maintaining him in old age. He did not want to treat him inhumanly, for humanity went for something even in the hard world of Rome: so he generously endowed the man with the dregs of himself, and got rid of a prospective encumbrance with an air of respectability that was eminently Roman. And the freedman remained bound to his old master by a strong customary tie. This might take the form of stipulated services or gifts on domestic occasions, but always included a general obligation to back up his patron in politics or the law courts. It was no small advantage to have the support of a number of such dependants, and we have seen above that the question of the freedmen's franchise was one of the most important political issues. Freedmen often continued in the employ of their patrons as

---

[1] From being *servus* of a *dominus* he became *libertus* of a *patronus*. The term *libertinus* properly connotes a man's public status, and includes the *libertus* of a patron and his son. In the third generation the son of a *libertinus* ranked as *ingenuus*. This is the literary usage. Strictly speaking, the man who had not himself been a slave was *ingenuus*. See §633, Mommsen *Staatsrecht* III 421—3.

agents, particularly in financial concerns.   The capitalist thus secured
an able representative, and even a senator like Cato could thus evade
the spirit of the Claudian[1] law and dabble in trade.   The mention of
Cato[2] may remind us that he was a typical Roman slave-owner,
business-like and hard, without a trace of sentiment.   He kept many
slaves, male and female, under strict discipline.   He even regulated
their pairing, and forbade promiscuity, doubtless with a view to
breeding, for the ranks of slavery were to some extent recruited by
this means.

662.   The great majority of slaves were bought in the market.
Of the two main sources of supply, the sale of prisoners of war was
in this period important, but it worked fitfully.   Alternations of glut
and dearth must have caused great fluctuations of prices.   A more
regular supply, though as yet probably less plentiful, was derived
from the time-honoured pursuit of kidnapping, which in the next
period[3] reached its height in the able hands of the Cilician pirates.
Frontier raids and wars, brigandage on the routes of travel by land,
descents on coast districts and robbery on the high seas, not to
mention occasional tragedies due to private hatred and revenge, all
left human beings at the mercy of ruffians who either had captured
their victims for sale or had an interest in selling them.   Once sold,
they passed from dealer to dealer till they found masters who wanted
them for their labour, and with the successive steps of the process all
hope (if any) of redemption faded utterly away.   We have seen what
became of them, good or bad, in domestic servitude.   Far worse was
the lot of those drafted off to work on some large country estate:
a degree worse still that of the poor wretches who, having been tried
as house-slaves and found unsuitable, were transferred to their lord's
familia rustica as a punishment.   We have already referred to the
disastrous changes that came over Italian agriculture in this period.
With the economic conditions in their favour, more and more of the
country was thrown into large estates (*latifundia*), to the growth of
which the elder Pliny[4], looking back from the first century A.D.,
traced the ruin of Italy.   Etruria in the northern half of the peninsula,

[1] See §§ 259, 397.

[2] The description of Cato's domestic life and his management of slaves and other investments, his pooling system against maritime risks etc., transmitted to us by Plutarch *Cato*
20—1, is a most interesting picture.

[3] Lange *RA* § 132 thinks that the *lex Fabia de plagiariis* was probably passed in 183, but
the date is quite uncertain.   In any case, to judge from the comments of later jurists in
Digest XLVIII 15, the man-stealing (*plagium*) forbidden in that law seems to have been
mainly the seducing harbouring etc. another man's slave with dishonest intent, not the
sale or purchase, knowingly, of a free man ; though that also was included.

[4] Plin. *NH* XVIII §§ 35—6.   Of course he was not the first to see this.   Compare the
famous passage of Lucan I 167—70, and Mayor on Juvenal XIV 159 foll.

with much of the South, particularly Lucania, were the chief seats of the new system. At the head of each rural unit was an overseer (*vilicus*), himself a slave, depending on the results of his management for the retention of his favoured position. He was under the strongest inducement to exact the maximum of work from the gang of slaves who formed his farm-hands: if he could at the same time rob his master a little, he would only be doing as others. The life of the common slaves reached the depths of human misery. Fed on the same principles as the other beasts used in agriculture, often compelled to work in chains by way of lessening the cost of super-intendence, shut up at night in noisome barracoons (*ergastula*), ever liable to the scourge and other tortures, their only hope of release lay in death, their only security for mercy in the fact of their being so much locked-up capital. A runaway slave had little or no chance of escape, and when caught he was branded on the forehead with an F (for *fugitivus*) or otherwise marked. Incorrigible contumacy might lead to his being sold to a trainer of gladiators for the edification of the Roman people; or he might serve as a warning to his fellow slaves by being burnt alive or crucified on the spot. The evidence of these last extremities comes from later times, but there is no reason to suppose that there was less barbarity in this period. Of course there were differences in the management of estates. Some masters were less heartless than others, or more early convinced of the poor economic results of labour carried on under conditions of despair. Such men would require their bailiffs to see that better work brought with it some small bettering of condition, and to double the effect of punishment by possibilities of reward. But the typical big landlord was a rich noble who wanted money for purposes of luxury or political ambition. He seldom if ever visited his distant estates, and in the splendid preoccupations of Rome took little thought of the horrors perpetrated with his sanction in the country side.

663. The brutal inefficiency of slave labour cooperated with the influx of cheap foreign corn to discourage the growth of cereal crops, and there was in this period a marked tendency to give up tillage for grazing. But in Italy nature enjoins a systematic change of pasturage, the hills in summer, the plain in winter. This shifting of quarters made the slave-herdsman difficult to watch, and introduced him to a large stretch of country. If he joined others to rob passers-by, his knowledge of the ground made it hard to find the offender. There was no rural police, and his master's bailiff was not concerned to protect travellers. Moreover the use of weapons, to guard his master's property (himself included) against wild beasts, roused in him feelings unsuited to a slave. Here we have the origins of the

brigandage with which Italy was infested in the next age, and which multiplied the fighting strength of the rebel gladiators under Spartacus. But much land was still under cultivation. The old population, living on and from the land, still remained in the mountainous districts of Central Italy, and the great plain[1] of the Po seems to have been full of prosperous farmers. But agriculture, at least on the estates of men of substance, was more and more turning to the vine and olive as sources of profit, and for the management of these crops great skill and patience were required. Clearly an estate of moderate size, not too far from Rome to enjoy the frequent inspection of the master's eye, was the best suited for this form of enterprise.

664. It would seem to be estates of this class that Cato had in view when he wrote his treatise on agriculture. The book has come down to us in a text perhaps modernized in respect of language, and probably not complete. At least the precept from which Vergil is said[2] to have borrowed his preference for intensive cultivation does not appear. It is a curious work, jerky and dogmatic in form, economical and profit-seeking in spirit; in short, Roman to the core. His advice as to the choice of a situation and the cautious observation of all local circumstances, including the condition of neighbouring farms, before buying the land, reeks of experience: so does his injunction not to overbuild but keep farm and farmstead (*fundus, villa*) in due proportion. Indeed chips of common-sense are not rare in the book. Sentiment is of course not to be expected. Everything not wanted for use on the estate should be sold off at once: with the rest of the surplus or worn-out live and dead stock thus got rid of are included slaves inefficient through disease or age. But nothing is more remarkable than the care interest and forethought[3] required from the master himself. If he kept an eye on all the points to which Cato calls his attention, he would be a busy man, a practical farmer with little time to spare for other things such as politics. Surely the portrait of the pattern *dominus* of this treatise is in the main that of Cato himself, for as to the merits of himself as a model the old censor entertained, and expressed, no doubt whatever. Proud as he was of his old-fashioned frugality, of which he boasted till men were weary of the subject, he is all for making the residential part of his country-house comfortable. 'If your country quarters are good,' he says,

---

[1] A letter (III 19) of the younger Pliny shews that in this district about 100 A.D. slavery only appeared in a mild form, and that the plantation-system with its chained gangs was unknown. This had probably long been the case, perhaps always.

[2] Servius on Verg. *georg.* II 412—3 *laudato ingentia rura, exiguum colito.* See Pliny *NH* XVIII §§ 35—7.

[3] Many of the instructions are meant for the *vilicus*, but it is clear that the *dominus* is to see that they are carried out.

'you will go there more often, and enjoy your stay.' He urges the wisdom of keeping on good terms with the neighbours—the landlords of course. Gossip said that he drank freely on convivial occasions: but to some persons in most ages this has been a phase of the simple life.

665. Even an imperfect list of details will give a better notion of the kind of farming contemplated by Cato. Of fruit trees he has the vine, olive, fig, apple, pear, and some nuts. Among other trees he grows or uses the oak, elm, pine, ilex, poplar, cypress, plane, and willow. The leaves of some serve as both fodder and litter for the live stock, but hay and other fodder-crops are not neglected, and the straw of wheat and barley furnishes litter. Cabbages, beans, and other vegetables indicate a productive kitchen garden. The milk of various domesticated animals is drunk or made into cheese: honey was the regular sweetener of ancient cookery. Among the live stock we meet with oxen, sheep, pigs, horses, asses, mules, geese, and fowls. We do not wonder at Cato's concern for the efficiency of the watch-dogs, or at the rations of his slaves being raised in the seasons of most labour and reduced in slack times. The elaborate variety of the work carried on is witnessed by the astounding catalogue of dead stock declared to be necessary for the business. The outhouses must have covered no small extent of ground. The machines, such as wine-presses, olive-presses, the endless tools for various purposes, the vats, jars, pitchers, buckets, basins, baskets, ropes and string, leathern thongs, and a host of other things, make up a bewildering list. The *vilicus* and (by the master's leave his consort) the *vilica* had no sinecure in the mere charge of all this plant, for nothing must be lost and everything must be in working order. In case of default this highly responsible couple would no doubt soon be reminded[1] that they (and their children) were slaves. Into the details of farming operations the writer goes minutely: ploughing, digging, sowing, harrowing, weeding, pruning, cutting and picking, and the rest. Irrigation is characteristic of Italy, and manuring includes the use of lime, accessible in most parts of the country. Grazing is important, and it may be profitable sometimes to have a pasture to let. Now and then you may find it well to get a job carried out by a contractor, perhaps the owner of a slave gang. Cleaning is constantly going on, and at most times of the year things are being made ready for coming seasons. Far-sighted activity and avoidance of waste appear everywhere. Household medicine is represented by a number of prescriptions for common ailments, and the veterinary side is not forgotten. The kitchen claims some receipts, and you are

---

[1] See Cic. II *in Verr.* III § 119.

told how to keep moths from the cloths and weevils from the corn. The goodwill of the gods is of course essential: but, speaking generally, this is the master's concern. The bailiff and his wife are to perform a few ceremonies at certain seasons, but beyond this they are to let religion alone. The importance of the right person doing exactly the right thing in the right way is recognised by prescribing the proper materials for purifications and sacrifices, and the proper forms of words to be used on several occasions. After all, buying and selling, though dismissed in few words, were certainly not the last thoughts of this close-fisted old Roman. He notes the various markets in which clothing waggons implements etc. are most advantageously to be bought: as for selling, one of his reasons for being on good terms with neighbours is that it is a help in disposing of your produce. One of his pithy sayings is that a landlord's business is not so much to buy as to sell.

666. Whether there were many estates of the sort and size to which Cato's treatise would apply, is just what we do not know. We can well imagine him, with his constitution of iron and energy that never flagged, hurrying from the city to his farm, auditing and overhauling, and posting back to Rome for a debate in the Senate, to address a mass meeting on some proposed legislation, or to take part in some trial. But Cato was a most exceptional person. Of two such lives as those led by him, one would be enough for most men, and it is probable that the country seats of Roman nobles were already as a rule more for pleasure and less for business than the ideal estate of Cato. Of course a man might own one or more large estates at a distance, besides having a pleasant *villa* within easy reach of Rome. In any case the slaves employed on farm work in gangs were a new and evil element in rural life. Their mere numbers made impossible[1] the old traditional personal relation between them and their masters. And they were a motley crew, Thracians Syrians Epirotes Sards Gauls and what not. Cato deliberately promoted jealousies and dissension among his slaves by way of facilitating their control. The saying *quot servi tot hostes* perhaps gained currency in this period, and of the rural slaves it would be true enough. Even under a kind master and an honest bailiff the total denial of choice was a brutalizing environment. It was reserved for the jurists of the Empire, under the influence of Stoicism, to guide imperial legislation to the announcement that a slave had certain rights. For the present slavery only came into touch with law as a form of property. But, while the domestic slave of the town house had a good chance of

---

[1] Plut. *Cato* 3 makes Cato work and take his meals with his slaves. But this refers only to his younger days, and was already so exceptional as to attract attention.

freedom and citizenship, the *familia rustica* were, with very rare exceptions, simply beasts, so much bone and muscle used up for the enrichment of their owners.   Nor did the action of the Senate, concerned to revive decaying agriculture, effect any real good.   After the taking of Carthage, the question arose, what was to be done with the Punic libraries[1] found in Africa.   There was no demand for Phoenician books at Rome, so the bulk of these collections were presented, not to the Punic towns such as Utica, but to the Numidian princes.   One work, the great treatise of one Mago on agriculture, was kept and translated into Latin by a body of expert scholars. But the Carthaginian farming was a system based on slave-labour, and this was the canker of Italy.   That the book was of some use to somebody may be gathered from the Greek versions and adaptations[2] which were made somewhat later, but as a cure for the evils of the *latifundia* it was useless.   One precept[3] of Mago's is cited: 'when you buy a landed estate, sell your town house,' that is, become a resident landlord.   But this was just what the up-to-date Roman noble had no intention of doing.

667.   We have shewn how slavery was driving out free labour in the country.   The same was taking place in the manual trades, though we hear less of it.   Rome had never really been an industrial centre of importance, and old prejudices against bodily labour other than agriculture helped to give over handicrafts to the slave-artisan. The freeman is never found to work contentedly beside the slave. Slaves were no doubt increasing in numbers, and it seems that some decrease of the free population was in progress.   If our records may be trusted, there was a drop in the citizen roll[4] at the census of 174—3, and again in 159—8, 154—3, 147—6, 136—5.   Though ignorance of the number of births and deaths, of manumissions, of the actual working of the measures for excluding Latins, forbid any exact conclusions, we may fairly accept the tendency to decrease as a fact.   Indeed if we try to discover what were the occupations of ordinary Roman citizens in this period, we come upon three lines of life, (*a*) soldiering with an eye to profit, (*b*) finance, including a certain amount of commerce, (*c*) acquiescent pauperism.   The first was to some extent compatible with the other two: the second was a possible development, the third a means of vacation.   This leads us to the question of the city mob.   The genuine Roman element in it seems to have consisted mainly of migrants from the country districts and disbanded soldiers, loth to turn to regular industry in

---

[1] Pliny *NH* XVIII § 22.   [2] Varro *de re rustica* I § 1.
[3] Pliny *NH* XVIII § 35.
[4] See the discussion in Beloch's *Bevölkerung der Griechisch-Römischen Welt*, chapter 8.

time of peace. By what odd employments these men may have eked
out a living we do not know. It is probable that the later form of
clientship, the mere dependence of the poor as poor upon the rich
as rich, the quest of corporal sustenance rather than social protection,
was already beginning. Cheap corn was naturally in great demand,
and to keep the hungry mob quiet it was provided at half or even
one fourth of the market price by the curule aediles even so early
as the years 201—196. This corn-supply was destined to become
one of the most ruinous burdens on the state treasury, and a ready
weapon of demagogues. An occasional means of profit might be
found by the pauper citizen in the sale of his vote, as the laws against
bribery attest. But this would in practice not come to much. And
we must not forget that for a large part of the year the warmth of
the southern sun makes a full diet unnecessary if not distasteful.
There were no doubt some men of better mould who got tired of idle
indigence, and could tear themselves away from the city for the sake
of a more active life elsewhere. The student of Roman history would
be glad to know more particulars of the colonial foundations of
this period; what classes of citizens took part in them; how far they
served to relieve the pressure of the Roman mob; whether a single
individual, once thoroughly habituated to urban life, was willing to
exchange its various distractions for the dead monotony of some
coast-town in the South or the cultivation of a farm in Cisalpine
Gaul. But on these points our record is silent. We know that Latin
colonies had to be given up, and that even citizen colonies were not
always easy to fill. We may perhaps fairly guess that the men who
went were on the average better than those who remained in Rome.
To the thinning-out of the better citizens of Roman parentage and
Roman traditions, to the corruption of the urban residuum, coupled
with the increase of the freedman element, we may probably assign
the chief part in the undoubted degradation of what passed for the
Roman people. Whether the draining of the Pomptine marshes,
undertaken[1] in 160, was really carried out, and, if so, whether any
poor citizens were provided with farms there, we cannot tell: at any
rate the land was swamp again in the time of Julius Caesar.

668.   But the populace of Rome had not only to be fed somehow:
it was idle, and had to be amused. The first beginnings of shows[2] or
games (*ludi*) at Rome were very ancient. Tradition carries them

---

[1] As stated in Livy epit. 46.

[2] The two festivals included in the earliest calendar celebrated with *ludi* (horse races),
the *Equirria* and *Consualia*, were in honour of the gods Mars and Consus, protectors of
horses. See Friedländer in Marquardt's *Staatsverwaltun*ℊ, Vol. III, and W. W. Fowler,
Roman Festivals, index.

back to the Regal period. The public *ludi* were a form of religious festival, connected with appropriate rites, and even the earliest may have begun as 'votive' games, performed in fulfilment of a vow. Such seems to have been the case with the great games with which we are here concerned, for occasional festivals tended to become annual. They were as follows—

Festival	Founded	Superintended by
(1) *ludi magni* or *Romani*...	in Regal period	consuls till 366, then transferred to curule aediles.
(2) *ludi plebeii*	220	plebeian aediles.
(3) *ludi Ceriales*	before 202	plebeian aediles.
(4) *ludi Apollinares*	212, regular from 208	city praetor.
(5) *ludi Megalenses*............	204	curule aediles.
(6) *ludi Florales*	240 or 238, regular from 173	curule aediles.

We observe that the establishment of these public festivals falls chiefly in the period after the first Punic war and during the second. Rome was already a great power, but underwent great trials. Probably the religious motive was dominant. What took place in the period 201—134 B.C. was not the multiplication of festivals, but the increase of the duration and splendour of those existing. This arose from the practices (*a*) of adding days to a festival, thus permanently increasing its length, (*b*) of renewal (*instauratio*), a repetition of the whole or part of a festival on the ground of some flaw in the formalities of a performance, (*c*) of humouring the growing appetite for magnificence and excitement. The last of these was from time to time stimulated by the splendour of the great triumphs of conquering generals: the masses were less easily pleased nowadays, and he who would win their favour must content them. Extensions too and renewals were promoted by the same interest, more and more as religion became the servant of politicians. Thus the *ludi Romani*, originally lasting one day, rose to ten days in the first half of this period, afterwards to more. As for the events, we can only note here that horse and chariot races composed the show in early times: scenic displays began in 364, and became regular since 240, when Livius Andronicus began to exhibit. Other shows were added later. But the introduction of spectacular novelties generally began, not in the regular yearly festivals, but in the games vowed by generals in momentous campaigns, and often carried out some little time after

the triumph. They were usually very splendid, and served to remind
a forgetful multitude of achievements already somewhat stale. We
hear[1] of the first appearance of Greek athletes in 186, and of a wild
beast fight or hunt (*venatio*) at the same time. Both these novelties
were at votive games. The military show[2] or tournament was not
improbably introduced on some such occasion; perhaps also the
Greek 'artists,' singers and dancers and the like, gathered from
Eastern lands. The regular place for these shows was the Circus.
An attempt to erect a permanent theatre for scenic representations
was made more than once in this period, but without effect: it seems
that the Senate[3] thought this move contrary to public morality, and
what was built was pulled down again. So temporary wooden erections
were the rule for about a century more.

669. Demoralizing many of these entertainments surely were,
as for instance the indecencies of the actresses (slaves under orders)
at the *ludi Florales*. But nothing was so bad as the blood-shows
of gladiators (slaves again) set to kill each other. These were, and
long remained, an irregular private affair. They took place[4] at a
funeral, and were essentially a survival of a very ancient notion that
such offerings contributed to the honour and comfort of the dead.
We have noted their first introduction from Etruria in 264. No
spectacle so quickly and completely took the fancy of the Roman
populace as this, and to give an exhibition of the kind was a sure
road to the favour of the mob. We hear[5] that at a performance of
the *Hecyra* of Terence a rumour of gladiators emptied the house.
Stray notices shew that this form of 'sport' was being greatly
developed in this period. More shows were given, and on some
occasions the number of pairs fighting was very large. At the funeral
of Flamininus in 174 his son provided a great solemn feast for the
people, including meat: he gave a dramatic entertainment: above all,
he exhibited 37 pairs of swordsmen. We hear[6] that in a space of
three days 74 men fought; whether survivors of the first pairs were
pitted against each other, and so on, we are not told. Clearly this
horrible custom was now well established, and regular schools of
fencing, with elaborate training on a full diet, already existed, as in
the following period. Perhaps it was already a mode of investing
capital to buy up numbers of able-bodied captives and keep them,

---

[1] Livy XXXIX 22.   [2] See Livy XLIV 9.

[3] See the details in Marquardt Vol. III. This demolition is particularly attested in the
case of the year 154. Livy epit. 48. I suspect the use of theatres in Greek cities as convenient places for demagogues to address mass meetings had something to do with the
Senate's view.

[4] See in particular Polyb. XXXII 14.   [5] Prologue to *Hecyra*.

[6] Livy XLI 28. See also XXXI 50, XXXIX 46.

ready trained, to meet a demand certain to occur before long. For a good swordsman was not made in a day, the wastage was great, and politicians seeking office were ready to pay long prices for a finished article. The time was coming when the exploits of a successful gladiator would be one of the commonest topics of conversation. We have seen that Antiochus Epiphanes, by way of creating a Roman atmosphere in his capital city, transplanted this institution to Antioch. There were as yet no amphitheatres in Rome: the regular place of these shows was the Forum.

670. What strikes us in these blood-shows is their brutalizing tendency. Roman opinion rather viewed them as a means of educating the people to look death in the face, and in Roman literature the gladiator appears as an example of manly courage. That this entitled him to the treatment of a man rather than a brute was a conclusion not to be drawn under a system such as ancient slavery, and not reached in effect until dominant Christianity introduced new standards to determine the value of human lives. But to Roman statesmen of serious views the cause of anxiety was rather in the public games held in the name of the state, and this on the ground of expense. The treasury contributed large sums for the purpose: in 200 the sum was not even fixed in the case of some votive games, but this careless policy was not long maintained. In 179 a consul had a vow of this kind to discharge after victories in Spain. He had some money in hand, he said, subscribed by Spaniards. In voting a sum from the state chest the Senate followed its own precedent of 187, limiting the amount to about £800 of our money. Furthermore they ordered him[1] not to transgress a recent decree of the House, passed in 182 to prevent the exaction of contributions from Allies in Italy and subjects in the Provinces. The offender on that occasion had been the aedile Gracchus, afterwards consul in 177 and censor in 169, one of the best Romans of the day. If he wrung money out of the Allies to promote his own political ambition, what must bad men have done as provincial praetors? The exaction of these 'voluntary' gifts towards Roman shows tended to cause discontent and so make trouble for the government. But the practice continued, and in the next period became a crying evil. It was not confined to lands directly administered by Rome: dependent kings and states had subscribed[2] towards the games given by L. Scipio Asiagenus in 186. But most serious of all was the outlay from the private purses of the givers of all these shows. The aedile spent far more than the state allowance, and the private exhibitor had no allowance at all. To prevent this mad competition in extravagance was impossible. Fortunes were

---

[1] Livy XL 44 with Weissenborn's notes.   [2] Livy XXXIX 22 §§ 8—10.

wasted in this way, and the need of recouping themselves for their outlay only served to impel the Roman nobles to further acts of extortion abroad.

671. A very few words must suffice as to the outward aspect of Rome in this period, and the habits of the people. No doubt the houses of the rich were gradually becoming larger and finer as wealth poured in and social life was affected by foreign influences. But this change would be almost wholly internal: so far as the streets went, the appearance of the city was probably as yet homely enough. The paving of roadways with blocks of lava (*silex*) was begun. A small stretch of the Appian way outside the walls was laid in 189, and a considerable extent of city streets in 174. The piers[1] of a new bridge over the Tiber were built in 179, but the arches were not added till 142. Perhaps a temporary gangway of wood from pier to pier served for use in the meantime. The left bank of the river, below the Aventine and outside the walls, had probably long been a favourite spot for discharging the cargoes of vessels brought up stream. In 193 a quay was built there, and to accommodate the growing volume of business the place[2] was in 174 paved with flags (*lapide*, probably travertine), and the river-wall made good and fitted with steps. The great trade in imported corn had its centre here. Various improvements in the city markets during this period shew that the food-supply of Rome was becoming a more and more urgent care. Of aqueducts there were already two, the Appian of 313, and that from the upper Anio of 272—270. In 179 an attempt was made to construct a third, but the refusal[3] of a landlord to let it be carried through his estate wrecked the scheme. In 144 the *aqua Marcia* was built, and delivered water at a higher level than the former ones. The public convenience was consulted in the erection of Halls (*basilicae*) close to the Forum, the centre of public life, the *Basilica Porcia* in 184, the *Fulvia* or *Aemilia* in 179, the *Sempronia* in 169. A public Hall served as a sort of Exchange for buyers and sellers, and at one end it was customary to rail off a space for the accommodation of courts of law, with a platform for the president's seat (*tribunal*) and benches (*subsellia*) for all persons concerned in the case before the court. The Greek name indicates the quarter from which the suggestion of such buildings was derived. These Halls became the resort of loungers. A *porticus* or colonnade erected in 167 seems to have been mainly a shelter or waiting-place. In this period too we hear of the erection of arches (196, 190) (*fornices*), apparently as approaches to public places, adorned with sculptures and no doubt inscribed with the founders' names. These were not as yet 'triumphal' arches, but we may see in

[1] Livy XL 51 § 4.   [2] *emporium*. Livy XXXV 10, XLI 27.   [3] Livy XL 51 § 7.

them the germ of what was in later times a favourite form of Roman monument. Temples were also being built, and in them or on them were placed dedicatory offerings, pictures, statues, inscriptions etc. But with the exception of the Greek works of art, spoils of war, it does not seem that much was done to beautify the city. Greek influences were no doubt modifying the architecture as everything else, but the Romans never acquired the Greek sense of proportion, and the splendour obtained by colossal size, and the use of gorgeous materials from distant lands, belongs to a later age. The increase of the urban population must surely have led to the building of more dwelling-houses. The tall stacks of flats characteristic of the later Rome were probably not known in this period. It is likely that increased accommodation[1] was gained by building an upper storey of wood on a ground-floor of unbaked brick. The lower part would be in danger from floods, the upper from fires; and we hear of great destruction, from the former cause in 193, 192, 189, from the latter in 192 and 178. That fire was a constant menace to the city we need not wonder. Beside the roofs of public buildings, benches and other fittings, there were great numbers of booths stalls and tables, particularly in the centre of the city and near the Forum. And the timber used for temporary stands and scaffolds would often be lying about: the turbulent mobs of the next period seem never to have been at a loss for wood, whether to break heads or to burn the body of some party hero. Round the city ran the old 'Servian' wall, which had been repaired in 212 to withstand Hannibal, but with the growth of Roman supremacy was gradually losing importance as a means of defence.

672. A few details are recorded relative to personal and domestic habits, indicating the growth of smartness and refinement, comfort and luxury. Shaving had been long introduced as an occasional thing, but Scipio Aemilianus[2] set the fashion of a daily shave. Washing for cleanliness sake was hardly yet turned into a luxury. In private houses a supply of warm water was provided by putting a bath-room next the kitchen, with a pipe through the intervening wall. If we may believe Seneca[3], the actual bath-room used by Scipio Africanus in his villa at Liternum was still existing nearly 250 years later. He describes it as a dark and stuffy little hole, moralizes on the simple ways of those good old times, and reminds us that it

---

[1] Diodorus fragm. XXXI 18 § 2 says that Ptolemy Philometor, when expelled from Egypt in 195, came to Rome to seek help, and lodged in a cramped upper chamber, because rents were so high in Rome.

[2] Pliny *NH* VII 211.

[3] See the very interesting passage, Seneca epist. 86 §§ 1—13.

was not customary in Scipio's time to wash all over every day. Arms and legs were washed daily, every eighth day (*nundinae*) was often enough for a full bath. Such were the men of old, hardworking in war and peace, a manly breed. A small beginning was perhaps already made in the way of public baths, which appear[1] as established institutions in the next period. We have heard of one in luxurious Capua at the time of the Hannibalic war. They seem to have entered Rome in very simple forms, one heating apparatus serving two rooms (for men and women) divided by a party-wall. They were worked by lessees, who charged a small fee for their use. Thus another appliance of Greek civilization found its way into Roman life, and the *balneum*[2] (βαλανεῖον) began to supersede the old wash-room (*lavatrina*). An important change in the food-department came in after the war with Perseus: baking, formerly a duty of the women[3] of a household, began to be a regular trade in the city. Not only was the bread got from the baker, but confectionery in the hands of specialists became a profitable art. Great houses might afford a skilled slave to do their baking at home: most people would be glad to be rid of a domestic nuisance. A notice[4] of rather doubtful authority implies that about the middle of this period there was a good deal of drunkenness among the common people, and that the scandal of numbers appearing drunk at public meetings was one of the causes that led to the *lex Fannia* of 161. That is to say, that the extravagance of rich men's banquets was attacked because of the evil effects of their example. We may at least believe that the bad example did harm. But guzzling and swilling were come to stay among the wealthy classes of Rome; and it was not for nothing that one of Ennius' miscellaneous works was a poem on dainties, called 'the art of pleasant eating' (ἡδυφαγητικά), or that in his writings and those of his contemporaries we begin the long long series of Roman references to the gout.

673. To turn to Literature. The fashion of writing history in Greek, set by Fabius Pictor and Cincius Alimentus, still continued. Gaius Acilius, who interpreted in the Senate for the three philosophers' embassy in 155, seems to have written a history of Rome from the earliest times, which was afterwards translated into Latin. Of others we need only mention Postumius Albinus (consul 151), who was foolish enough to claim indulgence for any bad Greek that might be detected in his work: upon which Cato remarked that no one had compelled him to write in Greek at all. But the use of Latin for narra-

---

[1] See Wilkins on Cicero *de Orat.* II § 223.

[2] For *balneum* and *balneae*, private and public baths in the strict sense, see Varro *de lingua Lat.* IX § 68.

[3] Pliny *NH* XVIII § 107.　　　　[4] Quoted by Macrobius *Sat.* III 17 § 4.

tive purposes was established in this period by Cato, the father of Latin prose. His book, called *Origines*, dealt with the foundation and early history of Rome. But his view was not limited to Rome: he himself came from Tusculum, a town long incorporated with the Roman state as a *municipium* but probably still conscious that it had once had a history of its own. So he included in the work the 'origins' or early history of the other peoples of Italy. This would have been a valuable store of ancient traditions, but unhappily only a few fragments[1] of it remain, and many of them not direct quotations. It was clearly a many-sided work, like its author. In the later books it of course became more Roman, and included the Punic and other wars down to the year 149. The bias of the writer no doubt was strongly marked. His spirit appeared in the omission of the names of the generals in some of the later wars, an implied censure of the self-advertisement of the Roman noble families and the vainglory of their records. Beside this work and his book of the farm, Cato wrote Advice to his son, treating of many subjects, and a Collection of good sayings. Like Cato, Cassius Hemina and L. Calpurnius Piso Frugi wrote histories in Latin: the latter was reckoned one of the best authorities among the Roman annalists. Among the great lawyers[2] of the period, in which jurisprudence seems to have made great strides, were a number of remarkable men, such as Sex. Aelius Paetus, called *Catus* (shrewd), M. Junius Brutus, M'. Manilius, P. Mucius Scaevola, and several others, some of whom lived on into the next period. Whether the great Cato is to be reckoned a jurist or not, is a matter of doubt: that he understood the law as a matter of ordinary practice seems certain. That he was one of the great orators of his day is universally admitted. What with politics and the law courts, his tongue was ever busy. He left behind him a number of speeches, 150 or more, which commanded readers for several centuries. Forty-four times, it is said, his enemies brought him to trial, but he won his case every time. Indeed it was probably as an orator that he was best known to the mass of his contemporaries, and some of the little fragments remaining give a vivid notion of his rugged power. His red hair, his grey eyes, his strength of lungs, have been duly recorded by tradition, for all the world saw and heard him. Our danger is rather of forgetting that there were many other great speakers, and that this age was a worthy prelude to the next. Oratory was an art that came to its greatest perfection in Rome during the period from the Gracchi to Cicero. Whatever evils beset the falling Republic the lack of free speech was not one of them. The loss of the works

---

[1] Collected in Jordan's *Cato*.
[2] For these see Roby, *Introduction to Justinian's Digest* chapter VII.

of the Roman orators has probably given us a very unfair view of Roman literature, by removing its most vigorous department from our ken.   Of M. Cornelius Cethegus, who died in 196, we only know that Ennius called him the 'marrow of persuasion.'   Of Scipio Africanus and Gracchus the censor of 169, father of the two reformers, we have the general tradition of eloquence, and the same is the case with Aemilius Paullus, Sulpicius Gallus, and others.   All these men gained their distinction in other ways ; it was not by public speaking that they came to the front.   In the latter half of the period we find the same state of things : indeed it was necessary for any Roman taking part in public life to be able to deliver his opinions in an effective manner.   We hear of Scipio Aemilianus and his friend Laelius, of their political opponent Metellus Macedonicus, of Galba the faithless butcher of the Lusitanians, and others.   A few small fragments[1] of some of these speakers are preserved, just enough to shew that their reputation was probably not beyond their deserts.

674.   Great as was the influence of Hellenism in this period, it is clear that the fear of this movement running to excess, and the effort to keep it within bounds, were not confined to Cato.   One form of this effort may be traced in the interest which was being taken in the Latin language.   The already pregnant vocabulary of this noble tongue was being cleared and enlarged, and its syntax made more flexible : it was fast developing into a literary instrument of the first order.   It seems to have been early in this period that a certain Spurius Carvilius[2] kept a school in Rome.   This man is said to have revised the alphabet, and to have introduced the letter G as a distinct symbol from C.   Of the plays produced by Titinius, bearing Latin names and with the scene laid in Italy (the so-called *togatae*, opposed to those drawn from Greek life, the *palliatae*) we know hardly anything.   National dramas (*praetextae*) with plots drawn from Roman history, first essayed by Naevius, were also produced by M. Pacuvius (220—132) and L. Accius, who was born in 170 and lived far into the next period.   But most of the work of Accius consisted of adaptations from Greek tragedy, and a real national drama never came to ripeness in Rome.   But it is time to leave these scattered notes and turn to the origin of the one department of literature that the Romans claimed as their very own.

675.   The literary career of Gaius Lucilius[3] belongs it is true to

---

[1] See Wordsworth, *Fragments and Specimens of early Latin.*

[2] Freedman of Carvilius, supposed to have been the first Roman to divorce his wife on the ground of barrenness.

[3] The Prolegomena to F. Marx's edition of the remains of Lucilius are a monument of ingenuity and learning.   I have accepted his dates and borrowed several details from him. A few points seem too readily assumed, but the main facts in the life of the satirist are most skilfully established.

the next period. But it was in the present period that he grew up and developed into the man he afterwards shewed himself. He was born at Suessa Aurunca, a Latin colony in the borderland of Latium and Campania, of a wealthy family. Whether he was a Latin[1] himself or not, may be doubted: his brother, the father of Lucilia mother of the famous Pompey, was not only a Roman citizen but a senator. The date of his birth is not certain, but it is now generally[2] placed in 180. When Scipio Aemilianus (born 185) came into his adoptive father's property, he owned estates not far from Suessa and the estates of Lucilius. Scipio had already perhaps the sympathy with the Italian Allies of which he gave proof later. Anyhow it seems certain that he and Lucilius drew together. Scipio was of course the chief in this friendship, and Lucilius the follower: we need not suppose that they were patron and client in the strict sense. When Aemilianus was sent out in 134 to end the Numantine war, he took no legionary levies, but a number[3] of volunteers. Some were sent him by foreign allied states and kings, some were clients from Rome or personal friends. Of the last he formed a trusty bodyguard, and it seems to have been in this select corps[4] that Lucilius served. They were mounted men (*equites*). In the fragments of Lucilius traces of military slang and stable phrases are supposed to be identified. They were no doubt as a rule men of property. The Senate had provided no ready money from the treasury, and Scipio had undertaken the campaign in reliance[5] on his own resources and those of his friends. During the weary siege of fifteen months the wealthy volunteers would be often in contact with the leader of their choice, and Lucilius in particular seems to have become more and more intimate with Scipio. After the fall of Numantia they returned to Rome in time to witness the overthrow of Tiberius Gracchus. Scipio did not approve the scheme of that reformer, and became unpopular with the mob. But he was indisputably the first man in Rome and the circle of his friends was the most brilliant of social coteries. Of this company Lucilius was now a regular member. He lived in good style in a house formerly built at the cost of the state as a residence for young Antiochus (IV, Epiphanes) when that prince was a hostage for the loyalty of his father, Antiochus the Great. He seems to have been a very free-living bachelor, and he denounced marriage as a hateful institution, a

---

[1] Marx thinks so, but his reasons do not seem conclusive. Proleg. pp. xviii, xix, xxv. Marius, with whom Marx classes him, was surely a Roman citizen.

[2] Jerome's date (148) is now generally regarded as an error. Munro in *Journal of Philology* VIII 214—5 corrects the text and arrives at 168.

[3] Appian *Hispan.* § 84.   [4] Velleius II 9 § 3.

[5] Plutarch *apophthegm Scip. min.* § 15, p. 201.

view which the spectacle of Scipio, unhappily mated[1] with an ugly woman, would only serve to confirm. After his friend's death in 129 he remained in Rome till 105, when failing health drove him to retire to Neapolis. There he died in 102 or 101, and was honoured with a public funeral. So many points in his life serve to illustrate the history of his times that no excuse is needed for speaking of it at some length.

676. Whatever was the age of Lucilius when he returned from Spain in 133 B.C., he soon felt the impulse[2] to write. The same head-quarters-gossip that bred mischief in Jugurtha may well have suggested to the future satirist a choice of topics. For the man was a patriot to the core, and the secret history of many a public and private scandal would stir his indignation. His admiration for the incorruptible Scipio would only add fuel to the fire of his wrath. Be this as it may, the testimony of later writers and his own surviving fragments entitle us to say that the staple material of his utterances was praise and blame. Blame of course preponderated, and this at once involved the question, in what form it was possible to deliver personal attacks. Mere generalities would perhaps command assent, but would certainly miss their mark. On the other hand, personalities easily run into libel, and defamatory writing was a recognized form of outrage (*iniuria*), and could as such be made the subject of an action at law. In the present state of the Roman legal system the private opinion or bias of the *iudex* appointed to try the case went for a great deal. For instance, to attack any one by name in a play was an outrage. But what was meant by attacking (*laedere*)? We hear[3] that Lucilius himself was attacked thus, and brought an action against the offender, whom the judge acquitted: while Accius, when placed in the same position, but before a different *iudex*, won his suit. To find some form of writing less easily made the subject of an action was desirable. Miscellaneous writings, the 'occasional pieces' of Ennius, and perhaps of other writers, seem to have been called *saturae*, whether in verse or prose. For whatever reason, this kind of free and easy writing commended itself to Lucilius. He kept to verse, trochaics iambics and hexameters: the last metre appears to have been his final choice. That he called his pieces *saturae* seems probable, but the name does not occur in the fragments: he refers to them as 'talks' (*sermones*), and in this respect was copied by Horace. The framework

---

[1] Appian *bell. civ.* I 20.

[2] Marx places his literary activity in the years 132—106.

[3] Of course we do not know the merits of these disputes, but they are cited as stock cases in *Rhet. ad Herenn.* II § 19. Marx thinks that Lucilius' own written personalities were the ground on which the *iudex* decided against him. This I doubt.

of his poems varied greatly; descriptions, dialogues, comments
imaginary scenes, all served as the vehicle of his criticism.

677. It has been well remarked[1] that 'the intensity of the
Roman temper tended to produce those one-sided types of character
which have been the favourite subjects of comic and satiric portrai
ture.' Lucilius had no doubt plenty of material ready to hand in the
mere foibles and follies of his contemporaries, such as the awkward
affectation of Greek ways, or in the opposite excesses of extravagance
and avarice. Starting from a patriotic platform, he would have a
Roman be a Roman, not in a narrow sense (for he is in favour of
education and wide interests), but to follow the Roman tradition
of dignity and virtue. Superstition, credulity, cheating, hypocrisy
empty rhetoric, were treated as bad and un-Roman. The language
too was being corrupted, and comments on spelling and etymology
shew the satirist's wish to keep it pure. But his earnest temperament
found its most congenial occupation in the ethical and political sphere.
On the glutton and debauchee he laid a heavy hand, and exposed the
abominations[2] of public life. He often referred to the subjects of his
attacks by name, and we naturally wonder how he managed to do
this with impunity. Probably the great influence of Aemilianus had
a good deal to do with it, and the Scipionic circle could always furnish
good advocates if one of the company were troubled with a lawsuit.
But we do not hear of such emergencies, and it is not unlikely that he
chose his victims carefully, and that they let him alone, fearing to
challenge him to produce his evidence in support of his charges. And
the master-bias of Roman courts was a tendency to find for the
defendant, whether from good or bad motives. Horace thought that
the bold personalities of Lucilius were inspired by those for which the
Old Comedy of Athens was famed. There may be truth in this view,
but we are hardly in a position to judge. Warm political passions
are characteristic of both, and the resemblance of the two is not to be
traced in detail.

678. With the literary characteristics of Lucilius we have here
little concern. The heedless fluency and disregard of finish, which
enabled him to compose verses of a kind at a surprising rate, is
blamed by Horace. In itself this might well be taken for a sign
of youth, and the frankness and warm feeling displayed in the fragments
are consistent with such a view. A marked feature of his style was
the introduction of Greek words into his Latin verses. How far this
was due to mere laziness, taking the first word, Greek or Latin, that
came to hand, and pushing on in feverish haste: how far the practice

---

[1] Sellar, *Roman poets of the Republic*, chapter VI.
[2] Marx thinks that his satire grew milder as time went on.

may have been deliberately adopted, in ridicule of contemporary affectation of Greek culture: these are points on which we have not enough evidence to attain a decisive conclusion. No doubt Lucilius was himself in most respects a man of the period. In private life we find him the mouthpiece of the low opinion of women that was becoming prevalent. In his relations to the public, he declared that he sought his readers among neither the learned nor the ignorant: the average citizen, or even the imperfectly Latinised people of southern Italy, were to be his audience. This probably refers to his desire of a wide influence. When he prefers the approval of the few wise men to that of the mob, he no doubt has in mind the Scipionic circle and their general sympathy with his views. Of Scipio he wrote in terms of panegyric, and laid the lash upon his political opponents, such as Metellus Macedonicus, Lentulus Lupus chief of the Senate, P. Mucius Scaevola chief pontiff, and others. Hostilius Tubulus an infamous scoundrel was another victim. Nor did he spare contemporary writers, such as Accius: he even made fun of the defects of Ennius who died in 169 and was already a venerated figure of the past. That we have not a single complete piece of Lucilius' writings is greatly to be regretted: the references to him in later authors shew clearly that his works contained a full picture of the variegated life of the day, painted with strong lights and shadows. His example stimulated Horace Persius and Juvenal to write satires in the various styles suited to their characters and the different conditions of their several times. In him we have lost perhaps the most truly Roman of all the Roman poets.

679. In treating of Lucilius we have had to look forward into the next period. It is time to bring this discussion of Roman affairs in the period following the second Punic war to a close. To sum up the main points briefly. We have reached an epoch at which power, efiective sovranty, was centred in the city of Rome to an unprecedented degree, while the old Roman characteristics were dying out. Under Greek influences the nobles were becoming more cosmopolitan in their ways of thought, but the race for wealth prevented them from improving the condition of subject peoples: the empire was their means of enrichment. The lower orders, pauperized and idle, their numbers constantly recruited by the manumission of alien slaves, were far on the way to become the mongrel mob, hungry turbulent and politically worthless, that we find them in later days. The class of capitalists, now becoming a power in the state, were a party of material interests without past traditions of ancestral virtue or present sense of responsibility: it was hardly in their greedy shrewdness that a thoughtful patriot would look to find the backing needed for a real

reform. Yet reform was a crying need: the decline of agriculture was laying waste great tracts of land in Italy, and the freeman giving place to the slave. The position of the Italian Allies was changed for the worse, and was fast becoming intolerable, yet in military emergencies Rome was more than ever dependent on their loyal aid. The central government was in effect the Senate, that is the Roman nobles, but in law the sovran power belonged to the Assembly, and the Assembly consisted normally of the city populace. This populace could not govern, but it had to be kept in a good humour: by its votes it could at least enforce the necessity of its own corruption: corruption was costly, and the governing class had necessarily to plunder the subject in order to amuse or bribe the citizen. And citizenship, now regarded as conferring rights rather than imposing duties, was not a thing to be shared with more partners, and extension of the franchise to the Allies was treated as beyond the range of practical politics. In short it was not clear from what quarter reform could come, or what direction it might profitably take. If a leader should arise, his first task would be to organize a force on which he might rely for support, in other words, to regenerate the Roman people. It is not too much to say that this was impossible. Among the nobles he might be sure of some backing, if only from a motive of party-spirit or jealousy. But to carry reforms for the general good without alienating these noble backers would be most difficult, particularly if he touched the complicated land-question. As for the Assembly, to rely on it for steady support was to lean on a broken reed. There was no great free industrial class to give steadiness to a popular movement. Even had such a class existed, there was no machinery for the effective expression of their will, for the principle of 'one vote one value' was unknown to their voting Assemblies. There remained physical force, which can achieve, or seem to achieve, any political end. It had indeed come to this, that no privilege could be successfully assailed or defended without resorting sooner or later to the use of the sword. And military revolution meant ı.ıonarchy. That the situation could not be clearly understood at the time was only natural, but a wise man could already discern the dangers inevitably attendant on reforming efforts under present conditions. Gaius Laelius the younger, friend of Scipio Aemilianus, was an able and cultivated man, kindly, patriotic, popular, and nicknamed the Wise (*sapiens*) on account of his judgment and learning. He was alarmed at the depopulation of Italy, and when tribune in 151 made an attempt to get the people back to the land. How far he got with his agrarian scheme we do not know; probably the opposition of the 'men of influence' took place in the Senate, and he found himself in a minority. Anyhow the discreet tribune[1] dropped his project of reform. We may fairly infer that he shrank from playing off the Assembly against the Senate, clearly seeing that a law so carried would be rather the beginning than the end of troubles. Force would be needed to make it operative, so he stood aside and let matters drift. No doubt this pleased the nobles, *optimates* and *populares* alike. An attack on their privileges was for the present averted, and they were well content to let things stand still. But human history knows no standing still: that which does not get better soon gets absolutely or relatively worse, and the thwarting of Laelius was but the omen of a coming storm. And yet there were still sound elements among both the nobles and the populace, and the strength of the old constitution, though the balance of its parts was upset and its mechanism obsolete, was still remarkable. To effect its final overthrow was the work of the civil broils and bloodshed of a hundred years.

[1] Plutarch *Tib. Gracchus* 8. Jesting remarks upon this instance of his reputed wisdom probably gave rise to the story that his nickname was derived from this withdrawal.

BOOK VI

THE REVOLUTION. (*a*) THE GRACCHI TO SULLA

CHAPTER XXXV

THE SICILIAN SLAVE-WAR 134—132 B.C.

680. THE division of history into periods is arbitrary, but necessary as a matter of convenience. When an event clearly overlaps two periods, transmitting effects of the earlier as causes to the later, it serves to remind us that the course of history is not a succession of leaps but a continuous march. Such an event was the great servile war in Sicily. In it we see the results of the slovenly organization of the Roman Provinces and the morbid growth of rural slavery. By its bloody suppression of the rising the Roman government did not remove the causes of evil. Good provincial governors were still hampered by the influence of capitalists interested in maintaining abuses, while the bad ones were under no sufficient control. The horrors of the slave-system remained, and bore their fruit in later slave-wars, in Sicily and elsewhere. The capitalist and the slave are the representative figures of the Roman revolution : they may stand for the forces that ruined Italian agriculture, cankered republican patriotism, and turned the citizen army into a body of professional swordsmen, the ready tool of ambitious leaders. The first steps in the process had been already taken. The period of revolution saw the gradual development of the inevitable result, the subjection of the Roman world to the rule of a single master.

681. The system of great estates worked by gangs of slaves was spreading fast in Italy : in Sicily it was already established throughout the island. The confiscations and settlement, which followed the restoration of Roman authority during the second Punic war, had greatly increased the amount of Sicilian land held by Romans and favoured Allies. In the course of some 70 years capitalists from Italy had doubtless bought up a good deal more : the few highly-favoured[1]

---

[1] See Cic. II *in Verr.* III §§ 93, 108, and § 252 above.

natives to whom the right of *commercium* within the province had been granted had probably done the same, and others of inferior privilege formed large estates within the boundaries of their several communities. It is clear that the land in general was held by a few landlords in large blocks, and worked by slave labour on a colossal scale. Luxury and the power of wealth were growing, and no moral or legal check restrained the master in his dealings with the slave. Long peace and security had led Sicilian masters to believe that in the island all was safe, and that greed and cruelty need fear no punishment. Their barbarities were beyond the common standard of slaveowners. Their niggardly selfishness made them blind to the folly of not allowing their human chattels enough food and clothing: and by conniving at robbery of travellers by their slaves they filled Sicily with daring brigands, who only needed a leader to become an army. Thus the country side was made unsafe, and the position of the remaining[1] small farmers, exposed to the depredations of their neighbours' slaves, was made worse. Meanwhile the dispossessed natives (all that was left of them) looked on in sullen disgust. Their means of livelihood were gone, the slaves had taken their place on the land. Yet the slave was not to blame: he did not come of his own free will. It was the fault of the accursed system under which a few slaveowners lived in wanton luxury. And these slaveowners had the ear of the Roman governors, who were constantly changing, and whose main object was to get through their term of office with profit to themselves, and not to provoke the resentment of powerful capitalists whose ill will might make itself felt at Rome and ruin the political career of a disobliging governor. There was thus no hope of redress for wrongs inflicted by the slave-gangs and their owners. Under such conditions, if the slaves should turn upon their masters, Italian or Sicilian, it was most unlikely that the poorer Sicilians would shed their own blood in defence of the hated capitalists.

682. That these capitalists, few and scattered, were in urgent need of protection, is clear enough. But the Roman government did not provide it. They had no standing army. Even when actual war broke out, it was not always easy to raise an army for service beyond the seas. A praetor with a small guard and a few thousands of local militia could not do much. And the Senate was not easily convinced of the existence of a state of war. To levy troops was not a popular measure, and the Fathers had their own reasons for not lightly resorting to a measure which might remind the populace of other grounds for discontent. Nor would the Sicilian landlords be forward to invoke the presence of a Roman army. Booty was in

[1] See note on § 1354 below.

these days the first object of the soldier, and in discriminating between the goods of friends and enemies he was apt to be careless. On the other hand, the quality of the Sicilian slave-gangs as fighting material was perhaps undervalued. They were all able-bodied men: the weakly were not worth importing. Whether employed in tilling the rich Sicilian cornfields, or in tending flocks and herds on the wilder lands, they lived a hard and healthy life and were always in good condition. True, they were mostly Orientals, drawn from Syria and Asia Minor, with traditional submissiveness to power. But this community of origin and ideas made it all the easier for large numbers to act together, and the cunning and cleverness of the hellenized Oriental were equal to most demands. And from the East they had brought with them a tendency to exciting superstitions, a readiness to accept imposture, to look for a deliverer and to follow a leader. Most of them could remember the days when they were freemen, some probably persons of consideration, in the far-off land of their birth: now, branded as cattle, some of them in chains, ever in danger of brutal punishment, they toiled to enrich cruel masters. Death, their only prospect of release, could for them have few terrors. Once convinced that no change in their condition could be for the worse, it was easy to conclude that it might be for the better, and in sheer despair even the patient Orientals rose at last.

683. The defects of our record[1] leave the chronology of the rising very obscure. That there was serious trouble in Sicily from about 140 B.C., and that the praetors one after another were unable to cope with the rebels, seems to be the fact. P. Popilius (praetor, according to Mommsen, in 135) put it on record that he sent back runaway slaves to their masters. This does not look like a thorough suppression of the revolt. We hear of other praetors in these years being utterly defeated by bands of slaves, but these may have been only cases of failure to put down unusually large and active bodies of brigands. Whether the main rising began before the end of the year 135 must be left doubtful. It was at least about that time that the dilatory Senate, convinced against their will that they had to do with a real war, woke up and sent a consul with an army to recover the granary of Rome. The first outbreak of the great rising occurred at Enna. The town occupied the flat top of a steep hill in the middle of the island, and was a fortress only to be taken by treachery or

---

[1] The chief authority is the fragmentary book XXXIV of Diodorus Siculus. The brief notices of Orosius v 6, 9 §§ 4—8, are probably drawn from the lost books of Livy. See Livy epit. 56—59. A little may be gleaned from Strabo VI 2 § 6 (pp. 272—3), Valer. Max. II 7 § 9, IX 12 § 1 (*ext.*), Frontinus *Strat.* IV 1 § 26, Florus II 7 (III 19). The last three also rest on Livy, and the lost history of Piso is probably at the back of them all. The inscription of Popilius referring to restitution of runaway slaves is in Wilmanns 797. Wordsworth p. 221.

hunger. The important personages of the place were a few rich men. Among them was one Damophilus, who was preeminent for wanton luxury and brutal cruelty: somewhat inferior, but of the same detested class, was Antigenes. Both seem to have been Sicilian Greeks. The latter had a Syrian slave named Eunus (εὔνους = well-wisher, kindly). He seems to have been a domestic, but the domestics of these capitalists seem often to have suffered from the barbarity of their owners, and in heart sympathized with the herdsmen and field-hands on the country estates. Eunus was versed in the superstitions of his native land, and was also a skilled juggler. By conjuring tricks, breathing fire and the like, by pretending to receive messages from Heaven, and by occasional success in prophesying, he gained among the Syrian slaves around the reputation of supernatural powers. So when the slaves of Damophilus were conspiring against their master they consulted Eunus, who promised them divine favour and bade them set about the business. The slaves rose and seized the town of Enna, where they massacred obnoxious persons and were joined by the local slaves. Damophilus and his equally cruel wife Megallis were fetched from their villa hard by, and put to death. Artisans able to take part in the making of weapons were spared and set to work, the rest of the Ennaeans slaughtered in cold blood. One exception shewed that even brutalized slaves retained some traces of human feeling. The young daughter of Damophilus had always been kind to her father's slaves and relieved their sufferings to the best of her power. In return for this compassion the rebels spared her life, protected her from outrage, and sent her away safely to friends at Catana.

684. The 'well-wisher' had been the leader and guide of the party that seized Enna. He had a lucky name, and his predictions had so far been fulfilled. The slaves now chose him to be their king. Monarchy came naturally to men of eastern traditions, and Eunus responded by following oriental precedent. He took the style of King Antiochus, declared his concubine. Queen-consort, and with a body-guard and household establishment aped the seclusion and luxury of an eastern court. To his rebel army he gave the name of Syrians: perhaps the body first assembled were all of Syrian race. Worthless rogue though he was, he had gleams of common sense. He chose a royal council of the ablest among his followers, and in particular placed great confidence in an Achaean Greek named Achaeus, to whose talents and bravery a good deal of his successes were probably due. Recruits now came pouring in, and the rebel army soon rose to 10,000 men, armed with any weapons they could get. Detachments in the Roman service were attacked and routed, and captured arms supplemented the output of the workshops of Enna. The praetors could make no headway. Just at this time another rising occurred in the western parts of the island. A herdsman of Cilician extraction named Cleon, a daring brigand, raised an army of slaves, seized and plundered Agrigentum, and overran the country round. All hope that the two rebel leaders would fall out and destroy each other was disappointed: Cleon gave in his allegiance to king Antiochus, and became his chief general. The revolted slaves soon reached the number of 20,000. The praetor Hypsaeus met them with 8000 Sicilian troops and suffered a defeat. The rising now took a more solid form. It was probably at this stage that the leaders managed to stop wholesale devastation of the country. Immediate need of supplies was no doubt the first motive of this policy, but it may well be that they hoped for a lasting success and the establishment of the slave-power as an independent kingdom of Sicily. The number of their host is said to have reached a total of 200,000. Anyhow it was very large, and Rome had now on her own territory and through her own fault to deal with a most serious war.

685. The Roman government must have been well aware of the danger of servile risings. Stray notices[1] of local conspiracies in Italy have come down to us. In 198 we hear of a contemplated outbreak near Rome, said to have been planned by the slaves attending on the Carthaginian hostages detained at Setia. Other slaves had been collected there, and a combination was formed with the object of seizing the town. Betrayal of the design, and prompt action of the authorities in Rome, dispersed the danger. But no small effort was necessary to clear the country round, and even Praeneste was threatened by the rebels. Two years later there was trouble in Etruria, where the plantation-system was probably already being introduced. This rising too was put down, but not until the slaves had been defeated in a battle. In 185 the slave-herdsmen of Apulia rose. But there was then a praetor with some troops at Tarentum, and this movement also was suppressed in blood. Years went by, the number of rural slaves increased greatly, and their treatment grew worse. About the time of the Sicilian slave-war there were several outbreaks[2] in different parts of the Roman world. At Rome itself a conspiracy of 150 slaves was discovered and crushed, but at Minturnae and Sinuessa a much larger number were involved, and hundreds were crucified as a warning. More than 1000 of the slave-miners in the silver mines of Laurium rose and threatened the peace of Attica, and at Delos, the great centre of the slave-trade, there was

---

[1] See Livy XXXII 26, XXXIII 36, XXXIX 29.
[2] See Diodorus and Orosius, cited above.

a riot: but the local authorities were prompt and the outbreaks were suppressed at once. If we may believe Diodorus, there were several other risings in various parts. But none of these movements attained the dimensions of a war. The affair of Aristonicus in Asia, also largely a rebellion of slaves, will be dealt with below. All were symptoms of the horrible disease at work beneath the surface of an unsound civilization. The record of them comes to us in scattered references consisting of very few words. From the slaves themselves we have of course not a word to shew us what so many thousands, nay millions, of the human race had to endure in those days of the bondman's agony.

686. Meanwhile the Sicilian insurrection had become a pressing danger, and there was the possibility, not likely to be ignored in view of past experience and while Numantia still defied the Roman arms, that the freemen under Roman rule might follow the example of the slaves. In Sicily itself, if the rebels gave up devastation and devoted themselves to extending their conquests, the poorer Sicilians, in deep discontent with their own lot, formed bands[1] and ranged the country plundering and burning the farms. The condition of the island was indeed deplorable. Lilybaeum and Syracuse were most likely still held for Rome: at least we do not hear of their fall, and the slave-power had no fleet. Whether Messana was lost is at least doubtful. But it is certain that the bulk of Sicily was in the hands of the insurgents, and the regular provincial government in abeyance. At last the Senate took matters seriously in hand. In 134, while Scipio went to Numantia, the other consul C. Fulvius Flaccus was sent with an army to Sicily, but we do not hear of his effecting anything. He was succeeded in 133 by the consul L. Calpurnius Piso Frugi, the author of the *lex Calpurnia de repetundis*, who was no doubt deeply interested in provincial affairs. Of his proceedings we learn from a passage of Orosius that he took some town[2] with great slaughter of the rebels, and that he crucified all those who fell into his hands alive. It would seem that he at least held the enemy in check, but it was not his fortune to end the war. We hear of his disgracing the commander of a detachment of cavalry, who had surrendered when hemmed in by a superior force. If, as it would seem, he restored the tone[3] of the army, it was his successor in 132 who reaped the fruits.

---

[1] See § 800.

[2] Hardly Messana, to judge from Oros. v 6 § 4. The name *Mamertium* in 9 § 6 is most likely corrupt. That he attacked Enna is not proved by the sling-bullets marked with his name found there. That he had a corps of slingers appears from Valer. Max. II 7 § 9. That his bullets would be recast by his successor is surely most improbable. See below § 688 (*l*).

[3] See the story Valer. Max. IV 3 § 10.

This was P. Rupilius[1], elected consul through the influence of his friend Scipio. He appears to have found the insurrection so far weakened that the sieges of two strongholds were the chief part of his task. These were Tauromenium and Enna. Neither of these rocky fortresses could be carried by assault, and the defenders had no hope of mercy. But supplies soon failed in Tauromenium under the pressure of blockade, a ghastly interval of cannibalism protracted resistance for a while, and betrayal did the rest. The remnant taken alive were put to death with torture. It was now the turn of Enna. Here much the same phenomena were repeated. On the least precipitous side of the town some fighting took place in which the brave Cleon met his end. Hunger and treachery, wholesale executions in cold blood, marked the closing scenes of the siege. The war was at an end, but the chase of isolated fugitives probably took a little time yet. In particular, the juggler-king had escaped from Enna before its fall. With him were his body-guard of 1000 men and a few personal attendants. Rupilius gave chase, and the guards, seeing that capture was imminent, slew each other to avoid a worse fate. Eunus took refuge in a hole, with his cook, baker, bath-attendant, and jester. He was dragged out and cast into a dungeon, where he soon rotted to death. Such was the end of King Antiochus. Brigandage was now quickly put down, fresh slaves filled the vacancies caused by the insurrection, and the working of the great estates was resumed. For a time the island was at peace, but no doubt the tradition of the slaves (who had at least not been tortured for nothing) still lingered in the country side.

687. Reconquest did not materially differ from conquest, and the usual measures for organizing a province were accordingly applied to Sicily. The consul was continued in command as proconsul, and a commission of ten senators were sent out to act as his *consilium*. The new charter or organic statute for Sicily, the *lex Rupilia* of 131, was their work. It regulated the administrative machinery of the province, particularly matters of taxation and legal procedure, and was no doubt an improvement on previous arrangements. But the evils inherent in the provincial system still remained. The capitalists interested in abuses were still influential at Rome, and the Roman government, even if willing, was still unable to exercise an effective control. For the time the capital city was content again to draw corn from its island granary: of the losses of the Sicilian landlords we can form no estimate.

---

[1] Rupilius is said to have been once a *publicanus*.

688. Note on inscriptions.

In the 2nd century B.C. inscriptions begin to have considerable importance as confirming the literary record in several details and attesting its general truth. The following specimens will serve to illustrate this statement. The abbreviations used are *CIL = corpus inscriptionum Latinarum* and W. = Wilmanns' convenient *exempla inscriptionum Latinarum*. Small letters in italics indicate the broken or erased letters restored by Mommsen and other expert scholars. Small Roman letters are supplements of abbreviations, and one longer inscription is given in that form.

(*a*)   P · SCIPIONI · COS · IMP · OB · RESTITVTAM · SAGVNTVM · EX · S · C · BELLO ·
PVNICO · SECVNDO

At Saguntum. Experts pronounce this to be a restoration, probably a copy, made in the Imperial age. Saguntum was restored 207 B.C., but Scipio was not consul till 205, which is thus the earliest possible date for the inscription. *CIL* II 3836, W. 653. Livy XXVIII 39.

(*b*)   L · Aimilius L · f · inpeirator decreivit utei quei Hastensium servei in turri Lascutana habitarent leiberei essent: agrum oppidumqu[e] quod ea tempestate posedisent item possidere habereque iousit dum poplus senatusque Romanus uellet. act[um] in castreis a[nte] d[iem] XII k[alendas] Febr[uarias].

On a bronze tablet found in southern Spain. It is a decree of Aemilius Paullus granting certain rights to a body of liberated serfs. It probably belongs to the time just after Paullus' victory over the Lusitanians. The date is the 19th Jan. 189 B.C. *CIL* II 5041, W. 2837, Wordsworth pp. 171, 415. Livy XXXVII 57.

(*c*)   (1)   M · FVLVIVS · M · F · SER · N · COS · AETOLIA · CEPIT

(2)   M · FOLVIVS · M · F · SER · N · NOBILIOR · COS · AMBRACIA · CEPIT

The first found at Tusculum, the second at Rome. Fulvius was consul 189 B.C., and the inscriptions are in dedication of spoils taken in the Aetolian war. *CIL* I 534, W. 26. Polybius XXI, Livy XXXVIII.

(*d*)   *p · cornelius · p · f ·* SCIPIO · AFRICANVS · COS · BIS · CENSOR · AEDILIS ·
CVRVLIS · TRIB · MIL

Found in the Sabine country. The inscription is of later date, set up by some successor in honour of a famous ancestor. Scipio was military tribune in 216, curule aedile 213, consul 205 and 194, censor 199. *CIL* I 280, W. 615. Livy and Polybius, indices.

NOTE. A considerable number of these inscriptions recording the deeds of great ancestors, sometimes in detail, have survived. Interesting specimens will be found in Wilmanns among Nos. 610—630.

(*e*)   (1)   M · AEMILIVS · M · F · M · N · LEPIDVS · COS · CCL · XIIX

(2)   *m* . AEMILIVS · M · F · M · N · LEPID · COS · CCXXCVI

Two milestones found near Bononia, giving the distances in miles from Rome, 268 and 286 respectively, on the *via Aemilia*, made by Lepidus when consul in 187. Mommsen holds them to be genuine copy-restorations of a somewhat later date. They are of columnar shape. They had been moved from their original places and used to mark distances on some other road near by. Hence other numbers had been cut on the sides for this purpose. On the *via Aemilia* the distances were afterwards reckoned from Ariminum. *CIL* I 535, W. 806, Wordsworth pp. 220, 473. Livy XXXIX 2, Strabo V 1 § II (p. 217).

(*f*) L·MANLIVS·L·F·ACIDINVS·TRIV·VIR·AQVILEIAE·COLONIAE·DEDVCVN-
DAE

Found at Aquileia. Among the *triumviri*, appointed in 183, who in 181 conducted the colonists to Aquileia, the name of this man appears. *CIL* I 538. W. 650. Livy XXXIX 55, XL 34.

(*g*) M·CLAVDIVS·M·F·MARCELVS·CONSOL·ITERVM

Found at Luna, on the pedestal of a statue. Luna was founded in 177 (§ 559). This Marcellus was consul for the second time in 155, when, as appears from the *Fasti Triumphales* (ed. Henzen), both consuls enjoyed triumphs. Scipio Nasica, the other consul, triumphed over the Delmatae (Livy epit. 47): it was conjectured by Henzen that the enemy conquered by Marcellus were Ligurians. A further scrutiny of the mutilated record in the *Fasti* revealed letters that confirmed this. It seems that the Luna inscription refers to an honorary statue erected by the *coloni* of Luna in 155, or at least not later than 153, for Marcellus was a third time consul in 152. *CIL* I 539, W. 651, Wordsworth p. 220.

(*h*) S·POSTVMIVS·S·F·S·N·ALBINVS·COS·EX·GENVA·*Cremonam*

A columnar milestone from the *via Postumia*. Mommsen thought this to be a later copy of an original. Like the stones in (*e*) above, it seems to have been adapted afterwards for use on some other road. This Albinus was consul in 148. *CIL* I 540, W. 807. Tacitus *hist.* III 21.

(*i*) The six dedicatory inscriptions of L. Mummius (Achaicus), given in *CIL* I 541—6, W. 27 are very interesting, but too long in the total to quote. He was consul 146. The offerings probably belong to the year 144. See Bücheler's *Carmina epigraphica* No. 248. Wordsworth pp. 220, 473.

(*k*) The Puteolan inscription known as *lex parieti faciendo* is a restoration of the imperial age copied from an original dated by the consuls of 105 B.C. It speaks of this as the 90th year from the foundation of the colony. This agrees with Livy XXXIV 45. *CIL* I 577, W. 697, Wordsworth pp. 222, 476.

(*l*) L·PISO·L·F·COS

Moulded sling-bullet from Enna. *CIL* I 642, W. 2821, Wordsworth pp. 226, 482, checked by an original in my own possession.

These inscriptions are referred to in the notes on the passages of preceding chapters in which the several events are narrated.

CHAPTER XXXVI

TIBERIUS GRACCHUS 133 B.C.

689. IF we place ourselves in imagination at the beginning of the year 133 B.C., we find the situation[1] of affairs in Rome to be as follows. From Spain and Sicily reports are coming in from time to time, but as yet no news of decisive success in either quarter has removed the uneasiness that weighs upon the public mind. In home politics, most men are conscious that something is wrong with the state, some are able to point out this or that abuse in particular, a very few have formed some notion of this or that well-meant remedy. But every abuse has grown by slow degrees, and many men are now interested in its continuance: moreover, the majority of the leading men are narrow-minded or timid, and accordingly opposed to change. One of the new tribunes has entered on office pledged to take the long step from negative discontent to positive reform. Meanwhile the first man among the Roman citizens, the leader around whom is grouped most of the talent of the day, the moderator to whom contending partisans might look to appease passions or end a political crisis, is at this juncture far away, doing the government's dirty work in the siege of Numantia.

690. The machinery to be controlled by a statesman bent on reform was hardly such as to promise a successful result. Of the defects of the constitution, in parts or as a whole, we have spoken above. We have seen that the practically governing body, the Senate, was in the hands of a class of nobles steadily degenerating under the influences of the age,—luxury, the race for wealth, crude Hellenism, often assimilated only in its worst forms, and a vast

---

[1] The main authorities for this chapter are Appian *bell. civ.* 1 1—17 and Plutarch's *Life of Tib. Gracchus*. These are both fuller and fairer than Velleius II 2—4 and the scattered references (see index to Halm's text) in Valerius Maximus. The latter pair draw from highly prejudiced sources, and their rhetoric holds up Gracchus as a fearful example. Diodorus fragm. XXXIV 5—7, and Livy (to judge from epit. 58, 59), seem to have had the same anti-Gracchan bias. The numerous references to the reformer in Cicero occasionally witness to some detail or other (see Ciceronian indices), but his views vary with the needs of advocacy, and are of little weight. In his later life attachment to the Senate and Equites led him to take a very unfavourable view of Gracchus. The works of contemporary writers, now lost, are traced and discussed in Holden's Introduction to *Plutarch's Lives of the Gracchi*.

imperial expansion with which their old Roman traditions had not fitted them to deal. We have seen that the old regular magistracies remained, still bearing the old names, still nominally possessing the old powers. The magistrate was irremoveable and irresponsible during his term of office, checked only by the intervention of an equal or superior officer. Rare instances of wilful disobedience have shewn that in practice the Senate controlled them all. We have seen that the popular Assemblies, the legal source of sovran power, were now wholly unfitted for its rational exercise in the name of the state. They no longer even approximately represented the real opinion of the mass of Roman citizens. The most active men were scattered far and wide in Italy, or were abroad, serving the state or engaged in their private business: the mob of Rome, ever more and more mongrel in its composition, generally dominated the voting of the Tribes. How many voters still lived in the rural districts, we do not know, but we have reason to think that they seldom came to vote. The mere distance disfranchised many. Others would be unwilling to spend time and money in coming to attend an Assembly which after all might never be held. Farmers could not afford to leave home for several days in busy seasons of the year. So the city mob was able to establish by degrees a claim to cheap corn and to a number of splendid shows freely provided by those concerned to win its favour. For of their sovran rights none could deprive them, and these rights commanded a price, a price which ever tended to rise, and was soon to include wholesale bribery. But, among the various corruptions that were already affecting the Roman state, the ancient respect for law and order had as yet kept bloodshed out of politics. If the ordinary citizen had hitherto with few exceptions been a soldier, he had learnt discipline together with the use of the sword. But we have seen that since the overthrow of Hannibal discipline had been declining, while brutality and greed increased. A careful observer would surely have viewed with alarm the formation of a military class, unused to peaceful industry and civil life: the appearance of slave-attendants, escorting their noble owners in the streets, might with good reason have caused him no less misgiving.

691. The situation then was full of danger. The Senate had, as we remarked above, virtually usurped the government of Rome. The merits of that body, merits that had enabled and indeed entitled it to assume an unconstitutional power, had steadily been growing less under the temptations and disturbing influences that accompanied the great extension of Roman supremacy. Only its effective control of the magistrates, particularly of the tribunes, had enabled the Senate to remain in the seat of power. But in law the position of the tribune

was still what it had been in the days when the Plebs used the
tribunate as a weapon to exact concessions from the Patricians.   At
any moment when discontent was rife, and a popular leader bent
upon reform, the tribunician power lay ready to hand as a means
of thwarting the Senate and initiating legislation.   But two circumstances made it unlikely that the ensuing struggle would be conducted
with the stubborn patience of the olden days, and that it would have
a peaceful issue.   In the first place it was not likely that the governing
nobles of these days would quietly submit to the inevitable.   They
had tasted the sweets of empire, and were beginning to see what
a mine of wealth lay open to them in the provinces.   The existing
land-system of Italy offered a ready means of investing their plunder,
and suited them very well.   They could rely on a strong majority
in the Senate, and it was hardly to be expected that they would
surrender their privileges without a fight.   Secondly, though the
tribunes while in office retained their old powers, it was no longer
lawful[1] for them to be immediately reelected from year to year.   Thus
the engine employed with irresistible effect in the time of Licinius
and Sextius was no longer available.   A succession of determined
leaders filling the tribunate year after year was the only plan by
which that office could be made to serve the purpose of giving effect
to the continuous pressure of a movement for reform.   Now there
was in fact no such supply of willing and fit persons: nor, even if
there had been, was there any longer a popular Assembly with the
incorruptible loyalty and grim patience necessary to support them.
To achieve lasting results was under such conditions an impossibility:
to attempt to change the conditions by violence would be the first
step in a revolution.

692.   These considerations seem clear enough now in retrospect,
but even at the time of which we speak they must in some form have
been present to the minds of many.   They did not however deter
Tiberius Sempronius Gracchus from coming forward as a reformer.
He was the elder of the two surviving sons of the distinguished consul
and censor of the same name.   His mother Cornelia was the daughter
of the great Scipio Africanus, and his sister was married to Scipio
Aemilianus.   Thus the noblest strains met in his birth, and powerful
connexions offered him the certainty of a splendid public career, if he
would but accept it on the ordinary terms.   But his widowed mother,
famed as the model of a great and large-minded Roman lady, had so
trained her sons as to combine Roman virtues with Greek enlightenment.   Tiberius developed his gifts of speech under the care of the
first living rhetorician, Diophanes of Mitylene, but the teacher who

---

[1] Livy epit. 58, Cic. *in Catil.* IV § 4.

probably influenced him most of all was an Italian Greek, Blossius of Cumae. This man was a friend of the Stoic philosopher Antipater of Tarsus, who thought highly of him. He seems to have been a man of lofty principles, which he was disposed to put in practice without making allowance for the circumstances of a degenerate age. To his guidance it was most likely due that the brave and high-minded lad grew up more of an eager patriot than a prudent statesman. Gracchus would probably be introduced to Greek literature bearing upon politics, in which the Reformer was not seldom a fascinating figure. In the house of his brother-in-law he may have listened to the talk of Polybius without imbibing the judicious moderation of the old Achaean. In any case the political experience of little Greek states was ill suited to furnish an equipment for a youth whose ambition was to solve the most complex problem of contemporary Rome.

693.   However much Gracchus may have misjudged the situation in other respects, he was right in recognizing the land-question as the fundamental problem of the state. If the decline of the rural population was to go on unchecked, the Assemblies could only go from bad to worse, the army must suffer for want of sound recruits, and Italy, now the seat of a great empire, be given over to the capitalist and the slave. The conquest of Italy had left large tracts of forfeited land[1] at the disposal of Rome. This *ager publicus populi Romani* had in course of time been reduced by allotments to Roman colonists on the foundation of colonies (*ager colonicus*) or to individuals when no colony was founded (*ager viritim divisus* or *viritanus*). Of these the former were strictly private property (*ager privatus optimo iure*), the latter mostly if not always so: at least it does not appear that the state reserved the right of resumption. The rest, probably much the larger part, may be classified under two main heads. One class includes all the state property administered by the state through the censors. Such were cultivated lands (as in the Campanian plain), broad 'runs' (*saltus*) used for pasture, and various rights in woodlands mines fisheries and the like. All these paid a rent in some form or other, the collection of which was generally if not always let to contractors (*publicani*). The revenue derived from these was the most regular income of the Roman treasury, and to take any step likely to lessen this revenue was obviously beyond the range of practical politics. Beside these, and perhaps the largest class of all, were the lands of which the state still retained the property, but which were held in effective occupation (*possessio* as opposed to *dominium*) by individuals or communes. Those under cultivation are said by

---

[1] See Marquardt, *Röm. Staatsverwaltung* II 151—161.

Appian to have been subject to a single tithe of corn or a double tithe ($\frac{1}{5}$) of fruit according to the crops. Another common form of recognizing the ground-ownership of the state was the payment of a small quit-rent. But it would seem that these tithes and quit-rents were collected carelessly, whether through not employing *publicani* or for some other reason, and they soon began to fall into arrear. Evasions increased, and by 133 B.C. the Roman people was drawing little or no revenue from this source. The lands held by individuals had passed without question from father to son or been transferred to other hands by bequest or sale. Long freedom from disturbance had caused the precarious nature of the tenure to pass out of sight: if the state had not surrendered its rights, it had allowed them to lapse. Accordingly the boundaries between private properties and *possessiones* had been allowed to disappear, buildings tillages and other improvements[1] had gone on promiscuously without regard to the varieties of title by which the parts of an estate were held, and in division of an estate the parties had ceased to take account of an apparently obsolete distinction. It is said that large financial interests were now involved in the *possessiones*, some lands being pledged as security for debts, while in others the capital of dowries had been invested: in short many more than the present occupiers were concerned in the permanence of the existing state of things. And behind these interests of individuals stood those of the various communities to which grants of the same kind had from time to time been made. It was of course a great boon to them thus to receive lands in addition to their own proper territories, and not only citizen colonies but Latin and other[2] communities of Allies had been thus endowed or rewarded. How much land had been thus granted we do not know. But, little or much, it was in practice viewed as tenable during good behaviour, and in the great wars of the past century the Allies in particular felt that they had served Rome only too well. Probably the enjoyment of these land-grants had chiefly benefited the wealthy: that however would be a local affair, for Rome did not interfere in the communal arrangements, nor, if she had done so, would she have thwarted those whom it was her traditional policy to conciliate. It will be seen that any attempt to tamper with what had by lapse of time and non-

---

[1] Ferrero I p. 49 lays stress on the improvement of vine-cultivation in recent years, referring to Pliny *NH* XIV 94. But I do not think this very important from the standpoint of Gracchus, though the prospect of disturbance would of course irritate the capitalists who had embarked on this form of rural speculation.

[2] Beloch, *Ital. Bund* p. 220, holds that the non-Latin Allies had no share in this privilege, and refers to line 31 of the *lex agraria* of 111 B.C. (see index), where they certainly are not mentioned. I find this very hard to believe. If we accept it, we must reject the evidence of Appian *civ.* I 10, 18—21, altogether. Cf. Cic. *de republ.* III § 41.

assertion of sovran rights come to be regarded as a permanent settlement would inevitably call forth indignant protest, and the outcry of individual Roman 'possessors' would find an echo among the Allies in Italy.

694. But the bold tribune (at this time a man of 30), who had led a storming-party at Carthage and saved a Roman army by negotiation at Numantia, was not the man to draw back in fear of opposition. His scheme was a simple one. It was evident that the broad estates now formed in Italy by absorption of public land were the result of wholesale violations of the laws carried by Licinius and Sextius in 367 B.C. The main provision of those laws had been to fix a scale-limit for *possessiones agri publici*. No individual was to occupy more than 500 *iugera* (about 310 acres) of the public land. This law, evaded from the very first, Gracchus resolved not only to reenact but to enforce. He saw the principal cause of its failure hitherto in the lack of proper machinery for putting it into execution. This machinery he would provide in the form of a standing land-commission, whose duty it should be to recover for the state the lands now held by possessors in excess of the Licinian scale, and to distribute the same in allotments to the poor. He would also meet the danger of a relapse into the present abuses by forbidding the sale of the parcels when allotted: a significant admission. Small farmers had for some time past been selling their farms and taking to urban or military life. These men if restored to country life might repeat the process, and born townsmen planted out on lonely farms were even less likely to endure with patience the unfamiliar monotony and toil. But the doctrinaire is ever confident in his nostrums, and Gracchus thought his remedy sufficient. And he was in a hurry. It is said that on his way to Spain in 137 he travelled through Etruria, where the plantation-system was in full swing. He observed the desolation of the country side, and the displacement of the native population by gangs of barbarian slaves horrified the young man's patriotic soul. The story is given on the authority of his brother Gaius, and it is a far more probable explanation of his hasty action than any of the contributory causes suggested by Plutarch. Velleius declares that what moved him was irritation at the repudiation of the treaty that he made with the Numantines, a story which seems to be the echo[1] of contemporary calumny.

695. The election of tribunes took place in the summer, usually in July. Gracchus then was elected some time in the middle of 134. He would enter on office on the tenth of December. He had thus at

---

[1] Transmitted through Cicero, *Brutus* § 103, *de haruspicum responso* § 43. It reappears in Orosius v 8 § 3, who probably got it from Livy, and Dion Cassius fragm. 83.

least five months in which to prepare his measures. The general scope of his intentions, land-reform in some shape, was well known, and it is said that the common people wrote up sentences on the walls, urging him to go ahead with his undertaking. A more effective stimulus was given by the approval of two eminent men. These were P. Licinius Crassus Mucianus (a Mucius adopted by a Licinius) and his brother P. Mucius Scaevola. Both were skilled lawyers, and helped him with their advice in drafting his bill: Crassus was an open supporter. The tribune was also backed by his father-in-law Appius Claudius. When Gracchus entered on office, Scaevola was probably already consul-elect for 133, but he was too cautious for the tribune to be able to rely on his support as consul. However, the Sicilian slave war was now affording an object-lesson in the evils of the plantation-system: take it all in all, such an opportunity for a reformer was hardly likely to recur.

696. Of the famous land-bill now laid before the people, no doubt a long and elaborate measure, we only know a few main points. It reenacted the Licinian limit, and set up an executive commission. But it also contained an important concession to present occupiers. Each 'possessor' was to be allowed 500 *iugera* for himself, but a further allowance of 250 *iugera* for each of his sons was thrown in. It would seem that the possessor of less than 500 *iugera* in all was nowise affected by the bill. On this point we have no record, which is much to be regretted. Not only would the difference between 499 and 501 be immaterial (perhaps no more than a surveyor's error), but the circumstances of acquisition might put a different colour on the two cases. True, this mechanical precision might remove the immediate fears of the smaller possessors, but the possibility of further legislation would leave them suspicious and hostile: while the treatment of all cases as on exactly the same footing would, however necessary, be somewhat of an abdication of the moral enthusiasm which was no small part of the strength of Gracchus. Another obscure point is the compensation offered to the disturbed possessors for any unexhausted improvements effected during their tenure of the land. It is sometimes stated[1] that this was in the form of a payment from the state treasury, an unlikely assumption unsupported by direct evidence. We should probably view the compensation as consisting in the guarantee, offered to the possessors by the bill, of secure possession of what was left them after surrendering the excess of their holdings, in the freedom from quit-rent in the future, and in the

---

[1] Compare Holden on Plutarch *Tib. Gracchus* 9 § 2 with Strachan-Davidson on Appian *civ.* I 11 § 5. The word τιμήν in Plutarch, which causes the difficulty, is rendered 'value' by Long.

tacit or express abandonment of any claim on the ground of past arrears. But to all these privileges the possessors conceived themselves to have acquired by long usage an indefeasible right. Gracchus was generously giving them what they regarded as already their own, and this accounts for one source of the dissatisfaction that certainly prevailed. For with the publication of the bill the inevitable storm broke out. The difficulties sketched above were all raised as fatal objections, backed by appeals to sentiment on grounds such as the desecration of family tombs, and the tribune's policy was denounced as revolutionary. On the other side we are told that the needy urged the necessity of the measure, if they were to have the wherewithal to rear families for the good of the state, and claimed the right to share the state lands won with their own and their fathers' blood. Gracchus harangued them boldly. He told them that they were the heirs of empire, but none of them owned a single clod of earth, much less an ancestral tomb: the wild beasts of Italy all had their dens and lairs, while the soldiers who fought for Italy had nothing but the sun that warmed them and the air they breathed: were they to go on facing battle and death that others might live in luxury? What percentage of his hearers were genuine representatives of ill-rewarded Roman manhood, is a detail which we have no possible means of guessing: but on our view of this detail our judgment of the moral value of the Gracchan agitation must largely depend.

697. The question is not a simple one. We are told that the hopes raised by the news of Gracchus' design drew streams of rural voters into Rome. Whether it was through their support that he was elected tribune, we do not hear. Probably not, for we know that in the summer months the farmers were busy on their farms. We must rather conclude that the mass of these country folk streamed into the city when Gracchus was already in office, for the purpose of voting for the bill. Rome would thus be filled to overflowing: many of the non-resident voters would be in great discomfort for lack of accommodation, and all would long to return home. Impatience of opposition and delay would be the dominant feeling, and would wax in intensity as the days went by. In some such state of tension we may reasonably find an explanation of the irregular proceedings that followed. The absence of statistics reduces us to guess-work. How many rural voters came in we cannot tell: how many of those who came were actual farmers, men still on the land in spite of the recent changes in the economics of rural life, how many were men recently displaced who had found a retreat in some country town, are points[1] upon which we can get no light. Perhaps it is

---

[1] See Diodorus fragm. xxxiv 6.

safest to observe that if their total numbers were no more than 10,000, this would probably be enough to turn the votes of all or most of the 31 'rustic' Tribes, so long as the solid 10,000 remained within call. When these men scattered to their homes, the best part of the reformer's following was gone. The support of the four city Tribes, even if their mob-voters stood firm, was of no avail. The 31 rustic Tribes would at once resume their normal character, of which we may try to form some general notion. We must bear in mind that dwellers in the city did not necessarily belong to any of the city Tribes. Men with landed property were placed on the roll of a Tribe in the district of which their land (or some of it) lay. But if a man with land in a rural district came to live in Rome, he still, unless degraded by a censor, kept his name on the roll of his original Tribe. Moreover, the primitive identification of land-owner (*adsiduus*) and citizen was now long out of date. The tribe-connexion had become a personal one, and the immigrant could now keep his Tribe though he had parted with his land. On ordinary occasions the voters in a rustic Tribe would probably be made up of the following classes.

1. Landowners (mostly rich men) resident in Rome.
2. Their sons.
3. Landless immigrants, often ex-soldiers.
4. Their sons, liable to military service.
5. A few wealthy freedmen, admitted by censors of the new school.
6. A few genuine country voters, who for any reason happened to be in Town.

If this be anywhere near the truth, it is clear that Gracchus could not reasonably expect much help from the first two classes, or from the fifth. Classes 3 and 4 would perhaps mostly support him at first, but many of them would be dependants of the rich nobles and other capitalists, whom in the long run they could not afford to disobey. The last class alone were capable of indefinite increase, when the farmers were roused: but in ordinary times they would be mainly well-to-do citizens from colonial and municipal towns, whose interests might or might not fit in with the project of Gracchus. Truly the reformer had but a slippery footing, once the farmers were gone. And we have in this tentative calculation made no direct allowance for the possible effects of calumny bribery and force.

698. The protests of the 'possessors' against the bill were soon backed up by those of the various communes of citizens and Allies[1]

---

[1] Velleius II 2 § 2 says that Gracchus offered to give the Roman franchise to the whole of Italy. This is probably a confusion between the schemes of Tiberius and Gaius. If there

who saw their interests imperilled.   The excitement grew, party spirit was inflamed, and even the indifferent had to take sides.   The partisans of Gracchus, urged by his speeches to claim their share of what belonged to all, and to put soldier-citizens in the place of non-military slaves, stood firm.   It was clear that the bill would pass. At last the opponents induced one of the tribunes to block it, as he had a perfect right to do.   This was M. Octavius, a man of high character and friend[1] of Gracchus, who was loth to promise, but kept his word.   What followed is most obscure in detail.   Plutarch says that the reply of Gracchus to the opposition of his colleague was to bring in his bill in a less conciliatory shape, simply ejecting present possessors from lands occupied contrary to the laws, that is, the Licinian laws.   The two tribunes met in public debate without indecent violence.   Gracchus offered to buy out Octavius (who was one of those touched by the bill) at his own expense, but Octavius would none of it.   Gracchus then issued an edict by which he put a stop to all public business, and sealed up the treasury in the temple of Saturn.   This deadlock was quite within his powers: it was to last till the people had voted on the bill.   The possessors' party now aimed at assassinating Gracchus, but did not succeed.   In the Assembly voting was stopped by the tumult that arose, but a free fight was avoided, Gracchus consenting to refer the whole matter of the tribunes' dispute to the Senate.   Of course nothing came of this.   The wealthy had an overwhelming majority in the House, and no doubt they were angry that their sanction had not been asked ·in the traditional way before giving notice of the bill.   And now it would seem that the necessity of haste forced the hand of Gracchus. He could not afford to wait, and he had gone too far to drop the whole scheme, which he might never be in a position to revive.   So he made up his mind to depose his stubborn colleague.   There was no legal means of doing this.   He proposed that a vote of the Assembly should be taken to decide whether he or Octavius should resign, but Octavius declined the unconstitutional offer.   Gracchus declared that a tribune only held office to carry out the people's will, and put the question of the dismissal of his colleague to the vote. When the vote of the first Tribe was announced in favour of this proposal, he paused to give Octavius one more chance.   But Octavius also had gone too far to retreat, and the men to whom he stood pledged were looking on.   When 17 Tribes had voted the same way, Gracchus paused again, but with the same result.   The 18th Tribe

is any truth behind it, we may guess that it refers to some verbal promise made at this stage to soothe the Allies.

   [1] Dion Cassius fragm. 83 represents him as a rival.

followed suit, and the first act of the Roman revolution was complete.

699. The bill, apparently the whole bill as first drafted, now became law without delay. But the rage of the rich possessors was extreme. Octavius did not admit that he had ceased to be tribune, but his place was at once filled by a Gracchan nominee. Plutarch says that he was haled away from the platform by a freedman of Gracchus, and that he narrowly escaped rough handling by the mob. The commissioners elected to carry out the new law were Tiberius Gracchus and his brother Gaius, not yet returned from Spain, and Appius Claudius the father-in-law of Tiberius. This family party offered a mark for hostile critics, and many men no doubt felt that things were going too fast. The rural voters went home, and Gracchus was left to face embittered foes who spared no pains to chill the cooling enthusiasm of the fickle populace and promote a reaction. When he applied for the equipment usually supplied by the state to its commissioners, the Senate shewed its spite by voting an insufficient allowance. And just then a friend of Gracchus died under suspicious circumstances. The cry of poison was raised, and for a while party-spirit flared up again. The tribune declared his life in danger, and begged the people to protect his sons[1]. Appian says that the opposition were threatening vengeance on the author of sedition so soon as he went out of office. This probably refers to an intended prosecution for high treason before the Assembly of the Centuries. But events took another turn. It seems from the epitome of Livy that Gracchus dealt with the question of jurisdiction in a separate[2] law, giving the commission full powers to decide all disputes as to boundaries between public and private land. This may have been carried at this time, when the Senate was unpopular. And now an envoy from Pergamum arrived in Rome, bringing official news of the death of Attalus III and bearing the king's will. The last of the Attalids, a cruel tyrant, left the Roman people his heir. This business by immemorial custom belonged to the Senate, but Gracchus saw in it a grand opportunity for a popular stroke. He gave notice that he would propose a law that the king's treasure should be appropriated[3] to enable the recipients of the land-allotments to stock their farms. The Senate was of course indignant: but according to Plutarch Gracchus also expressed his intention of following up

[1] For their number and fate see Valer. Max. IX 7 §§ 1, 2.

[2] This is very doubtful. The neglect of such a point in the original draft is a hardly credible oversight.

[3] Orosius V 8 § 4 says *populo distribueretur*, but the epitome of Livy 58 agrees with Plutarch.

this law by another, determining the treatment of the newly acquired territory. It was now clear that the tribune would spare no part of the constitution that hindered the fulfilment of his will: between Senate and demagogue it was henceforth war to the knife.

700. Moderate men (probably not many in all) had hitherto supported the tribune, attracted by his virtues and impressed by the magnitude of the evils that he was undertaking to remove. These now began to fall away, while his enemies waxed bold. One man asserted that Gracchus had received [1] the crown and royal robe from Pergamum, another charged him with encouraging license and disorder by parading the streets at night with an escort. A third challenged his action in deposing a fellow-tribune. Gracchus in anger ordered his arrest and began to denounce him before a popular meeting. But when the man said 'tell me now, suppose you want to lay a penalty on me, and I appeal to one of your colleagues for protection, and he comes to my aid, will you treat him as you treated Octavius?' the bold and ready tribune was at a loss for an answer. Indeed there was no satisfactory answer, and it was beginning to be widely felt that nothing could justify the undeniable weakening of the tribunate. Gracchus was thus driven into a position most unfavourable to a popular reformer, that of appearing in public as his own apologist. The heads of his speech are preserved by Plutarch. He urged (1) that the inviolability of a tribune did not cover treasonable and anti-popular acts, (2) as even a consul may be arrested by a tribune, so a tribune may be deposed for thwarting the will of the sovran people, (3) the rights of the people override all else, as the expulsion of the Tarquins shews, (4) even the most sacred of persons, the Vestal virgins, are put to death for acts destructive of their sacred character: and other less trenchant arguments. How many of his hearers were satisfied with his justification we do not know: his enemies would at least be pleased to have put him on his defence. They had employed the time-honoured device of representing him as aspiring to unconstitutional power, and indeed he had been borne in that direction by the course of events. If they asked a man in the street 'who is the Tarquin now?' there was but one possible name to mention. Even the man who replied 'nobody' would go on his way thinking.

701. The friends of Gracchus were now alarmed, and insisted on his standing for immediate reelection. In truth it was a sheer

---

[1] The pretext for this assertion may have been that the envoy paid his respects to Gracchus, as he would to all Romans of influence. That he approached Gracchus in particular with some special object in view seems an improbable conjecture. Attalus died in 133, and all Gracchus' acts have to be placed in the first half of the year. In the hurry of this time negotiations of a serious kind are not likely.

necessity, and scruples about the constitution were by this somewhat out of date. No land-allotment had as yet taken place, and the election of tribunes for 132 must have been close at hand. Gracchus announced his candidature, and called upon the rural voters to come and support him. But they were busy with their farm work in the summer, and it appeared that the attendance would be small. He was thus driven to rely mainly on resident voters, now much divided in sentiment, and his popularity with whom had been undermined by the intrigues and calumny of his foes. He strove to gain his former ascendancy by announcing further projects of legislation. According to Plutarch, one law was to have reduced the term of liability to military service: another to have granted the right of appealing from the decisions of the juries in the law-courts. But for citizens the army-service was no longer so frequent a burden as it had been of old, and the proposal bears the stamp of a demagogue in despair. As for the juries, made up of senators, their powers were derived from the Assembly of the Tribes, and we have already seen that no appeal from their verdicts was constitutionally possible. To allow such appeals would be revolution gone mad. Besides, the persons brought before the courts then existing were persons of importance accused of extortion: the ordinary citizen would not care about what did not affect himself. The statement may be wrong: the further one, that Gracchus intended to make half of each jury[1] consist of *equites*, is surely no more than the echo of some loose talk on his part.

702. When the election came on, and two Tribe-votes had already been recorded for Gracchus, the opposition objected that he was not legally eligible. The presiding tribune Rubrius shrank from overruling the objection. Mucius or Mummius, the successor of Octavius, offered to take the chair, and Rubrius made way. But the other tribunes claimed to decide the presidency in the usual way, by lot. An unseemly squabble took place, and the Assembly had to be dismissed for that day. It was now clear to Gracchus that he was fighting for his life. Many of the poorer citizens, ashamed to leave their leader in the lurch, responded to his entreaties by guarding his house all night. Very early in the morning the Gracchan party occupied the great Capitoline temple, in the open space before which the Tribes were to vote. The tribune himself was detained by evil omens. He and his friends were nervous, but the rationalist Blossius scorned the notion that such things should turn the people's champion from the path of duty. So forth he went, and his supporters greeted him with cheers. The proceedings began with tumult which

---

[1] Dion Cass. fragm. 83 says that he proposed to transfer the *iudicia* to the *equites*.

brought voting to a stop: Gracchus, it was said, gave a preconcerted sign and set it going. The frightened tribunes, who appear to have declined to back up their colleague any longer, made their escape; the priests closed the temple doors, and all order was at an end. Rumours passed round, that Gracchus was deposing the rest of the tribunes, or that he was declaring himself tribune for next year without the form of election. Meanwhile the Senate was in session hard by, waiting on the turn of events. A friendly senator, M. Fulvius Flaccus, slipped out and warned Gracchus that the rich opposition had armed their slaves and friends: if the consul presiding (Mucius Scaevola) would not put himself at their head, they meant to take matters into their own hands and murder their arch-enemy. Gracchus repeated the news to his partisans, who armed themselves with every stick they could get, and prepared for a fight. A misinterpreted gesture was reported to the Senate as proving that the tribune was asking for a crown. Even so the consul refused to take the lead or shed the blood of a Roman citizen uncondemned, but promised to hold invalid any illegal resolution of the Assembly. But the furious Fathers were in no mood to listen to a lawyer. Scipio Nasica, who had all along led the opposition[1] in the Senate to the policy of Gracchus, called on those who wished to save the state to follow him, and led them in a body, senators and attendants, to the attack. We are told that the throng made way for this rush of reverend Fathers and even allowed them to snatch their rude staves from their hands. It is far more likely that the ill-armed mob, deserted by their tribunes, were cowed by the stalwart slaves, armed with proper clubs, who escorted their wealthy masters to the fray. Onward sped the representatives of property and order, and fell upon the faithful band still gathered round Gracchus. Overpowered and routed, the Gracchans perished to the number of 300 or more, among them Gracchus himself. Bloodshed wrought by sticks and stones had asserted the majesty of the Roman constitution. To deny burial to the dead was a wanton outrage on religious sentiment, but the victors had the corpses cast into the Tiber under cover of the night.

703. The whole story is a convincing proof of the utter political helplessness of the Roman government at home now that it was supreme abroad. When he comes to the critical moment at which the senators rose with Nasica to put down Gracchus by force, Appian says 'I wonder they never even thought of having recourse to a Dictator.' We have already explained why the dictatorship[2] had

[1] According to Diodorus fragm. xxxiv (xxxv) 33 § 7, he gloried in his share of these transactions.

[2] For the right of Appeal against the Dictator in the city see on §§ 149, 293.

been allowed to drop out of the Roman system. It had done good work in earlier and simpler times. Now the jealous nobles would not place such absolute power in the hands of any one man. Nor can we judge whether the office would now have served their turn. The obvious man to nominate would have been Aemilianus, but he was not yet returned from Spain. When we reflect upon the reform-movement of Tiberius Gracchus, we can hardly help noticing many phenomena that remind us of Greece. The impatience, the tendency to appeal to general principles without making enough allowance for obstacles, the extremities of party spirit in which the sacred tribune becomes a Greek demagogue and the Roman Tribe-Assembly resembles a stormy Greek Demos, the final scene of bloodshed worthy of an Argos or Corcyra,—all these traits suggest the factious discord (στάσις) that was the canker of the Greek city-states rather than the old-fashioned 'parting' (*seditio*) or 'withdrawal' (*secessio*) of the aggrieved that had once marked reform-movements in the politics of Rome. Sedition, the term used by one party to describe the proceedings of the other, must henceforth connote factious violence and the probability of massacre.

704. The wealthy landlords who swayed the Senate had indeed made away with the reformer who threatened their possessions. Plutarch thinks that for the moment this was their object, a view borne out by their next measures. They soon got a special judicial commission appointed with power to inquire into the complicity of survivors in the Gracchan sedition, and to punish the guilty. It is said that some (probably in absence) were outlawed, and others put to death, Diophanes among them. Blossius admitted that he had obeyed Gracchus in everything. 'But' said Nasica 'suppose he had told you to set the Capitoline temple on fire?' 'He would never have given that order.' 'Answer my question.' 'Well, I should have obeyed him: he would never have ordered it had it not been for the people's good.' The cleverness of the Greek[1] is characteristic: he stood by his friend, and the blame rested on one now beyond the reach of punishment. The court let him go, and he withdrew to join the pretender now in arms against Rome, disputing the possession of the kingdom of Pergamum. The commission probably sat in the latter months of the year after the election of the consuls for 132, for they were members of it: P. Popilius Laenas, a bitter aristocrat, was its chairman. His colleague Rupilius went off early in

---

[1] Blossius was a friend of Scaevola, and of Laelius, who was a member of the court. Cic. *Lael.* § 37. This may have helped him, but it is clear that he did not feel comfortable in Rome.

132 to Sicily. But the wealthy nobles, though they had done to death their chief opponents, could not venture openly to tamper with the new laws. The lost leader was openly lamented and his murderers, above all Nasica, greeted with open expressions of hatred. Nasica had to be got out of harm's way, so the Senate found a pretext for sending him on a mission to Asia. Nobody seems to have wanted him: he went from place to place and died shortly after at Pergamum. As for the land law, it was thought politic to soothe popular feelings by letting the machinery get into working order. So the people were called upon to elect a commissioner to fill the place of Tiberius Gracchus, and his friend Licinius Crassus was chosen. To the proceedings of the commission we shall presently return.

705. Numantia fell in 133, and it must have been at the end of that year or the beginning of the next that Scipio Aemilianus came home to his triumph in 132. It is said that the news of his brother-in-law's death reached him while still in camp, and that he commented on it by quoting a line[1] from the *Odyssey*, the gist of which was 'serve him right.' At any rate this upright man and good citizen was definitely opposed to the action of Gracchus as a whole. Balance, rather than audacity, was characteristic of his temperament, and one who had patiently earned a great reputation was perhaps hardly the man to sympathize with an ardent reformer hurrying to attain a difficult end by a short cut. The return of Scipio and the chief members of his social circle to Rome was a powerful reinforcement to the conservative cause, strengthening its most respectable elements. The sequel of this home-coming is perhaps the strongest proof that there was among the city populace some genuine land-hunger, some lasting resolve to break the chains that bound them under the selfish dominion of the noble and rich, and in this we may see a justification of the rash enterprise of Gracchus. That such feelings did to some extent exist was shewn by the disgust that became general among the poor when the views of Scipio were known. He was too honest to give evasive answers to direct questions, and the Roman populace never forgave his approval of the death of Gracchus. The story runs that this utterance, made in a public meeting, was received with groans: whereupon Aemilianus turned upon the angry mob and said, 'silence, ye step-children of Italy: think ye that I, who brought you here in chains, will be daunted by you now you are free?' But the common people were not all freed-men, former prisoners of war. The meeting would consist of men

---

[1] *Odyss.* I 47.

who either resented or denied the truth of his words. Henceforth Scipio's place in politics was among the narrow-minded and self-seeking nobles, whose jealousy watched him and whose methods he at heart detested.

We have now dwelt long enough on the attempt of Tiberius Gracchus and his violent end. As an episode in Roman history it proved two things: first, that a popular leader must enjoy a continuity[1] of power, and secondly that he must find protection against the use of physical force. Under the present constitution neither of these requisites was ready to his hand.

---

[1] Compare Livy III 65 § 8.

CHAPTER XXXVII

706. THE interval of nearly ten years (132—123) between the death of Tiberius Gracchus and the tribunate of Gaius is marked by events less dramatic than the stormy political ventures of the two brothers. The importance of the events in Italy is however very great. The maladies of the state were developing fast, and by the time when Gaius came to the front the problems before him were more complicated, the means at his disposal more various, the consequences of failure or misjudgment more grave. Before we turn to these matters we must briefly consider what was passing abroad[1] during these years.

707. The bequest of the Pergamene kingdom, whatever suspicion some might entertain as to the genuineness[2] of the will of Attalus, was a fact. We may be quite sure that the governing nobles were nothing loth to add another sphere of operations to their present chances of enrichment and power, and the prospects of profit on the lines of Sicilian enterprises, in a country famed for its vast resources, would no doubt cause a flutter in financial circles. And it was peculiarly gratifying to have such a mine of wealth handed over for exploitation without the strain and disturbance of a war. But a young man named Aristonicus, who claimed to be a son of Eumenes II by a concubine, and so half-brother of the last king, refused to be put out of the succession. Failing in the attempt to win the support of the great Greek cities on the coast, he moved inland and raised a great following of slaves and some free barbarians. He soon controlled a great part of the kingdom, and the Roman government made its usual blunder of not acting with promptitude. What was supposed to be the business of Nasica in 132 we do not know, but clearly he was not in command[3] of an army. It seems to

---

[1] For external matters see Livy epit. 59, 60, Strabo XIV 1 § 38 (p. 646), IV 1 § 5 (180), III 5 § 1 (167), Plutarch *Tib. Gracc.* 20, 21, *C. Gracc.* 1, 2, Appian *civ.* I. 20, Justin XXXVI 4, XXXVII 1, Valer. Max. III 2 § 12, 4 § 5, VIII 7 § 6, Velleius II 4 § 1, Florus I 35, Eutrop. IV 20, Orosius V 10.

[2] The suggestion of forgery is found in Sallust hist. fragm. IV 69 § 8 Maurenbrecher, in the letter of Mithradates to Arsaces, B.C. 68, see Appian *Mithr.* 87, above § 581.

[3] He may have been one of the five πρέσβεις mentioned by Strabo, but it is doubtful.

have been late in that year that the Senate (perhaps owing to Nasica's reports) woke up to the fact of the war. P. Licinius Crassus Mucianus (the lawyer), consul in 131, was sent[1] with a strong force to end it. As governor of the friendly parts of the province he made a good impression on the Greeks by his familiarity with the various local dialects still spoken there. But in the field he was a failure. Early in 130, before his successor arrived, he met with a crowning disaster. Seeing all lost, and scorning captivity, he wounded a barbarian soldier and met the death he sought. Thus two chief pontiffs (for Crassus had succeeded Nasica in that office) died in Asia within a few months. When M. Perperna, consul 130, appeared, there was a change. He defeated and captured Aristonicus, who was sent to Rome and strangled. He also took over the royal treasure and shipped it to Rome, but himself fell sick and died at Pergamum. Manius Aquilius, consul 129, hurried to the province, hoping to have the glory of ending the war, but was too late. It was he however who with the usual ten commissioners regulated the boundaries and drew up the charter[2] for the new province. Its official name was Asia. It was the richest of all the Provinces of the Roman Republic, and was more systematically oppressed and plundered than any other. Speaking generally, it included Mysia Lydia and Caria with most of the adjacent islands. Rhodes still kept her little strip of the mainland, and a few rearrangements of minor importance were made.

708. Several points of interest meet us in the record of this war. The epitome of Livy tells us that Aristonicus 'seized Asia, though it had been bequeathed by king Attalus to the Roman people, and so by rights was free.' This remark reeks of Livy. It is the same old story as the 'freedom' granted to the Macedonians after the victory of Pydna. It meant that there was to be no King, no central ruler to unite and direct the forces of the realm, and perhaps to prove troublesome. So much of the territory as Rome thought rich and ripe for 'freedom' was to be a Province, and the people free both to do what Rome ordered and to pay for the honour. The more remote and up-country districts were less eligible for inclusion in the empire: they would cost more than they were worth. Such possessions were according to precedent suitable gifts for the friends of Rome, and any commission that might be levied on the transaction was so much to the good of the state or its able diplomatist. And it is remarkable that in this war for 'freedom' a large share of the burden had fallen on Asiatic monarchs. To put down one pretender, the kings of

---

[1] For his wealth. eloquence, etc. see the quotation from his contemporary Asellio given in Gellius I 13 §§ 9—13, where there is a story shewing him as a narrow-minded martinet.

[2] For Aquilius and the *lex Aquilia* see Orelli's onomasticon and *index legum* to Cicero.

Bithynia Paphlagonia Pontus and Cappadocia had all furnished contingents. Ariarathes of Cappadocia had himself fallen in battle for Rome; a contrast to Blossius of Cumae, who was with Aristonicus and shared his defeat, after which he committed suicide, knowing Roman freedom only too well. Another point of interest is the appointment[1] of Crassus. Both he and his colleague L. Valerius Flaccus, the priest of Mars, wished for the Asiatic command. Both were properly detained at home by their religious duties, for there was no precedent for the absence of a *pontifex maximus* on foreign service. But the new chief pontiff imposed a fine on this rival by the exercise of his authority, and the Assembly on appeal remitted the fine but would not release the *flamen Martialis* from obedience to his superior. The question now arose whether the command should not be given to Scipio, who was applying for the post. No doubt he was anxious to get away from Rome just then. The matter came before the Assembly. Perhaps the claims of a consul as against a private citizen helped to turn the scale, but it was doubtless to his connexion with the Gracchan movement that Crassus chiefly owed his success. But this preference of the actual holder of *imperium* before the skilled soldier was in accordance with tradition and more especially with the policy of the nobles: they can hardly have given hearty support to the claims of Scipio. Yet they could not like Crassus, whom they would regard as a traitor to the interests of their order. The report that the failure of Crassus in Asia was caused by his devotion to the treasures of Attalus rather than to the business of the war, whether true or not, was surely handed down with pleasure by some noble annalist. Of his successor Perperna[2] we have a strange story. It is said that he was an alien in Rome, elected consul without even being a citizen, and that, while he was retrieving Roman disasters in Asia, his father had been subjected to legal proceedings under some Alien Act and compelled to return to his Sabellian home. Thus the son's consulship was declared invalid by invalidating the father's citizenship. This tale is full of mystery, partly owing to the style of Valerius Maximus, who is a mere compiler, so busy with emphasizing contrasts and reflexions that he is

---

[1] See Cicero, *philippic* XI § 18.

[2] Or Perpenna. The name seems certainly Etruscan, but the father need not necessarily have migrated from Etruria proper. I suppose him to have got enrolled as a Roman citizen, and the son to have been put up for the consulship by the Gracchan party in a dearth of good military candidates. Then the other side hunted up the defects of his family record and procured men from his proper domicile to reclaim him under the Claudian law of 177 (see § 628). Perpenna's fellow-consul was a namesake, perhaps son, of C. Claudius Pulcher, who carried that law. The mention of the *lex Papia* by Valerius Maximus III 4 § 5 is either a blunder or a corruption in the text. See Mommsen, *Staatsrecht* III 200.

apt to slur over important facts. The above points in the record of this little war shew clearly how home and foreign policy tended to run together and be affected by the same influences. We have seen how Tiberius Gracchus claimed to dispose by legislation of the treasure and territory of Pergamum. To supersede the long established authority of the Senate in matters of foreign policy and finance was (as we can now see) a very questionable improvement in the machinery of government. But those who challenged the supremacy of the Senate could hardly have ignored these highly important departments: the pity was that the Assembly was already far gone in unfitness for governing at the time when the Gracchan movement roused it to governmental action.

709. These considerations are further illustrated by the proceedings in reference to the outlying provinces of the Pergamene kingdom. Aquilius and the commissioners had doubtless received instructions to deal with lands not included in the new Roman Province Asia as they thought best in the interests of Rome. So they served out rewards to the client-kings in the old style. The sons of Ariarathes were to have Lycaonia and the 'rough' Cilicia annexed to Cappadocia. So far well. It was more difficult to settle the disposal of the Greater Phrygia, an important district lying mainly to the east of Lydia. It contained a number of flourishing Greek cities, particularly in the southern portion of the country, and its position was strategically commanding. Nicomedes of Bithynia and Mithradates of Pontus were both eager to acquire it. The latter succeeded in inducing Aquilius to give it him: what means he found so effective, is not certain, but report said it was a bribe. Probably all such assignments of territory were made with a formal reservation of the final decision to the Senate and People of Rome. Fifty (perhaps even ten) years earlier the settlement of the commissioners would have been confirmed as a matter of course, but times were changed. Doubts and difficulties were raised, and we may be sure that the capitalist class, instructed by their agents in the East, did their best to decry the folly of letting a valuable property, acquired by Rome, pass to a foreign power and increase the resources of a possible enemy. It became a question of Roman politics, and the details of what happened are extremely obscure. It would seem that Mithradates enjoyed the overlordship for a few years, but was deprived of it before his death in 120, when Phrygia[1] was declared 'free' to be exploited by Roman capitalists. The resumption of the gift was resented by the great Mithradates (120—63).

---

[1] From Cic. *pro Flacco* § 65 it appears that by B.C. 59 it was part of the province Asia. See Marquardt *Stverw.* 1 pp. 333—5.

710. It is not necessary to dwell on the troubles[1] of the Syrian
and Egyptian monarchies. Rome had nothing to fear from these
quarters, and had enough to engage her attention elsewhere. Distracted Syria suffered from the intrigues of her neighbours, especially
Parthia, and revolutions and murders formed the staple history of the
declining house of Seleucus. Egypt under her fat-bellied tyrant was a
scene of horrors. Physcon was driven out in 129, but he had kept on
good terms with Rome, and returned to Alexandria in 127. He held
the throne till his death in 117. In general the reaction of the East
against western influences was going on, for the Graeco-Macedonian
forces had spent themselves, and Rome had not as yet taken these
countries seriously in hand. The little wars in the North and West
were unimportant in themselves but significant. In 129 the consul
C. Sempronius Tuditanus made a campaign in northern Illyria,
probably to quiet some restless tribes and keep the peace of the
Adriatic. The traffic from Brundisium to the East had to be protected. In Sardinia a rebellion of the upland natives kept L. Aurelius
Orestes, consul 126, busy for two years or more. Gaius Gracchus
served as his quaestor, and helped to overcome serious difficulties in
the clothing of the troops by his influence with the loyal provincials.
His simple life, just dealing, and freedom from greed, inspired in
them confidence and admiration, but his popularity with Rome's
subjects convinced the Roman nobles that the young man meant
no good. So Orestes was kept on as proconsul in order to keep
Gracchus away from Rome. His return before his superior was
quite against precedent: but he saw through the device. In another
quarter[2] the Romans made an important advance: for the little war
waged with the Salluvii or Salyes was really the first step in the
conquest of Transalpine Gaul. These people seem to have been a
powerful Ligurian tribe occupying the hill country north of Massalia,
and some of the lowland down to the Rhone. They were a thorn in
the side of Greek Massalia. The Massaliots at last appealed[3] to
Rome for help, as they had done thirty years before, when plagued by
tribes more to the East. The Senate well knew that Rome could not
afford to allow a strong power to be established in those parts. The
only land-route to their possessions in Spain lay that way, and they
can hardly have ignored the fact that whoever controlled those coasts
could at will render unsafe even the passage by sea. They therefore
responded gladly to the call of their old ally, and in 125 one of

---

[1] See Holm's *History of Greece* IV chap. 19.

[2] See an interesting monograph *The Romans on the Riviera*, by Mr W. H. Bullock-Hall.

[3] They had recently been appealing to Rome on behalf of Phocaea in Asia, which the
Senate meant to destroy for its support of Aristonicus. The city was spared as the mother-
city of Massalia. Justin XXXVII 1 § 1.

the consuls, M. Fulvius Flaccus, was sent with an army to their aid. He defeated the enemy, but he and other commanders had to carry on the war till 123, when the Salyes submitted and agreed to keep away from the actual seaboard. In 122 the proconsul C. Sextius founded the military station[1] of Aquae Sextiae at a spot where some hot springs rose: the post served to watch the restless tribes, and it commanded the most direct route to the North and West, avoiding the troublesome delta of the Rhone. But peace in these parts could not be lasting. Strong Gaulish tribes lay in front, uneasy and determined to resist the Roman advance: the collision was not long deferred, as we shall see below. In 123 the consul Q. Caecilius Metellus earned the name Balearicus by his successful expedition[2] against the Balearic isles, in the larger of which he founded two Roman settlements. Thus the sea-passage to Spain was further secured. We have before noticed that to occupy islands was a part of the imperial policy of Rome. To keep up an efficient fleet in times of peace was difficult, perhaps impossible, for a state with a clumsy system of finance and no large free seafaring population: but she could at least hold the best naval bases to the exclusion of possible enemies, and thus start with advantage if she were at any time compelled to reassert her sovranty of the seas. The employment of foreign auxiliaries, particularly light troops, was also becoming common in Roman armies, and these islanders were un-rivalled in the use of the sling.

711. Passing to events in Rome and Italy, we may begin with the land-commission. Appius Claudius, P. Licinius Crassus, and Gaius Gracchus were now its members. That they were not idle, at least in fixing the boundaries between public and private land, is shewn by a few inscriptions of landmarks (*termini*) bearing[3] their names. But in 130 Crassus fell in Asia, and Claudius died about the same time. The two vacancies were filled by M. Fulvius Flaccus and Gaius Papirius Carbo. Appian[4] tells us that the possessors did not make returns of their holdings, as we must assume the law required them to do. So the commissioners (now all three hot-headed reformers) put forth a notice inviting informations. This, says Appian, at once produced a mass of troublesome litigation. For the measuring of the public land raised all sorts of awkward questions as to purchases and divisions that had taken place in the past. It came to this, that

---

[1] Livy epit. 61.

[2] Orosius v 13, probably ollowing Livy, says that the islanders were giving trouble by piracy. Livy epit. 60.

[3] Wilmanns 859, 860, 861, give evidence both for these three and for the later colleagues, Gracchus Flaccus and Carbo.

[4] Appian *civ*. I 18—19.

everyone was called upon to shew his title to land, and evidence of title in the form of documents proving sale or allotment was not always forthcoming. Long freedom from disturbance had no doubt made people careless, and we are told that some of the documents produced were ambiguous. Original laxity in surveying, the old easy-going proclamations of early days, allowing any that chose to take unallotted land for tillage, and the changes brought about by lapse of time, were all causes of confusion. That the rich had been guilty of wrongful encroachments was certain, but to detect these in detail was no easy matter: and no man liked arbitrary dispossession and removals that might deprive him of what was perhaps the best part of his holding. So the outcry was great, and the communities of Allies to whom land had been granted in possession were no doubt alarmed at the prospect of having to contend against Roman informers before a court of Roman commissioners. Themselves helpless, they sought and found a powerful patron in Scipio. He was himself opposed to the Gracchan policy, and he owed much to the Allies. It was their hearty support that had enabled him to win military glory, and he now paid the debt. He procured the transference of the judicial powers of the commissioners to a consul. This was C. Sempronius Tuditanus, for his colleague Aquilius had left for Asia. But Tuditanus soon found the embarrassments of settling boundaries more than he could bear, and made the charge of the Illyrian expedition an excuse for leaving Italy. A deadlock followed, for the commissioners had no land for distribution, and could no longer expropriate present holders by rulings of their own. Of course the temptation to use judicial powers arbitrarily, in order to keep up the supply of land, was great, and Appian puts this argument into Scipio's mouth. But he makes him address it to the Senate, and seems to regard the transfer of judicial powers as the Senate's doing. It must surely have been an act of the Assembly, that is, if the bill of Tiberius Gracchus for conferring those powers had actually become law. But the epitome of Livy, from which we get our only account of this bill, merely says that he gave notice of it. The power of distribution was carried as part of the main land law. If the disturbances and the death of Gracchus prevented the actual enactment of the supplementary bill, is it possible that in the time of revulsion after his murder, when the Senate was anxious to conciliate the populace, they conferred judicial powers by a decree of the House, and that the usurpation, being in the interest of the reform party, passed unchallenged? If we do not form some such theory to account for the action of the Senate as implied by Appian, we must simply reject his version of the transaction.

712. That Scipio's action was highly unpopular with the mass of poorer citizens we can well believe. But we must turn back a little from the year 129 to consider some other affairs in which he had recently borne a part. It was a natural move of the Gracchan party to try and recover the old right of reelecting tribunes continuously. In 131 Carbo, who was then tribune, brought forward a bill[1] to secure complete freedom in this respect. It was supported by Gaius Gracchus; Scipio led the opposition. The approval of Tiberius' murder attributed to Scipio was probably drawn from him when haranguing a meeting (*contio*) on this matter, in reply to a question put by Carbo. Laelius also spoke against the bill. The Assembly threw it out, a result which Cicero (in the mouth of Laelius) attributes to the speeches. Considering the ordinary character of Assemblies in these days, we had better allow something for the possibility of other influences. And the rejection was not final: some time in the next seven years a measure of the same tendency[2] was carried, though perhaps of a less sweeping nature. Another event of the year 131 or 130 was the accusation of L. Aurelius Cotta, probably on a charge of extortion. Scipio led the prosecution; his great opponent Metellus Macedonicus, who had commanded with credit in Greece and Spain, spoke for the defence. Here too the acquittal which followed is variously[3] accounted for. Cicero, to serve the turn of a moment, declares that the jury resented the excessive influence of Scipio, but admits elsewhere that Cotta was an artful 'old hand.' It is more probable that, as Appian says, bribery was the true cause. After all, Cotta was more one of themselves than Scipio. But the scandal did not improve the tarnished reputation of senatorial juries.

713. In 131 censors were elected: for the first time[4] both were plebeians. The leading colleague was no doubt Q. Caecilius Metellus Macedonicus: with him was Q. Pompeius (consul 141). They were once enemies, but since Pompeius' quarrel[5] with the Scipionic clique they had become reconciled. Whether these censors could, if they had chosen, have contributed to the solution of the great questions, land-reform and enfranchisement of the Allies, may be doubted. At all events it seems that Metellus confined himself to preaching. In

---

[1] For this *rogatio Papiria* see Cic. *Laelius* § 96, Livy epit. 59, Wordsworth pp. 353-4, 633-4.

[2] Appian *civ.* I 21 § 6 with Strachan-Davidson's excellent note.

[3] Cic. *pro Mur.* § 58, *Brutus* § 82, Appian *civ.* I 22, Valer. Max. VIII I § 11. The last says that the trial was before the Assembly (*apud populum*), which is not likely.

[4] See Livy epit. 59, Cic. *de domo* § 123, Pliny *NH* VII §§ 142—6.

[5] See §§ 604, 621.

a speech[1] of which two small fragments are preserved he lectured the people on the duty of marrying and rearing children: they should submit to what was confessedly a nuisance for the good of the state. The roll of citizens shewed only a small increase upon the numbers of the last census (136—5): as compared with the lists of any other census for nearly 40 years, there was an actual decline. Yet there is no reason to suspect the present censors of exceptional[2] strictness. Preaching indeed was futile: the poor lacked the means of rearing families, and the rich preferred luxury to family cares. Metellus himself was not to blame. At his death in 115 he left four sons, all men of eminence, and he was long referred to as a striking example of the good fortune of a proverbially fortunate family. But he did not escape trouble in his censorship. In revising the roll of the Senate[3] he omitted the name of a tribune, C. Atinius Labeo. Now that the activity of the tribunate was reviving, this step was sure to be resented. Labeo brought the ancient powers of that inviolable office to bear on the censor by having him dragged off to be cast from the Tarpeian rock. The censor was saved by the interposition of another tribune, but this did not prevent Labeo from pursuing his revenge. With full religious formalities he 'consecrated' the censor's property, an ancient punishment consisting in the devotion of a man's goods to religious uses. There were probably other causes[4] of friction in this censorship, and it is easy to see that the political situation was very complicated. Between the party of strongly conservative nobles, such as Metellus, and the Gracchans, the position of Scipio and his friends must have been a difficult one, all the more since they sympathized with the Allies, and looked at things from a standpoint rather Italian and broadly imperial than narrowly Roman.

714. To return to Scipio's intervention on behalf of the Allies. He had reduced the commissioners to impotence, and they were furious. Mob-meetings and harangues followed. It was rumoured that the Gracchans meant to kill him, on which he is said to have remarked 'that is just what one would expect from the enemies of Rome.' One evening, after taking part in a debate, he was escorted home by a throng of admirers. On retiring to rest he put by his bedside a tablet, to be ready for jotting down the heads of a speech

---

[1] Revived by Augustus when engaged in a crusade of the same kind. Suet. *Aug.* 89, Gellius 1 6, notes in Wordsworth p. 631.

[2] Or Perperna and his father could hardly have got enrolled as citizens. See § 708.

[3] Livy epit. 59. Cic. *de domo* § 123.

[4] Lange *Röm. Alt.* III p. 25.

to the people. He had been much abused of late: it had even been said that he meant to organize a massacre and so make an end of the land-reform. But he was found dead in his bed next morning. The suspicion of murder was inevitable, and the body, according to one story, shewed marks of violence. Various rumours imputed the assassination to Gaius Gracchus, Carbo, Flaccus, or even to Cornelia mother of the Gracchi, helped (it was said) by her daughter Sempronia[1], Scipio's ugly childless wife, with whom he was not on good terms. Another suggestion was that he had taken poison in despair at the state of public affairs. Lastly, Cicero through the mouth of Laelius treats it as a case of natural death. We have no means of solving the mystery. The health of Aemilianus had always been uncertain. The way in which the death of the first Roman of the time was received[2] is most significant. No inquiry into the circumstances was held. The Gracchans were glad to be rid of an enemy, and to the mass of greedy nobles and capitalists his pure unselfishness had made him a somewhat embarrassing friend. The man of well-earned renown, who would neither lend himself to oppression and extortion abroad, nor bear a hand in revolution at home, was taken away from evil to come, and many rogues and fanatics breathed more freely. So the matter was allowed to drop, and it is even doubtful whether he had a public funeral. The character of Scipio has been variously judged. He was probably made to appear greater than he really was, for he stood out among rather a weak generation. A true patriot he was, no doubt, but the ability to see defects in both the contending parties was not an effective stimulus to vigorous action. What vigorous action was now possible without breach of the constitution, it is very hard to say. But the son of Aemilius Paullus was not the man to promote revolution: hence he could only incur the unpopularity of a moderator. It was no time for a patriot to whom the constitution in its present corrupted and perverted state was sacred. Scipio's honest scruples prevented him from joining the reform-movement, and made him the effective ally of greedy nobles and unscrupulous financiers, with whom he can have had no real sympathy. He was not blind to the internal evils of the state, generated or fostered by Rome's imperial development, but though clear in diagnosis he was timid in therapeutics, and nothing would induce him to resort to crude political surgery. Whether the knife of the Gracchans, firmly used for a continuous period of years, might have removed malignant growths and restored the Republic to health,

[1] A bold woman, to judge from the story Valer. Max. III 8 § 6.

[2] Dion Cass. fragm. 84 declares that he was regretted by even his opponents, and that his death left the land-commission free to ravage Italy.

is more than doubtful. That the process of checking movements without remedying evils, a course of revolution in compartments, was fatal, we know. That a man of Scipio's temperament and training, placed in such surroundings, should do as Scipio did, was perhaps inevitable, and it is neither possible nor necessary to form any more particular and final judgment of his public career. His virtues had earned him the respect and affection even of political opponents. It is reported that when Metellus Macedonicus heard of his death he turned to his sons and bade them attend the funeral, adding 'you will never see the funeral of a greater citizen.'

715. Of the events of the two following years we have little or no direct information. From the sequel we can gather that discontents were spreading. The *possessores* had to submit to resumption and distribution of the public land. But it would seem that little was actually done in this business. The commission could no longer clear the ground by its own decisions, and the present holders under various pretexts [1] contrived to make the work of dispossession move slowly. In particular the communes of Allies were uneasy at the death of their patron, and it was becoming clear to the reformers (the leaders, that is,) that something must be done to stifle their opposition. The outcome of this conviction was a movement to make all the Allies Roman citizens. It was hoped that they would set more store by this than by the land. According to Appian, the Allies were eager for the Roman franchise, and ready to accept this offer of the greater boon instead of the less. But the Senate would not hear of any such concession, and steps were taken to prevent it. It must have been quite early in the year 126, before Gracchus started for Sardinia, that the tribune M. Junius Pennus brought forward a bill [2] for the expulsion of aliens (*peregrini*) from Rome. Gracchus opposed it in a speech which he afterwards published. Pennus is said to have made great fun of his opponent in the debates that took place; indeed the young enthusiast may well have been easy game. But the proposal was a monstrous one, and sure to enrage the Allies, whom it was an object with the 'popular' party to conciliate. And yet it passed into law. Nothing could prove more clearly the worthlessness of Roman Assemblies than this result. We know nothing of the organization (perhaps including bribery) by which the senatorial managers brought it about: but we may safely say that a most instructive episode in Roman

---

[1] In Appian *civ.* I 21 § 1 I am rendering διέφερον ἐπὶ πλεῖστον 'were as long as they could be in putting it through.'

[2] For the *lex Iunia Penni* see Cic. *de off.* III § 47, *Brutus* § 109, Festus, article *res publicas*.

politics has here been lost to view. For the moment no doubt a number of Latins and other Allies, present in Rome to watch their interests, were forced to withdraw, but the franchise-question was brought no nearer a solution, and the wrath of the Allies burnt all the more fiercely as the news of the insult went round.

716. The complication of party aims was at this crisis extraordinary. Both sections of Roman politicians wanted to turn the influence of the Allies to account. The leaders of *populares* would admit them as citizens, if they would cease to help in obstructing land-reform: the *optimates* would cooperate with them in resisting resumption of the state lands, but would not give them the franchise. The reluctance to fill up the Tribes with masses of new voters was probably felt widely among both parties. Those who had mastered the art of managing the present Assemblies can hardly have wished for the trouble of learning the business over again, perhaps under less favourable conditions: the rank and file of the present voters were not minded to share privileges and perquisites with a larger number. To make the Allies, who filled the Roman armies, the tool of both parties in turn, and to cast them aside when done with, was to court terrible disaster. Yet this is just what was at this moment the political position. At this time (126) Aquilius returned from Asia, and the dissatisfaction[1] with the settlement effected by him took the form of a prosecution for extortion, including the bribes said to have been received as the price of certain transactions. But even the rank of his chief accuser, Lentulus, then *princeps senatus*, could not prevent the senatorial jury from acquitting him. Here was another case of judicial corruption: such at least was the general belief. But the Senate annulled at least some of his arrangements, particularly the cession of Greater Phrygia. The scandal helped to embitter party-spirit, and Gracchus was now absent in Sardinia. Flaccus and Carbo were leading the reform-party, and doing whatever was done in the name of the land-commission, probably not much. But the Gracchans were strong enough to elect Flaccus consul for the year 125, and this hot-headed ill-balanced man soon brought about another explosion.

717. He at once introduced a bill[2] for granting the Roman franchise to the Allies. It appears to have contained a provision that those communities, if any, which chose rather to keep their local autonomy, might do so, and receive as a separate privilege the right of appeal (*provocatio*) to the Roman Assembly. Thus a valued safeguard of the life and freedom of the individual would be gained,

---

[1] See Cic. *div. in Caecil.* § 69, Appian *civ.* I 22 § 2, *Mithr.* 12, 57, Justin XXXVIII 5 § 3.

[2] Appian *civ.* I 21 § 3, 34 §§ 4—6, Valer. Max. IX 5 § 1, Livy epit. 60.

and a grievance removed, without the loss of local self-government. We can see that this might suit the case of communities not in possession of Roman public land. Those that were possessors would surely want to have votes in the Roman Tribes as a means of preventing disturbance of their possession. The Senate were strongly opposed to the proposal, but Flaccus took no heed of their remonstrances. The strain of the situation was relieved by the consul's sudden abandonment of the bill, after raising hopes far and wide in Italy. It is probable that the mass of the Gracchan party had no stomach for sharing their civic privileges with a multitude of partners, and that Flaccus foresaw the failure of his project. The senatorial leaders would spare no pains to ensure its withdrawal. It was at least opportunely discovered that a consul with an army was wanted to support Rome's Massaliot allies. Whatever may have gone on behind the scenes, the upshot was that Flaccus set out to win glory in Gaul, leaving others to deal with the consequences of his misleading policy.

718. Fregellae[1] on the upper Liris, founded in the fourth century B.C. as a fortress and base of operations against the Samnites, was one of the chief Latin colonies, and its importance had been on occasion recognized by entrusting the delivery of views held by several Latin towns to the mouth of a Fregellan delegate. It had proved its loyalty by heading the 18 faithful colonies in the crisis of the Hannibalic war. News suddenly came that this model community of favoured Allies had thrown off its allegiance to Rome and declared itself independent. It was an alarming symptom of the state of feeling in Italy. We can hardly doubt that the revolt was undertaken with hope of some help from other Allies. But it seems to have been premature, and the inner history of the affair is lost. The Roman policy of isolating the Allies was a standing hindrance to their combining against their mistress, and the lesson that union was strength and the sword the only cogent argument had not yet been so learnt by them as to furnish an effective creed. The Senate did not dally: a force was raised under a praetor, L. Opimius, a leading member of the aristocracy, and sent to put down the rebellion. This did not take long, for the town was betrayed by a traitor within. Opimius destroyed[2] it (*diruit*), which seems to mean that he dismantled the walls and pulled down many buildings:

---

[1] Authorities. Livy epit. 60, Rhet. *ad Herenn.* IV §§ 13, 16, 22, 37, Cic. *de fin.* v § 62, *de inv.* II § 105, *ad fam.* XIII 76, Strabo v 3 § 10 (237), Plut. *C. Gracc.* 3, Velleius I 15 § 4, Plin. *NH* III § 64.

[2] Opimius even claimed a triumph for this exploit, but the Senate had the decency to refuse it. Valer. Max. II 8 § 4, Ammian. Marcell. XXV 9 § 10.

temples at least were spared, and ceremonies and markets were held there in the time of Augustus. As a city, a community with affairs of its own and local officials and senate, it ceased to exist. A severe judicial inquiry followed, not only into the guilt of the Fregellans. It was argued that the rash enterprise would never have been undertaken without some encouragement from Rome, and a determined effort was made to prove the complicity of leading Gracchans in this act of treason. Even Gracchus himself when he came home was forced to defend himself on this charge, which he did with success. No doubt some Fregellans were put to death: we have no details. Whether it was true that intriguers in Rome were in touch with the leaders of the revolt is a riddle past guessing: that it was the policy of the senatorial managers to assert it is obvious. To represent their opponents as men who would tempt others into acts of treason, and then leave them in the lurch, was a sure way of destroying their credit. To keep watch over the district a colony[1] of Roman citizens was planted not far from dismantled Fregellae. It is a fair inference that its territory consisted of land taken from the rebel Allies, and probably assigned as private property to Romans. This would offer a convenient opportunity of providing a maintenance for some of the most persistent professors of land-hunger, and so far would help to weaken the hands of the Gracchans. The new colony was named Fabrateria, from an old town near. So ended the shameful story of the revolt of Fregellae. No more isolated risings occurred. The event had served to remove all doubt as to the true position of the Allies: they had no choice but either to obey in silence or to be ground in the mills of Rome.

719. In 125 there were again censors, who left a monument of their activity in a new aqueduct, the *Aqua Tepula,* which delivered its water to the Capitol. In 124 Gaius Gracchus[2] returned to Rome. He had been very popular in Sardinia, and his reputation seems to have spread far. King Micipsa of Numidia sent corn to feed the army in that island. He did this expressly to oblige Gracchus. We must remember that Gracchus was a relative of the Scipios, to whom the Numidian royal house had been attached since the days of Masinissa and the first Africanus. Envoys arrived in Rome to report the king's meritorious act. The Senate sent them packing, and

---

[1] Lange *RA* III 27 thinks that the Senate at this time got the Assembly to grant the franchise to some Allies (as individuals, I presume, not to communities). Thus he accounts for the large increase of citizens at the census of 125—4. Beloch, *Bevölkerung* pp. 351—2, with reason rejects this view, and thinks the census numbers corrupt.

[2] Return and election of Gracchus. Plut. *C. Gracch.* 1—3 with Holden's notes, Appian I 21. The fragments of his speech before the censors are given in Wordsworth's *Fragm. and Spec.* p. 354.

arranged that the troops in Sardinia should at once be relieved by
new levies, while the proconsul, and with him presumably his quaestor
also, should remain.   Thus they hoped at once to keep the dangerous
young man at a distance and to prevent his creating a military following in the province. Gracchus saw the trap, and walked out of it. But,
when the censors came to revise the roll of Knights, he was called
upon to explain his conduct in leaving his official superior.   That
the step was contrary to custom he could not deny: but he pointed
out that by law he was only obliged to stay one year, whereas he
had stayed two.   He added that he had served twelve years in the
cavalry, instead of the required ten; and that, whereas other public
servants took out to their province jars full of wine and brought
them home full of money, he had gone out with a full purse and
come home with an empty one.   His justification was complete, and
he not only escaped the stigma of the censor but won much public
sympathy.   Here was a young man whom artifice could not constrain
nor opposition daunt, called to the front by popular enthusiasm and
his family traditions.   In the summer of 124 he stood for the
tribunate.   The news of his candidature drew voters to Rome from
the country, in immense numbers, according to Plutarch.   Appian
mentions the disappointment of the people at the recent stoppage
of land-allotment, and perhaps this may explain the presence of
a mass of rural voters at an inconvenient season.   Gracchus was
triumphantly elected, of course: but the change of circumstances
since his brother's election was shewn in a marked manner.   We
must remember that in the voting by Tribes, though the votes of
all Tribes were given at the same time, the announcement of the
results was made Tribe by Tribe, in an order decided by lot.
A candidate was declared elected so soon as 18 Tribes out of the
35 had voted for him.   It was an object of ambition to make up
the 18 Tribe-votes first, and so be first returned.   Gracchus had
counted on securing the first place, for his reception by the people
had been most warm.   But the secret influence of the senatorial
party had been strengthened by recent events, and he was only
returned fourth in order.

CHAPTER XXXVIII

GAIUS GRACCHUS 124—121 B.C.

720. THE great difficulties[1] that meet everyone who tries to form a clear notion of the acts of Gaius Gracchus, after his election to the tribunate, from the ancient writers, are generally admitted. Not only is the evidence often conflicting: it is sometimes, from the laxity of the expressions used, impossible to feel certain whether two statements do or do not refer to the same thing. Later writers have at times undoubtedly misunderstood the information gathered from predecessors now lost. This defect may be noted even in Appian, who, though painfully meagre, is at least dry-minded and calm. Plutarch is fair, but his contribution has the weaknesses of a biographic sketch: he is however our fullest surviving authority. The rest of the evidence is almost entirely hostile. When Cicero mentions Gracchus, he is generally more concerned to lend plausibility to some assertion than to observe historical accuracy, and the circumstances of each utterance must be weighed, sometimes with no satisfactory result. What little we have from Velleius, Valerius Maximus, and in a few scraps of Diodorus and Dion Cassius, is drawn from anti-Gracchan authorities, and must be received with great caution: in the revolutionary madness attributed to the great tribune we hear the echo of the prejudiced version of senatorial authors. The account given by Livy seems to have been equally unfavourable, to judge from what we read in the epitomes. From those of Florus and Orosius it may be gathered that a number of details were preserved by Livy that have not come down through other authorities, and that his version differed considerably from the others. It is a pity that we have nothing from Sallust[2] but

---

[1] Chief authorities—Plutarch, *C. Gracchus*, and Appian *civ.* I 21—26, The references in Cicero, some of them very important, are numerous. See an index. Livy is represented by epit. 60, 61, and Florus II 1, 3, 5, Orosius V 12, (Aurel. Victor) *de viris illustr.* 65, also no doubt by most of the passages of Valer. Maximus (Halm's index). Velleius II 6, 7, is rhetorical but not a copyist. Stray references in Diodorus XXXV fragm. 48—55, Dion Cass. fragm. 85. Speeches of Gracchus given in Wordsworth. Discussion of other evidence in Holden's Plutarch. Other references below.

[2] Sallust *jug.* 16, 31, 42.

a few stray references, which at least are of an anti-senatorial tendency.

721. The gravest defect, which applies to the whole of our record, is that we are not told in what order the acts of Gracchus took place. It is impossible to distinguish with any certainty the three stages of proceedings (*a*) informal announcement of an intended proposal (*b*) formal notice of a bill (*c*) its passing into law. To attempt any chronology of his measures is therefore out of the question. We may see (or seem to see) reasons for thinking that one measure came before or after some other measure, but the evidence is so imperfect that all such inferences must be quite uncertain. It is usual to divide the activity of Gracchus by official years, and to speak of this or that act as belonging to his first or second tribunate. Perhaps a truer principle of division would be found by taking the years from election to election (summer to summer) rather than the official years (winter to winter) as its basis. We can thus form some general idea of the tribune's career consistent with the record, though its imperfection defies reconstruction in detail.

A. First, there is the year from his election in 124 to his reelection in 123. This would include roughly six months of preparation— consultations, interviews, drafting of bills, assignment of parts to associates, and general arrangement of the plan of campaign. Also some six months of office, in which the formal steps were taken, and a series of measures passed into law. These measures would be carefully chosen with a view to attach the mass of voters to their leader, to weaken the opposition, and so to secure the reelection on which the tribune depended for carrying out his projects.

B. Secondly, there is the year made up of the second half of his first tribunate and the first half of his second. In the summer of 123 he had behind him the fresh achievements of the past half-year, while before him lay a whole year in which to carry out cherished designs that required more time than could be spared hitherto. If a year was not enough, he must be reelected again. There was great temptation to crowd into this year measures that commended themselves rather to the leader than his followers, and by so doing to encourage his opponents and risk the chance of defeat if he sought further reelection. That the leader might be right, and his followers wrong, was a matter of no importance from the point of view of practical politics.

C. Thirdly, there is the half-year (summer to winter 122) during which Gracchus, though still tribune, vainly strove to hold his ground as the leader of Roman policy. His prestige was broken by defeat at the election of 122, and the time was in sight when others would be in office and he but a private citizen. We must add a few days, after the new tribunes came into office on the 10th of December, for the beginning of the attack on his measures, his resistance, and the conflict in which he perished. This short space of time, during which his public position was that of a commissioner for founding a colony, brings us into the year 121.

722. Several of our authorities tell us that there was a considerable difference between Gaius Gracchus and his brother. Gaius was altogether of a more intense nature than Tiberius; a more brilliant speaker, appealing rather to indignation than to pity: in temper more passionate and bitter. In speaking he was liable at times to lose control of his voice and scream. To check this failing he would take with him a slave-musician, whose part was to stand behind his master, and to sound a lower note on a pipe whenever he observed his voice becoming shrill. Tiberius had been goaded into impatience by the obstruction of a colleague: Gaius was impatient and tempestuous from the first. In courage, magnanimity, and high moral character, they were alike: in feature and expression the difference of temperament was marked, for Gaius was eager and high-strung to look at, while his brother was comparatively gentle and calm. Both were sincere patriots, seeking their fellow-citizens' good: if the younger aimed at excessive power, and consciously or unconsciously took a long step in the direction of monarchy, it was because no other way seemed to lead to the attainment of his objects. The permanent obstacle was the existence of the Senate, virtually controlling the whole administration of the state. There was no prospect whatever that the Senate would initiate or support any serious movement for reforming the abuses of the age and checking the decay of the Roman people. If anything was really to be done, it must be by restoring the ancient popular sovranty, and putting an end to the Senate's usurpation. To effect this, a leader with great powers was a necessity, and to set up such a leader, able and willing to bring the popular forces to bear, was, whether Gracchus saw it or not, nothing less than a Roman version of the old Greek Tyranny. In the little Greek states the concentration of power in a single hand had often served as a means of bringing to an end the power of privileged nobles (ἀριστοκρατία) and thus as a stage in the development of popular sovranty (δημοκρατία). But no real democracy was possible in the Rome of Gracchus. The rule of the Senate had been a possible government: it had now become unbearable, and was going from bad to worse. The sovranty of the Assembly meant the rule of one man, and the power of one man, to be effective, must be

permanent. In a great imperial state the power of one man could only become permanent when other claims had been extinguished, and when the victor should be willing to change sword for sceptre and bear the burden of his fate. But Gracchus, with the failure of his brother before his eyes, still seems to have believed that he had only to be at the head of affairs for a few years, long enough to get a few measures passed and to put the Senate back into its old position as a mere Council, and then things would go well of themselves. There is surely no evidence that he aimed at a lifelong Tyranny: if not, we must view him as the victim of honest delusion, a not less pathetic figure than his brother.

723. When Gaius entered upon office at the end of 124, he at once set to work. No doubt he had already drafted a number of proposals. He had already made his mark as an orator, and no speaker of his time could compete with him in fiery eloquence. His first business was to secure his footing: to justify the acts of his brother (and so prospectively his own) as lawful assertions of popular sovranty, and to put a stamp of illegality on the acts of the government in punishing the supporters of Tiberius. He produced a bill to declare that a magistrate deposed from his office by a vote of the Assembly should be on that ground disqualified from holding any office in future. The effect of this would be that henceforth such deposition would become constitutional; it would also prevent Octavius from repeating his obstruction. But Gracchus never put this proposal to the vote. He gave out that his mother had persuaded him to withdraw it, but we know that the deposition of Octavius had alienated some of his brother's partisans, and it may well be that the withdrawal of the bill was not merely to spare Octavius. To force it through might have used up more popularity than it was worth. To condemn the acts of Popilius and his special commission, who had put to death or outlawed the adherents of Tiberius, was a necessity, and, once taken in hand, could not well be dropped. It was necessary to challenge the claim of the Senate to set up extraordinary judicial commissions competent to give decisions affecting the bodily or civil life (*caput*) of a citizen. We must remember that the court of *repetundae*, now in existence for some 25 years, owed its powers to the popular Assembly, and that men were now familiar with this method of delegation. Extraordinary judicial commissions had in former times often been appointed by the Assembly, that is, a magistrate had been selected as president, and he chose a board of advisers, the normal Roman *consilium*, the regular machinery for official action of a deliberative nature. Gracchus was very naturally resolved to keep such appointments in the hands of the Assembly.

He could not punish the Senate, but he could make the president of a commission liable for what he and his *consilium* might do. The chief provision of his bill was that no sentence affecting the *caput* of a citizen should be passed without the Assembly's leave (*iniussu populi*), and that any magistrate, who inflicted a capital penalty on a citizen without the sentence of a competent court, should be liable to be tried before the Assembly and outlawed. It perhaps also contained a clause altogether forbidding the execution of citizens: if so, this must have been an extension of the famous but obscure Porcian laws. We are told that the law (for it was carried) was aimed at Popilius, and this may be true. All that was needed would be to insert 'has' before 'shall have' (committed the act in question), a common and simple turn of wording[1] in Roman statute-drafting. Consistently with this we hear that Gracchus moved in the Assembly that Popilius be 'debarred from fire and water,' the regular form of outlawry. This motion he followed up with passionate speeches, rousing popular indignation by recalling the past. Popilius saw that to attempt a defence was vain, and took the usual course of going into exile. His friends could not save him, but escorted him to the gates of the city with tears.

724. The ground was now clear. The other nine tribunes had fallen into the background from the first, and Gracchus had no opposition to fear from them. And all officers of the state must have been impressed with the patent fact that the leading tribune was a man best let alone by all persons who valued their own security and peace. It is most probable that his next measure was the famous corn-law. Little is known of it in detail. It provided that the state should supply corn to Roman citizens in Rome, who applied for it in person, at a price about half of what it was fetching in the open market. The state was in short to buy and sell corn at 50 % loss, and to lose a larger sum the larger the population it supplied. The effect of this measure was to turn what had in the past been a temporary expedient, only used in times of dearth from failure of crops or the pressure of war, into a system of permanent poor-relief on a gigantic scale. True, all citizens had the right to apply, and Piso, the author of the law creating the standing court of *repetundae*, actually came forward as an applicant. But Piso might urge that in a general division of the common property he was entitled to claim a share: he could not do more than raise a laugh, for the law was popular, and not likely to be repealed. It was of course a heavy burden on the treasury. Cicero tells us that in his speeches for the bill Gracchus posed as the champion of the treasury, apparently on the ground

---

[1] Such as *jecit jecerit*, *cepit ceperit*, etc.

that his scheme was the truest economy. Modern admirers of the great tribune sometimes lend their ingenuity to attempt a justification of this view, unwisely. The corn-law had two fatal defects. First, it was a cause of vast unremunerative outlay. Secondly, it tended directly to neutralize the benefits of the agrarian reform. The state was compelled to buy corn at the lowest possible price, which meant the produce of slave-labour in Sicily Africa and elsewhere, delivered at Ostia by sea. It thus became the large and steady customer of the transmarine capitalist, and its interest in the rural development of Italy was left to depend upon the promptings of philanthropy, easily hushed, and in practice insufficient to maintain a continuous policy. Moreover, the life of a small cultivator, always hard, was now contrasted with that of the city idler, guaranteed a supply of cheap bread, possessed of a vote that would make the guarantee effective and perhaps turn to further profit, able (if content with poverty and dependence) to do without regular labour, sharing the public amusements, listening to the speeches of politicians from the platform or pleaders in the courts, and resting according to the weather in sunshine or shade. No wonder that the attempt to renew the race of small farmers, the cause in which the whole fabric of the state had been shaken and for which men had died, was a failure. We may reasonably doubt whether the need of increasing the rural population was as clearly grasped, and made a prime object of policy, by Gaius Gracchus as it had been by his brother. The corn-law gave Gaius a hold over the masses such as no leader had ever yet possessed. The already existing mob voted for their own bellies, and a stream of needy citizens from outside, increasing their numbers, probably began at once to run towards Rome. So was gradually formed the enormous city proletariate, the tool of demagogues, established and endowed by law as though for the very purpose of destroying what it had taken centuries of painful energy to build.

725. We shall probably not be far wrong if we place next the land-law. It must surely have been one of the earlier measures of Gaius. It seems to have reenacted that of his brother, and at the same time to have restored jurisdiction in matters of disputed boundary to the commissioners. Whether the right of receiving allotments was extended so as to include Latins, and this with a view to neutralizing the opposition of the Latin communities[1] by playing off the interests of the poor against those of the rich, must remain doubtful. At all events the commission was able to get to work again. Another popular measure probably carried about the same time was the

---

[1] Lange *RA* III 32—3. The evidence for this ingenious conjecture is hardly sufficient.

Army-law. His brother had talked of a bill to reduce the length of compulsory service, and there is no doubt that there was a good deal of discontent on that point. The bill of Gaius seems to have forbidden the enlistment of lads under 17, which happened now and then, though illegal; and to have provided that soldiers' clothing should be found them by the state and not out of stoppages from their scanty pay. Here we may trace the effect of his late experiences in Sardinia. It seems also to have met an anomalous grievance, if it be true[1] that a practice of granting a free outfit and food to Allies in Roman service, while citizen soldiers provided them out of their pay, was actually still in use. It seems to have been a concession dating from the dark days of the second Punic war.

726. It is far more doubtful whether the law dealing with the province of Asia belongs to this period, the first half-year of his first tribunate, before he was reelected in the summer of 123. It is not unlikely that it does. We have seen that the attention of his brother had been attracted to the rich new province, though he did not live to propose any legislation on the subject. Whether his design of using the treasure of Attalus to provide capital for stocking the new farms was actually carried out, we do not know. It is likely that a sale of the valuable plate had been held: the articles for which Gaius Gracchus paid a fancy price[2] are supposed to have been bought at this auction; but what was done with the money thus realized, and the rest of the cash from the king's chest, we are not told. At all events Gaius needed to find a source of income to meet the yearly charge imposed by the corn-law. ·If we are to believe the words which Appian[3] puts into the mouth of Antony at Ephesus (B.C. 41), the people of the new province had been free from taxation since they passed under the dominion of Rome, and the imposition of taxes was the work of Roman demagogues, that is, of Gaius Gracchus. But this is surely not to be taken for serious history. That a reduction of the dues paid to the kings took place is quite possible, and the local authorities may have been left to collect them. The important change introduced by the *lex Sempronia*[4] *de provincia Asia* seems to have been that the dues (tithes in kind for the most part) were henceforth to be collected by Roman contractors, to whom the censors were to farm out the right of collection for payment of a lump sum. The auction for this purpose was to be held in Rome. The *portoria* mentioned by Velleius are perhaps only a part of his Italian measures. In short, the law handed over some of the richest countries

---

[1] Polybius VI 39.

[2] Pliny *NH* XXXIII § 147, Plut. *Tib. Gracc.* 2 § 3.

[3] Appian *civ.* V 4.   [4] Cic. II *in Verr.* III § 12.

of that age to be exploited by companies of capitalists whose greed knew neither scruples nor bounds. Against the exactions of these blood-suckers the provincials had only one effective protection, the firm and just administration of upright governors. It was at best a lucky chance when such a man succeeded to the post and remained uncorrupted by the temptations of absolute power. An ordinary governor was unchecked by fear of the court of *repetundae*: acquittal could at need be purchased, and in provincial extortions it was easy to exact enough to meet incidental expenses of the kind. The system was scandalous, but the poor provincials had little to hope from any change. If the capitalist class should acquire the direct control of the Roman courts, they would be able to punish any governor who might try to stand between the greedy capitalist and his prey. And so the last state of the provincials would be worse than the first.

727. The amount of public speaking necessitated by all this legislative activity was no doubt considerable, and Gracchus seems to have published a collection of his chief speeches on these subjects, which long remained current as a part of Roman literature. A few fragments[1] survive. It is possible, but far from certain, that a debate on the Asiatic question, perhaps in connexion with the disposal of Greater Phrygia[2], was the occasion of a speech of which a fine passage, the best and longest of his remains, has come down to us. Mithradates of Pontus and Nicomedes of Bithynia were rival claimants for some favour or other, clearly the sovranty of some territory. Gracchus himself was for keeping it and making it a source of revenue. With merciless candour he exposed the selfish aims of the orators. Some were for Nicomedes, others for Mithradates, in either case working for a royal paymaster. More artful rogues were those who said nothing, having wrung money out of both sides by threatening opposition. These gentry were posing as incorruptible men, deceiving their fellow citizens, while the truth was they were practising an old Greek trick of getting paid for holding their tongues. 'I too' said the tribune 'have not come forward for nothing: I don't want money, but your good opinion and honour[3].' Unhappily we know nothing of the arguments used by him in support of his law for the province of Asia. We are left to guess how a man of high character, proud of his own self-control and honesty in Sardinia, came to hand over the people of Asia to the mercies of the *publicani*. He must, one would

---

[1] See the chief fragments in Wordsworth pp. 354—5. The passages preserved by Gellius x 3 seem to me to belong to a later stage of Gracchus' career.

[2] Wordsworth thinks that it was Cappadocia.

[3] *honorem*, perhaps = office, meaning reelection.

think, have known what those mercies were likely to be. If he did it simply to conciliate the tax-gatherers and get money to pay for feeding the Roman mob, we have indeed before us a striking illustration of the arbitrary limits of Roman philanthropy. The obscurity that hangs over the acts of Gaius Gracchus may be illustrated here by reference to a law which Cicero[1] attributes to him. It is defined very loosely as a measure to prevent any man from being 'come round,' that is, got into trouble and ruined, by or in a trial (*ne quis iudicio circumveniretur*). This has been interpreted as a clause in the previous law against extraordinary judicial commissions. Another view is that it was a separate law for the punishment of judicial corruption. The words of Cicero seem rather to favour the latter assumption. It is conceivable that it may have been an attempt to put down bribery and undue influence. If so, it must surely have been one of the tribune's earlier laws, aimed at the senatorial courts, before he transferred the judicial power to the Knights. The whole matter is full of doubt, and it cannot be confidently assumed that the words of an orator represent, even obscurely, a solid underlying fact.

728. It was probably at this stage of his official career that Gracchus displayed the administrative activity and talent for the despatch of business, of which Plutarch has preserved a picture. To carry out the corn-law it was necessary to provide storage, that the food of the sovran people might be forthcoming as required, and to avoid the risks of temporary scarcity when the corn-ships were delayed by foul weather. So granaries were built, which long bore the name of *horrea Sempronia*. The land-law too called for public works. Roads were needed in many places, to open up country districts and facilitate the movement of persons and produce. Hitherto road-making had been mainly governed by strategic considerations. Gracchus extended the road-system rather with the view of economic development. He also improved the roads by setting up better milestones, by providing mounting-blocks for horsemen, and by more scientific construction of the roadways. New bridges and embankments rendered the roads more passable in bad weather, and reduced some of the steeper gradients. Over all these works the tribune exercised a personal control, directing a host of subordinates. He was the centre of a throng of engineers contractors sub-commissioners foremen orderlies clerks and so forth, and the amount of detail got through, the manifold supervision exercised, the good-tempered and serious patience shewn in dealing with a variety of complicated affairs, paralysed opposition and caused general wonder. How far

[1] Cic. *pro Cluent.* § 151.

the various powers that he exercised were given him by the laws already passed, how far they were derived from supplementary enactments, or even conferred by decrees of the Senate, in which he for the time enjoyed a marked influence, is not clear. But it was noticed that the concentration of so many powers in one individual placed at his disposal a great number of subordinates accustomed to obey his orders and look to him for a lead. He was unquestionably the first man in the state, and to all appearance meant to remain so. He was reelected tribune, and with him his friend M. Fulvius Flaccus the ex-consul, who had won a triumph in Gaul. So great was his power, that he caused Opimius the destroyer of Fregellae to be rejected for the consulship in favour of C. Fannius Strabo, a nominee of his own. It is said that Gracchus was suspected of wishing to be himself consul and tribune at once, but this illegal ambition is probably no more than a malignant suggestion of enemies. No doubt there were those who took pains to call attention to the existence of an uncrowned king and to insinuate that the popular movement for reform was nothing less than a restoration of monarchy.

729. The law dealing with the jury-courts is placed by Appian[1] after the reelection of Gracchus. Plutarch puts it earlier, but his account is in other respects certainly incorrect. It falls naturally into this place if we regard it as a corollary of the law regulating the taxation of Asia. Gracchus was alive to the necessity of strengthening his position in every possible way, and in particular anxious to attach to himself the capitalist class. The prospect of vast fortunes to be made in the new province was no doubt intoxicating. But, the more splendid the opening, the more irritating would be the chances of disturbance. We may well believe that the possible interference of tiresome governors, either virtuously acting on principle or greedily eager to keep the plunder for themselves, was not left out of sight in tax-farming circles. In the view of the *publicani* a governor's proper function was to keep the provincials quiet under systematic extortion, to hold the sheep while they were being shorn. And to this view the prospect of fleecing submissive Asiatic Greeks must surely have given a fresh definiteness and strength. The scandals of the present courts of *repetundae* are said to have been put forward by Gracchus as calling for reform. But it is most unlikely that his speeches were the only form of agitation on this subject: it is far more likely that the capitalists shared, or even started, the outcry. Here was a public man, who already had made himself popular with the multitude, and

---

[1] App. *civ.* I 22. See discussion of a number of difficult points in Strachan-Davidson's notes on that chapter.

had shewn an inclination to court the tax-farming interest. To make prompt use of so favourable an opportunity to secure a further advantage was from their point of view an obvious step. It is hardly credible that these keen and unscrupulous financiers did not take it. In the first drafts of the jury-bill proposals for mixed courts of senators and knights, or for putting a number of knights into the Senate and thus effecting a dilution of senatorial juries (a plan which must soon have resulted in strengthening the enlarged Senate), may have found a place. Such provisions, attributed by some authorities[1] to the law of Gracchus, if ever actually proposed, evidently did not appear in the bill that became law. It simply transferred the right of sitting as jurors from senators to knights. The change would take the form of enacting that the praetor whose duty it was to prepare the list of qualified jurors (*album iudicum*) should choose them from a class of persons defined in a particular way, and the definition was so framed as to exclude both senators and common citizens. The effect of the *lex iudiciaria* was to put provincial governors at the mercy of a class of greedy investors, and incidentally to establish this class as a recognized rank or order (*ordo equester*). What their numbers were we do not know, but they were considerable, and community of interests and the experience gained by share-holding in companies (*societates publicanorum*) made the Equestrian Order a great power in the State.

730. The nobles had of course worked hard to defeat the bill, and the issue was not one likely to have much interest for the mob. We are not surprised to hear that it only passed by 18 Tribes to 17, but it may serve to remind us of the forces that were still working against Gracchus beneath the surface of political life. True, a law was a law, and there was no likelihood that this one would be a dead letter. The tribune had triumphed over the Senate. The state was henceforth two-headed, for the two privileged Orders faced each other in open rivalry, and in material power the Equestrian had for the present the upper hand. It is said that Gracchus boasted that he had found a weapon for senators and knights to hack each other with. Be this as it may, it is certain that the control of the *iudicia* became a bone of contention between the Orders, and thus introduced further discord into the already distracted Republic. It is hard for us to imagine a society in which the Judicature was habitually used as the organ of party vengeance or private gain, and in which the trial of a case on its merits was rather a professed aspiration than a reasonable hope. Such however was the state of things in Rome during the period of revolution. The writings of Cicero teem with references and allusions to

---

[1] Plutarch *C. G.* 5, Livy epit. 60. See note at end of this chapter.

this horrible abuse, and Appian, writing some 250 years after the death of Gaius Gracchus, interrupts his sober narrative to enlarge upon the evils that followed the legislation of Gracchus in this department of public life. In treating judicial reform as a class-question for party purposes the tyrant-tribune exposed the inherent weakness of his methods. How completely his power had superseded all others was shewn by the fact that the selection of the first list of equestrian *iudices* was by a vote of the Assembly entrusted to the tribune[1] himself, and not left to a praetor. All initiative was being concentrated in the hands of one man, whose activity transcended all official limits: and yet no effective step was taken to ensure that this managing director of the state should continue in possession of the power needed for the indispensable supervision and correction of his own creations. All was at the mercy of a party-system already degenerating into mere collision of factions, in a commonwealth where no strong and sound elements remained capable of maintaining a true republican government. The jury-law of Gracchus, which marks the zenith of his power, brings home to us the simple truth that he who would take on him the responsibilities of a monarch must first secure the crown.

731. It seems likely that the measures for foundation of colonies— citizen colonies of course—belong to this stage. Plutarch's story is that Gracchus saw that it was now war to the knife with the Senate, and noticed that Fannius (on whose support as consul he meant to rely) was shewing signs of lukewarmness. So he set to work to revive the attachment of the smaller capitalists[2] by colonial laws. The zeal of the masses had, it seems, been waxing cool, perhaps for want of interest in the question of the law-courts. The first proposal[3] was to send colonists to Capua and Tarentum. The former lay in the midst of a rich agricultural district mostly owned by the Roman state, and let out in farms to tenants. The Campanian rents were among the safest and most regular receipts of the Roman treasury, and with this valuable asset the land-laws had not ventured to tamper. There was also much eligible public land in the district of Tarentum, and the city was still a port of mercantile importance. Two more attractive sites could hardly be found, but it is clear that there were difficulties. Capua was no city at all, but a group of houses. The Campanians[4] were in the position

---

[1] Plutarch *C. G.* 6.

[2] Plut. *C. G.* 9 says τοὺς χαριεστάτους τῶν πολιτῶν, and Ferrero I p. 56 rightly argues that these colonies were meant rather to be trading-stations than refuges for mere paupers.

[3] See Marquardt, *Staatsvw.* I 107.

[4] See above § 625. When the Campani received the full franchise is not known, but it was before the great Italian or Marsic war. May it not have been granted during the reaction after the fall of C. Gracchus?

of half-citizens who had grievously erred in joining Hannibal, and had recently, after many years of disgrace, been restored to favour. But the confiscated land remained the property of the Roman people. The tenants of the farms would mostly, if not all, be Campanian half-citizens, probably hoping soon to be promoted to the full franchise. If a number of Romans were to be planted in Capua, some of the public land would surely have to be assigned to them, and this could not be done without ejecting present tenants. Gracchus can hardly have wished to add to his embarrassments by the discontents that such a disturbance was certain to provoke, and the Senate would hardly approve the financial loss implied in the sacrifice of rents. It does not appear that this colony was planted at all, and the above considerations may have helped to prevent the execution of an ill-designed scheme. The case of Tarentum was different. A body of colonists was sent there, and the official name Neptunia given to it, but the old Greek constitution was not suppressed. This may have been due to some action of the Senate after the fall of Gracchus: anyhow it was and remained a Greek city, in name only a Roman colony.

732. There seemed to be no end to the tribune's restless activity. Open opposition was vain, but the Senate well knew that passing laws and carrying them out were two very different things. So they now resorted to an artful policy of bowing to the storm, and waiting for the chances of better political weather, when their turn would come. M. Livius Drusus, a man of noble birth and high repute, was one of the tribunes, for Gracchus had not been able to fill all the places with his submissive tools. This respectable man was now put forward by the Senate to outbid Gracchus by larger and more showy proposals, and so to undermine his popularity. The Fathers rightly judged that the Assembly would swallow the bait offered by the sham demagogue. By this means they would get rid of the real one, and this was their present object. If Gracchus could be overthrown, the Assembly would relapse into helplessness: and if he resisted—well, many no doubt reflected that dead demagogues disturb no vested interests. The Livian laws of Drusus took a line parallel with the Sempronian. Gracchus provided for two colonies, Drusus for twelve, and these with less restrictions to ensure the choice of respectable[1] colonists: Gracchus provided that the recipients of allotments under the land-law should pay a quit-rent to the state, and this Drusus now proposed to remit. Gracchus had been talking of a bill to grant the Roman franchise to the Latins, and perhaps some privilege (possibly the 'Latin right') to the other Allies. Drusus

---

[1] τῶν ἀπόρων, says Plutarch.

cleverly proposed[1] to exempt the Latin soldier from liability to
scourging, that is, to extend to him the right of appeal in certain
circumstances which had been granted to the citizen soldier by one
of the Porcian laws. This concession would meet a real grievance,
and yet would not admit the Latin to a share of such perquisites as
corn-doles in Rome and land-allotments outside, rights which the
franchise would confer, but which the selfish populace of Rome preferred to keep for themselves. Here was a leader after their own
heart, who asked them for less than Gracchus did, and offered them
more. He gave the Senate the credit of this liberal policy, and
removed or lessened the suspicious antipathy with which the masses
were wont to regard the nobility: and the fickle and short-sighted
mob seem not to have perceived that this sudden devotion of the
Senate to the popular cause was insincere. The laws of Drusus
were of course not all carried at once, but were a series of attacks
on the popularity of Gracchus, and on the whole attained their real
object. For the genuine demagogue could hardly use his right as
tribune to block these bills: to do so would play into the hands of the
sham one. Thus the position of Gracchus was gradually weakened,
though he was by no means driven from power.

733. The obscurity hanging over the course of events is so great
that we cannot even tell whether the law for founding a colony at
Carthage comes before or after the intervention of Drusus. Assuming
it to be after this, it must have been at the beginning of the year 122.
Rubrius[2], a colleague of Gracchus, took charge of the measure. It
was a new move to plant a colony outside Italy, but the law passed.
Africa had been recently visited by a plague[3] of locusts, followed by a
pestilence and great loss of life. Whether the new scheme was in any
way connected with these local calamities, which had upset the province
a good deal, is doubtful. The famed fertility of the country round
Carthage was probably the main attraction, and Gracchus seems to
have paid no heed to the curse laid upon the site by Scipio. To this
subject we shall return later. We must now speak of a law which
almost certainly belongs to this year. It is generally identified with
a *lex Acilia* mentioned by Cicero, and the Acilius who was its author
is supposed to have been a colleague and follower of Gracchus. It is
a law reorganizing the court of *repetundae* with the new Gracchan
iudices and some changes of procedure. Apparently it was thought

---

[1] I can see no other way to get a real meaning out of Plutarch *C. G.* 9. The point must
be that the law was more acceptable to the Roman populace (not to the Latins) than the
scheme of Gracchus.

[2] See *lex agraria* line 59 (Wordsworth, pp. 198, 456), Plutarch, *C. G.* 10.

[3] Livy epit. 60, Orosius v. 11.

desirable to simplify and expedite the procedure of the court, the arrangements of the Calpurnian law of 149 being in some respects obsolete. The restitution required was in future to be double the amount of the established claim. A reference[1] to the *lex Rubria* shews that it was passed after that law. Senators are expressly excluded from the juries. Of the *lex Acilia repetundarum* a large part is preserved[2] on a bronze plate, and early copies of some of the lost fragments exist, made by scholars in the 15th century, when the plate was more perfect.

734. Another matter dealt with by Gracchus, probably in connexion with the law of *repetundae*, was the assignment of provincial governorships. By its control over this the Senate was able to control the magistrates, that is practically the consuls. If a consul was elected who had in any way defied the ruling nobles, they took care that no desirable post should be assigned as 'consular,' and so put within his reach. The *lex Sempronia*[3] *de provinciis consularibus* left the selection in the Senate's hands, but enacted that it should be made in each year for the year following, at some time before the consular elections. Thus instead of the Senate naming the provinces assigned to the consuls-elect, the Assembly would elect consuls to hold provinces already named. The Senate lost its position of vantage, and the consuls were under far less constraint to do the Senate's will. The measure was probably a wise and moderate one. In particular, it left to the Senate one useful power which no other body was fitted to exercise, that of keeping on a proconsul in his province whenever public policy required that he should be left to finish work already begun. By simply not naming the province as the department of a consul in the next year, the present governor held on until superseded, and in cases where a war was in progress this was most important. The Senate might not always use this power wisely, but Gracchus doubtless saw that there was really no alternative. The Assemblies were quite unfit to decide such points: and to injure Rome by democratic measures was no part of the tribune's conscious aim. To give the Assemblies themselves a more democratic character was of course an object. He is said to have brought forward a bill to change the order of voting[4] in the Assembly

---

[1] *lex Acilia*, line 22.

[2] See Bruns, *Fontes iuris Romani*, and Wordsworth's *Specimens*.

[3] See Sallust *Jug.* 27 § 3, 62 § 10, 73 § 7, Cic. *de domo* § 24, *pro Balbo* § 61, *de prov. cons.* §§ 3, 17. From the last passage it appears that tribunes were not allowed to veto the choice made by the Senate.

[4] Pseudo-Sallust *ad Caesarem de republica ordinanda* 2 § 8 *ut ex confusis quinque classibus sorti centuriae vocarentur.*

of the Centuries. The five Classes were to be blent together (*confusae*) and the order of voting to be fixed by lot on each occasion. This would do away with the precedence of the wealthy first Class, so far as it still remained. The lot might assign the first vote to any Century of young or old, rich or poor. And the tendency to follow the lead of the *praerogativa* made this of importance. No doubt the aim of Gracchus was to improve the chances of 'popular' candidates at the consular elections. We do not know that the bill ever became law. Our only authority for this proposal is a work published under the name of Sallust by some unknown writer of the imperial age. But this late rhetorician must surely have got the story from an earlier author to whom Classes and Centuries were still technical terms with a meaning: he can hardly have invented it.

735. It is probable that the rivalry of Gracchus and Drusus was now in full swing, the latter having the advantage of being free to block his opponent's measures by use of the tribunician power. The bill just mentioned may have been blocked by him. If Gracchus did meet any of his bills by *intercessio*, he would be quite ready to drop what was never seriously meant, and to turn the odium of obstruction on his opponent. But to Gracchus, who was in earnest, the opposition of a colleague was a deadly blow. The most important of his later measures was the bill for granting the franchise to the Latins. As to the details of this proposal we are very ill informed. From the confused accounts[1] of Appian and Plutarch it is generally inferred that the non-Latin Allies were to be raised to the present position of the Latins. To the Latins a choice was offered: either they might become full Roman citizens, or they might receive the right of *provocatio*, which would give them the same personal protection as was guaranteed to citizens by the Porcian and Sempronian laws. Under the latter alternative it was possible for a community to retain its local autonomy, and this seems to shew that the offer was made to communities, not to individuals. Thus it would follow the lines of the abortive bill of Flaccus. The alternative appeared also in the *lex Acilia*[2], but there as a reward offered to individuals who successfully prosecuted an offender in the court of *repetundae*: and it seems that, while this particular choice was restricted to Latins, the general offer of the citizenship as a reward was open to all. The right of voting in Roman Assemblies was a privilege of

---

[1] Appian *civ.* I 23, Plut. *C. G.* 8, 9. The language of Velleius, *dabat civitatem omnibus Italicis, extendebat eam paene usque Alpis*, is loose and rhetorical, and does not help us much. He had said much the same of Tib. Gracchus.

[2] *lex Acilia* 76—88. See note at end of this chapter.

very uncertain value, and might be bought too dear. The most absurd privilege[1] of Latins under existing rules was that they were allowed to vote in one Tribe selected by lot. It gave no effective power of influencing the result by votes. But the employment of Latins who happened to be in Rome, to influence results by agitation and uproar, seems not to have been unknown, and to keep them quiet or get rid of them was no doubt an object. Whenever the franchise-law of Gracchus came on for voting, it was pretty certain that the city would be crowded with Latins for days together. There was thus a good excuse for taking precautions to avert a riot. But the day of voting was delayed by the absence of the proposer.

736. Gracchus was one of the three commissioners for planting the colony at Carthage. Of course he had to take upon him such duties, particularly the unpleasant ones that others shirked, if the laws were to be carried out with good faith and energy. But he got little credit for undertaking what must have been an irksome charge. Drusus would accept no such appointment[2] under his own colonial law, trying to cast odium upon Gracchus as a selfish monopolizer of power. Gracchus then went to Carthage, leaving his proper field of action as a tribune, and worked at high pressure, travelling and surveying, marking out the site of the town and the divisions and boundaries of its territory, then back in haste to Rome, after an absence of only 70 days. Here he found that his enemies had gained ground while his back was turned. The agitation about the Allies was going on, and Flaccus, who according to Plutarch had stayed behind in Rome, was suspected of secret dealings with the Allies, encouraging them to claim the franchise by revolt. The consul Fannius had now gone over to the opposition, and Opimius the destroyer of Fregellae was known to be a candidate for the consulship of the following year. The populace were tired of burning questions. They had got their cheap corn, and plenty of promised colonies, if they cared to go to them. But many, it would seem, now preferred to stop where they were. Gracchus had found plenty of spare land round Carthage, so he had staked out 6000 allotments, a larger number than the *lex Rubria* had provided for. But the transmarine colony was not a popular project, and stories were soon circulated of the strange things that had happened when it was being laid out by the commissioners, signs ominous of evil to come. The superstitious masses were easily worked upon by these stories, spread by the industrious ill-will of the opposition. It is not surprising that

---

[1] Is it just possible that this arrangement may have been a device to get the visitors together and keep them quiet? See Livy xxv 3.

[2] Illegal, it would seem. See § 652 above.

Gracchus and his fellow commissioners invited colonists from all parts of Italy to make up the 6000. This probably means that Allies were offered the membership of a citizen colony, carrying with it the Roman franchise. The opposition to the scheme seems to have increased: why, is not clear, for it was in a fair way to take out of Italy some of the restless Allies. It may be suspected that the capitalists interested in the great African plantations used all their influence to prevent a new and wholesome element from being brought into the province. And the senatorial nobles may well have objected to the establishment of a Gracchan outpost in Africa. Gracchus was already in touch with the Numidian royal house through his connexion with the Scipios; it was not well that this connexion should be developed. So the demand for evil omens was great, and the supply rose: preparations were made for repealing the Rubrian law and bringing the Junonian colony to an end.

737. Three important issues were before the Roman people in the middle of the year 122. First there was the tribunician election. Gracchus was standing for a third term of office; reelection was his only chance of averting the ruin of his projects, indeed of saving his life from those bent on his destruction. Secondly there was the franchise question. This matter was becoming more and more urgent as the privileges and perquisites of Roman citizenship grew, and the Latins must have noticed in particular the tendency to legislate in favour of the city populace. Thirdly there was the question of colonies. At this time we hear nothing of the land-commission, and are almost driven to infer that colonial projects were more popular. No doubt the foundation of a colony seemed a simpler and more direct way of providing for poor citizens, and to be settled in a body as neighbours, with a town as their headquarters, offered a less dreary prospect than the comparative isolation of a plot of land in some lone rural district. The objection to the plan was that suitable places for colonies were not easy to find in Italy, and any attempt to carry it out on a large scale was sure to intensify the already widespread irritation among the Allies. In what order these three issues came up for settlement is very far from clear. It may be convenient to take them in the order followed below.

738. After his return from Africa Gracchus busied himself with preparations for laying various bills before the Assembly. The most important one was that for enfranchising the Latins. He now shifted his residence from the Palatine hill, where most of the nobles dwelt, to a street near the Forum, in a quarter occupied by the poor. If the corn-law had been still a thing of the future, perhaps he might have become once more the idol of the mob and master of Rome. But

the sense of gratitude was growing dull, and the illusive boons offered by Drusus had taught the fickle populace to look elsewhere for leading. The new franchise bill was not for them, nor were considerations of justice and sound policy likely to overcome their jealousy and bring them to share with the Latins what they wanted to keep for themselves. The corn-law as a thing of the past only made them less ready to back up its author. Gracchus was in great difficulties, but he went on with the bill. Much public speaking took place. It was probably in supporting this bill that Gracchus told three stories[1] illustrative of the cruel and tyrannical behaviour of the Roman nobles to the Allies. One of the chief reasons for desiring the Roman franchise was the prospect of escaping the liability to such treatment. Consuls, praetors, nay even young nobles not yet ripe for office, took upon themselves to have magistrates of allied towns publicly scourged for being somewhat slow in obeying the private whims of their aristocratic selves or their wives. A common citizen of the Latin colony of Venusia had been beaten to death by the roadside for a rustic jest on a stripling travelling in a palanquin (*lectica*), then a novelty. At Cales, also a Latin colony, the local authorities gave notice that, whenever a Roman magistrate arrived, the citizens must cease using the public baths until he was gone. It was in connexion with the baths that the chief magistrate of Teanum had been scourged, and the chief men of Cales had no mind for bloody backs. Ferentinum, an old Hernican town, had been the scene of a similar outrage. Was it wonderful that the Allies were anxious to change the state of things in which such enormities were possible? But all this was no more than an appeal to pity and philanthropy, feelings which a civilization based on slavery and tolerant of gladiatorial shows was little calculated to promote. On the other side the consul Fannius warned[2] the rabble that if they made the Latins Roman citizens they must expect to find themselves crowded out at all shows and spectacles. To this there was no effective answer, for it was patriotism up to date. Other speakers too opposed the bill, among them M. Aemilius Scaurus[3], who was already one of the rising men of the senatorial party. He had served under Orestes in Sardinia, where he may have come across Gracchus. From what we know of the two men it would seem that no sympathy between them could possibly exist. The Senate was of course watch-

---

[1] Quoted by Gellius X 3, text given in the introduction to Holden's Plutarch, *Gracchi*, and in Wordsworth.

[2] Cic. *Brutus* § 99. The passage referred to is quoted by the rhetorician Julius Victor in Halm's *Rhet. Lat. min.* p. 402. Lange *RA* III 43.

[3] These Scauri were patricians, but the family had been obscure for several generations, and was raised again by this artful man. See Cic. *pro Mur.* § 16, and Asconius, p. 22.

ing proceedings. Drusus was ready to block the bill, but they wisely preferred, if they could, to procure its rejection by the Assembly. A great concourse of Latins was expected in Rome at the time of voting, and Gracchus hoped in the confusion and pressure of the throng to carry his point somehow. To thwart him, the Senate induced Fannius to issue an edict requiring all persons other than full Roman citizens to keep out of the city, and at a distance of five miles at least, during the time of voting. The tribune angrily declared that he would protect any Allies who ventured to defy the consul's order. But the moral force supplied by popular enthusiasm was now lacking, and he did not venture to intervene when a case occurred. Indeed the tribunate, burdened with its long record of subservience to the Senate, and weakened by the recent deposition of Octavius and the murder of Tiberius, was no longer equal to so great a strain. So the collision of powers resulted in a moral victory for the consul and the Senate, the prestige of Gracchus was lowered, and he was not able to carry the bill.

739. In the course of these proceedings we hear nothing of the rural voters. Some of them were no doubt busy on new farms, and, having got their own desire, were indifferent to the claims of others. But in truth there was not much to rouse their enthusiasm in the movement for extending their privileges to others. Accordingly we find Gracchus, whose hopes now rested on the attainment of a third tribunate, confining his efforts to regaining his popularity with the city mob. A show of gladiators was to be given. It seems to have been customary to erect temporary stands for spectators, and magistrates in particular provided accommodation of this kind for themselves and friends. This selfish practice was of course resented as leaving insufficient room for the common people. A price was charged for the seats, and an invidious distinction created. On the present occasion Gracchus ordered the stands to be removed. No one paid attention to his order, so he gathered a party of the artisans whom he had at hand, and pulled down the stands on the night before the show. The populace, pleased with his resolute vindication of the rights of the poor, applauded the act: but the other tribunes, whose leave he had not asked, and who had probably engaged seats, were disgusted with their headstrong and high-handed colleague. Whether there was actual foul play with the votes at the election which shortly followed, was a disputed point: at all events the presiding tribunes were hostile to Gracchus, and he was not reelected. One at least of the new tribunes-elect was opposed to his policy, and his bitter enemy Opimius[1] was soon after elected consul.

---

[1] His consulship gave the name to the famous vintage of 121 B.C., which long retained its repute. See Pliny *NH* XIV 55, 94, and other references in Forcellini.

740. The prospect before Gracchus was black indeed. In the dead six months or so that followed his defeat it was impossible for him to effect anything of importance. The forces that had borne him to the height of power were manifestly spent. That any of his important acts belong to this unhappy time, we are not told, nor would such an assertion be credible. We may perhaps imagine him doing a little business as land-commissioner, or more probably trying to raise colonists for Junonia. His enemies were fully resolved to make an end of this colony, and their intentions were pretty sure to leak out. It is also likely that steps were being taken for founding a colony at Scylacium in southern Italy under the law of Drusus. This colony, named Minervia, seems to have been the only foundation[1] actually carried out under the *lex Livia*. On the tenth of December the tribunes for 121 came into office, and Gracchus became a mere commissioner under the provisions of certain laws. One of these laws was now openly attacked, and magisterial power in Rome was in other hands. On the first of January Opimius entered on office as consul. A date was soon fixed for the voting on the proposed repeal of the law for colonizing Carthage. Minucius, one of the new tribunes, was the proposer. What happened after this is told variously by our authorities. Several sets of details have come down to us, but, though differing in particulars, the accounts are not in any great degree inconsistent. It seems that Gracchus was anxious not to cause a riot, well knowing that the senatorial nobles sought occasion to destroy him. This surely means that he was ready to submit peacefully for the moment and to face the risks of a public trial (which assuredly awaited him), and that he still hoped for the reward of patience in a return of better times. But his friends, whose loyalty in the hour of trial is the best witness to his sterling qualities, in particular the hot-headed Flaccus, were for open resistance. It was agreed to attend the Assembly with concealed arms. Early in the morning both parties were astir, and all the points of vantage commanding the Capitoline yard were occupied by forces of one side or other. While the mass of people were assembling, an attendant of the consul came to words with Gracchus. Some of the ex-tribune's friends hastily fell upon the man and killed him. Gracchus was indignant at this criminal blunder, while Opimius exulted in the pretext furnished by the Gracchans for the use of force. For that day the Assembly broke up. Next morning a great parade of the attendant's corpse was held in the Forum near the senate-house: the senators, who were in session, adjourned to view it and express their horror at the murder: Minucius mounted the Rostra to address

[1] See Marquardt, *Staatsverwaltung*, p. 107.

the throng, and was interrupted by Gracchus, who wanted to offer explanations and express his sorrow. The cry was raised that he was 'calling away the meeting' from the tribune. This malignant interpretation served its turn, for *avocare contionem* was a dire offence, made penal in the early days of the tribunate, and Gracchus was now made to appear as one who had by his own act put himself out of the protection of the laws. The Senate reassembled, Opimius presiding, and they now ventured on a decisive step. By order of the House[1] they called upon the consul 'to see that the commonwealth took no hurt.' This famous form was in effect a strengthening of the executive by declaration of a state of siege. It may be[2] that the device was an ancient one, employed instead of a dictatorship for summary dealing with foreign or internal enemies of the state. We must in that case suppose that in the disuse of the dictatorship this power was tacitly reserved by the Senate for use in emergencies. Hitherto, during the long supremacy of the Senate, so extreme a step[3] as the so-called *senatusconsultum ultimum* had not been necessary: in the present crisis either an old claim was revived or a new precedent created. These two alternatives may come to the same thing, for the right of the Senate to grant dispensations from the laws was afterwards challenged[4] on the ground that originally the decree included a clause ordaining that a vote of the Assembly should be taken, which clause had fallen into disuse. Thus the revival of an old claim had by this omission created a new precedent. No actual statute existed empowering the Senate to act thus. But we must remember that in sudden emergencies the Assembly was useless. The Senate could always act as the *consilium* of the chief magistrate, and in Rome the presumption always was that the acts of a magistrate done with the approval of his proper advisers were valid. We shall see that the Senate held its ground, and even in the writings[5] of Sallust and Caesar, who represent the anti-senatorial party, the power is viewed as in itself constitutional, whatever may be thought of its exercise.

741. Opimius was now authorised to use force against the Gracchans as public enemies, and a bloodless end to the affair was hardly possible. In this moment of depression Gracchus still hoped against hope for a peaceful accommodation, but Flaccus was deter-

---

[1] It would seem from (Aurel. Victor) *de viris illustr.* 72 § 9 that the decree was approved on the motion of Aemilius Scaurus.

[2] See Livy III 4 § 9, VI 19 § 3. Whether these cases are anachronisms or not, I will not venture to say.

[3] See in general Mommsen, *Staatsrecht* III 1240—7.

[4] Asconius in *Cornel.* p. 57, Dion Cass. XXXVI 39 (22), Halm on Cic. *de imp. Cn. Pomp.* § 62.

[5] Sallust *Cat.* 29, Caesar *bell. civ.* I 5.

mined to fight. The houses of the two leaders were rallying-points of armed men all the night following: Flaccus drinking and boasting among a gang of desperadoes, Gracchus guarded by a band of faithful adherents taking turns of duty. The morning brought a summons for both to appear in the senate-house and give account of their conduct. The response of Flaccus was to occupy the Aventine hill with his ruffians. Gracchus followed, full of despair, for he was not the man to leave his partisans in the lurch. After this negotiations were opened with the Senate through a son of Flaccus. Opimius declined to treat with agents. The principals must come in person and surrender themselves to stand trial: the lad might report acceptance of these terms, otherwise he would only come again at his own risk. In spite of this warning the boy was again sent, upon which the consul seized and imprisoned him, and made dispositions for suppressing resistance by force of arms. His motley host seems to have included some soldiers embodied in the usual way, but an important part of it consisted[1] of wealthy citizens, each attended by armed slaves, and a corps of Cretan bowmen, whose arrows played havoc with the ill-protected Gracchans. A rout and massacre soon followed: Flaccus was dragged from a hiding-place and put to death: Gracchus was for killing himself, but two faithful friends compelled him to fly. While he crossed the river by the old pile-bridge, this devoted pair faced the pursuers and died to let their chief escape. Vainly, for he only got as far as a sacred enclosure hard by. There he ordered a faithful slave to kill him, which done, the slave slew himself over his master's corpse. A price had been set on the heads of the two leaders—their weight in gold. Report said that the weight of that of Gracchus was increased by substituting lead for brains, a trick of one of Opimius' friends: and another story was that those who brought in that of Flaccus, being common folk of no influence, got nothing. Many captured Gracchans were put to death by the consul's order, and with them the young son of Flaccus. He was a pretty lad, and many pitied his fate, but it was an hour in which the voice of mercy was unheard. The bodies of the slain were cast into the river. About 250 had fallen in the battle of the Aventine, and 3000 more were condemned[2] by Opimius afterwards. Women were forbidden to mourn the dead, the estates of Gracchus and Flaccus were confiscated, and with solemn rites the city was purified from the taint of civil bloodshed. To crown their glorious victory, the Senate instructed the consul to erect or restore a temple of Concord. This

---

[1] Plutarch, *C. Gr.* 14, 16.

[2] Whether these were all put to death is doubtful. See Plut. *C. Gracch.* 18 with Holden's note. The massacre was early in 121 B.C.

monument stood to remind men of what had happened : nothing, says Plutarch, irritated the multitude so much as this insolence. They mourned their lost leaders, and treated as holy ground the spots where the two brothers had fallen. But pilgrimages and offerings were but tokens of a vain regret : the Gracchi were gone, and their careers, whatever other effects they produced, had before all things proved that to rely upon the Roman People was to lean upon a broken reed.

742. When we pause to consider the condition of the Roman commonwealth after the death of Gaius Gracchus, we find ourselves in the presence of lamentable results produced by efforts on the whole well-meant. Every part of the state was changed for the worse by the events of the last ten or twelve years. The tribunate, once the organ of Plebeian interests, then of senatorial management, had done good work in its time. It had on the whole represented definite and serious aims, positive or negative. It was clothed with a peculiar sanctity. The tribune was essentially different from the traditional demagogue in the old Greek city-states. He was an official, with the powers and limitations of office: in particular, he was one of ten, each of whom could block proceedings. The power needed by a popular leader could only be created by the muzzling of his nine colleagues and his own reelection continuously and indefinitely repeated—in short, by the complete destruction of the tribunate, and the establishment of virtual monarchy. To work beneficially an office held by ten equal colleagues called for good sense and moderation at the best of times, but on the whole the sterling qualities of the old Romans had proved equal to the strain. Now conditions were changed; the great popular office was shaken, the relations of colleagues had lost their old reasonableness: what with bidding for the support of a degenerate Assembly, or serving as the tool of a frightened and malignant Senate, and corrupting public policy for temporary ends, the college had become a sphere for the quarrelling of its members and lost its usefulness and dignity. The later history of the tribunate is a chequered one, but evil throughout. It was reserved for the insight of Augustus to apply the only rational remedy. He absorbed the powers and left the office to others, for it was his policy ever to take out the nut with the least possible cracking of the shell. The consulate too was changed, not so much by the determination of the Senate to use it for restoration of what passed with them for order, the suppression of demagogy sword in hand, as by the new rule for assigning the consular provinces. The Senate could no longer directly favour particular persons, and it was now an easy step to make these provinces not consular but proconsular, and thus keep the two consuls

in Rome till their year of office was past. This meant that men, in their pursuit of wealth and glory, would come to regard the proconsulship, not the consulship, as the goal of their ambition, and that the regular crown of an official career would be a position monarchic in character and easily capable of extended tenure. An existing tendency was made normal. Great proconsuls with their satellite tribunes played the chief part in bringing the Republic to an end.

743. Nor was the Senate the better for its late experiences. In the use of force it had won a sort of triumph, but its power had been rudely shaken. It was not merely that some senators had been made to give up ill-gotten estates, that judicial functions had been transferred to other hands, or that bold tribunes had set at nought the authority of the House. The most serious falling-off was the general loss of moral force, of which these events were symptoms. The constitution of the Republic, clumsily constructed with many checks and balances, always in danger of a deadlock, had from the first only been workable through the presence of remarkable moral qualities in both the rulers and the ruled. As the dominion of Rome expanded, it was inevitable that the action of the state should more and more be directed by the great Council. And indeed, so long as the Senate sufficiently represented the old moral qualities by which Rome had risen, the respect for the Senate, though less and less justified by its merits, at least kept the Republic free from civil war. But the shock administered by the Gracchi had reminded Senate and People alike that the power of the senatorial nobility rested not on law but on prestige, and this prestige, once shaken, was never regained. And the worst feature of the situation was this, that to weaken a body no longer worthy of its great position profited the Republic nothing. For no new organ was found to take the place of the weakened Senate. To assert the sovranty of the Many against the domination of the Few was in itself but a barren demonstration. And when the Few, with the help of money, slaves, and mercenaries, destroyed the champions of the Many, this was no genuine restoration of their own power. Rather it foreshadowed the coming catastrophe, for they that took the sword perished with the sword.

744. Of the non-noble capitalist class, long active in Rome and ever growing in strength, we have to note that the judicial legislation of Gaius Gracchus first established them as a recognized Order. Military service of *equites* had now taken the form of supplying officers, and sometimes a special mounted corps in attendance on a general. The importance of the new Equestrian Order was mainly

financial. For a long time the struggle between Knights and senators for the control of the jury-courts was effective in keeping these two Orders apart. But the vital distinction of classes was now that between Rich and Poor, and the necessity of withstanding the crude violence of later demagogues eventually led the two Orders to combine. The remarkable thing is that the policy of Gracchus succeeded in keeping these natural allies apart so long.

745. The Roman Commons, whose gradual degradation we have traced, were all the worse for what the Gracchi had done. We shall see that the land-legislation had no permanent good effects : nature cooperated with the efforts of the rich to nullify this reform. But the corn-law of Gaius could not be set aside, and the mongrel mob of state-paupers, fickle and corrupt, was utterly unfit to enjoy the pre- rogatives of the Roman People. Of its legitimate sovranty there was as yet no power on earth to deprive it: fed and courted by the leaders of rival factions, it existed to sell its favours to the highest bidder. It had in this revolutionary age one, and only one, important function, that of conferring on a series of individuals an unrepublican power. By its votes adventurers obtained their opportunity and usurpers legalized their position. But this endowed disorder could not go on for ever, and with the restoration of order by Augustus the monstrous mob of Rome ceased to have a place in practical politics. Long before this end was reached, the resumed and continued decay of Italian agriculture seems to have made the free small farmers insigni- ficant from a voting point of view. The country districts still sent some voters in Cicero's time, but these were probably men of property, for the most part from the towns. The Roman husbandman, of yore the backbone of the *populus Romanus*, had for all public purposes disappeared.

746. If we admit that the several elements composing the Roman people were none the better for the acts of the two Gracchi, and all the worse for those of Gaius, what shall we say of the Italian Allies and the Provincials? In the former, hopes had been raised, and at once cruelly disappointed. The insolent rebuff administered to them in the edict of Fannius shewed them what they had to expect from the Senate: the fall of Gracchus shewed that nothing better could be looked for from the Assembly. Conscious of being the mainstay of the Roman State in war, it is wonderful indeed that they did not at once rise in rebellion. Want of a common organization was of course the reason, and the actual outbreak, in spite of their exasperation, was delayed for thirty years. As for the Provincials, the handing-over of Asia to the tender mercies of Roman capitalists, and the transfer of judicial powers to the same selfish class, were

marked changes for the worse. The existing evils were great, but oppression had at least been irregular and intermittent. The laws of Gaius Gracchus created a machinery, simple and effective, which made extortion and misgovernment regular and continuous, by giving the parties interested in their continuance the power to prevent reform. The provincial system was henceforth the most flagrant abomination of the Roman empire, and no change for the better was possible until the logical conclusion was reached, and the empire brought forth an Emperor. That a virtuous patriot, eager to do justice to the Allies, keenly interested in the welfare of the Provincials, should have left both these classes in a worse position than he found them, was a sad result. Circumstances were too strong for him : in haste to achieve unattainable ends he had to gratify the citizens of Rome by sacrificing her dependants. In the present state of Roman affairs no reformer could do any permanent good unless he himself ruled the executive machinery for a considerable period, and for this the time was not yet come. Among the ironies with which human history abounds it will not be easy to discover a more melancholy parallel.

747.   I have said that the reforms attempted by the Gracchi were impossible of attainment. The whole story of their acts shews that the means at their disposal were insufficient for the purpose. That there was miscalculation on their part must be admitted, but by their deaths they atoned for what was at least no ignoble error. It remains to present in a few words an outline of the main features of the situation, features that could not be discerned by contemporaries. Economic reform, which in the Italy of that period meant revival of agriculture, was impossible without abolition of slavery, and the minds of men were far from being ready to accept so sweeping a change. Political reform, the essential problem of which was the creation of a strong working government, able to view the affairs of the empire as a whole, to impose its will on all, and to relieve some parts of the empire from the tyranny of others, was now only to be accomplished by force of arms. Faction fights, in which the nobles with their dependants and slaves faced the rabble of the Roman streets, were of no more use in solving this problem than the votes of the Assemblies. Armed force could only be applied effectively by the army, and an army must have a leader. And in truth, though discipline and military spirit had greatly decayed since the defeat of Carthage had made Rome imperial, the army was probably the soundest part of the Roman state. And the army had at its back the logic of circumstances, for an emperor was necessary, and it was only from the army that an emperor could come.

748. If considerations such as these had been put before the Gracchi, even Gaius would surely have been horrified. Yet they must surely have been in some degree conscious that the institutions of the Republic were unsuited to the work in hand. The position of Rome at this time is unparalleled in history. Even regarded simply as a city-state, she cannot be compared with any Greek model so as to make the comparison instructive. Her patchwork constitution, full of inconsistencies, compromises, fictions, makeshifts of every kind, had none of the finish and precision that were needed to satisfy the artistic Greek. It was not an oligarchy, for every citizen possessed of civil rights had now political rights as well: the class of half-citizens had disappeared. It was not a democracy in any true sense, for group-voting differed fundamentally from mass-voting, and the greater part of the citizens, scattered in detached bodies all about Italy, could never record their votes. Yet popular sovranty was in the last resort more unchecked at Rome than it was even at Athens in her palmy days; if the Assembly could only be got to approve a bill, it was law. Regarded as a city-state ruling an empire, her position was neither that of Athens controlling Greek subjects nor that of Sparta at the head of her Greek allies. Her provincial subjects were tributary, but they were of alien races: her Italian Allies, technically alien, stood to her in a relation very different from that of the Peloponnesian confederacy to Sparta. Not only was she more of a mistress than Sparta till Sparta became supreme in Greece, but she was their leader in virtue of definite treaties: they had had no external policy of their own for some 150 years or more. And it is particularly to be noted that Italy was cut up into irregular blocks of Romans and Allies. A map[1] would shew a series of patches, where Roman territory and that of Allies lay side by side. In short, the citizen body in a ruling Greek city-state was as far as possible concentrated in or near the city, while the Roman citizens were largely planted out in distant townships, and non-resident in relation to the city whose franchise they enjoyed. And, if Rome differed widely from the ruling city-states of earlier Greece, so on the other hand her empire bore no resemblance to the Greek federations of more recent times. So far from being a league of equals, it was an aggregate of isolated inferior units, and all power was centralized at Rome. This centralization had once given to Rome a marked advantage in dealing with her loosely organized rivals in Italy. But she had now no rival in the Mediterranean world, and the system that had carried her through the ages of conflict was unsuited to an age of rest. It supplied no means for its own peaceful reform,

[1] See the map given § 842 below.

and was therefore doomed to progressive decline. The outside world, cowed and passive, could only look on and wait while the disease at the centre ran its course.

749. The lamentable result of the efforts of the Gracchi shews clearly that they miscalculated the forces at work in Roman politics. The error is I believe to be attributed to the influence of Greek ideas working on sanguine temperaments. Even so highly-trained an observer as Polybius in describing the Roman constitution views it formally rather than vitally. He delineates the fabric but does not ascertain its poise. The use of the Greek term Demos as equivalent to *populus* serves to obscure an essential difference. It is hardly too much to say that the Gracchi acted as if the Roman Tribe-Assembly were a compact resident civic body like the Ecclesia[1] of ancient Athens. One can hardly help suspecting that Gaius had before his mind the example of Pericles, in whose hands the formal democracy worked as a government by the first citizen. But it was the real Athens that was at the back of Pericles: it was not the real Rome that first raised to power, and then deserted, Gaius Gracchus.

[1] For the checks on the sovran power of the Athenian Ecclesia see Gilbert's *Handbuch der Griechischen Staatsalterthümer*, pp. 285—310 of Eng. trans.

NOTE ON CHAPTER XXXVIII

This chapter was written before I had read the two very interesting articles by Mr W. W. Fowler in the *English Historical Review* for 1905. I admit that C. Fannius (consul 122, see Index), who is known to have written a history, is very likely the ultimate authority for much of the doings of C. Gracchus. But as to the working value of this hypothesis in detail I am sceptical. And Mr Fowler wisely rejects the bolder parts of the theories of Kornemann and Meyer. The modern attempts to reconstruct the contemporary authorities from a study of the later writers whose works survive seem to me interesting but lacking the certainty that would make them a sound basis for further conclusions. See §§ 7, 1042. As to the famous corn-law, its motives and merits, the argument of Mr Fowler (pp. 223—7) is most instructive, but I am not yet fully convinced. So too in his account (pp. 420—1) of the problems of the land-commission. I am not persuaded that the actual territories of the Allies were in any way menaced by its powers and action. Lands granted them in possession are another matter. Nor do I believe that Gracchus put to the vote two bills (pp. 423—4) for extending the franchise, and carried the earlier one. I think Plutarch has made a law (cap. 5) out of what was merely a professed design. On the other hand, the reconstruction (pp. 427—31) of the traditions relative to the jury-law and the proposal to add 600 or 300 *equites* to the Senate is very tempting. So also is his theory that the so-called *lex Acilia* (p. 429) may be the jury-law itself. If I felt quite sure that no other standing court save that of *repetundae* at this time existed (see § 925), I should accept his view. As it is, I have let my chapter stand as written. The most important section (§ 721) reaches a conclusion practically identical with the views of Mr Fowler, and my chronological order of events is very slightly different from his.

CHAPTER XXXIX

FROM THE DEATH OF GAIUS GRACCHUS TO THE END OF THE JUGURTHINE WAR 121—105 B.C.

750. THE death of Gaius Gracchus left the remains of the 'popular' party without a leader. The law abolishing the colony of Junonia seems to have passed. There was thus no community planted on the accursed site of Carthage, but settlers to whom land-lots had already been assigned appear to have retained[1] their rights. Of the members of the Gracchan land-commission Carbo alone remained. But Carbo had probably been cooling down for some time, and he had now fully made his peace with the senatorial leaders. The commission was not for the present suppressed: it is likely that two safe colleagues were found for the survivor, and its activity indirectly checked in true Roman style. With quiet determination the nobles set themselves to upset the agrarian legislation of the Gracchi, and they easily found tribunes[2] to see measure after measure through the Assembly. In 121 or 120 the provision forbidding allottees to sell their allotments was repealed, and the old abuses revived at once. The rich man bought out his poorer neighbour: if he did not want to sell, the owner of a gang of slaves could soon bring him to a more compliant frame of mind. Not long after, perhaps in 118, the tribune Spurius Thorius carried a law to stop further assignations of land, thus doing away with the commission. The land was guaranteed to present possessors, and the quit-rents payable to the state were to form a fund towards the cost of corn-distribution in Rome. Thus the city mob was provided for, and only the man willing to till the soil was disregarded, a characteristic reversion to the old policy interrupted by the Gracchi, combined with the fatal blunder of Gaius' corn-law. As Appian remarks, it might be some comfort to the poor (that is, the pauper mob), but from the point of view of repopulating Italy it was useless. One more step yet remained to be taken, namely the abolition of the quit-rents and conversion of *possessiones* into private property. This seems to have been effected

[1] This is inferred from the language of the *lex agraria* of 111 B.C. See note in Wordsworth p. 456 on verse 45 of the law.

[2] See Appian, *civ.* 1 27 with Mr Strachan-Davidson's notes.

by an agrarian law passed in the year 111, of which large portions have come down to us in a contemporary copy. This part of the reaction against the Gracchan policy was now complete, and it left things in a worse plight than ever. The state chest was burdened with the cost of supplying Rome with cheap corn, and the rents recovered for it by the Gracchi, which might have gone some way towards meeting that cost, had been abandoned. Only the rich had contrived to get some advantage out of the agitations and bloodshed of the past twenty years. The formation of *latifundia* and the displacement of free farmers by slave-gangs could now go on unchecked, indeed with the virtual sanction of the law.

751. An attempt was also made to upset the Sempronian corn-law. For the present the reactionaries had to be content with a proposal for some modification[1] of the Gracchan plan. The tribune M. Octavius carried it through the Assembly. It was clearly nothing like a reversal of the policy of Gaius Gracchus, and its scope is uncertain; but it seems to have relieved the treasury to some extent. In this time of reaction nothing is more significant than the point at which reaction stopped. The laws for the benefit of the soldier, for the protection of the uncondemned citizen, for the farming of the revenues of Asia, for transference of judicial functions to the knights, for the early assignment of consular provinces, were left untouched. To tamper with the Gracchan settlement in any of these points would doubtless have evoked strong opposition, and the senatorial leaders were in no humour for raising an unnecessary storm. Their timidity is probably also to be traced in the fate of Carbo. In 119 the young orator L. Licinius Crassus impeached him, probably on a charge[2] of *perduellio*, in the interest of the 'popular' party. His utter lack of principle and his betrayal of all his associates made him generally hated, and he was the last man for whom it was worth while to make any sacrifice. So the nobles seem to have made no serious effort to save him. As Cicero[3] puts it 'he had come back to the Good but could get no protection from the Good.' He saw that he was a ruined man, and committed suicide.

752. In the year 120 the tribune P. Decius impeached[4] Opimius before the people. The trial was apparently held under the *lex Sempronia* of 123. Opimius had put to death citizens uncondemned. This offence was no doubt declared high treason by the law; the

---

[1] Cic. *Brutus* § 222, *de off.* II § 72.

[2] See Wilkins' *Introduction to Cic. de oratore* p. 8. In accepting the view of Mommsen, that the charge was high treason, we must regard the word *iudices* in Cic. *Brutus* § 103 as loosely used of the Assembly; as to which I have some misgivings.

[3] Cic. *de leg.* III § 35. The *boni* of course are the senatorial party.

[4] See Livy ep. 61, Cicero *de orat.* II §§ 106, 132, 165, 169—70, and Wilkins on § 135.

question to be decided by the Centuries was whether the case of Opimius was really covered by the law—was he *perduellis* or was he not? About the fact there was no doubt, but was not the order of the Senate in the circumstances of the moment a sufficient justification? The issue, important in itself, became peculiarly dramatic when the plea of justification was urged by the mouth of Carbo. That turncoat had gained the consulship, doubtless in the interest of the senatorial party, and now as consul spoke in defence of Opimius and procured his acquittal. This result certainly strengthened the hands of the Senate, for it virtually approved the claim of that body to proclaim a state of siege in emergencies. It also quieted the fears of others who had taken a prominent part in the suppression of the Gracchans, and who were in danger of being called to account. It is acutely suggested by Ihne that the impeachment of Opimius was a sham, got up by the nobility for the purpose of improving their position, and it is quite possible that this view may be the true one. It is thoroughly consistent with the usual policy of the Roman nobles, and the Assembly of the Centuries was capable of any amount of secret manipulation, particularly at such a juncture as the present, when the 'popular' party were discouraged and had lost their leaders. How completely the senatorial nobles felt themselves restored to power was shewn by the recall of Popilius, who had been in exile since 123. An obedient tribune, L. Calpurnius Bestia, procured a vote of the Assembly[1] for this restoration. So far all had gone against the defeated *populares*, but in 119 they began again to shew signs of life. Among the tribunes was a man of a rougher and less pliant type, who is said to have gained office partly through the support of one of the Metelli. This great house were now at the height of their influence, and their names constantly appear in the Fasti of this period. They belonged to the more moderate section of the nobility, but fully shared the desire of office and cheaply-won triumphs characteristic of the nobles of the day. So powerful a house had, besides its regular 'clients' in the strict sense, numbers of dependants. It was doubtless by attaching themselves to the great houses that citizens from the country *municipia* generally gave effect to their ambitions and overcame the disadvantages of a merely local reputation. The case before us is a striking one, for this hanger-on of the Metelli was Gaius Marius.

753. Marius[2] belonged to Arpinum, once a Volscian town, at the back of the Hernican country. After the Roman conquest the Arpinates were long in the position of Roman half-citizens, but received the full franchise in 188 and formed part of the Cornelian

---

[1] Cicero, *Brutus* § 128.   [2] Plutarch, *Marius*.

Tribe. Arpinum was now a *municipium* in the later sense, a community of full Roman citizens, a part of Rome, but with its local magistrates to manage purely local affairs. Outlying hamlets here as elsewhere formed part of the *municipium*, and in one of these, called Cereatae, Gaius Marius was born. His family were farmers of the old-fashioned close-fisted sort, hard thrifty people. That Marius worked on the land in his youth is likely enough: that he and his were mere day-labourers is a fiction[1] of later times. To paint a picture of striking contrasts was a temptation that moralizing rhetoric could not resist; it was not enough that he should be seven times consul, unless he rose to eminence from the plough-tail. He served as an *eques* in the army of Scipio at Numantia, and by his smartness and efficiency attracted the attention of his commander. One story represents him as a guest at headquarters, and even placed next the general at table. Life in the Roman lines no doubt taught the farmer's son many things. Ambitious he was by nature, but he had not the culture or elegant refinement that were now necessary for a man dependent on the favour of aristocratic cliques. But he did not despair. There was a great dearth of military skill and talent, and yet no quality was in more certain demand. Meanwhile money was always useful, and the influence of wealth was daily becoming greater. It seems probable that on returning to Italy he gave up farming the land, and took to employing his capital[2] in sharing public contracts. Many a Roman farmer no doubt had done the same thing before him, and the economical Marius was the very man to prosper in the trade of money-grubbing. This engrossing occupation is perhaps the reason why we hear nothing of him during the years 131—120. We may infer that he had at least some sympathy with the movements of the Gracchi, but he was not involved in the disaster of Gaius' fall. Now that he was tribune he soon shewed a determination to come to the front. He proposed and carried a law[3] introducing changes in the voting arrangements. By it access to voters while voting was made more difficult, and influential nobles resented a change that would hinder them in putting pressure on their dependants. A storm arose in the Senate, and the consuls (one of them a Metellus) headed the opposition: but Marius stood firm, and even threatened the consuls with arrest. The House had had enough civil broils for the present, and so gave way. It seemed as if a new demagogue had arisen, but the tribune surprised everybody by shortly after opposing a bill for

---

[1] See No. 10 of Madvig's *Kleine Philologische Schriften*. For the tradition of Marius' low birth see passages quoted by Mayor on *Juvenal*, VIII 245—53.

[2] δοκῶν γεγονέναι δημοσιώνης are the words of Diodorus fragm. XXXV 38.

[3] Plut. *Mar.* 4, Cic. *de leg.* III § 38.

further cheapening corn in Rome. The independent position to which he was apparently aspiring was however not easily tenable, and he seems to have lost the support of his aristocratic backers. He stood for the curule aedileship in 117. Seeing that he had no chance of this, he tried for the plebeian office, and failed. In 116 he succeeded in gaining the praetorship for the next year, but with difficulty, being the last in order of return. He was brought to trial for corrupt practices, and his condemnation appeared certain: but after several adjournments he escaped through the equal division[1] of the jury. We are clearly meant to infer that some hostile jurors had been mollified by bribes.

754. It is time to turn back and pick up the story of the Roman advance in Transalpine Gaul. The Roman government was determined to control the land-route to Spain. The sea-passage had been secured by the conquest of the Balearic Isles. Rome held all northern Italy, including Liguria, up to the junction of the Alps and Apennine. The coast as far as Massalia was either Roman or held by Massaliot colonies. For the purposes of a great military road towards Spain it was necessary to cross the Rhone above the delta, avoiding the impracticable country below. The problem was to reach and occupy a point convenient for crossing the river, without interfering with the territory of Massalia[2]. This was managed by starting from a carefully selected base on the coast at the spot afterwards known as *Forum Iulii* [Fréjus], and working westward. Thus the Romans kept to the north of the territory of their Greek allies. We have seen that Fulvius Flaccus and Sextius Calvinus defeated the Salluvii and other Ligurians in the district north of Massalia, but made no permanent conquest. The establishment of a military station at Aquae Sextiae [Aix] doubtless marks the line of their advance. The western Alps and other ranges on their right as they moved to the Rhone were held by free Ligurians. It was not the present object to subdue these: so long as Salluvii and Vocontii could be got to let Massalia alone, that was enough. Rome's business now was with the Gauls. That the advance to the Rhone was part of a deliberate plan is indicated in the time-honoured Roman manner. She was already allied with the Aedui or Haedui, a Gaulish tribe, who were on ill terms with their neighbours the Allobroges. The Allobroges were charged with having helped the Ligurians in the recent war, and with harbouring the beaten Ligurian chief. These pretexts served for a *casus belli*, but war with the Allobroges was a serious matter. At

---

[1] Plut. *Marius* 5. See below § 925.

[2] For the line of Roman advance and for the new roads see Mr Bullock-Hall's *Romans on the Riviera*, chapters 9 and 17.

their back were the Arverni, the most powerful of the warlike
confederacies of Gaul.

755. The geographical relations of these Gaulish powers shew
how exactly Roman policy at this time was in accordance with
ancient precedent. The great district roughly marked off by the
Liger [Loire] Garumna [Garonne] and Rhodanus [Rhone] may stand
for the south-central part of Gaul directly dominated by the Arverni.

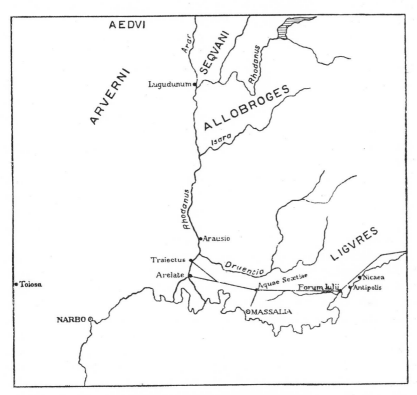

Southern Transalpine Gaul, shewing the probable line of the road from Italy to Spain,
avoiding the strip of coast belonging to Massalia.

Their influence extended further. As a great tribe enjoying a sort
of hegemony over weaker neighbours, it was to them that Gauls in
general looked in time of danger and stress as the natural leaders of a
common effort. Their own territory was a block of upland including
the highest ground in Transalpine Gaul, where their name yet lingers
in the mountains of Auvergne. On the left bank of the Rhone, in the
district between that river and the Isara [Isère], lay the Allobroges,
reaching up into the hill-country of modern Savoy. Of their dealings

with Hannibal nearly 100 years before we have spoken above. To the north-east of the Arverni were the Aedui, an important tribe, but weaker than their great neighbours. Roman diplomacy, acting on the information of the experts of Massalia, was at no loss for a policy. An alliance with Rome seemed to offer to the Aedui a chance of winning a more independent position. They took the bait, as many others had done before them. They too were destined to learn that relief from the oppression of their kinsmen was only to be bought by submission to the permanent sovranty of Rome.

756. The Senate knew very well that the contemplated advance beyond the Alps was an undertaking[1] not to be treated lightly, and accordingly took action in time. In 122 the consul Cn. Domitius Ahenobarbus arrived with an army and prepared for the inevitable war. Early in 121 the Allobroges seem to have taken the initiative by marching southwards. Domitius, now proconsul, met them at Vindalium, by the junction of the Sulga [Sorgue] and Rhone, and defeated them with great loss. They fell back to their own country, and waited for the coming of the Arverni. One of the new consuls, Q. Fabius Maximus, now came with a second army and took over the chief command. The generals made a combined movement up the line of the Rhone, and found the enemy massed in great force at the junction of the Rhone and Isère. The Arverni are said to have had 200,000 men in the field, and this round number apparently does not include the Allobroges. But their position was ill chosen and they were altogether outgeneralled. After a stubborn fight they broke, and were cut to pieces or drowned in the Rhone. Their losses were estimated at not less than 120,000 men. Submission followed, and peace was arranged. No extension of Roman territory to the North seems to have taken place, but the objects of Rome were fully attained. She had now a free hand in the South and went forward boldly. Meanwhile it was thought desirable to remove Bituitus, king of the Arverni, from contact with his excitable countrymen. The details of the story are variously given, but it seems clear that the Gaulish chief was induced to put himself in Roman power, and then treacherously detained in Italy with his son. One point of interest in the accounts of this war is the incidental reference to the wealth of the Gauls, or at least of their chiefs. We have before spoken of the practice of hoarding the precious metals in the form of ornaments and otherwise, common among the Gauls in Italy. The vast riches of the Arvernian kings and the splendour of the equipage of Bituitus are

---

[1] For this war see Strabo IV I § 11 (p. 185), 2 § 3 (190), Livy ep. 61, Velleius II 10, Florus I 37, Appian *Gall.* 12, Orosius V 13, 14, Cic. *pro Font.* § 36, Plin. *NH* VII § 166, Valer. Max. IX 6 § 3, Eutrop. IV 22.

mentioned. There were coins in Gaul, though perhaps we ought not to speak of a Gallic coinage. Greek coins in common circulation reached the natives through Massaliot traders and were rudely copied in the mints of Gaul. The presence of gold seems to have been partly due to local[1] mines. The display of wealth was not forgotten by observant Romans, and on more than one later occasion Gallic gold played a part in Roman history.

757. The importance of the recent victory was fully understood at Rome. Fabius assumed the title of *Allobrogicus*, and three decisive steps were taken shewing that the Romans were come to stay. First there was the construction of the contemplated road to Spain. The *via Domitia*, named after the active proconsul, seems to have run from the naval base known later as *Forum Iulii* to Aquae Sextiae the present headquarters, then to the passage of the Rhone [*Traiectus Rhodani*, now Tarascon], after which it followed an old trade-route, entering Spain by the eastern end of the Pyrenees. It has been well suggested[2] that Arelate [Arles], though at the head of the Rhone delta, was not chosen as the point of crossing, because it lay too near to Massalia and was regarded as naturally falling to the share of the Greek republic. This is far from unlikely, for the next step in the Roman advance was the formation of the southern part of Gaul into a regular Province. It was a long strip of country, enclosing the Massaliot territory, and reaching from the western Alps to the border of Spain. By its occupation Rome not only held the land-route but cut off the inland Gauls from access to the Mediterranean. No doubt every care was taken not to injure the interests or susceptibilities of Rome's oldest and most loyal ally. In 118 the third step was taken by founding a colony of Roman citizens at Narbo[3] [Narbonne] in the west of the new Province. It served as a fortress and military base for the protection of the western districts, and also not less efficiently as a Romanizing centre and a base for the operations of trade and finance. The fashion, prevalent[4] at this time, of naming colonies after some divinity, was followed in this case also, for the new colony was styled Narbo Martius.

758. Before we turn to the war with Jugurtha it will be well to refer briefly to some minor campaigns[5] in the North of Italy and adjoining lands. These movements were no doubt partly due to the triumph-hunting of the Roman nobles: how far they may have

---

[1] Strabo IV 2 § 1, 1 § 13. [2] By Mr Bullock-Hall, pp. 96—8.

[3] Velleius II 7, Eutrop. IV 23, Cic. *pro Font.* § 13, *Brutus* § 160.

[4] We have noticed Junonia, Neptunia, Minervia.

[5] See the *Fasti Triumphales*, Livy ep. 62, 63, 65, Strabo IV 6 § 6 (p. 204), Velleius II 8, Appian *Illyr.* 11, Dion Cass. frag. 88, Florus I 39, Eutrop. IV 23—4. Cic. II *in Verr.* III § 184, IV § 22.

served to keep restless tribes quiet by the display of Roman power, and so may be regarded as connected with the advance in Transalpine Gaul, is very hard to say. In 119 the consul L. Metellus had the province of Macedonia. He found some pretext for invading Dalmatia, though the natives are said to have done nothing to justify the attack. They made their submission and the consul wintered peacefully among them. It was enough to secure a triumph and the name *Delmaticus* to another of the Metelli. In 118 the consul Q. Marcius Rex made a campaign against the Stoeni or Stoni, a tribe dwelling in the northern Alps. He too earned a cheap triumph by a success of some sort. In 115 M. Aemilius Scaurus defeated the Carni, an Alpine tribe further to the East. These little frontier wars are unimportant and the details scanty and obscure. The fighting that took place in and about Macedonia with the Thracian tribes, particularly the Scordisci, was perhaps of a more necessary character. Rome had here to deal with large bodies of warlike barbarians, and any show of weakness might have led to very serious disaster. In 114 C. Porcius Cato was utterly defeated by the Scordisci, and lost most of his army, a disgrace which doubtless did much to secure his condemnation on a charge of extortion when he returned to Rome. Later governors restored the prestige of the Roman arms. We hear the names of M. Livius Drusus, who pushed the invaders back over the Danube, of Q. Minucius, and others, but our information is slight and doubtful: it seems that by about the end of 110 quiet was restored in those regions, at least for a time.

759. The comprehensive nature of Roman policy in the North is plainly shewn in the road-making enterprise of M. Aemilius Scaurus, who was censor in 109. His colleague M. Livius Drusus died in office, and he was constitutionally bound to resign. This he would not do until forced by the action of some of the tribunes. Nor was this unnatural, for he had begun the world as a poor man, though of Patrician descent: he had risen to the first position in Rome, and was unwilling to lose any chance of coming to the front. Already he had undertaken two important public works, the rebuilding in stone of the bridge (*pons Mulvius*) by which the Flaminian road to the North crossed the Tiber a little above Rome, and the *via Aemilia*[1] *Scauri*, which long bore his name. It started from Pisae or Luna in Etruria, and ran round the head of the Ligurian gulf, keeping near to the shore wherever possible, but turning inland to avoid the most difficult parts of that rocky coast, which the modern railway only penetrates by a series of tunnels. It thus provided a direct land-route to the port of Genua, where it made a junction with the *via*

---

[1] Strabo v I § II (p. 217).

Postumia by which communication with Cisalpine Gaul had been established forty years before. It did not however stop at Genua, but ran some 30 miles further to a spot on the coast called *vada Sabata* [Vado]. The importance attached to the connexion with the region of the Po was strikingly shewn by the construction of a second road, running from Vada Sabata to the north. It joined the *via Postumia* at Dertona, and thus the most difficult section of the journey between Cisalpine Gaul and the Ligurian seaboard was provided with two alternative routes. The new Aemilian road had the advantage of crossing the Apennine by an easier pass than the Postumian. The junction of the two at Dertona must have been

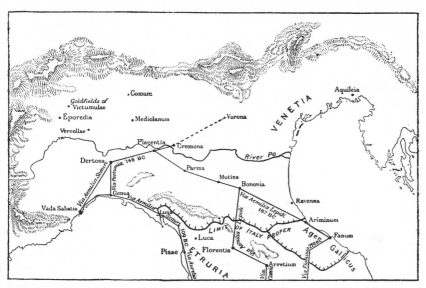

Cisalpine Gaul with Liguria about 100 B.C. Only the river Po and the chief roads are shewn. The advance of the boundary of Italy from the Aesis to the Rubicon [? 82 B.C.] is indicated. See § 921.

an important point, and it was accordingly occupied with a colony. The exact date is uncertain. If it was founded some years earlier, it was probably at least strengthened about 108. It was probably a citizen colony. Along the stretch of coast from Vada Sabata to the beginning of the *via Domitia* no regular military road was for the present constructed, and a local track was enough for local needs. Secure from pirates on the sea, the communications of Rome with the West and her footing in Transalpine Gaul were now well established. She held the islands and all the seaboard of the western Mediterranean, with the exception of the African coast belonging to the kingdoms of Numidia and Mauretania.

760. The matters of which we have been speaking are parts of a policy on the whole successful, particularly in Transalpine Gaul. Most of the business relative to this policy was doubtless transacted by the Senate. That body clung tenaciously to its power regained by the overthrow of the Gracchi. But it was nevertheless weakened. We have pointed out that the Popular party was reviving, and that the control of the jury-courts by the Equestrian Order gave to the financiers the means of putting pressure on the senatorial governors of Provinces. The weakness of the restored Senate is seen[1] in the affair of the colony of Narbo. The Senate, whose policy it had long been to check provincial expansion, were alarmed at the prospect of further ventures likely to arise out of so novel a step. A citizen colony abroad would have to be defended, and the new Province was hardly secure as yet. It is not unlikely that they had only undertaken the forward policy beyond the Alps with reluctance, as an outlet for popular energies. At any rate, even when the law for founding the colony had been carried, they still favoured a motion for its repeal. But the people rejected the bill. The capitalist class no doubt had their eyes on the prospect of profits to be made in a new banking centre, and the popular view was eloquently supported by the rising young orator L. Licinius Crassus. He was appointed chief of the commission for founding the colony, and the Senate had to make the best of its defeat. In short, things were not really comfortable in Rome; the parties, or rather factions, of *optimates* and *populares*, guided by the personal interests of selfish leaders, were still facing each other, while the equestrian capitalists, most self-seeking of all, were becoming more and more an organized body, able to turn the balance of power at any moment by throwing the weight of their influence into this or that scale.

761. Though the years 121—112 are marked by no great outbreak or movement, various stray notices[2] betray the truth that all was not well. The censors of 115 seem to have been wholly in the interest of the aristocratic party. They made Scaurus 'first man' on the senatorial roll [*princeps senatus*], a position which he enjoyed for more than 25 years. They struck out the names of 32 members, among them that of a recent consul, C. Licinius Geta, who was himself soon after [108] censor. They also endeavoured to check innovations in the public shows and amusements. It seems certain that under solemn pretence of a care for public morals they used their powers for party purposes, as others had done before them. The consul Scaurus carried a sumptuary law forbidding certain extravagant

---

[1] See Cic. *pro Cluent.* § 140, *Brutus* § 160, Wilkins' Introd. to *de Oratore*, p. 9.

[2] The references are given in Lange *RA* § 139 (III pp. 52—6).

dainties of the table, and one dealing with the old problem of the voting-rights of freedmen. But the relation of these enactments to the politics of the time is so obscure as to leave little opening for probable guess-work. The affair of Scaurus and P. Rutilius Rufus was no credit to the nobility. They were competitors in 116 for the consulship in 115. Rufus, a man of high character, was rejected, and thereupon prosecuted his rival for corrupt practices. Scaurus was acquitted, and retorted by prosecuting Rufus for the same offence. What happened to Rufus we do not know: probably he too was acquitted. Scaurus appears to have shewn himself a masterful consul, if the story is true that he humiliated the praetor Decius, even using violence, because of an act of disrespect to his official superior. But the scandal in connexion with the Vestals was perhaps the most serious sign of the rottenness underlying even the most respectable exterior of Roman high life. It was matter of common talk that three of these ladies had misconducted themselves with Roman Knights, and they were at length brought to trial in the chief pontiff's court. Only one was condemned, and public sentiment was greatly shocked at the laxity of the sacred tribunal. The case was of political importance, for, however much the spread of Hellenism may have emancipated the upper classes from religious terrors, the mass of the people still believed that the unchastity of Vestals carried with it the loss of divine favour and imperilled the existence of the state. So in the next year [113] the tribune Sextus Peducaeus proposed and carried a bill appointing a special court with full powers to deal with the matter. At its head was placed L. Cassius[1] Longinus, a man of the highest reputation for stern justice and incorruptibility. The conviction and punishment of the two other Vestals soon followed, though one of them, Licinia, was ably defended by the orator Crassus. Accomplices and persons in any way implicated then felt the severity of the court, which seems to have gone on sitting for some time. Among the accused was the orator M. Antonius, the rival of Crassus, but he made his own defence with success. The Sibylline books were consulted, and by way of expiating the recent abominations a temple was erected to Venus the 'turner of hearts' [*Verticordia*]. For dedicating the image of the goddess it was necessary to employ a lady of wholly unblemished character. The selection was entrusted to a committee of married ladies chosen (first 100, then 10 out of the 100) by the hallowed method of the lot. Punishment had it is true

---

[1] This man was the author (see § 647) of the *lex Cassia tabellaria* of 137 B.C., and also of the famous rule attaching a presumption of guilt to that party who profited by any wrongful or criminal act (*cui bono fuerit*, see Mayor on Cic. *Phil.* II § 35). Asconius p. 46. He was consul 127, censor 125. See Pauly-Wissowa under Cassii (No. 72), Drumann II 114.

overtaken all or some of the guilty, and sanctimonious scrupulosity truly Roman had effected public purification.   But these efforts, like the special court, were transient phenomena ; the lax jurisdiction of the pontifical college remained.   Not less significant of the evils at work among the ruling class at Rome was the passing of a new and more severe law of *repetundae*.   The Acilian law, inspired by C. Gracchus, had apparently proved insufficient.   The proposer of the new one was C. Servilius Glaucia, whom we shall meet again below.   This *lex Servilia* of Glaucia is probably[1] assigned to the year 111.   We hear that it was favourable to the order of Knights in some way, that it shortened procedure by cutting off the delays caused by the opportunities of repeated adjournment, and that the reward of Roman citizenship, offered in the Acilian law to any Italian Ally who successfully prosecuted an offender, was in the Servilian only offered to Latins. But this law, like its predecessor, was more notable as evidence of notorious evil-doing, and as putting power in the hands of the capitalist class, than as an effective check on extortion.   Of the reactionary land-law of 111 we have spoken above.   In general I may remark that these few details of which some record has come down to us are but the signs of the progressive decay in public and private life, of which we hear in general terms from such a writer as Sallust ; a decay vainly cloaked by hypocrisy, and which even honest attempts at reform were quite unable to arrest.

762.   At this point in our history we are no longer left to feel our way in the twilight of inference from a few details.   The incompetence and corruption of the ruling nobles is now glaringly illustrated by the story of the Jugurthine war.   This survives in the brilliant monograph of Sallust, one of the masterpieces of Roman literature.   Written some 70 years after the events described, by a partisan of Julius Caesar, its tendency is hostile to the nobility and favourable to the 'popular' party.   We must therefore make allowance for a partiality which the author is at no great pains to conceal.   In chronology and geography, even judged by the loose standards of antiquity, Sallust is abominably slip-shod and ill-informed.   But these defects, and other casual inaccuracies, chiefly affect the credit of his work as a mere history of the war.   His pictures of the political and social life of Rome, painted in striking colours, appear on examination to be less one-sided than one would naturally expect.   It will suffice here to remark that he is not blind to the merits of Metellus and Sulla or the shortcomings of Marius.   And it is for the light thrown on the condition of Rome (of course including the Roman army), not as a piece of military

---

[1] See Wordsworth, introduction to notes on *lex Acilia*, Lange *RA* § 139 (III p. 55).

history, that the 'War with Jugurtha' is especially valuable. In approaching the subject we must never lose sight of certain facts which give the clue to the meaning of a very strange series of events. In the first place we must remember that the kingdom of Numidia was practically independent. That Roman overlordship was recognized by Masinissa and his sons, and that at each demise of the crown Roman approval helped to arrange and guarantee the royal succession, does not imply any serious restraint on the freedom of the kings. Carthage was gone, and therewith the occupation of worrying and weakening Rome's old enemy. Now and then a contingent was asked for, and readily furnished. We have already spoken of the service of Jugurtha at Numantia, and of the impression made on the young prince's mind by the revelation of Roman corruption. We are now to see the serious consequences of his ambition, made reckless by his over-estimate of Roman weakness. Secondly, we must not forget the Roman traders and financiers who in quest of profit ever pushed forward into neighbouring countries. Numbers of these business-men, Roman or Italian, were settled in the chief towns of this favoured client-kingdom, and for Roman interests this peaceful invasion was enough. Here Rome designed no aggression : but on the other hand it was not safe to meddle with her merchants and bankers. Jugurtha seems hardly to have understood the change in Roman politics brought about by the rise of the Equestrian Order : if there was one influence that could still set in motion the dormant forces of the Republic, it was the bitter cry of outraged capital. Thirdly, there was in the system of the Roman Republic no standing army, only the small beginnings of intermittent professional soldiering. Trained officers were rare, and of generals, since the death of Aemilianus, there were none of high repute. That the smart trooper from Arpinum, whom he had met at the siege of Numantia, might reform and give efficiency to the Roman army, was hardly to be foreseen by Jugurtha. There were, now as ever, effective men in Rome, could they but come to the front. And so the miscalculation of Roman power, fatal to so many of her earlier enemies, was in the end fatal to the African. That it took six years of war for the giant Republic to crush a client-prince is the really important fact.

763. In 118 Micipsa the king of Numidia died. He had outlived his brothers who had shared the kingdom with him under the award of Scipio thirty years before. All three brothers had left legitimate issue, but the old king saw that no settlement had any prospect of permanence unless it satisfied the enterprising and popular bastard Jugurtha. A table will shew the genealogy.

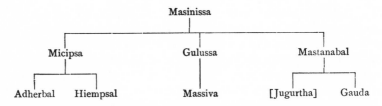

Micipsa then bequeathed the kingdom to his sons Adherbal and Hiempsal and his nephew Jugurtha, appealing to them to exercise the joint succession in loyal concord. Of course the plan was a failure. The high-spirited Hiempsal soon fell out with his cousin, and Jugurtha, served by his secret agents, quickly procured his murder. The milder Adherbal now stood on his guard, and sent an embassy to explain the situation to the Roman Senate. Meanwhile the kingdom was divided into two camps. In the ensuing conflict Jugurtha was victorious, and Adherbal fled to the Roman province Africa, whence he sailed for Rome. Jugurtha had no wish to bring upon himself a war with the Romans, and sent ambassadors well provided with money to counteract the possible effect of Adherbal's appeal. In a short time the upper circles of Roman society were convinced that there were two sides to the Numidian question. Adherbal might recall the long and faithful services of his fathers and declare his own perfect devotion to Rome. The emissaries of Jugurtha met his version of the recent events in Numidia with a very different story, and their lies found a favourable hearing. The majority of the Senate leant to the usurper's side, while a minority urged the obligation of doing justice to Adherbal, of avenging the murder of Hiempsal and the injured majesty of Rome. But, if we are to believe Sallust, the leader of this section, the irrepressible Scaurus, was influenced rather by the fear of burning his own fingers than by generosity or patriotic indignation. He would gladly have shared with others the gold of Jugurtha, but the affair had leaked out, and the scandal was the talk of the town. Respectability was a large part of his stock in trade, and he decided that it would not pay him to be detected taking a bribe. This debate in the Senate seems to belong to the middle of the year 116, and we should note that he was consul in 115 and was made *princeps senatus*. A man who was now well within sight of the highest honours might be loth to risk the crown of a virtuous career by the untimely gratification of an itching palm. The outcome of the debate was the appointment of a commission of ten, with instructions to divide the Numidian kingdom between Adherbal and Jugurtha. At the head of this body was placed L. Opimius, the destroyer of Fregellae and of Gaius Gracchus,

who had thus far not been one of Jugurtha's supporters. Once in
Africa, the chairman and most of his colleagues soon succumbed to
the artful temptations and lavish promises of Jugurtha. To him
they assigned the more fertile western part of Numidia, bordering
on Mauretania : Adherbal received the capital Cirta and the part
bordering on the Roman province.

764. The commissioners went home, leaving the two kings face
to face. Further trouble was certain, for it was now more than ever
clear to Jugurtha that everything at Rome had its price. According
to Sallust, when Scipio was sending back the foreign contingents
after the fall of Numantia, he gave the Numidian prince a bit of
advice. ' Keep on good terms ' he said ' with the Roman people,
rather than with individual Romans : don't get into the way of
giving presents : to buy from a few what belongs to many is a
dangerous game.' If anything of this kind was said by Scipio,
Jugurtha had at all events now lost all regard for the warning, and
soon set to work to carry out his ambitions. The years 114—3 seem
to have been devoted to encroachments and provocations of every
kind, till Adherbal, after vainly seeking redress by negotiation, was
compelled to resist his tormentor in arms. But a night-attack
skilfully directed by Jugurtha cut up and scattered his army, and
he could only take refuge in his capital and await a response to the
embassy which he had despatched to Rome on the outbreak of open
war. Meanwhile Jugurtha pressed on the siege with vigour, in hope
that, when the expected commissioners from Rome should arrive,
they might find him already in possession, and so have to deal with
a situation modified by the accomplished fact. But the city of Cirta
stood in a strong position on high ground, and a large part of the
walls were by reason of deep ravines fully protected from the siege-
engines of antiquity. Nor were defenders lacking. The population
was a mixed one, for to encourage the settlement of foreigners had
been the policy of the Numidian kings : in particular Micipsa had
induced a number of Greeks[1] to make it their home and develope a
many-sided urban life, as they alone knew how. It is not likely that
the city was devoid of the Phoenician element, scattered as that race
was all about the towns of the coast. But it was the imperial race,
Roman or Italian, that took the lead in the defence. They stopped
the first rush of the pursuers, and against the strong walls, when
properly manned, the assaults and batterings of Jugurtha were spent
in vain. Presently a Roman embassy appeared on the scene. Sallust
tells us that they were three *adulescentes*, young nobles no doubt, but
he does not take the trouble to give their names. Their mission was

[1] Strabo XVII 3 § 13 (p. 831).

to enjoin on both kings a cessation of hostilities and resort to arbitration, of course to be exercised by a Roman commission with full powers. The present trio of greenhorns were to all appearance little more than messengers, and Jugurtha treated them like children. He did not let them pass his lines, so they went back without having seen Adherbal at all. In reply to their message he took an injured tone, pointed to his own services and the approval of Scipio, declared that Adherbal was the real aggressor, and promised shortly to send an embassy to lay his case before the Senate. Foiled and perhaps mystified, the young men went home, and Jugurtha converted the ineffective siege of Cirta into a close blockade. Adherbal saw no hope but in Roman aid: his enemy was using every means to seduce or unnerve the motley garrison: but two daring Numidians, induced by rewards, succeeded in slipping through the blockading lines and bearing to Rome a pitiful letter of appeal.

765. The time was hardly favourable to any who at that juncture might implore Roman protection. In 114 C. Cato had lost one army in Macedonia, and the effort to redress the disaster was now occupying a second; in 113 Cn. Papirius Carbo, advancing to repel the northern barbarians threatening Italy from the north-east, was utterly defeated by them[1] at Noreia in the mountains of Noricum. True, no invasion followed at the moment, but the Romans were ever nervous at the approach of danger from the North. No doubt the general situation played into the hands of those who had taken the pay and represented the interests of Jugurtha. That the honour of Rome was deeply pledged to the rescue of a prince under Roman protection by the very fact of his appointment, was clear as clear could be. There was no reason to think that Jugurtha would be overawed by diplomatic action. But the combination of impotence and corruption that determined Roman policy at this crisis led to the despatch of another embassy. This time men of ripe age and high standing were chosen to go, with Scaurus at their head. Their instructions are not precisely recorded, but seem to have chiefly consisted in the threat that, if the Numidian did not quickly raise the siege of Cirta and leave Adherbal at peace, the Roman people would positively be angry. The envoys lost no time in setting out, for in Rome men were beginning to grumble at the mismanagement of the Numidian affair. They landed at Utica in the province Africa and at once wrote summoning Jugurtha to appear before them. He delayed long enough to make one grand assault, still hoping to confront the ambassadors with Cirta already in his possession. But he was again repulsed. He then hurried off to the conference, listened to the threatening message of the Senate,

[1] Livy epit. 63, Strabo v 1 § 8 (p. 214).

and by some means or other contrived to get rid of Scaurus and his colleagues without making any effective submission to the orders from Rome. He returned to Cirta, and the doom of the city was soon accomplished. The Italians were worn out, and there seemed no hope of relief. So they pressed Adherbal to surrender the town on condition of his own life being spared : for themselves they feared no hurt, trusting in the prestige and majesty of Rome. But to encourage a belief in the efficacy of Roman protection was no part of the policy of Jugurtha. Adherbal was tortured and put to death, and the garrison, Italians and natives alike, indiscriminately massacred. We can hardly doubt that this butchery was meant as an object-lesson to waverers throughout Numidia.

766. The fall of Cirta seems to have occurred in the summer of 112, before the election of consuls for 111. The news naturally aroused much indignation in Rome. To apply a modern metaphor, the tail of the Roman wolf had been twisted in contempt and defiance, for the edification of the outside world. Yet we are assured by Sallust that the indignation would have passed off in talk, worn out by the delays created by pro-Jugurthan obstructionists ; but the Senate was no longer left to dally with the matter. Gaius Memmius, tribune-elect for 111, took up the question from the point of view of the 'popular' party, denounced the corruption of the nobles, and forced the hand of the government. It was not desirable to provoke a conflict with the Assembly: the memory of senatorial impotence in the time of C. Gracchus was too fresh. War was perhaps not formally declared till the beginning of the next year, but Numidia was as-signed as the *provincia*[1] of one of the new consuls. Consuls were elected, and proceeded to draw lots. The Numidian command fell to L. Calpurnius Bestia, who at once set about his preparations for the campaign. Jugurtha soon got wind of these movements, and in alarm sent another embassy with plenty of ready money. But the Senate had gone too far to draw back, and the envoys, having no power to offer complete submission, were sent about their business, and the war began. Bestia, according to Sallust, was a competent commander. But he was, as an up-to-date Roman noble, intensely greedy of money, and chose as his staff [*legati*] various influential nobles, Scaurus among them, hoping that respectable company might cover and facilitate questionable acts. The last suggestion sounds monstrous, but there is nothing in the sequel to justify us in rejecting it. The consul landed in Africa, pushed on into Numidia, gained some successes, and took some towns. Then came a change. Jugurtha

---

[1] In point of form the province would probably be called *Africa*, as its base would be in the Roman province of that name.

lost heart and opened negotiations, of course on the usual footing. Confidential agents came and went, and the king, who at first only hoped to buy an armistice and gain time for further trafficking at Rome, was delighted to learn that the market-price of Scaurus himself had been found. He at once played for peace, and resolved to carry through the whole negotiation on the spot. In all the steps publicly taken the utmost propriety was observed. Jugurtha came under safe-conduct into the Roman camp. Before a full council of war he pleaded for forgiveness and made his submission. This was accepted, and he duly surrendered a number of elephants and horses and other material of war according to agreement. The more important financial transaction was carried out at a private interview with Bestia and Scaurus. So there was an end of hostilities in Africa, and the consul returned to Rome to hold the elections.

767. Bit by bit the news of this shameful business spread. That the consul and the first man of the Senate had sold the honour of Rome for their own profit seems to have been an unchallenged inference. The Senate was well aware that the peace could not be held good, but the influence of Scaurus was great, and his conversion added to the embarrassment of a body many members of which were already in the pay of Jugurtha. The common people, whose judgment was not corrupted by Numidian gold, were furious; and Memmius, who was still tribune, inflamed them still further by denouncing the nobility, their unconstitutional tyranny, and their infamous traffic in the rights and interests of Rome. He at length carried a motion for an inquiry. To prove a case against the chief culprits was only possible by using the evidence of Jugurtha. It was therefore resolved that the king should be summoned to Rome under a safe-conduct, and the praetor L. Cassius[1] was deputed to go and fetch him. No doubt Memmius was backed not merely by the city mob but also by the equestrian capitalists, to whom the massacre at Cirta would appear an even more serious matter than the sale of Roman honour. While these events were passing at Rome, Jugurtha was busy corrupting the officers whom the consul had left in charge of the army, and so recovering his strength for contingencies: in the absence of their principals he found the subordinates ready to do business like their betters. But when Cassius came, and pledged not only the good faith of Rome but his own for the king's safe return, he consented to obey the summons. He would seem to have been well informed on the characters of Roman public men. Moreover it is clear that contumacy would have proved the insincerity of his recent submission, and so have ruined Scaurus and Bestia. It was not to his interest

---

[1] This man was consul in 107. See § 785, and index. (Pauly-Wissowa No. 62.)

(looking to the future) to bring disaster upon those with whom he had dealings: besides, once at Rome, there was probably still much to be done with a full purse. That this forecast was sound the sequel quickly proved. Memmius protected the king from lawless violence, and brought him before a mass-meeting. He advised him to make a clean breast of it in respect of the recent transaction, and throw himself on the mercy of the Roman people. Jugurtha was called upon to reply, when another tribune, C. Baebius, forbade him to speak. In vain the crowd yelled and threatened the obstructive tribune: he stood on his legal right and would not be browbeaten. No doubt he had exacted a fancy price for facing the fury of the populace. But nothing more could be done, and the meeting broke up in impotent rage.

768. This was bad enough, but worse followed. Jugurtha was still in Rome when the consuls for 110 came into office. Of these, Sp. Postumius Albinus was to be the successor of Bestia in Africa, and he had no mind to see the war ended, and with it his prospect of a triumph. Massiva, son of Gulussa and cousin of Jugurtha, was staying in Rome as a refugee, for Numidia had of late been an unsafe residence for native princes. Sallust declares that the consul prompted him to put in a claim to the Numidian throne. Jugurtha saw that he must act quickly. To set aside this new competitor was beyond the power of his friends in the Senate: we may add that, if the resources of the kingdom passed to a new ruler, the goodwill of these friends would speedily follow. So he instructed his trusty attendant Bomilcar to make away with Massiva as soon and as secretly as possible. Bomilcar found assassins ready for the work, one of whom murdered the prince so heedlessly that he was caught. The frightened ruffian turned state-evidence against Bomilcar. Whether this person was or was not covered by the safe-conduct guaranteed to his master, is treated by Sallust as a very doubtful point. But he was brought to trial, and after the first hearing was forced to give fifty securities to go bail for his appearance later. It is astounding to read that the fifty were actually found among the friends of Jugurtha, who for his part brazenfacedly denied his own guilt in the matter. But he found that his friends could do no more for him, and for the sake of his prestige in Numidia it was indispensable to save Bomilcar. So he packed him off home secretly and left the fifty securities to pay the forfeit. At last the Senate was roused, and ordered him to quit Italy. Edifying tradition declared that as he left Rome he looked back and said 'For sale, a city—a city whose doom is only waiting for a buyer that can pay the price!'

769. The year 110 was now well advanced, and the consul's time

was short before the elections for 109, which he would have to hold,
his colleague Rufus being busy in Macedonia. So he hurried off to
the front, in hope to end the war by a short summer campaign. But
by ever-shifting movements and pretended negotiations Jugurtha
foiled him, till at last he had to return to Rome, leaving his brother
Aulus in command. Rightly or wrongly (for distrust of public men
was now general) his failure was imputed by many to a corrupt
understanding with the king. And he could not get his business
over quickly and rejoin his army, for a political deadlock[1] was
delaying all public affairs in Rome. Discontent was rife, and the
recent visit of Jugurtha had probably left suspicions and animosities
more bitter than ever. Two of the tribunes were making a push
to secure immediate reelection[2] [*continuare magistratum*]. Their
colleagues objected, perhaps on some constitutional ground. This
squabble was delaying the election of tribunes beyond the usual
time, and with it the other elections also. The difficulty seems to
have been got over[3] at length, but the year 110 was now spent and
Albinus (now proconsul) was still in Rome. His brother had meanwhile not been idle. In the heart of winter[4] he broke up his camp and
set out in hope of capturing a town which contained the king's treasury,
and so of at once enriching himself and ending the war. The position
of the place made a siege out of the question, and Jugurtha was not to
be frightened by feints. Soon he lured away the incompetent and
greedy Roman into the wilds on pretence of secret negotiations and
the hope of a profitable bargain. There he set himself to tempt the
weary and disgusted troops to desert, and, when discipline and
confidence were undermined, fell upon the Roman army by night.
Some Ligurian and Thracian auxiliaries went over to the enemy,
a few of the legionaries followed: a centurion betrayed his post on
the rampart, the Numidians burst into the camp, and all was lost.
On the morrow Aulus and the surviving fugitives were graciously
spared on terms dictated by Jugurtha. They were passed beneath
the yoke, and were allowed ten days to quit the territory of Numidia.

770. The disaster and disgrace were worse, if possible, than the
failure of Mancinus before Numantia. It was a repetition of the
Caudine Forks, an episode of the far-off past, when Rome was not
yet mistress even of Italy. Sallust tells us that the news aroused
in the Roman public not only shame and indignation but fear. It

---

[1] Sall. *Jug.* 37.
[2] The details of this affair are not given, and it is not easy to restore them by guessing.
For the conditions of immediate reelection see note on § 712 above.
[3] At least Mamilius seems to have been tribune early in 109, if not at the usual time
(10 Dec. 110). For times of elections see § 721.
[4] *mense Ianuario...hieme aspera.* Sall. *Jug.* 37.

may have been so: men's nerves were perhaps shaken by the defeats suffered in Macedonia and Noricum, and by rumours of coming invasion from the North. Albinus hastily raised[1] forces, but the tribunes forbade him to take them to the seat of war. He then hurried abroad himself, for the Senate had declared the treaty made with Jugurtha to be not binding. But he could attempt nothing, for the demoralized remnant of the beaten army was in no condition to take the field. At last however the limits of Roman endurance had been reached. It was probably at the very end of the year 110, when the new tribunes came into office, that the tribune C. Mamilius Limetanus brought forward a bill[2] for appointing a special commission to try persons who in recent years had corruptly favoured Jugurtha, had played into his hands in any way, or made terms with him. The bill seems to have become law early in 109. The nobles were greatly alarmed, and made a futile attempt to throw it out. But the votes of their dependants were not by themselves enough, and the Latins and other Allies whom they are said to have brought into town could after all not do much more than make a noise. The truth no doubt is simply that the Knights were working with the *populares* and the combination was irresistible. The exact machinery set up by the *lex Mamilia* is a matter[3] of some doubt. We learn that three Inquiry Commissioners [*quaesitores*] were to be elected: on the other hand we are distinctly told that the condemnations which followed were the work of jurors of the Gracchan model, that is, of the Equestrian Order. It seems then most probable that the form of the court was that of an official chairman with a *consilium*, but that the *consilium* was a real jury deciding cases by a majority of votes, not a merely advisory body. In short, the jury-system, existing since 149 in the court of *repetundae*, was become a normal type from which it was hardly possible to depart even in extraordinary commissions. The *quaesitores* might be senators, and perhaps all were. But why were three needed? It is hardly to be believed that there were three courts. The most important point surely was to guard against the risk of the attack failing through the sickness or death of a single *quaesitor*. A body of three, any one of whom was competent to act,

---

[1] When Albinus managed to hold the consular elections is not clear, but it seems to have been early in 109. We have no notice of the assignment of the consular provinces before the election, and it may have been deferred on account of the deadlock preceding. Then the return of Albinus to Africa is quite in order. The passage of Sallust (*Jug*. 43 § 1) is exceptionally inaccurate, as has been pointed out, *e.g.* by Mr Summers, Introd. to Sall. *Jug*. p. 15.

[2] For the *lex Mamilia* and its results see Sall. *Jug*. 40, Cicero *Brutus* §§ 127—8, *pro Balbo* § 28, *de nat. deor*. III § 74, Holden's notes on Plutarch *C. Gracc*. 18.

[3] See Mommsen, *Staatsrecht* II index (*quaesitor*).

was a practical precaution and not out of keeping with Roman ideas : and the recent constitution of the Gracchan land-commission seems to furnish a pattern in this respect. What happened on the present occasion agrees well with this view. Among the popular excitement and the panic of the nobles Scaurus kept his head and pulled the wires so cleverly that he actually secured his own election as one of the three commissioners. So says Sallust: from Cicero[1] we learn that, when Bestia was brought to trial, Scaurus appeared in court as a supporter [*advocatus*] of the accused. If Scaurus was not presiding at the trial of any particular case, there was nothing in Roman etiquette to prevent his acting thus, and the supposed inconsistency between the two authorities disappears. Sallust goes on to say that the inquiry was conducted in a harsh and arbitrary manner, under the pressure of party-spirit. The people had suffered from the excesses of the nobles in their hour of triumph, and now repaid them in their own coin. Among those named by Cicero as having been condemned in the course of these proceedings were the ex-consuls Bestia and Albinus, and the generally hated L. Opimius, who was at last reached by popular vengeance and died an exile[2] at Dyrrachium.

771.   Some time in 109, apparently about the middle of the year, the consul Q. Caecilius Metellus took over the African command. He stands on record as a man of high character specially remarkable for sincerity. A noble of nobles, of undoubted honesty[3] in an age of corruption, he was at once openly opposed to the popular party and not to be turned from doing his duty to the state. He knew very well that the war had to be begun afresh, and called for effective support. Backed up by Senate and people, by the Allies and the client kings, he set out for the seat of war, and men hoped for a blessed change under a leader impervious to Numidian gold. The task before him was not easy. He had to make his new army efficient, and to restore the morale of the old one, above all to prevent the latter from tainting the former. What he received from the luckless Albinus was a mob of slovens marauders malingerers and runaways. But he had foreseen his difficulties, and practical soldiers, not merely ornamental nobles, composed his staff. Among them were two remarkable men. P. Rutilius Rufus, an upright man who carried Stoic principles into practice, was consul[4] in 105, and distinguished himself

---

[1] Cic. *de orat.* II § 283, and Wilkins' note.

[2] Cic. *pro Sest.* § 140.

[3] Illustrated in the story that, when accused of extortion, and an amount was in dispute, he produced his account-book, which the jury refused to inspect, and took his word for the item in question. Cic. *pro Balbo* § 11, and Ciceronian index.

[4] Valer. Max. II 3 § 2. A gladiatorial show was then for the first time provided by

by reforming the soldiers' training. He was entrusted by Metellus with important duties, and was no doubt already giving special attention to matters of discipline and drill. Of Gaius Marius we have already spoken. In 114 he had been propraetor in the Further Spain, and had busied himself in the suppression of brigandage. What he had done was perhaps enough to have won the honours of a triumph, had he belonged to one of the great houses. But he was still outside the charmed circle. By this time he had probably acquired a considerable property, and this would not lessen the ambition by which his dark and jealous nature was inflamed. Metellus knew his value as an officer, but was in no hurry to put him to the front. In councils of war the position of the ex-farmer who had made money in state contracts was that of the tolerated professional[1] associated on an inferior footing with men of a class socially above him. In the work of restoring discipline, and making the army fit for campaigning and fighting, the consul doubtless owed much to these men. The fundamental difference between the two was destined to appear in the sequel.

772. The war now took another turn. Jugurtha made offers of submission, but Metellus intrigued against him, endeavouring to tamper with his envoys while pretending to negotiate. In dealing with a king this was a wily policy. Either some agent, tempted by the hope of reward, would murder or betray his master, and the war would be at an end ; or Jugurtha would find out the treachery, and not know whom to trust. By this move the republican consul was assailing the monarchy in its weakest point, the dependence on agents. An advance into Numidia followed, in which extreme caution was observed. The city of Vaga, a centre for Italian traders, was occupied and garrisoned as a military base, and fresh ambassadors from Jugurtha were received and tempted in the same manner as before. The king saw that he had got to fight, for it was absolutely necessary to check the progress of Metellus. He raised a great army and kept in touch with the enemy's movements, ready to take advantage of his local knowledge whenever he could catch the Romans in a bad position. The consul moved southwards along the line of the river Muthul, for it was a matter of the first necessity to be near a supply of water. He was therefore often compelled to march on low ground, and at last Jugurtha saw his opportunity and delivered his attack. A long and confused battle followed, in which the Numidian forces were greatly favoured by their superior mobility

---

magistrates, and the soldiers were taught gladiatorial swordsmanship. See Marquardt *Stvw.* III 555.

[1] Diodorus fragm. XXXV 38.

and the rough nature of the ground. Nothing but the steadiness of the Roman troops and the coolness of their generals averted a crushing disaster. In the end they beat off the enemy without losing their hold on the river: after a few days rest the army, allowing for losses in the battle, was still an organized force, ready to march and fight again. It was in short the army of a civilized power. Very different was the state of things on the side of Jugurtha. In close combat the Numidian soldier was no match for the Italian well drilled and well led. Trained to charge in a body, and at need to elude pursuit by scattering in retreat, the African who had once quitted the field was under little compulsion to return. He was in his own land, he had but small prospect of rich booty, even though victorious, in the pickings of a Roman camp, and he was tempted to make his way home. Hence a repulse differed little in its effects from a downright defeat, and the great army of Jugurtha melted away. The king however set to work to raise a new one, but according to Sallust he now drew his recruits from a less warlike class of the population. Metellus saw that the war was far from being at an end, and that success in pitched battles was very costly, so he changed his methods. Gradually and cautiously he advanced into the enemy's country, laying waste the land, capturing towns and forts, killing the adult males, and handing over the booty to his men. By these means he induced numbers of the natives to submit, and was able to feed his army on the local supplies. Garrisons were posted at important points, and Jugurtha was compelled to campaign as in hostile territory though he claimed it as his own. He resorted to a guerrilla warfare, cutting off foraging parties and waylaying small detachments with picked bodies of mounted men. The opposing generals had in fact now discovered, and were employing, the strategic methods best suited for making full use of the forces at their command.

773. After the dismal failure of the earlier leaders, it was natural that the successes of Metellus should be greeted with rejoicing in Rome, and that public confidence should revive. But the wary consul was concerned to expose his army to no risks. At the same time the plan of moving about and ravaging the country, with Jugurtha in constant attendance, picking up Roman stragglers and poisoning springs, was wearing and indecisive work. He therefore resolved to attack the city of Zama, an important stronghold and the chief place of eastern Numidia. If geographers have fixed the site correctly, it was not far from the frontier of the Roman province. We are told that the main object of Metellus was to force the king to come to its relief and so to fight a pitched battle. At this point we must notice a circumstance that throws some light on the difficulties of

Roman generals. Deserters from Roman armies were no new phenomenon, and in this war Jugurtha seems to have received plenty
of them. All or most of them were doubtless Italian Allies or men
of the foreign contingents. From deserters the king heard of the
design on Zama. He hurried off to the threatened city, encouraged
the inhabitants, and left with them a body of the deserters to stiffen
the defence. This done, he withdrew into the wilds and waited for
more news, which soon came. Marius had been detached with a small
force to bring up supplies from Sicca, a town more to the West now
held by the Romans. Jugurtha attacked the head of his column as
it issued from the gate, and a rising of the Siccans was imminent,
but Marius was a good workman and saved the situation by promptly
charging and routing the enemy. The Roman army now concentrated
on Zama. Into the fortunes of the siege we need not enter, though
the bloody assaults and desperate defence, the fierce attempts of
Jugurtha to relieve the place, the efficiency and resourcefulness of
Marius, are described by Sallust with unwonted clearness. In the
end Metellus had to raise the siege. He garrisoned various Numidian
towns and drew off the bulk of his army to winter-quarters in the
Roman province.

774. Not much had really been accomplished by the toil and
bloodshed of the past campaign. Once more Metellus resorted to
secret plotting. Bomilcar, the king's favourite agent, had served his
master faithfully in peace and war. But it now seemed likely that
Rome would win in the end: and Bomilcar saw that he stood no
small chance of being handed over to Roman vengeance. That
Jugurtha, to save himself, would sacrifice his friend, was not to be
doubted. He therefore leant a ready ear to the promises of Metellus,
who guaranteed him immunity if he delivered up his master alive or
dead. For the present matters got no further than an insidious
attempt to frighten the king into a complete surrender. Up to a
certain point the plan succeeded. Jugurtha was required to hand
over a large sum of money, all his remaining elephants, and a
quantity of horses and arms. This he did at once, and was then
ordered to surrender his Roman deserters: this also[1] he did, but
some had got wind of the negotiation, and had taken refuge in
Mauretania. The fate of the rest may be guessed. The king was
finally summoned to appear in person for orders. He saw the trap
set for him, and did not come. Gradually his shaken nerves recovered their tone, and in spite of all his fruitless sacrifices he
ventured to renew the war.

---

[1] Orosius v 15 § 7, probably after Livy, says that over 3000 were surrendered. The
Thracians and Ligurians referred to by Appian *Numid.* fragm. 3 perhaps belong to this
occasion.

775. In the arrangements for the year 108 the African province was left to Metellus as proconsul, and it seemed that he would be allowed to finish the war. But all was not well at headquarters, for the harmony between Marius and his chief was broken. Marius is said to have received from a soothsayer strong assurances of good luck. The man was devoured by ambition, and had set his heart upon attaining the consulship. He had been praetor and so was technically *nobilis*, but the traditional and generally successful policy of the great Roman houses was to keep the consulship for members of their own hereditary circle, who were *nobiles* in their cradles. Against this limitation—by custom, not by law,—Marius rebelled. The same self-control, which enabled him to bear the surgeon's knife[1] without flinching, had also enabled him to go on adding to the record of his merits without due recognition. But his patience was at an end. He asked Metellus for leave to go to Rome and stand for the consulship, and was refused. The noble commander could not rise above the prejudices of his class. But Marius persisted. The proconsul found that genial dissuasion was of no avail, and agreed to let him go as soon as he could be spared. Meanwhile he told him not to be impatient. It would be time enough for Marius to think of the consulship, when the young Metellus (a lad of about 20, then attached to his father's staff) could hold it with him. The suggestion that he should be content to wait more than twenty years was never forgotten or forgiven by Marius. It was not for such insults that he had toiled and fought. And it is clear that there were those in Roman society who took a different view of his merits, for he seems to have been already married[2] to Julia, a lady of an old patrician house. Well, he was not to look for help from Metellus: he grimly resolved to help himself, and not to be too nice about the means. Already he was popular with the men, whose labour and hardships he shared to the full. He now used his popularity to undermine that of his chief, by indulging the rank and file. He stirred up the wrath of the Roman financiers gathered like vultures at Utica, waiting to rush in and exploit the necessities of a conquered land. He hinted that the war was dragging on solely for the honour and glory of Metellus, who had no mind to retire into private life: and his hearers, chafing at delay, were only too ready to swallow the slander. He did not even disdain to court Jugurtha's half-brother Gauda, who was easily led to believe that the popular soldier, who flattered him, was more likely than the haughty noble, who snubbed him, to destroy Jugurtha and clear his way to the throne. The outcome of these disloyal intrigues was that letters and messages poured into Rome, the burden of them being

---

[1] See the story in Plutarch *Mar.* 6, Cic. *Tusc. disp.* II § 53.
[2] Plut. *Mar.* 6.

that change was needed and that Marius was the man of the hour. The court of the Mamilian commission had been at work: the nobility were depressed by the ruin of eminent members of their class: capitalists and mob were pulling together, and all was in favour of the new man.

776. Meanwhile Metellus was not idle. The first event of the campaign[1] of 108 seems to have been the revolt of Vaga. The town had for some time been in Roman hands, and was held by a garrison, the commandant of which was one Turpilius, an officer of engineers. He was a Latin, and owed his promotion to the fact that his family were old friends of the family of Metellus. Jugurtha had now got together a fresh army, and kept the war alive with restless energy. He induced the townsfolk of Vaga, who were sick of the Roman occupation, to surprise and massacre the garrison. Turpilius alone escaped, perhaps by a treasonable compact: in any case military tradition required that he should not desert his men. By a forced march and sudden attack Metellus recaptured the town and took a bloody vengeance. Turpilius was brought before a court-martial. Sallust tells us merely that his defence was not thought satisfactory, and that he was accordingly scourged and put to death: as a Latin[2] he had no protection against this summary execution. But, if Plutarch was not misled by a lying authority, there was more in the affair than appears on the surface. He says that Metellus was very unwilling to condemn the man to death, and that the finding of the court was due to the insistence of Marius. After this the proconsul could not help condemning his trusted officer and friend. Soon after the innocence of Turpilius was shewn, and Marius exulted in the grief of Metellus, on whose head rested the guilt of blood. What evidence there was to prove the innocence of the sole survivor of the massacre we are not told. The interest of this version is mainly as shewing what Romans were ready to impute to one another. All this while the plot against Jugurtha was going on. Bomilcar found his relations with the king less comfortable since the abandonment of the policy of surrender. He was in a hurry, and a letter written by

[1] This story is told in Sall. *Jug.* 66—9, Plut. *Mar.* 8, with important variations. The latter alone makes Marius implicated in the affair. Plutarch perhaps used Sallust, but certainly the memoirs of Sulla, which were bitterly hostile to Marius. It may be that the guilt of Marius is drawn from this tainted source. See H. Peter, *Die Quellen Plutarchs in den Biographieen der Römer.*

[2] Sallust's expression *civis e Latio* seems to be without parallel. But it can hardly mean anything more than 'a man of Latin status.' Mr Summers well points out that this man had received great power from Metellus, being even in command over Roman military tribunes. Latins sometimes appear in positions of great military trust. See Livy XLIII 18 § 10, 19 § 7, 21 § 2, and above § 283. In Appian Numid. frag. 3 the man is called a Roman (ἄνδρα Ῥωμαῖον), which is not definite.

him to a confederate, urging him to lose no time, fell into the hands
of a man who took it to Jugurtha. Jugurtha put Bomilcar and
others to death and kept the matter as private as possible. But we
may believe with Sallust that from that time he was as a hunted
man, able to trust none, beset with continual terrors by night and
day.

777. Foiled in his design against the person of Jugurtha, Metellus
addressed himself to the renewal of the war. The sulky temper of
Marius, and the mischief he was making in the army, made his
presence a nuisance, and the proconsul now yielded to the worrying
of his lieutenant. It seems to have been in the summer of 108 that
Marius started for Rome. Plutarch[1] says that there were only
twelve days to spare before the election, and that it took him two
days and a night of hard travelling to get on board ship at Utica.
But he arrived in time. His partisans, tribunes and others, were
inveighing against Metellus and pushing home the attack upon the
nobility, aided by the reports from Africa. Countrymen and townsmen alike rallied to the 'popular' cause, and the mass of the capitalists
were doubtless on the same side. On a genuine wave of enthusiasm,
however aroused, the 'new man' was borne into the consulship. The
victory was followed up by a further blow at the Senate. That body
had not assigned Numidia as a 'province' for a consul in 107. But a
tribune, disregarding the constitutional rights of the Senate, took a
vote of the Assembly on the question, who was to have the command
against Jugurtha, and the Tribes gave it to Marius. Thus another
joint in the Roman constitution was loosened. The great Council
that in ordinary times necessarily did most of the business of state
could not in moments of excitement hold its own. And indeed there
was ground for excitement. Metellus' colleague in the consulship
(109) had lately been badly beaten by the northern barbarians in
Gaul. The management of the wars at this time was not such as to
inspire confidence in the ruling nobles. Even nomination of generals
by the Assembly might be an improvement,—for a time. Marius had
boasted[2] that if elected he would make an end of Jugurtha, and he
was now to have his chance. Sallust pictures for us the rough
soldier-consul, or consul-elect, in the intoxication of his victory,
haranguing the people on the incapacity of the effeminate nobles
and his own merits. In truth no one could fairly say of him that he
was first elected consul and then began to 'cram' strategy in a Greek
text-book. If any man had learnt the art of war by a course of

---

[1] Plut. *Mar.* 8.

[2] Even Cicero *de offic.* III § 79 blames the conduct of Marius, and he was always inclined
to speak well of his fellow-townsman.

practical work, it was he. But his fierce attack on the nobility served
no useful end, and it certainly made their hatred of the upstart more
lasting and bitter: hence the malignity with which the name of
Marius was blackened by writers mostly belonging to the noble class.
The Senate at once voted everything he asked for the purposes of the
war. Their policy was to give him a free hand, and let him wear out
his present popularity in the enforcement of a great military levy.
But they were out of their reckoning. The common people believed
in Marius, and numbers of old soldiers, some of whom had seen service
with him already, responded to his call. This proof of confidence
was no doubt contagious, and the needy were attracted by hopes of
sharing some of the riches made notorious by the bribes of Jugurtha,
the restless by the prospect of taking part in a great and successful
enterprise. The consul was beset with volunteers, and there was in
the circumstances of the moment no power to prevent him from
forming his new army as he chose, without regard to precedent.
For the ancient principle, that the defence of the state was a burden[1]
on owners of property, Marius cared nothing. Practice had long
ceased to have any close connexion with principle, in this as in other
departments of public life. He meant to have an army devoted to
himself, for as a workman he knew the tools suited to his work, and
he would trample on anything, principle or sentiment, that stood in
his way. If the men without property, 'rated by the head' [*capite
censi*][2] had the making of soldiers in them, Marius would enrol them
in his legions. It was said that he was driven to this course because
he could not get the men of the property-classes to come forward:
others averred that he took the paupers by preference, as being more
likely to back him up in ulterior designs. These insinuations may
date from a later time, when Marius had become a name of terror;
but may have been contemporary, for the eye of jealousy is keen.
We may guess that among the destitute stratum of the Roman
population there was a proportion of old soldiers, good men-at-arms,
reduced to indigence by extravagance or misfortune. Beside the
citizen troops there were the contingents of Italian Allies and foreign
auxiliaries. The consul seems to have raised all he wished without
difficulty. In the end he found himself at the head of a force
considerably larger than that voted him; a fact which throws light
on the military system of the time and was ominous of the coming
period of civil wars.

778. Among the most important steps taken in view of a coming

[1] See Valer. Max. II 3 § 1, Gellius XVI 10. Marquardt, *Staatsverwaltung*, pp. 430 foll.
[2] Plut. *Mar.* 9 says that he even enrolled slaves, probably a slander derived from the
memoirs of Sulla, written after he and Marius were enemies. Sall. *Jug.* 86.

campaign was the appointment of a quaestor. He was generally the consul's right-hand man, and we can hardly doubt that the selection, under whatever form, was left to the all-powerful Marius. The man chosen was L. Cornelius Sulla, one of an old Patrician family that had seen better days. He was a man of great talents improved by education both Latin and Greek, and of a force of character as yet hardly suspected. His ambition had been clogged in youth by too much devotion to pleasures, and he was now 31, about 19 years younger than his commander, to whom he presented a striking contrast. His social gifts, his eloquence, his power of dissembling, his general capacity for dealing with difficult affairs, were all manifestations of the adaptability to circumstances which marked his career. Such a man, unscrupulous and adroit, was well fitted to succeed in business requiring deftness and a nerve different in kind from the somewhat clumsy force of the sullen unadaptable Marius. It was the war with Jugurtha that first brought into close contact the incompatible natures of these future rivals. For the present the quaestor stayed behind to complete the organization of the cavalry of the Allies, while the consul with the bulk of his army proceeded to the seat of war.

779. While Marius was carrying all before him in Rome, Metellus was chasing Jugurtha in Numidia. The king was constantly changing his plans, but at last the proconsul came up with his slippery adversary, forced him to give battle, and routed his army. Jugurtha took refuge in Thala, a royal stronghold, apparently situated inland to the south of the Roman province, and deemed inaccessible to a regular army by reason of a wide stretch of waterless desert dividing it from the outer world. Metellus resolved to shew that the Roman army could penetrate even there. By careful preparations, aided by good luck, he reached the oasis to the surprise of the enemy. The king, fearing to be pent up in the town, again took to flight with his family and treasures. But Thala only fell after a most stubborn resistance. A body of deserters made a last stand in the citadel, and ended by killing themselves to avoid falling into the hand of Rome. Little or nothing was gained by this exhausting expedition, probably because of the lack of vital coherence in the Numidian kingdom. To produce moral effects in a community where union is only expressed in the allegiance to a monarch, is naturally difficult. It is the king on whom impression must be made, and the impression on Jugurtha was merely a strengthened conviction that he had better keep out of the power of Rome as long as possible. But the city-community of Leptis, on the coast between Carthage and Cyrene, a place of mixed population, but in civilization mainly Phoenician, asked for and received a Roman

garrison. They were already allies of Rome. Whether the internal troubles from which they were suffering were directly connected with the Numidian war, is very doubtful. Metellus knew that his main business was to catch Jugurtha. At this point the narrative of Sallust is very unsatisfactory. We read that Jugurtha had taken refuge among the wild Gaetulians, who inhabited the upland country at the back of Numidia, and had never come into touch with Rome. Here he raised yet another army, to which he imparted a good deal of discipline and drill. He would seem to have been working westwards, for his next step was to seek the support of Bocchus, the king of Mauretania. At the beginning of the war Bocchus had offered himself as a Roman ally, but the money of Jugurtha was employed to procure the refusal of this timely offer. It was now the friends and favourites of Bocchus who were approached with Numidian gold, for that one of Jugurtha's wives was a daughter of Bocchus mattered little. The Mauretanian king at length was won over, and the combined army advanced into Numidia, of course from the West. We are told that their march was directed upon Cirta. Suddenly, without any record of its capture by the Romans, we find that Metellus is using that city as a depot for his booty (prisoners included) and stores. According to this version[1] of events, Jugurtha hoped either to win Cirta or to compel Metellus to advance to its relief. In the latter case he would give battle to the proconsul, and thus, whether victorious or beaten, secure the doubted loyalty of Bocchus by embroiling him with Rome. But Metellus seems to have heard of the alliance of the two kings before they came with the joint army. He encamped near Cirta, and waited to gain some experience of the new Mauretanian enemy before taking the risks of a general engagement. He had heard of Marius' election to the consulship. News now came that he was appointed to command in Numidia. It was a hard blow to the proconsul, who had borne the burden and heat of the day, and he complained bitterly of the humiliation of being superseded by his intriguing lieutenant. So he negotiated with Bocchus and warned him not to mix himself up with the lost cause of Jugurtha. The king would not abandon his ally, and much time was wasted in exchange of views. It is suggested[2] that this delay was intentional on the part of Metellus: if he was to be recalled, he would at least not exert himself now, to spare trouble to his successor.

780. Marius soon arrived and took over the army from the proconsul's legate Rutilius. Metellus had left this officer in charge and set out for Rome, to spare himself an unendurable scene. We

---

[1] Sall. *Jug.* 80—2.   [2] Sall. *Jug.* 83.

are told that on his return he found an unexpected welcome[1] from all classes. But we may well guess that the reaction was promoted by the nobles and their dependants, and was in part a demonstration against their hated enemy Marius. The new consul opened his campaign with raids made in force, and minor sieges and engagements, and greatly improved the cohesion and efficiency of his army. The two kings had separated for the time. Jugurtha hung round, waiting to catch Marius off his guard, but the chance never came, and in a battle near Cirta he was utterly defeated. Bocchus was all the while playing a double game, ready to profit by any turn of events: he could not throw over Jugurtha, but he kept up negotiations with Marius. Marius, like his predecessor, found that warfare on the small scale was wearisome and productive of little result. He resolved to strike a dramatic blow by the capture of a distant stronghold. The city of Capsa was even stronger and more difficult to reach than Thala: he would take this place, and outdo the recent exploit of Metellus. Capsa is identified with Cafsa, an oasis-city to reach which a long stretch of desert had to be crossed, devoid of water. But patient organization in detail[2] combined with promptitude of execution made the attempt a success. Capsa was surprised, for Marius had contrived to put Jugurtha off the scent. The capture of a number of natives outside the city walls led to some sort of surrender, which Roman policy interpreted by putting to the sword all adult males. Capsa had been favoured by Jugurtha, and it was not likely that local loyalty would be permanently overcome without a signal exhibition of Roman power. The fall of Capsa was followed by a number of minor sieges and the capture of towns. In Sallust these events only occupy about four lines of text: but, if the sequel be correctly given, these briefly-noticed successes must refer to nothing less than a march through the length of Numidia, some 600 or 700 miles, towns making submission with all speed as the Roman army moved to the West. For without any warning we find Marius not far from the river Muluccha, the Mauretanian frontier, busied with the siege of a stronghold containing some of Jugurtha's treasures. The westward advance is natural enough, for it was necessary to alarm Bocchus for his own safety. But it cannot have been crowded into what was left of the campaign of 107 after the fall of Capsa. We are left to guesswork. Probably the army

---

[1] He was allowed a triumph, and took the title *Numidicus*.

[2] The author of the *bellum Africum* (c. 32) tells us that Caesar in his African campaign (B.C. 46) was able to establish friendly relations with the Gaetuli owing to his connexion with Marius, whom they still remembered as a friend of their fathers. This gives us a glimpse of the policy of Marius in winning the support of the tribes of the hinterland.

wintered somewhere in eastern Numidia, and prepared for the general advance in 106. So long and perilous a march cannot have been undertaken without a strong force of cavalry, and Sulla with the cavalry from Italy must have already joined. The siege of the western fortress will then represent the farthest point reached in the campaign of 106. The place was only taken by a process of which history records many instances. While the defenders were repelling the main attack, the cliffs in rear of the fort, supposed inaccessible, were left unwatched. Marius was beginning to despair, when one of his Ligurian auxiliaries discovered a practicable path up the cliffs, of which effective use was made to turn the position.

781. For the present it would seem that no direct results followed from this successful expedition to the West. The proconsul was constrained to return eastwards in order to find winter quarters within reach of the coast, for he now depended upon sea-borne supplies. The retreat to Cirta was no easy matter. Jugurtha by lavish promises brought the wavering Bocchus once more into the field, and the numerous forces of the two kings followed the Roman army as it fell back, watching their opportunity. Twice they attacked it and inflicted considerable loss: but the coolness and energy of Marius, the steadiness of the Roman foot, and the skilful handling of the cavalry by Sulla, extricated the army from its danger. On the second occasion, not far from Cirta, the defeat of the barbarians was so severe that Bocchus again began to shew a willingness to treat for peace. At his request two trusty agents were sent to discuss matters with him, and the proconsul shewed his discernment by employing Sulla on this duty. The quaestor had turned out well. He had thrown off the man of pleasure, and applied himself with thoroughness to learn the military art. This he quickly did, and there was now no better officer. But he was much more than a mere soldier, and his steely temper, at once flexible penetrating and tenacious, never shewed to greater advantage than in the dangerous negotiations with Bocchus. The first conference was apparently abortive so far that the king talked of sending an embassy to Rome and did not do so. Sallust says that the influence of his courtiers, who were bribed by Jugurtha, again prevailed. But time and the advice of other counsellors told upon the barbarian's nerves, and Marius was not idle. He attacked a fort which Jugurtha had garrisoned with Roman deserters, took it, and doubtless put the whole party to death. Bocchus meanwhile sent ambassadors to make peace on the best terms they could get. These men, waylaid and robbed by wild Gaetulians, sought refuge with Sulla, then in command at headquarters as deputy of Marius. Sulla received and entertained them with far-sighted

hospitality, got out of them much useful information, and installed himself in the position of their personal friend and adviser. Some of them were sent on to Rome by Marius. There they did their errand and were told in reply that their master's offence might be condoned, since he now saw the error of his ways: if he wanted to be an ally and friend of Rome, he must do something to deserve the favour. The Mauretanian king was probably at no loss to interpret the inner meaning of this decorous answer. He wrote to Marius and begged him to send Sulla for a second conference.

782. Bocchus was clearly at this time back in his own country, and Sulla had to undertake a considerable journey. The escort[1] assigned him by Marius consisted of (a) some cavalry, probably Italian Allies, (b) a cohort of Paeligni, Italian Allies, not armed as heavy infantry but as light troops, (c) Balearic slingers, (d) bowmen, probably Cretans. The selection is interesting as throwing light on the composition of the Roman army, and the need of a highly mobile force for the business in hand. On the march there were alarms and fears of treachery, perhaps not without reason. Sulla could not be daunted or deceived into taking a false step. The mission safely reached the quarters of Bocchus with prestige unimpaired: no man knew better than Sulla how necessary it was to keep a moral advantage in dealing with barbarians. And now began a three-cornered struggle of wits and tempers: Aspar, Jugurtha's confidential agent, trying to induce Bocchus to seize the Roman and hand him over to Jugurtha as a security for obtaining a peace, while Sulla worked upon the fears of the king by pointing out that the only means of winning the favour of Rome was to catch and surrender the Numidian. The long wavering of Bocchus made a dramatic situation not neglected by the rhetoricians of later times. Of the two solutions of the problem he at length chose that offered by Sulla. Jugurtha was entrapped under pretext of a conference and handed over to the Roman, who lost no time in returning to headquarters and delivering his prisoner to Marius.

783. So ended the Numidian war. Of the settlement that followed little is known. Bocchus became an ally of Rome, and a large part of Numidia was added to his kingdom. The eastern portion, the former share of Adherbal, more or less, was placed under the rule of Mastanabal's son, the feeble Gauda. Rome had had enough of unprofitable war, and the kings were under no temptation to revive the ambitions of Jugurtha. Marius seems to have borne his part in the settlement of the affairs of northern Africa, and returned to Rome near the end of 105. Since the capture of Jugurtha his

[1] Sall. *Jug.* 105.

relations with Sulla had become unpleasant. The quaestor had all along been popular with the army, probably more so than suited the wishes of Marius. His cool dexterity had now achieved the one decisive success of the war. His friends and admirers, and all who were afraid or weary of the grim proconsul, made the most of his achievement. The news soon reached Rome, and passed from mouth to mouth: gradually moulded by the malignity of the proconsul's enemies into the saying that, as Marius had grabbed the glory of Metellus, so he was now robbed of his own by Sulla. Henceforth, though there was no open rupture, the two men were rivals. The elder jealously watched the younger, the younger saw that he could only raise and secure himself by the ruin of the elder. The new signet-ring of Sulla, the gem of which depicted Bocchus handing over to him the captive Jugurtha, was an ingenious form of automatic self-assertion. The seal of a man of position was in constant use, and every impression was a tacit challenge to Marius. Meanwhile it was Marius to whom the victory belonged, Marius who led the wretched Numidian in his triumph, Marius who sent him, dazed with agony and terror, to some horrible end in the cold damp dungeon beneath the Capitoline hill. The hard man of blood and iron who kept his promises was indeed at that particular moment Rome's most valuable asset. In the autumn of 105 news had come of a terrible disaster on the Rhone, imperilling the position of Rome in Transalpine Gaul. A conflict with the peoples of the North was a matter of life and death: a shudder, says Sallust, ran through the length of Italy. Rules and precedents were swept aside, and when Marius returned he found himself already elected consul for the following year and appointed to the chief command in the North.

784. The Jugurthine war enables us to peep for a moment behind the scenes and observe the inner decay and weakness of the Roman state, the lamentable inefficiency of its various parts. At home, noble cliques and the mongrel populace were each in their way corrupt; the financiers alone represented a consistent and effective influence, that of selfish capitalism. But in the matter of the war the present interest of the capitalists probably coincided with that of the state. Since the days of Masinissa and the first Scipio Africanus, the royal house of Numidia had owned the suzerainty of Rome. In 149 a settlement of the Numidian succession had been made by the younger Africanus. It was impossible to abdicate the overlordship without creating an exaggerated impression of Roman weakness, and in this there would be danger. To reject the appeal of Adherbal, and tamely submit to be defied by Jugurtha, would have been a public announcement of Rome's abdication, nothing less. If Rome

was to assert her suzerainty, she could not act too firmly or too speedily: the refusal of Bocchus' proffered aid, the shuffling pretexts for delay, the paralysing corruption at home and in the field, were aspects of a policy that sacrificed the permanent interests of the state to the temporary convenience or profit of individuals. When the Knights acted with the 'popular' party against the senatorial nobility and their dependants, when they punished scandals and insisted on a vigorous conduct of the war, they were right. It mattered not that their motives were mercenary, and that they were suspected of too great a readiness to condemn political opponents. It was necessary to restore the prestige of Rome and bring the wasteful war to an end. They pushed to the front the unamiable Marius, and Marius did what was required. Noble gossips and writers might strive to depreciate his services compared with those of Metellus and Sulla: we shall judge more fairly if we reflect that the success of Sulla's diplomacy depended on the fear inspired by the victories of Marius. The war also exposed defects in the Roman military system, which were partly remedied under the teaching of experience. In particular the importance of cavalry and light troops seems to have been more fully recognized. But these arms were made up of Allies and auxiliaries. The army was becoming less and less Roman, and the service of citizens in the legions was ceasing to be a duty and a burden on property. The pauper volunteer, serving for pay and plunder, was more and more becoming the characteristic figure of the legionary ranks, serving his general rather than the state. Nor was this tendency likely to decrease, for the time was come when Rome had once more to defend her existence with the sword. Efficiency at all costs had to be secured. An army of a new model might be a danger threatening the institutions of the Republic, but it was too late to dally over constitutional scruples when the dreaded northern barbarians were knocking at the doors of Italy.

NOTE ON THE GEOGRAPHY OF THE JUGURTHINE WAR.

The many obscure points in the narrative of this war are most fully dealt with in Dr Greenidge's *History of Rome* 133 B.C. to 70 A.D. vol. I (all that the author lived to publish), and a good map is given at the end of the volume. To discuss them in the text would have led me too far from my subject.

CHAPTER XL

785. THE relief felt in Rome at the successful ending of the Numidian war was all the greater because that war, in itself not a matter of life and death, was seen to be hindering the effective treatment of a far more serious danger. We must resume our sketch of events in the North, and shew, so far as our meagre information admits, the alarming situation with which Marius was now called upon to deal. The movement of the northern barbarians, of which we have spoken above, was evidently no sudden raid but a deliberate migration. They advanced slowly, changing their direction from time to time according as this or that country seemed to offer the most favourable prospect. The main body, known in our tradition[1] as Cimbri and Teutoni (or Teutones), were of German origin. It appears to have been the increase of their numbers in lands unable to support them that drove forth these mighty swarms, to wander in search of new homes and win them sword in hand. Like the Scythian hordes of the eastern steppes, they travelled with their wives and children, and a vast train of covered waggons (huts on wheels, in short) gave to their progress the air of a rude straggling city on the march. If we may believe the report handed down[2] by Julius Caesar, they crossed the lower Rhine into the Belgic part of Gaul. Here, in a district near the Mosa (Maas), they left all their less portable goods in charge of a strong detachment, and set out on their venture. By what route[3] they reached Noreia, where they routed Carbo's army in 113, we do not know. For the moment they turned to the West, and made for Gaul. Their movements are a mystery to us, but they seem to have drawn after them a large body of Tigurini, perhaps a Keltic tribe.

---

[1] The ethnology of the invaders has called forth much ingenious speculation. Some hold that the Teutoni, like the Tigurini, were Helvetian Kelts. See reference to the literature of the subject in B. Niese's *Römische Geschichte*, p. 159. Appian *Gall.* ιrag. 1, 13. For the name Kelts see below § 1091.

[2] Caesar *bell. Gall.* II 29. From the same book c. 3 we learn that earlier German migrants were already settled west of the Rhine. In those days Teutons and Kelts easily coalesced, and the distinction between them was not clearly marked by ancient writers. See Appian *civ.* I 29 § 2 with Mr Strachan-Davidson's note.

[3] For traditions oι their movements see Strabo VII 2, Plut. *Mar.* 11.

After they entered Gaul, the Ambrones[1], perhaps Ligurians or Kelts, appear in their company. In the dearth of satisfactory evidence we shall do well to affirm no more than that a mass of invaders, seeking a dwelling-place rather than plunder, in great part of Teutonic stock, were on the move in Gaul about 111 or 110, and came into collision with the Romans in 109. The Gaulish tribes seem to have been quite unable to meet them on equal terms[2] in the open field. On the other hand, when the Gauls shut themselves up in their strongholds, the invaders were foiled. They were unskilled in the siege of fortified posts, and they had not the patience, or it may be the means, to reduce them by blockade. Peaceful possession was hardly possible under such conditions; so they got tired of the undertaking, and the Gauls reoccupied their lands when the storm rolled by. In 109, when Metellus went to Numidia, his colleague M. Junius Silanus[3] held the command in Gaul. The leaders of the barbarian host sent ambassadors to him to ask for lands on which they might settle. He sent the deputation on to Rome, where the Senate refused their request. The outcome of this was a battle somewhere in the Rhone valley. The Roman army was defeated with great loss, and this disaster, so soon following that of Carbo, caused a panic in Italy. But again the enemy seem to have turned aside instead of pushing forward. For the present we hear of no invasion of the Roman province or direct threatening of Italy: the Cimbri and their allies were probably engaged in renewed attempts at conquest in the heart of Gaul. In 107 we find the Tigurini[4] far to the westward in the country of the Nitiobriges (north of the Garonne, between Bordeaux and Toulouse). The consul commanding in Gaul, L. Cassius Longinus, who advanced to check them and protect the province, fell into a trap and perished with a great part of his army. His surviving lieutenant C. Popilius only saved the remainder by agreeing to the most degrading terms.

786. The fortunes of Rome in Gaul were already at a low ebb, but as yet there was no turning of the tide. In 106 Q. Servilius Caepio was one of the consuls. He belonged to the party of the nobles, and was the proposer of a law which for a short time[5] restored to senators a share in the jury-courts. In this he was supported

---

[1] See Plutarch, *Marius* 19.

[2] See Caesar *bell. Gall.* II 4, VII 77 §§ 12—14.

[3] See Livy ep. 65, Velleius II 12, Diodor. fragm. XXXV 37, Florus I 38. In Eutrop. IV 27 the defeat of Silanus appears as a victory. From Asconius 68, a good authority, we learn that Silanus had procured the repeal of some recent laws by which the term of liability to service had been reduced. Probably a law of C. Gracchus was one. See § 725.

[4] See Caesar *bell. Gall.* I 12, Livy ep. 65, Orosius V 15.

[5] If indeed it was actually carried, which is very doubtful. See Lange *RA* III 67.

by the orator Crassus, the founder of the colony at Narbo, who was doubtless specially interested in the affairs of Gaul. It would seem to have been later in that year that Caepio went himself to command in Gaul. The army there had of course been reinforced, and Caepio was not wholly inexperienced in war, having as praetor in Spain put down a Lusitanian rising. But he was greedy and unscrupulous, like many of his contemporaries. At the back of Narbo was the land of the Volcae Tectosages, whose chief city was Tolosa. The place[1] had no doubt served as a military base in the campaign of Cassius, and a Roman garrison was posted there. Recent events had unsettled the people, who rose and overpowered the garrison. Caepio marched to recover Tolosa, which he did with the help of traitors inside. The town was famed for the great quantity of the precious metals stored there, chiefly as sacred offerings, in the temples, or sunk in the sacred tanks. The consul made a clean sweep of all he could find, and sent off the treasure to be in safe keeping at Massalia. So far he seems to have claimed it for the Roman treasury, at all events most of it. But the escort were waylaid and murdered on the road by persons unknown, and the treasure never came to hand. Unkind rumour hinted that the organizer of the robbery was the consul himself, but for the present nothing happened. We find Caepio in Gaul as proconsul in 105. The importance of keeping at bay the barbarians was now fully understood, and one of the consuls of the year, Cn. Mallius Maximus, was sent with a second army to ensure a successful result. Mallius[2] was a 'new man,' but people were heartily tired of inefficient nobles. Why he was sent to command in a serious war, having apparently no special qualifications for the work, is only to be explained by the chances of the lot. His colleague, P. Rutilius Rufus the military reformer, remained in Italy[3] busied with improving the drill of the reserve army. In particular he introduced more thorough sword-practice[4] on the gladiatorial model, and the Roman swordsman, highly trained in a school of thrust-fencing, learnt how to contend at an advantage with the clumsy giants of the North.

787. For the present however it was Mallius who went to the front, probably with raw troops, and was charged with the two difficult duties of stopping the advance of the barbarians and cooperating

---

[1] See Strabo IV 1 § 13, Orosius V 15 § 25, Gellius III 9 § 7, Justin XXXII 3 §§ 9—11, Dion Cass. frag. 90, 91. The legends to account for the gold in Tolosa are of no probability.

[2] Cic. *pro Plancio* § 12, *pro Murena* § 36.

[3] From Licinianus (Bonn ed. p. 21) we learn that Rutilius made all men liable to service (*iuniores*) swear not to leave Italy, and sent orders to the ports that no such person was to be allowed to embark.

[4] Valer. Max. II 3 § 2.

with Caepio. The details of what followed are variously given[1] in our fragmentary records, but the main outlines are clear. The enemy were pushing southwards along the Rhone, and the two Roman armies opposed to them were separated by the river and not effectively in touch. The jealousy between the two commanders was extreme: in particular the aristocrat Caepio resented the precedence of Mallius as consul of the year, and would not act in loyal concert with him. Mallius had with him as *legatus* an ex-consul, M. Aurelius Scaurus[2], who was commanding an advanced corps in front of the main army. The Cimbri attacked this body and routed it. Scaurus fell into their hands and was brought before the chiefs to be questioned, but his defiant bearing so enraged the barbarians that one of them slew him on the spot. Mallius sent an urgent request to Caepio to bring up his army. A concentration was indeed most necessary, but Caepio still held off, and was only induced by the clamour of his men to cross the river. But he only came to quarrel, and cooperation was as far off as ever. The barbarian chiefs, whose first object was to settle their people in a new home, sent once more to ask for lands and seed-corn. Their envoys addressed themselves first to Mallius, and Caepio, resenting the preference, would not receive them at all. Of the battle which followed we can only gather that the previous bickerings of the Roman commanders continued in the form of a selfish neglect of mutual support. Utter rout and slaughter left few to tell the tale of a defeat more disastrous than anything that had befallen Rome since the day of Cannae. Two armies had ceased to exist, and the defects of the military system and the political disorders of Rome were expiated in blood. The date of the battle[3] was the sixth of October, the place is thought to have been Arausio[4] (Orange). It was clear that nothing less than the best army Rome could raise, commanded by the best general to be found, offered any hope of averting the invasion of Italy. But again the barbarians turned aside[5] in their course. Some rumour seems to have led them to fancy that a Promised Land awaited them south of the Pyrenees. So they moved on into Spain, and left a breathing-space for Marius to restore the defences of Rome.

788. The want of clear and connected accounts of important changes is a familiar phenomenon to students of Roman history.

---

[1] See Livy ep. 67, Orosius v 16, Dion Cass. fragm. 91, Liciniani fragm. (ed. Bonn) p. 17.

[2] I can find no evidence that this Scaurus, when consul in 108, was commanding in Gaul and suffered a defeat, as is sometimes asserted. The loose reference in Tac. *Germ.* 37 certainly does not prove it.

[3] Plutarch, *Lucull.* 27.

[4] The name is due to Livy ep. 67, but the text is not wholly free from doubt.

[5] Plutarch, *Marius* 14, Livy ep. 67.

The military reforms of Marius are a striking instance[1] of this difficulty.   Some details are directly recorded, but much can only be arrived at by more or less certain inference.   The various changes cannot be placed in a strict order of time.   A beginning was probably made during the Jugurthine war: the wholesale enlistment of pauper volunteers has been spoken of above.   It is hardly credible that the consul dallied long in Italy in the early spring of 104, but much no doubt was done in that season of activity.   The rest of his innovations may well have been carried out gradually when he had reached Gaul and could devote himself to remodelling his army.   In general we may say that the Marian reforms were a practical recognition of the lessons of experience, an expression of tendencies long at work.   The distinction between the three lines of the legion had long lost its clearness and significance: Marius took away the spear of the *triarii*, and all alike now carried the *pilum*.   The Roman light troops disappeared, and the poorer citizens, from whom these *velites* had been drawn, were now accepted as heavy infantry.   In recent wars the larger unit [the *cohors*], employed in the contingents of Allies, had been found more convenient than the smaller one [*manipulus*] used in the Roman legions.   Marius, without abolishing the maniple or even the century, adopted the cohort as the effective tactical unit. Henceforth the normal strength of a full legion was 6000 men in ten cohorts of 600 each.   Each cohort, as formerly each maniple, had a standard, but Marius laid stress upon the essential unity of the legion by introducing a legionary standard.   This was a silver eagle on a staff.   We find it spoken of as the legion's god.   Before it religious ceremonies were performed in camp: to keep it safe, even on a stricken field, was the first principle of legionary honour. Perhaps we may assume that the eagle was only given to legions of Roman citizens: in other respects the assimilation of Romans and Allies seems now to have been complete.   From the military point of view this amounted to the organization of a great homogeneous Infantry of the Line.   Politically, it must have served to bring home to the Latins and other Italians the injustice of their exclusion from the franchise more forcibly than ever.

789.   But uniform bodies of foot, however well armed and drilled, did not make up an army.   I have pointed out that the Roman Knights had practically ceased to serve in the ranks as a mounted force.   From the young *equites* officers and a picked bodyguard for the general were still drawn.   But Latins would seem to have been finding their way by degrees into these close preserves.   From them and other Allies came the troopers of Italian origin.   But the need of

[1] See Marquardt, *Staatsverwaltung*, II 429—42.

a more numerous cavalry was now well known, and these had to be raised abroad. Some came from the provinces, others were supplied by client kings anxious to stand well with Rome. The practice was as old as the time of Masinissa. In the Jugurthine war we find Numidian and Thracian cavalry in Roman service, and these foreign contingents were employed more and more. But they were technically not *socii* but *auxilia*. So also were the bowmen and slingers and other light troops. A splendid light infantry, particularly for fighting in rough countries, was furnished by the hill-men of Liguria, the newly conquered Balearic isles sent their famous slingers, while bowmen were drawn from eastern parts, such as the restless communities of Crete. The mention of Crete may remind us (for Crete was still independent) that the use of sheer mercenaries was now a part of the Roman army-system, though we cannot connect it with Marius in particular. The pressing need of men at this crisis compelled the government to seek help wherever it could be found. After the defeats of Carbo and Silanus, in which great numbers of the youth of Italy had perished, the Senate had revived the tradition of the olden time, striving to keep public mourning within bounds[1] and calm agitation by setting an example of Roman dignity. But then came the crushing disaster of Caepio and Manlius, and none knew[2] what the immediate consequences might be. Marius was authorized to send over sea for aid, and it so happens that we have preserved to us a stray notice[3] of one of his applications. He called upon Nicomedes of Bithynia to furnish a contingent. The king replied that he could not do so, for he had not the men to send: more than half of his adult males had been kidnapped to supply the needs of the Roman capitalists and were now working in Roman provinces as plantation slaves. This might be a roguish exaggeration: at all events we hear that the Senate voted this enslavement of free allies illegal, and ordered provincial governors to see the grievance redressed. The results of this in the case of Sicily will engage our attention below: meanwhile we may note the story as revealing the state of piracy and man-stealing already prevalent in the eastern Mediterranean.

790. We have remarked that, ever since Rome began to exert her power beyond the seas, the old system of annual levies had become obsolete. The campaign for which a man took the military oath was no longer an affair of a year. It now became the practice to take the oath once for all, covering the whole period of service, and continuous service of 16 years was the normal term. The

---

[1] Diodorus frag. XXXV 37.
[2] It was felt that the very existence of Rome was in question, Cic. *de off.* 1 § 38.
[3] Diodorus XXXVI 3.

soldier was in short recognized as a professional. We have a story illustrating the importance attached by Marius to a high standard of professional training. In choosing between two men (probably candidates for the post of centurion) he passed over one who had already served (in the ranks) under Metellus and himself, and gave the preference to a smaller man[1] trained under Rutilius, because he was the smarter and more up-to-date soldier. To increase the mobility of large bodies of foot was another move in the direction of efficiency. The chief points calling for attention were the reduction of the baggage-train to the smallest possible compass and the avoidance of any arrangement by which soldiers on the march would be hampered in case of a sudden attack. Marius devised a plan by which each man carried his provisions and cooking-vessel packed in a bundle tied to an arrangement of sticks, which rested on his shoulders. Thus the load could be quickly laid aside in an emergency or during a halt, while the column of march was far less encumbered with beasts of burden and non-combatant drivers, all needing to be fed. In dealing with the barbarian hosts, 'trekking' in their lumbering caravans, the new kit-carriers were no small advantage: by the grumbling wags of the camp they were nicknamed[2] the 'mules of Marius.' In the selection of officers the consul no doubt exercised the greatest care. He was already jealous of Sulla, but he knew him to be a man of exceptional vigour and resource. Sulla therefore was taken[3] to Gaul, at first on the general's staff (*legatus*), afterwards as a legionary commander (*tribunus*), and the two pulled together—for a time. Another man who afterwards rose to fame, Quintus Sertorius, served under Marius in this war. He was one of the few survivors of Caepio's disaster, from which he had only escaped by swimming the Rhone with his arms. He was a good soldier, and by learning some Gaulish was able to do good service as a spy.

791. Before we go on to consider the doings of Marius in Gaul, we may glance briefly at the effect of the Cimbric invasion on the public life of Rome, as shewn in the trials[4] and punishments of the men held responsible for Roman defeats and disgrace. The first victim was C. Popilius Laenas, who in 107 had saved the remains of Cassius' army from the Tigurini by consenting to shameful terms.

---

[1] Frontin. *strat.* IV 2 § 2 *quia correctioris disciplinae arbitrabatur.* Skill in swordsmanship is no doubt especially referred to.

[2] For *muli Mariani* see Frontin. *strat.* IV 1 § 7. The stories in Plutarch *Mar.* 13 read like later inventions.

[3] Plut. *Sulla* 4, *Sertor.* 3.

[4] I omit the trial of T. Albucius in 103 for extortion in Sardinia. The man's history is interesting but hardly important. The index to Cicero will give the particulars, and the matter is fully given in Long's *Decline of the Roman Republic* II 36.

The people at home were probably unfair to the man at the front, who had had to choose promptly between two evils. Popular indignation was turned to account by a tribune, C. Caelius Caldus, a personal enemy of Popilius. He resolved to impeach him for high treason[1] and to do it in such a way as to bar all chance of escape. These treason trials before the Centuries were still decided by open voting, indeed the only survival of that method. Caelius proposed and carried a law introducing secret voting in this case also. He then gave formal notice of the accusation, and Popilius, now unable to rely on the open influence of his friends, went into exile without waiting for the result. Cicero declares that the author of the *lex Caelia tabellaria* ever afterwards regretted having injured the commonwealth in order to satisfy a private grudge. The next case[2] is that of Caepio, who to all appearance deserved condign punishment. A decree of the people deprived him of his *imperium*. For this course there seems to have been no precedent. But we must remember that strictly speaking he was not holding a magistracy: his *imperium* as proconsul only commissioned him to act in the stead of a consul (*pro consule*) for a certain purpose. The step taken, though novel, was perhaps hardly revolutionary : it disabled the man, but it did not depose a magistrate. This seems to belong to the year 105. In 104 the tribune L. Cassius, son of the Cassius consul in 107, in the course of a campaign against the nobility, carried a law by which any one condemned in a popular trial or stripped of his *imperium* by a popular vote was disqualified from sitting in the Senate. This was an open encroachment on the functions of the censors. In so far as it created a precedent for interfering with ordinary constitutional procedure, it was revolutionary. But after all the censors' power was derived from the people, and the reluctance of most censors to eject unworthy senators was notorious. This was not all. The tribune C. Norbanus[3] carried a law appointing a special commission to inquire into the affair of the treasure of Tolosa which had so strangely disappeared. The nobles did their best to burke the bill : two tribunes were procured to block it, but were prevented by force : in the riot stones were thrown, and the foreman of the Senate, M. Aemilius Scaurus, had his respect-

---

[1] A fragment of argument on the part of Popilius is given in *rhet. ad Herenn.* IV § 34. In I § 25 the charge is loosely called *maiestas*, but Cic. *de legibus* III § 36 clearly shews that it was *perduellio*.

[2] Caepio. See Livy ep. 67, Asconius 78, Cic. *de orat.* II §§ 124, 197, *de nat. deor.* III § 74 with Mayor's notes, *Brutus* § 135, Gellius III 9 § 7, Orosius V 15 § 25, Strabo IV 1 § 13.

[3] Norbanus was afterwards prosecuted on a charge of *maiestas* for his violence in this affair, and only escaped with difficulty. See Cic. *part. orat.* §§ 104—5, Wilkins' introd. to *de oratore* p. 15. The appointment of the commission is placed in 103, Wilkins p. 10. For the connexion of Saturninus with this affair see below § 823.

able head broken. Caepio was arrested and brought to trial before the commission. While he was in prison for safe keeping, and the trial apparently in progress, he was released[1] by a friendly tribune and went into exile. The confiscation of his property followed, and we may suppose that outlawry, 'interdiction from water and fire,' was decreed against him in the usual form. He is said to have ended his days in misery and shame. The 'gold of Tolosa' became a byword for ill-gotten gain, and an edifying legend grew up, that everyone mixed up in that business came to a bad end. A third case[2] was that of M. Junius Silanus. Five years after his defeat by the Cimbri the tribune Gnaeus Domitius Ahenobarbus brought him before the Tribes. If, as it would seem, the proposal was to fine him for his alleged misconduct as general, the charge was stale, and no wonder that 33 of the 35 Tribes acquitted him. Cicero declares that the real motive of the attack was personal, Silanus having wronged or offended a Gaulish friend of Domitius.

792. This same Domitius signalized the year 104 by a successful attempt to capture[3] the control of the state religion for the popular party. This move also is said to have been prompted by personal motives. I have pointed out that religion was still a force in politics, for the uneducated masses were superstitious. Domitius wished to fill a vacancy in the college of augurs. Scaurus, chief of the Senate, was an augur, and his influence in that close corporation caused the rejection of Domitius. The tribune charged him[4] before the Tribes with neglect of certain ceremonies to the hurt of the state. When the voting took place on the question of the fine named, Scaurus was acquitted by 32 of the 35 Tribes, though in some or all of the 32 the voting was very close. Domitius now proposed a bill[5] to change the method of filling vacancies in the principal sacred colleges. Hitherto cooptation had been the rule, but for some time past, probably since the third century B.C., the choice of one of the pontiffs to be *pontifex maximus* had been determined by the votes of 17 out of the 35 Tribes. The 17 were selected by lot: thus a popular election was avoided, 17 being a minority of 35; and the will of heaven, declared by the lot, prevented any possible clashing with the requirements of the divine law. This precedent was now adopted by the *lex Domitia de sacerdotiis*

---

[1] Valer. Max. IV 7 § 3. In VI 9 § 13 he gives another story, implying that Caepio was executed, which is unlikely.

[2] Asconius 80—1. Cic. *div. in Caecil.* § 67, II *in Verr.* II § 118.

[3] See Asconius 21, Cic. *de leg. agr.* II § 18, *epist. ad Brutum* I 5 § 3.

[4] Valer. Max. VI 5 § 5, Dion Cass. frag. 92, mention that a slave of Scaurus offered to give Domitius evidence of a very serious kind against his master. Domitius refused it, and handed him to Scaurus for punishment.

[5] See Lange *RA* II 501, 551, III 70—1, Greenidge, *Rom. publ. life* pp. 124, 254—5.

as the new method of appointing pontiffs augurs and *decemviri sacrorum*. Members of the colleges retained[1] a limited right of nominating candidates, and the admission of the chosen to actual membership still took place with due observance of the time-honoured forms. That Domitius should call Scaurus to account for alleged neglect of religious duties seems to have been quite unparalleled, a revolutionary invasion of the province of the chief pontiff. How serious a blow the *lex Domitia* had dealt at the Roman constitution was recognized 23 years later in its repeal by Sulla. If we may trust Suetonius[2], Domitius was impelled to this legislative venture by a second slight following on his rejection for the augurate. His father, the man distinguished in Gaul, died and vacated a place among the pontiffs. For the succession to this place he was passed over, whereupon he came forward with his law. But Suetonius confuses the son with the father in military matters, and this story is perhaps a mistake. Anyhow Domitius must have succeeded to some[3] vacancy, for in 103 he was himself raised to the chief pontificate.

793. These details will suffice to shew the tendencies of Roman politics during some four or five anxious years. There was trouble elsewhere in Italy, connected with the slave-system. But we will speak of this below, and for the present resume the tale of Marius and his doings in the North. There can be little doubt that he took his army to Gaul by sea. He encamped somewhere near the eastern mouth of the Rhone. The strategic point important for covering the direct approach to Italy was of course the passage of the river above the delta, but a base on the coast, communicating with Italy by sea and with the interior by river, was the first necessity. He formed a depot of stores, and employed[4] the respite allowed him by the absence of the Cimbric invaders in Spain in cutting an improved channel for the outfall of the Rhone. By this means he secured a better harbour and a navigable[5] canal, while he hardened his men. This great work must have taken a long time, and we have no reason to think that other departments of military duty were neglected. Stern discipline and strict justice, combined with full occupation, in due time made the tone of the army worthy of old Roman traditions. Not much appears to have been done at first in the way of up-country expe-

---

[1] Cic. *Phil.* II § 4, *Brutus* § 1.

[2] Suet. *Nero*, 2.

[3] Velleius II 12 § 3 puts the Domitian law in 103, probably by mistake.

[4] Plutarch *Mar.* 15.

[5] The famous *fossa Mariana* or *fossae Marianae* was afterwards handed over to the Massaliots and used by them for commercial purposes. See Strabo IV 1 § 8, Pomp. Mela II § 78, Plin. *NH* III § 34. A fine map of the district is given in Desjardins, *Géographie de la Gaule Romaine* I 176. See Bullock-Hall p. 100.

ditions, but we hear[1] of the capture of a Gaulish chief by Sulla. Marius was reelected consul for 103 in his absence. The popular party had no faith in any other general, and doubtless he had his special friends and agents who saw to it that no slackness of voters or intrigues of opponents should endanger the continuous tenure of his command. Another year went by in the same work of preparing for the coming struggle. Meanwhile things had been happening in Spain. We hear that the Cimbri, after laying waste a wide stretch of country, met with a repulse[2] in the land of the Celtiberians. This may mean that a war of sieges, for which they had neither means nor appetite, and the exhaustion of the districts traversed by them, made it impossible for the invaders to remain. They gave up their enterprise and returned to Gaul in the latter part of 103, no doubt weakened by their losses. Marius had to be in Rome to hold the elections for 102, in consequence of the death of his colleague. According[3] to Plutarch's account, which is credible enough, he was hankering after a fourth consulship. But there were several good candidates in the field, and none could tell what might happen. One of the tribunes of 103 was L. Appuleius Saturninus, a noisy leader of the popular party, who had the ear of the mob. Marius came to terms with him. The tribune went about singing the praises of the consul, and urged the people to reelect him once more. Marius affected a pretty reluctance: Saturninus insisted that duty to his country required Marius to give way, and he did. We are told that it was a clumsy farce, which deceived nobody. Whether this be the true version or a malignant slander, Marius was reelected. His colleague[4] was a popular noble, Q. Lutatius Catulus, a man of the highest character and great literary accomplishments, who had already stood for the consulship three times without success.

794. In the spring of 102 the situation[5] seems to have been as follows. The Cimbri were back in Gaul and in touch with their allies. None of the wandering peoples had succeeded in finding a land where they might settle down in peace. It was high time to find one, and nothing remained but to pierce the barrier of the Alps and take possession of Italy. The results of previous collisions with the armies of Rome gave hopes of a speedy conquest. A great concerted[6] advance was planned. The Teutoni and Ambrones were to

---

[1] Plutarch *Sull.* 4. The anxieties of Marius at this time come out in the story of the trap by which he detected disloyalty of Gauls and Ligurians, told in Frontin. *strat.* I 2 § 6.

[2] Livy ep. 67.   [3] Plut. *Mar.* 14.

[4] See Wilkins' Introd. to Cic. *de orat.* pp. 24—5.

[5] Campaigns of 102—1 in general. Plutarch *Mar.* 14—27, *Sull.* 4, *Sert.* 3, Velleius II 12, Liv. ep. 68, Florus I 38, Eutrop. v 1, 2, Orosius v 16, Dion Cass. frag. 94.

[6] The parts are differently assigned in Orosius.

enter from the West, passing through the Roman province, and coming down upon the Italian lowlands through the defiles of Liguria. The Cimbri and Tigurini were to work round at the back of the Alps and descend upon Italy from the North. From a strong encampment[1] Marius watched the Teutoni and Ambrones crawl slowly by, and neither the challenges and insults of the northern warriors nor the murmurs of his own men could induce him to give the order for battle. He knew that he could catch the enemy when he chose, and he meant to fight them in his own good time. To calm the growing battle-hunger of his troops he made a parade of taking the advice of a Syrian prophetess attached to his staff, on whom he professed to rely in choosing the lucky moment for fighting. Marius himself believed in divination, and had a profound trust in his own good fortune. But he knew that the army under his command, to perfect which had been a long laborious task, was the only effective force that Rome could put into the field, and his first object was not to waste it. So he quietly followed the 'trekking' barbarians. It was in the neighbourhood of Aquae Sextiae that his chance came. In two engagements he defeated first the Ambrones and then the Teutoni. The carnage[2] was beyond ordinary experience, for when the barbarians were driven back upon their camp the women in the waggons joined in the slaughter of the flying men and fought the pursuers. On the second day a good many prisoners were taken, but most of the brave wanderers perished by the sword. The heavy crops raised in after years on the blood-soaked soil, the hedges of vineyards made with bones of the slain, are details of the gruesome tradition preserved in Plutarch. The name of the village of Pourrières is said to be derived from *campi putridi*, the battlefield on which the remains of the dead rotted away. But the topography of the battles, the prodigies and other predictions that were thought to have foretold the victory of Rome, and many other particulars with which the tradition abounds, do not really concern us. The long and short of the matter is that Marius had done the work assigned to him and that one part of the great peril was at an end. Soon after the battle the news came that he had been elected consul for the fifth time. The strength of the popular belief in Marius may perhaps be further traced in the choice of a colleague. This was Manius Aquilius, the trusted lieutenant whom Marius had left in charge of his army at the time of his visit to Rome in the preceding year.

---

[1] Campaign of Aquae Sextiae. Bullock-Hall cc. 10, 11.

[2] The numbers given, 200,000 killed and 90,000 prisoners, are hardly credible.

795. This news would arrive some time in the autumn of 102. Plutarch tells us that it was quickly followed by bad news from the consul Catulus, whose charge was to protect Italy from the expected invasion of the Cimbri. It was thought that they would make their entry along the line of the Athesis (Adige) which issues from the Alps into the lowlands near Verona. Catulus did his best to prepare for a stout resistance, but he had neither the skill nor the prestige of Marius. He seems to have had an inferior army, and at the time of his first collision with the enemy his nervous troops had probably not yet heard how the victory of Aquae Sextiae had proved that the terrible barbarians were not invincible. That he did not add another to the roll of Roman disasters was most likely due to the presence of Sulla. That cool-headed and ambitious man had got tired of serving under Marius, whose jealousy no longer allowed him opportunities of distinction, and his skill and energy were now devoted to pulling Catulus through his difficulties. But the task before them was evidently more than they could manage. First the Alpine pass had to be abandoned, then the passage of the Adige was forced, and it was necessary to fall back westwards. Northern Italy now lay open to the invaders. How far they drove Catulus before them at that time, we do not know. But he probably retreated some distance and then formed a winter camp. The great battle of the next year was fought 120 miles to the west of Verona.

796. Marius came to Rome after his great victory, but did not for the present celebrate a triumph. For the campaign of 101 it was arranged that Catulus should stay on as proconsul, and that Marius should bring the victors of Aquae Sextiae to his aid. The consul Aquilius had work to do elsewhere. The army from Gaul probably came a short distance by sea to Vada Sabata or Genua, and crossed the Apennine by one or both of the roads leading by Dertona into the plain of the Po. We have a pictorial account of the scene when the junction of the Roman armies had been effected and the campaign began. The Cimbri were not minded to fight until their confederates appeared, but they sent envoys to demand lands. Marius, it is said, destroyed their hopes of the Teutoni by producing the chiefs captured in Gaul, and grimly informed them that their brethren in arms had been granted all the land they were ever likely to want. The last part of this story is a good specimen of the way in which the undeniably dramatic episodes of the Cimbric war were worked up as literary material for the honour and glory of Rome. The great battle, which rolled back the tide of barbarian invasion from Italy for some five centuries, was fought in the summer of 101 on ground known as *campi Raudii* near Vercellae, a town about half way between the

modern Milan and Turin. The highly coloured account of it preserved by Plutarch[1] is of small historical value, and the traces of an
authority hostile to Marius are unmistakeable. We may accept as
facts the fatal formation of the barbarian foot into a great solid
column acting by weight, a formation ill-suited to warriors whose
chief weapon was the heavy cutting sword: the superiority of the
Roman tactics, of their cavalry, and the exhaustion of the northerners
caused by the dust and heat: and the closing scene of bloodshed,
when the furious women turned upon their husbands and children
and themselves, and escaped slavery by indiscriminate slaughter.
The army of Catulus is reckoned at 22,300 men, that of Marius at
32,000. The Cimbric host is not to be guessed, owing to the presence
of the women and children. The slain are said to have been 140,000
or 120,000, the prisoners 60,000: but we cannot trust these figures.
A second time Marius had saved Italy by annihilating[2] the invaders.
They had indeed come to stay, and the cruel irony of their fate was
worthy of some ancient legend of the fulfilment of a Greek oracle.
The close of the Cimbric war was followed by a wise measure of
precaution. A colony of citizens was planted at Eporedia[3] (Ivrea)
on the Duria (Dora Baltea), at the point where an important pass
opens out on to the lower country. A fortress and military base was
thus established for the better watching of the western Alps.

---

[1] Plut. *Mar.* 25 gives Marius the credit of an invention by which the Roman *pila* were
made to entangle the enemy when lodged in their shields. But Frontin. *strat.* II 2 § 8
attributes to him important acts of generalship.

[2] According to Florus the Tigurini were not in the battle, but holding the Alpine pass as
a reserve or rear-guard, and so escaped.

[3] Velleius I 15 § 5.

CHAPTER XLI

THE SECOND SICILIAN SLAVE-WAR AND EXTERNAL AFFAIRS
105—92 B.C.

797. WE have seen that the northern invasion placed the power of Rome in serious danger, and that the danger was only overcome by great exertions and by the unrepublican position given to one individual. But it is not until we look inside the imposing fabric of the Roman system, and note the evils at work within, that we become fully conscious how great the danger really was. The changes of the past hundred years had filled Italy and Sicily with slaves, and a successful invasion would surely have brought in its train the horrors of a servile rising. The second Sicilian slave-war is contemporary with the long command (104—101) of Marius in the North, and no doubt the strain of this internal anxiety made it easier for the popular party in Rome to carry the reelection of their champion as consul year after year. But Diodorus[1], our chief authority on the Sicilian rebellion, points out that that rising was preceded by several small local outbreaks in Italy, from which we may get some notion of the unsound state of affairs. First a conspiracy of 30 slaves at Nuceria was quickly suppressed, then 200 broke out at Capua and were also put down without delay. The third case, also at Capua, was a much more serious business. A Roman knight, named Vettius, got into debt in connexion with a mad amour. Being unable to meet his liabilities, he procured on credit 500 suits of armour, armed his own slaves, and set up as a king. In this character he put his creditors to death, and went about raising and arming slaves. These he formed into companies as soldiers, and established a regular camp. Recruits came in, and he at length got together a force of over 3500 men. The news reached the Senate, who at once grasped the urgency of the danger, and sent the praetor L. Lucullus[2] to deal with it. He raised men in Rome and on the road, and was able to attack Vettius with 4400 men. Even so he was at first beaten off,

---

[1] He was a Sicilian himself, and these Sicilian affairs not too far removed from his own time are among the best portions of his narrative, fragm. XXXVI 1—11. The passages of Florus II 7 and Dion Cass. frag. 93 are of little value.

[2] If, as it would seem, this is the Lucullus whom we find praetor in Sicily, the date of the suppression of Vettius will be early in 103.

and only succeeded by the help of a traitor. The madman killed himself, and the slaves all perished. But, if such things could happen in the cities of Campania, we may guess what would have happened if a barbarian invader had penetrated into the heart of Italy, and the slave-gangs of the great plantations had been let loose upon the country side. The old rural economy of a century earlier, and the men whom that system produced, had now for the most part disappeared. If the Roman government could not and would not grant lands in Italy to the would-be settlers from the North, it was not because Italy was full to overflowing with a free native population. The evil of the *latifundia* was growing worse, and the discontent with existing conditions, silenced by the overthrow of the Gracchi, even found expression in an agrarian bill. It was in 104 or 103 that the tribune L. Marcius Philippus[1], an eloquent and independent man, brought forward a proposal of uncertain scope, perhaps a scheme for undoing the work of the agrarian law of 111, by which a quantity of *possessiones* had been converted into private property. It was a radical measure, and in advocating it Philippus let fall the remark that there were not among the citizens 2000 men who could be called men of property—an utterance pointing to communistic action, on which we find Cicero commenting with pious horror. But things had gone too far for any serious step in that direction: the bill was thrown out, and Philippus took its rejection very calmly.

798.   Since the ending of the first slave-war in 132 Sicily had been quiet.   The capitalists resumed their sway, vast numbers of new slaves were imported, and the plantation-system with all its abominations was reestablished in the island.   But like conditions tended to produce like results, and it only needed some occasion of excitement to bring about another rebellion.   In 104 C. Licinius Nerva[2] was governor.   He seems to have had at his disposal only a small force of inferior troops.   All the best soldiers were wanted elsewhere, and that Sicily was ripe for another explosion was probably not suspected by the Roman Senate.   The authority of the praetor must have been resting mainly on moral force, when the order[3] for the liberation of freemen wrongfully detained in slavery came into his hands.   Nerva at once issued notices in accordance with the order, and investigated claims.   In a few days he had set free more than 800 persons, and the whole slave population of Sicily were in a state of wild excitement.   A number of leading men, slave-

---

[1] See Holden on Cic. *pro Plancio* § 52, *de off.* II § 73.

[2] If this is the man whom Cicero, *Brutus* 129, calls *civis improbus*, we may guess that he belonged to the popular party.

[3] See above § 789.

owners no doubt, took alarm. They hurried to Syracuse, and the
governor, moved by their representations, dropped the inquiry and
ordered the rest of the claimants to return to their several masters.
The disappointed slaves took refuge in a sanctuary up the country,
and there discussed projects of revolt. The first result was a small
isolated outbreak in the West, but even this Nerva could not put
down by force. By a promise of pardon he induced a brigand under
sentence of death to do his dirty work. The fellow had been used to
murder freemen and spare slaves: the rebel slaves now trusted him,
and he betrayed their stronghold. So Nerva for the moment vindicated
the majesty of Rome.

799. The force employed on this service seems to have consisted
mainly of local militia, who were dismissed to their homes. We may
assume that the praetor had a small guard left, but he was clearly in
no position to deal with any serious rising. News soon came of another
outbreak. Prompt action was impossible, and when the governor did
take the field the enemy were already too strong for him, and their
numbers growing fast. He drew 600 soldiers from the garrison of
Enna, and sent an officer with them to attack the rebels. In the
rout and flight that ensued a number of men were lost, and the arms
of fugitives and fallen served to equip more slaves. The rebel army
soon rose to over 6000 men. They elected as their king one Salvius,
noted for the practice of divination and orgiastic rites. A large part of
central Sicily evidently now lay at their mercy: they collected horses,
and in a short time had more than 20,000 foot and 2000 horsemen
trained and fit for service. They even ventured to besiege the town
of Morgantia. Nerva with 10,000 Italian and Sicilian troops advanced
to raise the siege, but the rebels fell upon his army and routed it with
a loss of some 600 killed and 4000 prisoners. The capture of arms
again strengthened the slaves, and the siege of Morgantia was resumed.
The defenders of the place were largely slaves to whom their masters
had promised freedom. But when, after a successful defence, they
claimed the fulfilment of the promise, the praetor forbade the emancipation, and thus added another reinforcement to the rebel army.
At this stage the forces under Salvius seem to have been about
45,000 men. Meanwhile another rising had taken place in the West,
headed by a Cilician overseer named Athenion, a daring fellow,
skilled in astrology. He too took the title of king, and shewed
remarkable forethought by organizing an agricultural service to
provide food for his troops. When he had over 10,000 men under
arms he rashly undertook the siege of Lilybaeum, but soon discovered
his mistake, and drew off under pretext of a sign from heaven. In
his retreat he suffered some loss, being attacked by a body of bar-

barians from Mauretania, who had come to strengthen the garrison. Such it seems were the succours on which Rome was now driven to rely, doubtless the firstfruits of the loyal allegiance of Bocchus.

800. All order was now at an end: save for a few walled coast-towns and other fortresses held for Rome, the slaves were masters in Sicily, and the bloody tragedy ran its course. As in the former[1] war, the freemen impoverished by the spread of the plantation system turned to account the troubles of the time. They ranged the country in bands, robbing and murdering without distinction of persons or parties. The administration of justice had ceased, and there was nothing to hinder their depredations, adding to the tale of suffering. Rich refugees in the cities were powerless: they owned for the moment nothing beyond the city wall, and no master knew what the domestic slaves about him might do next. For the rising shewed as yet no sign of a collapse. Salvius, who now took the style of king Tryphon[2], ravaged the country up to the rich Leontine plain in the East, and presently moved off to occupy the stronghold of Triocala in the West. Here he summoned Athenion to join him, and the western leader came and submitted to his command. All hope of the rebellion failing through the jealousy of the ringleaders had to be abandoned. Tryphon established himself as monarch in true Eastern fashion, with a palace and guards and royal council, and in raiment and ceremonial reproduced in Sicily the externals of a Syrian court.

801. The Senate was now alarmed, and took steps to furnish the new praetor L. Licinius Lucullus with a sufficient force. Lucullus seems to have been governor in 103, but he perhaps arrived rather late, owing to the affair of Vettius in Italy. He brought 14,000 Romans and Italians, 800 Bithynians Thessalians and Acarnanians, 600 'from Lucania,' apparently a corps already[3] embodied, and 600 others. Tryphon had imprisoned Athenion on suspicion of disloyalty, but now released him, and on his advice gave up his intention of standing a siege in Triocala and marched to meet Lucullus with 40,000 men. A fierce battle, in which the brave Athenion was wounded and left for dead, ended in the rout of the rebels with the loss of 20,000 of their number. The praetor's force doubtless suffered heavily, and when he pushed on and invested Triocala the attempt was a failure. The slaves, downcast at

---

[1] See § 686.

[2] The name was perhaps copied from that taken by the usurper who ruled in Syria 142—138. As in the former war, Oriental slaves took the lead. Strabo XIV 5 § 2 says that it was the Syrian Tryphon who first formed the Cilician pirates into a confederacy; and Athenion at least was a Cilician.

[3] Were these perhaps a force raised in view of an expected rising in the Lucanian *latifundia*?

their defeat, had been half inclined to surrender, but the desperate section prevailed, and their spirits rose again when the baffled Lucullus withdrew. He was accused of lacking energy, and even of taking bribes; from whom, is not clear, but corruption was at this time regularly imputed as a cause of failure, and Lucullus had failed. He was afterwards brought to trial[1] and banished, which was not surprising, if the story, that he disbanded his army and destroyed his camp and engines of war in order to cripple his successor, may be received on the authority of Diodorus. The new governor (102) was C. Servilius. He effected nothing, possibly for the reason given above, for it is not likely that fresh troops could be spared just then. But it is probable that the resources of the island were by this time nearly exhausted, and that this made campaigning impossible. Tryphon died, and under the vigorous Athenion the slaves besieged towns and overran[2] the country at will. Servilius was punished[3] in the same way as Lucullus on his return home.

802. The year 101 opened more favourably for Rome. Marius had destroyed the Teutoni, and the worst of the great panic was now over. While he and Catulus faced the Cimbri, the consul Manius Aquilius was sent to Sicily, and no doubt furnished with men and means to put down the insurrection. So frightful was the devastation of that fertile land, already regarded as a principal granary of Rome, that the faithful cities were suffering from famine. Corn, in quiet times the staple product of the country, had to be imported from abroad, and we are told[4] that Aquilius among his other cares had to provide for their supply. In the field he was successful. The rebels were no longer able to make good their losses with fresh recruits, and the consul defeated them in a great battle, where he is said to have killed Athenion with his own hand. He went on to capture their strongholds and hunt down their roving bands, till the rising was fairly suppressed, and Sicily once more reverted to the horrors of what passed for order. The last party of the rebels surrendered, and were sent to Rome to fight with wild beasts and amuse the populace. There were 1000 of them. The story ran that they died by one another's hands, and cheated the bloodthirsty mob of the varieties designed for their entertainment. Aquilius seems to have stayed on as proconsul in 100 and not to have finished his work till 99. In 98 he was brought to trial on a charge of extortion. His

---

[1] This trial is probably referred to by Cicero II *in Verr.* IV § 147.

[2] Perhaps they even reached Messana. Dion Cass. frag. 93.

[3] The trial is referred to in Cic. *div. in Caecil.* § 63.

[4] Cic. *de leg. agr.* II § 83 *mutuum frumentum dedit.* It was a loan, not a gift, and very likely the cases were few.

later career shews him to have been one of the greedy sort, and Cicero[1] asserts that his guilt was certain. But he was defended by Crassus' rival the orator M. Antonius in one of his finest pleadings, and the exposure in court of his breast covered with scars gained him acquittal. The second slave war had lasted about five years, and is said to have cost the lives of 100,000 men. Sicily now settled down into its normal condition of peace with misery, and so remained, with minor alternations[2] of better and worse, till the coming of Verres. There is no good reason to mistrust the main outlines of the narrative of Diodorus on the ground of suspicious similarity[3] to the same writer's account of the first war. Like causes operating under like conditions naturally produced like phenomena. Both wars were events of the deepest historical significance. They afford us some means of judging how far the Republican government of Rome in its degeneration was contributing to the good order and happiness of the world. We get a glimpse of the means by which the unhappy province was henceforth kept quiet and the rights of property secured. In the time of the next praetor, L. Domitius, a wild boar of great size was killed, and forwarded to headquarters as worthy of the governor's table. Domitius asked who the sportsman was that had performed the feat. On inquiry it turned out that the hero was a slave-herdsman the property of some Sicilian landlord. The praetor ordered the man to be fetched, and he came with alacrity, in hope of a reward. 'How did you kill this huge beast?' said the praetor. 'With a hunting-spear' said the man. He thus stood self-convicted of breaking the strict police regulation then in force, that no slave might go armed on pain of death: and the governor had him crucified without delay. Cicero[4], who tells the story nearly 30 years after, genially admits that this was a harsh proceeding, but he points out that Domitius had to practise unfeeling severity at the call of duty. To let his feelings get the better of him would clearly in the orator's opinion have been a dangerous laxity. And the sequel had proved that Domitius chose rightly, for during the war of the Allies in Italy (91—89 B.C.) Sicily was at peace. Sicily in short was 'well able to provide for her own protection': the rules of the province were enforced, the slave had ceased to hope, and the sorely-tried slave-owner was at rest.

[1] Cic. *pro Flacco* § 98. For the story of the trial see Wilkins, Introd. to Cic. *de orat.* p. 15. Livy epit. 70.

[2] See Cic. II *in Verr.* III § 125, V §§ 5, 14.

[3] A curious parallelism is the rising of slaves in the Attic mines, contemporary with the second war (see Posidonius in Müller *FHG* III 264, No. 35) as with the first war (Orosius V 9 § 5). But it is not certain, as Long II 86 has to admit, that one of these records is an error.   [4] Cic. II *in Verr.* V §§ 7, 8.

803. When we turn to other parts of the Roman dominions we find trouble there also. In Spain, with the exception of one or two small local disturbances, things had for some time been fairly quiet. But during the Cimbric and Sicilian wars Rome had enough to do nearer home, and the Iberian peninsula was neglected. The Cimbri penetrated into Spain, a large part of the country suffered from their ravages, and the check put upon their advance was due to the resistance of the natives, and not to protection afforded by the sovran power. It was only natural that the retreat of the invaders should leave behind it a feeling of elation and unwillingness to bear tamely the yoke of rulers whose armies had not guarded Spain and had been cut up by the northern warriors in Gaul. Rumours of the inefficiency

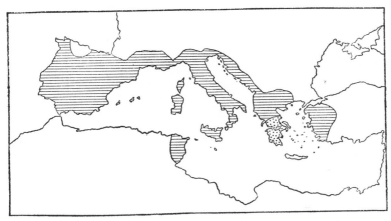

Roman dominions about 100 B.C. Greek protectorate dotted.

displayed in the Jugurthine war were probably not lacking: and by the time Marius and Aquilius had once more freed the hands of Rome the rebellious spirit was already dominant in central Spain. In the far West D. Junius Silanus put down a revolt of the Lusitanians in 102, but only for a time, for in 98 we find L. Cornelius Dolabella celebrating a triumph for victories won over them. It was in 97 and 96 that the chief struggle[1] took place, in the Celtiberian country. T. Didius, a 'new man,' no doubt of the popular party, commanded there[2] as proconsul. The war was carried on with brutal ferocity, and it is evident that Roman supremacy in Spain was seriously threatened, for one of the consuls of 97, P. Licinius Crassus, was appointed to the Further province. But Didius broke the resistance of the Celtiberi,

---

[1] See the *Fasti triumphales*, Livy ep. 70, Appian *Hisp.* §§ 99, 100, Plutarch *Sert.* 3, Frontin. *strat.* I 8 § 5, II 10 § 1.

[2] Didius had as praetor in 114 done some good service in Macedonia. In Spain Sertorius served under him.

and his successor ended the war. Crassus had some work to do: Didius and he had triumphs in 93. Mr Long well suggests that the captives in these wars found a ready market in depleted Sicily. Of Crassus we learn[1] that he took an interest in the western tin-trade and sailed over to the Tin-islands (Cassiterides), thus opening up the trade to private enterprise. The state of things in Macedonia was also one of unrest. Our information is very scanty, but it seems that inroads of barbarians, chiefly from Thrace, disturbed the province for many years. I have referred above to the defeats and victories of earlier governors. In 92 we find a time of greater pressure beginning, and in 88 the invaders penetrated so far into Macedonia and Illyria that they were able to enter Epirus and plunder the temple of Dodona. It was the time of the war with the Allies, and Rome was already embroiled with Mithradates. The governor of the province C. Sentius[2] was left to make what shift he could year after year. There are traces of an attempt of a pretender even to revive the old kingdom of Macedon. But Sentius seems to have got the better of his troubles mainly by good government; a striking illustration of what it was possible for a Roman governor to effect by virtuous conduct in circumstances of great difficulty. We shall return to the invasions of Macedonia in connexion with the Mithradatic war.

804. Now that Rome had dependencies beyond the seas, she was more than ever concerned to maintain peace along the waterways. For the security of commerce it was necessary to treat the Mediterranean as a province. Roman protection and regulation should by rights have been permanently organized, but it was not. This was not for want of knowledge, for in earlier times Rome had put down Illyrian piracy with a strong hand. It was mainly due to the slackness and inefficiency of the Roman government, and this in turn was due rather to the deadlock produced by the conflict of competing interests in politics than to the pressure of external wars. And Rome had now to face the consequences of her former harsh treatment of Rhodes. That island republic had in its palmy days acted as an unofficial warden, trusted by other powers and encouraged to maintain in the common interest the peace of the eastern seas. Rhodes was now only Rome's humble subject-ally, and the vast slave-trade now centred at Delos had made the presence of a strong naval peace-keeper more and more necessary. The immense demand for slaves,

---

[1] Strabo III 5 § 11. Where the Tin-islands are to be sought is beyond our concern here. It is hard to believe that a voyage to Britain is meant. See Elton, *Origins of Eng. Hist.* p. 18.

[2] See Livy ep. 70, 74, 76, 81, 82, Plut. *Sulla* 11 § 4, Orosius v 18 § 30, Diodor. frag. XXXVII 5a, Dion Cass. frag. 101, Cic. II *in Verr.* III § 217, *in Pison.* § 84. Sentius finds no place in the rhetorical passage of Florus I 39. For the Scordisci, who bore a part in the inroads, see Strabo VII 5 §§ 11, 12.

created by the spread of the plantation-system and the waste of lives
in war, could no longer be met by buying from dealers in Syria or the
ports of the Euxine. Kidnapping became a profitable business, and
the seaboard of the Euxine, Aegean, and eastern Mediterranean was
exploited for this purpose wherever convenient. Nests of pirates soon
were formed in the creeks and bays of Cilicia[1], and to the captures
made in raids on land were added the captures of voyagers by sea.
Ruffians of all races reinforced these bands: a contingent of the
corsair forces certainly came from Crete. As was to be expected,
piracy became a terrible nuisance, but Rome shewed no inclination
to undertake regular police work. This was partly owing to the
inveterate Roman habit of neglecting to keep up a navy in time of
peace. But something is surely to be allowed for the influence of
the capitalist class in politics. The pirate interest was closely in
touch with the slave-dealing interest whose headquarters were at
Delos, and the slave-dealers with the central body of capitalists in
Rome. No doubt many a rich financier drew profit directly or
indirectly from the transactions on the Delian exchange, and the
circle that followed his lead would be ready to look on the mis-
demeanours of the corsairs with an indulgent eye. The methods of
those gentry might at times be rough and inconsiderate, but after all
they were an efficient part of the machine that ground out fortunes
for respectable citizens. In offering this explanation to account in
part for the slackness of the Roman government we are imputing to
Romans of this age nothing more than we have on record in other
connexions, as for instance in the affair of Jugurtha. It would be
strange if the classes interested in the slave-trade had entertained
purer views of patriotic duty than the nobles whose aims in life were
principally the attainment of public office and the enjoyment of
plunder and bribes. At last however the sea-robbers went too far.
We do not know the details; probably some Roman interest was
endamaged or menaced by their excesses. In 103 the praetor
M. Antonius[2] was sent out with proconsular powers. His *provincia*
was to suppress Cilician piracy, but he may have had wider instructions. That this step was taken at a time when Rome was still under
the strain of the Cimbric and Sicilian wars proves that the matter
was urgent. No doubt the forces assigned him, being naval, were
raised among the allies, chiefly Greek, who were liable to furnish
such contingents. He appears to have taken several pirate strongholds on the coast of western Cilicia and to have checked piracy for

---

[1] The western or Rocky Cilicia. Strabo XIV 5 §§ 1, 2.
[2] This is the famous orator. See Cicero *Brutus* § 168, *de orat.* 1 § 82, and Wilkins'
Introd. p. 14, Livy ep. 68.

a time. Whether he annexed[1] a large territory, including Pamphylia Pisidia and the Greater Phrygia, as a regular Province, and whether this, together with the charge of the Cilician seaboard, was officially styled *provincia Cilicia*, are points not so certain: but it is probable that something of the kind took place. Roman governors of these parts begin to be mentioned. But the mountain districts of Cilicia Pamphylia and Isauria were not touched, and the later history of piracy shews that the naval demonstration in these waters was not developed into a permanent control.

805. While speaking of affairs in the East a very brief reference[2] to Syria will be enough. Intrigues and murders, revolutions and partitions, were reducing to insignificance the once great Seleucid empire. Its weakness was more and more a temptation and an embarrassment to its neighbours, and the house of Seleucus was clearly hurrying to an inglorious end. In Egypt the Lagid monarchy was also fast decaying. After the death of the fat tyrant in 117, his widow for nearly 30 years directed the palace intrigues of Alexandria. Rome was busy elsewhere, and for the present had no mind to interfere with the empire of the degenerate Ptolemies. But a part of this empire, the Cyrenaic[3] province, had on occasion been under the separate rule of some prince of the Lagid house, and since 117 a certain Ptolemy Apion had held it as an independent kingdom. In 96 Apion died, and left the Roman people his heir. But the Roman government did not care just then to take over the kingdom as a Province, with all the responsibility for order and defence therein implied. What they did for the present was to accept the inheritance of the royal domains, and to fix the dues payable by tenants to the Roman treasury. The five city communities, which with their subordinate townships and territories made up what was known as the Cyrenaica, were recognized as so many free states. It was a renewal of the old old Roman policy. We shall see that it was a failure, as indeed it was certain to be. But Rome shirked the duty of taking over the country as a Province for more than twenty years.

806. If the decrepit kingdoms ruled by the wretched descendants of the great Alexander's marshals were in no case to cause the Romans anxiety, in another part of the East vigour and ambition were laying the foundations of a strong monarchy. Given a Great Leader to inspire and control, the peoples of the East had by no means lost

---

[1] See Marquardt, *Staatsverwaltung* I 379—381. It is pointed out that these districts had not been included in Asia, and that Phrygia is in 88 spoken of as a province, Livy ep. 77. Hence a settlement on these lines by Antonius in 102 is probable.

[2] For Syria see Bevan, *House of Seleucus*. For Egypt, Mahaffy, *Empire of the Ptolemies*.

[3] See Marquardt, *Staatsverwaltung* I 457—9.

the capacity of producing a Great Power. And in this period a great leader at last appeared. The situation in Asia Minor may be very briefly outlined thus. In the northern part of that country there were the two kingdoms of Bithynia and Pontus, and between them Paphlagonia, a district of small principalities. Along the coast lay a number of Greek or semi-Greek cities, centres of trade and a superior civilization. These outposts of Hellenism were generally on good terms[1] with the potentates on whose seaboard they were planted. They brought wealth, and kings found their ablest ministers and generals among the clever Greeks: in particular, if a naval power were ever to be created in the Euxine, it could only be organized by the skilled sea-captains of the Greek cities. Most of these cities were colonies founded long ago in the golden age of free Hellas; at the present time, though overshadowed and partly controlled by continental powers, they seem in general to have had at least as much local autonomy as their mother-cities, now all in the grasp of Rome. They were not confined to Asia Minor, but scattered all around the shores of the Euxine. One group clustered about the strait of Kertch and sea of Azov, and carried on trade with their restless neighbours the Scythians of the steppes. To become the protector and overlord of these Greek cities, which often needed protection, was to become the master of the Euxine and of the mouths of great rivers from the Danube to the Don. It meant the control of vast resources, and was well worth the making an effort to obtain. On the land side there was much to draw the attention of an enterprising and ambitious king. Paphlagonia in its divided state was certain to fall into the hands of some strong power. Galatia, tribally[2] divided, might not be easy to conquer, but could easily be influenced, and it was a nursery of brave mercenaries. Cappadocia, since king Ariarathes had died in battle for Rome, was in a state of confusion, and seemed likely to be an easy prize. Now the two kingdoms of Bithynia and Pontus stood, by the mere fact of geographical position, in very different relations to the countries just mentioned. Bithynia was a neighbour of Rome, and Rome would certainly not favour projects of Bithynian aggrandisement. There was now no great Syrian monarchy to be watched, as had been the case when she enlarged the Pergamene kingdom for that purpose. If Rome had her hands free, she would hardly allow a Bithynian annexation even of Paphlagonia. Cappadocia was far

---

[1] It had for some time been the policy of the Pontic kings to acquire the Greek cities on the coast of Paphlagonia. The father of the great Mithradates made Sinope his capital.

[2] For the Galatians and their subdivisions under 12 tetrarchs (4 in each tribe) see Strabo XII 5 § 1 (p. 566). For the tribes §§ 417, 485 above. We find them later united under a single ruler, the old divisions having died out.

away. In dealing with the Galatian tribes the king of Bithynia was at no advantage as compared with the king of Pontus. And the king of Pontus had many special advantages. He was as yet nowhere in actual contact with Rome. His ancestors had been friends of the great republic, and any unfriendly designs on his part might for a time pass unsuspected. He touched Paphlagonia on its eastern side, the side away from Rome. He was comparatively speaking close to the inland Cappadocia. The country now known as Pontus had once been known as Cappadocia on the Pontus (that is, the Euxine): ethnological and traditional affinities still existed, and the one crying need of both countries was a strong king. To the south-east rose the great mountain land of Armenia, a land hard to enter, whose mighty rivers discharge their waters south-eastwards. The Armenian king had beyond him again the great Parthian monarchy, with which he often had uneasy or hostile relations, and he was therefore likely to wish to be on good terms with his Pontic neighbour. Between the great Armenia and Pontus lay a mountain district known as the Lesser Armenia. Generally ruled by local princes, it was sure in the end to form part of some larger unit. The Armenian king did not need it so much as the king of Pontus, to which it formed a convenient and profitable Hinterland.

807. If the kingdom of Pontus[1], as compared with Bithynia, was in a far better position for becoming the seat of a Great Power, it was at no less an advantage in respect of the qualities of its king. Nicomedes II was a cunning rogue; Mithradates VI Eupator was a cunning man of large views, well fitted to impress the imagination of eastern peoples by his exceptional powers of body and mind. Nominally succeeding to the Pontic throne on the murder of his father in 121, he found himself, a boy of 11 or 12 years, in the midst of perils, and early learnt to walk warily. In particular he is said to have used precautions against poison. At length he sought safety in flight, and for some years was a wanderer, seeing many peoples and enduring much hardship. About 114 or 113 he returned to Sinope, the Greek city which his father had made the capital of Pontus, and assumed the government. He was now at the age of about 18 a man of extraordinary strength and endurance, and had learnt many things in a thoroughly practical school. Under the rule of his mother and her associates the kingdom had lost ground

---

[1] For Mithradates and the expansion of Pontus see a good brief account in Holm's *History of Greece*, IV chapter 25. Strabo book XII has various details of interest concerning the countries referred to. Justin XXXVII, XXXVIII, gives a sort of continuous account, but confused and rhetorical. Strabo was himself a native of Amasia, the earlier capital of Pontus.

in various quarters. Mithradates made up his mind to revive and extend it. How great was the scope of his ambition at this time we do not know, but he had from the first a grudge against Rome on the ground that Phrygia had been promised to his father and the gift afterwards[1] resumed. With the help of competent Greeks he formed an efficient army, and the sequel shews that he had a naval force as well: so that, when the Greeks of the Bosporan kingdom sought his aid, he was able to undertake expeditions beyond the sea. The ruling dynasties in those parts were for various reasons no longer able to hold their own against their warlike barbarian neighbours. The king of Pontus was called in to save the Greek civilization now in imminent danger. On the east side of the so-called Cimmerian Bosporus (Strait of Kertch) lay Phanagoria, on the west side stood Panticapaeum (Kertch), the capital of the kingdom: further west, on the coast of the Tauric Chersonese (Crimea), was Theodosia. West of this again was Chersonesus (Sebastopol), a republic. The generals of Mithradates in several campaigns accomplished their task, and by about 106 he was recognized as king or protector of these outlying Greek cities, endowed with a large yearly revenue, and able to extend his influence in the north-western coast-lands of the Euxine. The south-eastern seaboard from Colchis round to the frontier of Pontus soon fell into his hands. With the speedy acquisition of the Lesser Armenia he had reached a stage at which he might seriously undertake the prosecution of more dangerous designs.

808. His first decided step towards the fulfilment of his ambitions was taken in 105, when he induced Nicomedes of Bithynia to join him in a partition of Paphlagonia. An appeal was made to Rome, but in that critical moment all the Senate could do was to send embassies to the two kings and request them to withdraw. This they did not do, but established a sort of joint overlordship in Galatia. After this the two fell out over the affairs of Cappadocia, on which country Mithradates had his eye. Nicomedes entered Cappadocia and claimed the sovranty by marrying the queen in possession. Mithradates drove him out. Upon the murders and changes that followed we need not dwell. Rome was again appealed to, and fraudulent pretenders produced. The Senate's decision was to order the evacuation of both Paphlagonia and Cappadocia, and to declare both countries free—that is, not subject to kings,—as had been done formerly in such cases as that of Macedonia. This seems to have been about the year 96. The kings withdrew, and the Cappadocians, who of course knew no other form of government than monarchy, were shortly after allowed to suit themselves with a king of their own.

[1] The Greater Phrygia. See Index.

But meanwhile Mithradates had come to an understanding with Tigranes the new ruler of Armenia. He gave him his daughter Cleopatra in marriage, and induced him to invade Cappadocia. Ariobarzanes the new king fled to Rome (? 93 B.C.). In 92 Sulla came out as propraetor of the Cilician province, with orders to restore Ariobarzanes. This he did, though his forces were inadequate. Thus the future conqueror of the Pontic king first came to blows with his great enemy: for the general acting for Tigranes was in fact an agent of Mithradates. In this bold expedition Sulla reached the Euphrates, where he was met by an ambassador of the king of Parthia. Plutarch, who is ever on the watch to record characteristic traits, preserves the story[1] of the dramatic interview in which the restored king of Cappadocia, the envoy of the Parthian king, and the Roman propraetor, sat together on three chairs. It was the first meeting of Roman and Parthian. No doubt each power was anxious to impress the other, and the Oriental is hardly likely to have erred by too unassuming a demeanour. But the man who had mesmerized Bocchus was not to be overawed by pretensions. He coolly took the middle seat and thereby silently asserted the primacy of Rome in the face of the ceremonious East. Party critics in Rome took different views of Sulla's action. The king of Parthia put his ambassador to death for acquiescing in the slight. For the moment the position of affairs was this: the Armenian forces were driven out of Cappadocia and Ariobarzanes restored, but the person really thwarted was Mithradates. He could only regain his dominant position in Cappadocia by force of arms, and for this he thought it wise to wait a little longer. It is possible that he was well informed of the coming storm in Italy. At any rate he knew that the power of Rome was not as strong as it appeared to be. In 91 Sulla was back again at Rome, and Rome had her hands full with a struggle that left her no leisure for intervention in the East.

---

[1] Plut. *Sulla* 5, with Holden's notes.

CHAPTER XLII

809. Our information as to affairs in Rome during the years 104 to 91 is, with the exception of one or two striking events, very scanty. Side by side with the degeneration observable in public life, the morals of private life were not likely to improve. Such glimpses[1] as we get— a son murdered by his father in 104 and a mother by her son in 101— at least give no favourable impression. We are in a time when politics were nothing but a struggle between[2] *optimates* and *populares*. These parties were alike politically worthless. They were rather factions than parties, for they served to promote the interests of leaders rather than to assert principles. Bribery was becoming common: whether the rich man bought votes, or the demagogue sacrificed the good of the state to please the corrupt and idle mob, made little practical difference. It is the time of L. Appuleius Saturninus and C. Servilius Glaucia. Whether these two 'popular' leaders would have come so much to the front if it had not been for the immense importance of military matters in the years 105—101, and the dominant position of Marius, is more than doubtful. It was the strength of the popular faction that they had as their figure-head the first soldier of the hour. In themselves the two demagogues were not men of great weight. If tradition (from hostile sources it is true) may be trusted at all, they were a disreputable pair. Saturninus when quaestor had been allotted the department of superintending the corn-supply of the city. Recent legislation had tended to increase the demand for corn in Rome and with it the importance of keeping up a regular supply. The dissolute young quaestor neglected his duty, and the Senate took the exceptional step of transferring[3] the charge to the mature and respectable Scaurus. No doubt they were glad to disgrace a young opponent who already shewed signs of being troublesome, and the interest of the hungry mob in the efficiency of the department was a practical guarantee that this interference would not be resented. Saturninus

---

[1] Cic. *pro Balbo* § 28 (Reid), Orosius v 16 §§ 8, 23—4, Livy ep. 68, *rhet. ad Herenn.* I § 23.

[2] The definition in Cic. *pro Sestio* §§ 96—8 is interesting, though coloured by the oratorical needs of the case, 56 B.C.

[3] Cicero *pro Sestio* § 39.

was thus left in the humiliating position of an official without a sphere
of action. He now threw himself with energy into a course of opposition to the Senate, and became the most turbulent leader of the popular
faction. In 103 he was tribune, and is said to have carried a land-law
granting allotments in Africa to the veterans of Marius. This record[1]
of a late author, if genuine, must refer to old soldiers of the Numidian
war, but it is perhaps a confused version of a later proposal. He is
said to have driven away a colleague who meant to block the bill by
getting the mob to pelt him with stones. That Saturninus sought to
follow in the footsteps of the Gracchi, and that mob-violence was a part
of his regular method, we need not doubt. His coalition with Marius
and support of the general's election to a fourth consulship have been
mentioned above. Glaucia was a man of lower type than Saturninus.
His ready and pungent wit and his popularity with the Equestrian
Order, to whom his law restoring to them the control of the courts was
most welcome, gave him a certain importance. But he was a man of
most abandoned character, and a speaker of the day once called him
the 'waste-product[2] of the Senate.' Both men were bold and effective
mob-orators, unscrupulous and turbulent, true children of the revolutionary age.

810. In the year 102 there was a census. The censors were
cousins, both Metelli. Of these Metellus Numidicus, the one superseded by Marius in Africa, was a noble of the highest reputation,
an honourable man of sound culture and respectable eloquence, whom
it was the fashion to esteem if not to imitate. He was not the man to
spare the disreputable leaders of the popular faction. Cicero says[3]
that he affixed the censorial mark (*nota*) of disapproval to the name
of Saturninus. But, when he wanted to strike both him and Glaucia
off the roll of the Senate, he was thwarted by the refusal of his
colleague. So the two remained senators, and Metellus had now
embittered these enemies, who were likely to stick at nothing. Marius
already hated him, and Marius, sour and self-made, was not one to be
mollified by the virtues of a noble whose very presence he felt as a
hindrance and a rebuke. In 101 came the destruction of the Cimbri
and the great triumph of Marius and Catulus. At this time, among
all the signs of rejoicing, public life in Rome must have been seething
with intrigue. We find traces[4] of it in the conflict of evidence as to

---

[1] [Victor] *de vir. illustr.* 73. From Sall. *Jug.* 84 Ihne infers that this was the fulfilment
of promises made by Marius in 107 when enlisting volunteers among the poor.

[2] *stercus curiae*, Cic. *de orat.* III § 164. For Glaucia's gifts see the *Brutus* § 224, and
index to Cicero.

[3] Cic. *pro Sest.* § 101, Appian *civ.* I 28, Orosius V 17 § 3.

[4] Plut. *Mar.* 25—7.

the respective shares of credit due to the victorious generals. We see it also in the various stories[1] as to the joint triumph—that the Senate insisted on including Catulus, that Marius shared his triumph with Catulus, that Marius dared not triumph alone with his own army because the army of Catulus would not have taken quietly the exclusion of themselves and their commander. No doubt the nobles in general glorified Catulus, and no one was a more active spreader of anti-Marian gossip and criticism than Sulla. But Marius was the hero of the hour. As consul he ranked above the proconsul Catulus, and the credit of the first great victory was all his own. But north Italy (Cisalpine Gaul) was the province of Catulus, and this point in favour of the proconsul was assuredly not overlooked by Romans addicted to legality and precedents. Marius was rightly recognized as the material saviour of Rome. Unfortunately he was also the man who dealt the Roman constitution its most fatal blow. He had already held five consulships, four of them continuous: he was now eagerly desiring a sixth. There was now no great emergency to justify the continued disregard of constitutional law. The reelection of Marius would mean a wanton abandonment of republican principles. But things were tending in that direction. Saturninus was all for a course of new legislation on Gracchan lines, and to some extent[2] his policy may have been sincere: but a blind rage of antagonism to the senatorial nobility was now the most powerful motive of his actions. Quite recently he had been in violent collision with the Senate over the reception of an embassy from Mithradates. The scandals connected with Jugurtha were fresh in men's minds, and it was said that these men were agents for bribing senators in the interest of the king of Pontus. Of this view Saturninus was doubtless the chief spokesman. He in some way insulted the envoys, and the leading senators in some way retaliated on him for what was at least represented to be outrageous conduct towards ambassadors of a friendly power. We hear of the demagogue being brought to trial and reduced to solicit public sympathy by the adoption of foul raiment and abject entreaties, as accused men usually did: it was true he was acquitted, but only through the moral pressure exercised by the mob gathering round the court. The details[3] are untrustworthy and confused, but the collision with the Senate is not to be doubted. Moreover both Saturninus and Glaucia were eager to deal a blow at Metellus: Marius wanted to rid himself

---

[1] Cicero *Tusc.* v § 56, Valer. Max. IX 12 § 4, Plut. *Mar.* 27, Juvenal VIII 253.

[2] That the memory of Saturninus was not all bad may be inferred from the guarded language of Cicero *pro Sest.* § 37, *Brutus* § 224.

[3] Diodorus frag. XXXVI. 15.

of a sturdy and incorruptible opponent. By joining forces[1] they could command the support of the mass of ordinary voters, and control the whole situation. The coalition resulted in the election for the year 100 of Marius as consul, Glaucia as praetor, Saturninus as tribune.

811. The utter disorder of public life in Rome was illustrated by the episode[2] of the sham Gracchus. A certain L. Equitius laid claim to the honoured name, giving himself out to be a son of Tiberius. The fraud was easily exposed, for the fate of all Tiberius' sons was known, and the censors of 102 had refused to register this person as a citizen. He was said to be a runaway slave. The pretender came forward as a candidate for the tribuneship, and Saturninus, ever ready to catch the flavour of Gracchan traditions, supported him. This seems to have been a little too much for Marius, who is said[3] to have arrested the fellow and locked him up. But the populace broke open the prison and carried him off in triumph. He did not however become tribune on this occasion. Riot succeeded riot, and it is even said that one strong rival candidate was done to death[4] by partisans of Saturninus. There are several stray details that have come down to us in relation to the elections of this year, faint side-lights that shew us how very little we really know about the currents and counter-currents of Roman politics at this critical moment. First, we are told[5] that Marius, with all his popularity and prestige, had to bribe voters in order to gain his sixth consulship. Secondly, there is some reason[6] to infer that Glaucia and Saturninus were not too cordially united : after they were both in office, the tribune took offence at a real or supposed slight on the praetor's part, and avenged the majesty of the tribunate by roughly interrupting proceedings in the praetor's court. That the two demagogues were civil to Marius only because and so long as they enjoyed his help, does not call for much remark. Lastly, we find it stated[7] that in carrying legislation during his second tribunate (100) Saturninus found his chief support among voters whipped up from the country, mostly old soldiers of Marius. In the free fights, which were now the ordinary procedure

---

[1] The coalition. Cic. *pro Sest.* § 37, Plut. *Mar.* 28—9, Appian *civ.* I 28—31 with Strachan-Davidson's notes.

[2] Cic. *pro Sest.* § 101, *pro Rab. perd.* § 20, Appian *civ.* I 32—3, Florus II 4 § 1, Valer. Max. (index *Equitius*), [Victor] *de vir. illustr.* 73.

[3] This story may belong to the elections for 99, when Equitius was elected tribune.

[4] Appian puts this after the rival was already elected tribune, and makes Saturninus succeed to the vacancy created by the murder. But just here his narrative is full of inaccuracies.

[5] Plut. *Mar.* 28, on the authority of Rutilius.

[6] [Victor] *de vir. illustr.* 73.   [7] Appian *civ.* I 29—31.

of Roman Assemblies, these men quieted the opposition of the city populace with sticks and stones. Who these men from the country were, whether Roman citizens or Allies or both, is uncertain. If both, we must suppose that military[1] comradeship, now that soldiering was becoming more and more a profession, had already done much to efface the distinction between Citizen and Ally. That the men from the country were all Allies is hardly credible: surely a great political convulsion must have taken place then and there. The help of Allies, not by voting but by preventing opponents from voting, is conceivable. In any case it is possible that friction between the different factions may have existed already at the time of the election, and may have some bearing upon Marius' resort to bribery. That Marius was just then not universally popular was partly due to an act of his to which persons jealous of his fame would doubtless call attention. Some of the Allies in his army shewed conspicuous bravery in the battle with the Cimbri, and Marius promised[2] them the Roman citizenship as a reward. There were two whole cohorts of them (probably over 1000 men). It would seem that the Assembly confirmed the gift, but there was no precedent for so wholesale a bestowal of the franchise by a general in the field, and many people objected to it. When challenged on the point, Marius evaded constitutional scruples by saying that in the din of arms he had not heard the voice of the laws. But there were probably those who reflected that for every one rewarded there would be many more unrewarded, and that the excluded ones would feel their own exclusion all the more bitterly. And this state of things was really dangerous, for the Allies all through Italy had long been fuming with discontent.

812. The exact details[3] of the stormy political year 100 cannot be recovered. Among the various memoirs relating to this period the most trustworthy no doubt was the autobiography of P. Rutilius Rufus. But he too was an enemy of Marius, and his version of events can hardly have been a sufficient antidote to the venom of the memoirs of Sulla. We have to depend on later writers, who used some of the contemporary writings: but we cannot accurately gauge the extent to which our record is affected at any particular point by this or that bias. Cicero, our earliest surviving witness, is subject to two conflicting influences. For the demagogues, and the popular party generally, he has no mercy, but he deals in a different spirit with Marius, his own fellow-townsman of Arpinum. The following

---

[1] See Diodorus frag. XXXVII 15, a passage relating to the early part of the Italian war.

[2] Cic. *pro Balbo* §§ 46, 50, Plut. *Mar.* 28, Valer. Max. v 2 § 8.

[3] In general see, beside references above given, Livy ep. 69, Velleius II 12 § 6, and indices to Cicero and Valer. Max.

account is an attempt to combine such evidence as has come down to us, and to make allowance so far as possible for the partiality of the original witnesses. Of the three leading figures, Marius was from the first in an embarrassing position. By his own victories in the field he had made himself as a soldier less necessary to the state. Great military services had been rewarded with great honours. He must now follow up these with great political services, or the tide of popular gratitude, already slackening, would surely ebb. But the hard soldier was not at ease in the part of a civil magistrate. Consumed by ambition, he could not do without popularity, and to combine popularity with dignity, always a difficult task, was far beyond the abilities of Marius. Moreover, to a consul in residence the support of the Senate was in practice indispensable, much more so than to a tribune. Nor must we forget that Marius had in his earlier life belonged to the class of *publicani*. He probably shared the prejudices of the capitalists, and was at least loth to displease them. In dealing with the common people it was unfortunate that the consul was not a ready orator, and that the nerve unshaken in battle failed him when he had to face the irreverent humours of a mass-meeting. He lacked versatility, and his two associates did not make things easy for him. Each wanted to use the others for his own ends, a situation which places the head of a coalition in a dilemma. Either he must prevail, which means monarchy; or he must be the puppet of his juniors. Marius had no clear scheme of policy, and accordingly wavered and drifted to political ruin. Saturninus had some definite aims, and in him at least there was no wavering. He was a disciple of Gaius Gracchus, but without his master's scruples. He too was to illustrate the truth that to carry through a policy of any considerable scope was not possible without aiming at unconstitutional continuation of power. We have no authority for believing that he was at all reluctant to adopt such a course. Yet we should remember that our accounts of him are entirely derived from hostile witnesses. Of all the Roman demagogues none was more hated by the nobles than he; and what passed for Roman history was chiefly written by men of the noble class.

813. It was Saturninus who took charge of the measures now brought before the people. So far as we can gather from our scanty information, the *leges Appuleiae* were as follows. First, a land-law[1] dealing with lands in northern Italy which had been conquered and laid waste by the Cimbri and reconquered for Rome by Marius. Whether those lands the Gaulish occupants of which still survived

---

[1] *lex agraria.* Cic. *pro Sest.* §§ 37, 101, Appian I 29—31, Orelli *onom. Cicer.* III 136.

were included in the scope of the bill, or whether it concerned only those vacant by deaths, we are not told. In any case what had been held by Rome's Allies the Cisalpine Gauls was now viewed as Roman state property by right of conquest. This land was to be assigned, apparently[1] in allotments to individuals (*viritim*). We hear nothing of *possessio* or quit-rents, and it would seem that in accordance with the prevailing tendency *ager publicus* was to be converted into *ager privatus* once for all. It is likely that some of the soldiers of Marius may have cast longing eyes upon the rich lowland famed down to our own times for its fertility and high cultivation. How far this law was carried out we do not know, but it passed and was turned to party purposes. A clause in it required all senators within five days to take an oath to observe it : any defaulter was to lose his seat in the Senate and incur a heavy fine. The spirit displayed in this provision was in general a determination to prevent the nobility from procuring the repeal of this law as they had done in the case of the laws of the Gracchi. But it was especially aimed at Metellus Numidicus. The story, perhaps with some exaggeration, goes on to say that Marius now by means of a dirty trick prevented any possible failure of the design. He declared in the Senate that he would never consent to take the oath, and Metellus said so too. Metellus was now in the trap. Marius at the last evaded his promise by a dishonour-able equivocation : he and the rest swore as required, and Metellus alone persisted in his refusal. Saturninus then gave notice of a bill of outlawry against the recusant. We are told that the city people sympathized with Metellus, and that the support of Saturninus chiefly came from the country mob, Marian soldiers. The exact truth is not to be made out from our partisan versions. The great family con-nexion of the Metelli and their dependants would of itself furnish sympathizers enough to lend colour to the story as we have it. But it does not seem to have been the case that Saturninus had lost all influence with the city mob. Metellus would not allow his supporters to defend his cause by rioting. He withdrew into exile rather than let the state suffer hurt, and found a congenial retreat among the intellectual society of Rhodes. Saturninus then carried through his bill, and Marius as consul had the pleasure of proclaiming his honour-able opponent an outlaw.

814. The next measure was a corn-law[2] to please the city populace. The sale of corn to the people below the cost-price under the law of C. Gracchus was already a heavy drain on the

---

[1] For past precedents see Livy XXXI 4 (200 B.C.) with Weissenborn's notes, Polyb. II 21 (232 B.C.).

[2] *lex frumentaria*, known from *rhet. ad Herenn.* I § 21.

treasury.   Saturninus proposed to lower the price to a merely nominal[1] amount, less than $\frac{1}{7}$ of the Gracchan figure.   The city quaestor, Q. Servilius Caepio, perhaps a son of the disgraced proconsul, reported to the Senate that the treasury could not possibly stand the cost of such a scheme.   The Senate passed a resolution that if Saturninus went on with the bill he would be acting against the interest of the state, and found tribunes ready to block it. Saturninus disregarded their veto and put the bill to the vote. Caepio tried to break up the Assembly by rioting, but was not able to stop the bill from becoming law.   For this attempt to interrupt proceedings by force he was afterwards brought to trial on a charge of lowering the 'majesty' or dignity of the Roman people.   A third law[2] was that for the foundation of a number of colonies outside Italy.   The only point on which we are at all well-informed is that the law authorized Marius to bestow the Roman franchise on a few Allies (or Latins at least), three for each colony.   If a late writer is to be trusted, the capital required for starting these colonies was to be found in the 'gold of Tolosa' lately recovered[3] by the state from Caepio.   The outcome of this measure is characteristic of the period. The colonies[4] were never founded, but Marius had at once dispensed the patronage at his disposal, and a delicate question afterwards arose, whether the grant of citizenship made under this clause in the law was or was not invalidated by the failure of the condition on which the clause was based.

815.   These laws were clearly the work of one inspired by the acts of Gaius Gracchus, but altogether inferior, narrower in views and more ripe for violence, than the great reformer, and inclined to push imitation to the verge of caricature.   The most interesting question about the Appuleian laws is that of the *lex de maiestate*.   The notion of the 'greatness' of the state as a real thing which it was possible by definite misconduct to lessen (*minuere*) was surely not new.   How long it had been developing we do not know, nor does it greatly matter.   The old trials for *perduellio* before the Centuries were meant for the worst forms of treason, and the penalty was death.   Convictions were hard to secure in ordinary cases of less serious guilt, and the procedure before the Tribe-Assembly, where the penalty was

---

[1] *semissibus et trientibus* ($\frac{1}{2}+\frac{1}{3}=\frac{5}{6}$ of an *as*) instead of *senis et trientibus* ($6\frac{1}{3}$ *asses*) per *modius*.   I confess to some doubt as to this immense reduction, but Mommsen and Marquardt *Staatsverw.* II 114—5 seem to accept it without misgiving.

[2] *lex de coloniis deducendis.*   [Victor] *de vir. illustr.* 73, Cic. *pro Balbo* §§ 48—9.

[3] See § 791.

[4] It is most unlikely that Eporedia (§ 796) was one.   Lange *RA* III 80 regards it as a product of an attempt of the Optimates to outbid Saturninus as they had outbid C. Gracchus by the schemes of Drusus.   This is only too ingenious, and rests on no evidence.

a fine, practically[1] superseded the more primitive and harsher method of dealing with treason against the state. The next stage was the appointment of special judicial commissions (*quaestiones extraordinariae*) with power to try offenders. This amounted to a temporary delegation of its powers by the Assembly, and it is clear that in referring a case to the decision of such a court a marked importance attached to the precise terms of the reference. Nor is it wonderful that a loose phrase, capable of wide application, should be employed. The strict definition of crimes is a slow growth. Whether the acts proved against an offender amounted to a lessening[2] of the inherent greatness (*maiestas*) of the Roman people, was left for the court to decide. The word *maiestas* had long held an important place in Roman phraseology, especially in treaties[3] with the communities leagued with Rome on an inferior footing: these were bound to uphold the 'majesty' of the Roman people, and of their conduct in this respect the Roman people was in effect the judge. As in external, so in internal affairs, the decision of cases[4] that arose was certain to generate definition. As treaty-rights hardened into the complete subjection of allies to an imperial mistress, so isolated decisions at length produced a new treason-law with some attempt to define the classes of acts grouped under the conception of what was now regarded as a special public crime. This result was attained a few years later in the legislation of Sulla. That the acts of Saturninus in some way or other contributed to the movement in this direction is most probable. But whether a complete general law of *maiestas*, establishing a standing court (*quaestio perpetua*) for such trials, formed part of the legislation of the year 100, is very doubtful. If with Mommsen[5] we identify Cicero's *lex Appuleia de maiestate* with the law appointing a special commission[6] to try Caepio in 103 (Saturninus' first tribunate), we must answer in the negative. In that case we may still believe that the law, though creating a special court for a particular trial, did something in the direction of definition. But the connexion of Saturninus with the trials of Caepio[7] and others, however probable, rests on very slight and dubious evidence. On the other hand Lange[8] points out that it was undoubtedly an object with

---

[1] The old procedure for *perduellio* was not abolished. See Madvig *Verfassung und Verwaltung* II 274—5.

[2] Tacitus *ann.* I 72.   [3] See Marquardt *Staatsverw.* I 46.

[4] See the questions raised in Cic. *part. orat.* §§ 104—5.

[5] Mommsen *RH* (Eng. trans.) III 196.

[6] Ihne V 149—151 puts it in 103, but treats it as a separate law.

[7] The proconsul, not the quaestor mentioned above. The evidence is a passage of Licinianus, probably genuine (Bonn ed. p. 21) but pretty certainly out of its place.

[8] Lange *RA* III 81—2.

Saturninus to put a stop to the violent opposition which impeded the action of demagogic tribunes. He had had experience of this hindrance, and the old methods of procedure were too clumsy to serve as an effective means of removing it. And it must be granted that the references[1] to an Appuleian law of *maiestas* fall in more naturally with Lange's view, that Saturninus was indeed the author of a law by which this offence, like that of *repetundae*, was placed under the jurisdiction of a standing court.

816. Whatever be the true version of the disputed point just discussed, there is no doubt that all the legislation of Saturninus was carried by violence. Violence was sure to provoke a reaction, particularly among the capitalist class, never well disposed to disorder. They had been useful supporters of Marius, and their growing dislike to the methods of the 'popular' leaders no doubt made the consul uneasy. The signs of a split between Marius and his democratic partners began to appear. Saturninus and Glaucia could no longer rely on his steady support, but, if they could secure their own continuance in office when he retired into private life, they might perhaps do without him. We hear that it was now the object of Saturninus to get reelected to a third tribunate, while Glaucia was to stand for the consulship. That he could not legally do this (being still praetor) mattered not in this time of confusion. Force was still to be the means to the desired end; the democratic leaders indeed knew no other. But in the use of force they had been largely dependent on the disbanded soldiers of Marius, and the estrangement of Marius must have lost them many of these doughty politicians. The nobles on the contrary were beginning to breathe more freely. The worst of the democratic storm was past. Men of experience were watching events, and, when the disgust of the Knights and the hesitation of Marius were noted, the wary Scaurus and others saw that their chance was come. As the canvass for the consulship proceeded, it became clear that M. Antonius the orator was certain of the first place, but that Glaucia would probably be beaten for the second by C. Memmius, who as an active tribune had distinguished himself on the 'popular' side in exposing the scandals of the Jugurthine war. Saturninus had Memmius beaten to death. The voting Assembly broke up in confusion, and all order and decency were at an end. But it would seem that most people had now had enough of Saturninus and Glaucia as exponents of popular government. Their enemies were preparing to attack them openly, and they could only get recruits by bringing in more ruffians from outside. They seized the Capitol. The Senate dallied no longer, but on the motion of their

[1] Cic. *de orat.* II §§ 107, 201.　See below § 818 on the trial of Titius.

foreman Scaurus passed the 'last order' in the regular form, calling on the consuls and other magistrates to save the state. Marius of course was meant, and he could see no way out of his difficulties. Slowly and reluctantly he served out arms and embodied all available men, to save the state by civil war against his own associates. No doubt the force arrayed under his command consisted largely of rich senators and knights, each with his band of dependants, including[1] freedmen and slaves. Cicero, speaking 37 years after in defence of a client accused of having borne a leading part on this occasion, makes out that every man of position in Rome responded to the consul's call; and in a sense this was perhaps true enough. Never had the wealthy classes enjoyed such an opportunity. The blunders of the revolutionary leaders had delivered them into the hand of their enemies: the consul whom the nobility hated was by the irony of fate driven to be their agent in the destruction of his own political allies, and to bear the greater part of the odium of civil bloodshed. In the fighting which followed Saturninus and his party were driven back upon the Capitol, and compelled to surrender by the cutting of the pipes that supplied them with water. The leaders trusted that Marius would save them, and Marius is said to have guaranteed their personal security on behalf of the state. But things had now passed the point at which even a Marius could control their course. The rich were in no mind to let slip an opportunity that might never return. The story is variously told, but all agree that a massacre of the prisoners took place. Among them were a praetor (Glaucia) a tribune (Saturninus) and a quaestor (Saufeius), wearing their robes of office. Another of the many victims was the sham Gracchus, who had entered on the tribunate that very day. We thus learn that the day of the massacre was the tenth of December.

817. Rome was now one stage further on the road of revolution. Tiberius Gracchus, still a magistrate, had perished in a riot. Against Gaius Gracchus, no longer in office, and his partisans, the Senate had employed a consul of their own colour to levy civil war. Now the Senate had the supreme good fortune to find a tool in a consul who had risen to power as a democrat, and through his aid was able to slaughter troublesome magistrates with surprising ease. On the surface it might appear that the Senate had now only to occupy the recovered seat of power, and be more than ever the real government of Rome. Thrice the popular party had gathered force to withstand the nobility: for the third time their attempt had been

---

[1] Cic. *pro Rabirio perd.* §§ 20—31. In § 31 he asserts that a slave was rewarded as the actual slayer of Saturninus. On the other side we hear of Saturninus calling slaves to arms, Valer. Max. VIII 6 § 2.

foiled and their leaders slain. And now their hero Marius had gone over to the enemy. But it is the position of Marius at this juncture that enables us to form a truer appreciation of the state of affairs. He is to us the outward and visible sign of the incapacity of the Roman Republic to achieve its own reform. He could not be leader of the 'popular' party, whose leaders he had patronized and betrayed. He could not be leader of the 'good,' as the rich and noble called themselves; for the nobles hated him, and he despised them. They chuckled over their luck and skill in turning him to account and leaving him politically impotent. The saviour of Rome had none to trust him now; and it was a galling reflexion that he was outmanœuvred and discredited by the very men whom he had once successfully defied. Now it was the case that ever since Rome had ceased to have a rival the parts of the Roman state had degenerated in the absence of a salutary fear. Senate and Assembly alike were ineffective unless led by great leaders, whom the times could seldom produce, and who could do little or nothing without unrepublican continuation of office. In the present crisis the need of a leader was more marked than ever, and Marius had broken through the rules of the constitution pretty thoroughly. But he could not be leader himself, while he was a fatal obstacle to the leadership of another. No means existed for the recognition of military services apart from political life. That the first public man in Rome should be politically extinct was in itself a mischievous thing. Power was wanted to drive the worn-out machine of government, and in the presence of Marius no one else could accumulate the necessary driving-power. The situation was indeed intolerable, and so Marius himself found it. There were three ways in which it might be relieved. He might withdraw, and leave the field clear for smaller men; or he might find the means of reviving his prestige by victories in another war; or his glory might be obscured by the rising of some newer or brighter star. Marius, it is said, did the first in hope to bring about the second, but we know that it was the third alternative that in the end relieved the political strain and gave a fresh start (delusive, it is true) to the constitution. Saturninus had completed the proof, begun by the Gracchi, that a popular leader could safely defy the Senate so long as he could retain his office. The Senate had proved that the only effective check on demagogues was in the last resort force, and their use of force had tended to become more and more of a military kind. The action of both parties was familiarizing the minds of men with the notion of empowering individuals to disregard precedents and override the law. Monarchy in short was not only in the air, but the manner of its coming was already foreshadowed. As

Mommsen puts it 'the sword had begun to appear by the side of the crown.'

818. For the moment the victorious Optimates turned their attention to getting rid of the Appuleian laws. Pretexts were not hard to find, for formalities had been lightly treated and omens disregarded: one law at least had been carried by votes taken after a peal of thunder. The Senate refused[1] to recognize them as valid. But it was perhaps felt unwise to do nothing at all for the disbanded soldiers who had given so much trouble. For it would seem to have been[2] in this year or early in 99 that a colony was founded on the coast of Corsica. We read of it as *colonia Mariana*, founded by Marius. We hear of men rebuked by Marius for complaining of the smallness of the allotments which were in his opinion (and he was an authority on the point) sufficient for their maintenance, a story which probably refers to the same event. This appears to be the first of those regular military[3] colonies, as distinct from the allotments to individual soldiers, which meet us henceforth in the history of the Republic and the Empire. A very proper desire was also manifested to recall Metellus. In the remaining days of his consulship (11th Dec. to end) Marius prevented this, and in the year 99 one of the tribunes, P. Furius, blocked the bill for his restoration, so Metellus had to wait. But Furius seems to have lent himself to the reaction[4] against Saturninus, if it be true that he procured the confiscation of the estates of the slain leaders. The house of Saturninus[5] was demolished. But no campaign of prosecutions against his surviving followers is recorded: perhaps the wealthy classes, now strong in union, felt their position more secure than the nobility had done after the fall of the Gracchi. That the *populares* were by no means suppressed is clear from the fact that the tribune Sextus Titius carried through a law[6] for allotment of some lands in spite of opposing colleagues and the occurrence of a prodigy. It was however soon after annulled on a religious pretext. When the tribunes for 98 came into office, the bill for recalling Metellus was at once carried through, and the noble exile enjoyed a triumphant restoration. The reaction against the revolutionary movement expressed itself more freely in the prosecution of Titius. The trial[7] seems to have been

[1] Cic. *de legibus* II § 14.

[2] Lange *RA* III 84, citing Pliny *NH* III § 80, Seneca *ad Helviam* 7 § 9, Pompon. Mela II 7 § 122, Ptolemy III 2, Plutarch *Crassus* 2.

[3] Velleius I 15 § 5.

[4] Orosius V 17 § 10. From Dion Cass. frag. 95 we learn that he had joined and deserted Saturninus. [5] Valer. Max. VI 3 § 1.

[6] Cic. *de leg.* II §§ 14, 31, Obsequens *de prodig.* 46. For Titius see Cicero index.

[7] Cic. *pro Rabir. perd.* §§ 24—5, *de orat.* II § 48, Quintil. VI 1 § 49. If the charge was *maiestas*, it follows that Saturninus did carry a law establishing a court for such cases, and that (as Lange *RA* III 84 says) this law had not been cancelled.

held before a regular court with an equestrian jury. The charge is not recorded: what it can have been, other than *maiestas*, is very hard to see. The possession by the accused of a bust of Saturninus is said to have been a piece of damning evidence in the eyes of the capitalist jurors, who condemned him. On the other hand, when C. Appuleius Decianus accused[1] Furius before the Tribes, an outbreak of popular wrath took place. It is said that the hated turncoat was lynched by the mob, and that the accuser (on what charge and by what court is not stated) was afterwards punished for having expressed sympathy with Saturninus. These obscure affairs are important as illustrating the cross-currents producing confusion in Roman politics at this time. Of the prosecution of M'. Aquilius for extortion in Sicily we have spoken above, and also of that of L. Licinius Lucullus. The latter case gave rise to one of those hereditary[2] accusation-feuds which were a feature of the life of the upper classes in Rome and contributed to intensify the partiality of Roman tribunals.

819. As it was the desire of demagogic tribunes to brush aside all formal hindrances to speedy legislation, so it was the aim of the conservative *optimates* to keep all checks on hasty action in good working order. The consuls of 98, Q. Caecilius Metellus Nepos and T. Didius, the latter a 'new man,' carried a law[3] (*lex Caecilia Didia*) in which old rules governing the lawful action of the Assemblies were stringently reenacted. The combination in a single enactment of clauses dealing with matters having no essential connexion[4] with each other—'tacking,' as we call it—had for some time been forbidden. And the period of 24 days[5] (the *trinum nundinum*, three Roman eight-day weeks) had from very early times been the legal period of notice required for public business meant to be laid before any Assembly in the ordinary course. The purport of the new law was to declare the former practice definitely illegal and the latter absolutely necessary. This law, taken in connexion with the rules for observance of signs from Heaven (*lex Aelia Fufia* etc.), left the Senate in a strong position for impugning on occasion the validity of an unacceptable statute. We may also reflect that all checks upon the prompt action of the Assembly tended to reserve the power of dealing

---

[1] Cic. *pro Rab.* § 24, Valer. Max. VIII 1 § 2, Appian *civ.* I 33, Dion Cass. frag. 95. Decianus is said to have fled to the East and joined Mithradates. Cic. *pro Flacco* § 71 and Schol. on § 5.

[2] Plut. *Lucull.* I.

[3] Cic. *de domo* §§ 41, 52—3, *pro Sestio* § 135, *philippic* v § 8, *ad Att.* II 9 § 1. That the common object of the clauses known was to prevent the people being tricked and hurried into voting for something they did not really approve, is clear. See note of Tyrrell.

[4] Mommsen *Staatsrecht* III 336, 377.

[5] Mommsen *Röm. Chronol.* p. 243.

with emergencies to the Senate; a power of which the House in its
palmy days had made free use, and the free use of which it would
undoubtedly wish to recover. The passing of this law clearly marks
the strength of the reaction against the revolutionary movements of
recent years. For a time the wealthy classes could enjoy themselves
according to their bent. No immediate peril menaced the owners of
land and slaves, and the equestrian financiers, secure in the control
of the jury-courts, might carry on the robbery of Rome's provincial
subjects undisturbed. But the difficulties in the way of just and
consistent administration were as great as ever: the constitution of
a city-state supplied no fit machinery for governing a vast empire.
At present there was concord between the Senate and the Knights.
But the two wealthy Orders might fall out, and the renewal of their
discord would leave little prospect of any return to a better state of
things on a republican footing. Meanwhile it seems not to have been
understood how serious was the disaffection of the Italian Allies; and
it was perhaps impossible with the information at disposal to gauge
truly the danger of the storm now brewing in the East.

820. When the return of Metellus Numidicus was already assured,
but had not yet taken place, Marius left Rome, a soured and discredited
man. The natural sequel to his career of consulships would have been
that he should hold the censorship in 97. But now he feared rejection,
and found some pretext for not being a candidate. As for leaving
Rome, he gave out that he had vowed to sacrifice to the 'Great
Mother,' and must visit Galatia and Cappadocia for the purpose.
According to the story preserved by Plutarch[1], this excuse covered
a design of very different scope. If Marius was to regain his former
preeminence, it must be by service in war. For civil life as a field for
distinction he had no gifts. At the time of his Numidian triumph he
had come straight from the ceremony into the senate-house wearing
his triumphal robe, outraging the proprieties of Roman etiquette.
And, now that the barbarians from the North were dead and buried,
his manners were no doubt a standing offence to men who were his
superiors in polish and who deemed him no longer necessary. In
short Marius was clumsy and boorish, though crafty: he did not
succeed as he perhaps might have done if, though bluff, he had been
also dexterous. We are now told that his object was to make trouble
in the East, and in particular to stir up Mithradates to declare war,
solely in order to create for himself an opportunity of coming to the
front once more. He is even said to have visited the king of Pontus,
and to have been most honourably received. But no attentions could
induce him to be even decently civil; with brutal frankness he told the

---

[1] Plut. *Mar.* 31. The story may have been taken from Sulla's memoirs.

king[1] either to try and conquer the Romans or to hold his peace and do their bidding—a flat provocation which sounded a warning in the ears of Mithradates. Truly a strange story, and one not lightly to be believed on the single authority of a Greek compiler who is known to have drawn some of his gossip about Marius from partisan and hostile sources. But if the withdrawal of Marius to the East was a significant step, surely not less significant to us, looking back and trying to form some notion of what was passing in Rome, is the absence of information as to the doings of Sulla. Even in the list of names of the men of mark who took part in putting down Saturninus (and Cicero mentions not a few) his name does not appear. Whether the orator, speaking in the year 63, thought it bad advocacy to cite the participation of Sulla as justifying the participation of his client Rabirius, whether Sulla held back, perhaps from reluctance to follow Marius, or whether he was employed at some other point and so missed the attack on the Capitol, we do not know. In the year 100 he was a man of 38, and had greatly distinguished himself in the recent wars. Yet we lose sight of him till he stands for the praetorship, perhaps in 95, and fails. In 93 he was *praetor peregrinus*. That this bold and aspiring man restricted himself for some six years to private luxury and debauchery is hardly credible. We may guess that he was no inconsiderable figure in the background of public events, gaining experience and studying men and matters, making friends, and waiting for his hour to come.

821. With the year 95 we reach an act of public policy destined to hurry on what was probably the most momentous crisis in the history of the Republic. In that year two eminent men were consuls, L. Licinius Crassus the famous orator, and Q. Mucius Scaevola, afterwards[2] chief pontiff, who as a jurist was even greater than his elder namesake and cousin the augur Scaevola, father-in-law of Crassus. The old trouble of the interference of Latins and other Allies in Roman Assemblies had been often felt in recent years. It would seem that at every census a few contrived to get their names on to the register of one or other of the Roman Tribes and passed for Roman citizens. Previous attempts to stop this practice had failed, as commonly happens when the effective working of strict regulations depends upon the prevention of evasions by constant human vigilance. But a far more serious nuisance than the surreptitious qualification of

---

[1] Kiene, *Bundesgenossenkrieg* p. 243, takes this speech, if genuine, as a warning meant to deter rather than provoke.

[2] He was a pontiff already, and must have become head of the college on the death of Domitius, some time between 92 and 82. He is sometimes referred to by anticipation as Pont. max.

non-citizen voters was the introduction of non-resident aliens to bear a hand in the noise and rioting which was becoming normal in Roman Assemblies. The evil was great, and the wish to put an end to it was consistent with the most purely patriotic motives. The consuls tried to deal with it by a law for the regulation[1] of citizens (*de civibus regundis*). It was a fundamental principle of Roman law that no man could be a citizen of two or more communities at the same time. It is to be lamented that we have no exact account of the provisions of the new law, for that it was a mere 'get you home' order addressed to Allies then present in the city is not likely. In the first place, any whose names were on the roll of citizens owed their registration to the censors of the year 97. Unless some machinery were provided for trying questionable cases, these names would remain as those of citizens until the next census at least. Registration by the censor did not create[2] a legal right, but recorded the fact that a man passed himself off for a citizen and that his claim was approved or unchallenged at the time. And a man whose citizen rights were beyond all question might be out of reach abroad at the time of the census, and so be missed out. Again, the census, even when most regularly held, came only at intervals of five years. It is most unlikely that a citizen returning (say) after absence from home was debarred from the exercise of civic functions until the completion of the next census. And the censors might lay down their office without having performed their duties. It has been pointed out that in the next generation[3] this happened several times, and a notable instance occurred in the year 89. Whether there was any direct relation between the censors' register and the exercise of voting in Assemblies, is not clear: but to be placed on the register was at least *prima facie* evidence of citizenship. Our information is very imperfect, but it leaves no doubt that the difficulty of ensuring that none but the legally qualified should take part in the voting was at all times enormous.

822. It may be gathered from the words of Cicero[4] that a special commission was appointed to try cases of illegal assumption of citizenship. The question is, what were their powers and how did they use them? According to one[5] authority, they were empowered to order

---

[1] For the *lex Licinia Mucia* see Cic. *pro Cornelio* I frag. 10 and Asconius' note, *pro Balbo* §§ 48, 54, *de off.* III § 47, *pro Sestio* § 30 with Scholiast, *Brutus* § 63. The emendations (*redigundis* for *regundis* etc.) are I think rightly rejected by the Berlin editors of Asconius. Roby *Justin. dig.* chap. 8 keeps *regundis*, and gives an admirable account of Scaevola and of this law.

[2] See Cic. *pro Archia* § 11, Mommsen *Staatsrecht* II 361—2.

[3] Reid, Introd. to *pro Archia* p. 15.

[4] *pro Balbo* § 48 *acerrima de civitate quaestio......in iudicium est vocatus.*

[5] Schol. Bob. ad Cic. *pro Sest.* § 30, *ut redire socii et Latini in civitates suas iuberentur.*

Latins and other Allies to return to their several cities. Asconius[1] says that the aim of the law was to put each individual back into the right of his own city. The former seems to imply actual removal of the persons, and we need not doubt that the commission had this power. The latter does not necessarily imply more than a constraint put upon individuals to renounce publicly all claim to a franchise (*civitatis ius*) not properly theirs, and to revert to their own. This constraint would very likely in some cases take the form of compelling a man to return to his own city. But it need not be inferred that the only aliens allowed to remain in Rome were those who were not Italian Allies. So extravagant a supposition is not to be entertained, and the passage in which Cicero[2] criticizes the law from the standpoint of civic courtesy surely tells the other way. Perhaps we may in general conclude that the Allies wrongfully registered as citizens were all disfranchised, but only a few of them ejected from Rome; and that any wholesale ejection that took place was no more than the getting rid of the non-citizen roughs who, having been brought in to promote disorder, would have little inducement to hurry back home and quit the state-fed idleness of the great city. One thing seems clear: those who had acquired the Roman franchise in any legal way were not affected by the law. It only remains now to account for the intense irritation caused throughout Italy by this law. If it was mild compared with the alien acts of earlier date, how came it[3] that 'the leading men of the Italian communities were thereby so set against Rome that this act was the chiefest cause of the great rebellion of Italy'? Why did Cicero[4] declare that, though Crassus and Scaevola were the wisest pair of consuls of his time, it was universally agreed that their law had done the state not only no good, but a great deal of harm? We may reflect that the return of the rough element, not improved by their sojourn in Rome, was not likely to promote content or loyalty to Rome in their native towns. Nor would local magistrates be over-pleased at having to replace on local registers names of men whose claim to be Roman citizens had been suddenly disallowed. These men had but the other day been men to be imitated: they were the advance-guard of the enfranchisement of Italy, the pioneers of a movement justified by a reasonable hope. For Flaccus and Gaius Gracchus had both made definite proposals to this end. The Allies had patiently acquiesced in their failure. Recent wars had made the service of the contingents of Allies vitally necessary to Rome; they had been her mainstay in the

---

[1] Ascon. cited above, *ut in suae quisque civitatis ius redigeretur.*

[2] *de offic.* III § 47.   [3] Asconius.

[4] *pro Cornelio* cited above.

hour of danger. Men from their cities had been passing for citizens of Rome; others had been inculcating a liberal policy by a vigorous coercion of the Roman mob, and this with the countenance of Roman politicians. And now the expectations naturally roused by the course of recent events were at one stroke dashed to the ground. It was clear that the Roman nobility and the selfish city populace had been emboldened to take this step by the generally peaceful aspect of affairs. The possible good intentions[1] of the consuls were nothing to the Allies, and the conviction spread fast that the attitude of Rome could only be modified by war.

823. That the overthrow of Saturninus and the feeling of security enjoyed by the rich and noble were not leading to much improvement in the state of Roman society is indicated by stray details relating to these years. The wanton growth of luxury went on, and the prices[2] of the objects of gluttony and other vices were ever rising. Men were more and more losing the strenuous temper of the early Romans. We have before noted cases of a disposition to shirk arduous and unremunerative duties. At this time we hear of one bearing the name of Scipio[3] who backed out of a Spanish province allotted to him. The Senate passed a vote of censure on his conduct, which it was easy to do: probably those who censured him had themselves little stomach for duty in an ill-equipped and impoverished province. Nor must we see evidence of great virtue in the decree of the Senate[4] passed in 97 forbidding human sacrifices. It was easy to gratify a few enlightened and scrupulous men by such a vote. But superstition was not really checked by the protest, and the use of human victims for purposes of divination seems to have occurred sporadically down to much later times. A man named M. Duronius[5] had when tribune procured the repeal of a sumptuary law. In 97 the censors struck him off the list of the Senate. He retorted by prosecuting one of them, Antonius the orator, on a charge of *ambitus*; before what court, does not appear, but it seems to have been merely a method of annoyance, as was often the case at Rome. In 95 we come to a notable[6] political trial. The *optimates* saw their way to dealing a blow at C. Norbanus, who had nine years before effected

---

[1] For views as to the real aims of these moderate and sagacious men see Wilkins' Intr. to *de orat.* p. 11.

[2] Diodor. frag. XXXVII 3.

[3] Valer. Max. VI 3 § 3. Whether he gave the excuse attributed to him, *quod recte facere nesciret,* may be doubted.

[4] Pliny *NH* XXX 12.

[5] Valer. Max. II 9 § 5, Cic. *de orat.* II § 274.

[6] The accuser was the talented young P. Sulpicius Rufus, who afterwards went over to the Marian party. The references to this case are collected in Wilkins' Introd. to Cic. *de orat.* pp. 10, 15, 17.

the ruin of their friend Caepio. Norbanus had been an ally of Saturninus, whose law on the subject of *maiestas*, passed since Caepio's trial, had made penal[1] the informalities and violent proceedings now laid to the charge of Norbanus. A conviction seemed likely, for the Knights were still in harmony with the nobility, old Scaurus gave evidence against the accused, and Crassus took some part in the prosecution, justifying Caepio, and so indirectly accusing the author of his ruin. But Norbanus was acquitted, not wholly through the eloquence of Antonius who defended him. Caepio had attempted to wrest the control of the law-courts from the Knights, and the equestrian jury would not encourage the enemies of their Order. As a piece of 'straight voting' this episode well illustrates the general spirit of Roman juries. Whether the ostensible charge was substantiated or not was hardly the point. In the crude state of criminal jurisprudence, and with the tradition of the old trials before the Assembly, it was far from easy to exclude irrelevant considerations; and both condemnations and acquittals were apt to be decided on the simple issue 'do we mean to punish this man or do we not?' This trial must have been held early in the year, for the consul Crassus soon went off to his province in the North of Italy, and tried to get an excuse for a triumph[2] by worrying some wretched Alpine tribes. Such were even the better nobles of this period. The Senate consented to grant the triumph, but his colleague Scaevola was man enough to veto the order and prevent the scandal.

824. Speaking of scandal, we now come to what was perhaps the most infamous scandal[3] recorded in the history of Rome. The victim was a noble whose spotless character and public services were a credit and support to a class fast degenerating and keen to exploit the merits of its best members for the advantage of the less respectable. Hence the noble historians, extreme to mark the delinquencies of a rival Order, pilloried with much gusto the shameful act of an Equestrian jury, and the secondary writers of later times could not help echoing the bitter cry. Add to this that Cicero[4], to whom a man of surpassing excellence, driven into exile for the offence of being better than his neighbours, appeared the very prototype of

---

[1] We may say that by this time charges of *maiestas* had become a regular political weapon.

[2] References in Wilkins p. 11.

[3] Case of Rutilius Rufus. In general see indices to Cicero and Valer. Max., Livy ep. 70, Velleius II 13, Diodorus frag. XXXVII 5, Dion Cass. frag. 97, Florus II 5, Orosius V 17 §§ 12—3, and other references in Lange *RA* III 93—4, Holden on Cic. *pro Plancio* § 52, Wilkins' Intr. to *de orat.* p. 20.

[4] See index to Cicero. It is to be noticed that nearly all his references to Rutilius occur in works written after his own exile. In *pro Fonteio* § 38 (28), an earlier speech, we read of slanders uttered by the accuser. This was a debauched fellow named Apicius.

himself, made free use of his talents to crown the injured Rutilius with glory. These considerations will account for the great number and close agreement of the versions of the story that still survive, and the many references[1] to it as an instance of ill-rewarded virtue. But there is no ground for doubting that the hero of the story was a great and good man, or for attempting to whitewash the black infamy of Roman capitalists.

825. P. Rutilius Rufus, soldier lawyer and upright patriot, a painstaking but dry orator, was a man of wide reading, deeply imbued with the principles of Stoicism, which were the active guide of his life. We have met him many times in the foregoing pages : perhaps no fact is more to his credit than his aversion to the crafty and muddle-headed ambition of Marius. He was an intimate friend of the pontiff Scaevola, also a follower of the Stoic school, which had a peculiar attraction for Roman lawyers. When after his praetorship Scaevola went to rule the province Asia as proconsul, Rutilius went with him as his *legatus*. When Scaevola after nine months of governorship returned to Rome, he left Rutilius in charge as his deputy, so that the latter was acting governor until a successor arrived. To the infinite disgust of the farmers of revenue (*publicani*), money-lenders (*negotiatores*), and other financial vermin, whose agents swarmed in the province, these two good men revolutionized the administration by converting it from what it really was to what it was in theory supposed to be. It was not enough to refuse bribes and presents themselves, and exhibit a priggish but harmless virtue in dealing with Rome's subjects. Their frugal lives were nobody's loss but their own. It was another matter when the law-courts under their direction did equal justice between the natives and the representatives of Roman financial companies. News soon reached Rome that it had become impossible, in the richest province of the Roman dominions, to exact more than the legal dues, that the attempt to use force or fraud for any such purpose, so far from being winked at or even backed up, now met with immediate punishment, not to be averted by influence or corruption. Shares in the companies had no doubt been taken up on the supposition that normal conditions would prevail during the period for which the concession held good. The two Stoic lawyers had upset the calculations on which capital had been invested. Dividends were certain to be poor, and we need not wonder that the rage of the shareholders[2] broke out in abuse of Scaevola. But it was probably impossible to take their revenge on him in any practical manner, for there was no legal way of getting at

---

[1] Especially in the writings of the Stoic Seneca.
[2] Cic. *pro Plancio* § 33.

the pontiff. So the outraged capitalists waited for a good chance to strike at Rutilius. In 93 or 92, some six years after, when there was general peace abroad, the chance came. The offender was brought to trial under the *lex Servilia* of Glaucia on a charge of *repetundae*. Rutilius scorned to bid for pity by the common tricks of mourning-clothes and unwashed person, nor would he call the eloquence of Antonius and Crassus to his aid. Scaevola and his own young nephew C. Aurelius Cotta were allowed to take part in his defence, but the most important speech was no doubt his own. The famous example of Socrates[1] was probably present to his mind, and it would seem that he did no more than disprove the charge. Of course the jury found him guilty. Dion Cassius says that the blame for this was partly laid at the door of Marius, to whom the presence of the man who 'loved righteousness and hated iniquity' was an eyesore. Whether Rutilius was outlawed in the usual form is not clear; probably not, even if the law allowed this penalty. But the claim of money declared to have been extorted had to be met, and it was now discovered that the whole estate of Rutilius did not by any means amount to the sum named. In poverty and disgrace he withdrew from Rome, and passed the rest of his days as an honoured resident in the very province alleged to have been the scene of his extortions. Driven from Mitylene by the Mithradatic war, he finally settled at Smyrna, where he became a citizen. Philosophy and literature were his occupations, and he wrote[2] on Roman history in Greek. Sulla afterwards offered to restore him to his position in Rome, but the offer was declined. In the year 78 Cicero, then travelling for study in Asia, paid the old man a visit. Such is the instructive story, full of light on the state of Roman society, of the man whom Velleius, writing under Tiberius Caesar, called the best man, not merely of his own generation, but of all time. The fate of Rutilius left behind it a general uneasiness. All men were afraid of the law-courts, for it was evident that even the most perfect innocence was no protection against ruin.

826. The year 92 was marked by the discord[3] of censors, and by the beginning of a movement for a change in the constitution of the public courts. Of the censors, Crassus the orator was a lively and somewhat vain man with a turn for modern refinements and display: Domitius the chief pontiff was a man of the old-fashioned school, hard and unsympathetic. Domitius expressed himself freely in disapproval

---

[1] Seneca repeatedly couples him with Socrates; whether from a true instinct, or from some indication in Rutilius' memoirs, or from Cicero *de orat.* I §§ 227—233, I know not. The imitation is plainly asserted by Cicero.

[2] See H. Peter, *Histor. Rom. Fragm.* pp. 120—4.

[3] The censors. See Cic. *Brutus* § 164, *de orat.* III §§ 93—5 and Wilkins p. 12, Sueton. *Nero* 2, *de rhet.* 2, *de grammat.* 6.

of his colleague's luxurious ways: Crassus retorted by a witty defence, and raised a laugh against his critic. The pair seem to have got through their official business somehow. In one act of corrective policy they agreed. Teachers of rhetoric had for some time been established in Rome, where all great issues were now decided, and where the necessity of effective speaking created a growing demand for systematic training in the art. Hitherto the teachers had been Greeks, whose wider culture was improving the education of the leisured class of Romans. But now some Latin rhetoricians had begun to set up schools. The training given by these men was much inferior to that of the skilled Greeks: to Crassus, if Cicero gives his views aright, they seemed no better than quack practitioners: whatever the future might have in store, for the present the hour of a purely Latin rhetoric was not yet come. The censors put forth an edict ordering the suppression of these Latin schools. One of the teachers followed Rutilius to Asia. But it was not possible to carry out the prohibition permanently. The practice was almost immediately resumed, and the city soon echoed, and continued to echo, with the declamations of pupils on conventional themes.

827. This however was a matter of importance chiefly as the beginning of an influence destined to have a bad effect on the later literature of Rome. The matter of the law-courts was of immediate importance, and through all the lamentable obscurity of surviving notices we can discern that the movement for a change, though it failed, had most serious results, not only undesigned but wholly unforeseen. The Equestrian Order had been placed in possession of the courts by Gaius Gracchus in order to weaken the Senate. The former senatorial juries had corruptly acquitted guilty men of their own Order: the Knights improved on this record by corruptly condemning innocent men of the senatorial Order. The recent scandal was flagrant, and the best and most moderate of the nobles resolved to make an effort to reform the courts. No such plan as the appointment of trained lawyers as permanent judges to preside over courts of law was within the horizon of the men of that day. Even in the civil courts, where strictly legal issues were tried, the legal skill available was a purely private affair. If a praetor happened to be learned in the law, it was only by accident; but he could, if an amateur, resort to a learned friend for help, and there was no lack of competent technical advisers. In the public or (as we may loosely call them) criminal courts the question was one of fact, at least on the face of it, or rather how a given fact should be regarded: and in the lack of precise definition it was possible conscientiously to hold very different opinions. The absence of a trained judge left an honest jury to be

swayed this way or that by the partisan speeches of counsel : with a dishonest one the verdict was dictated by personal or party interests and passions, including bribery.   We must picture to ourselves a money-grubbing class of men, habitually seeing all things from the standpoint of the dealer or speculator anxious to make a profit, and used to none but material considerations.   The only reform conceivable by a Roman of the time was to provide better jurors.   But, as the class now in possession were peculiarly liable to use their power badly, so they were most unlikely to surrender tamely a monopoly of which they were just beginning to enjoy the full profits. The situation in Rome was one of unsuspected danger.   The struggle for the control of the courts was of itself serious enough to call for the highest qualities of statesmanship.   But it had on the face of it no connexion with the claim of the Allies to the franchise.   If however the two questions should in any way become connected, the ensuing complications might lead to calamities the extent of which none could forecast.

828.   The cause of judicial reform was taken in hand by M. Livius[1] Drusus, who is supposed to have been the son of his namesake the opponent of C. Gracchus.   He entered on office as tribune in December 92, and at once came forward as a legislator.   A young man of good character and patriotic aims, his career resembles those of his forerunners in illustrating the ineffectiveness of the yearly tribunate as an engine of reform.   For every question of importance was complicated by the number of interests to be conciliated or encountered, and the inevitable growth of a reformer's programme was a fatal obstacle to his success within so short a space of time.   But Drusus, unlike the Gracchi and Saturninus, came forward as a champion of the Senate : unlike his father, he was not merely the Senate's tool.   His first object, in which he had the support of the nobility and their dependants, was the abolition of the Equestrian juries.   But here he found himself face to face with two difficulties.   Some means of conciliating the populace must be found, and the bitter opposition of the Knights must be overcome.   To meet the former of these Drusus resorted to the old expedients of a colonial bill, to carry out previous plans for colonies in Italy and Sicily which were still in abeyance, and a bill for extending the facilities for getting cheap corn at the expense of the state.   Over these proposals there does not seem to have been any great struggle: men were by this used to seeing such legislation carried, and pretexts could be found for preventing it taking effect.   But the transfer of the judicial power,

---

[1] Drusus.   Indices to Cicero and Valer. Max., Livy ep. 70, 71, Velleius II 13, 14, Appian *civ.* I 35, 36, Florus II 5, Orosius V 18 §§ 1—7, [Victor] *de viris illustr.* 66.

once carried, would assuredly not remain a dead letter, if the Senate could help it. A rearrangement of political forces quickly took place, and other vigorous combatants now appeared upon the scene. Of these the most prominent was L. Marcius Philippus, whom we have met in his earlier character of a radical tribune of communistic tendencies and a reckless tongue. He had now changed his line of policy, perhaps partly from a conviction that there was really nothing to be done in the direction of colonies and land-allotments in Italy. Indeed there was little or no land to be got for such purposes without dispossessing somebody, and the evils of disturbing present tenures would be greater than the prospective benefits. But he had probably other reasons for opposing Drusus. He was a man of passionate intensity, and a most ready and forcible orator. He was now consul, and was in every respect a dangerous adversary. Another leader of the opposition was Q. Servilius Caepio, the man who had withstood Saturninus. He was married to a sister of Drusus, but the brothers-in-law[1] were now at loggerheads. He had no sympathy with the claims of the Allies, and his prosecution for *maiestas* had been conducted by an orator from Asculum; his own reply (for he was no great speaker) was made in a speech composed for him by a professor of rhetoric. But he was cunning and restless, and at this juncture it suited him to throw in his lot with the capitalist class. These two had at their back the solid support of the Equestrian Order. The popular masses were hardly concerned with the question of the juries, and any attraction that colonies might have for some of them was already weakened by the rumour actively circulated, that Drusus meant to enfranchise the Italians and swamp the present citizen body by giving a share of their privileges to this alien multitude. The result of the coming struggle was likely to depend in no small degree upon the line taken by the Senate. The pick of that body, Scaurus Antonius Crassus and others, were with Drusus, but that the rank and file of the senatorial nobility would stand by him was by no means certain. A split in the Senate would wreck the schemes of Drusus, for the *equites* were pretty sure to hang together.

829. Whatever were the details of the colonial bill, it was not likely to find favour with the landed interest, instinctively suspicious of change. Nor was the average senator likely to welcome any proposal by which the close character of the body would be modified and his own importance proportionately lessened. And the judicial bill of Drusus[2] seems to have had this tendency. The Senate at this

---

[1] The quarrel, attested by Dion Cass. frag. 96, is said by Pliny *NH* xxxiii § 20 to have started from their both bidding at an auction for the same ring !

[2] With much reluctance I dissent from the conclusions of Mr Strachan-Davidson on Appian *civ.* 1 35 and adhere to the common view.

time contained no more than about 300 members. If we allow for those at any time sick or absent on public or private business, the number was none too large[1] to secure a full House, and that the House should be always ready to meet at short notice was an essential principle of the constitution. Mere reasons of convenience pointed to the need of raising the total number, if the senatorial Order was to furnish the large juries[2] usual in the public courts. We are told that Drusus proposed to enlarge the Senate by adding to it 300 picked men of the Order of Knights and to transfer the judicial function to the Senate thus enlarged. He may have hoped by this mixture to weaken the opposition, but it would seem that he rather[3] strengthened it. Those of the Knights who might hope to be selected for promotion were perhaps content with the prospect, but their promotion would mean the passing over of the rest of the Order— probably a far larger number—who would have nothing to console them for the loss of a privilege the market-value of which was at times considerable, and which was a security for good returns on their provincial investments. Little it seems was gained in the way of breaking up the solid array of the capitalists. In the Senate a serious discontent was aroused. Some wished it is true to recover for their Order the control of the courts, but held that the addition of 300 new members was too great a price to pay for it. The old members would gain a half-share in the juries, but they would in the process lose half of the general power of directing the administration. This, their ancient prerogative, they had no mind to share with as many more. There might be formed a regular new-members' party, a Senate within the Senate, and the influence of the House would in consequence suffer. True, there were still many good men who backed up Drusus from belief in the necessity of the proposed reform: but the support of men acting on conviction, and ready for a policy of give-and-take, was not enough in the circumstances of the time to carry out effectively a compromise distasteful to the rank and file of the parties concerned.

830. In short the bill for reforming the *iudicia* set going such cross-currents of interest and opinion as to make the progress of the movement more difficult as time went by. Perhaps nothing

---

[1] For the questions about a Quorum see Mommsen *Staatsrecht* III 989. A member could call for a count (*numera!*).

[2] In the *lex Acilia repetundarum* a total *album iudicum* of 450 (*equites*) was prescribed. Out of 100 named by the claimant, the defendant could reject 50. And there might be more than one trial going on at once. Kiene, *Bundesgenossenkrieg* p. 163, thinks that the 300 Knights were not to be put in the Senate, mainly because of the objection of the Knights to be made punishable for judicial corruption. But their objection was natural in any case from their point of view.

[3] Appian *civ.* I 35, [Victor] *de vir. illustr.* 66.

strengthened the opposition more than the further proposal[1] of Drusus to make jurors liable to punishment for taking bribes. Judicial corruption was no new thing, and Gaius Gracchus had tried to check it by a law under which offenders could be prosecuted before the Assembly. But this clumsy procedure did not work, and the law, carried in the days of senatorial juries, was plausibly maintained not to apply to their Equestrian successors. Drusus seems to have proposed to render all jurors liable, and probably to set up a new standing court to try offenders. If such a scheme had been carried out, the result would most likely have been corruption in this court also: for the present every man, Senator or Knight, who might have a conscience to sell, entertained the sincerest objection to the design. Rome was now a scene of political confusion, and it seems that much public speaking in mass-meetings went on during the spring and summer of 91 without any vote of the Assembly being taken on the bills. The tribunician veto and the resources of religion were doubtless employed to obstruct progress. The patience of Drusus was overtaxed, and he was once provoked to order the forcible arrest and confinement of the consul Philippus. But the very virtues of the honourable tribune gave vantage in this teasing and wearisome struggle to his less scrupulous adversaries. The stories told of him[2] depict him as a man of candour and high principle, living honest in the sight of all men. It was in the moral atmosphere of his house that his nephew M. Porcius Cato, the hero of the falling Republic, passed his early childhood. One story implies that Drusus was already in negotiation with the leading men of the Allies. Another credits him with having forewarned his enemy Philippus of a plot laid against his life by Italian conspirators. The position of the tribune was evidently one of immense difficulty. He had on the one hand to keep quiet the Allies with the hope of a peaceful settlement of their claims, while on the other his influence was being undermined by malignant allegations that, if it were not for him, the Allies would be quiet enough. Other attacks[3] were made upon him, probably groundless, and old Scaurus suffered also for supporting him. Calumny soon developed into violence, and the whole city was divided into opposite camps. In a mad moment of irritation Drusus is said to have threatened to have Caepio thrown (like a criminal) from the Tarpeian rock. This was reviving the ancient powers of the tribunate with a vengeance.

---

[1] See in particular Cic. *pro Cluent.* §§ 150—5, *pro Rabir. Post.* § 16, Appian *civ.* I 35 §§ 5, 9.

[2] Velleius II 14, Plutarch *praec. de republ.* 4, Valer. Max. III 1 § 2, Plut. *Cato min.* 1, 2, Florus II 6 §§ 8, 9, [Victor] *de vir. illustr.* 66 § 12.

[3] References in Lange *RA* III 100, 101.

831.   At this point it is remarked that we have no direct tradition of any counter-proposal intended to supersede and get rid of the *rogationes Liviae*.   But we do hear of a certain Remmius as having been a colleague of Drusus in the aedileship.   It is ingeniously suggested[1] that this man was probably also tribune in the same year as Drusus, and was the author of a *lex Remmia* which was in operation[2] in the year 80 and seems to have remained in force for centuries.   It added another to the list of 'public' or criminal offences.   An accused person could declare that he was the victim of a false and vexatious charge.   If he was acquitted, his accuser was dealt with by the same jury on a charge of malicious prosecution (*calumnia*), and subjected, if found guilty, to severe penalties.   Whether this law is to be assigned to the year 91 must be left as a matter of conjecture.   But it can hardly be denied that it has the air of an attempt, whether sincere or not, to improve the working of the courts by holding, not the jurors, but the prosecutors, liable for miscarriages of justice only too likely to occur. Such an attempt would surely commend itself to the Equestrian Order generally.   Nor was the measure, whenever carried, in itself bad; but like other laws it was, in the hands of corrupt juries, open to abuse.

832.   The time was passing by in unprofitable bickering, and when September came[3] Drusus had accomplished nothing.   Indeed he was losing ground.   He still had a majority in the Senate, but it was probably getting weak.   The consul Philippus in a speech to a mass-meeting openly declared that he could not carry on the business of the state with a House like the present; as things stood, he would have to seek advisers elsewhere.   This was a hard saying, for the Senate was the proper advisory board of the consuls.   After the great *ludi Romani* (4—12 Sept.) were over, Drusus summoned the Senate, and strongly protested against this indecent behaviour.   He was followed by Crassus, who outdid his own reputation in the brilliancy of his invective, and met the consul's threats with defiance.   But the exertion was followed by a fatal chill, and in a few days the great orator was dead, taken away, says Cicero, from the evils to come.   So this effort to stiffen wavering senators against the bullying consul was not successful for long.   Soon after came the election of tribunes for the next year: Drusus did not seek reelection himself, and those candidates who would have continued his policy were defeated by men standing in the interest of the opposition.   Of these one was

---

[1] See Lange *RA* III 101.

[2] Cic. *pro Rosc. Am.* § 55 with scholiast, *Digest* XLVIII 16 1 § 2.   For *calumnia*, Asconius 55.   For Remmius, [Victor] *de vir. illustr.* 66 § 2.

[3] See Cic. *de orat.* III §§ 1—12, 1 §§ 24—5.

a man named[1] Q. Varius, destined to cause trouble. He was partly of Spanish origin, and it was doubtful whether he were by rights a Roman citizen at all. It was now clear that Drusus had only the remainder of his own year of office, a little over two months, in which to carry out his intended legislation. He put a brave face on his misfortunes, and made some change in his plans, but in truth his case was desperate. The exact detail of his later proceedings is lost in the loose expressions of rhetorical writers and stray notices of isolated facts devoid of the needful setting. To Appian[2], who gives us a kind of continuous narrative, the whole episode of the Livian legislation is only interesting as an event connected with the civil wars. Hence his account is so meagre as to be of little use, and his occasional inaccuracies leave it very doubtful whether he had any clear notion of the state of affairs in the Roman Republic more than 200 years before he wrote. The following version of the story is put together from various sources. It must be admitted that it is a strain[3] upon our powers of belief.

833. Drusus, beside his jury-bill, had on hand a bill for founding colonies, probably also one for further cheapening the state supply of corn. He now added to these a bill for land-allotments. But this was not enough. Whether to make good omissions in this scheme or for some other reason, it was followed up by another *lex agraria* proposed by one Saufeius, apparently a tribune. We hear also that Drusus debased[4] the currency, apparently in the hope of covering by this means some of the financial deficit resulting from the corn-law. This implies a *lex nummaria*. From an inscription[5] it appears that he was actually appointed a commissioner under the two land-laws. Ordinances forbidding such appointments had been already overridden in the cases of the Gracchi. The general tendency of the laws is inferred from the reported saying of Drusus that the dirt and daylight (*caelum et caenum*) were all that was now left for distribution. The difficulty of carrying all this legislation in so short a time by constitutional means was enormous, probably quite insuperable. Drusus had now entered on the demagogic path of his predecessors, and every step he took only proved more clearly[6] that he and the Senate must part company. He had to find supporters somewhere. The Equestrian Order was against him. The city mob, ever a broken reed to those

---

[1] Valer. Max. VIII 6 § 4, Cic. *de orat.* I § 117 and index.

[2] Appian *civ.* I 35, 36.

[3] The time at the disposal of Drusus seems insufficient.

[4] Not by alloying it, but by issuing plated *denarii* at face-value, according to Mommsen.

[5] Wilmanns 611 d, Orelli 544. See above §§ 652, 736.

[6] Pseudo-Sallust *de rep. ordin.* II 6 lays stress on the inability of the meaner nobles to appreciate the disinterested aims of Drusus.

who trusted it, was very susceptible to the influence of money and other means of personal solicitation, sure to be unsparingly used by his opponents. To the citizens from the country and the municipal towns the prospect of colonies and land-lots might appeal, at least to the landless and poor among them. But this was not enough, and it seems certain that Drusus in despair was driven to convert the friendly understanding between himself and the leaders of the Allies into a close political compact. At this time there was put into circulation a form purporting to be the solemn oath taken by a number of these men. A Greek version[1] of it is preserved, and its publication in Rome is attributed to the consul Philippus. Whether it was a fabrication or not; whether, if genuine, it is accurately rendered in the Greek; what were the exact terms of the promise doubtless made by Drusus on his part; these are questions on which opinions do and must differ, for certainty is beyond our reach. In this form as we have it the leaders of the Allies bind themselves by the most solemn oaths to have the same friends and enemies as Drusus, and to spare neither life nor child nor parent in following the common cause of Drusus and those bound under the same oath. If they are made citizens by the law of Drusus, they will look upon Rome as their country and Drusus as their greatest benefactor. Each undertakes to administer this oath to as many as he can[2] of his fellow-citizens, and invokes on himself, if faithful, a blessing, if faithless, a curse. Whether we do or do not accept the oath as a genuine document, the situation[3] implied in it is probably a fact. And that Drusus undertook to procure the Roman franchise for the Allies is in the face of our tradition not to be doubted. But he had ceased to represent the views of the majority of the Senate. In so manifest a revolution they were not ready to bear a part. The reform of the juries was what concerned them, and the jury-bill of Drusus was in itself hardly to their mind. To the rest of his schemes they were opposed, and the tribune was driven to rely on non-resident voters and a host of non-citizen rioters, that is on force used in defiance of the laws.

834. But after arousing so many expectations and enmities it was not possible for him to stop. It appears that he tacked several bills together, that he disregarded reports of unfavourable auspices, and carried the combined measure by force. In it were included (1) the

---

[1] Diodorus frag. XXXVII 11 [ὅρκος Φιλίππου].

[2] That is, in the community to which each of the original associates belonged.

[3] The story in Diodor. fragm. XXXVII 13 of the march of Pompaedius Silo with 10,000 men on Rome, and of his turning back at the friendly admonition of a certain Domitius, who begged him not to put pressure on the Senate, already well disposed to the claims of the Allies, is in several points obscure. I do not see my way to drawing any safe inferences from it.

judiciary law, (2) probably the colonial and agrarian laws, (3) perhaps the corn-law. What connexion there was between his schemes for colonies and land-allotments is far from clear. We hear of Italian opposition, particularly in Etruria and Umbria, to his colonial proposals, apparently[1] on the part of rich Allies, who still held parcels of state domain-land, and feared disturbance. On the passing of the combined law, Philippus summoned the Senate, intending to have the act declared invalid. Drusus still kept a bold front to his enemies, but they now had drawn over all the weak and wavering members to their side. Prejudiced and alarmed, the House upheld the religious and constitutional scruples urged, and declared[2] that the *lex Livia* was not binding on the people. It is said[3] that Drusus did not as tribune choose to veto this decree: if the Senate would not accept his proposals, they would surely bear the consequences. He went on to keep his promise to the Allies by arranging to put the law for their enfranchisement to the vote. But he was not destined to carry out this part of his policy. He had lately had one of the epileptic fits to which he was subject, and the prayers and vows of Italy shewed at once what a value the Allies set upon their champion's life. Many in Rome were known to desire his death, and he now seldom went abroad, but did his business at home. His house would accordingly be filled with visitors: and one evening he suddenly cried out that he was wounded. So it was, and he died of the wound, but none knew[4] who did the deed, nor was any public inquiry held. Suspicion fastened upon his enemies, in particular on some of those[5] whose names have been mentioned as bitter opponents of his policy. There can be little doubt that we have here a case of deliberate murder perpetrated in the interest of faction; nor shall we do much injustice if with Mommsen we regard the nameless assassin as the representative of the Roman capitalists.

835. Such was the end of Drusus, young, high-born, rich, cultivated, brave, and still holding the great inviolable office of tribune. That he was a sincere and unselfish patriot is beyond doubt. His death left unsolved the problems with which he and his forerunners attempted to deal. The social questions of land and colonies were never really solved, nor was any real solution possible in a civilization based on slavery. The corruption of the jury-courts, and the oppression of Rome's provincial subjects, were evils that nothing but the establish-

---

[1] If we may believe Appian *civ.* I 36.
[2] Cic. *de legibus* II §§ 14, 31, *de domo*, §§ 41, 50, Asconius 68.
[3] Diodorus XXXVII 10.
[4] Cicero *pro Milone* § 16 compares this case with that of Scipio in 129 B.C.
[5] Varius, Philippus, Caepio.

ment of a strong central power could mitigate. While the Republic lasted, the complication of party interests and private ambitions nullified all projects of reform. The great problem of the Allies was immediately solved in the only way now possible, by the sword. But its solution brought neither peace nor health to the body-politic. For the Republic was past mending, and it could not be ended without a long and terrible agony. Drusus was the last of the civilian reformers. Rome was just now engaged in no great war, and it is to be noted that we hear nothing of Marius in connexion with the agitations of this troubled year. Sulla had gone to the East in 92, but with the never-failing good luck on which he prided himself he was back at Rome in time to win the chief glory in the coming war. The movement of Drusus was thus independent of the great military leaders. But the recent disbanding of large and highly-trained armies had scattered over Italy a vast number of soldiers, most of whom had little means of subsistence and probably less taste for agriculture, and were awaiting in idleness the call to arms.

CHAPTER XLIII

THE GREAT ITALIAN OR MARSIC WAR 90—87 B.C.

836. THE last hope of a peaceful settlement[1] of the claims of the Allies was removed by the murder of Drusus. Ever since the passing of the *lex Licinia Mucia* in 95 negotiations had been going on between the leaders of the various Italian treaty-states in preparation for the last necessity of war. So far had their agreement been carried that, when war broke out, these detached communities, isolated by all the ingenuity of Roman statecraft, appeared at once as a League with a ready-made constitution. We even hear[2] of a body of 10,000 men marching on Rome in the lifetime of Drusus to support the tribune in his proposal to extend the franchise, and only induced to return home by assurances of the Senate's goodwill conveyed through a Roman emissary. At any rate military preparations were already far advanced when Drusus fell, and the revolt began without delay. The first outbreak occurred at Asculum in Picenum. A Roman officer, sent to quell disaffection, provoked the rage of the people. His murder was followed by a general massacre of all Romans present in the town. The sword was now drawn, and in a few days the Marsi Paeligni Vestini Marrucini Samnites and Lucani were up in arms. In short, all the chief military peoples of north-central and southern Italy were arrayed against Rome for the express purpose of becoming Romans. We are not to suppose that any theories of the rights of man, or any desire to bear an active part in the general direction of government, were the motives of this rebellion. It was practical needs, the urgency of which had been impressed upon their minds by long and bitter experience, that drove the Allies unwillingly to war with Rome.

837. The time had been when Rome, content to win and keep the headship of Italy, had followed a wise and moderate policy towards the conquered. Some of them she incorporated as inferior members of the Roman state, to others she granted treaties, more or less favourable according to circumstances. Her aims and motives

---

[1] Kiene, *der Römische Bundesgenossenkrieg* (Leipzig 1845), is a most learned and ingenious treatise. I think it sometimes too ingenious, but desire to confess no small obligations to it. I have not accepted the name 'Social war,' for which there is little authority.

[2] Diodor. fragm. XXXVII 13.

were selfish, but on the whole she kept good faith, and her practice as Leader was certainly no worse, probably much better, than that of other powers whose conquests form part of the history of the ancient world. That some power should take the lead in Italy, and that the weaker or less competent communities should bear their share of military burdens, renouncing the lust of internal warfare, were necessary conditions, if Italy was to work out its own destinies free from external interference. Against the Gauls, against Pyrrhus, against Hannibal, Rome successfully asserted her protectorate, and the failure of the invaders had been primarily due to the solidity of her organization. To her the Italian peoples owed that their strength was made effective and able to stand the strain of disaster. So far she had done well by the peninsula, and the service of the allied contingents was but a moderate contribution to the defence of a common interest. To interfere in the internal affairs of the treaty-states was no part of Roman policy; but in any rearrangement of relations necessitated by events care was taken to place the pro-Roman party in a position to control the local government. That the party thus favoured was that of the wealthy was due to no peculiarity in Roman statesmanship. A minority consisting of men with something to lose was more likely to act loyally by the leading power than a reckless and indigent majority. The local autonomy enjoyed by the Italian Allies was greatly prized. The offer of full Roman citizenship was not always[1] accepted as a reward: the half-citizenship had often been imposed as a punishment. But with foreign policy the Allies had nothing to do. Rome was their one representative, and it was with Rome as the Head of Italy that the powers abroad engaged in peace or war.

838. Foreign conquests, and the change in the relation of Rome to her Italian Allies, were alike inevitable. Kingdoms and Federations, tribes and city-states, were overthrown. Various settlements, temporary or permanent, were made for the government of the various countries; but foreign allies, provincial subjects, protected areas, and client-kings, all saw their mistress in Rome. Rome had become an imperial power. The day of Pydna disclosed the truth that she was the one imperial power. To this height she had risen by a skilful use of the forces of Italy, but the profits of empire were monopolized by her own citizens. It was natural that the Allies should wish to share the privileges and perquisites of Romans, but Romans were now less disposed to share their advantages with Allies on whom, as virtually subjects, they looked down with contempt. The gradual admission of half-citizens to the full Roman franchise only deepened the gulf

---

[1] See above §§ 192, 310, 624, 735.

between Citizen and Ally. All the irritating and injurious distinctions in respect of military punishments remained, and were more and more felt as a practical grievance, while the unpopular service in such countries as Spain was more and more reserved for the contingents of Allies. Even the sound old practice of equal rewards to those who had taken part in the same campaign was no longer to be relied on. Moreover both Citizens and Allies were profoundly affected by the growth of the Provincial system. Pride luxury and greed were fostered in numbers of Romans, while political morality was sapped by the temptations of absolute power. The Allies on the other hand might see how little Roman nobles cared for the wishes and interests of those subject to their rule, and the object-lesson can hardly have been lost upon them. Nor was the cheapening of corn in Rome at the cost of the state calculated to please those who viewed it from outside. Not only were they themselves without share in the privilege, but the decay of Italian agriculture was of no advantage to any of the Allies, and probably did harm to some. The growth of the city mob and its political significance cannot have escaped the notice of Italian observers. At any moment some measure injuriously affecting the Allies might be carried by the votes of a rabble ever becoming more mongrel in its composition and more unfit to decide political issues. With the grievous change in their position relatively to Rome the Allies could not possibly be contented. But there were considerations that might check bold spirits capable of seeking redress by force. There was the fact of local autonomy guaranteed by treaties, the use of Roman state-lands granted to some at least of the subordinate communities; moreover some of the men might hope to improve their status[1] by migration. But the Roman nobles began to act in an arbitrary manner towards the Allies, and tyrannical disregard of treaty-rights became a possibility too often realized in practice as time went on. The attempts of ordinary Allies to settle in Latin towns, and so to acquire the special privileges of Latins, and of Latins to acquire the Roman franchise, were firmly checked. At last Roman reformers began to tamper with the existing arrangements in the matter of the public land, and it was probably the wealthier men among the Allies, the very class on whose interested loyalty Rome had relied, that were most directly affected by the change.

839. There could no longer be any doubt that the only road to relief from present oppression and to security for the future lay through the attainment of the Roman franchise in its most effective form. Once fairly enrolled in the 35 Tribes, the sorely-tried Italians would find their troubles cease. This became their first object, and

[1] See above § 628.

the frequent presence of large numbers of *socii* in Rome was probably
in part the result of this conviction. But the confusion and corruption
of Roman politics were ever growing, and formed a fatal obstacle to
the peaceful and reasonable settlement of their claim. If they trusted
to reforming tribunes, the senatorial nobility were against them ; and
the reformers too could not do without the city populace, who viewed
the claim of the Allies with selfish jealousy. Then came the inquiry
of Crassus and Scaevola, by which illegal usurpation of citizen rights
was sternly repressed. A fraud that had been winked at was thus
put a stop to, but this meant that force was to be the only remedy.
Last of all came the hopes and disappointment of the well-meant
movement of Drusus, supported though it had been by the best of
the Roman nobles, who saw the necessity of concession at the
eleventh hour. Patience could go no further. Thanks to the efforts
of their leaders, the difficulties in the way of combined action by the
Allies had been overcome, and it was not their confederated units,
but the centralized Roman government, that was taken unprepared.
The considerations set forth above were doubtless present to the
minds of the Allies in general. But in one part of Italy at least
the effect of practical grievances was greatly intensified by sentiment.
In their hill-country, remote from the main lines of traffic, the dalesmen of Samnium, still speaking their Oscan dialect, retained much
of the old habits and traditions of their fathers. They and their
territory were but the relics of the once great Samnite confederacy,
of old dismembered by Rome. To them Pyrrhus and Hannibal
might appear to have been not enemies repulsed but deliverers that
had failed, and their connexion with Rome would seem not so much
the due allegiance to a welcome protector as a bondage associated
with ancient memories of wrong.

840. At Rome the news of the outbreak in Picenum and the
spread of armed rebellion, accompanied of course by suitable prodigies, caused the profoundest alarm. The gown of civil life was
commonly discarded for the military cloak: it was felt that this was
no ordinary war, but a war at their very doors, a *tumultus*, and that
not, as of yore, the work of invading Gauls, but a life-and-death
struggle with the best and bravest peoples of Italy. Yet such was
the miserable state of Roman public life that even the panic of the
hour did not induce the dominant politicians to waive or defer
vengeance on their beaten opponents. Even nobles were found[1] to
lay the blame of having brought matters to the present pass on the
dead Drusus. But this cowardly lie was not enough for the party
now in power, of which the Equestrian capitalists were the kernel.

[1] Pliny *NH* xxv § 52.

They had carried the elections for the year 90, and some (probably a majority) of the new tribunes were in their interest. Entering on office in December 91, one of them, the mongrel Q. Varius, proposed a bill[1] to appoint a special court to inquire into the responsibility of persons accused of having caused the rebellion of the Allies. A tribune blocked it, but the *intercessio* was disregarded, not for the first time, and the Assembly, coerced by the presence of armed men, passed it into law. It only remained to choose the scapegoats, who were quickly found among the supporters of Drusus. The charge was one of treason (*maiestas*), and some of the best men in Rome were put on their trial as betrayers of their country. Among them was old Scaurus, the venerable *princeps senatus*. Varius had recently, in the first flush of his tribunate, summoned him to trial before the Assembly, but he is said to have escaped this danger by calling attention to the absurdity of the situation: was he, a Roman of Romans, to be declared a traitor at the instance of a Spanish half-breed? And now also, under the Varian law, his bitter enemy Caepio seems to have been unable to procure his condemnation. But for men of less influence there was no mercy. Some were condemned, some found safety in flight, few were acquitted. Among the victims was one of the associates of Drusus, C. Aurelius Cotta, who had stood for the tribunate and been rejected. Thus, while the rebellion was spreading, and armies being raised hastily to meet it, the capitalist juries were busied with the congenial task of driving their opponents into exile. In the Senate too their party had gained the upper hand. Taking advantage of an opportunity, the House passed an order suspending the action of the ordinary law-courts during the continuance of the present crisis. Only the proceedings of the Varian commission pursued their course.

841. Before we speak of the campaigns that took place in the Italian war we must consider the nature of our authorities and the geographical situation. Of the former all historical critics agree that they are most unsatisfactory. The loss of the work[2] of L. Cornelius Sisenna, which contained a narrative of the war, is irreparable. Not only was he a contemporary (119—67 B.C.), but from the praise bestowed on him by Sallust we may infer that his sympathies were rather with the democratic or Marian party than with Sulla and the senatorial nobles. He may have been fairly impartial: at all events

---

[1] For *lex Varia* and the commission see especially Cicero *Brutus* §§ 304—5, *pro Scauro* § 3, *pro Cornel.* frag. 29, Asconius pp. 22, 79, Appian *civ.* I 37, and indices to Cic. and Valer. Max.

[2] The fragments of Sisenna's history are collected in Peter *hist. Rom. fragm.* pp. 175—189. Very little can be gleaned from them in detail, but they constantly bear witness to the stubborn fighting in the war, and sometimes to the internal troubles of Rome.

his account would have given us some solid matter to check the versions now current, tainted as these all are more or less by the influence of writings representing the views of the side victorious in that civil war which grew out of, and was indeed a part of, the war with the Allies. For as time went on the line of party cleavage in Roman life and literature became more and more that between democratic and reactionary factions, and a calm impartiality in treating of the recent past was hardly possible. Now in our surviving notices of the Italian war it is clearly the Sullan tradition that holds the field. To make a fair allowance for the corruption of truth arising from this influence, and yet not to allow too much, is a most delicate and difficult task. Plutarch in his biographies of Marius and Sulla says hardly anything of the war in detail; his general statement, that it lowered the reputation of Marius and raised that of his rival, is probably gathered from Sulla's own memoirs. The loss of this part[1] of Livy's history has no doubt deprived us of a great mass of facts that would have thrown light on many a dark place. From the surviving epitomes, and the echoes of his work in the brief summaries of Florus Eutropius Orosius and others, we can dimly see that he too was under the influence of the Sullan tradition. A few remarkable details relative to the war are preserved in the fragments[2] of Diodorus, and in particular the account of the constitution set up by the confederates. Our fullest narrative[3] comes from another Greek writer, Appian. He seems to be honest enough, and indeed a historian writing in the second century A.D. had no concern with the passions that had distorted the story of this war. But the omissions, and the occasional blunders occurring in his work, make it necessary to use his evidence with peculiar care. What little we have from Velleius[4] is of value, though mainly confined to generalities. Himself of Italian extraction, he puts on record the loyal services of an ancestor to Rome in this crisis, but asserts with authority the justice of the confederates' cause. In other writers we have only detached references to particular events. The value of Cicero's utterances as usual varies with their occasion and setting. The geographer[5] Strabo, Pliny the Elder, the anecdotes of Valerius Maximus and Frontinus, supply a few notes. Of this part of the history of Dion Cassius[6] two small but significant fragments remain.

---

[1] Livy ep. 72—77, Florus II 6, Eutropius v 3, Orosius v 18, [Victor] de viris illustr. 63, 67, 72, 75.

[2] Diodorus XXXVII.

[3] Appian civ. I 38—64, with notes of Mr Strachan-Davidson.

[4] Velleius II 15—18, 20 § 2, 21 § 1, 29 § 1.

[5] Strabo v passim, VI 1.

[6] Dion Cass. fragm. 98, 100.

In this miscellany of tradition many discrepancies[1] occur. Events are grouped round different persons and different places, and in one important constitutional point we have a conflict of evidence which modern ingenuity has never been able to reconcile. Still on the whole the agreement of our authorities is far more remarkable than their divergence. The meagreness of the evidence is the great obstacle to the extraction of the truth. We move as in a twilight, and the intermittent gleams of certainty serve rather to dazzle the eye than to aid us in finding the right path through the darker and broader intervals between.

842. We will now take the map of Italy[2] and work down it from North to South, tracing as best we can the ways in which the physical features of the country and the political geography resulting from past history affected the strategic situation at the time when the rebellion broke out. It will be convenient to divide the long peninsula into blocks, and to prefix the letter A or R to each, according as the part under consideration was a stronghold of the Allies or of Rome.

With Cisalpine Gaul and Liguria we have little or nothing to do. The strong Latin and citizen colonies, and the settlers planted on confiscated lands, could probably have held the country for Rome in any case, and growing prosperity tended to keep it quiet. Individual Gauls served on the side of the Allies, apparently as mercenaries; but some of these at least may have come from beyond the Alps. Whether Rome drew any recruits other than Gauls from the Cisalpine lands is not certain, but she had for some time past enlisted Ligurians in her armies, and probably did so now. Italy proper began at the Aesis on the N.E. coast and the Macra on the S.W.

(A) The northern parts of Etruria and Umbria were still mainly in the hands of their old population. Their position was that of Allies. The old Etruscan nobility, and the cities in which they chiefly dwelt, were much decayed, but a considerable force could still be raised in the country. The Etruscans had never in historical times been famous for effective cooperation. The Allies in Umbria held for the most part a hilly district, and the Apennine range must have rendered communications difficult. That there was no lack of discontent in these parts was proved in the sequel. For the present the Etruscans and Umbrians had not declared against Rome.

---

[1] A good instance in detail is the siege of Pinna. In Diodor. XXXVII 19, 20, it is bravely held for Rome, but Valer. Max. V 4 ext. § 7 makes the Romans the besiegers. The former is probably right. That there were two sieges of Pinna is improbable. See *rhet. ad Herenn.* II § 45.

[2] In this section many hints have been taken from Beloch's work *der Italische Bund* (with map), and the maps of Italy in the Müller-Grundy series (Murray).

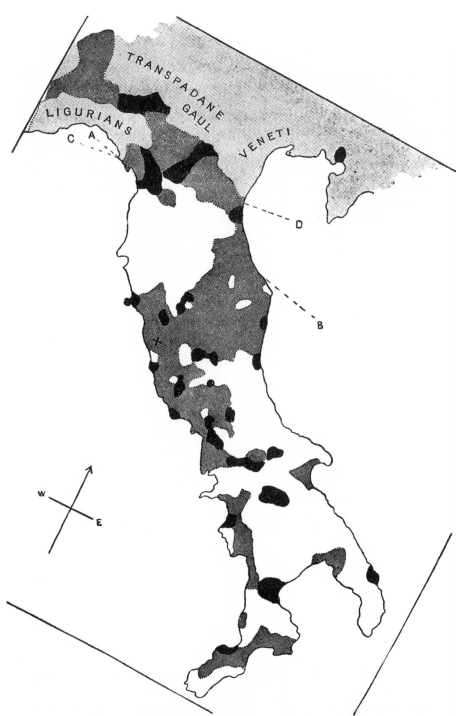

Map of Italy 90 B.C., shewing Roman territory in dark-hatching (Rome is marked with a cross), the Latin Colonies of the Roman People in black, and the territory of Treaty-states in white. The dotted line AB is the official limit of Italy proper, from the Macra (West) to the Aesis (East). CD is the line from the Macra to the Rubicon. For the question of the advance of the official limit see § 921. The map is adapted from that in Beloch's *Italische Bund*.

(R) We next come to a great belt of Roman territory extending across Italy from sea to sea. On the N.E. coast the Latin colonies of Ariminum to the N. and Hatria to the S. mark the limits of a piece of seaboard all actually or virtually Roman. On the S.W. coast the stretch from the Latin colony of Cosa down to Ostia was strongly held by citizen colonies. Inland, the large districts of southern Etruria, eastern Umbria, and Picenum, were in general *ager Romanus*, held either by great landlords as plantations or by Roman settlers on rural allotments, or by the old inhabitants, at first made half-citizens but now enjoying the full franchise, or towards the N. by citizen colonies on or near the coast. To these we must add several Latin colonies, once outposts of the Roman advance northwards. Imbedded in this block of territory held for Rome were a few communities of Allies, such as the Umbrian Camerinum and the Greek or half-Greek Ancona, the chief seaport of the N.E. coast. These two remained faithful to Rome, but a third, the Picentine Asculum, was a hotbed of rebellion. Its isolation compelled the rebel leaders to make great efforts for its relief, and its position made the Romans desire its capture. For it lay on the line by which alone the confederates could establish a military connexion with the Allies in Umbria and Etruria, and to prevent this connexion was the object of Rome. South of Asculum lay the mountainous land of the Sabines. But Sabines as such had disappeared: they had long been full Roman citizens, and their hills were a stronghold of Rome. Thus to pierce the Apennine or pass to the N. of that range to stir up or support an Umbro-Etrurian rising was a matter of extreme difficulty. It only seemed possible to the confederate generals because of the present weakness of Rome.

(R) Continuous with this important belt to the N. of Rome were the districts E. and S.E. of the city, in which the Roman power had long taken deep root. To the E. were the Latin colonies of Carsioli and Alba, watching the northern frontier of the Marsi, and some states of old Latin and Hernican Allies, all greatly Romanized and true to Rome. Mixed up with them were stretches of *ager Romanus* held by communities long since merged in the Roman state, and some of the Latin colonies founded in early days. Rome's advance southwards and her old wars with the Samnites were recorded in the Latin and citizen colonies guarding the coast and the roads into Campania. Moreover in all this country the old leagues and tribes were long extinct: whatever might remain of Aequi Volsci Aurunci Sidicini was now all Roman. Long internal peace and the changes in agriculture had perhaps somewhat impaired the military strength of the free population here as in southern Etruria: but these districts were still a formidable bulwark barring the approaches to Rome.

(A) To the E. and N. of this Roman block lay a solid mass of the minor hill-peoples, Marsi Paeligni Vestini Marrucini, reaching from the Apennine to the Adriatic seaboard. South of these again were the remaining Samnites and the Frentani along the coast to the E. of them. They seem to have been still in loosely federated groups of cantons much as their fathers of old. As Allies they had been invaluable, for the flower of the Italian infantry was drawn from this region, and they had upheld the power of Rome on many a hard-fought field. Armed and trained in the Roman manner, led by good officers of their own, no better fighting material could be found. But it is not likely that their generals had as much practice in handling large bodies of troops as some of the more experienced Roman commanders. Nor could it have been easy for them to attain all at once the effective unity of action that successful strategy requires. Of the northern division of these peoples, the Marsi were nearest to Rome, and from them the struggle was commonly spoken of as the Marsic war. It was their task to keep Rome employed with a northern campaign, and if possible to call the Umbro-Etruscan Allies to arms. The southern or Samnite division had work in other quarters. Into the Samnite country projected the Latin colony of Aesernia, a fortress which became a bone of contention, offering as it did great advantage to the side that held it.

(R) South of this group of peoples, the headquarters of the rebellion, lay the rich land of Campania. Here was a considerable stretch of *ager Romanus*, held by state-lessees, as in the district of Capua, or by citizen colonies on the coast. In the middle were a number of important cities of Allies from Nola and Nuceria inland to Neapolis and the other towns that fringed the bay. Here was a meeting-ground of civilizations. The descendants of the old Samnite conquerors were numerous, and the Oscan tongue and Sabellian traditions by no means extinct. Greek influences were still strong in the maritime districts, and doubtless told in favour of Rome. But they had probably hindered the Romanizing of the inland districts, the loyalty of which proved doubtful, and caused this neighbourhood to become one of the principal seats of war. Still Campania as a whole was at first in Roman hands, and the confederates could only win control of its resources by force. This they had every inducement to do. To the S.E. of the shrunken latter-day Samnium lay the Latin colonies of Beneventum and Luceria, and between them a settlement of transplanted Ligurians. This was a creation of Roman policy, a barrier between the northern Samnites and their kinsmen the Hirpini and Lucani beyond. To turn and isolate this Roman barrier-block, or to pierce and conquer it, was no doubt an object with the leaders of the rebels.

(R) The southern coast of Lucania and the isthmus, from Paestum to Copia (Thurii), was held by Romans or faithful Allies, and the mixed arrangements of the Bruttian peninsula need not detain us, as they do not concern our present purpose.

(A) The Hirpini and the inland Lucani were descended from the Sabellian invaders of old time, a sort of continuation of Samnium, conquered isolated and turned to account by Rome. Their rebellion added a very large area to the territory of the confederacy. Whether their military support was proportionately valuable is not so certain. The great Latin colony of Venusia was a thorn in the side of these southern rebels, and to capture that fortress was a prime object.

(A ?) To the N. of these peoples lay the country of which we hear by the general name Apulia. In it were remains of the primitive race or races driven southward by the Sabellians. Its population was thus not homogeneous, and it seems never to have been easy to unite the diverse sections in common action. A patch of *ager Romanus* and the citizen colony Sipontum broke up the continuous mass of Apulian Allies. There was discontent in Apulia as elsewhere, but the presence of a confederate army and the capture of Venusia were necessary if the embers of discontent were to be fanned into flame.

(R) The S.E. heel of Italy lay outside the range of the war. The Latin colony of Brundisium and the citizen colony at Tarentum mark the Roman possession of these all-important ports. And in this connexion we may pause to observe that all the centres of maritime traffic were in Roman hands. Rome had no special anxiety in reference to sea-port towns. Those held by Allies, such as Neapolis and Rhegium, were at least largely Greek, and looked to Rome as their head.

843. In considering the geography of Italy from the point of view of the great rebellion, we have had to indicate the main necessary aims of strategy on the side of the Allies. The chief points of Roman policy in encountering these aims may be summarized as follows.

(*a*) To keep the Etruscans and Umbrians apart from the original rebels, and to prevent or quickly suppress a rising in those parts. The means used were the northern campaigns, the siege of Asculum, and the *lex Iulia* of 90 B.C.

(*b*) To cover Rome. This was best done by taking the offensive, particularly against the Marsi and the rest of that group of rebel Allies.

(*c*) To hold Campania and hinder the combined action of the Samnites and their confederates further South. This was the object of the southern campaigns, only effected after the failure of the rebellion in the North.

(*d*) To prevent help reaching the rebels from abroad, while drawing as much foreign help as possible for the cause of Rome. This was secured[1] by the control of the sea-coast.

(*e*) To weaken the rebels by promoting desertions. This was effected by the *lex Plautia Papiria* of 89 B.C.

844. For the revolted Allies some centre was necessary as the headquarters of the confederate government. This was found at Corfinium in the Paelignian country on the eastern side of the Apennine. It was renamed Italia in honour of the movement, and became a central depot of arms money and stores. The political constitution contained the time-honoured elements of Senate and Magistrates. If we may trust the details as given by Diodorus, the Senate consisted of 500 members, and was entrusted with absolute powers. By whom, our informant does not say, but they were in some way delegates[2] from the confederate peoples, and that every unit of importance sent delegates is not to be doubted: the limited number can hardly be otherwise explained. This omnipotent Senate was a common organ for dealing with a great emergency. It was thus *de iure* what the Roman Senate was *de facto*: we are not however to assume that they were meant to retain such extensive legal powers in time of peace. No doubt they were picked men, the leaders of their several states. We are told that they were expected to make appointments out of their own number; appointments of magistrates (that is, generals), and a select council[3] to deliberate on the common interest. At this point they clearly began to copy Roman models. The Senate adopted the system of 'collegiality.' There were to be two yearly consuls and 12 praetors. For purposes of the war Italy was to be divided into two consular provinces, and each consul was to have six praetors in his department. The chief command in the northern district was entrusted to Q. Pompaedius Silo the Marsian, the chief promoter of the rebellion: C. Papius Mutilus the Samnite held the corresponding position in the South. Precautions had been taken to secure the adhesion of communities suspected of Roman

---

[1] The importance of this point is also well brought out by Nissen (*Landeskunde* I 340) in connexion with the rebel capital. Corfinium was a strong fortress, but it was three times as far from the sea as Rome was.

[2] It is tempting to follow Kiene p. 190 in speaking of this institution as the beginning of a real representative constitution, but I think he assumes too much.

[3] I can see no other meaning to be got out of the words οἱ προβουλεύεσθαι δυνάμενοι in Diodor. XXXVII 2 § 5. In Dionys. Hal. IV 76, V 1, we find πρόβουλος used to translate *consul*. No doubt the consuls were included.

leanings, by taking hostages from them. The unity of the confederacy was symbolized in a common coinage, the legend on which was either Latin or Oscan, according to the dialect prevailing in the northern or southern parts. For the present the unity was real enough: leaders and peoples worked together for a common cause. But the sequel betrayed the truth, a commonplace in the history of rebellions, that the ringleaders of the movement were prepared to go further than their followers. Many thousands simply looked upon the war as the only road to the Roman franchise. If others, such as Pompaedius and Papius, aimed at setting up a new Italian compound state, their ambition would not appeal to men of more limited views, and Rome, compared with any new venture of the kind, exercised the attraction of her successful past. If the minor peoples, unable to stand alone, must merge themselves in some larger unit, not a few would prefer to form part of a system long established. And to those who cast a greedy eye upon the perquisites of empire it might occur that, if they overthrew Rome, they were not likely to win that empire for themselves. In short, the present unity was at any moment liable to be loosened by a reasonable hope of Roman concessions. For battles the confederacy was strong in the bravery of its hardy soldiers. For a protracted war it was not so strong as it looked. Only the Samnite element was inspired by the grim hatred able to endure the strain of sacrifices and the ups and downs of war.

845. Before the regular campaign of the year 90, in the winter of 91—90, a good deal was done on both sides. The fate of Servilius at Asculum had shewn that the Allies were no longer to be overawed. A state of war now existed, and the rebels found the firstfruits of their rising in a way that illustrates the relations of imperial Rome to her Italian Allies. A Cilician pirate-captain[1] had fallen into Roman hands, but had somehow managed to compound for his life. Following past precedents, the Roman Senate packed off the troublesome prisoner into the charge of the magistrates of Asculum. The man was known to be skilled in irregular warfare. He was now set free, and entered the rebel service. In a short time he was at the head of a robber band, and did much damage in Roman territory. The case of Servilius was not an isolated one. Another Roman emissary[2] was seized by the Lucanians when the revolt spread to the South, but escaped with his life through a woman's pity. Probably the same sort of adventures occurred in other parts. Q. Sertorius[3] was quaestor in Cisalpine Gaul, and orders were sent him to raise troops for the

---

[1] Diodorus XXXVII 16, Orosius V 18 § 10.
[2] Livy ep. 72.
[3] Plutarch *Sertor.* 4, Sallust fragm. I 88 Maurenbrecher.

war now imminent. This he did with energy, and a strong Gaulish contingent was added to the available forces of Rome. Meanwhile the Latin colonies[1] were responding to the call for aid. This must not be taken to include them all. The far-off Aquileia can hardly be meant, and Venusia can hardly have sent away troops, with the enemy on all sides threatening her safety. But the support of the Latins was no doubt general. Among the Allies, beside Greek cities, a few stood by Rome. The town of Pinna in the Vestini was an example; not even to save the lives of their children (hostages, of course) would they join the rebels. But such cases were clearly very rare. In the Hirpinian district a local noble[2] raised a legion for Rome, whether just at this juncture is uncertain. This too was exceptional, nor do we know what prospects he may have held out to his recruits. We do however hear that foreign troops fought for Rome in this war. For instance, a Numidian[3] corps is mentioned, and there were in all likelihood others. Ihne truly remarks that Roman writers were never prone to admit how much Rome depended on external aid; and in this war the temptation to conceal unwelcome facts would be even greater than usual. The story of the Cretan bowman[4] indicates the presence of mercenaries on the rebel side. He was higgling with a Roman consul for the price of treacherously deserting his present employers at a pinch. At the offer of Roman citizenship he laughed: such nonsense had no value for a Cretan, and the Roman was forced to promise him 1000 drachmae payable on due performance of his share of the bargain. In short, the efforts made to raise forces adequate to maintain what all saw to be a desperate struggle were far greater and more widespread than our fragmentary record tells us in detail. The general statements as to the immense scale of this war and its momentous results are not to be received as exaggerations.

846. An embassy from the confederates[5] appeared in Rome with a statement of the past services and present claim of the Allies. But the Senate could not now give up the Roman position by negotiating with them as an independent power. They refused to treat with them unless they were prepared to lay down their arms. So war went on, and according to Appian the confederate field-army amounted to 100,000 men beside the separate local forces of the several states. The Romans managed to put about the same number into the field.

---

[1] Livy ep. 72. [2] Velleius II 16.

[3] Appian *civ.* I 42 §§ 5, 6. He calls them Νομάδας Μαυρουσίους, but the context rather implies that they were Numidians. See below §§ 847, 852. The story of two ships from Heraclea Pontica serving Rome in this war is too much mixed up with geographical error to be taken for certain. Memnon in *Fragm. hist. Graec.* III p. 540.

[4] Diodorus XXXVII 18. [5] Appian *civ.* I 39.

The rebels were already besieging Alba and Aesernia, and the relief of these two fortresses was urgent, when the consuls of the year 90, L. Iulius Caesar Strabo and P. Rutilius Lupus, started for the seats of war. Each commander was provided with a staff of five *legati* competent to act as generals of division in case the war (as seemed likely) led to scattered operations at many points. Among those who served under Caesar in the southern department was Sulla, with Rutilius in the northern were Cn. Pompeius Strabo, consul in the following year, and the veteran Marius. The choice of the ten *legati* seems to have been made solely on the ground of military skill. But the consuls themselves had been appointed by popular election as usual, and were probably nominees of the political party that over-threw Drusus and were opposed to the Italian claims. Party-feeling was of course by no means extinct in Rome. Open strife was for the moment hushed, but the concessionist nobles who had favoured Drusus were continually reminded of painful memories by the pro-ceedings of the Varian court of treason. Political differences between men of different sympathies might impair the mutual confidence of high officers, and it is not unlikely that such influences did actually at times corrupt the harmony of the camp.

847. The southern campaign of this year was disastrous for Rome. The consul Caesar seems to have marched to relieve Aesernia. After a defeat he threw himself into the town, but soon had to leave it to its fate, and was beaten again as he withdrew. The siege was resumed, and before the end of the year famine compelled the sur-render of the place. Meanwhile a Roman force operating in Lucania suffered a severe defeat, and an invasion of Apulia by the rebels brought over a number of places to the side of the confederates, some of them without the use of force. Chief among these, if we may believe Appian[1], was the great Latin colony of Venusia: at all events it was lost to Rome. But, while his lieutenants were winning victories on all sides, the most serious blow to Roman power and resources was delivered by Papius himself with his main army. He burst into Campania, where there would seem to have been no Roman force able to hold him in check, and where many sympathized with the rebellion. Nola was won by treachery, the Roman officers killed, and the garrison taken into the confederate service. He even reached the coast, and took Stabiae and Salernum. Nuceria[2] stood firm for Rome, and the devastation of its lands was the penalty. Other towns now joined him, and added a reinforcement of 11,000 men, freemen and slaves, to his army. The slaves were probably the property of rich men, either Romans or partisans of Rome. He next under-

---

[1] Appian *civ.* I 39 § ·, 42 § 7.   [2] See map in § 310 above.

took the siege of Acerrae, and Caesar, now strengthened by a strong corps of Gauls and some Numidians, advanced to oppose him. Here we get another peep into the ways of Rome in Italy, and the complications of her imperial position. It had been necessary to remove from Numidia a son of Jugurtha. He was made a state prisoner and placed in the custody of the local authorities of Venusia. The chances of his ever being troublesome to Rome were apparently very small, but with the surrender of that town he fell into the hands of the rebels. We next hear of him in the camp of Papius, who made use of him[1] to entice Caesar's Numidians to desert. The armies lay facing each other, and the name of Jugurtha was still great among his own people. The Roman consul found his African corps melting away, and thought it wise to send the remainder home. The Samnite commander seems now to have attacked the Romans in their camp, and to have been repulsed with loss. This success is said to have revived confidence in Rome. But it does not seem to have been followed up. Caesar retired, probably northwards, and the siege of Acerrae went on. The rich Campanian plain[2] lay open to the rebels, and the probable loss of its resources threatened ruin to the Roman government, already in great financial difficulties. Moreover the fall of Aesernia soon led to the betrayal of Venafrum. By the end of the year it might seem that the cause of Rome in southern Italy was lost. But the imperfection of our record leaves us in much doubt. It is strange that we hear nothing of Sulla, whose exploits were soon to change the aspect of affairs. It is possible that the failures of this year may have been exaggerated in order to heighten by contrast the successes of the next. In any case much has been lost, and a dim uncertain outline of events is all that remains.

848. In the northern campaign also the Romans met with grave disasters, but on the whole held their own far better than in the South. Rutilius, opposed to Pompaedius Silo, needed every advantage of efficiency and discipline. Unluckily there were among his officers[3] some nobles whom political differences had inclined him to view with suspicion. It became clear that the Marsian general was receiving information of intended Roman movements. Eventually the leakage of news was accounted for by the detection of Marsian spies within the Roman lines, but the incident had meanwhile caused uneasiness and hesitation at headquarters. The consul's lieutenants suffered several defeats: Perpenna lost most of his army, so the consul

---

[1] Appian *civ.* I 42.

[2] Cic. *de leg. agr.* II § 80 says that in the failure of other sources of revenue it was the Campanian rents that enabled Rome to keep great armies in the field.

[3] Dion Cass. frag. 98 § 1.

dismissed him and added the survivors to the division of Marius. But he would not listen to the old soldier when he advised a waiting strategy, and fell into an ambush laid for him by P. Vettius Scato (or Cato) commanding a Marsian army. A great Roman disaster was the result, and the consul himself was among the dead. Marius, who was not far off, delivered a timely attack on the enemy's ill-guarded camp, captured their supplies, and forced them to retreat with loss from the scene of their victory. An election of a new consul could not be held, for Caesar was more than busy in the South, and there were generals to hand. The northern command was by the Senate's order shared between Marius and Caepio the recent opponent of Drusus. Evidently there was jealousy of Marius at work. Neither the dominant party nor the strict *optimates* liked him: the former probably suspected him with some reason of being in heart inclined to favour the claim of the Allies; as for the latter, Sulla was their man. But Caepio was no match for Pompaedius, who deceived him by a ruse, led him into a trap, and destroyed him with a large part of his army. Marius now received the remnant of the beaten troops. He soon won a victory over a force of Marsi and other rebels. This seems to be the battle in which, according to Appian[1], Sulla was present with a body of troops and bore an active part. Whether Sulla had been transferred for some reason (perhaps to watch Marius) from the southern department to the northern, or whether he and the consul Caesar had disagreed, or whether again the whole story is a fiction, designed to glorify Sulla, and innocently copied by Appian, we have no means of deciding. In other quarters the fortune of war was varying. We hear that a Roman general defeated the Paeligni, probably not in their own territory, for we have no report of an advance threatening the rebel capital at Corfinium. On the other hand Cn. Pompeius, who was operating in Picenum, was met by a concentration of three of the confederate leaders and driven back upon the Latin colony of Firmum. There he stood at bay, and Servius Sulpicius the victor of the Paeligni came to his aid. The enemy were routed and driven into Asculum, which had no doubt been the objective of Pompeius. This rebel town was marked out for early punishment, and the siege was at once begun. But the final success of Rome in the northern theatre of war was very doubtful, and it was probably a wise caution that guided the strategy of Marius. It is perhaps to this stage of events that the story preserved by Plutarch[2] belongs. Pompaedius sent the taunting challenge 'Marius, if you are a great general, come down and give me battle.' 'Nay' replied Marius 'if you are a great general, make me give battle when I don't choose to.' A characteristic and edifying anecdote, which might even be true.

[1] Appian *civ.* I 46.   [2] Plut. *Mar.* 33.

We hear later of his fighting a drawn battle with the Marsi. What were the circumstances of the affair we do not know, nor the numbers engaged. But we can see that to hold the main enemy in check was necessary for the siege of Asculum, and there is reason to think that already rumours of an Umbro-Etruscan rising were causing anxiety in the department of the North. The fair conclusion to be drawn from our meagre record is that the services of Marius were great, and that his retirement from command at the end of the year was due to other causes than the veteran's failure in capacity and vigour.

849. The nerve of the people at home had been sorely tried by the frequent bad news from the front. The funerals of the consul Rutilius and other men of note produced so painful an impression that the Senate passed an order for all bodies henceforth to be buried where they fell. In general, the great council seems to have kept its head; with all their faults, the nobles of Rome in face of deadly peril could still bear themselves in a way worthy of their fathers. And now, apparently in the winter of 90—89, the long-dreaded news arrived that the Allies in Etruria and Umbria had at last risen in arms. Whether they had hitherto furnished their usual contingents to Rome, or had openly or tacitly refused to do so, we do not know. Now at least they were in rebellion, and the Senate saw that it would be impossible to deal with an enemy thus strengthened in the North and at the same time to recover the ground lost in the South. Indeed the city itself would be endangered. We can see that to call in the northern forces by way of covering Rome was strategically impracticable. Not only would the siege of Asculum have to be raised, but all the moral and material advantages gained by taking the offensive would pass to the rebels, and the ruin of Rome could only be a question of time. The hour of concession was come. It seems to have been late in the year 90 that the necessity was fairly faced. The consul Caesar had returned to Rome to hold the elections for 89. The Umbro-Etruscan rising was no long-planned and well-organized movement, but a venture prompted by the apparent success of the confederates already in arms. Probably it had not as yet gone far. Forces were quickly despatched to repress it, and Roman tradition claimed victories in both districts. But these victories evidently did not mean much, and the true means of averting the new peril was found in legislation, not in the sword. A *lex Iulia* was proposed and carried by the consul offering[1] the Roman franchise to all communities of Allies that had as yet not rebelled or at once laid down their arms. The offer found general acceptance in Etruria, and quiet was at once restored in the North. But the effects of the

---

[1] Cicero *pro Balbo* §§ 19—21, Velleius II 16 § 4, 20 § 2, Appian *civ.* I 49, Gellius IV 4 § 3, quoting the jurist Servius Sulpicius, *tempus quo civitas universo Latio lege Iulia data est.*

Julian law were felt all over Italy. Wherever there was a Latin colony, or a treaty-state still loyal to Rome, there it now rested with the community to declare its formal acceptance of the boon, and so become Roman. If a Greek city like Neapolis hesitated to take this step, that was merely the result of attachment to local laws and institutions, and not of any sympathy with the confederate rebels. The concession in fact encouraged Rome's friends, confirmed the wavering, and raised even among the enemy hopes that tended to mitigate ferocity. No doubt it was generally assumed that admission to the franchise meant equality with the existing citizens of Rome, and that the new citizens would be fairly distributed among the 35 Tribes. But this was a matter for the next censors, and just now, with the war still going on, it is no wonder if such details, though important, passed unregarded. How the question of registration was afterwards dealt with we shall inquire below.

850. We are now come to the year 89. The new consuls were Cn. Pompeius Strabo, who was pressing the siege of Asculum, and L. Porcius Cato, who had just been in command against the Etruscans. Both consuls operated in the northern department. Perhaps they were both still in those parts, and had been elected in their absence. The southern campaign was under the direction of Sulla as lieutenant of Cato, at least in the Campanian region. To make all safe on the seaboard the Senate had garrisoned[1] the towns from Ostia to Cumae with bodies of freedmen. This seems to imply some fear for the communications with the South by the Appian way, and an intention to keep the communication by sea unmolested. To return to the North. The rebel leaders knew of the Umbro-Etruscan rising, and were eager to support it. News of its collapse had not yet reached them, when they sent a strong force to penetrate the wild hill-country in midwinter and cooperate in the revolt. The march was difficult, and Pompeius caught them and forced them to give battle. They were beaten with heavy loss, and in their retreat a number more perished of cold and hunger. What happened to Cato is obscure and variously told. His troops seem to have been mutinous[2], and he died somehow while operating against the Marsi. Another general, Sextus Iulius Caesar (consul in 91), who had taken over the siege of Asculum, died on service there. Marius disappears from command in the field. Plutarch says that he resigned on the ground of bodily infirmity. This is a most unlikely story in itself, and his enemies were eager to represent him as effete. It may be a fiction of theirs, but he was

---

[1] So Kiene p. 203, and this perhaps is the right view. But the words of Appian *civ.* I 49 need not imply more than cruisers patrolling the waterway.

[2] Dion Cass. fragm. 100.

now 67. A more likely explanation is to be found in his resentment at finding his recent services unappreciated. That he should fancy himself indispensable, as in the days of the Cimbric war, was not unnatural, and his temper had doubtless not improved with age. But nothing short of the last necessity would induce the Roman nobles to restore him to the dominant position from which he had fallen; and the democrats had surely not forgotten his desertion of Saturninus. If the year 89 had been disastrous for Rome in the North, it might have been necessary to place Marius in the chief command, but matters took a favourable turn. The pacification of the Etruscans and Umbrians not only set free the forces employed against them: it left them Romans, and the firstfruits of their new franchise would be service in the Roman legions. There was no need to call Marius to save the state, for the consul Cn. Pompeius did his work well enough. This man is an interesting figure, for his conduct in the northern command produced some curious results in later years. Cicero, then a lad of 18, served in his army, and has left us a description[1] of an interview in which the consul met the Marsian general between the opposing camps. The whole point of the story lies in the absence of bitterness on the part of the leaders, particularly the Roman. If we may believe Diodorus, an even more remarkable[2] scene had occurred in the previous year, when the armies of Marius and Pompaedius met and fraternized, and the two generals conversed as kinsmen. This sounds overdrawn, and it may have been purposely exaggerated in order to represent Marius as no true champion of Roman pride. At any rate conciliatory behaviour on the part of Pompeius, who possessed the full confidence of the Roman government, was a far more significant phenomenon. It must be taken in connexion with the *lex Iulia*, and with the certain fact that in his suppression of the Picentine rising he contrived to gain the goodwill of the conquered. He seems to have had the statesmanlike adroitness which Marius lacked. That his conduct was part of a general policy is further indicated by his being kept on as proconsul in 88 to carry out the final pacification of these northern districts. He had with him at headquarters his son Gnaeus, a youth of 17 or 18, learning the art of war. This lad was destined to reap the fruits[3] of his father's popularity in Picenum, to become a famous general, and to be known to after ages as Pompey the Great.

851. We hear little of the siege of Asculum, but it was undoubtedly the chief operation[4] of the northern campaign. Its fall would produce

---

[1] Cic. *philipp.* XII § 27.   [2] Diodorus XXXVII 15.   [3] Velleius II 29 § 1.
[4] Around Asculum a great number of sling-bullets have been found. A collection of their inscriptions is to be seen in the *Corpus Inscr. Lat.* I 644—680.

a great moral effect on the group of confederate peoples headed by the Marsi. Velleius tells us of a battle there in which 75,000 Romans engaged more than 60,000 Italians, and points out that there were at the time a number of armies engaged in other parts. It was probably some time in this year that Judacilius, a native[1] of the place who had commanded a rebel force in Apulia, tried to break up the siege. In this he failed, but cut his way through the Roman lines. Inside the town he found the state of things desperate; so, after putting to death the chief advocates of surrender, he killed himself. Towards the end of the year Asculum fell, and an example[2] was made of it, as a warning to rebels. The importance of the event was recognized by the triumph[3] granted to the consul, and held on the 27th of December. Meanwhile his lieutenants had been at work in the country of the Marsi and their neighbours, fighting and ravaging. One by one the confederate peoples submitted and sued for peace, in what order, and whether before or after the fall of Asculum, we do not know. That the sword alone did not bring about this collapse of the rebellion of these warlike peoples, we shall presently see reason to believe. But, though discontent was not at an end, and a corps of observation was still maintained in that region, the supremacy of Rome was no longer effectively questioned in the North. The confederate capital was shifted to Aesernia[4], and desperate rebels like Pompaedius Silo withdrew to share the fortunes of the Samnite South.

852. By what exertions the Roman government raised and equipped armies for the southern department in 89 we are not told. But three or four forces were put into the field somehow or other, and a naval squadron is heard of in the bay of Naples. The spirit of the troops was perhaps at first doubtful. The officer commanding the fleet[5] cooperating in an attack on Pompeii was murdered by his men. Sulla had to be content with calling upon the mutineers to redeem their credit by bravery in the field. He appears to have won a battle against the Samnites, and then to have gone to direct operations for recovery of the coast towns lost in the previous year. Meanwhile his lieutenants were facing the Samnites inland, and gained a great victory. Another rebel army was pushed forward to compel Sulla to raise the siege of Pompeii. Sulla beat them off for the time, but they were soon

---

[1] Appian civ. 1 48.

[2] In Cic. pro Cluent. §§ 21—24 we have the story of a youth captured at Asculum and made a slave.

[3] Fasti triumphales.

[4] Diodorus XXXVII 2 § 9. Of Bovianum Appian civ. 1 51 § 4 only says that it was a κοινο-βούλιον of the rebels.

[5] Valer. Max. IX 8 § 3, Plutarch Sulla 6, Appian civ. 1 50 § 3, Livy epit. 75, Orosius V 18 § 22, Velleius II 16 § 2, combined.

joined by a body of Gauls and returned to the attack. At this point we meet with a story[1] which illustrates the use of foreign auxiliaries in this Italian war. A huge Gaul came out and after the manner of his race challenged any one on the Roman side to single combat. It would seem that Sulla's old connexion[2] with Bocchus had enabled him to draw useful succours from the Mauretanian king. The challenge was accepted by a little Maurusian, who slew the clumsy braggart Kelt, and cooled the ardour of the rest. A timely attack drove the rebel army back in rout upon Nola with heavy loss, and the moral forces of success and full trust in their leader henceforth played their part in the war on the side of Rome. Sulla, deservedly saluted *imperator* by his men, now boldly advanced into the Hirpinian country. Compsa and Aeclanum fell, and his devastation of the land soon brought the Hirpini to their knees. By the promptitude of this advance he had forestalled an expected movement of a confederate army from Lucania. He had cut in two what was left of the confederacy, and the strategic situation was now all in his favour. In Lucania a Roman force under A. Gabinius more than held its ground. In Apulia C. Cosconius disputed the possession of the country with a Samnite general, and eventually recovered a large part of it for Rome. Sulla was now free to turn northwards. Taking an unexpected route, he burst into Samnium, fell upon the army commanded by Papius and routed it with great slaughter. Papius fled to Aesernia, and Sulla pushed on and took the important rebel centre of Bovianum by storm. There could not be much doubt that here was a general determined to crush resistance without delay. To him no suspicion of a secret sympathy with the Italian rising could be attached. The war, it is true, was not at an end; but Rome was no longer in any serious danger as an Italian power from the efforts of the Samnite league, stunned and disheartened by a succession of defeats. News from the East proved that danger did seriously threaten her from that quarter as an imperial power. The masterful Patrician saw a more glorious and congenial task opening out before him. He went to Rome, determined to win the consulship, and with it the command against Mithradates.

853. For the purpose of marking so far as possible the connexion of events in these momentous years, it has seemed best to group them year by year. But the exact chronology is not to be recovered. We will now turn to the internal history of Rome, legislation and other matters that seem to belong to this year 89.

---

[1] Appian *civ.* 1 50 § 5.

[2] From Plutarch *Mar.* 32, *Sull.* 6, we gather that Bocchus had recently erected in Rome a work of art which revived memories of his surrender of Jugurtha to Sulla. This renewed the feud between the latter and Marius.

First come the laws dealing with the extension of the franchise. Of these there were three. The *lex Calpurnia*[1] of L. Calpurnius Piso empowered the generals in command of troops to bestow the Roman *civitas* on their men. Once the policy of concession had been begun by the Julian law, it was clear that Allies fighting for Rome were entitled to the benefits. The *lex Plautia Papiria*[2] of the tribunes M. Plautius Silvanus and C. Papirius Carbo was potentially an extension of the Roman franchise to the whole of Italy. Any man might become a Roman citizen, provided (*a*) that he was already on the register of some state connected with Rome by treaty, (*b*) that his regular home (*domicilium*) was in Italy, (*c*) that he made formal declaration of his wish before a praetor within 60 days. So says Cicero. We have not got the text of the law, and it is quite clear from the notices of extension of the *civitas* to Italians in later years that all Italy did not in point of fact receive it now. We are expressly told[3] that the Samnites and Lucanians did not receive it at this time. Probably some definition excluded the members of states still in rebellion : indeed a state in arms against Rome could hardly count as a *civitas foederata*. But the resumption of friendly relations with Rome may have qualified any member of the state so submitting itself to take advantage of the law. In earlier days a treaty would have been forfeited by rebellion and renewed after submission on more onerous terms. Now no renewal of a treaty was in contemplation. The road to the Roman franchise was opened to Allies, but it is not likely that Roman statesmen were in any special hurry to see the new policy take practical effect. There was undoubtedly an immediate object of great urgency, to weaken the rebels by creating disunion in their ranks. If we knew the exact dates of the passing of this law and of the earliest submissions of revolted Allies, we should probably find some connexion between the two, at least some practical explanation of the time-limit of 60 days. That the submission of the Marsi may have been hastened by internal dissension is obvious : it is perhaps no mere accident that the news of the Roman offer would have ample time to penetrate into every corner of their territory, and to invite the acceptance of all who were weary of the war. If then to those peoples who were still in arms at the end of the year we add those who submitted, but not in time for their members to benefit by the Plautio-Papirian law, we can fully account for the continuance of the franchise-agitation after the Italian war had apparently come to an end. It was not likely that those who were late in making their

---

[1] Sisenna fragm. 120 Peter, Mommsen *Staatsrecht* III 135, Kiene pp. 224—6.
[2] Cicero *pro Archia* § 7, Mommsen *Staatsrecht* III 132, 179.
[3] Appian *civ.* I 53 § 2.

peace would quietly acquiesce in exclusion ; nor was the line drawn by the time-limit a satisfactory one, even from a Roman point of view. But for the present this law appears to have met immediate needs. So far however we have only been concerned with Italy. But it seems to have been thought necessary to deal with the questions raised in Cisalpine Gaul by the changed situation in Italy proper. A *lex Pompeia*[1] of the consul Cn. Pompeius was the result. The country naturally fell into two divisions. That south of the Po contained the Latin colonies of Placentia and Bononia, beside the citizen colonies of Parma and Mutina, and districts assigned to Roman settlers, with the market towns (*fora*) and other local centres (*conciliabula*) founded for their convenience. The Romanizing of the district was fairly complete. It seems certain that all the inhabitants not already Roman citizens received the franchise at this time, and Cispadane Gaul (as it was still styled) became henceforth virtually a part of Italy. In the Transpadane district were the Latin colonies of Cremona and Aquileia, which no doubt received[2] the Roman franchise like the rest of their class. But a large part of the country was still occupied by Gauls. It was desirable to bring them under an organization of an Italian type as a step in the further Romanizing of this rich and populous region. The plan followed was to establish urban centres, each city with a suitable territory, and to bestow on each the constitution and privileges of Latin colonies. No new colonists[3] were sent : the Gauls seem to have been civilized enough to use considerable powers of local government, and perhaps it might not have been easy to find colonists at a time when every available man was wanted in Italy or in the East. The ruder Gauls and Alpine dalesmen were divided into batches and placed in subordinate and tributary relations to the cities near which they severally lived. So for the time Cisalpine Gaul was regulated. We have only to remark in passing that the grant of citizenship by special vote of the Assembly to persons who had done Rome good service was distinct from these general laws. It was of course no new thing.

854. But to grant the franchise by legislative acts was one thing ; to make this incorporation politically effective was another. In the matter of voting in the Assemblies the question of registration was of immediate importance. We need not wonder that the new citizens felt an interest in this question. It is true that residence at a distance would debar most of them from the active and frequent exercise of

---

[1] Marquardt *Stvw.* I 14, 62.

[2] By the *lex Iulia*, or by an extension of its scope, if that law applied only to Italy proper. There was a Latin colony at Carteia in Spain, but this does not seem to have been included.

[3] Asconius p. 3.

their votes in Rome. But the events of recent years had shewn that, on occasions when public feelings were stirred, the power of far-resident voters was a force to be reckoned with, and the pacified Allies had no mind to lose their old local autonomy without gaining an equality of privilege as Romans. Now in the Roman system the vote of an individual counted only towards determining the vote of a group, Tribe or Century as the case might be, and his enrolment as member of a Tribe or Century was the work of the Censors. And, whatever may have happened in the case of old citizens accidentally absent from a census, but well known to belong to this or that group, the new citizen must have been in a peculiarly helpless position until a place had been found for him in some recognized division. But, while the new citizens wanted to know in what groups they were entitled to vote, the old citizens were in no mind to expose themselves to the risk of being outvoted by the new. The risk was no mere fancy, though perhaps exaggerated ; but those who had rejected the just claims of the 'Italians as Allies would naturally be jealous of them at first as fellow citizens. How to deal with the details of the present enfranchisement of such masses of men was clearly a burning question in the year 89, but our wretched authorities give us no account of the views current at the time. In this year there were censors, L. Iulius Caesar the consul of 90, and P. Licinius Crassus one of his lieutenants in the campaign of that year. That they were not lethargic[1] is shewn by their activity in various ways. They re-vised the senatorial roll, issued some sumptuary edicts, and closed the *lustrum* according to custom, and in particular endeavoured to meet the financial needs of the state by selling for building-sites some valuable parcels of land hitherto occupied by members of the sacred colleges, on the Capitoline hill. But they did not carry out the chief business of the census, the registration[2] of the whole body of citizens. That duty had never been more urgent than it was at this moment, and the reasons for neglecting it must have been strong. It must indeed have been on purpose to carry out the provisions of the Julian law that they were appointed, for it was not five years since the census of 92. And yet Cicero says quite plainly that no registration took place.

   855. Velleius[3] tells us that the *civitas* was granted to Italy on the understanding that the new citizens were grouped as tribe-members (*contribuerentur*) into eight Tribes, the object being to prevent them from outvoting the old citizens, whom it was desired to protect from such a slight. In default of any indication to the contrary, it is very

---

[1] References in Lange *RA* III 113.   [2] Cicero *pro Archia* § 11.
[3] Vell. II 20 § 2.

properly assumed that he means 8 of the 35 Tribes. Appian[1] says that the new citizens were enrolled in 10 new Tribes created for the purpose. These new Tribes voted after the 35 old, and their votes were often useless, for the votes of the 35 already given were more than half the total. He does not say that this arrangement was prescribed by the Julian law, nor need we interpret the 'understanding' of Velleius as implying anything of the kind, in itself surely improbable. Neither writer mentions the censors, perhaps assuming that those officers must have been concerned in the matter. An obscure fragment[2] of Sisenna, referring probably to the year 90, speaks of two new Tribes, but breaks off just at that point, so that we learn little, not even whether such a plan was ever carried out. No more vexed question has engaged critics than the attempt to extract some reasonable conclusion from this defective evidence. No satisfactory solution of the problem has been found. The following is a new attempt. We must begin by remarking that whatever was done now did not long remain in force. Also that there was precedent for letting Latins present in Rome vote in one Tribe chosen[3] by lot, that the Tribes voted simultaneously, but the declaration of their votes took place in an order settled by lot. So soon as 18 Tribes had voted one way, the declaration ceased. The number 18 was therefore the one mainly to be noticed; it was the traditional majority-number. We have now to suppose that the Tribe-order for the day has been settled, and that the new citizens, not yet entered on any Tribe-register, have been told off to vote in the eight Tribes last in the order of the day. We see that if 18 old-citizen Tribes vote one way, the 8 mixed Tribes will have quite 'useless votes,' for they will never be declared at all. If the old citizens choose, they can decide any issue. Even when voting is closest, and the last Tribe gives the decisive vote, the position at best is 17 old on one side and 10 old plus 8 mixed on the other. Even if the 8 mixed all vote solidly in the majority, they are still only a minority of that majority. The old-citizen tribes are still 'more than half.' Now let us suppose two new Tribes added to the 35. The position is so far changed that the traditional 18 is no longer a majority. In a division of 18 old on one side, and 9 old plus 8 mixed plus 2 new on the other, the new citizens may have determined 10 votes out of 19. They are not only in the majority of 19, but they are a majority of that majority. We may be inclined at first sight to think

---

[1] App. *civ.* I 49, 53.

[2] fragm. 17 Peter, *Lucius Calpurnius Piso ex senati consulto duas novas tribus*.......

[3] Livy XXV 3 § 16. The case of freedmen in XLV 15 § 5 is perhaps a more permanent arrangement, at least in intention.

the difference between the two positions trivial. But we may remind ourselves that there were issues, not regarded as trivial, namely the pontifical[1] elections, that were decided by 17 Tribes only. It will be observed that as 17 was a minority in 35 so 8 would be a minority in 17. Now add 2 to 35. The corresponding minority-number will be 18. It is quite possible that the two new Tribes may be among the 18 selected by lot, and the new citizens not in these two are assigned by lot to 8 other Tribes. Here we have them able to control 10 votes, a majority in the total of 18. That the possible effect on pontifical elections was a leading consideration with contemporary statesmen, it would be rash to suggest. But that such considerations as the way in which an arrangement might work in practice were familiar to the Roman mind, is as certain as anything can be. It is submitted as a probable solution of the problem that, in default of censorial registration, presiding magistrates let the new citizens vote in Tribes chosen by lot, that these Tribes were eight in number and last in the order of returns, for the reasons given. Further, that two new Tribes were created, probably to contain some special batch of new citizens, perhaps the soldiers enfranchised under the Calpurnian law. Lastly, that Appian has confused the ten Tribes in which the new citizens voted with ten new Tribes, whereas there were but two. If he did, it would be no more than he has done in other passages ; certainly he had no clear notion of the politics of the Roman Republic. In any case the arrangement was of such short duration that error was not easily to be avoided in referring to it.

856. So far I have spoken only of the suffrage in connexion with the Tribe-Assembly. The system of Classes and Centuries, in which the voting of the Assembly by Centuries took place, was in the sole power[2] of the censors. The presiding magistrate might allow a man to vote in this or that Tribe, but he could not assign him to his proper Class or Century. It seems an irresistible conclusion that the new citizens could have no vote in the Centuriate Assembly until the censors took their case in hand. In the matter of legislation this exclusion was of no importance, for that work was in practice done by the Tribes. But the election of consuls and praetors was important. The new citizen was entitled to have an equal chance with

---

[1] See above § 792.

[2] The censor grouped the people in *classes* according to property, and the *classes* (of each Tribe, since the reform, see §§ 257—8) in *centuriae* according to age. This principle of grouping was traditionally military. The censor did not in point of form give a man a vote, but the vote in *comitia centuriata* followed from the assignment of a place in a *centuria*. The process of forming the *classes* and *centuriae* took time, and could not be done in haste without inquiry. The arrangement held good till the next Census. Hence the phrase *exercitus quinquennalis*. See Mommsen, *Staatsrecht* II 399—400, III 268.

the old of attaining those offices; this he would hardly have until new and old voted side by side. The agitation that followed is partly to be explained by the irritation of this remaining disability, which would be especially galling to the most active and ambitious among the newly-enfranchised.

857. Some time in this year the monopoly of the Knights in the jury-courts was attacked by the tribune Plautius in a *lex Plautia*[1] *iudiciaria*. He was backed up by the nobles, to whom the proceedings of the Varian commission were giving great offence. No other criminal court was sitting, and it may be that the new law only applied to these trials for *maiestas*. It introduced a new principle of appointment. Each Tribe elected 15 of its own members, without limitation of Order or quality, and the 525 men thus elected formed the list of jurors out of whom for that year juries were to be chosen. Thus senators could be, and were, put on the list. Even common citizens not belonging to the privileged orders found a place, but it seems that the Equestrian Order still kept a majority. The law did not remain in force long. But it marked a reaction against the party who had destroyed Drusus and precipitated the war. Q. Varius himself was brought to trial and condemned under his own law. Even so the commission did not come to an end, for Cn. Pompeius was tried before this court when his term of office expired, but was acquitted. In this same year a *lex Papiria*[2] *nummaria* reduced the weight of the copper *as* to $\frac{1}{2}$ *uncia*. It was in any case only a token coin and the *semuncia* was a common weight for the small-change of Italy. At the present juncture the state was, as we have said, in financial straits. But the scarcity of ready money expressed itself in a serious crisis. Many owed money, and could not pay, by reason of the general disturbance of business through the war. The creditors resorted to the civil courts. The debtors found a protector against their creditors in the praetor[3] Asellio, who raked up old obsolete laws against usury, and contrived to obstruct recovery. The enraged capitalists retorted by murdering him in broad daylight when wearing his official robe and engaged in sacrificial duty. For this no one was punished. Such was law and order in Rome; but worse was coming.

858. I have said that Sulla returned to Rome to stand for the consulship. His splendid victories had given him an overpowering claim to this, and also to the command against Mithradates. But

---

[1] Cicero *pro Cornel.* fragm. 29, Asconius p. 79. See Madvig, *Verfassung und Verwaltung* II 222, Greenidge, *Rom. Publ. Life* 385—6, Lange *RA* III 115.

[2] Marquardt *Stvw.* II 18.

[3] Livy ep. 74, Appian *civ.* I 54, Valer. Max. IX 7 § 4.

Marius had the same desires, and he had been now in Rome for months past, doubtless not idle. We hear nothing of him beyond the general gossip of Plutarch, drawn from hostile sources. Marius is represented as taking part in manly exercises on the Campus Martius in order to display his vigour and activity, in short his fitness for the coveted command. But we are told that age corpulence and rheumatism made his efforts ridiculous. We may at least be sure that the nobles who slighted his services in the Italian war did not hesitate to depreciate him now, and that Sulla's memoirs recorded all disparaging traditions in the most venomous form. No doubt Marius wished for another consulship, but we have no reason to think that he was actually a rejected candidate for office in 89 or 88. It is more likely that he did not stand, not finding sufficient support. Into the maze of Roman politics at the end of the year 89 we can see but dimly; but the three parties, of which the capitalist Knights the moderate and the stiff-necked nobles were respectively the leading elements, can be traced. The first were in an ill humour because of the invasion of their judicial monopoly by the Plautian law. The second were smarting under the loss of some of their best men, now in exile. The third had gained at the expense of the other two. They had not, like the first, to bear the odium of the Varian commission, and the favourable turn taken by the Italian war had strengthened them and weakened the concessionists. The situation was expressed in the consular election. Sulla was elected together with Q. Pompeius Rufus, a man of the same political colour. But their success was probably due to the lack of cooperation between the other parties, and a new disturbing element was brought into public life by the election of P. Sulpicius Rufus as tribune. This man, a great orator[1] in an age of great orators, had been a friend and supporter of Drusus. He belonged to the concessionist nobility, like Cn. Pompeius, under whom he served with distinction in the campaign of 89. It was perhaps his absence at the front that saved him from the Varian commission. He was now a leading member of his party, and he was evidently in strong opposition to the anti-Italian views of the section represented by the new consuls. Q. Pompeius had been[2] one of his most intimate friends, but friendship now gave place to a bitter enmity. Sulpicius came of an old Patrician house, and it is not likely that in order to qualify himself for the tribunate he became a Plebeian without good reason. From the first he meant to carry on the policy of concession to the Italians. The attack on his old commander Cn. Pompeius would intensify his hostility to

---

[1] Cicero *Brutus* §§ 182—3, 203, etc., Wilkins Introd. to *de Oratore*.
[2] Cicero *Laelius* § 2.

the nobles now in power. He could only hope to give effect to his policy by a coalition with the capitalist Knights. Discontented and suspicious of the extreme section of the nobility, they were ready to sink differences. A mediator and figure-head was needed to bring about the somewhat incongruous combination of sections so essentially different. The man was found in Marius.

859. The recent banishment of a number of public characters, first the supporters of Drusus and then Varius himself (and perhaps others with him), had left the friends of both these groups anxious to recall their own associates. At the end of 89 one of the new tribunes brought in a bill for the restoration of the exiles who had not had a hearing, that is, a fair and regular trial. Perhaps Varius or some of his crew were meant. Sulpicius at once blocked it. But his negotiation with Marius changed his tone. The terms[1] of the coalition seem to have included the recall of the exiles (probably of both parties), the complete equalization of new and old citizens, and the appointment of Marius to command in the East. Of course we find this represented as an utter abandonment of principle on the part of Sulpicius. It was surely not more so than what happens in all coalitions; but the new programme placed the tribune in open antagonism to the greater part of the nobility, encouraged as they were by the military glories of Sulla. They saw in the new consul a leader after their own heart, to whom all the democratic movements of recent times were an abomination, and who had relieved them from the necessity of trusting Marius. So they made the most of his victories, and advised Marius to try the baths of Baiae for the cure of his infirmities. Sulla with his usual luck had drawn the lot for the command in the East. His army, trained in the Italian war, and devoted to their general and their hopes of plunder, lay before Nola, which had not yet surrendered. He was himself still in Rome when Sulpicius, backed by Marius, began what was nothing less than a revolution. The *leges Sulpiciae*, for recall of the exiles, and for distributing the new citizens and the freedmen among the 35 Tribes, were a complete reversal of the policy pursued for the last two years, and meant the triumph of the rebellion now so nearly suppressed. The opposition was of course strong and bitter. Violence in the Assemblies was now quite normal, and Sulpicius prepared to carry his measures by force. He formed a body-guard of 600 young men of the Equestrian Order and with these and other armed ruffians he bore down all opposition. The consuls were addressing a meeting in the Forum: the tribune and his gang broke it up. The consuls fled for their lives. Q. Pompeius got away himself, but his son was

[1] Rhet. *ad Herenn.* II § 45, Livy ep. 77, Plutarch *Mar.* 35, *Sulla* 8, Velleius II 18 § 2.

murdered : Sulla found refuge[1] in the house of Marius, where no one thought of looking for him. Such were the methods by which laws were to be carried. To stop the voting on the bills the consuls had proclaimed a suspension of public business (*iustitium*). This legal but vexatious hindrance they were compelled to remove. Sulla went off to his army in Campania, and Sulpicius at once carried through his laws and transferred the Eastern command from Sulla to Marius by vote of the Assembly. The whole affair was revolutionary. We cannot suppose that a free vote of the Roman Tribes would have cancelled the appointment of Sulla. He was consul, and everything was in order. By their action his opponents placed the game in his hands. Sulpicius might be hot-headed and the course of events might lead him further than he had meant to go. But Marius well knew the nature of the armies of the new model, his own creation : if he imagined that such a man as Sulla, at the head of such an army, would surrender his own prospects and the desires of his men at the dictation of a gang of rioters in Rome, it was a fatal delusion. An army no longer served the state, but their general. Marius had never had a clear eye for politics. That the army was the one great political force, that the true centre of Roman power at that moment lay in the camp before Nola, seems to have escaped him. He seems to have thought that his irregular commission from Rome would suffice to place him in command of an army that was not his own. This was in effect to rely on the moral influence of reverence for Rome as the centre of citizenship and seat of government, a reverence which his own career had powerfully tended to destroy.

860. In the short interval before the breaking of the storm Sulpicius appears to have carried through a few more measures. The command in northern Italy, where things had not yet settled down, was entrusted to Cn. Pompeius[2] as proconsul, thus excluding the new consul Q. Pompeius, who was a partisan of Sulla. A law for removing from the Senate members whose finances were embarrassed perhaps also belongs to this time. But the importance of the moment is this. The votes now taken were the last in which the Roman Republic as a political organism expressed itself, however violently and corruptly, still free at least from constraint actually or potentially applied by military force. Henceforth, though statesmen might do and undo, though the mob might riot, though Assemblies might vote, though financiers and nobles might intrigue, the real power lay with the masters of the legions whenever they had a mind

---

[1] From Plutarch *Mar.* 35 it appears that Sulla was at some pains to explain this episode away.

[2] Plutarch *Sulla* 8 (but see Holden's critical note on the text in § 4).

to use it. The virtues and abilities of great and good citizens might fitfully and partially illuminate the unreal spectacle: the fierce collisions of public life might call forth literary activity and discover the bent of Italian genius. Whether men saw the truth or not, whether they confessed it when seen or pretended to ignore it, Rome was no longer the vital centre of a free Commonwealth, but an Imperial capital waiting for an Emperor.

861. If Marius had misjudged Sulla and his army, Sulla at least had taken the measure of Marius and the forces at his back. When the news of his deposition from command reached him, he addressed his troops, coolly telling them what had happened, and leaving them to draw their own conclusions. They saw that Marius might prefer to take other soldiers to enjoy the loot and license of the East. Doubtless the centurions had good reason for fearing that they at least would lose the reward of previous good service under Sulla. The solid army, divining the real wishes of their leader, called upon him to lead them to Rome. Presently two military tribunes arrived with orders from the Senate that they were to take over the army and conduct it to Marius. The soldiers stoned them to death. Sulla now broke up from before Nola and set out for Rome with six legions, about 35,000 men. The rulers of the city were busy making away with some of Sulla's partisans and seizing their goods. As the consul drew near, embassies were sent to warn him not to approach nearer than five miles. The soldiers insulted them: Sulla affected to obey, but resumed his march. Most of his chief officers had left him, horrified at his proceedings, but other men had left Rome to join him, his colleague Q. Pompeius among them. The two Roman consuls, at the head of a nominally Roman army, soon forced their way into defenceless Rome. The futile discharge of tiles and stones from housetops was overcome by setting fire to the buildings. Marius and Sulpicius did what they could with the swordsmen at their disposal, and vainly appealed to the slaves to rise in arms. Overpowered and routed, they and their chief partisans fled in all directions for their lives. So by nightfall Sulla was master of Rome, and had already taken some steps to restore the appearance of order.

862. The victor had now to choose between three alternatives. He might stay in Rome and establish himself as head of the state virtually or openly. But for this the time was not yet ripe. It would be a slow and delicate business, and failure would be his own destruction. He could not expect his army, thirsting for the plunder of the East, to stay in Rome or Italy merely for the purpose of asserting his supremacy. Nor would he win a firm footing in Italy if he abandoned Rome's eastern interests and possessions to Mithradates. His place was already assigned him as his country's champion abroad: if he shirked the duty, he was no better than a brigand at home. Another plan might be to stay at home himself and send another general abroad. But he would thus bear the blame of failure, while success would probably raise up a new rival to oust him as he had ousted Marius. The third course open was to patch up things at home so as to leave his own partisans in power, and at all risks to make good the authority of Rome against the foreign enemy. The Italian war was not at an end. He probably guessed that his supporters at home would not prove equal to dealing with the complications that might arise. But something must in any case be left to fortune, and Sulla, fortified with omens and dreams, was a firm believer in his star. He boldly decided to go, and began making arrangements in Rome without delay.

863. After a public address, lamenting the necessity of his recent action, he set himself to carry through the measures, personal and constitutional, by which he hoped to keep things quiet during his absence. First of all, Sulpicius, Marius and his son, and nine others, were by order of the Senate declared public enemies, and outlawed in the usual form. They could now lawfully be put to death. In the hue and cry after them Sulpicius, betrayed by a slave, was murdered. Roman principles were vindicated by manumitting the slave and then executing him. These proceedings shocked and alarmed many. In the Senate the aged augur Scaevola stoutly protested against the outlawry of Marius. Plutarch suggests that Sulla's conduct in setting a price on the head of Marius, who had so lately spared him, was thought ungenerous by both Senate and people. But Sulla was not a man of illusions or sentiment. His present task was to remove obstacles, and he no doubt rightly judged that he had seen the last of the mercy of Marius. The next business was to make some repairs in the constitution, to enable the strained and shaken fabric to hold together for a time. The ground was cleared by repealing the Sulpician laws, which indeed had been so carried as to have no claim to respect. There were now three main points to aim at (1) the Tribunate and the Tribe-Assembly (2) the Magistrates (3) the Senate. Appian[1], our only witness, evidently had no clear notion of the meaning of the measures described in his authorities. The following is an attempt to extract the truth from his confused account. First, it was enacted that nothing was in future to be laid before the Tribes without the previous sanction of the Senate. This revived what had been the law of the constitution down to 287 B.C., and a wholesome custom down to the time of the Gracchi (but recently disregarded by

[1] App. *civ.* I 59.

demagogic tribunes), and apparently fixed it by statute. This, provided the Senate were strong enough to use their power, would be some check on troublesome mob-leaders; we are told that the tribunes were weakened in other ways, but we do not know how. Another law dealt in some way with the Assembly by Centuries. The drift of the law was in general to place more power in the hands of the wealthy. But by what changes in detail this result was arrived at, whether the present relation of Tribes and Centuries was in any way interfered with, ingenious criticism has not been able to ascertain. The likelihood of consulships praetorships and censorships falling into the hands of revolutionary men would be lessened. Thirdly, we are expressly told that in order to strengthen the Senate, which was thinned and consequently weak, 300 new members, chosen from the 'best men' (aristocrats), were added in a body. This was no doubt made regular by another law. That some reactionary changes in the direction here indicated were introduced by Sulla at this time is hardly to be denied. We cannot set the testimony of Appian aside altogether. That most of them were revived and extended a few years later during the supremacy of Sulla is no ground for doubting their introduction now. That these changes could only become effective through a vigour and moral force, assumed but non-existent, in the Roman nobility, was the weak point in the situation. Neither the patchwork of 88 nor the great reconstruction of 81 was able to stand the strain of facts.

864. The revolution of Sulpicius had probably been carried out with the help of masses of new citizens, drawn to Rome by his agitation, and unsettled through the devastation of Italy. Sulla would want to get rid of this element. · It is possible that an obscure reference[1] to his founding colonies may be a trace of his compelling them to return to their homes. He sent forward his army to Capua, and for the present remained himself in Rome transacting public business. But in the capacity of mere chief-magistrate he no longer inspired universal awe. Partisans of wealthy exiles clamoured for their friends' recall; the Senate was sulky; the common people, disgusted at being driven to give their votes under the eye of an army instead of being flattered or bribed, took heart and shewed open hostility. At the consular elections Sulla could not bring in his nominees. He had to be contented with securing one place for Cn. Octavius, a pronounced aristocrat, as colleague of L. Cornelius Cinna, who belonged to the opposite faction. He made the best of it: the people, he said, were shewing their appreciation of the freedom he had won for them. He felt that it was time to be gone. So he bound Cinna by most solemn

---

[1] Livy ep. 77, so interpreted, but emended, by Kiene pp. 289—90.

oaths[1] to be faithful to the policy of his settlement (a proceeding which he must have known to be a farce), and set out to rejoin his army, leaving his colleague Q. Pompeius to his fate. The repeal of the acts of Sulpicius had restored to him, as to Sulla, his military province. He had left Rome to take over the northern army[2] from the proconsul Cn. Pompeius. But the soldiers mutinied and murdered him, and the proconsul resumed the command.

865. At the beginning of the year 87 there were three Roman armies on duty in Italy, beside the army of Sulla, bound for Greece. There was that of Cn. Pompeius in Picenum guarding the peace of the North. It seems that the Vestini and Paeligni[3] were still restless, and had to be compelled to make a final submission. Appius Claudius commanded in Campania, with headquarters at Capua, but a considerable force lay before Nola. When the siege of that town ended is not clear. In Apulia Aemilius Mamercus, and after him Q. Metellus, carried on an active campaign. But there can be little doubt that the pick of the strictly Roman troops went with Sulla, and that the armies serving in Italy were less homogeneous. It is clear that they owned but a doubtful allegiance to the unstable government in Rome: on the other hand no one popular general had them all at his disposal. There were evidently a large number of the new citizens in the ranks. This was in itself a serious danger at a time when the main issue dominating Roman politics was the question whether the new citizens should be registered in all the 35 Tribes or not. Partisanship inevitably found its way into the camps, and the recent capture of Rome by Sulla had made a precedent for civil war waged by Roman armies under Roman standards. Meanwhile the war with the Allies, the Italian rebellion proper, was coming[4] to an end. The Samnites and Lucanians had not laid down their arms. In Samnium, since the withdrawal of Sulla in 89, the organization of the rebels had been remodelled. Pompaedius the Marsian had disdained to share the submission of his own people. He was now made commander-in-chief of the Samnite forces, and under his leadership the shrunken confederacy gained some success. Meanwhile it was clear that help from abroad was urgently needed, and an embassy was sent to invite Mithradates to Italy. This was indeed a counsel of despair. As allies

---

[1] In his anxiety to get Sulla out of Italy Cinna is said to have induced a tribune to threaten him with a prosecution. This attack Sulla (no doubt on the authority of his own memoirs) is said to have treated with contempt. See Plutarch *Sulla* 10 § 4, Dion Cass. fragm. 102 §§ 1—4, Cicero *Brutus* § 179.

[2] Livy ep. 77, Velleius II 20 § 1, Appian *civ.* I 63, the last very confused.

[3] See Kiene pp. 294—5. I think he rightly holds that Livy must have included some events of 87 (early) under 88.

[4] Diodorus XXXVII 2 §§ 9—14.

of the great king of Pontus they could have had no chance of winning the independence for which they longed; victory would have been as fatal as defeat. This was of course hid from their eyes. But Mithradates, like a true Great King, sent back word that he was just now busy settling affairs in Asia: as soon as he had leisure he would invade Italy. This meant that no help would reach them in time, and the hearts of the Samnites sank, while the Roman armies were gaining ground in Apulia. We hear of a battle in which Pompaedius was beaten by Mamercus, and in an engagement with Metellus the great champion of Italian independence himself fell. With him fell the cause. We hear of some Italian leaders making an expedition into Bruttium and even aiming at the occupation of Sicily. But the arm of Rome was too long for them. The governor of Sicily raised a force and defeated them while busied with the siege of Rhegium. The Italian armies as such disappear from the scene. It is in the corruption and disorganization of Roman public life that we must henceforth seek the cause of the perils that beset the Roman state. Italy was in no mood to settle down and be at rest: whatever burning questions the strife of Roman factions might kindle, the fire would burn more fiercely and more widely through the rage of sullen survivors in a wasted land.

The *Guerre sociale* of Prosper Mérimée (1844) is a brilliant narrative of the war, with its causes and its sequel in civil war. But it gains no small part of its vividness from accepting a number of details that seem to me doubtful or immaterial.

CHAPTER XLIV

MARIUS AND CINNA[1]. 87—86 B.C.

866. THE dramatic and biographical tendency, which has for some time past been stealing over the history of Rome as transmitted to us, at this moment appears with striking clearness in the story of the adventures of Marius. While the other fugitives were exposed to much the same dangers, and the head of Sulpicius was wasting, affixed in horrid irony to the speakers' platform in the Forum, the human interest gathers with tragic intensity round the hairbreadth escapes of the exile who had once been the saviour of Rome. This may have been to some extent the case at the time. But what has come down to us is the product of later moralizing and declamation: to Roman poets and historians, alike rhetorical, the poignancy of contrasts in the life of Marius offered an irresistibly attractive theme. The old man's perilous voyage along the Latin and Campanian coast, his unwholesome refuge in the swamps of Minturnae, the wavering policy of those who had him at their mercy, afraid to spare yet ashamed to betray him, the tale of the German or Gaulish slave who would not venture to kill Gaius Marius, his eventual escape to Africa, where the conqueror of the Cimbri sat among the ruins of Carthage, his unfailing belief that he would yet return and be a seventh time consul:—these and many more details form a romance based on fact, leading up artistically to the horrors of the sequel. They became part of the stock-in-trade of Roman literature, and it is chiefly for this reason that they are briefly referred to here.

867. No sooner was Sulla's back turned, than Cinna began to upset the arrangements which he was under oath to maintain. Bills were brought before the Assembly for a general distribution of the new citizens and the freedmen among all the 35 Tribes, and for recalling the exiles outlawed by Sulla. Octavius the other consul, backed by' some tribunes, opposed him stoutly, but Cinna prepared

---

[1] The general authorities for this chapter are Livy ep. 79—83, Velleius II 19—24, Appian *civ.* I 60—76, *Mithr.* 51, Plutarch *Mar.* 35—46, *Sertor.* 4—6, *Pomp.* 4—5, *Crass.* 4, Florus II 9 §§ 3—17, Orosius V 19, Eutropius V 7, Obsequens 56, [Victor] *de vir. illustr.* 67, 69, and the fragments of Diodorus XXXVIII 1—5, Dion Cass. 102 §§ 5—12, Licinianus ed. Bonn pp. 23, 25, 27, 29. The chief references to Cicero and Valer. Max. are given in separate notes. See generally Cic. *philipp.* VIII § 7, *de nat. deor.* III §§ 80—1.

to carry the bills by force in the now usual way. He was of course in league with the new citizens (scandal declared that he had received a heavy bribe to take up their cause), and great numbers of them swelled the host of ruffians at his disposal. The mass of old citizens rallied to Octavius, who in the fight that followed dexterously broke up the enemy and drove them out of the city. Both sides were armed with daggers, and much blood was shed. Cinna and his associates fled. The Senate pronounced him a public enemy, not a citizen, and therefore no longer consul. The place declared vacant was filled up by the election of the priest of Jupiter, L. Cornelius Merula. But they had not done with Cinna. He doubtless knew that the bulk of the troops left in Italy, consisting largely of new citizens, were in sympathy with his movement, and he set out to find himself an army. That of Appius Claudius at Capua[1] was his choice. The general himself was suspected, it would seem, for we hear that a vote of the Assembly[2] had been taken to deprive him of his command: the men were probably ill pleased at not having been taken by Sulla to the eastern war. Cinna knew how to work upon them. They quickly recognized him as still consul, and took to him the oath of military allegiance. He then went on tour among a number of the allied cities, where the new citizens welcomed him as one that had suffered wrong in their cause. He raised money and troops so readily that he was soon able to march on Rome at the head of thirty[3] legions, while many men interested in a revolution joined him from the city.

868. We need not try to define exactly at what point the war with the Allies as such ends and the civil war begins. The one is the continuation of the other. The strength of Cinna lay in the fact of his representing the ex-Allies, the new citizens, who were determined to accept nothing short of equality. The struggle of the old citizens to keep as much as possible of their privileged position was hopeless without the direction of a great leader, and their great leader was far away. Octavius and Merula strengthened the defences of Rome, but what they most wanted was an army. They sent to raise troops in the Italian communities not yet committed to the cause of Cinna, and in Cisalpine Gaul. But these measures were insufficient in the face of Cinna and his host. They were driven to call upon Cn. Pompeius, who still commanded an effective army in the North. He was a doubtful character, and had condoned if not actually prompted the murder of his intended successor, the Sullan consul of the previous year. His interest was not bound up with that of the nobles and old citizens who held the city, and seems to have been in the main purely

---

[1] So Appian, at Nola according to Velleius.
[2] Cicero *de domo* § 83.   [3] This number is hardly credible.

selfish. He is said to have aimed at the consulship for 86, and, being at the head of the only well-organized force available, he seemed able to dictate his own terms. He dallied in his advance, and his attitude was so ambiguous that each faction suspected him of intriguing with the other. His position was a difficult one. The Sullan party had good reasons for hating him, and did, while to Cinna he would appear as an unwelcome rival for the favour of the new citizens. His delay in coming was mischievous. Cinna had time to get his raw troops into order, and to make connexion with Marius, who now reappeared upon the scene.

869. Marius had heard of Sulla's departure and Cinna's rising, and started for Italy with some fellow exiles and a few troops raised in Africa. Landing in Etruria, he proclaimed himself in favour of the claim of the new citizens. He attracted many, and by enrolling also a number of plantation slaves soon was at the head of a considerable force. He soon came to terms with Cinna, who had with him Q. Sertorius, an officer of tried courage and capacity, and the turbulent Cn. Papirius Carbo. No wavering or dissensions marred their union; but it seems that Sertorius, though bitterly hostile to the Sullan faction, had grave doubts as to the wisdom of combining with Marius. He mistrusted the old man, who went about dirty and unkempt, and whose fierce scowl suggested intentions of a terrible revenge. But Cinna could not set Marius aside. Though he was consul and Marius a private citizen, the conqueror of the northern barbarians was necessarily the first figure of their company, and the revolution took its colour from his presence. The four leaders now advanced upon the city, Cinna and Carbo facing it, Sertorius from the North, and Marius, who had something of a fleet, attacking Ostia. Cn. Pompeius, who was encamped outside the Colline gate, now made up his mind to support Octavius in earnest. But it was too late. He fought a bloody but indecisive battle with Sertorius. But his men had no interest in the cause of the old citizens, and discontent spread fast in his camp. Meanwhile Marius had taken and plundered Ostia, and cut off the supply of corn to the city. He overran the towns of the Latin coast and advanced to bear a part in the capture of Rome. The forces in the city were not equal to their task. The Senate in their despair had offered the citizenship[1] to those Italians who had been conquered by force of arms and had as yet not been allowed the benefit of the laws extending the franchise. But the hope of substantial support from this quarter was disappointed. When Metellus, who was watching the Samnites, tried to carry out his orders to come to terms with them and march to relieve Rome, he found the Samnite claim to

[1] Livy epit. 80, Licinianus p. 27 *dediticiis omnibus*.

perfect equality more than he could accept. The Marians had no such scruples, and the Samnites accordingly joined them. All Metellus could do was to hurry off to Rome with a detachment, leaving the main body of his army under a lieutenant, only to be cut up by the Samnites. The succours actually received by the Senate from the Italians were only some 8000 men. The expected reinforcements from Cisalpine Gaul were held in check by a column despatched by Cinna: Placentia, held for the Senate[1] by one of Octavius' officers, was besieged and taken.

870. The details and order of events are painfully obscure. It would seem that Marius made his way into the Transtiberine quarter of Rome, aided by treachery, but was soon driven out by Octavius and Pompeius. The success was not followed up, owing to the caution of Pompeius. He was indeed an evil counsellor throughout. By his advice negotiations were opened with Cinna, whose faithlessness was notorious, and who was bidding for the help of the slaves. Delay was all in favour of the Marians, for the stock of corn in the city was running out, and desertions weakened the defending army. Some of Pompeius' own men conspired to murder him and were only thwarted by the vigilance of his son; others left him and went over to the enemy. An epidemic broke out in his camp, and many died. The proconsul was perhaps himself one of the victims, but his death at this juncture was attributed to a stroke of lightning, which sounds like the official version hushing up an assassination. He died universally hated; the populace insulted his corpse at the funeral. But the loss of their best general was a blow to the cause of the Senate. Octavius had not the confidence of the soldiers. He was a high-minded patriot, too refined and scrupulous to be an effective leader in a crisis that called for qualities of a very different order. He would not offer freedom to the slaves, and left them to yield to the seductions of Cinna. But he was consul. And, when the soldiers begged Metellus to take the command, that worthy man scolded them and bade them obey the consul's orders, whereupon they passed over to the enemy in disgust. Desertions and the near approach of famine brought the defence of the city to an end. Cinna would not treat with the Senate save in the capacity of consul, so Merula had to be deposed from office. He would not swear to put no one to death, so he had to be admitted into Rome on a mere assurance that he would shew all possible mercy. He at once entered the city, and went through the form of procuring a vote of the Assembly annulling the outlawry of the men expelled by Sulla. Marius, who had refused to enter Rome until solemnly recalled, now

[1] Valer. Max. IV 7 § 5.

condescended to appear as a citizen. Octavius declined to abandon
the post of duty, though warned to fly. Seated as consul with his
lictors around him, he calmly waited for his murderers. Metellus[1]
seems to have taken a chief part in negotiating with Cinna, and to
have been viewed as more or less of a traitor by Octavius. At all
events he escaped to Africa, to reappear later as a partisan of Sulla,
and did not, like the consul, offer an ill-timed exhibition of clumsy
virtue.

871. And now began the infamous massacres which the grim
bearing of Marius had led the trembling citizens to expect. The
pent-up rage of the old man was beyond control, and he took
vengeance for his sufferings in the swamps of Minturnae and elsewhere in a way that was never forgotten. While his old colleague
Catulus and the deposed Merula were summoned to trial before the
Assembly, and committed suicide to escape inevitable outlawry and
certain death, Marius paraded the streets attended by his company
of liberated slaves. A sign, even the mere omission of a friendly
greeting, was enough to instruct these ruffians to cut down any
chance passenger not favoured by their master. Headless and
mutilated corpses lay about in public places, and none dared to
bury them. Marked men were hunted down by pursuers, and the
betrayal of refugees by friends and the treachery of informers added
mutual mistrust to the agony of the time. For five days and nights
the general butchery went on. The heads of senators were stuck up
in front of the Rostra in requital for the treatment of Sulpicius.
Among the distinguished victims—two Caesars, two Crassi, and
many more—none impressed the public mind more than the aged
orator M. Antonius, one of the leading men of the period, who was
betrayed by an informer to the deadly enmity of Marius. Yet there
was a reverse to this terrible picture. We are told[2] that the practice
of procuring the death of a citizen in order to get his estate had
not yet found its way into Rome, and that even the plunder of the
houses of the dead was declined by the healthy sentiment of the
rabble. We hear too that slaves did not always[3] betray their masters;
one striking case, in which the master was saved by the cleverness
of faithful slaves, is recorded in detail. But of the brutalities and
robberies committed by the monsters who followed Marius it seemed
there would be no end. Sertorius loathed them, and Cinna was sick
of bloodshed, at least of a purposeless kind. So they fell upon them

---

[1] Diodorus XXXVIII 2. This Metellus, called *Pius*, was the son of Numidicus.

[2] Velleius II 22 § 4, Valer. Max. IV 3 § 14. The words of Appian *civ.* I 73 § 4 cannot
outweigh this evidence.

[3] Plutarch *Mar.* 43, Appian *civ.* I 73.

in their sleep with a band of Gaulish soldiers, and rid the city of a pest.

872. Political revolution had also its share of the victors' attention. The Senate, that is, its surviving members who had not fled from Rome, obediently declared Sulla a public enemy, and this was followed by the confiscation of his property, the demolition of his house, and the annulling of his laws. But the year 87 must now have been far spent, and the election of magistrates for the coming year had to be made. It is said that Cinna simply declared himself elected with Marius for his colleague, which is perhaps merely an exaggerated description of an election that was a farce. Marius had now reached the goal of an ambition said to have been originally roused by the soothsayers' interpretation[1] of a strange occurrence in his boyhood. Such influences were as powerful as ever, for the decay of the public religion had little or no effect upon popular superstition ; indeed the growth of disbelief in divine interference had rather cleared the ground for the worship of Fortune. But it was noted[2] that a blind trust in divination had led the consul Octavius to his doom, and the confidence of Sulla in Fortune's favours was a singular comment on the lucky destiny of Marius. No wonder that the ingenuity of Etruscan specialists was concerned to offer theories to account for the variations of success and failure in the art of prophecy. As for Marius, his revenge was still not glutted, but his end was near. On the Ides (13th) of January he died. Fiction gathered thick about the story of his last days and the scenes of his death-bed. The Sullan tradition is an awful picture of drunkenness and delirium, of mad terror at the rumoured return of Sulla, of dream-battles in the coveted Mithradatic war. Fragments of a very different version rather suggest that the dogged and dangerous old man, inured to hardship from his youth up, but worn out with recent sufferings and the canker of continued fury, succumbed to an attack of pleurisy. One of his satellites, the ruffianly soldier C. Flavius Fimbria, signalized his funeral by an attempt to murder[3] the highly respected chief pontiff Scaevola. But the great lawyer escaped with a wound, only to be murdered later.

873. The death of Marius brought a lull in the storm of bloodshed. Cinna is not known for his merits, if any, but his vanity and ambition at least looked rather to advancement in the future than revenge for the past. He took L. Valerius Flaccus as his colleague, and some progress was now made with the work of the political

---

[1] Plutarch *Mar.* 36, Appian *civ.* 1 75.

[2] Plutarch *Mar.* 42, *Sull.* 7, Diodorus XXXVIII 5.

[3] Cicero *pro Rosc. Am.* § 33, Mayor on Cic. *de nat. deor.* III § 80.

revolution. The general course of this was a return to the policy of Sulpicius, but with modifications and additions. Sulla's laws being annulled, and the new government hostile to the Senate, it was probably now that the Knights (by repeal of the Plautian law) regained their control[1] of the public courts, which we find later on taken from them by Sulla. One of the most pressing needs of the moment was to find some way of dealing with a great financial crisis. Events in Rome had of course unsettled the money-market. Credit was destroyed, for everyone wanted to realize and to recover his loans. Ready money, portable and easily concealed, was in abnormal demand; and on the top of this came the panic[2] among the capitalists caused by the Mithradatic war and the sudden stoppage of remittances from Asia. To meet the difficulty, the consul Flaccus carried a law[3] enabling debtors to get discharge by paying only 25 % of their liabilities. This perhaps saved some from actual bankruptcy, but confidence could not quickly be restored by a remedy so closely akin to the disease, and the stringency in the money-market continued, silently aggravating the troubles and anxieties of the time. The need of money was pressing not on individuals only, but on the state chest. It was no doubt in connexion with this lack of resources that the young Cn. Pompeius[4] was put on his trial. It was alleged that his father had taken a great share of booty at the time of the capture of Asculum, and had never accounted to the treasury therefor. The son was now required to make good to the state what his father had embezzled. His defence seems to have been that the property in question had been carried off from his house by some of Cinna's men. But it was more to the point that he secured a friendly understanding with the praetor presiding over the court, and that among his counsel were not only the rising orator Q. Hortensius but the strong Marian partisan[5] Cn. Papirius Carbo. He was acquitted, and in a few days married the praetor's daughter. The financial situation was further complicated by the state of the currency. Ever since it had been tampered with by Drusus, the number of bad *denarii* had been on the increase. Bad coin tends to drive good out of circulation, and we can form some faint notion of the confusion and distress arising from this cause alone and the extent to which astute bankers and moneychangers[6] profited thereby. No man, says[7] Cicero, could tell

---

[1] See Cicero I *in Verr.* §§ 37—8, Velleius II 32 § 3.

[2] Cicero *pro lege Manil.* § 19, *pro Caecina* § 11.

[3] Cic. *pro Quinct.* § 17, Sallust *Cat.* 33, Velleius II 23 § 2.

[4] Plutarch *Pomp.* 4, Orosius V 18 § 26.

[5] Cicero *Brutus* § 230, Valer. Max. V 3 § 5.

[6] Asconius p. 90 says they were nicknamed 'pouchers,' *saccularii.*

[7] Cic. *de off.* III § 80, Pliny *NH* XXXIII § 132.

what he was worth. Something had to be done. The tribunes conferred with the praetors, and drew up a joint edict dealing with the matter. The details are far from clear, but it seems that provision was made for assaying coin and withdrawing the base pieces from circulation. Who bore the expense of this reform is not stated. From the great popularity gained by the praetor who drew all the credit of it to himself by forestalling his colleagues in announcing the decision, we may guess that it fell upon the public treasury. If so, those who then held the reins of power in Rome must for a time have been more than ever embarrassed by want of funds. But a regular system of assaying was in itself a good check on counterfeiting, and we learn from Pliny that it became a profession, and bad *denarii* curiosities.

874. The registration of the new citizens was of course a matter not to be neglected. We find censors in office 86—5 B.C., thus again appointed before the five years interval had expired. These censors, L. Marcius Philippus, the former opponent of Drusus, and M. Perperna, seem to have carried out the registration; on what principles, is not clear. Probably the new citizens were distributed over all the 35 Tribes, according to the promise of Cinna, but that an approximately equal number were put into each Tribe we have no reason to think. Local considerations and personal influence had perhaps more weight than notions of symmetry. But the census, if the numbers[1] recorded are correct, can hardly have been complete. No doubt a large number were abroad, for instance the army of Sulla, and it is most likely that full advantage had not as yet been taken of the recent franchise-laws. Cicero tells us too that some of the praetors whose duty it had been to receive applications (in 89) had been very careless[2] in keeping their lists. But the business was carried through somehow, and Cicero elsewhere[3] remarks on the way in which some men of note managed to keep on fair terms with Cinna at this time; a fact worth mentioning, because many of the senatorial nobles had fled to Sulla[4] in hope of present safety and future restoration. As time went by, news of Sulla's victories reached Rome, and the government became more and more uneasy at the prospect of his return. They had no leader with ability and nerve to match Sulla: even Sertorius was not up to that standard, and he was apparently kept in the background by Cinna and Carbo, who were wholly unequal to their

---

[1] In 86—5 only 463,000, an absurdly small increase on the 394,336 of 115—4. Beloch, *Bevölkerung* pp. 348, 352, would emend the figure for the census of 86—5. Lange *RA* III pp. 135—6 thinks that this return was incomplete, which is a milder and perhaps equally probable explanation.

[2] Cic. *pro Archia* §§ 9—11.   [3] Cic. *ad Atticum* VIII 3 § 6.

[4] Velleius II 23 § 2.

difficult task. Whatever competence there might be among the still-resident senators, the times were not suited to the leadership of co-operative commonsense evolved in a debating council. A Man was wanted, and was not forthcoming. He was certainly not to be found in the consul Flaccus, who seems to have been no soldier and a man of bad character. But Cinna made the gross blunder of sending him out with a force to take over from Sulla the command against Mithradates. To cover his defects, Fimbria, who was at least a soldier, was sent with him as chief of his staff (*legatus*). The hot-headed and desperate subordinate was to enable the corrupt and incompetent consul to supersede the best living general in the command of his devoted army, the most efficient force of the day. This absurd scheme, in which all the most important elements were left out of account, enables us to gauge the incapacity of Cinna. How Fimbria made away with Flaccus, and afterwards with himself, we shall see below. Meanwhile the Marian or new-citizen party remained dominant in Italy, and sent out governors of their own colour to various provinces. Cinna and Carbo are said to have declared themselves[1] consuls for two years (85, 84), a step which has been thought inconsistent with their position as heads of a movement professedly democratic. Unwillingness to trust the Assembly by Centuries may perhaps have been the cause of this arbitrary proceeding. If the censors by the end of the year 86 saw no prospect of including a large number of new citizens in the Classes and Centuries (surely not an extravagant supposition), the old citizens would control a great majority of the Century-votes. To hold an election, and force the Centuries at the sword's point to vote as directed, would have been as tyrannical as the course actually taken, and more likely to renew civil war, not to the interest of the men in power. The remark of Cicero[2], that in the interval between the departure and return of Sulla constitutional government was in abeyance, is not far from the truth. There was no hope of better things while the commonwealth was ruled by force, in the hands of men with no clear aims beyond their own advancement, devoid of foresight discretion and consistent vigour. Their alarm at the prospect of Sulla's return, the negotiations with him, the futile preparations to encounter him, the murder of Cinna, the rule of Carbo and the younger Marius, and the overthrow of the Marian faction, must be spoken of in connexion with the proceedings of Sulla, in whom the main interest of Roman history was now to be centred for several years.

---

[1] Perhaps some form of popular election was observed (see Strachan-Davidson on Appian *civ.* I 77 § 4), but I doubt it. The whole proceeding is revolutionary.

[2] Cic. *Brutus* § 227, *sine iure fuit et sine ulla dignitate res publica.*

CHAPTER XLV

875. IN a former chapter we left Mithradates at the point where he made submission to the orders from Rome delivered by Sulla, and allowed Ariobarzanes to be restored to the throne of Cappadocia. This was in 92 B.C. He was merely biding his time, and the discontent of the Italian Allies, of which he was no doubt well informed, seemed likely to give him an opportunity of renewed aggression by tying the hands of Rome. In the East itself no serious opposition was to be feared. Egypt, where the Lagid house was utterly degenerate, and Syria, where the later Seleucids fought over the little remnant of that once huge empire, were alike powerless abroad. In Armenia Tigranes had enough to do in consolidating his own kingdom, and he was an ally of the king of Pontus. Cappadocia was disorganized and weak, and certain to be controlled by whatever might become the leading power in Asia Minor. The warlike Galatians still clung to their system of tribes and cantons: the lack of a strong central power and their constitutional fickleness, a compound of cause and effect, made them more suited to strengthen the armies of their neighbours than to develop a policy of their own. The present king of Bithynia, Nicomedes III, was a base tyrant, and a brother named Socrates, who had for a time been the ruler of Paphlagonia, had designs upon the Bithynian throne. It was only the support of Rome that upheld Nicomedes. The western parts of Asia were either under a Roman protectorate, as Phrygia and other districts and cities, or included in the Roman province of Asia. The province swarmed with Romans and Italians, farmers of the revenues, financiers investing money in loans and watching the investments, merchants seeking bargains, and the freedmen and slaves in the employ of these various

---

[1] The authorities for this chapter are better and more copious. The chief ones are Appian *Mithr.* 10—63, Plutarch *Sull.* 11—27, *Lucull.* 1—4, Livy ep. 74, 76—8, 81—4, and the fragments of Memnon (*Fragm. hist. Graec.* III pp. 540—4), Posidonius (*FHG* III pp. 265—70), and Licinianus (ed. Bonn pp. 33, 35, 37). See also Velleius II 23—4, Diodorus XXXVII 22, 26—8, XXXVIII 6—8, Dion Cass. fragm. 99, 101, 103—5, Valer. Max. v 2 (ext.) § 2, Justin XXXVIII 3—7, Florus I 40 §§ 6—14, Orosius VI 2 §§ 1—12, Eutropius V 5—7, Obsequens 56, (Victor) *de vir. illustr.* 70, 74—6, Zonaras X 1, Sallust *hist.* IV 69 § 12 (Maur), Appian *civ.* I 75—8, and indices to Cicero, Strabo, and Pausanias.

worthies. The real centre of these enterprises was in Rome. The officials in the province, even the governor, could do little or nothing to check the illegal extortions of the tax-gatherers. If they ever felt impelled to stand between the oppressed provincials and the agents of Roman capitalists, the presence of the exile Rutilius in Smyrna might remind them of the fate in store for those who depreciated the shares of Roman companies by exhibiting Roman virtue in Asia. And so local industry and skill were being bled to death by cruel extortions usury and fraud. Unable to achieve their own deliverance, the wretched people sighed for a deliverer. Any single tyrant would indeed be less burdensome than this system. A whole civilization in the West was being built up on their ruin.

876. Mithradates was firmly seated in his kingdom of Pontus. He had annexed the Lesser Armenia and the eastern districts of Paphlagonia, and was now overlord of the tribes of Colchis and powerful in Galatia. To the Greeks of the Tauric Chersonese (Crimea) he was a welcome protector. He had a full treasury, a strong fleet, and a well-trained army. Able Greeks filled the chief posts in his civil and military services, and on receipt of news of the Italian war he was ready to take advantage of the crippled state of Rome. To win Bithynia and the Roman province was his immediate object. Accordingly he lent an army to the pretender Socrates, who drove out Nicomedes and assumed the Bithynian crown. He sent another force to occupy Cappadocia. Ariobarzanes had again to fly, and Ariarathes, son of Mithradates, once more took his place. The ejected kings appealed to Rome, and the Senate ordered that they should both be restored. To execute this order they despatched an embassy to Asia, and instructed the governor of the province, who had a small force under his command, to cooperate with the commissioners. It was a delicate business, for Rome was not in a position to send out a strong army from Italy to enforce her will: so the notorious responsibility of Mithradates was so far ignored that he was himself invited to lend a hand in expelling the usurpers. This he would not do, but he seems still to have shrunk from open war, and the two kings were restored. But M' Aquilius the head of the Roman embassy, was a man greedy of gain, as his conduct in Sicily had shewn, and his avarice is probably to be traced in what followed. The kings had been made to pay large sums to the commissioners and generals on account of their restoration, and had been driven to borrow the money from Roman financiers, doubtless on no easy terms. It was suggested to them that to plunder the territory of Mithradates would not be a step unfavourably viewed at Rome. The kings held back, knowing too well the strength of Mithradates, and

probably distrusting the immediate efficacy of Roman aid. But Nicomedes was in the toils of a truly Roman conspiracy. To keep faith with his creditors he had to invade the Pontic Paphlagonia, where he made great booty. Mithradates offered no resistance. But he had now got what he wanted, a good pretext for forcing on the inevitable war. He sent a Greek envoy to expostulate with the Romans and make specious offers. But Aquilius and the rest had made up their minds to back up Nicomedes. Mithradates reoccupied Cappadocia and sent his envoy again, to lay the blame of a rupture upon the Roman ambassadors, and to claim the reference of the whole dispute to Rome. But they would not consent, and insisted on full and prompt obedience. No understanding could be reached, and about the end of 89 B.C. the war was actually begun.

877. Aquilius and his colleagues evidently underrated the power of Mithradates. Beside his fleet, and a mass of warlike auxiliaries from his barbarian allies, he had a well-trained army of his own amounting to some 300,000 men. The Romans had few Italian troops at hand. Hastily they raised a force of Asiatics (among them Galatians of course), which they organized in three divisions. The governor of the Cilician province led one to Cappadocia ; the others, under Aquilius and the governor of Asia, operated in connexion with the army of Nicomedes. All seem to have been inefficient, and they had in case of defeat the disaffected province of Asia in their rear The Greek emissaries of the king of Pontus were probably at work secretly in the cities of the province. The maritime republics, such as Rhodes Byzantium[1] Cyzicus and Heraclea Pontica, generally stood by Rome. But the fleet stationed at Byzantium to guard the mouth of the Euxine was no match for that of Mithradates. The king made short work with his enemies. He routed and dispersed their armies and took possession of Bithynia. The cities of Asia nearly all rose against Rome and joined him, Aquilius and Oppius the governor of Cilicia fell into his hands, while Cassius the governor of Asia escaped to Rhodes. Mithradates made a triumphal progress through the Roman dominions, dragging about with him the wretched Aquilius, bound on an ass, till he reached Pergamum. There he is said to have closed the exhibition by pouring molten gold down his victim's throat, the comment of an oriental potentate on the greed of Roman statesmen. The effect of his complete success on land was felt on the water. Many of the islands came over to his side : the Roman squadron on the Bosporus scattered or surrendered, and the king's navy was for the time supreme in the Aegean. The news of these events reached Rome some time in the year 88. War was

[1] For services of Byzantium see Tacitus *ann.* XII 62.

declared against Mithradates, but immediate action was delayed, first by the difficulty of finding an army disengaged, and then by the dispute as to the command, as has been set forth in a previous chapter.

878.   Meanwhile Mithradates felt that his next task was to sweep the Italians out of Asia and to secure the full control of the sea. The first object was gained by ordering a general massacre of the Romans and other Italians in the cities of the province.   Here and there a man was spared, for instance[1] Rutilius; but some 80,000 Italians are said to have been butchered.   The provincials were by their own act deeply committed to the king's cause.   He was henceforth under little necessity of consulting their wishes.   From the spoils of the slain and treasures found in various places he appropriated[2] vast sums of money.   For the present he was popular.   By easing their financial burdens he had relieved the provincials liberated from Rome, and his liberal treatment of Asiatics taken prisoners in battle had given him a good name far and wide.   To command the sea it was first necessary to reduce Rhodes.   But the brave and skilful islanders, though greatly outnumbered, beat him off.   Neither in sea-fights nor in siege operations could he make any impression on their resistance, and he had to retire with serious loss of time and money, to prosecute other designs.   But he still dominated the Aegean, and the absence of a Roman fleet no doubt tempted him to take the step of extending his conquests to Greece.   Athens in her old age, ever dreaming of past glories, the seat of schools of philosophy, had no substantial ground for complaining of her treatment by Rome.   A favoured and idle city, she had sunk into a paradise of talk, out of touch with the realities of the age, and fitfully cherishing vain aspirations.   The reports of the success of Mithradates aroused hopes of a new era in which Athens, no longer a mere University town, the habitat of professors and resort of students and tourists, might recover somewhat of her departed greatness.   The king of Pontus was well known as a patron of Greeks, and had old friendly relations with Athens.   A certain Aristion, a man of mixed origin, but a citizen, was professor in the Peripatetic[3] school.   He saw his chance of power in the present excitement, and got himself appointed ambassador to Mithradates.   The king received him with much

[1] See Cicero *pro Rabir. Post.* § 27 for his escape from Mitylene.
[2] Among them 800 talents in Cos, sacred money belonging to the Jews.   Strabo hist. fragm. 5 (*FHG* III 492), cited by Josephus *Ant.* XIV 7 § 2.
[3] So says Posidonius fragm. 41 (*FHG* III 266—7), whom I follow, agreeing with Holm. Appian *Mithr.* 28 says that he was an Epicurean, which Mommsen seems to accept. Posidonius calls him Athenion, which may be a nickname, or an error of Athenaeus, in whom the citation occurs.

honour, and his letters soon held out prospects of royal bounty and a return to the extended franchise of yore when the Demos of Athens was in its prime. The flighty Athenians persuaded themselves that the power of Rome was broken, and Aristion on his return from the king's court was welcomed with a triumphal procession. He now carried all before him. Nominally the democracy was restored; in effect Aristion, at the head of a board of generals nominated by himself for election, was tyrant of Athens and Attica. The phenomena of such revolutions in Greek cities soon were reproduced here. To raise money by robbing the wealthy was the first care. In Athens as elsewhere men of property in general inclined to Rome. Attica swarmed with the tyrant's satellites, tracking and arresting those who tried to escape. Executions tortures and judicial murders served to fill his treasury. He coined money with the Pontic symbols to mark the alliance now concluded with Mithradates and the repudiation of the treaty with Rome. He had designs upon the temple-treasures of Delos, but a mismanaged expedition sent to seize them only led to an exchange of bloodshed to the advantage of the Roman garrison. A large colony of Italian traders, slave dealers and others, resided there without adequate means of defence. Soon the king's fleet under Archelaus, bound for Athens, appeared at Delos. The little island was speedily conquered, the Italian colony destroyed by killing the men and selling the women and children into slavery. In Delos and other island strongholds claimed by Athens some 20,000 men were massacred. The Delian treasure was sent to Athens, and a Pontic garrison placed in the city. The Piraeus was garrisoned also. Mithradates was now fully committed to a policy of aggression in Greece, and Archelaus soon induced the Greek states with very few exceptions to declare for his master.

879. We have seen how the Italian war was dying down in the year 88, how internal struggles still hindered the assertion of Roman supremacy in the East, and how Sulla for the moment settled matters at home and sailed for Greece early in 87. The situation awaiting him there needs some consideration. Even allowing for the control of the sea, the army of Archelaus was far from its base, and not strong enough to hold its ground on land without support. The declining states of the old Hellas could do little of themselves, even less than in the days of Antiochus. Mithradates therefore with good reason sent a second armament under Metrophanes, which operated by landings and ravages in Euboea and on the Magnesian coast of Thessaly. But he met with a resistance perhaps unexpected. The Roman governor of Macedonia, the propraetor C. Sentius, had remained at his post for a number of years; why, we are not told,

possibly because nobody was eager to take over an arduous duty with small prospect[1] of self-enrichment. He was an honest and capable man; and had dealt successfully with a Macedonian rising and recently with a Thracian invasion. The eastern and northern frontiers of the province were always a source of anxiety owing to the restlessness of warlike tribes on the border. Sentius now detached his lieutenant Bruttius Sura with a force to hold in check the generals of Mithradates. Sura beat Metrophanes in a small sea-fight, and shortly advanced to meet the Pontic armies now concentrated in Boeotia. Here he brought them to battle, with results variously reported, but at all events stayed their progress. At this point Sulla appeared with his army, and Sura, probably at the order of Sulla, withdrew to Macedonia. The enemy fell back, Archelaus to the Piraeus, Aristion to Athens. As the famous Long Walls no longer existed, the two cities were separate fortresses. Both were strong, but only the former could receive supplies by sea in the event of a siege. Sulla pushed on into Attica and began the siege of both cities. The need of a fleet was manifest, so he sent his able lieutenant L. Licinius Lucullus[2] to collect one. This mission led Lucullus all round the coasts of the eastern Mediterranean from Cyrene to Rhodes. Disappointed of an Egyptian contingent owing to the timidity of the reigning Ptolemy, and unable to seek alliance and support in the cities held by the pirates, he could only pick up ships slowly here and there. After many adventures and some losses he succeeded in raising a respectable fleet, but was not able to get to work in the Aegean till the summer of the next year. Meanwhile Mithradates was playing the Great King at Pergamum, rewarding and punishing, instructing satraps, and caressing a young Greek wife whom he had lately added to his harem. He does not seem to have understood that the coming of Sulla had completely changed the situation in Greece. After a first assault, in which he was beaten back from the old stone walls of Pericles, Sulla withdrew for a time to Eleusis to make full preparations for a fresh attack. This he seems to have begun in regular form during the winter of 87—6, while Rome was in the hands of the Marians, and he was being deposed from his command. Archelaus had been reinforced, and held Piraeus strongly. Another and larger Pontic army was advancing slowly by way of Thrace and Macedonia. It was certain that the party of Cinna would not leave the deposed

---

[1] According to Cic. II *in Verr.* III § 217, Sentius in the end made money indirectly by commuting his food-allowances for cash when corn was dear. For Sentius see § 803.

[2] According to Strabo fragm. hist. 6 Lucullus was specially accredited to the Jewish colony in Cyrene. Jewish friendship with Rome dated from the rising of the Maccabees. Josephus *Ant.* XIV 7 § 2 cites the words of Strabo.

proconsul to carry on the war unmolested.   But Sulla's mind was
made up, and he set to work upon the double siege in earnest.   That
the general, completely master of his own army, could defy both the
enemy and the home authorities, was a proof of astounding moral
force and military efficiency, but it announced the fall of the Roman
Republic.   Looking back to the days of Aemilius Paullus, the student
of Roman history must feel that he has travelled far.

880.   Blockade and hunger were the chief means used to reduce
Athens.   On the Piraeus Sulla brought to bear all the resources of
military art, and the defence was not less ingenious and stubborn.
The need of timber led the Romans to cut down the trees in the
famous gardens haunted by the philosophic schools: the need of
money caused Sulla to send round collectors to temples and lay hands
upon the sacred treasures of Greece.   Famine did its work in Athens,
and on the first of March a weak place in the defences was found,
and the Romans burst into the city.   Massacre and plundering
followed, but in deference to the entreaties of Athenian exiles and
Roman senators the slaughter was presently checked and the city
not given to the flames.   Soon the Acropolis fell also, and Aristion
and his guards were put to death.   Sulla now attacked Piraeus with
renewed vigour, and at length carried the main defences, but Archelaus still held his ground in its acropolis Munychia, where a small
harbour kept him in touch with his fleet.   Meanwhile the great army
coming from the North under Taxiles had driven before it the weak
Roman force in Macedonia, and added a number of Thracians to its
motley throng of various nations raised in Asia Minor.   According
to Appian it amounted to 120,000 men.   Sulla was expecting L.
Hortensius[1] to join him with a reinforcement from Italy, and was
alarmed for his safety; the troops he was bringing were only a little
over 6000.   The scene of war was now shifted to western Boeotia.
Archelaus effected a junction with Taxiles.   A part of their army
was probably detached to hold Euboea, which since the abandonment of Munychia would be their naval base on the Greek coast:
their fleet commanded the strait.   When their land-army met Sulla
near Chaeronea they still outnumbered[2] the Romans enormously.
Indeed the difficulty of feeding this great host was one of their chief
embarrassments, and led to relaxation of discipline in the quest of
supplies.   By campaigning in the comparatively level country to the

---

[1] Probably a brother of the famous orator. How, in the state of affairs in Italy, he could
raise a force there and bring it to Sulla, is far from clear. See Plutarch *Sulla* 15 § 3, Appian
Mithr. 43, Memnon in *Fragm. hist. Graec.* III 542.

[2] Memnon puts their total at over 60,000, but the other writers much higher. Sulla,
according to Plutarch, had not more than 16,500.

west of the lake Copais they gained a better field for the tactical operations of their cavalry and chariots, but they lost connexion with the shipping by which they had been drawing stores from Macedonia through the port of Amphipolis.   To Sulla on the contrary, with fewer mouths to feed, the change from exhausted Attica to Boeotia[1] was a relief from commissariat anxieties.   But he could not afford to dally, for by this time he could guess that somebody would be sent to supersede him; he must have done with the Pontic army before he could face a Roman rival.   The battle that ensued was decided by the superiority of the Romans in all the qualities vital to military success; a cool and determined general, officers of readiness and nerve, and the genuine unmechanical discipline of the rank and file. Only about 10,000 of the enemy escaped from the field, among them Archelaus, and found safety at Chalcis.

881.   The news of this great disaster roused Mithradates to fury. He was less popular with the Greeks of Asia now that they had experience of his despotic rule.   With or without reason he suspected his new subjects of an intention to turn against him, and arrests and executions, confiscations fines and enslavement, were his methods of forestalling revolt.   He treacherously murdered a number of Galatian chiefs, and then turned upon Chios.   He had been dissatisfied with the Chian squadron in the sea-fight off Rhodes the year before, and he now made an example of the unhappy islanders.   Concession after concession was extorted from them, till they were left helpless, without money or arms, in the hands of a Pontic commander.   Then they were put on board ship (in charge of their own slaves, according to one version[2] of the story) and carried away captive.   It is said that they were to be transported to Colchis.   But, if the historian[3] of Pontic Heraclea is to be trusted, the seamen of that Greek republic captured the convoy as it sailed by their shores; and the Chians, thus rescued and relieved, were afterwards restored to their native land.   The armament employed against Chios then went on to Ephesus.   The Ephesians, seeing the fruits of obeying orders in the case of Chios, took heart and murdered the king's general, put their city in a state of defence, and declared for Rome.   Tralles and some other cities did the same.   Mithradates now had to waste his forces by sending an army to put down the revolters.   Wherever he succeeded, the rebels were punished with horrible barbarity.   But it was his desire to have a strong party in each city interested in his cause. To this end he proclaimed a general cancelling of debts, thus setting

---

[1] Boeotia, as in the war with Antiochus, was ever doubtful in its allegiance, and suffered in consequence.   For the severities of Sulla see Appian *Mithr.* 54, Pausanias IX 7 §§ 4—6.

[2] Posidonius fragm. 39 (*FHG* III 265).   [3] Memnon fragm. 33 (*FHG* III 543).

the poor or thriftless against the rich, who had or were thought to have a preference for the government of Rome. He also gave the franchise of each city to aliens resident there, thus outraging sentiments deep-rooted in the Greek mind; and set free the slaves, a step which in effect would not so much give freedom to the bondman as secure the slavery of the freeman. The indignation of the wealthy soon led to conspiracies, followed in due course by betrayals, espionage, tortures, executions. It was more than ever important to keep the Romans busy in Europe, for their presence in Asia might give a new and unfavourable turn to an already disappointing war. So the king raised yet another army 80,000 strong, and sent it to Greece under his general Dorylaus.

882. Flaccus and Fimbria had landed in Greece before the coming of Dorylaus, and Sulla moved northwards to meet them. Their force was not large, and the men had no stomach for a profitless civil war. Flaccus was hated by his troops, and Fimbria with difficulty kept them in hand. An advance-guard deserted to Sulla, and the main body were therefore conducted towards Asia by the northern coast-route. Sulla did not follow them, for news came that Dorylaus had landed, and he had to deal with the enemy in his rear. The armies met near Orchomenus, where level ground gave advantage to the strong Pontic cavalry. But the camp of Archelaus, who was again in chief command, was close to the great Copaic marsh. Sulla hindered the movements of cavalry by digging trenches, but with the utmost exertions could hardly make head against the enemy in a battle fought against great odds. He succeeded however in forcing them back upon their camp, which he then approached with renewed spade-work and finally carried by storm. Immense numbers were slaughtered or driven to perish in the swamp. Again Archelaus escaped, and collected the remaining fugitives at Chalcis. The victory of Orchomenus must have been won early in 85 B.C., for the campaign that followed led Sulla over a vast expanse of country, and would occupy many months. Meanwhile Flaccus and Fimbria were pursuing their troubled way. When they at length crossed to Asia Minor they quarrelled, and Fimbria murdered his superior and assumed command of the army. He was an energetic soldier, and pushed on southwards, met and defeated the forces of Mithradates, and drove the king into Pergamum. To be shut up in that city would not suit Mithradates, so he fled to the sea-port of Pitane, where he got together some ships, in hope to escape that way. But the waterways were no longer clear of the Roman naval power. With great efforts Lucullus had at last raised a fleet, and was now cruising in the Aegean. He had recovered Cnidus Cos Colophon

and Chios for Rome, when Fimbria, hearing of his doings, sent him an urgent request to blockade Pitane and share with himself the glory of capturing the arch-enemy in a trap. Through loyalty to Sulla or dislike and distrust of Fimbria, or for some other reason, Lucullus refused, and the king slipped away to Mitylene. But Lucullus kept on to the northward and was victorious in a great sea-fight off Tenedos, over what seems to have been the main fleet of Mithradates under Neoptolemus. As ever, the Greeks were to the fore in naval matters, and Lucullus (who himself spoke and wrote Greek) owed his success largely to Rhodian skill.

883. The balance of advantage was now clearly in favour of Rome, notwithstanding the trouble in Italy and the lack of co-operation among her forces abroad. Sulla's wife Metella (she was his fourth) joined him in Greece, having managed to escape the Marians, and urged him to return and help his friends in Italy. But Sulla had other work to do first. Archelaus, perhaps acting under direct orders from his dejected master, felt his way to an interview and offered suggestions of peace. He tried to secure favourable terms by a proposal of assistance from the king in subduing Sulla's Italian adversaries. In reply Sulla invited him to throw over Mithradates and desert to Rome with his fleet. No doubt Sulla's memoirs are the source of this story ; but it may be true, for these two able men were like wrestlers feeling for the grip. They soon came to business. Sulla named his terms, which were these. The king was to surrender the fleet under Archelaus, and all Roman officers[1] and other prisoners of war, with deserters and slaves; to restore deported peoples to their homes; to withdraw all garrisons and evacuate Asia Bithynia Paphlagonia Galatia and Cappadocia, remaining content with his ancestral kingdom; and to pay 2000 talents (over £450,000) as costs of the war. A special provision was to be made for the benefit of those Macedonians who had been faithful to Rome and had probably been carried off by the agents of Mithradates. The smallness of the war-indemnity is surely a sign of Sulla's eagerness[2] to end this war, and be free to turn his attention to Italy. But the king's need of peace was even greater. Sulla offered to procure him forgiveness for the past and readmission as an ally of the Roman people, but he had of course no authority to make such an offer. Mithradates did not at once accept the terms; in particular he objected to give up Paphlagonia. The cool hard Roman decided to

---

[1] According to Licinianus p. 35 Bonn, Oppius and Aquilius were specially named. But the latter was dead.

[2] According to Memnon (*FHG* III 544) the first move towards peace was actually made by Sulla.

let him think the matter over, and meanwhile to improve his own position. In Asia the pressure of Fimbria was playing his game. He marched northwards, taking with him Archelaus, who had withdrawn his garrisons, and was treated with great favour. Indeed he was so rewarded that he incurred some suspicion of having purposely misconducted the campaigns in Greece; but this is not likely. When an answer came from the king rejecting the terms as too severe, Archelaus was at his own request sent to renew negotiations, and Sulla pushed on into Macedonia. Here he made an expedition against the northern tribes and restored order in the frontier regions. All hopes of Mithradates based on troubles in that quarter were thus at an end, and the Roman army, now in touch with the fleet of Lucullus, moved eastwards by the coast-route and safely made the passage into Asia Minor. The king, who had vainly tried to put pressure on Sulla by hinting that he might prefer to negotiate with Fimbria, now sought a personal interview, which took place at Dardanus in the Troad, not far from the ruins of Ilium, the traditional Troy, which Fimbria had barbarously destroyed.

884. After some bickering (for Mithradates still tried to evade a full compliance) the terms of Sulla were agreed to. The sum of 3000 talents named by Memnon perhaps marks a raising of the indemnity in consequence of the additional trouble and expense incurred by Sulla since he made his first offer. The same writer tells us that there was a stipulation that those Greeks of Asia who had transferred their allegiance to Mithradates should not be punished, a bargain not kept in the sequel. Sulla's next business was to settle accounts with Fimbria. This did not take long, for on the approach of Sulla Fimbria's men began to desert, and their leader killed himself. The victory of Sulla was now complete, his present objects being fully attained. But the Pontic kingdom was not destroyed. Mithradates withdrew to his own land sullenly meditating revenge, and set to work at once, reestablishing his authority and organizing fresh forces for a renewal of the war as occasion might serve. Sulla assumed the control[1] of Asia. He rewarded those who had fought or suffered for Rome; on the disloyal he laid a heavy hand. His proclamations provoked local risings, which were put down with bloodshed. He levied on the province[2] a contribution of 20,000 talents, the taxes of five years, to be paid at once, and (if we may trust Appian) a war-indemnity as well.

---

[1] His meeting the exile Rutilius has been already referred to (§ 825). See also Plutarch *Pomp.* 37, Appian *Mithr.* 60. For loyalty of Smyrna, Tacitus *ann.* IV 56.

[2] For Sulla's settlement of Asia see Marquardt *Stvw.* I 337 foll. He seems to include the war-indemnity in the 20,000 talents. Lange *RA* III 140 treats this sum as standing for the indemnity only.

The wretched provincials could not raise the amount without recourse to loans. Far and wide the public property of the cities was mortgaged. The capitalists whom the news of Sulla's victory had brought to Asia reaped a rich harvest, and for many a year, beside the normal oppression and extortion, the curse of poverty and hopeless debt rested on what had been one of the most prosperous regions of the ancient world. But for the moment there was a further infliction. Sulla's men are said to have grumbled at the peace. Mithradates, they thought, had been let off too easily. Perhaps the opportunities of plunder had not come up to their expectations, and no doubt the king had skimmed the cream of local opulence. To reward their exertions and prepare them for following their leader in the coming civil war, he put them into comfortable winter-quarters in provincial cities. No doubt the most disloyal cities were selected to bear the greater part of this detested burden. The local treasuries had to pay their tormentors at a rate four times the military wage: even the common soldier received 16 drachmas (about 13*s*.) a day. The householder on whom he was billeted had to feed the soldier and his guests, and to put up with constant violation of all he held most dear in private life. Many were thus reduced to beggary, and there is no doubt that in the winter of 85—4 the Asiatic provincials drained the cup of misery to the dregs. But, whatever their sufferings, they had to bear them as best they might. So long as the Roman Republic lasted, the financial interests of individuals stood in the way of any material alleviation of their lot. The administrative arrangements of Sulla mostly remained in force for several centuries: the farming of tithes in kind, the chief field of extortion, was only exchanged for a system of fixed tribute by the wisdom of Julius Caesar.

885. Sulla had now plenty of ships, so he began the homeward journey by transporting his army to the Piraeus by sea. The legions of Flaccus and Fimbria were left behind under L. Licinius Murena with Lucullus as his quaestor. For the time Mithradates was quiet, and there was peace on land. But the disorder caused by the war had encouraged a great development of piracy, with which the combatant powers were too busy to interfere. Corsair squadrons raided the islands of the Aegean and towns on the seaboard of Asia. Sulla had objects to him more important than the suppression oi this evil. The losses fell almost wholly on Asiatic Greeks, whose protection could safely be deferred. So he let this matter slide, and wintered in Greece, where he had enough to do, what with settling local questions, organizing preparations for a descent on Italy in the coming spring, and taking the waters to relieve a touch of gout. His residence at Athens is the occasion of a story[1] too famous to be omitted here. It is said that the library bequeathed by Aristotle to Theophrastus, and by Theophrastus to Neleus of Scepsis in the Troad, had been carried off to Scepsis. To elude the search of the Attalid kings of Pergamum, who were book-hunting for their great library, these literary treasures were hidden away in a cellar, where the indifference of the heirs of Neleus left them till they were seriously damaged. Among them, beside the works of Theophrastus, were the only extant copies of the more abstruse and technical writings of Aristotle; for the later Peripatetics had no knowledge of the profounder doctrines of their master, and did what they could with popular treatises and diluted tradition. In the Peripatetic school at Athens was one Apellicon[2] of Teos, who was more of a book-lover and antiquary than a philosopher, and who in the quest of curiosities was not above filching documents from public record-rooms at Athens and elsewhere. This man got to know of the hoard at Scepsis, and bought it of the owners for a good round sum. In the process of deciphering and copying the books he ventured to repair by conjecture the ravages of damp and worms; and it was no wonder that errors abounded in the hastily-restored texts, or that multiplication of copies led to variation. Apellicon died about this time, and Sulla took possession of his collection, which he afterwards transferred to Rome. And there, to finish the story, curious scholars (Greek, so far as we know,) obtained access to it, and copying went on apace. Many careless copies were made without being duly collated with the original. And so the authentic works of Aristotle, with numberless errors and variants, were spread abroad[3] among the learned of the civilized world. That some truth at least underlies this singular and romantic tale, is I think generally admitted; that many particulars in it are unsatisfactory, can perhaps hardly be denied. What concerns us here is the interest shewn by Sulla in what passed for an unique find of masterpieces, a trait quite consistent with his character and with the tastes of the time. While in Greece, he consorted with actors and musicians, and procured initiation into the Eleusinian Mysteries. Athens, to which cultivated Romans were now again resorting, had probably many

---

[1] Strabo XIII 1 § 54 (p. 609), Plutarch *Sull.* 26, and Posidonius fragm. 41 (*FHG* III 269). A good brief modern criticism of the story is in Mr Newman's *Politics of Aristotle*, vol. II pp. III, IV.

[2] We learn from Posidonius that this man had been a trusted satellite of Aristion.

[3] Varro *de re rustica* II 5 § 13 speaks of certain persons, authorities on a curious point in cattle-breeding, as 'readers of Aristotle.' He seems to refer to Arist. *gen. animal.* IV 1 §§ 18—21. This treatise may thus be an instance of a work recovered at this time, for Varro is writing after Caesar's death. So too many of Cicero's references may be to rescued works. But in *de inventione* II §§ 6, 7, he must refer to books already known, if he is writing (Wilkins' *de orat.* p. 56) during Sulla's absence.

attractions for Sulla, busy though he was. In particular we here meet with a notable figure, the young Roman knight[1] T. Pomponius Atticus, destined to play a rare and conciliatory part in the days of bitter jealousies and factious collisions that accompanied the break-up of the Republic. His policy in life was to take neither side in a quarrel, but to do good turns to individuals on both sides. He had already lent money to the younger Marius when an outlaw fleeing from Sulla. But Rome under Cinna was no place for him, so he escaped from Italy, and was now at Athens. He was soon high in the favour of Sulla, and used his influence[2] in favour of the unhappy Athenians. The state was in great distress for want of money, and financiers would only lend at usurious rates. The wealthy Atticus came forward with a loan at reasonable interest, and shewed his insight into the Athenian character by not allowing them to postpone re-payment beyond the day fixed for redemption. His many acts of generosity, and his gentle affability to men of all sorts and conditions, endeared him greatly to the people, but the highest honours pressed upon him he declined. A follower of the quietist sect[3] of Epicurus, he is the most striking illustration of the charm which the dogmas of that school possessed for some of the most refined natures and culti-vated minds of Rome. Sulla tried to induce Atticus to accompany him to Italy; Atticus excused himself on the ground that he had already left Italy in order to avoid taking part with the Marians, and now did not wish to take part against them. So he stayed behind, out of the hurlyburly of Roman politics, and resided at Athens for more than 20 years.

886. Early in the year 83 Sulla put to sea with five legions, 6000 cavalry, and a few Greek auxiliaries, about 40,000 men[4] in all, and landed safely at Brundisium, where he had a friendly reception. This wonderful man had managed to keep the devotion of his soldiers unimpaired. They must have known that they would have to face fearful odds in Italy, where the Marian faction had been in power for nearly four years. But these seasoned veterans knew that numbers do not make an army, and voluntarily took an oath to stand by their fortunate and skilful leader. Military superstition is proverbial, and

---

[1] See Life of Atticus by Cornelius Nepos. Boissier, *Cicéron et ses amis*; Strachan-Davidson, *Cicero*; Tyrrell, *Corresp. of Cic.* I pp. 44—6. The last takes a very unfavourable view of his character, too much so to be a fair description of him when young.

[2] Sulla restored the constitution of Athens as it was before the revolution of Aristion. That is, the franchise was limited and placed again on a property-basis. See Appian *Mithr.* 39, Plut. *Sull.* 14.

[3] The Epicureanism of Atticus was doubtless an adhesion of temperament and interest rather than of intellect and conviction.

[4] So Appian. Velleius says not more than 30,000.

the luck of Sulla was able to provide suitable omens of victory. The chief himself, cool and clear of purpose, had in 85 written to the Senate recounting his past services, protesting against the treatment of himself and his partisans, and announcing his intention of returning and executing judgment on his adversaries. From Asia he had sent home a report of his proceedings, ignoring the fact that he was technically an outlaw and not a representative of Rome. He had let it be known that he did not intend to persecute the new citizens as such, probably meaning that he would not upset the settlement of the franchise-question arrived at, under the direction of the Marian leaders, by the censors of 86. This engagement[1], designed to mitigate the hostility and soothe the suspicions of the Italians, he appears to have repeated later in a more solemn form. We have now to consider the situation in Italy, the measures taken by the Marians, and the instructive story of the civil war.

---

[1] Compare Livy ep. 86 with Appian *civ.* I 77 § 2.

CHAPTER XLVI.

CINNA, CARBO, SULLA, AND THE CIVIL WAR[1]. 85—82 B.C.

887. IN Italy the year 85 was a time of great uneasiness. The Marian party under Cinna and Carbo were dominant, but painfully preoccupied with schemes for securing the retention of their power. It was not under such rulers that distracted Italy could find rest. Men of rank were still leaving the country and in most cases taking refuge with Sulla in Greece; Metellus was preparing to assail the Marian interest in Africa, and young Crassus was hiding in a cave in Spain. Among the members of the Senate still in Rome there were some, such as the chief pontiff Scaevola, who were notoriously hostile to the present government, and probably few sincere in its support. That Cinna could not fully trust the new citizens scattered about Italy, was soon shewn by the action of his successor Carbo. In Samnium and Lucania large numbers of men were still in arms, either gathered in armies or ready to be embodied at short notice. In truth armed force was in these times the only effective power, and armed force had not as yet been able to set up a government in the stability of which all might feel confidence and to which even the dissatisfied might finally submit. Carbo and Cinna began to make preparations for the civil war now in prospect. They raised troops, collected money and supplies, posted garrisons in coast towns[2], got together a fleet, and exerted themselves to secure the cooperation of leading men throughout the country. The letter or manifesto of Sulla addressed to the Senate emboldened that body to open negotiations with him in hope of preventing civil war. Why Cinna let them take this step is not clear; perhaps he did not at the moment feel strong enough to forbid it, or he may have thought that Sulla, by refusing the terms offered (as he surely would), would place himself in the

---

[1] Authorities. Appian *civ.* I 76—94, Plutarch *Sulla* 27—30, *Sertor.* 6, *Crassus* 6, *Pomp.* 5—8, Livy ep. 83—8, Velleius II 24—9, Diodorus XXXVIII 6, 9—20, Dion Cass. fragm. 107—9, Florus II 9 §§ 18—24, Eutropius V 7—8, Exsuperantius 4, 5, 8 (a late writer, perhaps early in 5th cent. A.D., echoing the lost history of Sallust, but confused, especially in chronology), Orosius V 20, Strabo V 3 § 11, 4 § 11. In the fragments of Sallust *hist.* are many scattered passages bearing on this time, but the reference has generally to be ascertained from other authorities.

[2] Probably Neapolis was one. See Appian *civ.* I 89 § 6.

position of a public enemy, and arouse general apprehensions of the vengeance likely to follow his return. Meanwhile, until his answer arrived, preparations for war had an air of provocation, and the Senate went on to order the consuls to suspend them. They affected to comply, but a just estimate of approaching danger led them to disregard their promise. They went about raising troops, and began sending them over in detachments to the Illyrian coast. There was probably a good deal to be said in favour of the plan of not waiting to be attacked. But a loyal and contented army was an indispensable condition of success. Before them lay the toils of a long march through a mountainous country, if they meant to strike at Sulla, and there was small prospect of plunder to tempt their men to desire an enterprise of the kind. The advantage of taking the offensive was a consideration not likely to weigh much with the men. To them civil war was but a last resort, an evil to be avoided if possible: the motive of retaining power would not appeal to them as it did to their leaders: and the newly-raised troops had not the cohesion of a veteran army, or the devotion to their commanders that is the fruit of time and victory. Cinna was not popular, and a disaster to the second convoy in an Adriatic storm produced a mutiny in the camp at Ancona. The cry was raised that he had murdered young Pompey, who was missing, having slipped away, suspecting the intentions of Cinna. In the riot that followed Cinna was killed.

888. The murder of Cinna took place at the beginning of 84. Carbo was thereby left sole consul. He was busy collecting and organizing the army at Ancona, having given up the project of a transmarine campaign, and appears to have had no great desire for another colleague. He did not respond to the request of the tribunes that he should come to Rome and hold an election. They had to threaten him with a bill for his deposition from office before he would act. But seasonable portents broke up the Assembly on two occasions, and the attempt to provide him with a colleague was dropped. He was noisy and ambitious, and according to Cicero[1] a thorough scoundrel; certainly he was not fit to be at the head of the state in a time of gathering dangers, for he was deficient in nerve. The weakness of the government in Italy at this juncture was probably beyond our power of imagination to conceive. There was the Senate, in which the reactionary party was reviving, but uncertain how far it might venture to go without provoking another massacre on Marian lines. There was the consul, rash and insufficient, flustered and endeavouring to make up for lost time in organizing the means of resistance to Sulla. There was the Assembly, consisting mainly of

---

[1] Cicero *ad Jam.* IX 21 § 3, and index.

the city populace, interested in its own food-supply and amusements, and becoming conscious of its own impotence through the bloody revolutions of the last four years. And all over Italy were the great mass of citizens new and old, who either distrusted the good faith of the Roman government or doubted its stability. The fear of a reaction brought about by the return of Sulla seems to have been on the whole the predominant feeling, but this feeling could not find effective expression in the lack of a strong and inspiring leader. Such was the situation when Sulla's answer to the Senate arrived. They had offered to facilitate the reconciliation aimed at by providing for his personal safety on return to private life. He replied that he and his army would see to that matter. Thus he announced that he did not mean to disband his army on landing in Italy, but to use it for his own ends. He declined to be reconciled to the leaders of the Marian faction after all they had done, but grimly added that if the state saw fit to grant them their lives, he would raise no objection. He demanded the complete restitution of all properties positions and privileges, not only to himself but to all the distinguished refugees for whose safety and restoration he had made himself responsible. On these understandings, but not otherwise, he was their humble servant. In other words, he meant to be their master, and the cool irony of the message was assuredly not lost upon those who knew the character of Sulla. Everyone had now to decide upon a course for himself; the hour for trimming and dallying was past.

889. In the Senate there was a strong inclination to accept the terms offered, but Carbo and his associates managed to prevent this, doubtless by threats of violence, and the last hope of avoiding civil war was at an end. Carbo and the Senate were now pulling different ways. The consul wanted to bind all the towns of Italy to the Marian cause by taking hostages from them; the House refused to vote him authority for the purpose. On the other hand the Senate passed an order 'granting the suffrage to the new citizens,' as the epitome of Livy[1] puts it. This must mean allowing them to vote in any of the 35 Tribes. The same authority adds that the freedmen were divided among the 35 Tribes. These measures mark a return to the policy of Sulpicius and Marius. We know no details. That the Senate had no power[2] to decide on the voting-rights of the new citizens need not make us doubt the general truth of the statement. No doubt some attempt of the kind to satisfy the new citizens was made at this critical moment. The promise made in Sulla's first

---

[1] Livy epit. 84 *novis civibus senatus consulto suffragium datum est.*

[2] Perhaps, as Lange *RA* III 141 thinks, the order was formally carried out by a *lex Papiria* of Carbo.

manifesto, that he would bear no grudge against citizens new or old, had of course become widely known, and this was a countermove. That it had some effect is probable from the subsequent action of Sulla. We hear also of an order passed by the Senate that all armies wherever serving should be disbanded, and that it was carried under pressure from Carbo and the Marians. This can only have been a desperate move, meant to bring into clear relief the illegality of Sulla's position. He would not obey it, as they very well knew, and their own preparations went on. The consuls elected for 83, L. Cornelius Scipio Asiaticus and C. Junius Norbanus, were Marians, and both men of energy. Carbo went to Cisalpine Gaul as proconsul, to raise more troops and make sure of the North. We find him trying to exact hostages[1] at Placentia. A sign of the times may be traced in the behaviour of his cunning quaestor, the afterwards notorious C. Verres. This rogue foresaw the ruin of the Marians, so he robbed the military chest[2] and went off to join Sulla. At the end of 84 the newly-elected tribune M. Junius Brutus, one of the men outlawed by Sulla in 88, carried a law[3] for a colony at Capua, doubtless a military base for the operations of the war.

890. When Sulla landed at Brundisium, the Marians had several armies in the field. One under Norbanus was in Apulia, another under Scipio in northern Campania. We hear from Appian that the consuls and the Marian cause generally were well supported by 'those in the city,' who feared the intentions of Sulla, embittered by the wrongs and insults heaped upon him, and not the man to forgive or forget. They must win, or destruction awaited them. Probably this refers to the Knights in particular, among whom the Marian element was strong; and capitalists instinctively dread revolutions. But, as usual in times of peril, old prophecies of evil import were recalled and prodigies reported, and a wave of nervousness passed over Italy. Sulla for his part, superstitious like others, had a happy knack of imposing his own interpretation on such things, and he had not been ashore long before he received solid proof of Fortune's favours. Metellus had suffered defeat from the Marian governor of Africa, but he seems to have brought off a good part of his force, with which he now joined Sulla at Brundisium. Presently still better news came from the North. Young Pompey had made up his mind to do the same. In Picenum, where his father had made himself popular, he had estates and a wide connexion. He now raised a legion and brought it to Sulla, and soon after made up two more.

---

[1] Valer. Max. VI 2 § 10.
[2] Cicero I *in Verr.* § 11, II *in Verr.* I § 34.
[3] Cicero *de leg. agr.* II §§ 89—99.

Thus not only was the invading army strengthened in numbers and encouraged by the adhesion of fresh and willing allies; the brain-power was augmented at a critical moment by the accession of skilful and efficient generals. And Sulla knew how to get the most out of his supporters. No scruples or pedantry hindered him from humouring the vanity of Pompey; a striking contrast to the way in which the capacity of Sertorius was being wasted by the neglect of the Marians. To notice this is important, for the events of the next 40 years were to shew that the steady stream of tendencies in the falling Republic was on the whole adverse to the reactionary move-ment represented by Sulla. That he triumphed for the present was due to the personal superiority of the leader and his lieutenants and soldiers over their blind or half-hearted opponents. Sulla advanced into Apulia, defeated Norbanus near Canusium, and drove him over the Apennine to take refuge in Capua. He then turned upon Scipio in northern Campania. It was said of Sulla that he was a compound of lion and fox, and that the latter element was the more dangerous of the two. It was now the fox's turn. Scipio's army was reported to be in low spirits and indisposed to fight. Sulla made pretence of wishing to negotiate for peace, and Scipio, disregarding the warnings of Sertorius, consented to an interview. They met between Cales and Teanum, and Cicero[1] tells us that they discussed the franchise and suffrage questions and the position of the Senate in the constitution. In fact Sulla drew from Scipio an authoritative version of the political programme of the Marians, so far as they had any, which was to him useful material in shaping his own policy. Meanwhile the real busi-ness was quietly being transacted behind Scipio's back. His troops, grumbling at a piece of what seemed to them mismanagement (Scipio having disclaimed a bold act of Sertorius), were exposed to the temptations of Sulla's men, who thoroughly understood their part. Soon the consul's army went over in a body, and Sulla found himself the captor of a force twice the size of his own without striking a blow. Scipio and his son, deserted and helpless, refused to join him, so he let them go. They were an object-lesson to dishearten the other side, and to clemency judiciously invested Sulla had no sentimental repugnance whatever. After this Norbanus would receive no envoys, fearing not unreasonably a repetition of the same experience. Ser-torius, who was already appointed to a governorship[2] in Spain, but

---

[1] Cic. *philippic* XII § 27, XIII § 2.

[2] Exsuperantius 8, drawing from Sallust no doubt, says it was the Hither Spain, and adds that the Marian leaders sent him away to be rid of a critic, perhaps to provide a strong ruler for a restless province.

had stayed in Italy for the war, now left for his province, disgusted
with the blundering of his superiors, which he was powerless to prevent.
The war to the south of Rome for the rest of the year took the form
of raids, each side laying waste the lands belonging to the partisans
of the other.

891.   The results of the first campaign were in Sulla's favour.
It was to little purpose that Carbo had hurried to Rome and induced
the Senate to issue its 'last decree,' and declare Sulla and all senators
acting with him to be public enemies.   It came to this, that the consuls were empowered to do what they could not do.   Sulla had with
him a number of senators, some of them useful men, to whom his
victory would mean restoration.   Among those who had joined him
since he landed in Italy was P. Cornelius Cethegus, a man of bad
reputation, but clever and adroit.   He had been a violent opponent
of Sulla, and in 88 joined old Marius in Africa, and shared his
return.   His judgment of the prospects of his faction in 83 brought
him over to Sulla, who pardoned his offences and found him useful.
He became[1] infamous and influential, and his career is of interest as
illustrating the sinister influences at work on and beneath the surface
of Roman life.   His keen forecast was not at fault, yet the Marian
forces on foot at the end of the year still far outnumbered those of
Sulla.   Several armies were in the field, and the fear that Sulla would
not, if victorious, confirm their privileges lately conceded, kept the
mass of the new citizens loyal to the Marian cause.   Carbo had
played upon their fears, and had been able to raise immense forces in
Etruria and Cisalpine Gaul.   In Rome itself the burning of the
temple of Capitoline Jove alarmed many, as ominous of coming
disaster.   Who set it afire, nobody could tell : emissaries of Carbo or
Sulla[2] were hinted at, but the purpose of the act was not explained.
The opening of the campaign of 82 found Sulla still an invader, and
the resources of his opponents practically unimpaired.   Accordingly
at the beginning of this year he seems to have taken a wise step.
He negotiated by means of agents with such Italian communities as
were willing to treat and within reach.   Wheedling or threatening,
with use of promises and even bribes, he induced some at least to
enter into a compact[3] or treaty (*foedus*) with him, in which he pledged
himself not to disturb them in their political privileges.   Their part

---

[1] See Appian *civ.* I 80 § 6, Plutarch *Lucull.* 5, 6, Sallust *hist.* fragm. I 77 § 20, Cicero
Brutus § 178, *pro Cluent.* §§ 84—5, *paradoxa* § 40.

[2] Pliny *NH* XXXIII § 16 seems to imply that young Marius was concerned in the affair,
at least as a robber of treasure from this and other temples. Tacitus *hist.* III 72 says
fraude privata.

[3] Livy epit. 86.

of the bargain can only have been an undertaking, if not to help him, at least to stand neutral.   We are not told what communities made terms with him thus.   The later course of events shews that the Samnites and Etruscans can hardly be meant.   It is not easy to point out any block of country, not too distant, and at the same time occupied by newly-enfranchised Italians, to whom this negotiation can with reasonable probability be referred.   Perhaps the Marsi[1] and the peoples of that central group are as likely as any.

892.   The campaign of 82 included much serious fighting.   In his advance towards Rome Sulla fell in with the army under C. Marius the younger, who was consul in this year with Carbo.   The battle took place near Signia, at a spot called Sacriportus.   The steadiness of Sulla's veterans and the desertion of some of the consul's troops at a critical moment turned the stubborn fight into rout and massacre, and Marius only escaped with a remnant to Praeneste.   The pursuit was hot, and many prisoners taken; all Samnites found among them were put to the sword.   Sulla could not dally before the walls of a fortified town, so he left his lieutenant Q. Lucretius Ofella to besiege Praeneste, and pushed on himself to Rome. There horrors had already begun.   Before the siege-lines closed round him, Marius, who had at least inherited the bloodthirsty side of his father's character, sent orders to L. Junius Brutus Damasippus the city praetor bidding him to put to death certain nobles known to sympathize with Sulla.   On some pretext the Senate was summoned to meet.   Armed ruffians were brought into the House, and some of the marked men murdered then and there: others fled and were cut down outside.   The most illustrious victim was Scaevola[2] the chief pontiff, who through all these evil times had bravely remained at his post in defiance of his Marian enemies.   The Senate thus purged was a miserable body.   To have been spared by Damasippus was to be marked out for the vengeance of Sulla.   When Sulla appeared, all the chief Marians fled, and he entered the city unopposed.   The mere occupation of Rome was undoubtedly a moral gain, but he could not afford to linger there, so he made temporary arrangements for public business and placed partisans of his own in charge, made a reassuring speech to the people, and marched northwards into Etruria, now the principal seat of war.   In Umbria and Picenum fighting had been going on between Metellus and Pompey on the Sullan side and various Marian leaders.   The latter were generally beaten, and Carbo had to bring up fresh forces from Cisalpine Gaul.

---

[1] The recruiting expedition of Crassus (Plut. *Crass.* 6) in the Marsian country seems to support this view.

[2] See Mayor on Cicero *de nat. deor.* III § 80.

So far as can be made out from our very meagre authorities, the Sullan commanders cooperated more effectively than their opponents. Sulla himself had the upper hand in Etruria.   When Carbo crossed the Apennine range, a great drawn battle near Clusium was a moral victory for Sulla, who was gaining ground elsewhere.   Metellus invaded Cisalpine Gaul and occupied the low country about Ravenna. Pompey and Crassus won a victory in Umbria, though various causes prevented them from following up their advantage.   Far away to the South, in a night attack aided by treachery, the Sullans killed most of the garrison of Neapolis and seized the fleet of that city.   Meanwhile food was running short at Praeneste, and to raise the siege was now the first object of the Marians, whose weakness would stand exposed if the town were allowed to fall.   A force sent by Carbo to relieve it fell into an ambush and suffered heavy loss, and those who escaped for the most part dispersed to their homes, disgusted with the incapacity of their leaders.   Then a large army of Samnites and Lucanians attempted the relief from another side, but found the way blocked by Sulla.   They could not join hands with Marius, who for all his efforts could not break out.   Nor was a later attempt, made by Damasippus under orders from Carbo, any more successful.

893.   In the North also the Marian cause was failing.   Mismanagement led to distrust.   When Carbo and Norbanus rashly attacked Metellus in Cisalpine Gaul, the result to their army is given[1] as follows ; killed, about 10,000 ; went over to enemy, 6000 ; retreated in good order to Arretium, 1000.   The rest of what was evidently a large army were scattered in flight.   A legion of Lucanians on the march to join them, hearing of their disaster, went over to the Sullan general.   Their commander protested, but in a few days wearied of his own loyalty.   He secretly got from Sulla a promise of his life, if he earned it by some meritorious service.   He invited Norbanus and other Marian leaders to dinner, murdered those who accepted his hospitality, and in virtue of this achievement withdrew to the camp of Sulla.   Norbanus had missed this entertainment, but he saw the cause going to ruin, towns and bodies of troops going over to the enemy, and no friend whom he could safely trust.   He took ship and made his way to Rhodes.   When Sulla was in supreme power, he sent to demand the extradition of Norbanus, who in despair took his own life while the answer of the Rhodians was still in debate.   The Sullan forces gained another victory near Placentia, and all Cisalpine Gaul soon made submission to what was now clearly the more powerful side.   Yet Carbo had still a strong army in Etruria, and his Samnite allies were making great efforts for the sake of the cause.

[1] Appian *civ.* I 91.

He chose this moment for leaving them in the lurch, and fled to Africa with a few friends. Of his end we shall speak below. The army deserted by him was defeated by Pompey near Clusium with great loss: most of the survivors dispersed: a part, under three desperate Marians who could expect no mercy from Sulla, made their way to the Samnite army. That army was now in a dangerous position. Sulla himself barred the way to Praeneste, and Pompey was now free to come up and complete their destruction. They were led by brave men who meant to fight to the last, among them Pontius Telesinus, a namesake and perhaps a descendant of the Samnite hero of the Caudine Forks. Rather than sit still and wait to be destroyed, they resolved to stake all upon one desperate venture. They broke up by night and marched upon Rome. Samnites, Lucanians, and the remnant of the beaten Marians, they may have amounted to 80,000 men, the number given by Velleius. And this was a real fighting army. The moment was one on which the imagination of later generations loved to dwell. Pontius, calling on his troops to assert Italian freedom by destroying the lair of the Roman wolves, is the Hector of the scene. By great exertions Sulla and his army reached the city just in time. The famous battle of the Colline gate, fought under the walls of Rome on the first of November 82, ended in the final overthrow of an already lost cause. Here was at last a real death-struggle worthy of the occasion. Not until midnight did Sulla know that he had won, for his own wing of the army had been beaten. The losses of both sides in the battle are put at 50,000 men.

894. There was now no need of clemency as a means of conciliating opponents or attracting waverers. The fruits of victory were gathered with ease, and with Sulla the day of mercy was past. In the good faith of surrenders he had no belief: a dead enemy was at all events unable to rebel. Some of the beaten army he promised to spare if they would kill others; this done, he killed them. Six thousand[1] were butchered in a body by his order, and the ears of senators (for the House was in session hard by) were alarmed by the shrieks of the victims. Sulla invited members to attend to the business before them, and not be distracted by a little matter of punishment. Heads of captured Marian leaders were sent to the lines before Praeneste and exhibited to the beleaguered garrison. The place soon fell. Marius tried vainly to escape by way of a drain or underground passage, and committed suicide. The leaders were put to death: of the common soldiers the Romans were spared, Praenestines and Samnites slaughtered like cattle. Norba too was

[1] According to Appian, 8000.

held for the Marian side, and still resisted for a time; but some traitors let the Sullans into the town, and the defenders, sooner than trust the good faith and humanity of the conqueror, killed themselves or each other, having first set fire to the buildings. The civil war in Italy was at an end. That there was still work to be done in some of the Provinces we shall presently see. This may remind us that Rome was no longer a merely Italian power, and warn us that any attempt to ignore facts, to reorganize the Roman empire on any other than an imperial basis, was doomed to fail. For the present one thing seemed clear, that the Marian party, with its democratic connexion and its championship of the claims of the new citizens, was utterly crushed. To contemporary observers it can hardly have seemed possible that it would ever again revive; still less that *populares* would triumph over *optimates*, and place a greater than Sulla in the seat of absolute power. Yet there can be little doubt that in their hearts the majority of the citizens, new and old together, even now inclined to the party which, in however confused a succession, was heir to the democratic tradition, and associated with the movement, however clumsy and wasteful of blood, which had brought about the incorporation of Italy in Rome.

895. The ruin of the Marians had been accelerated by their opponents' military skill, but this was only a secondary cause. No leader on their side stood out above the rest so far as to be able to devise and carry out a consistent policy with the help of loyal subordinates. Delay and hesitation, slackness and inefficiency, marked and marred their proceedings. Of personal vanity and ambition there was enough and to spare, enough to prevent them from producing a monarch or even turning talents to the best account; and this when a central control and the best use of available resources were the pressing needs of the hour. Against a Sulla, accepted as a master by willing servants, using only the capable in positions of trust, strong in the logical unity of a policy directed by a single mind, the Marians had no chance. The pick of the governing nobles sympathized with him; Metellus, Pompey, Crassus, and others ran great risks to support him, far-sighted rogues like Cethegus and Ofella went over to him in time to claim the merit of a judicious treason. Desertions of troops, treachery or flight of leaders, are the characteristic phenomena of the Marian side in the actual war, the outcome of a political condition fundamentally unsound: the staunch loyalty of the Samnites was essentially anti-Roman, and was displayed too late. For good or for evil, Italy had not humbled Rome, but the Roman city-state had absorbed Italy. Yet this absorption had left the Republic as a form of government more helpless than ever.

When the civil war, epilogue of the Italian war, was over, Rome and all that belonged to Rome lay at the disposal[1] of a single will.   Men might disguise the truth by the make-believe of forms and phrases, a process ever congenial to the Roman mind.   But the truth remained.   Whether the monarch had or had not come to stay, the principle of monarchy had triumphed.

[1] With Appian *civ.* I 97—8 compare Cicero *de harusp. responso* § 54 (of Sulla) *tum sine dubio habuit regalem potestatem, quamquam rem publicam recuperarat.*

CHAPTER XLVII.

SULLA[1]. 82—78 B.C.

896. WHAT has been said of the biographical tendency in the history of the later Republic finds no more striking illustration than the supremacy of Sulla. The personality of this strange man is everything. His temperament and tastes, his fierce energy coupled with a passionate longing for luxurious repose, his cool cynicism and freedom from illusions joined to a superstitious fatalism, punctilious scruples in some things, utter unscrupulousness in others, a mixture of unbending cruelty with easygoing indifference—the blend of contrasts in the person of one possessed of supreme power in the greatest state of the ancient world is enough to justify the assertion that the man and the situation together were unique. The decay of civil government and the growth of military power, the differentiation of citizen and soldier, had indeed made the appearance of a despot not only possible but inevitable. But that the despot should do what Sulla did was surely in the highest degree improbable. In short the man was not more the creature of the situation than the situation of the man. Hence the stray notices of Sulla's life and habits, preserved by Plutarch and others, are of great importance in enabling us to judge not only his personal character but the spirit of his public acts.

897. Among the various opinions concerning Sulla only one calls for special consideration. Some ancient writers[2] speak of him as having undergone a marked change at the moment of attaining supreme power. He had upheld the prestige of Rome abroad and put down the tyranny of the Marians at home. So far well; he had 'recovered the commonwealth.' But it was a shocking thing that he should at once have set up a tyranny more crushing than that of the Marians, that he should have outdone their irregular atrocities by a deliberately organized course of murders and confiscations, and that in liberating Rome he should merely have set people free to tremble

---

[1] General authorities. Appian *civ.* I 80, 95—106, Livy ep. 88—90, Velleius II 28, 30 § 4, 32 § 3, 41—3, Plutarch *Sull.* 30—8, *Crass.* 6, *Pomp.* 9—15, *Caesar* 1—3, *Cato min.* 3, *Cicero* 3, 4, Sallust *Catil.* 5 § 6, 11, 16 § 4, 21 § 4, 37 § 6, 47 § 2, 51 §§ 32—4, *Jug.* 95, *hist.* frag. Maur. I esp. 55, Florus II 9 §§ 25—8, Eutropius V 9, Orosius V 20—2, Dion Cass. fragm. 108—110, Diodorus XXXVIII 19, 20, Augustin *de civ. Dei* II 24, III 27—30.

[2] Plutarch *Sull.* 30, Dion Cass. fragm. 109, Velleius II 25 § 3.

before himself and submit in patience to whatever he might inflict or enjoin. And shocking it was, no doubt; but surely it does not indicate any change in Sulla. From first to last the love of pleasure was his ruling passion. Banqueting and wantonness, in the company of actors and actresses, dancers and buffoons, with enough wit and culture[1] to season the entertainment and distinguish these social gatherings from the gratifications of the pigsty, were the joys of his youth. For them in his last years he renounced the responsibilities of government and the pomp of power. How far he can strictly be called ambitious is a more doubtful question. The vigour which gave zest to a many-sided debauchery also expressed itself in a determination to emerge from the restraints of poverty and a subordinate position. Patriotic he was in a narrow sense, and he did Rome much good service; but he was assuredly under no delusion as to the state of politics in his day. From Marius he learnt most of the art and practice of war, and the lesson that an army now belonged not to the state but to a successful general. The republican system implied competition, but the real competitors now were not magistrates as such, who might or might not be commanding armies, but generals of armies, who might or might not be magistrates, as the transfer of the eastern command in 88 from Sulla to Marius sufficiently proved. Once Sulla had entered into competition with others, there was under the conditions of the time nothing to be done but to fight it out to the bitter end. Each step led to something further: the higher he rose, the less likely were enemies to spare him if they once got him in their power. The point was reached at which it was only possible to secure his safety and a return to his interrupted pleasures by utterly destroying his enemies. This he did without scruple, with characteristic thoroughness, and went back to his old pleasures as a matter of course. In politics he did not see his way to doing anything without a cleaning of the slate; so he washed it in blood, drew on it a reactionary scheme of government, and laid it aside, obviously sick and weary of the whole business. Whether his failure as a political reformer was more directly due to indolence or to lack of insight is a subject on which views may differ. It matters little. To reform the constitution on republican lines was probably quite impossible. The indirect but effective way in which he provided for his own security shews that he was not likely to take shadow for substance, and his reform of the judicature was a real advance in the right direction. Sulla was ever thoroughgoing, whether in work or

---

[1] Pliny epist. v 3 § 5 names him among the eminent men who used to throw off light copies of verse not always decorous. In Nicol. Damasc. fragm. 81 (*FHG* III 416) his 'satyric comedies' are mentioned.

pleasure: good or evil, what he found to do, he did with his might. He is said to have written his own epitaph, to the effect that whoever had done him a good or bad turn had been repaid in full. Outlaw or despot, he always knew what he wanted, and went straight to its attainment: if men or institutions stood in his way, they had to go. The acts in which this policy expressed itself were horrible enough, all the more so for being deliberate. But we are not entitled to say that, given Sulla's conditions, any gentler being could have done better than Sulla and died in his bed. So far as he succeeded, it was because he was a Sulla and not a Caesar.

898. The speedy execution of the captured Marian leaders and the butchery of the Samnite prisoners struck terror into the citizens. Sulla addressed a public meeting, promising reforms for the public good, but threatening dire vengeance on his enemies. It seemed that it was not enough to submit to the conqueror. Was he not going to spare his fellow-citizens now that he had them in his power? Murders were occurring daily, and it was clear that Sulla allowed them. At last a question was put to him in the Senate—What were his intentions? How were men to know whether they were his enemies or not? The questioner was one of his own partisans. Sulla consented to relieve the strain of uncertainty, and accordingly began to issue a series of black-lists. Day by day the notice-board appeared with a list of names of men doomed to die. Rewards were offered to those who killed or betrayed any of the *proscripti*, while those who concealed or protected them were menaced with penalties. The property of the victims was to be confiscated, and their sons and grandsons disqualified from ever holding public office or sitting in the Senate. Cold-blooded and methodical as this procedure was, it did not allay the nervous tension produced by uncertainty. If a man's name were not in the first batch, it might appear in the second, and so on; supplementary lists were posted at intervals for some months, to meet the cases of those overlooked in the first hurry. Of the total number done to death in the Sullan proscriptions we have no accurate statistics. Probably there never were any, for in that epidemic of murders no doubt many perished unobserved. One writer[1] asserts that 4700 names were actually recorded in the lists. We have no reason to suspect that the sickening pictures[2] of the Sullan reign of terror are overdrawn to any great extent. We read of the utter demoralization of Roman society under the influence of continued panic and temptations of every kind. In the frantic

[1] Valer. Max. IX. 2 § 1.

[2] The *locus classicus* for the epic-rhetorical treatment of the Marian and Sullan horrors is Lucan II 68—232.

endeavour to save their own lives men and women betrayed their nearest relatives and dearest friends. Once a man was doomed, the main question was to whose profit or loss the inevitable murder would turn. The presence of informers would cause everybody to suspect everybody else, and the threatened punishment of the faithful was not likely to remain an idle threat. Was it necessary to share the fate of a friend whom it was impossible for loyalty to save? To some at least it seemed that a timely act of betrayal was the less of two evils. To these general considerations we must add the special dread that weighs upon slave-owning societies. In many a household the turn of events had made the slave the master of his lord. The fear of retribution to follow, always an active element in servile fidelity, was quite inoperative in face of the firm supremacy of Sulla. Nor could much be hoped from offering the slave his freedom. Sulla confiscated and manumitted them wholesale. If the slave accused and destroyed his present owner, he had the prospect of becoming a freedman of the most powerful of patrons. And in this dreadful time even the readiness to emancipate his slaves exposed a man to the imputation of acting from a motive of conscious guilt. As for the black-lists, to shew a marked interest in them or to avoid looking at them was alike dangerous.

899. What made the Sullan proscriptions so horrible was not the mere fact that the victor put his enemies to death without trial. Such executions were no new thing, but a time-honoured means of disarming hostility. In Greek party-strife they had been normal, and to waive the right was a signal exhibition of clemency. To eastern courts they were the simple and effective method of removing persons whose presence was not desired. Rome herself had in these latter days seen the bloody vengeance taken by Marius in his hour of victory. Nor again was it the confiscation of the victims' estates that shocked public sentiment so deeply; it was not without precedent. That the innocent sometimes suffered with the guilty was sad, but it might happen at any time of revolution in hot-blooded haste. What impressed contemporaries, and remained a nightmare to generations of Romans, was rather the awful truth that it placed all the best elements of the population at the mercy of the worst. The slow and systematic procedure of Sulla gave every scoundrel time to understand how great were the opportunities for paying off old scores, for procuring indemnity for past crimes, for ridding himself of encumbrances, and for enriching himself by the ruin of his neighbours. In the Rome of 82 B.C., a Rome that had lost its old simple ideals without acquiring sound new ones, a Rome given over to the worship of wealth however acquired, and for the last fifty years torn by civil

discords leaving behind them a heritage of feuds, there was no lack of persons to whom the present opportunities were an irresistible temptation. To get the name of an enemy posted on the list was no very difficult matter, and he could then be murdered without risk at a convenient season. An improvement on this was soon devised ; the man was killed first, and his name posted afterwards. The next development was when a man who had murdered another before the proscriptions began now got his victim's name placed on the list. It is said that the afterwards notorious L. Sergius Catilina, who had made away with a brother during the war, received indemnity in this form by grace of Sulla. Still the number of public and private enmities gratified by the proscription-lists could hardly have been so great, or the memory so bitter and lasting, if hatred and jealousy had not been quickened by greed. The hope of sharing the plunder of the slain, or of buying up forfeited estates at less than their real value, was a powerful stimulus to crime. The capitalist whose foresight or luck had ranged him on the side of Sulla now saw before him the chance of acquiring untold wealth by judicious purchases in a market glutted by forced sales. The Equestrian Order had generally inclined to the Marian side, and a great number of them fell victims to Sulla's vengeance. Thus a vast amount of property now changed hands, while the number of likely purchasers was lessened. The man with ready money, whether senator or Knight, could pick up valuable houses and landed estates[1] with the practical certainty of making profitable bargains. Many did so, among them M. Licinius Crassus, the millionaire of the next generation, who built up his colossal fortune by thus picking the bones of his brother capitalists.

900. It is easy to see that the result of this infamous transfer of property would be to interest an influential class in the maintenance of the Sullan settlement. At the moment it had the further effect of encouraging crime. A man need not himself procure the proscription and murder of a wealthy citizen : if he profited in any way by the occurrence, he was not in a position to raise awkward questions. Indeed a growing lust of wealth might easily tempt him to bear an active part in extending his own opportunities. It is said that Crassus proscribed (and presumably killed) a man in the Bruttian country, solely for the purpose of enriching himself, and that Sulla, who thought ill[2] of the proceeding, withdrew his confidence from

---

[1] Sulla's lavish generosity to his partisans was notorious, but some are said to have declined to profit by it, or by the forced sales. See in particular Cicero *de off.* I 43, and Asconius p. 18.

[2] Compare Cicero's account of his treatment of the greedy turncoat Verres, II *in Verr.* I § 38.

Crassus. But, if we may believe our authorities, the case was by no means singular. It was indeed a horrible thing that men, innocent even of resistance to Sulla, should be done to death merely because others coveted their estates; but, once the thing was done with impunity, all the worst hangers-on of the victorious faction scrambled for a share of the booty, and the last traces of scruple disappeared. Sulla himself presided at auctions of confiscated property, and Cicero tells us that he spoke of it as his booty (*praeda*), a military term for the goods of a conquered enemy. Romans were thus brutally informed by a fellow citizen that they were slaves. They saw him putting to death whom he would, and lavishly rewarding his adherents and worthless minions of both sexes out of Roman spoils. The artful Greek freedman, serviceable to a tyrant in need of ministers bound to fidelity by hopes and fears, but terrible to citizens whose aspirations were not compatible with his existence, now appears: a sinister figure, destined to reappear again and again in the days of the Empire as an instrument of administration, and to wield enormous power. The Romans of Sulla's time, particularly the nobles, did not lack the pride which saw in the Roman, or even in the Italian, an essential superiority to the supple and cringing Greek. Nothing can have brought home to them their servitude more clearly than the predominant influence of such creatures as Sulla's freedman Chrysogonus. It was bad enough that they dared not raise their voices against the bloodshed and robbery with which all reasonable men were now disgusted; but to have to fawn upon freedmen was the very crown of their shame. We need not wonder that the agony of the Sullan proscriptions lived on in a copious and vivid tradition; written large and ghastly in the literature of Rome.

901. To give any notion of the surroundings in which people had to live at this time, we must not shrink from recording horrors. Among those who fell into Sulla's power was the praetor M. Marius[1] Gratidianus, the man who had gained great popularity two or three years before by his action in respect of the currency. He was by adoption a member of the Marian family, and Sulla, whose rule was to pay off all scores in full, now chose him as a victim to atone for the death of Catulus. Old Marius had forced his colleague of the Cimbric war to commit suicide: Sulla, having caught a live Marius, had him put to death[2] at the tomb of the Lutatii, by the refined process of piecemeal dissection known to readers of books on China as 'death by the

---

[1] His father was M. Gratidius, who was by a marriage connexion Cicero's great-uncle. The relations of the three respectable families (Marii, Gratidii, Tullii) give us a glimpse into the municipal society and politics of Arpinum. See Cicero *de legibus* III § 36, *Brutus* § 168, Wilkins on *de orat.* I § 178.

[2] See Q. Cicero *de petit. cons.* § 10, and Tyrrell's note.

1000 cuts.' Catiline, his brutal henchman, is said[1] to have done the deed with his own hand, to have brought the victim's head to Sulla sitting in the Forum, and to have rinsed his bloody hands in a sacred basin of purificatory water hard by. We read of tortures inflicted at Sulla's house, and the production of heads of eminent victims stored there. We are told[2] that young Cato, when brought by his tutor to call on the great man, was so infuriated by the horrid sight that he asked for a sword to kill the tyrant then and there. Even the dead were not left in peace. The remains of old Marius were taken up and cast into the river Anio, and the trophies of his victories in the Cimbric war were pulled down. After these performances the show of heads on the Rostra and the corpses drifting down the Tiber sound commonplace and according to precedent. But we must not forget that the scope of the proscriptions was not confined to Rome. All Italy was affected. Not only were trackers of blood[3] abroad, hunting down fugitives from the city: the same horrors on a minor scale were repeated in country towns, wherever a notorious Marian was detected or an influential Sullan cast greedy eyes upon a desirable estate. Of the punishment of whole communities we will speak below. Even in the Provinces and allied kingdoms and republics there was no safety for the proscribed, for none cared to provoke the despot in Rome by harbouring a refugee.

902.   In giving a sketch of the atrocities of Sulla I have delayed considering the question of the authority by which he did these things. Just at first, while Marian forces were still in arms at Praeneste and Norba, he acted on the right of the sword as conqueror, and a good deal of the slaughter seems to have been carried out on that simple footing. But with the fall of these fortresses open resistance was at an end in Italy, and Sulla was too much of a Roman not to have a turn for formalities. He had never laid down the proconsular powers under which he had taken his army in 87 to the East. Strictly speaking, his entry into Rome had extinguished his *imperium* ; in any case he had no right to be there with his army save for the purpose of a triumph, and then only in virtue of a special law granting the right. He began to legitimize his position by a decree of the Senate[4] confirming all his acts as consul and proconsul. Of course anything he chose to order was passed at once. Whether this was at once embodied in a law and carried through the Assembly,

---

[1] See Holden's note on Plutarch *Sull.* 32 § 2. The last detail may be a bit of later colouring, but I see no ground for doubting the rest of the story.

[2] Valer. Max. III 1 § 2.

[3] See a good instance in Cic. *pro Cluentio* § 25.

[4] Appian *civ.* I 97 § 2. I think Lange rightly (*RA* III 149) refers this to the Senate.

is not clear; somewhat later at any rate a law[1] was carried which gave him full powers for the future, combined with retrospective clauses. Our authorities are too vague to enable us to distinguish the exact course of proceedings. A fully-gilt equestrian statue, to be set up in the Forum, was voted him. He now assumed the title of 'fortunate' (*felix*) as an extra surname, which in Greek he rendered by 'favoured of Aphrodite' (ἐπαφρόδιτος), the goddess of good luck with the dice-box. His wife Metella about this time bore him twins, boy and girl. These he named 'lucky' (*Faustus* and *Fausta*). To impress the world with the irresistible might of his fortune was a part of the drama not neglected by one deeply conscious of other men's superstitions and willing to parade his own.

903. Fortune had indeed favoured him. Outside Italy there was little to cause him uneasiness. In the East, where he had triumphed over every obstacle, the news that he was now absolute master at home was sure to have a quieting effect. In the West there was Sertorius, who meant to hold Spain in the Marian interest. His military skill made him dangerous, and Sulla sent the praetor Annius to expel him. This was soon done, and Sertorius could not for the present make good his footing in that country. Sardinia seems to have been wrested from the Marians during the war by the old turn-coat L. Marcius Philippus the opponent of Drusus, who had begun public life as a radical with leanings to communism and was now a minister of the reaction under Sulla. The corn-producing island was important to the ruler of Rome; even more important were the provinces of Sicily and Africa. The present governor of Sicily, M. Perperna, was of the Marian faction. In Africa there seems to have been no regular governor. The man appointed by Cinna, C. Fabius Hadrianus, had made himself so obnoxious to the Romans settled at Utica that they raised a mob against him, blockaded him in his official residence, and burnt the house, governor and all. But the Roman community, who were probably for the most part capitalist Knights or their agents, seem to have been on the Marian side. When that cause was failing in Italy, Carbo joined them, but soon left again for Sicily with a fleet that he had somehow got together. The present head of affairs in Africa was Cn. Domitius Ahenobarbus, another proscribed Marian fugitive, who induced Hiarbas the king of Numidia to support him with a native army. To clear up these remains of the civil war, and doubtless to reopen the corn-supply, now more than ever necessary in the exhausted state of Italy, Sulla chose young Pompey. He was now barely 24, and had held no office, but Sulla knew his man. The obedient Senate were charged with his appoint-

---

[1] Cicero II *in Verr.* III § 82, *de leg. agr.* III § 5. See below § 905.

ment, and he was formally invested with the *imperium*. But before the young general left for the South he had to submit to a rearrangement of domestic relations at his master's orders. He put away his wife[1] Antistia, a lady against whom nothing is alleged, and who had lately lost her father. We have seen that the Marians, just before they evacuated Rome, murdered several senators suspected of a leaning to Sulla. Among these was P. Antistius, doomed because of his son-in-law. But Sulla had no consideration for the daughter's feelings. Pompey too did not let her stand in the way of his own advancement. She had to go, and her mother was so upset by these sorrows that she killed herself. Meanwhile Pompey married the lady assigned him by his chief. This was Aemilia, daughter of Sulla's own wife Metella by a former marriage with M. Aemilius Scaurus the well-known statesman. A family connexion was thus set up. Sulla's object was to attach to himself a young man likely to prove useful in furthering his designs. One of these designs was no doubt his own secure retirement; and he probably detected in Pompey that vanity and appetite for honours which in him took the place of masterful ambition, and which in the end led him into a position from which he could not escape. Aemilia was already married to M' Acilius Glabrio, and was big with child. But Sulla cared for none of those things. Aemilia was divorced, and remarried to Pompey, in whose house she was shortly afterwards confined, and died in childbirth.

904. Such were the liberties that Sulla allowed himself to take with the relations of private life. 'The affairs of this marriage were suited to a tyrant's court' says Plutarch. That is, all other considerations gave way to dynastic convenience. But the use of marriages as an appliance of policy, though known to Greek tyrants, was positively normal in the kingdoms of Alexander's Successors. If we must needs find a parallel, perhaps a suggestive precedent, for Sulla's cold-blooded rearrangements, it is quite as reasonable to seek it at Antioch as at Syracuse, and Plutarch's words may possibly not exclude this alternative. But the heads of Roman houses habitually paired off their children with wives or husbands chosen for them on the principle of securing good value in the form of the best obtainable alliance. The analogy of the house-father's power in the Roman family was probably enough for Sulla, when his interest guided his will, and his will was law in Rome. But there was another young man who proved less pliant than Pompey. C. Julius Caesar, a youth of old Patrician stock, now between 20 and 21, was in danger from his connexion with the Marian leaders. He was married to Cinna's daughter Cornelia, his aunt Julia had been the wife of the great

[1] A similar case of compliance (M. Piso) is given in Velleius II 41.

Marius, and her son the younger Marius was thus his cousin. When only just of age (14) he had been put into the office of priest of Jupiter (*Flamen dialis*) by Marius and Cinna. Sulla now ordered him to divorce Cornelia. This he refused to do, and the autocrat then confiscated that lady's marriage portion. All the acts of the Marian government had been declared void, so Caesar's priestly office went with the rest. It is a wonder that he escaped with his life; indeed powerful friends found it hard to induce Sulla to listen to intercession on his behalf. They pleaded for him as a gay careless lad engrossed in pleasures and dangerous to nobody. Sulla, who saw deeper, consented to spare him, but warned[1] his aristocratic advocates that no good would come of this clemency, for there was more than one Marius in the skin of Caesar. Caesar thought it safest to leave Rome.

905. The affair of Caesar must be placed late in the year 82 or early in 81, for it appears to have happened after Sulla became dictator. Of this step we must now speak. A mere military despotism was not to Sulla's taste. It was of course laborious, and it had the defect common to all tyrannies, that the way into the position was far easier than the way out. Sulla wanted to establish the constitution on lines traced by himself, with the power in thoroughly conservative hands: this done, he might lay aside the worries of government and take his ease. Some means, as constitutional as circumstances would allow, had to be contrived by which he should have autocratic power, apparently elective, for as long as he needed it. Meanwhile it was necessary to set the old machinery going as soon as possible, with the view of facilitating his own retirement. The device that he adopted was a curious blend of the scrupulous and the revolutionary, of the formal and informal. There were no consuls to carry on the administration. Marius was certainly dead; Carbo, if still alive, was a fugitive outlaw. Acting on instructions from Sulla, the Senate chose an *interrex*. The choice fell on L. Valerius Flaccus the foreman (*princeps*) of the House. Appian says it was expected that an election of consuls would be held. But Sulla, who had withdrawn from Rome for a time, sent Flaccus his views, or rather orders, by letter. He advised that a dictator should be appointed, not for the traditional term of six months, but to hold office until such time as he should have composed present troubles and brought the storm-tossed ship of state safely into port. All knew for whom these ample powers were designed, but Sulla frankly recognized his own past services by adding that the best thing for Rome would be that he should

---

[1] Suetonius *Jul.* 1. The truth of this story has been doubted, without good reason, as it seems to me.

continue to serve it in the capacity suggested. There was of course nothing to be done but to obey. Flaccus accordingly brought the matter before the Assembly in the form of a bill for conferring on[1] Sulla, with the title of Dictator, the powers demanded. This was duly passed as a *lex Valeria*, and the declaration of Sulla's appointment was accompanied by a favourable sign[2] attesting the judicious complaisance of Heaven. We learn from Cicero that every act of Sulla was confirmed in advance by this law. Law set him above the law as absolute autocrat, with a show of popular election. When he was called to be dictator for drafting statutes (*legibus scribundis*) and setting the commonwealth in order (*rei publicae constituendae*), it was not for him to decline the mandate of the Roman people. It is highly probable that the law was also retrospective, declaring his past acts valid and relieving him of all responsibility in connexion therewith. How far the powers of ordering executions and confiscations, of founding colonies, of regulating the succession to client-kingdoms and the status of communities, and so forth, of which we read in general terms, were included in special clauses, is hardly to be determined. There is no doubt that after the passing of this Valerian law Sulla had power to do any of these things without any effective restriction whatever. Decency had been observed after a fashion. Cicero denounces the law as shameful, violating as it did every sound principle of legislation—that is, in a free state. But he admits that Flaccus could not help himself; the law, he says, was not the measure of its proposer, but of the times.

906. It is quite clear that the position in which Sulla was placed was essentially different from the dictatorship as known to the earlier Republic. The time-limit of six months was of the essence of the old office, in which the republican principle of 'collegiality' was suspended and a brief monarchy set up to deal with an emergency. Nor had the old dictatorship been elective. The dictator was named (*dictus*) by a consul, and the existence of a consul able to perform the act was presupposed. Now, whatever the exact forms observed in appointing Sulla, it was really an election, unwilling though the electors might be. The election[3] of Fabius in 217, not to mention the interference of the Assembly in giving him Minucius as a colleague, had been felt to have taken away the utility of the office for its proper purpose. Hence, as we have seen above, the Senate saw to it that there were no more

---

[1] I believe that Sulla was mentioned by name. It is possible that only a dictator was mentioned, and Sulla named afterwards by Flaccus, but this seems less likely. See Cicero *de leg. agrar.* III § 5, *de legibus* I § 42, Appian *civ.* I 99, Plutarch *Sull.* 33.

[2] Pliny *NH* II § 144.

[3] See Mommsen *Staatsrecht* II 141—2, and §§ 289, 293, above.

dictators after the second Punic war. A democratic elective dictatorship would have been simply a Tyranny. Moreover, in the case of a
dictator specially appointed for some formal purpose, ancestral custom
of binding moral force enjoined that the holder of the office should lay
it down so soon as that purpose was fulfilled, it might be after a tenure
of a few days or hours. In the case of Sulla the special purpose was
one requiring considerable time. If not identical with that of the
Decemvirate[1] of 451, it was closely analogous to it. But in 451 ten
commissioners held office for one year only; those of 450 were not the
same body. And the Decemvirate with its absolute powers had not
been found satisfactory. That episode had been closed by legislation
sternly forbidding the election[2] in future of any magistrate not subject
to the right of appeal from his decisions. Sulla was a single magistrate
appointed for an uncertain term, to which only death or his own will
could put an end ; that he was eager to have done with the business
and return to his pleasures was probably guessed by none. Therefore the situation, with its Interrex and the vote of the Assembly,
perhaps most of all resembled the proceedings on the vacancy of the
throne in the old days of the kings. The three essential elements of a
single nomination, popular acceptance, and appointment for life, are
all there, though of course with some slight differences in detail.
Whether Sulla's decisions were in formal language declared to be not
subject to appeal we do not know: that this was the practical effect of
the powers conferred on him, is not to be doubted. When therefore
we find his power spoken of as regal (*regnum, tyrannis, βασιλεία*), the
expression has more accuracy than we are, in our suspicion of
rhetorical exaggeration, at first inclined to admit.

907. Sulla kept up the fiction implied in the title Dictator by
appointing a Master of the Horse. But the abnormal character of his
power could not be concealed, nor was he at much pains to conceal it.
Of course he had 24 lictors, but he was attended by the whole number
in the city as well as outside, which was a significant novelty. He
seems also to have used other precautions, perhaps even a bodyguard,
for the safety of his person. That there was an irregularity[3] in the
action of Flaccus as *interrex* does not seem to have troubled him
in the least. He now set about his great project of remodelling the
institutions of the state. His policy was in essence revolutionary but
in form largely reactionary. To restore so far as possible the state of

---

[1] See the two described in order, Mommsen *Staatsrecht* II 682—4.

[2] The word *creare*, used by both Cicero *de republ.* II § 54 and Livy III 55 § 5, does not
apply to the dictator, who is *dictus*.

[3] The first *interrex* was not properly competent to hold an election. And there seems to
have been at least no precedent for an *interrex* proposing a law. See Mommsen *Staatsrecht*
I 637—8, Lange *RA* I 553.

things existing (or as he conceived it to have existed) before the movements of the Gracchi, was in effect to ignore the history of the last fifty years. It was a shortsighted attempt to turn back the tide of tendencies, to defeat the irresistible. Sulla was not exempt from the blindness that is apt to fall upon leaders of reaction. They stand too near to the issues of contemporary politics, and are led to miscalculate the forces at work by tacitly assuming that in human affairs the strength of the ebb is not less than that of the flow. Sulla may have known that his political reforms could only last a short time, but it is far more likely that he misjudged, excusably enough, the problem with which he attempted to deal. Those parts of his work in which he started from things as he found them, and moved forward, were just the parts that were lasting: the flood-tide of democracy, sweeping on to monarchy, quickly submerged the rest.

908. The year 82 must have been far spent by the time when Sulla assumed his so-called dictatorship. His triumph was celebrated on the 27th January 81. The last months of 82 and the first days of 81 must have been a season of intense activity, if all the measures placed before the triumph by Livy (epit.) and Appian were really carried through in the interval. At all events they surely belong to the early part of his dictatorship, for they mostly dealt with fundamental points of policy, which can hardly have been left to wait. Most of them seem to have taken the form of laws, the mere drafting of which must have taken a good deal of time. The Senate always contained men able to draw up orders of the House and other documents in the technical phraseology dear to the Roman mind. Sulla no doubt employed the services of such men to put into statutory shape the principles laid down by himself. One of the first, if not first of all, was the law for the future regulation of the tribunate. This office, as we have seen, evolved as an organ of the Plebs for the protection of its members, instrumental in gradually winning for Plebeians equal rights with Patricians, was afterwards captured by the Plebeian nobility and sank into being a convenient tool of the Senate. In the hands of the Gracchi and their successors it had been restored to importance as an engine of reform more and more revolutionary as time went on. To weaken it, to put it as nearly as possible into the humble position of its early days, was the fixed purpose of Sulla. Whatever limitations he had imposed on the power of tribunes in his hurried legislation of 88 had been swept away by the Marians. He now dealt with the matter thoroughly. He enacted[1] that no

---

[1] See in particular Cicero *de legibus* III §§ 19—26, I *in Verr.* § 38, II *in Verr.* I § 155, *philippic* II § 53, *pro Tullio* §§ 38—9, Caesar *civ.* I 7, Asconius pp. 66, 78, 81, Livy ep. 89, Appian *civ.* I 100 § 4, Velleius II 30 § 4. The heading of the *lex de Termessibus* (Bruns p. 85) is a contemporary witness, see note in Wordsworth p. 462.

tribune should be competent to propose a law to the Assembly without the sanction of an order of the Senate. He took away the tribunes' right of seizing a man (*prensio*) and bringing him to trial before the people, at least without the Senate's leave. Thus the tribunate as a great office, leading the popular Assembly in its legislative and judicial character, was destroyed. The power of *intercessio* he did not take away in general terms. But there were already matters excluded from its operation either by law or imperative custom. He added to the number of matters thus reserved, and enforced a definite statutory prohibition by statutory penalties. The original purpose of 'intercession' was held to have been 'succour,' the *auxilium* protecting Plebeians from the *imperium* exercised by magistrates who in those early times were of course Patricians. To this function the once formidable negative power of a tribune was now practically restricted. But it was not only the possession of great positive and negative powers that made the tribunate attractive to men of this revolutionary age. It was an office in which it was possible to earn popularity, and so to have a better chance of rising to the praetorship and consulship in due course. For this purpose, if less effective than the aedileship, it was at least far more easy to gain (there being 10 places as against 4), and more economical to hold; the tribune had no costly shows to provide. Sulla made the tenure of the tribunate an absolute disqualification for any curule[1] office. Thus it lay no longer in the path of ambition, and men of enterprise no longer sought it. No wonder Velleius says that only the shadow of it was left by Sulla; no wonder the restoration of its lost powers was the first aim of the *populares*, when their party began to revive.

909. In order to bring the working of the constitution back into the grooves of 200—150 B.C., when the Senate was really the government, it was necessary to lay down strict rules for the magistracies. This had been recognized by the *lex Villia* (*annalis*) of 180, but many irregularities had occurred in recent years. Thus the younger Marius had been consul at the age of 26, while the rules against reelection and continuation of office had been broken again and again. The old rule had required ten years military service before a man became qualified for the quaestorship, and by a scale of succession with certain intervals between office and office a series of age-limits was indirectly established. But the condition of the ten years service was no longer observed, and the failure of this rule destroyed the effectiveness of the rest. The separation of civil and military life had

---

[1] The notion that Sulla made only senators eligible for the tribunate (Lange *RA* III 154) does not seem borne out by the evidence adduced. I translate Appian *civ.* I 100 § 4 in the way implied in Mr Strachan-Davidson's note.

apparently gone too far to make the renewal of the old condition practicable. An age-limit to govern the succession of offices (*cursus honorum*) had to be fixed in some other way. This Sulla seems to have done by a *lex Cornelia*, of which some provisions are certain, while other details are most doubtful, and have given rise to much difference[1] of opinion. Only ex-praetors were to be eligible[2] for the consulship, only ex-quaestors for the praetorship. The general scheme of age-limits[3] seems to have worked out in practice as follows

Age at time of election	Office	No. of places under Sullan system
30	quaestorship	20
(36)	(aedileship)	(4)
39	praetorship	8
42	consulship	2

That is, in a case where a man was elected at the earliest date when he was eligible (*anno suo*). The aedileship, for reasons already given, could not be included in the necessary course, but a rising man would generally find it worth his while to hold it. If, as is commonly assumed, Sulla fixed a minimum age for the quaestorship, and regulated the others in relation to this fixed point, it would seem that 8 clear years had to run between quaestorship and praetorship, and 2 between praetorship and consulship. It is not unlikely that, if a man did hold the aedileship, an interval of 2 clear years was required between it and the praetorship. But why was the gap between quaestorship and praetorship made so large? Perhaps partly in deference to past usage: men would in practice generally have held not only the aedileship but the tribunate also in the interval, and, though this last, as a plebeian office, had not belonged to the *cursus* or followed its rules, still an interval of some sort was required. Sulla was clearly anxious to raise the minimum ages all round, and to increase the power of the Senate. By making the quaestorship confer membership of that body, he effected two things: first, all men in the prime of life who had experience of public affairs were included in the Senate; secondly, all senators had to have some experience of affairs. The members gave a character to the body, and so did the body to its members. That the latter influence would operate most effectually

---

[1] See Mommsen *Staatsrecht* I 548—53, Madvig *Verfassung und Verwaltung* I 336—9.

[2] Appian *civ.* I 100 § 3.

[3] The case of Cicero, who prided himself on his series of elections *anno suo*, illustrates this. He was born on 3rd Jan. 106 B.C., so that he completed his 31st year at the beginning of 75. His dates are, quaestor 75, aedile 69, praetor 66, consul 63.

during the earlier years of membership was a point not likely to escape the observation of Sulla; and we may perhaps fairly suppose that an arrangement by which a number of young ex-officials were for several years brought under the guidance of the elder senators, and enabled to catch the tone and tradition of the House, was in accordance with his views. But, while Sulla was anxious to prevent the early promotion of hot-blooded young men, he desired also to hinder a few prominent leaders from monopolizing official power. He therefore re-enacted that the same office should only be held a second time after an interval of ten years. Thus he strove to keep open the flow of promotion, and give a chance of the consulship to as many as possible. To let another Marius or Cinna hold that office year after year would be to disappoint the reasonable ambitions of a number of men whom his system was designed to ripen and encourage. And the system of Sulla was intended not to develope a Ring but to establish a ruling Caste.

910. The next thing was to fill up the Senate. We are told that Sulla had done this in 88 by adding 300 new members. We now hear[1] that he added 300 chosen from the 'best knights.' That is, no doubt, from those members of the Equestrian Order who were lucky enough to have taken the side of the aristocratic reaction. It is an obvious suspicion, that the story of the earlier addition is a mere anticipation, due to a misuse of authorities by Appian, from whom we get both stories. The course of recent events, so far as we know it, hardly justifies this sceptical attitude. If Sulla added 300 in 88, the existing number being then under 300 (for they were barely 300 in 91 at the time[2] of the proposal of Drusus), the state of things in 82 or 81 would appear thus

A. Old senators. Of these, some had fled to Sulla in the East or to other refuges, and now returned in his following. A few moderate men, out of those who remained in Rome, probably survived. The dead, Sullans murdered by the Marians, and Marians and turncoats now proscribed by Sulla, beside suicides and those who fell in the wars, would account for a large number of vacancies.

B. New senators (Sullans of 88 and probably a few Marians added since). Of these the only survivors who would dare to appear in Rome would be those Sullans who had fled and now returned, with perhaps a few who had posed as moderate men during the rule of the Marians.

[1] See Appian *civ.* I 59 § 5, 100 § 5, Livy ep. 89, Cicero *pro Rosc. Am.* § 8, Dionys. Hal. v 77.

[2] Appian *civ.* I 35 § 4.

In default of direct information we are driven to loose generalities based on guess-work. We do not even know whether the censors of 86 had ventured to eject from the Senate any of the new members put in by Sulla. But in any case it appears probable that the total number of senators available in 82 B.C. was not more than enough (after allowing for absentees sick or on duty) to make a fairly full house. Now Sulla meant to make the Senate more than ever the real Governing Body of Rome and her empire. He meant also to restore to senators the judicial functions of which C. Gracchus had deprived them. Moreover, he meant to increase the number of the jury-courts, and a larger number of qualified jurors would have to be found. That he should now add a second 300 new members to the Senate is therefore not a story that we need regard as matter for surprise. The wastage had undoubtedly been very great, and we are not to assume that in a space of six years no deaths had occurred in the ordinary course of nature. For the moment the House was filled: it was, as we should say, a strong body on paper, and ready for the duties and powers about to be entrusted to it. The exact form in which the appointment of these 300 was carried out is not clear. The men were of course in truth Sulla's nominees, but we are told that he caused the Tribes to vote on each individual case. Perhaps a formal polling of the Assembly by Tribes would not take very long when the attendance was small and no one dared to vote No. But 300 such pollings are hardly conceivable. A suggestion[1] that, on the model of the election of jurors under the *lex Plautia* of the year 89, each of the 35 Tribes separately voted on a certain number of names, may deserve consideration, for that Plautian law was itself a piece of senatorial reaction. Fortunately the matter is not important in itself, for no sure conclusion can be reached. Sulla's arrangement for the regular filling-up of the Senate in future will be described below.

911. The *lex Cornelia iudiciaria* next demands attention. Ever since the time of C. Gracchus the Knights, formed by his legislation into an *ordo equester*, had supplied the juries of the public courts. The attempts to deprive them of this privilege had failed. The Servilian law of 106, if ever passed, had soon been repealed; the Plautian law making jurors elective seems not to have worked so as effectually to weaken their hold, and had probably been repealed by the Marians. For about 40 years their tenure had been practically continuous. Sulla now took away[2] from them the control of the courts, and gave

---

[1] Lange *RA* III 156. The court of the *centumviri* (really 105) were at least appointed 3 from each Tribe. In the *lex Licinia de sodaliciis* of 55 B.C. the Tribe appears as an element in the selection of jurors. See Holden on Cicero *pro Plancio*.

[2] Cicero *div. in Caecil.* § 8, Tacitus *ann.* XI 22.

it to the senators. This blow came on the top of two others; first, the loss of 300 of their Order, now drafted into the Senate, and second, that of a far greater number in the proscriptions. Sulla left them a thinned and weakened body, and no doubt hoped that he had crushed them for good as a political force. But the real tendency of the times was in their favour, and in a few years they had revived and were once more, under new conditions, a power in the state. The senatorial juries seem to have begun work[1] in the year 80.

912. In rebuilding the constitution to accommodate the Senate it was impossible to leave out of account the sacred colleges. Their powers touched politics at many points; indeed their importance was now wholly political. It was a thorn in the side of the senatorial nobles that since the *lex Domitia* of 104 they had lost control of the appointments to these bodies. Sulla now did away with the peculiar form of election[2] introduced by Domitius, and restored the old method of cooptation. It was a part of his general scheme that the bodies with whom it lay to increase or lessen the friction of religious scruples and formalities in public affairs should be close corporations, hostile to change. He also enlarged the membership, raising the pontiffs and augurs each from 9 to 15. The *decemviri sacris faciundis* probably[3] became *quindecimviri* at the same time. Thus a larger number of individuals bore a part in the dignity and power of these colleges.

913. The business side of the proscriptions, confiscations sales and so forth, had to be regulated. Whether this was done by a special *lex Cornelia*, or by a decree of the dictator acting under the provisions of the *lex Valeria* of Flaccus, seems uncertain. The evidence[4] is on the whole in favour of the former alternative. The black-lists were probably still appearing in the last days of 82, when Sulla was already dictator, and legislation was actively in progress. The most important step was the fixing of a date (1 June 81) after which all proceedings connected with the proscriptions were to come to an end. It may be that the disqualification of the sons of the proscribed for holding public office was included in the same statute. Possibly the emancipation and enfranchisement of a large number of picked slaves was enacted or confirmed at the same time, for of course they were a part of the confiscated estates. If so, it probably took the form of conferring on Sulla full power to make the selection

---

[1] Cicero *pro Rosc. Am.* §§ 11, 28, Gellius XV 28.

[2] Whether he also abolished the old system of choosing the chief pontiff by vote of 17 Tribes (§§ 792, 855) is not certain. Mommsen *Str.* II 29 is inclined to think he did, and Cicero *de lege agr.* II §§ 16—19 seems rather in favour of this view.

[3] Marquardt *Stvw.* III 380—1.

[4] See Cicero *pro Rosc. Am.* §§ 125—8.

and to grant the franchise. They became freedmen of the great dictator, and according to custom took his gentile name. These freedmen *Cornelii*, 10,000 in number if Appian[1] may be trusted, were an element in the city population on which he could thoroughly rely; not only as voters, but (for Sulla picked out young sturdy fellows) as exponents of his policy by force. In the auctions of the goods of the proscribed, which were now frequently taking place, he did not shrink from presiding in person[2] and behaving as a victorious general holding a sale of spoils. The property of Roman citizens was thus, in Rome and by a Roman Patrician, treated as prize of war.

914. If we leave the legislative and administrative measures of Sulla for a while and turn to other matters, the mixture of different topics will fairly correspond to the crowding and jostling of events at this trying time. Everything had to be done, and done quickly. Sulla was a hard master, but a master he was, and Rome was by no means in such a state as to be able to do without one. This shewed itself at the election of consuls for 81. Among the candidates was Ofella[3] the former Marian, who had joined Sulla and had directed for him the siege of Praeneste. This man had not held the praetorship or even the quaestorship. Sulla, whose law forbidding such candidatures was doubtless announced, if not already passed, sent him orders to withdraw. The foolish man, relying on his recent services, continued his canvass, as though Sulla were the man to put up with this sort of thing. The dictator sent an armed centurion, who found Ofella among the throng in the Forum, and killed him then and there. Murmurs arose, but an appeal to Sulla was useless. He told the people that the murder had been done by his order, and warned them to mind their own business. This brutal frankness jarred upon Roman nerves, and the shocking story was eagerly handed down as a specimen of Sulla's tyranny. We need not defend the character of the man. But the Roman people of that time needed a sharp lesson. The better elements of the citizen body, the respectable burghers of municipal towns, counted for little in the public life of Rome: the resident elements, senators knights or common folk, were mostly corrupt. They were only fit to obey; and Sulla scorned to dissemble the unpleasant truth. To use Cromwellian language, the murder of Ofella did no doubt 'tend to prevent the effusion of blood for the future.' Needless to say, the consuls and praetors elected were men approved by the dictator. It may be well at this point to say

---

[1] Appian *civ.* I 100 § 6.

[2] See in particular Cicero *pro Arch.* § 25, *de leg. agr.* II § 56, II *in Verrem* III § 81, Plutarch *Sull.* 33, *compar. Lysandr. et Sull.* 3.

[3] Ofella. Livy ep. 89, Plutarch *Sull.* 33, Appian *civ.* I 101, Asconius p. 92.

a few words about the Assembly[1] by Centuries. In 88, before leaving for the East, Sulla had in some way changed the existing organization, of course on reactionary lines. With the return of the Marians all his acts had been annulled. After Sulla's time there is no trace of any such change being in force. It seems probable that in 82—1 he let this matter alone. Indeed it was one of great difficulty and intricacy, and his other changes would, if they had only been lasting, have sufficed to effect his objects.

915. While Sulla was thus busy with affairs of state, the preparations for a grand ceremony were going on. His triumph for victories over Mithradates (27 Jan. 81) served to remind the public that he had in spite of every disadvantage upheld the majesty and dominion of Rome in the East; that, before he made himself master of his fellow citizens, he had struck down the common enemy abroad. The triumph was a splendid show, as was usual when the pageant was adorned with oriental booty. But the procession of restored exiles in honour of their great restorer was the distinctive feature of this as compared with the common run of triumphs. Surely it must have crossed the minds of many spectators that the restoration of exiles was the result of the civil war, not of the war with Mithradates. Their presence was a powerful advertisement of Sulla, but of Sulla as conqueror of Rome. He avoided a direct and formal triumph over Roman citizens, and that was all. Meanwhile the last embers of the civil war were being stamped out. Pompey's expedition[2] was going well; it was apparently in 82 that he caught Carbo in Sicily and put him to death. At the beginning of 81 he seems to have been engaged in Africa, recovering that province also from the refugee Marians and their allies. This he did in a workmanlike manner. Domitius and his army were cut to pieces, Numidia invaded, king Hiarbas captured and reserved for a triumph, and Hiempsal installed on the throne. Of Pompey's return and his relations to Sulla we will speak below.

916. In connexion with the triumph we may speak of the great games[3] instituted by Sulla in 81, though they belong to a later part of the year. These were the *ludi Victoriae*, intended to commemorate the 'crowning mercy' of the first of November 82, the victory of the Colline Gate. The festival lasted seven days, beginning on the 26th of October, and was a most elaborate[4] affair. The usual contests

---

[1] That he employed the *comitia centuriata* for acts of legislation appears from Cicero *de domo* § 79.

[2] Plutarch *Pomp.* 10—12, Livy ep. 89. His cruelty to his benefactor Carbo throws light on the true character of Pompey. Appian *civ.* 1 96, Valer. Max. v 3 § 5, IX 13 § 2.

[3] See Marquardt *Stvrw.* III 502, 585.

[4] It included a *venatio*, in which for the first time lions were turned loose in the circus. Seneca *de brevitate vitae* 13 § 6.

in the Circus, races and so forth, were supplemented by performances
of Greek athletes fetched for the purpose. The *ludus Troiae*[1], perhaps
a survival of ancient military training, was performed by youths of
good family, among whom the young Cato took a leading part. It
consisted of evolutions on horseback. A notable feature of the games
was the appearance of members of noble families as drivers in the
chariot-races. This, which was a shock to Roman notions of propriety,
was done in deference to the wishes of Sulla. Why he, who was
concerned to restore the nobility to power, should have promoted this
lowering of their dignity, is not explained : we should probably understand it better, if we knew the circumstances of particular cases. The
precedent was followed by some of the least worthy of the Roman
emperors, but with them to encourage the degradation of the nobles
was part of a consistent policy. A general feasting of the people,
lasting for several days on a most lavish scale, is also a foreshadowing
of imperial extravagance: the waste is said to have been immense.
By this time the proscriptions and sales were over, and the dictator
ushered in the advent of a more cheerful dispensation with a display
of jollity. At this point we get another peep into his private life.
Metella was ailing ; her recent confinement had been too much for
her. At the time of the festival she was sinking fast. Sulla was
a pontiff, and for a pontiff's house to be polluted by the presence of
a corpse was contrary to religious law. He therefore formally divorced
his dying wife, to whom he seems to have been sincerely attached,
and had her removed to die in another house. But her death was
a great grief to him. He had lately been legislating in restriction
of extravagance in funerals and entertainments, but these rules he
now disregarded utterly, and tried to drown his grief in the wine-cup.
The story is recorded by Plutarch. It is credible enough, and all of
a piece with the character of Sulla. Roman scruples drew their line
sometimes at even stranger places[2] than this. A few months later
he yielded to the advances of a pretty and coquettish lady of good
family named Valeria, whom he married. But the devotion to drink
and low company remained with him to the last.

917. The year 81 was altogether a time of astounding varied
activity on the part of the dictator. The work done in Italy was
clearly immense, but we have only fragmentary references[3] from
which we can gather a detail here and there. A number of communities were punished for their support of the Marians in the civil
war. From some he exacted fines and contributions ; others had

---

[1] This is the first mention of it that we have. The *locus classicus* for it is Vergil *Aen.* V
545—602. See Marquardt III 525—6.
[2] Tacitus *ann.* VI 4.   [3] See in general Appian *civ.* I 96, 100.

their fortifications dismantled; local adherents of the Marian party were hunted down[1] by proscriptions. But the most general form of punishment was the confiscation[2] of land wholesale. For this there were two powerful reasons. In the first place, Sulla had no intention of keeping up a standing army. Most likely he never thought of such a thing. It would have been wholly contrary to republican precedent, and Sulla, who knew Roman armies only too well, was not the man to devise such a novelty. He had therefore an army to disband, amounting at the lowest estimate[3] to 23 legions, say over 100,000 men. There was no means of pensioning them off save by grants of land. Secondly, it was important not to plant them all in one district, but to scatter them up and down the country. He would thus in all parts establish formidable garrisons of men able and willing to maintain the Sullan settlement, on the permanence of which their own rights depended. It was in fact more of an object to get hold of large blocks of land in suitable places than to punish opponents and make sure of punishing the right ones. As individuals, innocent even from the Sullan point of view, or even a few partisans of Sulla, were made away with in the proscriptions, so it is likely that some communities suffered confiscation of territory on slight or false pretences, principally to suit the conqueror's convenience. Anyhow the wholesale evictions by which landed property, private or communal, was transferred to new holders left behind them a legacy of intense bitterness. The old owners were turned out to make room for soldiers whom years of fighting alternated with looting and debauchery had unfitted for a life of patient husbandry. For them in most cases there was nothing but ruin and despair. If the idle soldiers parted with their allotments rather than till them, the buyers would generally be some of the capitalist land-grabbers already gorged with the spoils of Rome. To prevent the sale of the allotments a special prohibitory clause[4] was put into the laws dealing with the Sullan colonies. Tiberius Gracchus had taken the same precaution; but (not to mention possibilities of evasion) it had been proved by the subsequent history of the land-laws that such a prohibition could not be kept in force. In this as in other matters Sulla shewed that he either could not or would not learn by the experience of the past. The soldiers were marched off in bodies and planted in the regular way either in existing towns or as new colonies. There may be exaggeration or inaccuracy in the story (preserved by Florus[5]) that

---

[1] See Cicero *pro Rosc. Am.* § 16.

[2] See Cicero *de lege agr.* II §§ 68—81, III §§ 6—13. The *liber coloniarum* (in Lachmann's *Gromatici veteres*) contains several traces of the land-settlement.

[3] Appian *civ.* I 100 § 7. In Livy ep. 89 the number is 47, perhaps an error in tradition.

[4] Cicero *de leg. agr.* II § 78.   [5] Florus II 9 §§ 27—8.

whole municipalities were put up to auction, but it may be true; as also that the Paelignian town of Sulmo was sentenced to destruction. Most of the notices of Sulla's land-settlement[1] are either references to the quarrels between the old burgesses and the Sullan intruders, as at Puteoli and Pompeii, or cases in which some special punishment was inflicted on the town. Of these latter the most notable[2] was that of Volaterrae in Etruria. The district had been one of the last to adhere to the Marian cause. The city was a strong fortress. Some of the proscribed had found refuge there, and they and their friends resolved to resist the ordinances of Sulla. They rose and killed Sulla's governor, and managed to get together four legions. Of course they were soon besieged in their stronghold, and Sulla himself[3] came for a time to direct operations; but they held out till early in 79, and then only surrendered on terms. Meanwhile Sulla had passed a law by which, in addition to the loss of territory, the Volaterrans were deprived of their rights as Roman citizens and placed in the status of those later[4] Latin colonies (268—181 B.C.) which had *commercium* with Rome and no more. Arretium[5] in the same district suffered in the same way. But it was not only in Etruria that force had still to be used. Though the agents of the proscriptions had cruelly searched[6] the dales of Samnium, and though many thousands of their people had perished in battle or the Sullan massacres, we hear of a Samnite force still holding Nola. But on the approach of a Sullan army they surrendered. It seems probable that the dictator himself visited Samnium to stamp out a few remaining sparks of open discontent. The Marian colony at Capua, if ever really established, was now suppressed, and the *ager Campanus*[7] reverted to the Roman state, to be leased out for the benefit of the treasury. But at no great distance from Capua Sulla found the means of planting one of his settlements, the *colonia Urbana*[8], on some of the rich Falernian land. We hear of only one Sullan colony beyond the limits of Italy, that at Aleria[9] in Corsica. It may be remembered that there was one Marian colony in Corsica.

---

[1] Plutarch *Sull.* 37, Cicero *pro Sulla* §§ 60—2.

[2] Cicero *pro Caecina* § 18, *de domo* § 79, *pro Rosc. Am.* §§ 20, 105, *ad Att.* I 19 § 4, Strabo v 2 § 6, Licinianus p. 39 Bonn.

[3] That Sulla's settlements extended beyond Italy proper into Cisalpine Gaul is probably to be inferred from the town of Forum Corneli (Imola) between Ariminum and Bononia. See Prudentius *peristeph.* IX 1, Pliny *NH* III § 116, index to the Itineraries, inscriptions 4406, 5210, in Orelli-Henzen.

[4] See above § 221.   [5] Cicero *pro Caecina* §§ 95—8.

[6] Strabo v 4 § 11, Livy ep. 89, Licinianus p. 39.

[7] Cicero *de leg. agr.* II § 81.

[8] Pliny *NH* XIV § 62, Beloch *Campanien* p. 309.

[9] Pliny *NH* III § 80.

918. These few surviving details give us but a very faint notion of the extent to which the Sullan settlement unsettled Italy. Coming as it did at the time when a peaceful return to normal industry offered the only chance of recovery from the utter exhaustion of the Italian and civil wars, it was to many thousands of Italians, the soundest elements of the population, the consummation of economic and social ruin. Their utmost exertions could not have restored Italian agriculture to the prosperity of earlier days, but they would surely have done something to arrest its further decline: the Sullan settlers did not even try. The evils of the *latifundia*, which reformers had vainly striven to check, now resumed an undisputed sway, and in a short time the land of Italy was in fewer hands than ever. In the next twenty years the government was face to face with three great forces of disorder, ever threatening and sometimes breaking the public peace. There was the old peril of the slave-gangs, more serious than ever owing to the increased demand for gladiators. There were also two sections of the free population; the 'Sullan[1] men,' that is military settlers, impoverished by their own lack of industry and thrift, and those whom they had displaced, the 'men stricken with the disaster of the time of Sulla.' From beggary to brigandage was for many an easy step. Some no doubt drifted into Rome, adding a dangerous reinforcement to the Roman mob. But wherever these ruined men were found, there was a discontented element, disgusted with law and order, a ready instrument of revolutionary designs. These results took a few years to become fully effective. The Sullan settlers as a means of maintaining the Sullan settlement did at least last Sulla's time.

919. Our information as to the financial arrangements of Sulla is also lamentably meagre. The assertion[2] in a rhetorical fragment of Sallust, that the Roman people had no longer left to them as much sustenance as slaves receive from their masters, is borne out by a fragment of Licinianus (perhaps based on Sallust) from which it appears that after the retirement of Sulla the practice of providing the people with corn below cost price was resumed. It seems then that the dictator put an end to it for a time. Appian[3] tells us that he imposed special taxation on the provinces and client-kingdoms, and did not respect the immunities enjoyed by some cities under treaties or grants, the rewards of good service in the past. But he wanted money to carry on the business of state. We learn from Cicero[4] that

---

[1] See Cicero *in Catil.* II § 20, *pro Mur.* § 49, Sallust *Cat.* 16 § 4, 28 § 4.

[2] See Marquardt *Stvw.* II 116, Sall. *hist.* I 55 § 11 Maur., Licinian p. 42.

[3] Appian *civ.* I 102.

[4] Cic. *de off.* III § 87. Compare Plutarch, *compar. Lysandri et Sull.* 3.

he trafficked with some tributary cities, selling them exemptions from fiscal burdens for sums of ready cash. The Senate of course knew that this forestalling of future revenues was unsound spendthrift finance, but the House had to pass orders confirming the bargains. In another passage[1] Cicero asserts that Sulla, in virtue of his autocratic power, favoured certain persons by writing off a part of the sums owed by them to the treasury. This had at the time been authorized by the Senate, but the House afterwards cancelled its order, and required payment to be made in full. We are, he adds, maintaining the Sullan settlement in other respects, because to upset it would only lead to worse confusion still; but it has been agreed that in thus remitting debts to the state Sulla exceeded even the extraordinary powers conferred on him by special law. On the other hand there are indications[2] that Sulla took steps to improve private credit, which had been much impaired by the Valerian law[3] of Flaccus and made worse by the recent troubles. The general impression left by these fragmentary notices is that the financial arrangements of Sulla were of a wayward and shortsighted character, much what one would expect from a temporary despot. He himself applied large sums of public money as he chose, and was thought to have appropriated a good deal. After the overthrow of his constitution attempts were made to recover[4] some of this from his son Faustus, but without success.

920. We now come to the important changes in the regular magistracy introduced by Sulla. It will be best to speak of these in connexion with the great departments of policy which they severally illustrate. First, it was a defect in the arrangements of the imperial Republic that the Home magistracies and the Provincial governorships had never been properly correlated to each other. Praetors ruled provinces abroad or discharged departmental duties at home. In case of a foreign war, such as those with Jugurtha the Cimbri or Mithradates, the practice was to send out a consul. The frequent necessity for extension of commands had long been turning promagistracy into a normal appliance of Roman government, for which it had not been intended. In short it was largely a matter of chance whether a magistrate or a pro-magistrate at any given time presided over any given Province. The praetors at home had enough to do, and Sulla had in hand schemes that would find employment for

---

[1] Cic. II *in Verr.* III §§ 81—2, written in 70 B.C.
[2] See Lange *RA* III 162.   [3] In 86 B.C.   Velleius II 23 § 2 (§ 873 above).
[4] See Cicero *pro Cluent.* § 94, *de leg. agr.* I § 12, Asconius p. 72. For the similar attempt to recover the price of confiscated estates, remitted by Sulla, see Sallust fragm. IV I Maur. (Gellius XVIII 4 § 4).

several more.   He undertook to get rid of the inconveniences of the present haphazard practice by a reform which offered a simple and logical solution of the difficulties.   He accepted the pro-magistracy as the normal status of provincial governorships: a man was to serve first as magistrate at home, then as pro-magistrate abroad.   This meant the creation of an imperial Provincial service beside (or rather above) the Home service.   The former would be the crown of the latter, the consummation of an official career.   It was a momentous step, for it openly recognized the imperial character of the Republic as its most important quality.   But Sulla can hardly have foreseen the inevitable consequence that, while the Provincial service tended to become more and more imperial, the Home service would tend to become more and more municipal.

921.   There were at this time nine Provincial governorships to be provided for, (1) Sicily, (2) Sardinia and Corsica, (3, 4) two Spains, (5) Macedonia, (6) Africa, (7) Asia, (8) Narbonese or Transalpine Gaul, (9) Cilicia.   To these it is almost certain that Sulla added (10) Cisalpine Gaul.   For he enlarged the *pomoerium*[1] or sacred boundary of Rome, which was a privilege traditionally reserved for those alone who added to the *ager Romanus* in Italy.   The advance of the limits of Italy proper (from the Aesis to the Rubicon on the eastern coast and possibly[2] from the Macra to the Varus on the western) was therefore the work of Sulla.   The conversion of the country north of the Rubicon into a regular Province was in all likelihood[3] carried out at the same time.   It was a peculiar Province, the Roman and Romanized elements in the population being exceptionally strong.   The scheme of Sulla provided that the number of praetors should be raised from 6 to 8.   With the two consuls there would thus be ten regular magistrates with *imperium* every year.   These ten were all to spend their year of office in Rome, discharging administrative or judicial duties ; after this their *imperium* was to be prolonged, and they were as proconsuls or propraetors to fill the ten Provincial governorships.   The Senate was to decide which Provinces were to be proconsular, and which propraetorian, for the year following, and the consuls and praetors were to apportion each class respectively among themselves by lot or private arrangement in the usual way.   Various provisions were added[4] to smooth difficulties

---

[1] See Seneca *de brevitate vitae* 13 § 8, Gellius XIII 14.

[2] This is a doubtful point.   See below § 1217.

[3] Pointed out by Mommsen.   See the note in his *History* III 387, Marquardt *Stvw.* I 218—9.   The arguments of Mommsen are to me convincing.   The district known as *ager Gallicus* had been called the province *Ariminum*.   It extended from the Aesis to the Rubicon, and the charge of the Po-country was added to it as *Gallia Cisalpina.* See Livy XXVIII 38 § 13, XXIV 44 § 3, XXVII 7 § 11, Nissen, *Landeskunde* I 78.

[4] Marquardt *Stvw.* I 523—4.

incidental to the regular goings and comings that this system pre-supposed. Thus the outgoing governor was to stay in his Province until his successor came to take over the government. On the arrival of his successor he was to quit it, but a space of 30 days was allowed him to complete the preparations for his journey. His *imperium* did not lapse until he reentered the city on his return, but this was in view of a possible triumph, for after handing over the Province to the incoming governor he had no sphere of his own in which to exercise it. There were also provisions to protect the provincials from undue burdens in the way of requisitions for the governor's staff or of costly testimonials to the governors themselves. All these latter regulations were well-meant improvements, and remained in force, at least in theory. The military model of the succession-scheme is unmistake-able. As to the general principle of the reform we must observe that the Provincial pro-magistracy rested on the immediate continua-tion of the urban magistracy. If an interval were ever introduced[1] between the two, the Provincial service would inevitably become more and more a service independent of the urban. In about 30 years time this result actually followed. Again, it was not likely in the various chances of human affairs that the successions could always be carried out in exact accordance with the scheme. Wars upset the most careful calculations, and commanders could not be changed from year to year as in the simple old days when a campaign was a suburban operation. Moreover, any increase in the number of Provinces would call for more governors. Then either the Home service must be increased for reasons other than its own requirements, or extra governors must be found by some method other than imme-diate continuation of urban magistracy in the form of pro-magistracy. In short, the *lex Cornelia de provinciis ordinandis*, like many another elaborate reform, needed to be worked with many adaptations and developments. To work it thus with success a central authority, supreme and uncorrupted by private interests, concerned to promote efficiency at all costs, was indispensable. No such authority could be created out of the materials at the disposal of Sulla, and the failure of the republican system was not perceptibly delayed by his ingenious scheme.

922. Another piece of Sulla's policy comes out very clearly in his law[2] providing for the yearly appointment of 20 quaestors. It not only raised the number of these junior magistrates: it enacted that every quaestor as such was entitled to a seat in the Senate. It

---

[1] See Marquardt *Stvw.* I 522—3, below §§ 1178, 1185.

[2] A fragment of this law actually remains on a bronze tablet at Naples. Text in Bruns p. 82 ; it seems to have been passed in the Tribe-Assembly, see note in Wordsworth p. 460. Tacitus *ann.* XI 22.

is a good instance of the defects of our record that no direct statement survives to attest this. But it is a certain inference[1] from the
fact that we find persons in the Senate who had not been introduced
by censors but who had been quaestors. Sulla had by adding 300
new members filled up the House for the time: by providing for an
accession of 20 in each year he kept it full. This automatic arrangement superseded censorial action so far as the Senate was concerned.
It seems that Sulla looked upon the censorship with marked dis-
favour. In another department of the work of that office, the public
contracts, the duties of censors[2] were in 80 and 75 discharged by the
consuls. It has been pointed out[3] that the interval of five years
(*lustrum*) stamps this as a deliberate step, and there can be no doubt
that it was an outcome of the policy of Sulla. For several reasons
it was natural that he should dislike the censorship. Its capricious
action might at any time undo part of the work he was now doing
with great pains. It might, under the sway of a democratic movement, be used to make a material change in the composition of the
Senate. There had been radical censors in the past, and there might
be others in the future. Sulla therefore arranged for the filling-up of
the Senate and the letting of contracts by other means. But how
about the roll of citizens? Was this to be neglected, or did he make
other provision for the performance of this duty also? We do not
know. But we have reason to think[4] that in his eyes the enrolment
of new citizens in the Tribes (and still more in the Centuries) was
not a thing to be encouraged, and that anything tending to hinder
that result would appear a positive gain. And we know that after
the Marian censors of 86 no more were appointed till 70, and that the
revival of the activity of that office was one of the symptoms[5] of the
break-up of the Sullan constitution. Sulla did not abolish the
censorship any more than the tribunate; but, as he muzzled the
latter, so he arranged to do without the former. No doubt the increased number of quaestors was in itself a convenience, for in the
Roman Republic there had always been a tendency to keep the staff
of officials below the strength required for the prompt despatch of
public business; and the departments in which a quaestor was
required were many and various. The way in which the three
objects, the supply of junior officials, the supply of senators, and the
practical disuse of the censorship, were effectively attained by one
coherent act of policy, was an achievement in Sulla's best manner.

---

[1] For this matter see Mommsen *Staatsrecht* III 863, Lange II 341—2.
[2] Cicero II *in Verr.* I § 130, III § 18.   [3] Mommsen *Staatsrecht* II 325.
[4] See Kiene, *Bundesgenossenkrieg* pp. 328—9. Cf. Sallust *hist.* I 55 § 12.
[5] Cicero *div. in Caecil.* § 8.

But so far as the censorship was concerned it had only a very brief success.

923.   We will now turn to the greatest and most permanent work of the dictator, the reconstruction and development of the public courts, which was the foundation of a regular criminal procedure, and out of which a true criminal jurisprudence was destined to grow. The subject can here of course only be treated in outline, and for clearness sake we must start from the two distinct notions of compensation and punishment. The aim of the former is to give satisfaction to the individual aggrieved: the latter is the act of the community for its own protection. The notion of revenge is present in both, as a deterrent from future wrong-doing; for compensation, beside the material form of a payment of money or restitution in kind, might in early times appear as a guaranteed right of retaliation[1] (*talio*). If A breaks B's leg, B may do the same by A, with the full sanction of custom which embodies itself in law. Whether compensation or punishment be the matter in hand, it is the sign of an organized community that the magistrate bears a part. But his part is under the Roman system very different in the two cases. When A makes any claim against B, it is the magistrate who hears and decides the dispute, or rather (for this stage was early reached) refers it in the form of a plain issue to the decision of a *iudex*. With that decision the case is ended. But if any man has done something for which in the magistrate's opinion he ought to be punished, then the magistrate, representing the state, names the penalty he is prepared to inflict. This he proceeds to enforce, but is met by an appeal to the people in Assembly. This amounts to a denial that the magistrate is truly representing the state in this particular matter. Whatever the details of procedure, the action of the Assembly is practically the same in judgment as in legislation. It is a vote of Aye or No, accepting or rejecting, and the issue before it is that raised by the action of the magistrate and the challenge of the defendant. Thus in the case of compensation the magistrate defines the legal point at issue, and his definition is final. What the *iudex* decides is merely whether, on the evidence produced, this point tells in favour of plaintiff A or defendant B. In the case of punishment, it is the character of the defendant's act, quite as much as the fact of its commission by him (indeed more so), that is judged by the Assembly. Here endless varieties of moral valuation may come into play. The man may be clearly guilty, and the penalty named by the magistrate clearly no more severe than the act taken by itself deserves ; yet pity, expediency, gratitude for former good service, and other motives, may

_____
[1] See XII Tables (VIII 2) and note in Wordsworth.

lead the people to acquit him. This result need not imply any censure of the magistrate's action as hasty or extreme, but it is a reversal of that action none the less. Rude and clumsy though the procedure of trials by the Assembly (*iudicia populi*) was, in their admission of moral considerations they contained the germ of criminal law.

924. I have already on several occasions referred to the appointment of special judicial commissions[1] (*quaestiones extraordinariae*). If we may believe tradition, these courts date back into the early days of the Republic. Nor is this incredible. Cases would occur in which an inquiry could only become efficient in the hands of a small body, able to act with despatch and at need with secrecy. It is probable, but not certain, that there was no appeal from the sentence of such a court. At first the appointment was made by the Assembly on the proposal of the Senate, but in course of time the Senate seems to have assumed the right to act independently in this as in other matters. The court might consist of a small body (*tres viri* etc.) named in the terms of appointment, or of a magistrate or magistrates (e.g. one or both consuls) who would call in a few competent helpers to act as *consilium*. The transition from this system of occasional courts to permanent courts came about in a remarkable way, through the reaction of the Provinces upon imperial Rome. Rebellions provoked by greedy governors were too costly not to suggest the necessity of checking extortion. We have seen[2] how an attempt was made to redress the wrongs of Spanish Provincials in 171, and how it was rendered abortive. This was a case of compensation sought by a civil action, not of punishment. We have seen that the abuses continued, and that in 149 a standing commission was created to try cases of *repetundae*. In this court also simple compensation was the thing aimed at. It was in fact a civil court dealing with imperial issues. But the change of procedure was momentous. The court was a jury presided over by a praetor. This magistrate sat with them, and announced their decision; but this decision was not that of the magistrate on the advice of a *consilium*, but the verdict of a voting jury. From it there was no appeal. By passing the statute for establishing the court the Assembly had abdicated any right it might have to interfere. Nor is it clear that at this stage of progress they had any such right ; for there was as yet no question of punishment, and the decisions of the ordinary civil[3] courts were never subject to the *provocatio*. The *intercessio* of an equal or higher magistrate could be invoked as against[4]

---

[1] A fuller treatment of this topic will be found in Greenidge's *Legal Procedure of Cicero's time*, pp. 380—5.

[2] §§ 556, 639 above.

[3] Mommsen *Staatsrecht* III 353.   [4] Greenidge pp. 287—91.

some action of the praetor during the preparatory proceedings of a trial, but this is a point of small importance here. A well-marked stage of development was reached in the *lex Acilia repetundarum* of 122. Certain features of the old civil procedure are removed, the sum to be recovered is twice the amount extorted, and security is taken for the payment of the money to the quaestor of the treasury, by whom the claims of the parties to be compensated are met. Here we have got beyond mere compensation: punishment is beginning to appear, in the form of double restitution, and the state collects the money. The *lex Servilia* of 111 made certain changes in procedure, and enabled proceedings to be taken not only against the governor himself, but against any persons into whose hands[1] any part of the plunder could be traced. This was the law in force at the time when Sulla undertook his great reform.

925. Even in the laws dealing with extortion, designed to protect the Provincials, we find marked indications of the change from the notion of compensation to that of punishment. We are moving from the conception of a wrong or 'tort' (*delictum*)[2] towards that of a charge or 'crime' (*crimen*). The plaintiff or claimant (*actor* or *petitor*) is giving place to the prosecutor (*accusator*). But in the standing courts the accuser need not be a magistrate. Any citizen may come forward[3] to prosecute, unless he is under some special disqualification. This is a wide departure from the practice of the old trials before the Assembly. The fact that the first standing court was set up to protect the subject peoples, who had to plead through the mouth of a Roman protector (*patronus*), probably had something to do with this extension of the right to prosecute. But it is quite in harmony with the popular movements of the period 134—81 B.C., and the growth of standing courts to try cases where both the accused and the wronged party were Romans would be a further motive for allowing any willing citizen to act as prosecutor. It is a pity that the evidence for the existence of *quaestiones perpetuae* for cases other than those of extortion is very scanty and inconclusive. That a court sat in 142 B.C. to try a case of a criminal[4] character does not prove that it was a permanent court. That Marius was tried for corrupt practices[5] at an election in 116, and escaped only by an equality of votes, is not convincing. That Saturninus provided for the trial and punishment of treason[6] does not by itself prove that he established a standing court. All we can safely say is that offences calling for punishment, as

---

[1] Cicero *pro Rabir. Post.* §§ 8, 9.   [2] See Maine's *Ancient Law* chapter x.
[3] Greenidge pp. 11, 459.
[4] Cicero *de finibus* II § 54 speaks of a praetor presiding over a *quaestio inter sicarios*.
[5] Plutarch *Mar.* 5. See § 753 above.   [6] See above § 815.

distinguished from wrongs requiring compensation, were becoming more clearly recognized as matters for the state to deal with through the agency of juries. It is on the whole probable that some standing court or courts other than that for extortion[1] existed before the reform of Sulla, but it is not certain.

926. Sulla did not issue a general code of criminal law. The method followed was to pass a series of *leges Corneliae* each of which created a standing court for the trial of certain offences (which we will now call crimes), and imposed definite penalties on the persons convicted of the same. Of these statutes there appear to have been seven. Among these seven the jurisdiction in various classes of crime was distributed as was thought convenient. Probably one aim was not to overburden any particular court, but it is evident that an attempt was made to group together crimes of similar character. In the classification and drafting the dictator, himself an expert on many points, no doubt had the help of the most skilful lawyers of Rome. If we may infer from the passages quoted from one of these laws by Cicero[2] and Ulpian, the scope of each crime was defined in the usual concrete Roman style 'whosoever hath done or shall hereafter do' this or that. It was easy on this plan to combine practical definitions of several crimes in one and the same statute. The object was to make it clear what crimes came under the jurisdiction of the court established by this or that law, not to give a scientific definition of a particular crime. There was a possibility that an act might be regarded from more than one point of view, and that it might come under more than one law. In the offences connected with public life this was more especially the case. Thus *repetundae* and *peculatus*, or *vis*[3] and *maiestas*, might run so near together that in either pair it was not always easy to say under which of two laws the charge could best be brought. Such ambiguities could only be removed by the growth of a criminal jurisprudence. This growth was made possible by the Cornelian laws. For the present it was enough that a prosecutor had to name the law under which he proposed to bring the charge.

927. The courts of the *leges Corneliae* may be enumerated as follows

(1) *quaestio repetundarum.* The law was based on the *lex Servilia* of Glaucia, and the changes appear to have been slight. Whether the penalty was raised from restitution of twice to $2\frac{1}{2}$ times the amount

---

[1] In an inscription (Wilmanns 611 c) we find a man called *iudex quaestionis veneficiis, praetor repetundis*, and it is known that he was praetor in 95. Mommsen, *Strafrecht* pp. 174, 615, holds that murder trials came under a standing court before 142 B.C.

[2] Cicero *pro Cluent.* §§ 148—51, Digest XLVIII 8. Bruns p. 85 collects the fragments. The law is that *de sicariis et veneficis.*

For the *lex Plautia de vi* see below § 929.

extorted is doubtful, owing to the rhetorical character of the passage[1] from which this has been inferred. Whether outlawry (as a means of compelling resort to voluntary exile) was added is even more doubtful, for the same reason. But the words of Cicero[2], if taken seriously, certainly seem to imply that it was. And this is the more probable, since we do not hear of disqualification[3] for public positions and acts (*infamia*) as a result of condemnation.

(2) *quaestio peculatus.* That the misappropriation of state property was an old offence, and that steps were taken to punish it before the time of Sulla, is certain. But that a standing court for this class of cases existed is in the defect of evidence not to be assumed. We hear of it at work[4] in the year 66, and its establishment is probably to be attributed to Sulla. The effect of condemnation for this offence was at least[5] to enforce simple restitution. But it is very hard to believe that the condemned were not liable to *infamia* in some degree. In these trials, as in those for extortion, a second proceeding, the assessment of damages[6] (*litis aestimatio*), followed the conviction of the accused. This was carried out by the same jury, who often used their power[7] to mitigate the punishment of the guilty.

(3) *quaestio maiestatis.* The wide scope of the conception of treason has already[8] been discussed. It was probably not narrowed by Sulla, though he may have expanded it by means of more effective definition. Almost any public act capable of an unfavourable construction could be brought under this charge. It is practically certain that the penalty was outlawry (*aquae et ignis interdictio*).

(4) *quaestio de ambitu.* We have referred to various attempts to put down corrupt practices, which in the later Republic chiefly consisted of the purchase of votes and treating. Our word 'bribery' used in a large sense will fairly cover the meaning. The establishment of such a court seems to be assigned to Sulla on slight grounds. If the only direct mention[9] of a Cornelian law on bribery does refer to Sulla and not to some other Cornelius, the penalty consisted in a disqualification from office for ten years.

---

[1] With Cicero *div. in Caecil.* § 19 compare I *in Verr.* § 56, II *in Verr.* I § 27.

[2] II *in Verr.* II § 76.

[3] Mommsen *Strafrecht* p. 709 assumes that this was already included in the Servilian law, but cites no evidence. That other parties who had profited by the extortions of the chief offender were liable under both laws appears from Cic. *pro Rab. Post.* § 9.

[4] Cic. *pro Cluent.* § 147. See II *in Verr.* III § 83.

[5] Greenidge p. 509.   [6] Greenidge pp. 502—3.   [7] Cic. *pro Cluent.* §§ 115—6.

[8] See §§ 815, 818, 823. It is notable that Ammianus Marc. XIX 12 § 17 refers to *Corneliae leges* and *maiestas*, speaking of the protection of the emperor Julian. See Wagner's note.

[9] By the generally well-informed Scholiast of Bobbio, cited by Orelli *onomasticon* III 147. Mommsen, *Strafrecht* p. 867, refers it to Sulla.

(5) *quaestio inter sicarios*, established by Sulla's law *de sicariis et veneficis*. For convenience sake the court was styled 'among the assassins.' It dealt with all cases of assassination poisoning and murder generally, with arson, and (in the case of senators only) with judicial corruption leading to the wrongful infliction of a capital penalty. The penalty inflicted by this law was capital, that is outlawry. Only the murder of a near relative (known by the old name[1] *parricidium*) was actually punished with death. The manifest intent, as well as the completed act, constituted guilt, and aiders and abettors were on the same footing as principals. This *lex Cornelia* was the basis of criminal jurisprudence and supplementary legislation all through the Imperial period, and is markedly referred to in the Digest and Institutes of Justinian.

(6) *quaestio de falsis*. The law establishing this court[2] is also called *testamentaria* and *nummaria*. The cases included forgery coining and other modes of fraud. The penalty may have been[3] outlawry even in the *lex Cornelia* as Sulla left it. If not, it can hardly have been less than a high degree of *infamia*.

(7) *quaestio iniuriarum*. Of this very little is known. It seems to have dealt with cases[4] of assault and battery, defamation insult etc., so serious as to call for some penalty beyond the mere money-compensation obtainable through the civil *actio iniuriarum*. What the penalty was is unknown.

928. Into the details of procedure in these courts it is not our business to enter. What concerns us is that we have here a bold attempt to form a consistent system, and that it was henceforth easy to carry it on to a higher degree of completeness, either by bringing omitted varieties of crime under an existing statute, or by additional legislation creating as needed additional courts. Its place in the general scheme of the Sullan constitution is shewn by the composition of the juries and the arrangements for the presidency at trials. Of the eight praetors two[5] were always required for the charge of the civil jurisdiction. The other six were available to preside over six trials in the *iudicia publica*. It was of course uncertain how many cases would in any year come before each divisional court. An uncertain number of additional presidents were therefore required. Thus we find one

---

[1] Greenidge pp. 505—6. Mommsen, *Strafrecht* p. 615, holds that *parricidium* had come under a standing court before the reform of Sulla, but at a later date than simple murder.

[2] Mommsen, *Strafrecht* p. 669.   [3] Greenidge p. 507.

[4] The offence must not be confused with *vis publica*, which is more akin to rioting. Mommsen *l. c.* p. 785 does not include it in the system of *leges Corneliae* save in so far as they regulated the formation of a court.

[5] *Urbanus* and *peregrinus*. The 8 *provinciae* were assigned by lot.

trial presided over by a praetor, and another[1] by a *iudex quaestionis*. The function and the title are both older than the reform of Sulla. The juries were senators, that is, taken from those members of the Senate who were not absent or holding public office. The numbers empanelled for particular cases varied a good deal, perhaps according to definite rules. The choice of a jury was carried out by a combination of drawing lots (*sortitio*) and a right of the parties to challenge (*reiectio*) a certain number of jurors. The verdict of the jury was determined by a majority of votes. For condemnation this must be an absolute majority of the whole number. A vote might be either 'not guilty' (*absolvo*) 'guilty' (*condemno*) or 'not proven' (*non liquet*). Voting was generally secret, by tickets (*tabellae*) on which the initial letters A or C or NL were scratched. It is remarkable that Sulla allowed the accused, at all events in some[2] cases, the right to insist upon the votes being given openly, order of voting being then settled by lot. But this privilege, which enabled a man who had paid for votes to see that he got them, was soon taken away; in the year 66 it was obsolete.

929. It is hardly possible to avoid referring to the crime of *vis* (*publica*), though no law dealing directly with it is attributed to Sulla. Armed violence as a political engine had been often used in Rome during the last 40 years, and was destined to become an ordinary thing. It is doubtful when the *lex Plautia*[3] *de vi*, which we find in operation soon after Sulla's time, was passed. It has been variously assigned[4] to 89 B.C., during the great Italian war, and to 77 B.C., which brings it into connexion with the troubles after Sulla's death. The question is one that I see no means of solving satisfactorily. That Sulla ignored the subject is most unlikely. Perhaps he considered that he had sufficiently dealt with it in his *lex de maiestate* as a mode of treason. The *lex Plautia* was employed against P. Sulla in 62, P. Sestius in 56, M. Caelius in 56, who were all defended by Cicero. If the law was really passed in 77, it must be regarded as a supplement of the legislation of the dictator. We have a statement[5] that Sulla also legislated for the punishment of adultery, regardless of his own practice. But whether this extended beyond a clause in his law on

---

[1] The general term *quaesitor*, and the statute phrase *quei......quaeret*, can cover both.

[2] Cic. *pro Cluent.* §§ 55, 75.

[3] See Reid Introd. to Cic. *pro Sulla* §§ 25—7, Greenidge pp. 424, 431, Orelli *onomasticon* III 233—43.

[4] The latter date is the more probable. Mommsen *Strafrecht* p. 654 points out that Catulus, who was its real author (consul 78), could not himself as proconsul in 77 propose it. Hence it bore the name of the tribune who acted for him. See Cic. *pro Caelio* § 70.

[5] Plutarch *compar. Lysandr. et Sull.* 3, on the authority of Sallust.

murder, treating the homicide of the offender by the injured husband[1] as justifiable, must remain doubtful. That he was responsible for some sumptuary[2] legislation is certain. But on this futile effort, inconsistent with his own life, we need not dwell.

930. While Sulla was engaged in remodelling Roman institutions new causes of anxiety[3] had arisen in the East. We have seen that in 83 he left Murena behind in Asia with the two legions of Fimbria's army. This commander was no doubt instructed not to provoke another war, for Sulla had patched up a peace with Mithradates in order to have a free hand in Italy. But Murena was bent on winning the honour of a triumph, and soon contrived to bring about a collision. The king was busy reasserting his authority in the lands east and north of the Euxine, and had raised great armaments for the purpose. These preparations Murena affected to view with suspicion. Archelaus, hitherto the trusted lieutenant of Mithradates, had fallen from his master's favour, and fled for safety to Murena, whom he soon persuaded not to wait for the king but to go to war at once. An invasion of Cappadocia was begun, and much booty taken. Mithradates did not resist, but sent envoys to the Senate and Sulla, complaining of this unprovoked aggression. A commissioner was sent to order Murena to leave the king at peace. To this message Murena, who had (so gossip afterwards said) spent a riotous[4] winter in Cappadocia, paid no heed, and in the season of 82 moved northwards into Pontic territory. Mithradates now fell upon him and gave him a sound drubbing. The shattered Roman army was only able to reach Phrygia[5] with difficulty, and the prestige of Mithradates was fully restored. Sulla was now master of Italy. His own hands were full, and he was in a position to understand and discharge imperial responsibilities. He sent out a second commissioner with full powers. Murena now submitted to peremptory orders and returned[6] to Rome. Peace was renewed with the king, who by a fresh treaty gained an extension of his frontier in Cappadocia. Murena had the face to claim a triumph, and Sulla, busy and indifferent, let him have his way, and he had it[7] in the same year (81) as Sulla himself. The case of Pompey was more remarkable. He had speedily recovered Africa

---

[1] See Digest XLVIII 8 § 2, comparing § 9 on the case of a burglar.

[2] Plutarch *Sulla* 35, Gellius II 24 § 11, Macrobius III 17 § 11, Lange *RA* III 166. Ammian Marc. XVI 5 § 1.

[3] Appian *Mithr.* 64—6, Livy ep. 86, Cicero *pro Mur.* §§ 11, 15, 32, the last a grotesque misrepresentation.

[4] Cic. *pro Mur.* §§ 11—13.

[5] The brief account in Memnon 36 (*FHG* III 544—5) is less unfavourable to Murena.

[6] He was succeeded by M. Minucius Thermus, under whom young Julius Caesar served with distinction at the siege of Mitylene, which was only reduced in 80 B.C.

[7] See Henzen on the *Fasti triumphales*, year 673 (81).

and set up a new king in Numidia.   After this he wrote applying for
leave to bring home his army and triumph over Numidia.   He was
only a Roman knight, 26 years of age.   Sulla held by precedent,
which required that for triumphal honours a man must have been
praetor or consul.   But he did not want to have any unpleasantness,
and so stooped to evasion.   Early in 80, when he had become consul,
he solemnly introduced a bill to grant the request of Pompey as a
special privilege.   But he found an obedient tribune[1] to block it.   He
then sent the young general orders to disband all his army save one
legion, and wait at Utica till relieved.   Pompey was greatly vexed,
and his army furious.   For a time it was believed that Sulla would
have to deal with actual revolt, to fight with boys in his old age,
as he remarked.   But Pompey was not the man to push matters so
far, and Sulla gave way.   Gossip said that the youth was vain and
bold enough to remind the dictator that it was the rising and not the
setting sun to which mankind do homage, and that Sulla's comment
was 'let him triumph.'   And so the pliant husband, who had divorced
his wife at his master's bidding, stood firm in the cause of his own vainglory and triumphed over the Numidians, or rather over Sulla and
precedent, on the 12th of March[2].

931.   The year 80, in which Sulla was both dictator and consul,
was on the whole a quiet time.   Only in the West was there a cloud
gathering on the horizon, and for the present it might seem but small.
Sertorius had landed in western Spain, and was at the head of a
Lusitanian rising, of which we shall speak below.   Sulla's colleague
Metellus was sent to put it down.   The dictator-consul had time to
attend to public works, chief of which was the restoration[3] of the
Capitoline temple, and to religious functions.   The new law-courts
began their work with the senatorial juries.   And it so happened that
the first case in the murder-court was one of surpassing interest to
contemporaries, and that the speech of Cicero for the defence has been
preserved.   At the municipal town of Ameria in southern Umbria
lived a rich and respected citizen named Sextus Roscius.   He was a
partisan of Sulla, and is said to have served in the Sullan army
against the Marians.   He visited Rome at the time when proscriptions
and murders were in full swing.   One evening he dined with a friend,
and was waylaid and assassinated on his way home.   Cicero's story is
that the murder was committed by certain other Roscii, also from
Ameria and kinsmen of their victim.   They had been on bad terms
with him, and they had an eye to his property ; this however would in

---

[1] Sallust *hist.* frag. II 21 Maur. (Gellius X 20 § 10).
[2] That is, of the year 80.   Mommsen puts it in 79.
[3] Tacitus *hist.* III 72.

the ordinary course descend to his only son of the same name, to get rid of which obstacle was now their object. They turned to the powerful freedman Chrysogonus, who met their wishes by getting the name of the murdered Roscius entered on the proscription-list. Confiscation followed, and at the sale none dared to bid against Chrysogonus, to whom the whole estate was knocked down for a trifle; according to Cicero, for about $\frac{1}{3000}$ of its true value. The three villains now divided the spoils, the great man of course taking the lion's share. The two Roscii went as his agents to Ameria, took possession of the property, and turned the young Sextus Roscius out of house and home. The leading men of Ameria were horrified at these doings, and a municipal deputation was sent to Sulla, then engaged in the siege of Volaterrae, to petition for redress. But they were prevented from getting a hearing through the arts of Chrysogonus. As things began to quiet down, the three robbers became uneasy lest the surviving son might bring them to justice, and they resolved to put him out of the way. He fled to Rome, where he found shelter in the house of a kind lady, an old friend of his father. Here he was of course more dangerous than at Ameria. So they set themselves to work his ruin by accusing him of the murder of his own father. They reckoned on the prepossessions of a senatorial jury, interested in upholding the new order of the Sullan restoration, and on the improbability that any competent counsel would be found to dare the wrath of Chrysogonus by undertaking the defence. For at the back of the freedman[1] was his patron Sulla.

932. Crassus and Antonius, the great orators of the last generation, and many other able advocates, had died natural or violent deaths in recent years. The present leader of the Roman bar was[2] Q. Hortensius. A young man from Arpinum, M. Tullius Cicero, had lately ventured to face him as counsel in a civil[3] suit, and now, by appearing for Roscius while others held back, went on to challenge his preeminence in general. The defence as conducted by Cicero was a work of genius. To draw a broad distinction between the acts of Sulla and those of Chrysogonus, and to utilize the hatred felt by all (not least by the senators) for the too-powerful minion, were the two most effective points in the speech. As for the dictator, Cicero affected to believe that the horrible abuses of the proscriptions were the work of wicked agents deceiving a beneficent master, whose eye

---

[1] According to Tacitus *dial.* 40 Sulla allowed speakers to declaim against himself. This however is a different thing from letting them interfere in what might be regarded as a matter of policy. See Cic. *de off.* II § 51.

[2] For Hortensius and his elder rival Cotta see Cicero *Brutus* § 317.

[3] Cic. *pro Quinctio*, 81 B.C. Gellius XV 28.

could not be in every place beholding their misdeeds. It was not easy for Sulla to repudiate the suggestion, sarcastic though he might know it to be, without fitting an ugly cap to his own head. He was at this time most deeply concerned to bring troubles and worries to an end, and he might well view the humiliation of Chrysogonus with indifference or secret pleasure. Cicero judged him rightly, and assailed the favourite bitterly and boldly. He charged the two Roscii with the murder of their kinsman, and exposed the infamous conspiracy out of which the present charge of parricide had grown. He called upon the jury not to sacrifice his client merely that the three criminals might sleep sound on their ill-gotten gains. Was it for this that the Roman nobles had fought their way back into the seat of power? The well-planned defence was successful. Young Roscius was acquitted ; but any proceedings for recovering his father's estate seem to have been quite out of the question. The reputation of Cicero[1] was made. To a modern student of this period a careful reading of this famous speech is indispensable. It throws upon the experiences and feelings of the time a light such as only a contemporary utterance can give. Incidentally it may serve to remind us how small a part was still played by direct evidence[2] in the proceedings of the criminal courts.

933. With the close of the year 80 the second consulship of Sulla came to an end. He refused to be reelected for the following year. Shortly after the consuls of 79 entered upon office he called a public meeting, at which he announced his resignation[3] of the dictatorship, dismissed his lictors, and went home a private citizen, even submitting with good temper to the insults of a railing fellow in the street. His work, as he understood it, was done. He felt secure, and now he meant to enjoy himself. He had an estate in Campania, near Cumae and Puteoli, on which he found a congenial retreat. He took with him his own company, a chosen band of low parasites. But there was method even in these disorderly revels of Comus. A loathsome disease, fostered by his mode of life, demanded constant treatment, but he steadily went on writing his memoirs[4] up to two days before his death. His end was characteristic. The neighbouring town of Puteoli was troubled with internal dissension. Sulla was perhaps appealed to: at all events he could not resist the temptation to

---

[1] Cic. *Brutus* § 312.

[2] Not from want of recognition of its value. See Cic. II *in Verr.* I §§ 27—29.

[3] A favourite rhetorical theme in later times. See Quintilian III 8 § 53. So also the 'advice to Sulla' to seek retirement. Mayor ɔn Juvenal I 16.

[4] He dedicated these memoirs to Lucullus, whom he left as a sort of trustee of his fame, whether as writer or as editor, or both, is not quite clear. Plutarch *Lucull.* I.

restore order in their municipality. His profound self-confidence can only be appreciated when we observe that the affair belongs to the year 78, when signs of a counter-reaction in Roman politics had already begun to appear. Of the consuls for that year, M. Aemilius Lepidus had gained office mainly through the support of the popular Pompey, against the wishes of Sulla. He was openly aiming at the overthrow of the Sullan constitution, and was only held in check with difficulty by his colleague Q. Lutatius Catulus. But Sulla went on with what he had in hand. Ten days before his death he is said to have drawn up a new constitution for Puteoli. During the consideration of this scheme he learnt that the chief magistrate was delaying a payment[1] due to the fund for restoration of the Capitoline temple, hoping that the ex-dictator's death would enable the debt to be evaded. He at once sent for the man and ordered his slaves to strangle him. But in the transports of fury he broke a blood-vessel, and the next day he died.

934. It was natural that his partisans should wish to give a public funeral in Rome to the late master of the Roman world. A party headed by Lepidus tried in vain to prevent it. On this question he could not carry Pompey with him. Pompey knew where the real strength lay, and increased his own importance by shewing that he was in touch with the old soldiers of Sulla. Of the splendour of the funeral we have full accounts. The veterans came in great numbers, and in their presence all ranks of citizens felt or feigned extravagant mourning for the deceased. One part of the ceremony, the burning of the body on a costly pyre in the Field of Mars, called forth particular remark. Interment had hitherto been the unbroken custom of funerals in the Cornelian clan, and gossip, echoed by later writers, strove to account for the cremation of a Cornelius. To decide between the conflicting stories[2] is an unprofitable task. His will revealed the shrewdness of his judgment of men. Pompey was simply passed over, which in view of Roman usage[3] was a marked slight. His other friends were duly mentioned, and Lucullus, whose raising of a fleet under great difficulties in the East has been referred to above, was appointed guardian of his young son. Evidently the testator saw through the self-centred vanity[4] of Pompey, and preferred a more solid type of character.

---

[1] Valer. Max. IX 3 § 8, Plutarch *Sull.* 37 § 3.

[2] Cicero *de legibus* II §§ 56—7, Pliny *NH* VII § 187, Licinianus p. 43 Bonn (? after Sallust).

[3] See Mayor on Cic. *phil.* II § 40. Lucullus was once the victim of a like disappointment, Valer. Max. VII 8 § 5.

[4] Sulla and Pompey. Cicero *philipp.* v §§ 43—4.

935. A man of more iron will than Sulla, more cool hard and deliberate, perhaps never existed. He beat down all that stood in his way, as a man instinctively assured of the folly of hesitation and the irrelevance of mercy. He seized despotic power, and called it restoring order: he laid it down, and left the state drifting to anarchy. He left widespread ruin and unrest in Italy, and the seeds of evils germinating everywhere. Even before his death the signs of the coming collapse had become visible. The restoration of the senatorial nobility to power was no solution of the problems of the age. It was no longer possible[1] for a governing caste to work together in dignified and patriotic harmony as had been done of old, when it was necessary to compete with rival powers, and when a simpler aristocracy was not as yet corrupted and corrupting others with the plunder of an empire. It was true that in the Roman Republic of Sulla's day nothing could be done without the use of force; but to do any good much more than force was needed, and force as applied by Sulla was no remedy at all. The state was not yet so prostrated by public exhaustion as readily to acquiesce in a despotism, and Sulla was too narrow and unsympathetic to have in him the making of a great despot. He was also too self-indulgent, and, having lived hard for nearly 60 years, he was too old. Such a man could not supply any effective answer to the urgent and difficult questions of Roman politics. That answer had to wait for the coming of a greater man, large-minded and humane, a man of another mould than Sulla. It was necessary to move forward, not backward. The true master must not waste his efforts in setting back the clock, or abdicate his responsibility. He must be ready at whatever cost to take up the burden and bear it to the end.

---

[1] See the brilliant sketches in Tacitus *hist.* II 38, *ann.* III 27.

31505